A WOMAN'S VIEW

Joan Crawford, punching the time clock, at the start of *Mannequin*

A
WOMAN'S
VIEW

How Hollywood Spoke to Women, 1930–1960

JEANINE BASINGER

ALFRED A. KNOPF   NEW YORK   1993

This Is a Borzoi Book
Published by Alfred A. Knopf, Inc.

Copyright © 1993 by Jeanine Basinger

Library of Congress Cataloging-in-Publication Data
Basinger, Jeanine.
A woman's view : how Hollywood spoke to women, 1930–1960 /
Jeanine Basinger. — 1st ed.
p.   cm.
Includes bibliographical references and index.
ISBN 0-394-56351-4
1. Motion pictures for women.   2. Women in motion pictures.
I. Title.
PN1995.9.W6B36   1993
791.43'082—dc20   93-268   CIP

Manufactured in the United States of America

Published September 2, 1993
Second Printing, September 1993

ACKNOWLEDGMENTS

THIS IS A BOOK that could have gone on forever, and almost did. Once I observed the things I refer to, I found them in every film about women that I saw and wanted to write about them all. Time and space prevented the discussions of literally hundreds of movies that fit my format, and I regret I had no space for *Ruby Gentry*, *The Toy Wife*, *Torch Song*, *Marriage Is a Private Affair*, *Road House*, *The Star*, *When Tomorrow Comes*, *Random Harvest*, *Lost Angel*, *The Legend of Lylah Clare*, *All I Desire*, *There's Always Tomorrow* . . . and many more.

I thank all the people who found movies for me and shared them: Jeffrey Lane, Richard Teller, Toni Ross, David Kendall, Joe and Kit Reed (intrepid friends who'll watch anything), Richard Slotkin (always a generous and supportive colleague), Bernard Dick, Eric Spilker, and Leonard Maltin. Research help came from Sarah Projansky, Jeremy Arnold, Louis Maggiotto, and Susan Glatzer, and excellent hospitality as well as rare films were provided by Jan-Christopher Horak of Eastman House, Mary Lea Bandy at the Museum of Modern Art, Maxine Fleckner Ducey at the Wisconsin Center for Film and Theatre Research, and Jean Firstenberg of the American Film Institute. For help with photos and research, I thank Mary Corliss of the Museum of Modern Art Stills Department, Howard Mandelbaum of Photofest, and Robert Cosenza of the Kobal Collection.

I am grateful to Leith Johnson of the Wesleyan Cinema Archives for his support, and I am forever indebted to Claire LaPila, Administrative Assistant of the Archives, because without her this book would never have reached completion. She was invaluable. And anytime I undertake a project like this, I thank my husband, John, and my daughter, Savannah, who help with everything from ideas and organization to grocery shopping. I want to thank the people at Knopf who worked so hard and well on the book: Iris Weinstein, Karen Mugler, Andy Hughes, and Sarah Burnes. Finally, I must thank my editor, Bob Gottlieb, who, after suggesting the project, accompanied me willingly to far-flung places like upstate New York and Wisconsin, where we confronted that confounding thing known as "the woman's film." Without him, I would not have known about *Weekend Marriage*, *Sarah and Son*, and *Mountain Justice*, to name only a few, and I would have missed our riveting discussions about Ruth Chatterton and gold lamé.

CONTENTS

The Genre   3

The Woman Herself   2 4

Duality: "My God! There's Two of Her!"   8 3

Fashion and Glamour   1 1 4

The Stars Who Play Her   1 6 0

Ways of Seeing Her   1 8 8

The Woman's World   2 1 3

Men   2 5 7

Marriage   3 1 9

Motherhood   3 9 2

The Woman in the Man's World   4 4 5

Proof: Kitty and Angie and Janet   4 8 6

Appendix: Women at the Box Office   5 0 9

Bibliography   5 1 1

Index   5 1 5

A WOMAN'S VIEW

THE GENRE

WHEN I WAS A CHILD, powers of observation were needed, because no one told you anything. You were awash in a sea of noninformation, and it was up to you to paddle your own canoe to whatever shore of truth you could locate. There were no PBS shows in which friendly animals explained everything from the number 6 to sexual molestation, and there were no colorful little books about *Your Appendix and You*. We children all coped as best we could, sharing dubious shards of information, discarding them and keeping them as seemed fit. For instance, we all knew that Rae Greb's idea that her parents slept in the same bed so her father could do something odd with her mother was sheer nonsense, but we were reasonably interested in David Christensen's idea that a little man lived in the refrigerator to turn the light off and on. Since we lived in a world of alert mothers, we had limited opportunities to find out anything that might be useful to us later in life. We were forced back upon youth's most trusted form of information gathering: spying on adults by pretending to play paper dolls while secretly watching and listening. This didn't gain us much ("Hush! It's the children!"), but fortunately our research was aided by an unexpected, and largely uncensored, bonanza: the local movie house. In those days, parents felt safe sending their children, alone and untended, downtown to the movies. Fortified by Walnettos and popcorn, limited only by our own lack of courage in moments of horror and stymied only by our lack of data to apply to what we saw, we watched in peace and felt like grownups—a part of the action, a part of the decision-making process. Adults might have been going to the movies to escape, but we children went to get into the thick of things, to be in that place where the real world always said "No children allowed."

Thus it was that, like so many before me, I began doing my first

serious research into my future life as a female person by going to the
movies. I can't say it was an unpleasant job—far from it—but it surely
was a confusing one, because the truth is that the movies of those years
contained some highly contradictory information about the woman's life.
For instance, although women seemed to feel that husbands were the most
important thing in the world, men apparently were not to be trusted because
they were always dying unexpectedly, getting fired, and running off with
chorus girls. These movie women seemed to feel that it was desperately
important to be married, yet marriage was an economic disaster in which
women had to start baking pies professionally or taking in washing. Women
were supposed to be sexually desirable, knowing how to tempt and satisfy
men, but they were also supposed to be innocent and pure. How was that
going to work? Women needed to be glamorous and lavishly dressed to gain
the attention of men and the envy of other women (this latter being particularly important), but they were greedy little beasts if they coveted expensive clothes and jewelry. Instead of asking for things, they should create
stunning outfits out of the draperies or produce a cookie jar crammed with
about a million dollars' worth of egg money to hand over to their man when
his automobile factory went broke. Women needed protection because they
feared spiders, but they could survive Indian attacks and cholera and
fashion failures. They seemed completely capable of bopping villains on
the heads with frying pans, and although they screamed a lot, they could
run faster than the Wolf Man when he turned up on a moonlit night to try
to date them.

   None of this made much sense, but then neither did a lot of other
things I saw. For instance, movies also told me that all professors smoked
pipes, but none at our local college did. Bats were really vampires, but
people who believed that could also be talked into believing you could tip
over a cow. When you told off your boss, he loved you for it, and tomboys
grew up to be Lana Turner, two ideas clearly without merit. Justice would
always be done, because we lived in America, and that was the American
way. (No one who had Miss Bertha Norem for grade-school math would
ever believe *that*.)

   Even as children, we knew how much of what we were seeing was
untrue, wishful, escapist. What were we—idiots? I am always astonished
at how so much writing about old movies assumes that the audience believed
everything in them. Of course we didn't. We entered into the joyful conspiracy of moviegoing. We chose what we temporarily wanted to pretend
was true, and when real experience didn't provide a yardstick, we cautiously
wondered and questioned. We grew to understand and accept the great
secret of the Hollywood film: its ambivalence, its knowing pretense. You

were a fool to believe any of it, but you were a fool if you didn't. You could have it both ways, neither way, one way or the other. It didn't matter, because movies were really only about one thing: a kind of yearning. A desire to know what you didn't know, have what you didn't have, and feel what you were afraid to feel. They were a door to the Other, to the Something Else.

Nowhere is this more manifest than in the mysterious entity known in the 1930s, 1940s, and into the 1950s as the woman's film. Most of these movies have plots that no one could possibly take seriously. For instance, Barbara Stanwyck is sent to prison by her rich young lover's mother, and when she gets out and can't find a job as a waitress, she apparently has no choice but to become a famous Broadway star overnight (*Shopworn*, 1932). When Bette Davis's husband, who was presumed dead, turns up (and husbands are always doing that, as we all know), Davis thinks she'd better shoot and kill her current lover because he just might decide to spoil the husband's cello debut at Carnegie Hall (*Deception*, 1946). A little sensible talk is never allowed to sort things out. In *Paid in Full* (1950), when Lizabeth Scott accidentally backs her car over, and kills, her sister's child, she generously compensates by sleeping with the sister's husband so she can bear the two of them a suitable replacement. One oddball event after another piles up in *To Each His Own* (1946), in which small-town girl Olivia de Havilland (who actually won an Oscar for her trouble) bears the child of her dead war hero after their one-night stand. Not wanting to embarrass her father, de Havilland has the baby out of town, but concocts a scheme whereby she can keep it. On the very night that her best friend is giving birth, de Havilland plans to sneak out and leave *her* baby (which she has been hiding in her house) on her friend's doorstep. She will then just casually drop by, presumably to see how the childbirth is coming along, and then magnanimously volunteer to take this unexpected extra baby off her friend's hands. The plot assumes that there will be no questions, such as Hey! Where did this kid come from? or Why did de Havilland stop by? or Why does an unmarried young girl want a baby? or even Is an unwed girl going to be allowed to adopt? The movie just plows forward toward its key moment in which the friend's baby is born dead, and the desperate father gratefully scoops de Havilland's convenient substitute off the front steps, placing it in his grieving wife's arms just in time to keep her from going crazy. The audience is then asked to suffer over de Havilland's loss, and—although she does end up becoming a wealthy cosmetics tycoon—to see her life as a total tragedy because she never gets a chance to mother her own son until he is fully grown. The fact that all these events grow out of initial carelessness, all-around bad planning, and lack of honesty is swept aside. A crackpot plot becomes the excuse for one woman's life of intense suffering.

What's astonishing is that these plots work. Women's films are cautionary tales of a particularly desperate stripe, but they contain real passion, real anger. The lunacy verifies them. There's something fabulous about the craziness, a kind of appealing madness that is indigenous to both the literary and filmed world of women, but that we accept as noble in literature (*Wuthering Heights*), while condemning it as foolish in movies. Although many women's films are unquestionably demented, I salute their reckless plots, in which well-dressed stars act out the woman's form of heroism: living outside the rules of correct behavior, which in story terms is realized by living outside the rules of logical narrative construction.

No one ever suggests how unintentionally liberating a form the woman's film actually was. The stories were a kind of protective coloring, which allowed women to step outside the rules and thus be riotously freed. Wheeeeee! And it was a safe way to lift the restrictions, because the out-of-control plots were just too, too bizarre. Women in the audience could watch while their favorite female stars wore great clothes, sat on great furniture, loved bad men, had lots of sex, told the world off for restricting them, destroyed their enemies, even gave their children away. Women could ruin their lives—get free of everything—down at the movie house for twenty-five cents with butter on their popcorn. What was even more wonderful, no one cared. There were no articles written on the subject of "What Is Gold Lamé Doing to Our Mothers?" or "Will George Brent Destroy Civilization?" Society didn't feel threatened. When the end of the movie came around, the surrogate woman was usually dead, punished, or back in the fold, aware of the error of her ways. Since the stories were so obviously cracked, and since the heroines paid dearly for their unrestrained behavior, it all seemed a perfectly safe form of pseudoliberation for women to enjoy.

The woman's film was successful because it worked out of a paradox. It both held women in social bondage and released them into a dream of potency and freedom. It drew women in with images of what was lacking in their own lives and sent them home reassured that their own lives were the right thing after all. If it is true, as many suggest, that Hollywood films repressed women and sought to teach them what they ought to do, then it is equally clear that, in order to achieve this, the movies first had to bring to life the opposite of their own morality. To convince women that marriage and motherhood were the right path, movies had to show women making the mistake of doing something else. By making the Other live on the screen, movies made it real. By making it real, they made it desirable. By making it desirable, they made it possible. They gave the Other substance, and thus gave it credibility. In asking the question, What should a woman do with her life? they created the possibility of an answer different from the one they intended to provide at the end of the movie.

Thus, what emerges on close examination of hundreds of women's movies is how strange and ambivalent they really are. Stereotypes are presented, then undermined, and then reinforced. Contradictions abound, which at first seem to be merely the result of carelessness, the products of commercial nonsense. But they are more than plot confusion. They exist as an integral and even necessary aspect of what drives the movies and gives them their appeal. These movies were a way of recognizing the problems of women, of addressing their desire to have things be other than the way they were offscreen.

The woman's film is the slyboots of genre; or, to put it bluntly, the woman's a two-face. Of all the genres in Hollywood's history, the woman's film is the most deceptive, as appropriate to the sex that has had to achieve its goals partly through subversion. Everything the woman's film is, it also isn't. Everything it endorses, it undermines. Everything it destroys, it reaffirms. This is fundamental to a full definition of the woman's film, and it is also, I suspect, the main reason for its success. These are not films that tell a lie, like many of Hollywood's escapist dreams. These are films that tell the truth, but only because they are about the unhappiness of women. They'll tell all the lies in the world to make that one point clear.

How, then, can the woman's film be defined? What *is* "the woman's film"? As is true of all genres, its assumed definition seems to blur somewhat upon concrete examination of the movie evidence. Some people feel that the woman's film is the same thing as melodrama, but that equation would eliminate more than half of the films that are concerned with women and their fates, among them Rosalind Russell's career comedies, musical biographies of real-life women, combat films featuring brave nurses on Bataan, and westerns in which women drive cattle west and men over the brink. The truth is that the woman's film is not all that easy to define, being something contradictory, elusive, hypocritical, and deceptive.

Genres are usually defined by specifics: recurring characters, settings, dialogues, locations in time and place, plot events—all of which seem to serve some larger social or mythological purpose for the viewing audience. Although this purpose can be transformed over time in an evolutionary process that inverts it from good to bad, and the films may try to fool us by putting on new hats, the familiar conventions themselves (characters, settings, and so on) more or less remain fixed and recognizable. True to generic form in this conventional sense, the woman's film has its own familiar plots, predictable exchanges of dialogue, and recurring filmic techniques. For instance, music is likely to swell up on the sound track in key

moments, an aural equivalent to a woman's passion; or a beautiful young
girl will be lit from behind so that there appears to be a halo around her
head. Sometimes people actually *do* say "I'll need plenty of hot water"
when a baby is about to be born, and often enough, when a woman cries
out "I'm happy, so terribly happy; everything is perfect," she either immediately gets cancer, or her husband dies, or the economic roof falls in
on her head. Women's films tell stories of rags to riches, riches to rags,
unwed motherhood, spinsterhood, betrayal by a loved one, the battle of
the sexes, the other woman, the need for sacrifice, and plain old girl meets
boy in all its variations, including girl kills boy or boy kills girl. Movies
about women, which are often stories about sex, also find familiar visual
ways to signal to audiences that the leading lady is having a fulfilling
experience: fireplace flames, fireworks displays, and waves crashing to
shore. Repeated episodes about meaningful events in a woman's life appear
and reappear: fashion shows, parties and dances, weddings and proms.
And there is one unique convention that almost never appears anywhere
except in a woman's film, the Happy Interlude.

This sequence, which might also be called the Bliss Montage, is
familiar to anyone who watches old movies. In it, the leading lady can be
seen laughing her head off, dressed in fabulous clothes, racing across the
water in a speedboat, her yachtsman lover at her side. In an immediate
scene change, she is seen peering through binoculars at a racetrack, cheering wildly behind her furs while her horse romps across the finish line in
first place. Next, she's dancing cheek to cheek at a lavish nightclub, an
orchid on her satin shoulder, her suavely tuxedoed man in her arms. Finally,
she is all in organza, ruffled to a fare-thee-well, picnicking beside a stream,
her hand trailing in water while the moss drips, the willows weep, and her
cow-eyed lover strums a ukulele. This, of course, would be in the ritzy
version. In the poor-girl variation, she goes bowling or roller-skating, eats
a hot dog at a ballpark, holds hands in the upper balcony of the Roxy, and
rides the roller coaster at Coney. Her Happy Interlude is a woman's small
piece of action, her marginal territory of joy. It occurs between "after she
meets the man" and "before he lets her down or something really awful
happens." Its visual presentation, as a montage, finds the cinematic equivalent of its own meaning: the rapid and brief passage of time in which a
woman can be happy. (Note that one of the main events of the woman's
film is actually a nonevent, nothing more than a representational piece of
editing that allows her maybe two minutes' running time of joy.)

The Happy Interlude is presented as visual action, but it is actually
a static piece of information for the audience. Viewers do not see it as
"Janet and Ed went to the races," but as "Janet and Ed are happy."
Furthermore, they also grasp a secondary level of information: "And it isn't

going to last." Some trouble, however temporary, will threaten it. This is one of the major differences between the woman's film and more active male-oriented genres, like the western. The shoot-out or the cattle drive, two familiar conventions of the western, are story-driven active events. Action does not represent the woman's life in films the way it represents the man's. The ritual events of male films—taking an objective in combat, racing the bootleggers across the Canadian border, withstanding the Indian raid—are defined by the man's individual courage. The ritual events of female films—weddings, proms, births, and even the Happy Interlude— are defined by nature or society, and the woman is bound by the rules.

Considering the woman's film in these traditional genre terms, however, immediately poses some problems. For instance, there are huge differences among such titles as the screwball comedy *Unfinished Business* (1941), the murder story *Sudden Fear* (1952), the western *Johnny Guitar* (1954), the musical *Love Me or Leave Me* (1955), the film noir *The Locket* (1946), or the biographical *Madame Curie* (1943), yet each can be defined as a woman's film. In women's films, the fixed conventions, while they *do* exist, do not exist in quite the same way as in other genres. The woman's film isn't set in any one time or place, and its locale can be real or imaginary. It can be contemporary or historical. It can easily be a biography of a real person, and just as easily be a totally fictional account of a tomboy, a princess, a space explorer, or an ordinary shop girl. It may be purely a generic woman's film of the type most people envision when they think of women's films (a melodrama with a big-name female movie star), but it may also be a female variation of some other, presumably more "masculine" genre, such as a western or a gangster movie. The woman's film, ironically, isn't even always about a woman, the ultimate insult to a gender that has, in the words of W. C. Fields's mother-in-law in *The Bank Dick* (1940), "just had to take and take."

Thus, attempting to unlock a definition of the woman's film by identifying repeated plots, characters, and conventions fails to yield much beyond what one knew before one started, which is that a film about a woman, or about a woman's life, is going to be about love, marriage, men, sex, fashion and glamour, and the need to make a decision about having a career or not. Tracking out repeated plot developments leads into a labyrinth involving these issues. There are enough crazy, unpredictable plot twists in women's films to give anyone pause—as when Kay Francis in *Mary Stevens, M.D.* (1933) saves a small boy's life by ripping a bobby pin out of her hair and plunging it down the child's throat to keep him from choking to death. You don't see that one repeated very often. (A woman's action usually comes in response to trouble, or else it is an act of sudden emotional or irrational behavior. On the whole, the woman's film is passive, internal, psychological in its story and characterization.) This unexpected female action seems bizarre, memorable, dramatic, or comic simply because it *is* action, action being the man's prerogative and not the woman's.

Because of this, one cannot effectively define the woman's film the same way one defines other genres, or, more to the point, one *can* define it the same way, but then one has ignored its main characteristic, which is that rather than repeat active events as a ritual for the audience to experience and reexperience the woman's film juxtaposes in unrealistic ways two contradictory concepts: the Way Women Ought to Be and the Other Way.

Watching hundreds of women's films reveals how cleverly they contradicted themselves, how easily they reaffirmed the status quo for the woman's life while providing little releases, small victories—or even big releases, big victories. From movie to movie or within one single movie, opposing attitudes were voiced and demonstrated. Women could hear Rosalind Russell in *Rendezvous* (1935) saying, "It's a man's place to make the money for the house, and the woman's place to take care of the man when he comes home. A woman with a career wouldn't have time to bring up a lot of kids." However, she might also have heard Ruth Chatterton flatly remark that "some women like to have a man around the house . . . not me, I'd rather have a canary" in *Female* (1933) or Bonita Granville saying "I think every girl should have a career" in *Nancy Drew, Detective* (1938) or Hedda Hopper in *Rebound* (1931) demanding to know "Am I a failure because I didn't get married? Does marriage make a woman any better?" Cedric Hardwicke suggested in *Valley of the Sun* (1942) that "the way to a woman's heart is to take her *out* of the kitchen," but Mary Astor gushed in *Smart Woman* (1948), "I love my house . . . my garden." Walter Pidgeon paid tribute to the American woman in *Calling Bulldog Drummond* (1951) by saying she could do anything "from changing a baby to flying a Spitfire," but a little boy told a little girl in *High Barbaree* (1947), "Aw, you're nothing. You're just an old girl."

Even in the most appalling conversations, there can be a subversive undercurrent, as in one of the endless debates that can be found in the American movie in which men and women discuss their relationships with one another. As Lizabeth Scott pilots her expensive convertible down a Florida highway in *Dead Reckoning* (1947), she and Humphrey Bogart talk it over:

BOGART: You know the trouble with women is—they ask just too many
             questions. They should spend all their time just being
             beautiful.

SCOTT: [*ironically*] . . . and let the men do the worrying . . .

BOGART: Yeah. You know, I've been thinking. Women ought to come capsule size, about four inches high. When a man goes out for an evening, he just puts her in his pocket and takes her along with him, and that way he knows exactly where she is. He gets to his favorite restaurant. He puts her on the table, lets her run around among the coffee cups while he swaps a few lies with his pals . . .

SCOTT: [*astonished and amazed*] Why, I . . .

BOGART: . . . without danger of interruption. When it comes that time in the evening when he wants her full-sized and beautiful, he just waves his hand, and there she is, full-sized.

SCOTT: Why, that's the most conceited statement I've ever heard.

BOGART: Well, if she starts to interrupt, he just shrinks her back to pocket-size and puts her away.

SCOTT: [*suddenly confident*] I understand. What you're saying is, women are made to be loved.

BOGART: [*suddenly confused*] Is that what I was saying?

SCOTT: [*firmly*] Yes. It's a confession, really. A woman may drive you out of your mind. You wouldn't trust her. Because you couldn't put her in your pocket, you'd get all mixed up.

A man has confidently vocalized a horrible attitude toward women, but a woman has turned it around in a covert manner. If you can't control a woman through "love," indicates Scott, you can't cope and certainly can never master her. None of this is really what the movie is about, but a sharp listener hears something interesting. As it turns out, Scott is a murderess and has been ahead of Bogart every step of the way in all the other important matters of the film, too. For this, she will end up dead, but at least she had Bogart's number.

Over and over again, conversations take place about the woman's proper role in life. Questions are asked. Should she have sex while unmarried or not have sex? Should she have children or not have children? Should she marry for love or for money? Should she be dominated by men or should she take matters into her own hands? Should she kill the rat who ruined her life or just grin and bear it? By asking the questions, the film prepared an audience to find its own answers. It's obvious that seeds of unrest, even rebellion, were planted in some female minds by the evidence they saw on-screen, despite the conventional endings that turn a story into a cautionary tale. When morality has to dramatize its own opposite to make its point, the opposite takes on a life of its own. The film becomes accidentally ambivalent, contradictory. It sends two messages, though they're allegedly resolved by a hokey finale. This ambivalence makes the woman's film a quagmire. And a masquerade.

Often, an entire movie is about this contradiction, telling a story in which women are shown to live in society in one role while secretly preferring another. In *Now, Voyager* (1942), one of the most successful and moving women's pictures ever made, Bette Davis enacts such a story, well demonstrated by one key scene. Chic and self-assured, Davis goes to an elegant preconcert cocktail party with her betrothed, the rich and blue-blooded John Loder. She is woman's-film chic, dressed in sequined satin, suavely coiffed, and wrapped in luscious mink. On her fur she wears meaningful camellias, a gift from her secret married lover (Paul Henreid). Across the crowded room, she and Henreid unexpectedly spot each other, and Henreid is struck dumb by her beauty. The music swells. They draw together and brilliantly enact a double-layered conversation. On a highly audible level, they speak as casual strangers, making appropriate cocktail-party chitchat. "I believe we met on a pleasure cruise" and "Yes, I've been here for ten months now." Beneath this, in hushed tones, they communicate privately in a conversation heard only by them and, of course, the audience. "I had no idea you'd be here" and "I am so proud I could burst." This is a scene and a conversation about a woman who must live in polite society without what she really needs or wants. The idea is carried out through the visual metaphor of two people in a highly public social context trying to conform on the surface level to what is expected of them, but revealing in conversation and yearning looks what it is they really want and really feel. The success of *Now, Voyager* is no doubt partly related to the connection women in the audience felt with Davis's character. If they went to the local cinema to feed themselves on fantasies because they felt emotionally deprived or starved, here was a heroine just like them. Rich and glamorous though she is, she, too, is going to have to make do. She will have something, but it won't be what she dreams of or really needs.

This kind of saying one thing and showing another, or the raising of social questions within a safe context, is typical of all Hollywood movies, not just the woman's film. For instance, during Hollywood's transition-to-sound period, gangster movies were very popular, spewing out tough talk and machine gun bullets. When the censors became nervous about the glamorizing of gangsters, a crackdown took place. Hollywood immediately found a simple way to deal with the problem. It went on making gangster films, with all the same talk and the same bullets, but it killed off the bad guys at the end and announced: "Crime does not pay." Everyone seems aware of this ruse, and much has been written about the cheap attempt to make violence acceptable by a last-minute line of dialogue or character turnaround. Isn't it interesting, then, that when a woman's film shows a woman in power for eighty-five minutes and reverses that in the last five minutes ("Oh, Maude, give up your presidency. Come back to me and the children."), everyone seems to feel that this reversal defines the entire movie more than the rest of the film does? Why is this? If "Crime does not pay" is an FBI advertising slogan pasted onto a movie as an excuse for its celebration of violence, what is "I think I'll bake cookies instead of curing cancer"?

The most significant thing about the women's films of the 1930s– 1950s period is the way they display this consistently inconsistent purpose and attitude. The crazy plots, the desperate characters, and whatever settings and time periods the woman's film inhabits can be best considered under the umbrella of three main purposes:

- To place a woman at the center of the story universe ("I am a woman, and I am important")
- To reaffirm in the end the concept that a woman's true job is that of just being a woman, a job she can't very well escape no matter what else she does, with the repression disguised as *love* ("Love is my true job!")
- To provide a temporary visual liberation of some sort, however small—an escape into a purely romantic love, into sexual awareness, into luxury, or into the rejection of the female role that might only come in some form of questioning ("What other choices do I have?")

These purposes, which were no more understood or planned by the people who created them than those of any other Hollywood genre, are at once revealed to be at cross-purposes; they conflict with one another and contradict one another. These movies, like other kinds of Hollywood films, provided audiences with what they didn't have in a format that was related to what they *did* have, with a reconciliation between the two implied, however falsely, at the ending. For the woman's film, though, this contradiction is built solidly into the definition of the genre, and is, in fact, present as a motivating force in every story.

THE CENTER OF THE UNIVERSE:
"I Am a Woman and I Am Important"

MICHAEL WOOD writes in *America at the Movies*, "It seems that entertainment is not, as we often think, a full-scale flight from our problems,

Bette Davis in *Now, Voyager*. Before (with Claude Rains)

not a means of forgetting them completely, but rather a rearrangement of
our problems into shapes which tame them, which disperse them to the
margins of our attention."

Since a woman's problems were usually shoved to the margins of
society's attention, the woman's film did the opposite. It entertained women
by rearranging their particular problems and worries into shapes that released them onto the screen, putting them front and center as terribly
important and terribly real. Although a great many movies about women
were made—some positive and some negative, some serious and some
comic—one thing about all of them was consistent. In them, women were
not marginalized. They were what the movie was about.

In movies about women, all important historical and natural events
are translated into the terms of a woman's daily life. World War I is not
about the Allies versus the Kaiser. It's about how unmarried women become
pregnant when they have sex. The Depression is not about an economic
collapse. It's about runs in stockings, no money for carfare, and being
forced out onto the streets. Natural disasters like earthquakes and cholera
epidemics are defined by miscarriages and dying children. Everything is
couched in terms of what are presumed to be the major events of a woman's

. . . and After (with Paul Henreid)

life: love, men, marriage, motherhood, and all the usual "feminine" things. At the same time that big events are made small, personal, small events are made huge. A woman's purchase of a new hat becomes a significant and meaningful moment on which much attention is lavished. If she comes home with her hat and no one notices it, it is a catastrophe that can lead to argument, divorce, or even murder.

Whatever the plot, whatever the tone, whatever the outcome, the woman's film accomplishes one important thing for its viewers: It puts the woman at the center of the universe. Thus, the woman's film is a genre that generously empowers a sex that society has relegated to secondary status. The gigantic silver screen shimmers and glows, and on it women may be seen to be astonishing in their beauty, intimidating in their outfits. They talk, and everyone listens. They cry, and everyone feels sad. They laugh, and everyone perks up. They need a glass of water, and everyone fetches. Most important of all, men worship them. Rich and handsome, virile and exciting, powerful and dominating men get down on their knees and beg women to listen to them, to kiss them, to marry them, to go to the prom, to fly high in the sky in the ominously named Fokker Fighter. These men want to eat barbecue! "Eat barbecue with me," the men cry out, "oh, please, please, please. . . ." The women laugh gay little laughs, toss their heads, and, well, maybe they'll eat barbecue and maybe they won't eat barbecue. *They'll* decide. If. Who. When. Why. On the screen, in the woman's film, the woman will decide. She is important. She matters. She is the Center of the Universe.

Even before we meet the character of Charlotte Vale in *Now, Voyager,* we realize that, ugly and unloved as she may be, she is nevertheless the center of the universe. The film opens by dramatically setting the stage for Charlotte's entrance. There is heavy rain pouring down outside a city mansion. Inside is a world of wealth and luxury, vast halls and giant staircases. It is 4:00 p.m., teatime, as an anxious butler and nervous maid get ready to cope with the demands of Charlotte's imperious mother, played by Gladys Cooper. The arrival of a kindly psychiatrist (Claude Rains) and Charlotte's sympathetic sister-in-law (Ilka Chase) initiates a conversation that is all about Charlotte, who is not present. The whole point of the scene is Charlotte—who she is and how she behaves, and what's the matter with her, anyway? She is the reason Chase has come to tea. She is the reason Rains has agreed to come along. She is the reason Cooper is crabby, angry, unresponsive. Charlotte commands the frame without even being in it. Her power in the story line is clearly established and is thoroughly supported by the fact that she is played by Bette Davis, a huge star.

The way Charlotte is introduced physically into the film further under-lines her importance. A close-up of the mother's nervous, twisting hands fades into a close-up of Charlotte's capable hands, working with small tools on a design for an ivory box. Charlotte's face is not revealed, although the audience clearly knows *This is Bette Davis, the star.* Charlotte's hands jerk, spoiling the box, when she is told by the butler that she must come down the stairs to greet her mother and the guests. As the camera follows Charlotte by showing only her feet descending the stairs, her mother's voice is heard: ". . . a child of my old age . . . her father passed on soon . . . my ugly duckling." At these cruel words, Charlotte's feet stop suddenly and begin to back up. The audience still has not been allowed to see Bette Davis's face. A sense of power and control is thus imparted to her character, and the audience becomes intent on seeing her. How will she look? Is Davis really playing Charlotte? Who is Charlotte Vale and what is her story? We have already seen the faces of six characters, but none is as important or seems as intriguing.

When Charlotte enters the room, mute and hesitant, a viewer can see for the first time that she is overweight and badly dressed, wearing glasses over which her unplucked and shaggy eyebrows glower. She enters without glamour and without wardrobe, but even in the cavernous room over which her odious mother presides, every composition favors her, allowing the audience to focus on her insecure personality and her considerable anger. She says very little until she leaves the room, followed by both the camera and Claude Rains. The film has used everything it has to tell the audience that this woman matters. She has no beauty, no charm, no grace, but she is a woman and her troubles and woes are at the center of the universe.

This is how the genre exaggerates a woman, elevates her status. The great female stars of Hollywood who played these roles were themselves physical exaggerations, almost frightening in their intensity. Think of Bette Davis's bug eyes, which saw all there was to see, or Joan Crawford's wide shoulders, which filled the screen with a get-out-of-my-way insolence, and Betty Grable's legs, a cool million dollars' worth of insured merchandise via Lloyd's of London. The woman's genre does not have a character at its center who is meant to triumph over exaggerated events and be elevated to the status of hero, as in films about men. Instead, it presents an exaggerated character, played by an extravagant beauty, who is to be brought low by love for a man and returned to a state of normal, ordinary womanhood. Until that moment of normalcy, however, the woman is empowered. Her troubles matter.

REPRESSION: *"Love Is My True Job!"*

"A WOMAN can do anything, be anything," says Joan Crawford in the 1931 film *Possessed*, "as long as she doesn't fall in love." (Contrast this with Louis Wolheim in *Sin Ship*, also from 1931, explaining his masculine credo: "I don't say no prayers. I don't hit no cripples. And I don't fall in love.") No matter where the story is set, who stars in it, what other genre it's mixed with, or what happens in its plot, the woman's film reminds women that they have a biological function related to their role as women. Being a woman is a full-time job, and one they cannot easily escape. "That's one career we all have in common—being a woman," says Bette Davis in *All About Eve* (1950). It is a great stopper to female action and achievement. Mary Boland puts it perfectly in a song she sings in *The Women* (1939): "Oh, a man can ride a horse to the range above, but a woman has to ride on the wings of love." It's almost a perfect definition of the difference between male and female genres.

The movie approach to this problem is clever. Contrary to popular opinion on the subject, women's films—or movies in general—don't always suggest that women have no choice in life other than to become wives and mothers. In fact, movies show women doing all sorts of astonishing things. They fly airplanes, direct traffic, win elections, run businesses, edit magazines, perform brain surgery, and invent the safety pin. They are resourceful and amazing. A woman *can* be anything. She *can* do anything. She is as strong as the American man she stands alongside. But, oh, boy, if she *tries* to do anything or be anything! Yes, she may be a nuclear physicist flying a spaceship toward Mars, commanding her troops, but she still finds herself subject to the dangers that befall one because she is a woman: falling in love, becoming pregnant, giving birth, being victimized, and losing her lipstick. Someone could still accuse her of the worst crime known—"You're not a woman, Dr. Frisby. You're a machine."

The woman's film suggests to women that until they figure out what to do about the fact that they are women, they can't expect anything else to work. It further suggests that even when a woman thinks she has made a liberated decision she can find it coming back to haunt her. She will fall in love, and then what? The movies show women what will happen to them without the love of a man, and what will happen is not even always portrayed as bad. Some female movie characters lead useful lives as nuns and schoolteachers. Women can find adventure as Arctic explorers or eccentric detectives. They can invent things, save lives in Crimea, and wagon westward. Only then do these particular women discover that they can no longer be happy the way they used to be because love is their true job.

Thus the movies prettied up the woman's biological function as love. They were not necessarily telling women not to have careers; they were telling them that their best choice of career was love—not washing dishes, or cleaning house, or even having children . . . but love. Over and over again the answer to the question of what a woman should do with herself was wrapped in shiny paper and presented as love.

LIBERATION: *"What Other Choices Do I Have?"*

> *"Look, honey, why do you want to fool around with a*
> *career when you can go out with me?"*
> *"It's not the same thing, Buzz."*
> —Jack Carson answered by Joan Leslie,
> TWO GUYS FROM MILWAUKEE (1946)

EVERY MOVIE FEMALE has to confront the major action of the woman's film: making a choice. This means showing a viewer two opposite directions for a character to take, and that means giving substance to some form of liberation. First, the woman's film makes a woman important, and, last, it reminds her that her problem is that she *is* a woman; she can't escape the fact and thus ought to accept love. In between, however, comes the conflict and contradiction in the form of a visualized Other. Sometimes a woman is a young girl who finds romance (Love versus the Other). Other times she's a married woman trapped in an unhappy or unsupportive marriage (Marriage versus the Other). She can also be a parent, abandoned or without economic security (Motherhood versus the Other). The Other as shown in movies can be a lot of different things, from practicing medicine to flying the Pacific solo to singing "Put Your Arms Around Me, Honey" to an adoring audience. It's always the same thing, however. It's the Other.

By telling a story in which a woman has to make a choice, the woman's film found a convenient way to lure viewers, satisfy secret urges for a life other than the conventional one, entertain with all manner of "bad" female behavior, and still end up with the "love is your job" concept. Thus, in the woman's film, the woman has to choose, always choose. She is not supposed to have two of anything. She can't have both a career and a home. She can't love two men. She shouldn't have two personalities, and frequently she can't even have two children, because one has to die for her sins. What these movies tell an audience is that women have to make choices, and once the choice is made, they must live with the consequences. The way the plots shape up, the movies are frequently defining a no-win situation in which the choice is, in some fundamental way, always wrong:

- A woman chooses the right man, but he dies and she has to earn her own living.

- She chooses the right man, but he goes wrong and she has to earn her own living.
- She chooses the wrong man (although everybody warns her), and he turns out to be really, really wrong, and she has to earn her own living.
- She chooses the wrong man, but she thinks he's the right one because he's rich and she won't have to earn her own living.

She soon figures out that this last choice is wrong, because she shouldn't have married for money. She finds the right man, meaning a man who is not rich, but he can't earn a decent living. He does, however, give her lots of kids, a little house, plenty of love, and many opportunities to bake. This is right, although wrong, whereas it might be wrong, although right . . . or . . . well, she still may have to earn her own living. In other words, for a woman, a decision is frequently the same thing as a disaster.

However, there is a subtext attached to making all these choices. For instance, sometimes when the man dies, runs off, or deserts her for whatever reasons, a woman is then forced immediately to go out into the world on her own and do something to survive. She does this brilliantly, and not only survives but survives on a very posh scale. She gets *things*. She becomes glamorous and powerful, and new and better men suddenly want to marry her, even though she's in control of her own life and will not be dependent on them. This is subversive, but there it is, right up there on the screen, frequently in living color. To make this situation comfortable for everyone, this woman who has become something and has met a different, better man, suddenly has to face again the same problem she had in the first place: What choice should she make about love?

It is these contradictory purposes, with their accidentally liberating events, that must be considered in defining the woman's film. Put a woman at the center of the universe, show her making a choice that takes her outside of ordinary behavior, then put her back into the fold. This generates a useful working definition of the woman's film of Hollywood from 1930 to 1960:

> A woman's film is a movie that places at the center of its universe
> a female who is trying to deal with the emotional, social, and
> psychological problems that are specifically connected to the
> fact that she is a woman.

Whatever she chooses to occupy herself with in life will ultimately be influenced by that fact. Her problems are made concrete by various plot developments that are marked by bizarre actions and shifts her in her fortune. She is forced to make some kind of choice between options that

are mutually exclusive, and these options will be visualized as two contradictory paths, one of which will empower and/or liberate her in some
way, however minor, however temporarily, and one of which will provide
her with love.

THERE HAD TO BE a reward for women who came to these movies,
something that pleased them and drew them in, something to make them
happy or allow them to feel good about themselves. Movies certainly punish
women and put them in their place, but anyone who watches a great many
Hollywood films can clearly see that they also do something else. When I
was a little girl back there in the movie theater, I didn't fully understand
the rules of society's repression. For me, having a woman suddenly say at
the end of a movie, "Oh, Bruce, let me give up my life as a world-famous
international newspaperwoman and keep house for you and our kids" was
an abstraction. All I knew was that for eighty-five or ninety minutes, I had
seen a picture of a woman who was running the world. That interested me.

Let me cite one example. As a child, I saw *Ladies Courageous* (1944),
starring Loretta Young, Geraldine Fitzgerald, and June Vincent. It is a
story about women who ferry bombers during World War II, and despite
that promising concept it is hardly a feminist tract. The women keep falling
in love and forgetting to put their flaps down, and the film is not really
about war or even very much about aviation. It is actually a woman's
film—the story of several women whose personal lives are depicted in
flashbacks that explain just why each woman is flying airplanes. Where
are their men? Why do they not have children? How did they learn to fly?
Some of these explanations are relatively simple; for instance, one of the
women came from a family that owned a flying circus and grew up around
airplanes. There is one story, however, that has stayed with me from
childhood, and I can tell it from memory.

As June Vincent pilots a huge aircraft west, she flies over her hometown and begins to narrate her personal story through a voice-over. We are
shown a close-up of her lovely, delicate face as she sits at the plane's
controls and remembers how she was once a student down below in a
convent school. Her face fades away, and the image dissolves into her
flashback through a picture of ringing bells, which dissolves in turn into
a typical elementary classroom. An authoritative but kindly nun is leading
the schoolgirls in chorus. The camera moves back to frame a representative
group of half a dozen young girls, angelically singing, their faces obediently
turned toward the camera, a perfect image of two kinds of dutiful femininity.
First, there's the nun, sacrificial, dressed in her uniform, devoting her life
to God and to other people's children, a noble model of appropriate behavior

Ladies Courageous. Loretta Young (second from right) and allies

for women. Second, there are the young girls, also in uniform and obedient, following the rules and opening their little mouths to sing in unison, doing what is expected of them. However, the camera soon picks out one other girl, sitting in the back row. A slim and ethereal child, she is not singing, not obeying, not looking toward the front. Her face is turned toward a large window, and she is looking outward. This child, representing the young June Vincent, is wearing a Mona Lisa smile and watching the wind blow through the trees. She is looking upward into the sky, dreaming of flight.

Without any words being spoken, this film has already said a great deal. Here is an image of an adolescent young girl not following orders but dreaming dreams of glory, of freedom. She is full of imagination and hope, separated from the dark-haired, pudding-faced dutiful singers of her class-room. Viewers already know that she grows up to be an airplane pilot. It is not a question of whether any women in the audience might possibly identify with her out of some secret desire for escape. The film overtly invites viewers, both male and female, to make this identification and to understand its implications. As the story continues, the nun approaches the child to gain her attention. The little girl openly admits she was day-dreaming, and the nun sympathetically informs her that someone once said that only the dreamers in life are practical. There is no lecture about obedience, no warning that dreams are for men only. As the nun walks away, an amazing thing happens. A storm is approaching the school, which is why the child has been watching the wind in the trees. As she continues to look out the window, she suddenly sees an airplane coming in to land, barely ahead of the approaching storm. The bad weather has forced the pilot to risk a dangerous landing through the trees onto a grassy part of the school lawn. The children all run to the window, and our point of view is switched to outside the classroom, so that we are looking in at the frightened and astounded little faces that are behind the window. The plane makes it down safely, and as we observe the attentive children's faces watching the brave and competent pilot emerge from the plane, the little blond girl's lips part in total astonishment as she mouths the words, "*It's a girl!*" Out of the plane comes no other than Loretta Young, shaking loose her long hair, a brave woman coming down out of the sky to say "Dreams do come true" to the little girl in the classroom.

It would be nice to be able to add that, after this flashback, Vincent becomes a brigadier general in the air corps and wins World War II single-handedly. Unfortunately, she dies in an air crash, and I can't very well sweep that under the rug. However, I've never forgotten her story, her desire for freedom, and her moment of understanding in which she almost seems to conjure up the image of Loretta Young to be her role model.

This is a book about both the repressions and the hidden liberations in films about women; about what might have been under the surface as well as on it. This is a book that shows how movies about women were two-faced, providing viewers with escape, freedom, release, and then telling them that they shouldn't want such things; they won't work; they're all wrong. This book is about the phenomenon observed in *Ladies Courageous*, whose women pilots are supposed to look nice, fall in love, care about their men, marry or stay married. It is a woman's film with woman's film concerns. However, its females also ferry bombers; they are doing a man's job during wartime, and they are doing it well. To do so, they had to leave home, to learn to fly, to risk their lives. Would a girl or woman watching this movie want to fall in love, the way Geraldine Fitzgerald does, or would she want to grow up to fly airplanes and "go free . . . make a path through the sky . . . mark no trail . . . go as the lark goes," as Loretta Young tells June Vincent that women can do? I was seven years old when I first saw *Ladies Courageous*, and I know what *I* wanted.

THE WOMAN HERSELF

WHO SHE IS

> *The All-American man wears a coat of high finance,*
> *But the All-American girl wears the pants.*
> —Lyric from
> TAKE ME OUT TO THE BALL GAME (1949)

"I FORGOT how much trouble an American woman can be," says Alan
Ladd in *China*, and there's movie truth in those words. The American
woman on film is not a weak creature. She may have a weakness, and it
can bring her down; she may be confused and worried, which will cause
her to make foolish mistakes; but she is not weak and she is not stupid.
Men constantly have to cope with her. She can wreck their dinosaur models,
outshoot them in a rifle contest, poison their mushrooms, and reduce them
to gibbering idiots. She can, and she does. The American woman on film
is too hot to handle. Sometimes the movies make it look as if all of American
male culture is focused only on the task of figuring out how to control a
force that is stronger than it is, stronger than politics, stronger even than
nature—the force of the American woman, trying to establish a place for
herself, demanding equality. Not getting it, of course, but standing at the
center of the filmic universe as if she were entitled to have it. No female
character can be the leading role in a woman's film unless she has the

24

strength to be at the center of the universe, because that is also the center of the plot.

The primary thing about the woman herself in the woman's film is that she be strong, interesting, beautiful, or glamorous enough to be able to command center stage. These are films that glorify women, that say that women's problems matter. They exist to give substance to women's feelings. Although they surely invited viewers to admire fashion, glamour, and beauty, they also asked them to admire female strength and to respect female anger. Thus, the woman herself, the central figure of the genre, is always depicted as having strength and frequently as being very, very angry. Her ability to cope is remarkable.

In a superb obituary tribute to Bette Davis, *Time* magazine's Richard Corliss defines this strength, calling the actress "Hollywood's thoroughly modern woman: her independence born in neurosis, her strength forged in professional and domestic combat, her man of the moment an irrelevance or a desperate burden." Davis's roles throughout her career typified the kinds of females who populated the women's films—the strong women who, by coping, also prevailed and even sometimes dominated. No matter how the movie comes out in the end or what it purports to be about or even if its star says "Hold me, Charles, I'm no good without you," the strength of the American woman on-screen in the woman's film is an undeniable fact. "The woman herself," as the thriller writer Jim Thompson titled one of his books, is "one hell of a woman."

To accomplish the double goal of covert liberation and overt repression, the movies, whether intentionally or unintentionally, follow a format that is well defined by a character played by Joan Crawford in *Paid* (1931). Sent to jail for a crime she didn't commit, she learns early in life the terrible lesson that women are often judged erroneously by appearances. The woman who wants to get along has to go along. Vowing revenge, Crawford leaves jail and becomes a master criminal, one who says the way for a woman to win is to cheat and trick, but to stay "within the law." It's the perfect metaphor for how the woman's film works. By coming around in their final moments to saying that a woman's real career is love, and that women can find happiness only in marriage and motherhood, these movies stay "within the law." By allowing women to voice resentment and complaint, by letting them blow off steam about how men let them down, and by showing them losing their kids to geographically and socially distant people, they stay "within the law." The woman herself, the one the story is about, remains strong and central to all events. She is the vessel through which all this can pass, a person who temporarily challenges the law or who demonstrates how to live within it.

To show how the woman herself is portrayed as a strong creature, four films from World War II with different emphases make excellent comparisons. *China* and *Dragon Seed* stress freedom and independence, allowing their female stars to put aside the roles of motherhood, marriage, and love as they undertake activities that would more commonly be undertaken by men. Two other films, *The White Cliffs of Dover* and *Mrs. Parkington*, do exactly the opposite. They tell stories about women whose main interest in life has been the men they first fell in love with, the sons they bore them, and the lives they have led that might be called the woman's lot. Although two films are nontraditional and two are traditional, in all four cases the central woman character is strong, dynamic, determined, smarter than everyone else in the movie, capable, and almost ruthless in accomplishing her goals.

China (1943), the movie in which Alan Ladd complains about the troublesome American woman, is a clear example of how an ordinary little movie puts a woman in the midst of the male action and allows her to dominate the plot, thereby endorsing female strength. Its resourceful heroine, Loretta Young, verifies the positive attributes of women, because she is presented as an exemplary female except that she is, as Ladd says, not only trouble but also like a lion tamer he once knew, "always crackin' the whip." Young retorts that Ladd is simply "arrogant" and a lot like her father that way. (Aha!) Dialogue exchanges of this sort allow the film to present a tough, dominant woman as a romantic object, because they help to siphon off male resentment. They also alert experienced moviegoers to the fact that these two characters will, of course, end up in each other's arms. There is often an implication in Hollywood films that the macho American male needs his female equivalent for a suitable mate, and this is the source of the "meet cute" concept. But American film couples don't meet cute as much as they meet brute, clanging up against each other in mortal disagreement that becomes mutual sexual attraction. In fact, Young and Ladd do fall in love in *China*, but this does not diminish Young's strength, nor does it finally unseat her from a central position in the action of the film or deter her from her mission.

China turns out to be a subversive masterpiece of contradictions, a textbook case. It is definitely a story about a woman, dominated by a big-box-office female star who has the top billing, but because it is set in World War II and was released during the darkest days of the war, it is also a propaganda movie with a hybrid set of generic goals. It might be called a quasi-combat-romantic-action-woman's-propaganda picture. It has several agendas, one of which is to gain sympathy from the American public for our allies, the Chinese, because in addition to being a story about a brave woman it purports to initiate viewers into Chinese culture, to demonstrate the bravery of the Chinese people, and to establish their desperate need for American support as they fight oppression by a barbaric enemy (Japan). This agenda is effectively accomplished by using women as main characters. Young plays an American schoolteacher in charge of a group of Chinese girls, her former students. The issues that the film wants to teach the home audience of the day are packed into its story of a woman's journey across the wartime landscape of China. The use of women helps to soften the propaganda and sell it to moviegoers.

Loretta Young represents strong American womanhood, and she is at the center of the universe. What does an audience see her do? Although the film begins with Alan Ladd, an American who sells oil to the Japanese army, and his sidekick, William Bendix, Young makes a dramatic entrance. On a dark and rainy night outside an isolated village, she calls off a horde of Chinese peasants who are besieging Ladd and Bendix in their truck. Then she commandeers the vehicle herself. "Move over!" she barks at Ladd, who meekly slides aside while she climbs in and takes the wheel, steering cautiously but competently forward, getting them out of the mess they're in. Young takes charge of the situation by proving she can drive a large truck over difficult terrain in a torrential downpour. Bendix explains to her, however, that she will not be able to convince Ladd to take her where she wants to go. "When Mr. Jones [Ladd] gets his mind made up, nothin' short of beatin' his brains out will make him change it, and well, nobody ever beat his brains out yet."

"There's always a first time, isn't there?" says Young, smiling grimly.

Looking at her, Bendix answers, "Yeah, and you're probably just the one that can do it."

Young crisply replies, "There's no probably about it. I've got to." (The young girls laugh at Ladd behind his back, cheerfully calling him an insect.)

As the story unfolds, it is made clear that although these women have courage in a difficult situation, they cannot escape their fates as women. They will actively participate in stopping the advance of the Japanese army, but the contradiction common to films about women will befall them along the way. In one half of the story, the women find freedom from the usual feminine conformity. In the other half, the reinforcement of a traditional attitude surfaces in plot events that are designed to remind viewers that, after all, Young and her band of students *are* women. As such, they are subject to the biological and cultural events that are associated with their sex. No matter how brave they are, how independent they wish to be in shaping the "new China," they will be slowed down by three story developments that are related *only* to the fact they are women: rape, motherhood, and love.

Thus, the movie takes a direction it would not take if Loretta Young

and her students were males. Three events occur that are linked to the
female sex. First, there is a subplot involving an abandoned baby that has
been rescued by Bendix during an air raid. Ladd has told him to "ditch
the kid," but Bendix has hidden the child in the back of the truck. When
Young decrees that the baby needs milk, they stop at a family farm, so
that they can milk a cow. This delay due to the instincts of motherhood
ends up placing them directly in the path of the advancing Japanese.
Second, one of the girls is raped by soldiers and dies from the experience.
Third, Young inevitably falls in love with Ladd. The first two events are
linked both narratively and visually. When the baby is being washed at
the farm in a little tub, the females gather around the child, sharing the
joy as a significant moment in a woman's life. After one of their group is
raped and lies dying, they gather around her bruised and broken body,
grieving as women grieve in times of sisterhood, sharing the pain of what
they know to be also a significant moment in their lives, and one that they
too might be subjected to during wartime. The dynamic narrative push
forward of *China* is temporarily derailed by these two narrative events: the
feeding and caring for a baby, and a rape and resulting death.

As is typical of Hollywood's treatment of minorities, it is a Chinese
girl who is raped. Loretta Young, as the leading female star, is not subjected
to any event that might take her out of the plot line permanently. It is her
fate to be slowed by the third of the big three stoppers to female action:
love. To balance the story of Young as a dominant force acting against
Ladd's decisions, a romance is introduced into the plot, a familiar story
about a dynamic virgin with a goal who meets a tough-guy, low-class hero.
This situation was old long before *The African Queen* (1951) ever came
along, and *China* is a kind of *Chinese Queen*, with Young getting thawed
and Ladd getting initiated into the need for meaningful political goals.
Thus, a story about a woman is combined with both romance and war
propaganda. These additional attitudes free the image of the woman from
bondage, as it were, and allow her to behave in a dominant way. The
romance tempers that dominance, reassuring the audience that Young is,
after all, still a woman who will have to decide what to do about love. The
war has made her aggressive behavior acceptable, because in wartime,
anything goes. Besides, she's not next door; she's over there somewhere
in China.

In the love story, Young, who has at first not worried about how she
looks or what she wears, starts putting lipstick on in the truck. "That's
better," Ladd tells her, although he also points out that she's "not the
lipstick sort" and that her putting it on is "like a traffic cop powdering his
nose." Young's lipstick is a metaphor for her acceptance of Ladd, and the
two are soon wrapped in a tight clinch, locked lipstick to lip and vowing

eternal love. Young tells Ladd that "whenever men are in danger [women] are lighting candles even brighter than the stars. But not in shrines—in their hearts—for the men they love who've gone away." Ladd seems pleased.

One might think that is where the movie would end. Or one might think that Ladd would end up having to rescue Young and her group from some dreadful capture or threat of death. However, to complete its contradictory format, the finale shows two active combat episodes, the scriptwriters having apparently decided that the movie had met its romantic obligations satisfactorily. Young takes part in both. When her group joins some Chinese guerrillas in a plan to steal dynamite from the Japanese, she insists on accompanying the raid because she is one of only three who can drive the truck; if anyone is hurt, she might be needed. While she waits with the truck in hiding, the raid takes place. She tells the one commando who remained behind with her: "I'm not afraid . . . that's not true! I *am* afraid . . . but it's a woman's fear. The kind that comes to them while they sit waiting and helpless. I know now it must eat their hearts out." While Young offers this wisdom, she is calmly loading bullets into an ammo belt. Since most of the men are wiped out in the raid, Young and her girls have to help dynamite the ravine to permanently bar the progress of the enemy. During this action, the Japanese arrive sooner than expected, and while Ladd goes down to talk to them, keeping them stopped long enough for the charges to be set, Young and her girls help the few remaining guerrillas rig a trap across the road. While Ladd talks to the Japanese general, who like all Japanese generals in American films speaks excellent English, he is told the news about Pearl Harbor and America's entry into the war. Ladd takes action. Delayed in conversation, Ladd knows he has lost his opportunity to escape. He gives the signal to ignite the dynamite, realizing he will be killed in the resulting avalanche. He is sacrificed in the Robert Jordan tradition, dying in a "last stand" that allows Young, Bendix, and the Chinese to escape. For once, it is the man who makes the sacrifice instead of the woman.

Young continues her journey to deliver the Chinese girls to safety, because they are "the destiny of China." The film wraps up by using her to visualize the two contradictory levels of its story: the traditional portrait of a woman as a loving creature who does not fight wars, and the nontraditional portrait of a woman who blows up half of Asia on a successful combat mission. These two purposes are skillfully united. In fact, they are linked so successfully, and the transitions between them are made so smoothly, that an audience sees the two halves as being not only compatible but completely appropriate and logical. Loretta Young loads ammo into a machine gun that she can handle effectively, but she also prattles about the importance of love in a woman's life. Loretta Young weeps dramatically over the death of the man she loves, but she efficiently lays dynamite charges and sets them off. A woman is a lover is a soldier. A woman cries and dynamites and reminisces and marches forward.

China does not end in a close-up of a romantic embrace between Ladd and Young. It doesn't even end by lingering over the dead body of Alan Ladd, the sacrificial hero. It ends with a close-up of Loretta Young's face. To fulfill the woman's film tradition, she looks noble, beautiful, vulnerable, yet strong. The flag of China, representing the message "Well, it's wartime, and things can't be the way they always were," is superimposed over Young's image. In case we've forgotten about Ladd, William Bendix, his faithful sidekick, solemnly intones, "He was a great guy." He is, however, dead, and Young's lipstick is back in the pocket of her trench coat. And she's once again driving the truck.

An even more overt presentation of a woman's strength can be found in *Dragon Seed* (1944), starring Katharine Hepburn as a heroic Chinese woman. The movie has built into its dialogue and plot developments an actual argument for liberation, and certainly a respect for an independent, free woman who knows her own mind and acts on it. This appeal comes to an American audience in a safe guise, as it is set in another culture, far removed from the everyday life of most viewers. Furthermore, since the film is once again played against a background of open warfare, there is an excuse for nonstandard female behavior. However, *Dragon Seed*, a movie made in Hollywood for American moviegoers, discusses liberation within its plot and definitely questions what the woman's role in life should be. *Dragon Seed* was based on a novel by a woman, Pearl Buck, and was adapted for the screen by two women writers, Marguerite Roberts and Jane Murfin. Its advertisements told viewers it was "the glorious story of a girl with a fighting heart and the man who fought by her side." He fought by her side, not she by his.

The women in the film are used as metaphors. Jade (Hepburn) is a feminist, although the term is never used. This is established at the opening of the film when it is discovered that she is not at home doing women's work, the way she should be. ("The matchmaker cheated us on that one," comments her mother-in-law.) She is, instead, in the village at a political rally. Furthermore, she even dares to speak up, standing bravely, asking sharp questions and expressing her sentiments clearly. This shocks everyone, including her husband, who arrives to drag her home. ("You're not where a woman should be . . . at home waiting for her husband.")

Jade and her behavior are a constant topic of conversation. Since she does not give herself totally to her husband—or even, it is hinted, at all —he discusses this with his brother: "She is like the western wind. When

I reach for her, she's gone. She is mine and yet not mine. When I touch her, it is as if her spirit goes and only her body exists." When the men in the family advise him to beat her, his mother warns him that men must be sure that they are able to beat their wives before they try it. "These new-fangled wives," she advises, "are not so easily beaten."

Jade can read, which gives her power over her husband, who cannot, and which singles her out in the world she lives in. This ability is noticed by her silly sister-in-law, who for the first time in her life becomes curious. She wants to know about Jade's book. "You see," warns the mother. "An idea spreads. It is wrong to give a woman such a dangerous thing." Not only can Jade read, she can think. She sees what is coming regarding the war, and she educates her husband and his family. She leads the way, and her husband follows. She also explains to him that she wants sexual equality. "I think and feel, and not just that I give you children. I am not to just belong to your house, but to be yours." After finally turning to him at night of her own free will, Jade tells him that she now knows he will accept her for herself and not just treat her like someone to bear his children, do his work, make his food. Until she has been sure of this, Jade has kept herself private, separate from her husband.

As for the other women in the film, the strong ones survive and the weak ones die. Jade's mother-in-law (Aline MacMahon) disapproves of Jade at first, but comes to realize that they are not unalike. She, too, is strong and brave, although she is a more traditional peasant wife than Jade. By showing courage and resourcefulness, both of the strong women survive the war. Two others, both of whom are weak and silly, do not. One of these is fat and lazy, and her lethargy makes her easily caught and killed by the enemy, a lesson unto itself. The other is Orchid, the brother's wife. She is a great beauty, but very foolish and not terribly intelligent. She becomes a rape victim and is bayoneted to death afterward. Since she is the character who enacts the usual woman's role, she makes a noble sacrifice on behalf of her children. She is caught and raped largely because, instead of re-maining hidden, she chooses to stand up and show herself in order to draw the soldiers away from where her children are cowering. To save their lives, she runs far away, chased by the soldiers.

Dragon Seed, as is true of many films about women, includes endless discussions about the woman's position in life. Since Jade is rejecting a traditional role, and since she is the role model of the film, all the other characters in the movie continuously point out to the viewer that she is different. There is an ironic level of safety introduced, by which audiences are asked to participate in a pseudoliberated attitude. The film sets up a clever mode of identification: it is assumed that audiences are like Jade, liberated and wise, and that they will understand that these Chinese peasants need to wake up and be like us Americans, treating their women as equals. (The idea that American women *are* equals often appears in the wartime movies of the 1940s, a time in which democracy was stressed.)

Two important events complete the action of *Dragon Seed*. First, Jade gives up the child she has borne in order to go away with men and fight in the hills. (Even though she gives the child to her in-laws, the act is worth noting.) Second, Jade poisons the entire Japanese army, an action that clearly marks her out as stronger than the men around her. Throughout *Dragon Seed*, Jade constantly questions the role of women in society, but at the same time she loves her husband and bears his child. She becomes the main combat force of the movie, however, when she hatches her plan to poison the troops that are billeted in their village. ("Women ever must act while men indulge themselves in talk.") While the men are sitting around trying to figure out what to do, Jade walks into town with a hefty package of poison, the woman's weapon. Showing great courage, she enters the main hall, flirting with the guards until she can get to the kitchen and poison the soup so that the entire army keels over at a banquet that very night. Jade has accomplished her goals by taking action on her own. She takes "feminine" action by flirting with the soldiers to distract them; by her female ability to gain access to a kitchen; and by the fact that, since she is a woman, no one thinks she can do it. The biggest action of the film skillfully unites both its traditional and nontraditional attitudes. How well I remember the impression this scene made on me when I first saw the film as a child. A woman poisons the Japanese army! Perhaps I should learn to cook, after all. Because she flirts and because a woman belongs in the kitchen, Katharine Hepburn helps to win World War II.

China and *Dragon Seed* are not commonly found on lists of women's films, due to their settings in foreign countries during wartime. Since China was not known at that time as a country of liberated women, the setting provides a safe place for such notions, a kind of "and we all know this couldn't happen" reassurance.

To VERIFY the contradictory nature of the woman's film, one can consider the other two movies from the same time period: *The White Cliffs of Dover* (1944), starring Irene Dunne, and *Mrs. Parkington* (1944), starring Greer Garson. These movies are inarguably more traditional women's pictures than the war-oriented *China* and *Dragon Seed*. Yet *White Cliffs* and *Mrs. Parkington* are still portraits of women at the center of the universe, undergoing, yet strongly surviving, the problems that befall women. In 1944, both Dunne and Garson were at the top of their careers, established and respected stars of women's pictures. Garson was nominated for Best Actress for her role in *Mrs. Parkington* (she lost to Ingrid Bergman in *Gaslight*). Both movies were box-office successes.

The women portrayed in these two films are shown to have the human flaws of jealousy, fear, and doubt, but they are otherwise clearly to be recognized as strong, almost perfect women. This is not the same thing as saying that they are idealized. Many movies, most of which are about men, present a different kind of "perfect woman," a woman who is being put on a pedestal. These are often mothers (Beryl Mercer as James Cagney's mom in *Public Enemy*, 1931) or wives (June Allyson as Jimmy Stewart's wife in *The Glenn Miller Story*, 1954). They are seldom independent young women. The characters played by Dunne and Garson *do* have flaws, but they are supposed to be charming, understandable flaws or tragic, sympathetic flaws. For instance, Mrs. Parkington's curl keeps flopping down on her forehead so that she has to swaggeringly blow it upward in an unladylike manner (charming! understandable!), and the woman in *White Cliffs* goes into a decline when her husband is killed in World War I (tragic! sympathetic!). The two women are thus presented as true role models, "typical" women of the times.

The plots of these two films again illustrate how stories about women accomplish contradictory goals. First, each young woman has to be brave enough to leave behind the world she has been raised in to enter a strange new world where she will have to learn how to behave. These movies are dictated by the same motivation: the women fall in love. Greer Garson has been left an orphan by the death of her mother in a frontier-town mining accident, and she is removed from her provincial world by marriage to the wealthy, glamorous Colonel Parkington (Walter Pidgeon). Irene Dunne voluntarily separates herself from her father, a Rhode Island newspaperman, in order to remain in England to wed the man she loves (Alan Marshal). The men in both cases are slyly disguised forms of liberation, and women in the audience who had married to get out of difficult home situations no doubt identified strongly with the concept. These two films do not follow a format in which a weak man has to be rejected by a strong woman. Instead, they are truly conventional movies in which men are portrayed as foolish but lovable (*Mrs. Parkington*), and having to fight wars where they will die and leave the woman alone in life (*White Cliffs*).

In both films, the women represent vigor and energy. Garson is from the West, an open, honest woman without guile and without manners or style. Dunne is an American, too, which always means direct and outspoken in movie terms, who has to win over her wealthy British in-laws. *White Cliffs* is a story about wartime sacrifices, and *Mrs. Parkington*, the lighter of the two films, is more a story about how wealth does not bring happiness. Although the surfaces of these films seem not to have much in common, parallels may be drawn between them:

- Both begin in then-modern times and tell their stories through flashbacks.
- Both are based on literary properties, *White Cliffs* on a poem by Alice Duer Miller and *Mrs. Parkington* on a Louis Bromfield novel.
- Both are stories of young, inexperienced girls aging into elderly women over a long lifetime.
- Both women undergo loss and sacrifice, with *White Cliffs*'s heroine losing both her husband and her son to war, and *Mrs. Parkington* suffering a miscarriage and later the death of a son.
- Marriage removes both women from the world they know and takes them into a world of wealth and privilege that they were not born into.
- Neither woman has a mother.
- Both women find unexpected allies in relationships with other women who should have been rivals or adversaries. Garson finds true friendship and sisterhood with her husband's former mistress, a French woman played by Agnes Moorehead. Dunne finds a deeply devoted relationship with her husband's mother (Gladys Cooper), a woman who at first resents having an American daughter-in-law from a different class.
- Both women are strong, clever, and decisive—they are survivors.

These movies define their heroines in ways that both men and women could admire: as spunky, brave women who love their men and accept whatever fate deals them. There appear to be no real contradictions, and yet, as one watches the films carefully, one can see how clearly it is suggested that it is women who understand things and who must make all the decisions. This is particularly true in *Mrs. Parkington*, in which women are shown to be manipulating everything behind men's backs. The suggestion that women should be loving and dutiful, putting their men first, is undercut by the idea that women should be in charge of things. *Mrs. Parkington* has Greer Garson speak openly to her husband, saying that she is ashamed to be his wife. "I'm just a woman to you. Someone you can pick up and put down in your house. Someone you can turn on or off like gaslight. . . . I always felt that a real wife was a . . . well, a partner, who knows what her husband does and what he thinks . . ." She educates him to be a better man, one who can appreciate a fine woman such as herself. In both films, the heroine is told by another woman, "You're showing no courage. You must go on." Whereas Loretta Young and Katharine Hepburn had to go on because it was wartime and events required women to set aside feminine concerns, Irene Dunne and Greer Garson are forced to go on because they are women who have no other choice in life. Instead of dealing with the Japanese army, Dunne and Garson deal with the problems indigenous to the woman's world. Dunne faces the death of her husband in World War I, and Garson faces the loss of her son. Dunne is told she must go on for the sake of her newly born son, and Garson is told she must go on for the sake of her husband. Dunne and Garson face the female crisis: the men matter more than they do. And yet the two women, strong and central to all events in the film, end up fully in charge of the worlds in which they live. Mrs. Parkington ends her life as an imperious old woman, in full control of the family finances, happy enough with her memories, although disappointed by the weaknesses of her surviving children. She states the typical woman's motto: "There's nothing more important than being with the man you love." Irene Dunne's character ends her life as a woman running a Red Cross hospital during World War II. Neither woman has a husband any longer, and both will have had a son die before "The End" appears on-screen. They are essentially alone, but accept this fact with strength and optimism.

Within one year, American women could go to the movies and see Loretta Young, Katharine Hepburn, Greer Garson, and Irene Dunne determining the outcome of all events, overcoming all enemies, and prevailing through days of hardship and woe. In all four cases, whether the movie was liberating or restricting in its main surface story, the woman herself was a strong and intelligent creature, a positive identification point for female viewers.

STEREOTYPES

Some day my prince will come.
—Lyric from SNOW WHITE AND
THE SEVEN DWARFS (1938)

IN *Her Majesty, Love* (1931), Leon Errol offers the opinion that all females can be divided into three groups: "ladies, women, and cuties." Furthermore, he has advice for men on how to handle them. "Never mistake a lady for a woman, a woman for a cutie, or a cutie for a lady." After thinking about it awhile more, he adds thoughtfully, "Of course, there are ladies who behave like ladies, dress like women, but are cuties inside, and there are cuties who dress like ladies, but act like . . ." He has pinpointed one of the problems for scholars who want to find convenient labels for the characters women play in movies. There are all those subtle nuances of behavior . . . those sudden character changes and repentances . . . those whores who are really mothers, and mothers who are really whores . . . those nuns who put on lipstick when left alone in their cells . . . and all those tomboys and doctors and scientists who fit no easy category.

Most of the writing and thinking done on the subject of the image of women in movies has logically concerned itself with the considerable stereotyping of the woman's role that the screen has presented or with the unacceptable victimizing of women that occurs with such appalling regularity. Indeed, because women from the thirties through the fifties were being asked to conform to an accepted pattern of social and moral behavior in real life, it was inevitable that films would reflect those patterns. It becomes easy to label characters sexually ("virgin" or "whore"), parentally ("mother" or "daughter"), or connubially ("wife" or "old maid"). These labels provide a quick reference for viewers as to what the character's status is vis-à-vis men, marriage, and motherhood, the big three of the woman's world. What has not been written about often is how easily women in a single story could be *both* virgin and whore, or wife and daughter, or mother and whore, or daughter and old maid. Woman's mobility in terms of switching her labels is a fascinating aspect of popular movies. When a whore becomes a mother, she has traded up. When a wife becomes a whore, she has traded down. When an old maid is not a virgin, she is one kind of old maid; when she is a virgin, she is another, and so on.

Assuming that movie females were never anything but mothers, virgins, or whores overlooks the subversive agendas such roles may have contained, and it becomes an oversimplification of a complex visual world in which strong women were often seen struggling against such labels or complaining that those were their only options. Even if they *were* only mothers, virgins, or whores, they were often nevertheless intelligent, dynamic, and well aware that these labels were a sham, a cheat, and certainly a dead end.

Such an assumption also does not address the purpose behind the depiction of women. The function of the woman's film was to articulate female concerns, angers, and desires, to give substance to a woman's dreams and a woman's problems. This, as has been established, meant putting a strong woman at the center of things in order to carry the plot. Thus, it was easiest to label stereotyping of women through describing the secondary characters or by studying movies that presented multiple females in the plot rather than one dominant female character. This stereotyping was almost always linked to sex, to the woman's biological function, or to how she looked physically. In film after film, there were parades of fat women, bossy women, gossipy women, jealous women, mean women, cheating women, almost all of whom were presented as sexually unattractive, sexually overactive, or sexually repressed. It was when a woman was *not* the center of the universe but only a secondary character that one saw the true ugliness, the real repression. Even in films about strong women, negative stereotyping regarding secondary characters could appear. A good example of this is *Ladies of the Jury* (1932), in which the intrepid Edna May Oliver plays a society doyenne with top-drawer brains who sits on a jury and dominates the situation. Five other jurors are standard female types:

1. A plain, masculine woman, unmarried
2. An Irish washerwoman, a motherly figure
3. A cheap floozy, chewing gum
4. A mousy librarian type, sensitive and scared
5. A married southern belle, who talks about her husband all the time

Here we see a lineup of conventional attitudes toward women. If a woman is like a man, no one will marry her (1). If she is bookish, she will be mousy, and no man will marry her (4). If she is Irish, a man will have married her, but she will have tons of children, and they will define who she is (2). If she is a beautiful belle from the South, a man will marry her, but she will be stupid and dominated by her husband (5). If she is cheap . . . well, she will chew gum. What she really does cannot be shown on the screen, so gum chewing becomes an effective shorthand for: she does something physical with great enthusiasm (3). Hidden in the stereotypes, as the woman must hide, is the meaning society wants to impose. These secondary women are *not* the brave, strong creatures of the woman's film.

Ladies of the Jury presents these stereotypical women struggling to make a decision regarding a trial over a woman's crime. (Ex–chorus girl shoots husband.) Of all the women described, only Edna May Oliver has the brains to realize that the ex–chorus girl didn't really do it. She alone votes not guilty, but why does she vote not guilty? "Woman's intuition," she explains. *Ladies of the Jury* also presents the men on its jury as stereotypes. The male characters include:

1. A pathetic stutterer, who is dominated by his wife
2. A belligerent former soldier, married to a Frenchwoman he met in World War I
3. A sensitive poet
4. An academic, flowery-talking man

5. An Italian ethnic
6. The jury foreman, an ugly macho type who judges the chorus girl, calling her a fallen woman
7. A real estate salesman, a go-getter with a cigar always jammed in his mouth

In comparing the male and female stereotypes, one sees that both are defined by sex and marital relationships. Just as the women are defined by men, the men are defined by women. The Irish woman equals the Italian man for ethnic stereotyping. The masculine unmarried woman (hint: lesbian) is equated with the sensitive male poet (hint: homosexual). The man who stutters because his wife is bossy (she shouldn't do that) is offset by the jury foreman who cruelly and incorrectly judges the ex–chorus girl (he shouldn't do that). The gum in the mouth of the floozy equals the cigar in the mouth of the salesman. The gushing of the southern belle is the flowery talk of the academic. These things clearly mark *Ladies of the Jury* as a woman's film, because *all* the characters are defined by their attitude toward the woman's role or by their relationship to women.

In the end, the hero of the film, by process of elimination, is a woman, Edna May Oliver. She *is* the strong central woman of the film, a problem solver, and also the motivator of the action. This more or less proves that *Ladies of the Jury* is a woman's film. However, the covert subtext of the movie is a desire to prove certain stereotypes wrong and to suggest that judging people by them, or on false information, is a wrong thing to do. The courtroom trial provides a perfect metaphor for this. *Ladies of the Jury* effectively uses familiar attitudes among the viewers and knows it can count on the audience to respond to the plot in a specific way because of them. The irony is that stereotypes motivate and make possible a plot in which the idea of making a decision based on a stereotype about a woman is proved to be wrong. (The ex–chorus girl didn't do it. Edna May's intuition is right.)

A stereotypical presentation of the woman's role in life is seen through a single female secondary character in *The Cavern* (1966). When a group of men is accidentally trapped underground by bombs during World War II, one woman is entombed with them. Instead of becoming merely a love interest, this lone female provides the motivation for all the plot developments. She does this by playing all the possible female stereotypes in the book. One woman fits all. While the men sit and think and try to figure out what to do to escape, she bustles around taking care of business. She takes the following actions, each representing a typical female role:

1. Tends wounds (nurse)
2. Kindly repulses the shy advances of a very young boy (mom)
3. Causes fights between the men (object to be won and owned)
4. Repulses real sexual advances and potential rape (sex object, victim)
5. Falls in love (romantic object)
6. Cooks and cleans (servant)

She does not do any of these things willingly or meekly, however. While serving the men coffee as they play cards (thinking has worn them out), she screams, "Lice! Amusing yourselves at cards. And me, I cook and slave for all of us and I clean for you like a servant. And you don't even look at me or say thank you. Lice!" *The Cavern* reduces the woman's role to its essence: the bag of stereotypes that women are often forced into in movies. Yet one cannot help noticing that the woman isn't happy about it. Her constant objections form a pseudofeminist and very angry under-current, and an audience is invited to see that she's right and to agree with her.

Representative women are used to define the woman's various approaches to sex and marriage in *The Long, Hot Summer* (1958), a movie loosely based on stories by William Faulkner. Four women illustrate varying attitudes toward sex and what it brings or fails to bring them. Two have embraced and accepted their sexual roles. Two have no sex in their lives. These characters are presented with subtle shadings.

The two women who represent sexuality are played by Lee Remick and Angela Lansbury. Remick is a young woman who is not only luscious and sensual, but also good-natured and loving. Her interests are only in clothes and the admiration that wearing them well brings her. She is married to a young man (Anthony Franciosa) who is besotted with her, and who, when he is not at work, chases her around constantly. Their relationship is portrayed as purely sexual, with the implication that, because Remick is always willing, she can get anything she wants from Franciosa. Lansbury is an older woman who has been the mistress of Orson Welles, a wealthy landowner, for years. She functions as his wife, cooking for him and taking care of him. They, too, are happy together, and Lansbury is portrayed as fulfilled as a woman by this relationship.

Neither of these women is, however, completely happy with her lot. Remick complains to Franciosa that since he is after her all the time she can't even get her hair washed or her nails done. Finally she has to tell him, "I certainly wish you'd find another form of recreation," even though she feels bad saying it. Her status as sex partner on a night-and-day schedule has gotten to her. Lansbury is unhappy because she wants marriage. She isn't getting any younger and is not satisfied just being the hired help. She lays down the law to Welles, insisting on having her way. Both these women end up with what they want by being strong enough to redefine their sexual roles on their own terms.

The two women who fear or reject sexuality are the leading lady, played by Joanne Woodward, and a minor character who is the mother of the man Woodward is scheduled to marry. The latter is possessive of her son, domineering with him. She is hanging on to him, keeping him from a normal sex life and marriage so that he will remain the man in her own life. There is no husband or father in sight in the film, and this woman is clearly presented as antilife. It is suggested to viewers that this is not how women should be.

Woodward's character is more complex. She is intelligent, strong-minded, and attractive, although not openly sensual or sexily dressed. Although she is repressed, she knows that what she really wants in life is to have a home of her own with a loving husband in a happy marriage. However, she wants this arrangement on her own terms, by which she means a man who is "decent" and preferably "poetic." She hates men who push, she says—a telling phrase. Her fiancé is an appropriately mother-dominated, nonpushy male, and they somehow never get around to anything sexual. Woodward's life is upended when she meets a drifter who comes to town (Paul Newman) and is confronted by a man who has real sexual energy. Woodward tries to deflect Newman's open advances by telling him that she's twenty-three years old and has been saving up for a wonderful relationship. He tells her that she's just waiting for something to happen and explains that she doesn't have to wait: it's all right there for her with him if she wants it, ready for the taking and for the pleasure. He suggests that they both give a little and then they'll both get a little. It would be a perfect arrangement: free and easy and fair and equal. Woodward has to become strong enough to accept the risk of a *real* relationship with a man.

The Long, Hot Summer is a film that reflects the beginning of a change in sexual attitudes. By suggesting, as it does, that Woodward ought to free herself from repression and accept sex with a man openly and freely, for pleasure and not just for procreation or marital duty, it indicates the start of the sexual revolution. However, it continues the pattern of using secondary characters as sexual stereotypes.

These stereotypes, which have been covered in other books,* are used to make the point that, in fact, men and women are not really equal. That is, society does not afford them equal freedoms, equal choices, or equal mistakes, because they have different biological functions. Women

---

* See Bibliography, especially *From Reverence to Rape*, by Molly Haskell, *Popcorn Venus*, by Marjorie Rosen, and *On the Verge of Revolt*, by Brandon French.

have to be very, very careful about sex, and thus most of the stereotypes are grounded in simpleminded sexual attitudes. This attitude has its own subversive side. Because women have to be very, very careful, they frequently become very, very smart at handling and manipulating men. Furthermore, in order to compensate for this inequality, films often suggest the ways in which woman are superior to men. Men are not the emotional equals of women. They don't catch on to things. They don't see the future (the Cassandra syndrome). They don't smell danger. They don't love as deeply and completely, and thus are less human. And, heaven knows, they don't sacrifice themselves as much, the noble thing to do. Men don't have women's intuition! Stereotypes serve this ridiculous need. They are placed at the service of the concept that women are superior because they are so willing to be inferior. A con job to end all con jobs, and yet an invitation to female viewers that endorses their strength and superiority.

NONSTEREOTYPES (WOMEN AS HEROES)

They've got brains that work standing up, too.
—SHE HAD TO SAY YES (1933)

THE *New York Times* once reported a conversation overheard on a busy city street between two men. One said to the other, "Did you ever stop to consider how different Emma Bovary's life might have been if she'd lived next door to Lucy and Ethel?" This is wonderful, but it misses the point. Lucy and Ethel are modern-day Emma Bovarys, two bored housewives who don't have enough to do all day and who want something more out of life. Since they are the traditional troublesome American kind of women, they cook up schemes to change things in our great entrepreneurial tradition. Instead of taking lovers, they steal John Wayne's footprints from Grauman's Chinese Theatre. Instead of running up debts, they try to earn money by getting jobs in a chocolate factory. Instead of encouraging provincial theatrics, they pretend to be two women from Mars. Like Emma, they never quite get out of their daily rut, but they soldier gamely on in the woman's eternal fight for attention and equality. Lucy and Ethel are heroic. They take action. Where Emma Bovary tried to change her life by buying a new chair, Lucy goes out and pretends to *be* a chair. It's demented, but it's not passive.

Much of the stereotyping of women in movies is related to passivity

—to the fact that female characters are often not allowed to take action. When a woman in a movie is merely decorative, she can easily be used as a sex object or as a victim in the plot. If her only function in the story is to give birth or to take care of the male hero until he goes out to do his thing, she has nothing to contribute. Such characters provide little of the covert level of subversion common to the woman's film. Because the woman's genre is trying to appeal to women by embodying their concerns, it not only has to present strong women but often has to depict strong, *active* women; that is, women who actually take specifically heroic action in the plot. The chapter "The Woman in the Man's World" will address films in which women actually become pirates, western heroes, or swordspersons. However, there are other, less masculine forms of action that women take, and these actions, while peculiar, mark them out as heroic.

What kinds of "female" action do women take in movies? A good example is the weird decision Joan Crawford makes in *Strange Cargo* (1940). As she and the hero huddle upstairs in her room, trying to figure out how to get rid of the villains who await them downstairs in the saloon where she is a singer, Crawford brilliantly devises a female strategy for action. "I'll go down and song 'em off!" she declares. This is put forth as reasonable—the woman's form of fisticuffs, in which she slinks down the steps in a low-cut gown and sings and dances at them. The hero finds this an excellent suggestion instead of the nutty plan it actually is. Audiences are asked to assume it will work, which, of course, it does as Crawford vamps forward in a very good dress and songs 'em off. Way off.

The woman in the woman's film does what she can according to the limits of who she is supposed to be inside the genre that has been generously bestowed on her as her own. A perfect example of this occurs in *Gremlins* (1984), a horror movie in which a woman does battle with hideous little beasts in woman's terms in a woman's territory: She uses her kitchen appliances to destroy them. In this sequence, the mother of the film's hero first does what women in horror films always do. She hears a noise and goes to see what it is. Down to the basement, up to the attic, or out to the garage, women always go to see. They are never satisfied to leave it alone, so this is proper woman's action. But why does our culture approve this as female behavior? Are women supposed to be stupid, or are they brave? Are they used to getting no help from the men in their lives, so they know they'd better deal with the problem themselves? Or are they just nosy? Whatever the answer, we accept certain forms of action from women, and this is one of them, allowing women to fulfill plot expectations by willingly going forward to become victims, eternally useful for their damage value.

As Mom "goes to see," she realizes there is trouble. She picks up a carving knife and advances toward her kitchen. Peeking around the corner, she sees one of the wretched gremlins eating the head off a gingerbread man. When the little beast bends down into her mixing bowl to eat the remainder of the cookie batter, Mom rapidly reaches around the corner and turns the machine on full force. He's mixed and blended, whipped and pureed. As one of his pals starts to throw dishes at her, Mom picks up a TV tray and advances on him, wielding her knife menacingly, using her tray as a shield. When she turns her back and is attacked from behind by yet another gremlin, she quickly grabs some household spray off the counter and sprays the creature, driving him backward toward her microwave oven. Then she shoves him inside and nukes him. This is an impressive combat sequence, in which a woman defends her domain, the kitchen, by using the woman's weapons, common household appliances that she operates every day: a set of sharp carving knives, a mixer and blender, a microwave oven, and one very durable TV tray.

These actions, of course, reflect the desperation of screenwriters as much as they define the role of women in society. There are serious movies in which women actually take on heroic dimensions, bursting forth from the boundaries of female behavior to become "female heroes," rather than "heroines." These characters are not stereotypes, even though some elements of their lives might be labeled as stereotypical.*

My definition of a hero who happens to be a woman is the same one I would make for a man. In an article for *Women and the Cinema*, written in 1977, I defined a positive portrait of a woman that could place her in the position of hero in the following way:

- A woman who defies conventional rules and redefines her life on her own terms, even if she opts to become a wife and mother (the process of questioning is what is of value)
- A woman who defies not just convention but society itself, never settling for less than possession of her own life, even if she is destroyed

---

* There is a subtle distinction implied here. Many brave and noble women are depicted in women's films who are heroines, not heroes. For instance, Claudette Colbert portrays a real woman in the stirring *Three Came Home* (1950), an excellent picture that depicts the lives of women incarcerated in a Japanese prison camp in North Borneo during World War II. Colbert is brave, and she withstands hardship and risks danger to sneak to a meeting with her husband (who is in the nearby men's camp). She shows exceptional courage in meeting her husband, in caring for her sick child, and in standing up to deprivation and bad treatment. ("I never knew you were a woman of steel," she's told, and she wryly replies, "I'm not. I'm a woman of tin foil.") However, she is brave as a woman is brave about things that are presumably a woman's concerns. She does not organize a prison escape or take action that might be considered the prerogative of a male movie hero. The film is based on real life, and Colbert plays the role honestly. As a narration says, "The men waited because it was their duty; the women because it was their choice." The women I am referring to as heroes go farther toward a liberated viewpoint or toward a defiance of restrictions.

in the fight (a man who fights this way is called a hero; why not a
woman?)

- A woman who, by choice or by accident, finds herself in a situation
  or profession that would be commonly restricted to male participation,
  and who functions ably in this situation (she must not be caricatured
  as choosing this endeavor because she is "unwomanly" or "frigid")
- A woman who forms and maintains a positive sisterly relationship or
  a healthy mother-daughter relationship

Typical examples of each of these categories exist. Two women who
defy conventional roles are Barbara Stanwyck in *My Reputation* (1946) and
Jane Wyman in *All That Heaven Allows* (1955). Both are young widows who
are encouraged to accept lives of quiet boredom, belonging to women's
clubs or perhaps remarrying dull, acceptable suitors. Both are also encouraged to live for their children, only to discover that the children have
their own lives, their own friends. Both live in wealthy homes and are
surrounded by a country club social set; but with no real role to play in
life, they feel alone and alienated. Both films clearly depict how women,
still young and attractive, find out just how much of a man's world they
had really been living in. Suddenly, they are "extra" women, prey to smarmy
husbands of friends who try to instigate affairs (in Stanwyck's case) or to
cruelly gossip (in Wyman's case). The social world is organized around
couples, and women of good manners and respectable breeding aren't
supposed to go places alone. They become trapped in their beautiful,
elegant homes. Stanwyck's mother does not approve of her having dates,
and Wyman's children smugly believe that her job is to sit home by the
fire and be Mother rather than a sexual partner for someone or a person
with her own interests. In a terrifying scene, they present her with a gigantic
television set, companion enough for her old age. As they leave for their
own busy social lives, Wyman sits alone, dejected, her face reflected in
the empty screen of the huge set. Both widows choose to defy society,
embarking on love affairs with what their group would consider inappropriate men. Stanwyck becomes involved with a military man (George Brent)
whose morals are no better than they should be. He is not really interested
in marriage, but would enjoy having a mutually satisfying sex relationship
with Stanwyck, and he makes his intentions clear. Wyman falls in love
with her gardener (Rock Hudson), a man who is not only younger than she
is, but who clearly is not on her social level. Neither woman caves in to
pressure from family, and, although their choices are about men and love,
they are questioning the traditional lives women are asked to lead and
exhibiting bravery in rejecting these lives.

Female heroes turn up in strange places, played by unexpected actresses. Consider a film in which the following argument takes place between a young man and woman, regarding how he feels when she refuses to quit her job or give up attending suffragette meetings:

HE: It's an indication. Cynthia, you *must* consider my feelings in this. It's different now. We're going to be married. If you continue to work and be a suffragette leader as my wife, I'll be the laughing-stock of Boston.

SHE: Is it so important what people say?

HE: . . . they [women who are wives] have to be willing to give up outside interests.

SHE: But *why* is it always the woman who has to change her way of living and thinking? Equal rights is not a habit like biting your nails. It's a principle, and you don't give up principles overnight. This concerns a handful of women who are devoting their lives to an ideal, because they believe in it, deeply, fervently. I can't let them down.

HE: Oh, it's nothing but a lot of childish nonsense, run by a collection of frustrated old maids who haven't got anything else to espouse.

SHE: . . . This is a fundamental difference in the way we see things . . .

HE: But we're going to be married! You'll be Mrs. Pritchard!

SHE: You keep saying that as if you had just bought me in the slave market. I have no intention of becoming anyone's chattel. I'm exactly the same person I was before you proposed. I have the same hair, the same eyes, the same voice . . . and the same unshakable conviction that women should have equal rights!

Who would one imagine enacting this discussion? Spencer Tracy and Katharine Hepburn? George Brent and Bette Davis? Clark Gable and Joan Crawford? Cary Grant and Rosalind Russell? It happens to be a serious, straightforward argument between Dick Haymes, the singer, and Betty Grable, the pinup girl of World War II, in a Technicolor musical comedy called *The Shocking Miss Pilgrim* (1947). Its leading lady, Cynthia Pilgrim, is a hero. And she never gives up.

The movie begins with a title card that announces "On July 4, 1776, men became free. On January 1, 1863, slaves became free. On June 10, 1874, women became free . . . or at least independence winked at them for the first time. Not because Congress passed a law, but because of the newly invented typewriter which was called most impractical . . . and a handful of daring young ladies who were called . . . any number of things." The movie then introduces Betty Grable, the woman graduating Number One in her class at Packard Business College, where a group of eighteen (both men and women) are the first people in the world to have been trained to use typewriters. The head of the college, a man, tells them about their responsibilities in this regard, adding that "on you ladies falls an additional responsibility. Until now, the business world has been a man's world. If you fail, it will remain so. I hope you succeed. Godspeed."

Grable is sent to Boston, where she encounters masculine prejudice from her boss, Dick Haymes, who wants to renege on the hiring. However, his aunt, who owns the company, insists that Haymes keep Grable on for a trial run. Grable cleverly and patiently wins her male coworkers over through her sense of humor and her thoughtfulness, but mostly she succeeds by being good at her job. There *are* small touches that pander to a traditional audience, as when Grable's ankles are exposed or when she lifts her skirts to fix a run in her stocking, giving the audience its only brief glimpse of her famous legs. On the whole, however, Grable is presented as intelligent, strong, and heroic in her determination to represent women well in the job market and to help others to achieve the same goal. Grable is never humiliated or ridiculed. She voices her philosophy about suffrage: "You can't force suffrage down men's throats. You can't gain equality with brass bands and speeches. Women have got to earn equality. That's why I became a typewriter. To show men that women can do men's work. But equality in the office isn't all. It's not enough. Women have to go into other fields of endeavor and gain equality there, too, and then suffrage will be a natural conclusion." When her boss suggests that she not wear her severe dark blue outfit to work anymore (a fashion note!), he tells her that "it gives you a domineering quality and a severity that I've just discovered is not only misleading, but quite untrue." She explains that "the girls in New York discovered that if they dressed attractively, the men never thought they had any brains. They consider all women unintelligent, and a typewriter even more so."

Although Grable and Haymes fall in love, singing romantically to each other, the plot mainly reveals how she does a splendid job in his office, and how she becomes very active in the suffragette movement, speaking at rallies around the state. One of these meetings is shown in detail, and the women are presented as gentle caricatures. They are mostly odd sizes, odd shapes, and odd faces. They sing a silly but triumphant song: "Stand up and fight! We've got the right. Like it or not, men have got, to take the view, that women are people, too." They ask musically why women can't be judges, engineers, and book reviewers, building to their final question: "Aren't women human beings?" One sees how movies, by setting such issues inside musical comedy and expressing them through lyrics sung by funny-looking women, pull the punch out of strong messages of liberation. However, *The Shocking Miss Pilgrim* actually steers a straight

Betty Grable at the typewriter in *The Shocking Miss Pilgrim*.
Gene Lockhart oversees.

course toward its main point, which *is* equality for women and, indeed, that women are people, too.

Since the movie is a love story, Cynthia is shown trying on her suffragette sash (over the severe blue dress Haymes objected to) to prepare for a meeting, but instead of seeing herself in her mirror, she sees Dick Haymes, singing, "For you, for me, forevermore." In a traditional film, this would be an indication that Grable would eventually give up her job for him, but *The Shocking Miss Pilgrim* is not really a conventional film in its presentation of its heroine, although it is a conventional musical in every other way.

After Grable and Haymes fall in love and he proposes, they have the argument described earlier. As a result, Grable leaves his office, and Haymes hires a series of incompetent men, followed by a series of unattractive women. Finally, in despair, he and his office manager go to a newly opened secretarial school to find someone suitable. Once there, Haymes is asked to respond to a questionnaire. A prim young woman asks him, "Do you have any objection to hiring a married woman?"

"No," he replies, "I've come to the conclusion they have a perfect right to work if they want to."

As the questions continue in this vein, and he admits each time that he has accepted the idea of women as equals, he suddenly becomes suspicious. Who made up these questions, anyway? The general manager of the school, Miss Cynthia Pilgrim. Grable is running the school and waiting for him inside. "You knew I'd come around to your thinking, didn't you?" he asks, and to conclude the film on its own generic terms, they sweetly reprise an earlier love song, in which he sings, "Unfortunately we had to break up," and she sings, "Eventually I knew you'd wake up," and they both sing, "But aren't you kind of glad you did?" It's musical sugarcoating, but Cynthia Pilgrim has won the day. She has *not* given up her work. She has *not* said she'll marry him and forget all about women's rights. She has made him see it her way. She is a hero.

Another heroic woman is Pamela Thistlewaite, the strong character played by Katharine Hepburn in *A Woman Rebels* (1936). This movie, set, as audiences are told, "in the middle of the Victorian era," clearly establishes itself in feminist terms. "Don't let him make you cry," Hepburn advises her sister, played by Elizabeth Allan. "No matter what he says, don't. That's what he likes." These words are an admonishment from one female to another not to take it from a man. In this case, the man (Donald Crisp) is father to the two young girls, and he instructs their teacher and chaperone to read aloud to them from Mrs. Ell's *True Daughters of England*. She reads:

> As women, the first thing of importance is to be content to be inferior to men, inferior in mental power in the same proportion that she is inferior in physical strength. A really sensible woman feels her dependence. She is conscious of her inferiority and therefore grateful for support.

These words, as foolish as they are ungrammatical, do not sit well with Hepburn. "I don't believe it! It's nonsense!" is her comment. Sent to bed without her supper, Hepburn pursues this line of thinking, pointing out to her more timid sister that she isn't afraid of her father. In fact, she doesn't even like him. The two sisters support each other, aided by their faithful old servant, Betty (Lucile Watson), who sneaks food in for Hepburn. The three women are a unit of sisterhood, both literal and figurative.

A Woman Rebels tells the story of Pamela, who like many other movie women mistakes love for freedom and a man for salvation. When Hepburn becomes pregnant from an affair with Van Heflin (who forgot to tell her he was married), she goes to Italy where her now-married and also pregnant sister, Elizabeth Allan, lives, the faithful Betty accompanying her. In a set of plot complications that can only be called convenient, Allan's husband is killed, and she falls down the stairs when she hears the news, terminating her own pregnancy. Just before dying, Allan makes Hepburn promise to return to England with her baby, who Hepburn can claim is her niece.

Hepburn takes up this ruse, which allows her to keep her child. As she travels homeward, Herbert Marshall, a new man in her life, tells her she's "different from any woman I've ever known. Honest. Forthright. Independent. Nothing helpless about you." Hepburn replies, "Don't you think that 'dependent' myth about women is one that men created for their own protection?"

When she tells him she will live alone in London, he says, bewildered, "Well . . . uh . . . what will you do?"

"Work," she says.

"*Work???*" Marshall is incredulous.

"Why not? You do," Hepburn softly comments, adding, "I'll tell you a secret, Mr. Lane. Even though I'm a woman, I have brains and I intend to use them."

The next third of the movie is devoted to the story of how Hepburn takes over a little newspaper about needlepoint and cooking, *The Ladies' Weekly Companion*, and turns it into a feminist publication called *The New Woman*. She herself writes the articles "Why Can't a Woman Be a Mother and Still Have a Career?" and "Why Must Women Be Denied the Benefits of Healthy Exercise?" and "The Woman of Today" and "Against Child Labor." She has been inspired to devote her life to this cause by meeting another young unmarried woman who has borne a child. After this poor creature kills herself because she does not have the money (or the plot developments) to get away with it as Hepburn herself has, Hepburn finds her true calling in helping other women. She refuses to marry her faithful suitor, Marshall, even though she does love him, in order to accomplish her feminist goals. "I need no one," she has said. "I'll go on by myself." And she does. Of course, Marshall remains at her side over the years, even though he lives in Italy, and she has her child, even though she can never tell anyone the little girl is actually hers and not her dead sister's. ("You can't, my dear," Betty has told her. "That is your punishment.")

Hepburn's story in *A Woman Rebels* is truly one of a woman who rebels strongly against society and against the restriction of a woman's life. The film is openly on the side of a liberated life for women. Yet it still maintains the theme of sacrifice, in that Hepburn feels she cannot marry Marshall because if the truth about her ever comes out, it might ruin his career. In the end, a scandal erupts involving Hepburn and her former lover Heflin, and Hepburn allows her own name to be tarnished in order to protect her daughter from the taint of illegitimacy. By that time, the girl

is a grown woman, and Marshall and Hepburn have gone twenty years
without love. Marshall simply tells the girl that she is really Hepburn's
daughter, thereby violating one basic rule of the woman's film, which is
never to tell the truth. As Hepburn finally agrees to marry Marshall, and
the daughter accepts her as her true mother, Hepburn goes to Marshall
near tears. "These modern women are so weak," he says in an ironic tone.
"Aren't they?" she replies, equally ironic.

Despite her rebellion, Hepburn does have to live the usual woman's
life, in that society finally punishes her, having missed its chance while
she was young. "Leader of Women's Movement in Society Scandal," say
the headlines. Her father, who suddenly reappears in the movie, is angry
with her, but she tells him off. "It's time that you learned that women are
human beings. Have feelings. Get lonely. It's because you wouldn't make
allowances for that that this has happened. You had nothing but coldness
and indifference for Flora and me because we were girls. . . . Women are
beginning to have some standing. Not enough. But some." She takes credit
for at least some of that change and feels satisfied with what she has chosen
to do with her life.

Although Hepburn finally agrees to marry Marshall at the end of the
movie, she has done so on her own terms, after devoting her life to her
own career and to helping other women realize their potential. She has
been decisive, brave, and independent all through the film, including the
moment when she had to face her single pregnancy alone. She qualifies as
a strong hero, taking life on her own terms and fighting for the things she
believes in whether society agrees with her or not.

Perhaps the oddest female hero in the history of movies is a character
who probably no one would define as a hero, but one who, nevertheless,
fits the bill. She is Rosa Moline, the grotesque creature played by Bette
Davis in the much maligned *Beyond the Forest* (1949). If Paul Newman in
Cool Hand Luke (1967) is a hero because he knows he'll lose but fights
the system anyway . . . and if T. E. Lawrence is a hero because he leads
the Arabs to violence and destruction . . . and if Charles Laughton is a
hero when he murders his horrible wife in *The Suspect* (1944) . . . then
Rosa Moline, a murderous fighter who wrecks the lives of people around
her, is a hero, too.

Beyond the Forest begins with one of those title cards that women's
films often use to advise the audience of the proper attitude it should take
toward what will follow: "This is the story of evil. Evil is headstrong—is
puffed up. For our soul's sake, it is salutary for us to view it in all its
naked ugliness once in a while. Thus may we know how those who deliver
themselves over to it, end up like the Scorpion, in a mad fury stinging
themselves to eternal death." This superb statement justifies our enjoyment

at watching "evil," which in this case is nothing more than a woman who refuses to accept the role society defined for her. An evil woman, it seems, is "puffed up." In other words, she is uppity, a female who rejects her natural job of wife and mother.

The story takes place in a perfect woman's world, the small town of Loyalton, Wisconsin, a sawmill town where, if the residents have bedrooms that face the mill, they have to draw black shades at night to keep the glow from the sawdust incinerators from keeping them awake. As the film opens, a trial is taking place, and the narrator explains, "The women of the town are all here, all wondering if at last they're going to learn the secret of Rosa's life. What makes her different from the rest of them?" These women have left their housework, their dirty dishes in the sink, their unwashed children, to come downtown to hear the truth about Rosa Moline. She is a woman who has the finest house in their town (which is not a very fine house; in fact, it is the place that inspired Davis's famous line, "What a dump!"). She even has a maid, a sullen Native American played by Dona Drake. However, she is on trial for murder, and everyone agrees she is "different." Why? they want to know.

As the trial begins, a flashback takes a viewer five months into the past to learn Rosa's story. She is, quite simply, a woman bored to the breaking point with her dull marriage to a kindly country doctor (Joseph Cotten). Rosa wants more from life. "Life in Loyalton," she says, "is like sitting in a funeral parlor waiting for the funeral to begin. No. Not sitting. Lying in the coffin and waiting for them to carry you out." Her husband does nothing but work, she says, implying that they have no sex life. She is different, she says, from all the other women in town, and this seems to be her only hope: If she truly *is* different, as she believes, she can get out of town and also out of the woman's traditional role of wife and mother. From the moment the flashback begins, with the sight of Rosa plucking her eyebrows beside a rushing river while her husband and a pal happily cast for fish, it is made clear to viewers that Rosa is obsessed with escape. When the men throw a small fish back in the water, she cries out, "Go, go, little fishie . . . while you've still got the pep to get somewhere." This determination to get free is the thing that makes her different.

Unbeknownst to either her husband or his pal, Rosa has engineered a tryst with a wealthy Chicago industrialist, played by David Brian, who frequently comes up to Wisconsin to hunt and fish from his posh lodge ("20 rooms, 18 bathrooms"). Davis and Brian effectively enact a pair of cheap lovers, both of whom have fought to get more out of life than their low-level upbringing meant them to have. In Brian's case it has been a successful fight, because he is a man. He is rich and powerful and ruthless, greatly admired for his money and success. Davis, however, is both ridiculed and treated with contempt for her desires. "You're something for the birds, Rosa, something for the birds," her husband's pal (Minor Watson) tells her. Brian and Davis demonstrate what it is that brings them together in a brief exchange that represents their sordid, sadomasochistic, but passionate affair. When Davis abruptly and harshly demands, "I want you to marry me," Brian laughs. His laugh is full, open, cruel, and demeaning. It comes from deep inside him as if he has just heard the world's funniest joke. Without hesitation, Davis moves to him and slaps him, giving him a truly hard crack across the face. Immediately following this exchange of contempt and anger, they sweep together into a hot and steamy kiss.

Later, Brian asks Davis why, if she wants out of Loyalton so badly, she hasn't simply gotten out on her own. "What as?" she asks. "A telephone girl? A stenographer? A waitress?" She understands the limitations of the jobs available to women like her. "You could get me out," she says, realizing that it would take his kind of money and his kind of power to elevate her out of the situation she is stuck in through the simple fact of being a woman.

Rosa Moline never shuts up about how limited she thinks being a woman is. When her husband proudly tells her, "I just saved a woman's life," she snaps, "Saved her for what?" Although she constantly remarks that she is different, that she is proud to be different, that she is unlike the other women in her world, Rosa's problem is that, like Emma Bovary before her, she has a very narrow idea of what being different might mean. With no education and no role models, she assumes that getting out or being different means serving chicken à la king on toast and having a mink coat. "If I don't get out of here, I'll die," says Rosa. "If I don't get out of here, I *hope* I die. And burn."

When Rosa finally gets to Chicago, where, she believes, she will join her lover and get free of Loyalton forever, she finds that David Brian has fallen in love with a young society woman. "She's like a book with all the pages uncut," he gushes. "Yeah! And nothin' on them," replies Davis. When Brian finally offers Davis money to terminate their affair, she cries out in rage, "I came here! Dragged myself on my hands and knees with no pride. Me! Rosa Moline! And you don't want me. I'm not good enough. You taught me my place, all right." She gets out of his car and walks in the rain, telling herself, "Any other woman would have taken the money. But I'm not just any woman. I'm Rosa Moline." Over and over again in the film, Bette Davis's character states that she is Rosa Moline. The constant repetition of her name becomes an attempt to empower herself as more than just a small-town woman, to make herself into somebody.

Rosa's tragedy is that her trip to Chicago ends in a nightmare of rejection as she tries to sit in a bar but is told that she cannot be there without an escort . . . as she walks on the street and a low-class man approaches, trying to pick her up by saying he's got "a coupla bucks" . . . and as she bumps into a policeman while an old whore laughs at her terror. Defeated and broken, she returns home. As her husband takes her back and puts her to bed, she says coldly, harshly to him, "I want you to kiss me." When he hesitates, she says, "Don't you want to?" He forcefully embraces her, and as they kiss, the image dissolves into the sudden shock of an ax cutting into a tree with a terrible thwack! This direct editing introduces a scene in which Davis tells Cotten she is pregnant. She begins by telling him how she realizes the trees stand proud and tall for a time until someone comes along and puts "the mark of death on them." As she sits, looking broken and sad, she muses, "Someone says, it's your turn. Wonder if they know?" Cotten says that people never know, and she asks him, "See it on me?" When he looks blank, she continues, "Don't you see it? I'm going to have a baby." She has called her pregnancy "the mark of death," which is what it will turn out to be for her. After he digests this information, they go on with their conversation:

HE: Aren't you glad?
SHE: Not glad and not not glad.
HE: I should think a baby would make you happy.
SHE: Will it, Louis?
HE: It ought to. Why should you be different from any other woman?
SHE: I always thought I was. Now I'm like all the rest.

Rosa, however, gets another chance at her version of happiness. David Brian suddenly turns up in her life again, his young society belle having found him too crude, too ill-bred and unmannered for her taste. He has returned to his own kind, the passionate and low-down Rosa Moline. They plan to run away together to be married after a quickie divorce, but her husband's fishing pal becomes aware of their plot and won't let it happen. He tells Rosa that he will inform David Brian about the impending child unless she tells him herself. Rosa's solution is to go along on the hunt planned for the next morning and shoot the pal dead. It has been established throughout the movie that Rosa is a crack shot who has known how to hunt since she was a child.

The film then returns to present time, picking up Rosa's trial for this killing. The verdict is brought in as death by accident, and Rosa is allowed to go free. Brian then tells Davis that the two of them must wait "a couple of months" before they run away, because he doesn't want any dirt clinging to them. He does not know that Rosa shot the man on purpose, nor does he know she is expecting a child. Desperate, Rosa tells her husband that she and Brian are lovers and that she murdered his friend. "I've got more brains in my little finger than you've got in that whole stupid head of yours," she explains. Cotten, however, is determined. He wants his child. "You can go where you want to and do what you please . . . after you've had the baby." Rosa Moline says she'll kill herself first. True to her word, she lunges out of their car and throws herself down a cliff in an attempt to abort the child or die trying.

The next morning Rosa Moline wakes up in her bed with a satisfied, sensual smile on her face, her equivalent of the Scarlett O'Hara morning after. Realizing that she has indeed aborted and can now marry her lover, she moves deliciously in the bed and picks up her mirror and lipstick to make herself presentable. Her joy is short-lived, as she soon begins to "burn up" inside. After making herself up like a grotesque caricature of a woman, she staggers downtown to board the night train to Chicago in one last attempt to get out of Loyalton, Wisconsin, and to get free of a typical female life. As she approaches the station, the train sits on the tracks, smoking and hissing and belching like the Train to Hell rather than the night train to the Windy City. The train appears to be waiting for her, but like the treacherous male symbol it is, it pulls out and leaves her, abandoning her to her fate. After the train moves out, viewers see Rosa, lying dead alongside the track, having died from the pain of being a woman. In a perceptive article on the film's director, King Vidor, Eric Sherman says that Vidor "seems not at all concerned that we understand why she [Rosa] is this way," meaning why Rosa Moline is evil, desperate, murderous. Sherman is correct, but from a woman's point of view I would say that females in the audience understand exactly why Rosa Moline is "this way." No construction of an explanation is necessary other than her being a female character played by a woman. Rosa Moline didn't want to make her husband's nice dinner. She didn't want to have her husband's little child. She didn't want to be nothing or nobody. She was Rosa Moline, and she insisted that meant something. She fought on to the end, gallant but misguided, unwilling to accept repression and restriction. She's like Michael Corleone or Frankenstein's monster or Cody Jarrett. She may kill. She may look ugly. She may be something for the birds. But she never quits. Rosa Moline is an American hero.

THE RULES OF BEHAVIOR

You can't get away with things.
You're a girl, not a man.
—THE SINGLE STANDARD (1929)

THE WOMAN HERSELF in the woman's film, whether she is a stereotype or not, is a surrogate for the women in the audience. She lives through all kinds of plot shenanigans, representing female strength and enacting female anger and disappointment, and she also accomplishes one other important thing: she shows women what will work for them in the man's world and what will not work for them. Her experiences form a rule book of acceptable behavior for women, a kind of social survival kit. The whole point of the woman's film is not really represented by whether or not the woman character can be labeled "virgin" or "whore," but whether or not she is behaving by a larger set of rules for women. A virgin can be bad if she poisons men, and a whore can be good if she has a heart of gold, by which it is meant that she will step in front of a bullet meant for a man, sacrificing her life to save his.

The woman's film rule book of behavior tells women to be good or else. To accept their jobs as women or else. "Or else" is the plot. The basic rules are simple:

1. A woman must be a good sport. (Sacrifice is everything.)
2. A woman will need to lie in order to survive. (Deception is acceptable.)
3. A woman must not be evil. (Being evil for women means becoming powerful in some way.)
4. A woman must be initiated into what it means to be a woman. (She has to give up any power she was born with or assumed, become a good sport, lie as needed, and live by the rules of behavior.)

All this, of course, is subverted from film to film as is common to the genre.

Taking these things one at a time, one can ask the question: How does a woman become a good sport? She pretends everything is okay. When the man she loves marries another woman, her job is to go on loving him quietly in the background, bringing him pie and waiting for him to come to his senses. Love and pie are the same thing in the woman's world.

Donna Reed has to be a good sport in *Green Dolphin Street* (1947)

when the man she loves writes home from New Zealand, sending for Reed's
sister (Lana Turner) to journey out and join him to become his wife. Actually, he loves Reed, but he always did get the two sisters' names mixed
up! Imagine his surprise when Turner arrives. He has to be a pretty good
sport himself and marry her, but Donna Reed *really* has to be a good sport,
and so she becomes a nun, an appropriately religious form of good sportsmanship for women. (Others include volunteering to be a guinea pig for
any new serum developed, or becoming the first victim of my personal
favorite among movie inventions, the "inertia projector" from the last of
Ronald Reagan's Secret Service movies, *Murder in the Air*, 1940.)

Ginger Rogers has to be an awfully good sport when her beloved Joel
McCrea suddenly marries a rich bitch in *Chance at Heaven* (1933). Rogers
goes on cooking dinner for McCrea afterward. She also decorates his house,
helps him with his business, and brings over care packages containing his
favorite foods while his wife is out aborting the child he wants, without his
knowledge. Carole Lombard has to be a good sport in *In Name Only* (1939)
when Kay Francis refuses to give Cary Grant a divorce, even though she
really can't stand him, and Marsha Hunt has to be a good sport while Susan
Hayward sinks into alcoholism in *Smash-up, the Story of a Woman* (1947),
instead of helping her husband's career the way Hunt would do. Margaret
Sullavan has to be a good sport when her husband falls in love with Joan
Crawford in *The Shining Hour* (1938). To demonstrate her good attitude,
Sullavan makes close friends with Crawford, complimenting her on her
clothes and hair and posture, and then runs into a burning house merely
in order to die and remove herself from the competition. (Crawford's also
a good sport, though. She runs in and rescues Sullavan. It's a woman's
world one-upmanship.) So pervasive is this attitude that women even have
to be good sports after they die. In *Sentimental Journey* (1946) (remade in
1958 as *The Gift of Love*) and *No Sad Songs for Me* (1950), wives leave
behind plans for how their husbands can find love again without them,
ghoulish good sports reaching out from the grave. Good sports Joan Fontaine
in *Letter from an Unknown Woman* (1948) and Margaret Sullavan in *Only
Yesterday* (1933) are seduced and left pregnant by men they spend every
day waiting for and dreaming of, only to find that within a year or two these
men, when encountered, don't remember them. The ultimate in good sportsmanship is the woman who sacrifices her life for her married lover, so he
can maintain his good name, his beautiful home, and his children. Barbara
Stanwyck does this for Adolphe Menjou in *Forbidden* (1932) even donating
their child to his wife, and Irene Dunne, Margaret Sullavan, and Susan
Hayward, in varying degrees of loss, do this in the three filmed versions
of Fannie Hurst's *Back Street* (1932, 1941, 1961), a story that remained
popular with women for more than four decades.

What the many films that present such good sportsmanship on the part of women are really doing is showing that the woman herself, the central strong figure of the woman's film, is expected to sacrifice her own desires to those of a man or of society. This is part of the rules of behavior that women have to learn in order to survive, or at least to get along in the world. Those who do not become good sports but who fight circumstances (and many films show us that behavior choice) will suffer the consequences.

The strange thing about this sacrificial good sportsmanship is that in some perverse way it puts the woman in control. The female character is tough enough to survive the many disappointments that men who can't get names straight inflict on her. By choosing not to confront Lana Turner and tell her the truth, Donna Reed controls the destinies of both Turner and the man she goes out to wed; without consulting either of them, she determines that they will both be stuck in a loveless marriage for the rest of their lives. What the woman's film always accomplishes, even at its lowest and most depressing level, is the empowerment of a female figure who gets to decide how things will be. Martyrdom, yes, but perverse control.

There is one interesting subdivision of good sportsmanship that lets a woman out of her dependence on men—nobility. Such a woman goes out among mankind and does good instead of marrying. It is a form of sacrifice that makes a curious parallel to that of a male hero who runs into a burning building to save women and children or who remains alone, firing at the enemy, until he, too, dies in a last-stand form of nobility. The noble male either triumphantly survives, having performed a deed that reinforces his maleness and coincidentally performs a social function, or he dies to prove his bravery. The noble-woman form of the woman's film usually does not present her as either dying or saving the situation. Instead, she is presented as slogging on . . . and on and on. Thus, the noble woman is an eternal mother, or wife-in-perpetuity, destined to serve, sacrifice personal happiness, and devote herself to others through causes that are deemed suitable for the feminine presence. She loves and serves all men instead of just one, so it is all right for a woman to reject men and love if, suggest these movies, she has a higher purpose in mind, something that will serve other women, small children, or all humanity. Women of noble purpose are to be admired by everyone—not necessarily emulated, but admired. When a woman sacrifices her life as a woman to a higher purpose, movies step back and ask an audience, "Isn't she noble? Isn't she fine?" These movies tend to be biographical, as in stories about Florence Nightingale, Elizabeth Blackwell, Edna Gladney, and others. A typical example is the story of Nightingale made as *The White Angel* (1936), starring Kay Francis as the Heroine of the Crimea.

The White Angel begins with a title card: "Towards the year 1850,

England was at peace with the world. Her men were following her ships to the four corners of the earth, building the great empire that is Queen Victoria's monument. Women were only permitted to nod weak approval. In all England, only Her Majesty has the right to express herself with the independence of a man."

This will be a movie that clearly says that women's not being allowed to express themselves is wrong, wrong, wrong. Throughout its running time, it will clarify the issue of the woman's place in society by suggesting that those who try to restrict a woman, prevent her from doing meaningful work, are hopelessly misguided and, what's more, slowing the progress of civilization. All this is, however, placed within a very safe setting. It isn't "now," it's "then." It isn't Americans who are blocking a woman, it's the British. And it isn't the average woman who wants to do this, anyway; it's Florence Nightingale, a saint, a paragon, and certainly not the average woman—nor is she meant to be. She is noble. She is exceptional. She is fine. If another one like her comes along, we shall all be happy to welcome her contributions, but in the meantime, ladies, just take a look at how she suffers and ask yourselves if this is for you. How do *you* like the Crimea?

Nightingale's story is told through a series of long speeches and specific episodes that represent her advancement toward noble sacrifice and away from the conventional woman's life. The speeches trace the character's questioning of what she is being asked to do as a woman:

> *Regarding her piano lessons:* "I can't be satisfied with just playing well. It would be [a satisfaction] if I had a purpose in life. As it is, I never feel so useless, so devoid of any purpose as when I get up from the piano."
>
> *In response to being told that marriage will give her a purpose and she'll still have time to visit the poor:* "Yes, I suppose I could visit the poor as a hobby for a little while. In the end, when you're at the embassy [speaking to her prospective husband] I should be swamped with house, servants, and children. Mother likes it. That's why they can't understand me."
>
> *Commenting on the woman's life:* "Half our life is spent in waiting and doing nothing! That's supposed to be the whole duty of a woman!"
>
> *On being told she'll forget about nursing after she's married:* "I shall never be anybody's wife!"
>
> *On woman's need to work:* "How I envy the Queen, the only woman in England who does a man's work and is allowed a man's point of view."
>
> *On her choice to be a nurse:* "This is a whole-time job. It's my life. I chose it. I must give my life to humanity."

On being told she is out of place in the Crimean war zone, because it is a world of soldiers: "We are all soldiers."

The responses Florence Nightingale gets to these sentiments range from "Well, suppose we all go to bed and see how things look in the morning" to "Flo, dear. No opinions tonight." *The White Angel* expresses the idea that where most women's passion goes into love and marriage and motherhood, Florence Nightingale's goes into a higher cause, that of nursing. The impulse is the same, hers is just directed differently. She is not like a man, nor is she really different from other women, just pointed in another direction. She has decided to be noble, but it's okay because the way she has chosen is to be a nurse and take care of men. The rules of behavior allow this.

An ordinary woman who wishes to sacrifice herself to the greater good of society often has a more difficult time of it. With no historical real-life model to follow, the film can drop its nobility motif and shift the woman's desire to help into a somewhat more critical mode. An example of such a story is *Mountain Justice* (1937), starring Josephine Hutchinson as a mountain girl who becomes a nurse in order to form the Mountain Health Clinics, where children can be properly treated for medical problems.

Mountain Justice is a classic example of how a film accomplishes the two opposing purposes basic to the woman's film. Its heroine, the intrepid Ruthie, is placed in a story that initially defines her rebellion in terms of a father-daughter conflict. Her father wants her to remain ignorant and marry a rough mountain man he has selected for her. However, Ruthie has been away to school, partially completing a nursing course, and she has other ideas. She has her own acre of land that her grandfather left her, and she wants to sell it to start a clinic. Her father flat out says she cannot do this. His sentiments are echoed by the townspeople, who at various times remark, "'T'ain't seemly for a young woman like you to make yourself so forward among your elders" and "There's no holdin' that gal since she come home from nursin' school full of ideas." Ruthie's life changes in the way women's lives usually change. A man "from the outside" enters her life in the form of Paul Cameron, played by George Brent. (Sometimes it seems that the figure of George Brent *is* the figure of man in the woman's film.) He is a lawyer who has come to town to attempt to prosecute her father for shooting a man. No one takes this trial very seriously, since the jury members are all close friends of the father, and this form of killing is "the mountain way." However, Brent makes use of Ruthie's testimony against her father and wins his case. Her father is sentenced to six months in the county jail, with the sentence reduced to three before he even leaves town.

Mountain Justice: Josephine Hutchinson and Robert Barrat

Brent and Hutchinson fall in love, but he goes away to return to his work. While her father is in jail, Hutchinson sells her acre to fix up their mountain shack for herself, her mother, and her little sister. The shack becomes feminized with flowers, a phonograph, piano, little knickknacks on shelves, and photographs and reproductions on the walls. In a tragic and rather terrifying scene, the father cruelly and viciously destroys all this when he comes home from jail. This scene, in which a brutal man destroys female things, is a strong antimale commentary. The father (Robert Barrat) also demands that his daughter give him all the money left from her land sale, and then he strikes her.

Shortly after this, Brent returns to the mountains and proposes to Hutchinson, but she refuses him, saying that she simply cannot marry. She has to build her clinic. Later, she tells her mother about Brent's proposal and her refusal. Her mother advises her. "Why did you send him away? There's nothing more important to a woman than love. Nothin' . . . You're wrong, terribly wrong. You love Paul [Brent]. In your heart that's what you want, not the other. Get out of this place now. Marry Paul. It's the only way you'll ever have true lastin' happiness."

This mother's advice is a piece of cleverly constructed dialogue. It clearly defines love as the woman's career in the usual manner, reminding the young woman that marriage is her only chance for happiness. At the same time, it defines marriage as an escape hatch, the only one open to women. The mother's words "Get out of this place now" explain the real reason for Ruthie to marry. Escape. Couched in traditional romantic terms, the argument nevertheless hints at something more subversive. Furthermore, it is delivered by a woman who obviously has had nothing but misery in her marriage and whose advice by example isn't worth dirt.

After Ruthie is viciously whipped and beaten by her father, she and her mother sneak out in the night to the town's kindly doctor figure (Guy Kibbee) and his lady love, a spinster played by Margaret Hamilton. (This relationship, in which Kibbee keeps finding a way to postpone his marriage to Hamilton, is a comic subplot that is finally resolved by Hamilton's taking charge and publicly forcing the ceremony.) The two friends donate the money they've saved over twenty years for their marriage to Ruthie to finance her trip to New York to finish her nursing course. When Ruthie says she simply can't use their money, her mother takes charge in a speech that contradicts what she has said earlier about marriage:

> You can, Ruthie. You've got to. All my life, I've slaved, wantin' things, wantin' to do things. Never doin' 'em. Plannin'. First for myself and then for you. I never complained because they didn't come to me, but I prayed and prayed that they'd come to you. Ruthie! Don't let life cheat you like it has me. [*Turning to her friends, she pleads.*] She's got to go, Doc. Phoebe! Make her!

The three friends secretly put Ruthie onto the night train, and they watch her departure; the faces of the two women are a study in grief and female forbearance. Two older women who've accepted their fates and their disappointments have put a younger woman on the train to freedom.

Brent and Hutchinson are reunited in New York through the efforts of Mona Baris, the actress born to wear a necktie. Brent keeps begging Hutchinson to marry him, and she keeps on refusing "till my job's done." When Hutchinson even hurries back to the settlement house from a glamorous and romantic date with Brent, Brent complains to Baris about this dedication: "You women can rattle around more nonsense in your skulls." Baris replies, "Can't you realize that the sooner she gets this out of her system the sooner you'll be telling bedtime stories to little Camerons? Why don't you get smart?" Baris, who is independently wealthy, agrees to finance

Hutchinson's mountain clinics, and before departing, Hutchinson tries once again to explain to Brent why she simply can't marry him. "Paul, if I married you, I'd try to be happy, but an important vital part of me would be frustrated. Don't you see? I've just got to get it out of my system." He replies, "Well, maybe I'm stupid, but, Ruth, why don't you ensure your own happiness first?" She won't.

In this way, *Mountain Justice* works back and forth between delivering direct statements of a woman's need for independence and career fulfillment, and treating these things as something she should get out of her system. Although telling a story about a dynamic woman who fights to build a set of clinics and who bravely educates herself to do so, it is telling this story in the context of "but this is what she'll do while the faithful suitor who will never get tired of waiting waits."

Mountain Justice ends with Ruthie killing her father accidentally when he beats her savagely because she has tried to rescue her little sister, Bethie, from the same horrible marriage her father once tried to inflict on her. While the masculine Baris runs their string of clinics for her, Ruthie is tried for the murder, defended by George Brent. This time, he's not very successful, and she is found guilty and sentenced to twenty-five years in prison. When Brent first comes to help her, saying he will be her defense lawyer, Hutchinson suddenly crumbles, weeping on his shoulder and saying, "Ever since that night in New York, I've thought of nothing but you, wanting you. Wanting to feel safe and protected and loved. When I think that we might have been together all this time!"

The audience, of course, has seen no evidence of this on the screen during the time between the scene in New York and this scene in prison. Rather, it has observed a determined and strong Hutchinson build not one, not two, but three clinics and make them enormously successful. She has her own car, is well dressed, commands respect and attention, and she has gamely fought off her father's dastardly attack. (This is a truly brutal scene, not prettied up in its physicality.) She has also repaid the loan that Kibbee and Hamilton have made her, and she and Baris have a productive and mutually respectful friendship as they work alongside each other. None of this, however, apparently mattered. Unbeknownst to the viewers, she has been thinking of nothing but Brent.

When Brent pleads his case for Hutchinson before a hard-faced group of mountain men, he asks them how it would be if her father were on trial for killing her instead of vice versa. What would their verdict be then? Brent points out that an autopsy shows that her father did not actually die of the knocks on the head she administered to him in her struggle, but of a heart condition that had been stressed to its breaking point in the fight. He tells the men that, had he not had the heart attack, Ruthie's father surely would have succeeded in killing her. "What would your verdict be?" seems to focus them. They convict her.

Mountain Justice ends with a bizarre amalgamation of its divided loyalties trumped up as a rescue. When a lynch mob forms to string Hutchinson up, Phoebe rounds up the town's women to support her, reminding them of how she had saved their children with her health clinics. Brent, Guy Kibbee, Kibbee's best friend, and an unidentified father of one of the "saved" children join the lynch mob. They break into the jail with the group and rescue Ruthie, putting her in one of her clinic's vehicles and saying they'll drive her to the lynching site. (Since all the men are masked, no one knows who they are.) Instead, they drive her to a waiting airplane, where the townswomen, who helped plan the rescue, put her on the plane to fly away with Brent. "I hope you won't hold it against us for what some of the menfolks tried to do," their spokeswoman says. Ruthie's sentence is then commuted by the governor, and she and Brent prepare to marry.

"Darling, are you satisfied now—got it all out of your system?" asks Brent. Baris is running the clinics full-time, and Hutchinson seems cheerfully appeased. "If they [the clinics] succeeded, that's all I ever wanted." Brent hands her a gift, which she sees is called *The Wishing Book*. Inside it are the things he is giving her that represent the traditional woman's life:

1. Photographs of the two of them together, taken in a booth at the carnival the night they first met (love and romance)
2. A marriage license, with their names filled in (marriage)
3. The photograph of the posh and spacious home he has purchased for them (the setting for their potential family life)
4. Two tickets to Europe (proof they are about to have a Happy Interlude, an extended honeymoon trip)

Mountain Justice has come full circle, restoring itself to a conventional ending and a conventional attitude toward what will make a woman happy in life. In the mind's eye is the memory of the vicious father beating his daughter nearly to death and destroying her lovely things. In the memory linger her mother's words, "Ruthie! Don't let life cheat you like it has me!" and Ruthie's own comment, "Paul, if I married you, I'd try to be happy, but an important vital part of me would be frustrated." *Mountain Justice* has put the woman herself front and center to provide a covert voice of anger and liberation . . . and has reaffirmed the status quo for women. It is a real woman's film, its attempt at the nobility option aborted by true love.

• • •

GOOD SPORTSMANSHIP and its variation, the noble life of renouncing marriage for the greater good, are linked directly to the second rule of behavior for women, which is that of deception. In the movies, women always lie. In fact, one of the worst things any woman can do is tell the truth until the absolute last possible minute, at which point it becomes her moment of weepy confession, worthy of forgiveness. The need to deceive is indigenous to the woman's world. Deception is the makeup a woman puts on her own life story. Because of society's restrictions, women are often forced to live a lie, as polite society would shut them out if they knew the truth. For instance, in *Lady of Secrets* (1936) Ruth Chatterton pretends that her illegitimate daughter is her younger sister. Does the truth ever come out? Yes, late in Chatterton's life, but the decision is made not to tell the "sister" because it would be "too upsetting." The unwed Ann Harding gives her baby up for adoption in *Gallant Lady* (1934). Some years later, she accidentally meets the child and learns that his adoptive mother is dead. Does she try to reclaim her child in any sensible way? No, she hatches a scheme in which she can meet the adoptive father, Otto Kruger, and woo him into marrying her so she can become her own son's mother. When Kruger and Harding actually *do* fall in love, does she tell him that his son is really her own child? She considers it, discussing it with her faithful adviser, a drunken doctor played by Clive Brook. "You dope!" cries out Brook at the suggestion, appalled that she would be so foolish as to tell the truth. Harding marries Kruger and doesn't tell him. Of course, it is a waste of time to expect logic or truth in a film like *Gallant Lady*, which features an illegitimate birth, euthanasia, a decorating business, a singing Italian count, a bucket of fish, a chapel, and a plane crash; obviously, anything goes. But "Live a lie" does seem to be its best advice to the women in its audience.

Sometimes the chicanery is downright appalling, particularly when it is presented as if it were charming and lighthearted, as in *Every Girl Should Be Married* (1948), starring Cary Grant and Betsy Drake. The story is yet another of those Grant films in which his life is shattered by an irresponsible but allegedly lovable woman, as in *Bringing Up Baby* (1938) and *Monkey Business* (1952). Drake plays a shop girl whose spare time is spent looking for a perfect husband. She first spots Grant at a magazine stand in a drugstore. He looks to her like an ideal choice for a husband because, well, because he looks like Cary Grant. She does detailed research on him, finding out he is not married, is wealthy, and is a respected pediatrician. ("I know it's dreadful," she says about her determined library research, "but it's the kind of thing men force us to do. It's for his own good.") She finds out all his sizes, his likes and dislikes, his college and year of graduation, his hobbies and his daily schedule—and sets off in pursuit.

Every Girl Should Be Married makes comedy out of the idea that women are determined to marry and men want to avoid it. It suggests matter-of-factly that the only way to resolve this difference is for women to trick men. Women must use what power they have available, such as sex and home cooking, but they must have a *plan*. Women must treat the pursuit as if it were a business deal, all research, cleverness, deceit, and outmaneuvering the opponent.

In a key moment in *Every Girl Should Be Married*, Betsy Drake challenges Grant openly at a lecture he is giving. She delivers a speech that is an oddball mixture of feminist determination and a paean to a woman's right to cheat and lie as a basic rule for her behavior. When Grant tells her that she is objecting to man's old privilege of choosing his own mate, she gallantly responds:

> Who made that rule? Men, that's who. All the women in this room who admit to the fact that they deliberately went out and trapped their husbands without the men ever knowing it, please stand up. [All the women stand, laughing joyously at the opportunity to admit the truth.] Don't be too upset, Doctor. Women have found it necessary to use subterfuge and their own feminine devices for centuries, we just never thought it quite a good idea to tell you men about it.

Naturally, Grant ends up marrying Drake. In thinking about how this entanglement evolved, I am reminded about Alan Ladd's definition of a love affair in *Appointment With Danger* (1951): "It's what goes on between a man and a .45 pistol that won't jam."

According to the woman's film, the woman's life is almost always a life of deception. Deception is the woman's power maneuver, one of the few tactical weapons she has at her disposal no matter how rich or poor she might be, no matter how beautiful or unattractive. Telling lies and playing roles help her achieve her goals. This is a metaphor for the woman's world: to live a lie, repressing all instincts that are not considered appropriate, "feminine," or correct, so that the woman who deceives, who sets up an elaborate, lying scheme, is actually carrying out a basic metaphor of this world.

The double-edged meaning to the rules of good sportsmanship and deception is not only that they turn out to be the same thing, but that they both accomplish the same goal. They put the woman in control. Movies tell us that women should be good sports, sacrificing themselves to the greater needs and desires of men, and also tell us that they can lie in order to do this. Both strategies allow a woman to know more than any man about what is going on and to make the decisions regarding his life. Thus, such movies place women in the audience in the position of observing both their own repressions and their own paths to empowerment or freedom.

THE GOOD BEHAVIOR / bad behavior format is polarized in films about two types of females, the tomboy and the evil woman. They are opposites in that the tomboy is a female who can do all the things men do and frequently do them better. She realizes through the course of the film that she must relinquish her skills and accept her femininity. The evil woman uses her femininity against men or for the wrong purpose. She acts out rule number three, which teaches that women should not be evil. The tomboy acts out rule number four, as she shows viewers how a woman is properly initiated into her female life.

An evil woman may be defined as a female who, whatever the plot variation may be, is actually taking power into her own hands. She may kill, maim, or hurt men, or she may reject motherhood. She refuses to do her job as a woman. In other words, she is refusing to conform to the accepted standards of good behavior for women. She is not going by the rule book. She is *Bad*. That is to say, she does not do what society expects from a woman. She does not behave herself. Whereas it's okay for Katharine Hepburn in *Dragon Seed* to poison the Japanese army while the men stand around, it is not okay for Joan Fontaine in *Ivy* to poison her husband. Whereas it is okay for a woman to marry rich, it is dangerous for her to have her *own* money. Wealth creates a nightmare woman, even if she's basically a nice person. When Brian Aherne criticizes Joan Crawford in *I Live My Life* (1935) for spending "hundreds a year just on [her] fingernails," Crawford, a rich girl, scornfully retorts: "Hundreds? Hundreds? *Thousands!* And my eyebrows are hand-plucked. What of it?" The movie asks us all to stop and contemplate the sheer horror of this. When women have money, eyebrows will get properly plucked, but Armenians will starve. Of the many, many films about evil women, an excellent example is the little-known *Wicked As They Come* (1957), which I admit I have chosen for its perfect title.

In *Wicked As They Come*, Arlene Dahl plays a girl from Tenth Avenue who audiences can see is very, very bad from the opening moments of the film, partly because they are told "All she thinks about is clothes." Here is another of those ironies. On the one hand, the woman's film does nothing but glorify fashion, reminding women that they must dress not only well but in feminine finery in order to be appreciated. On the other hand, a villainous woman is often partially defined by her desire to have *Too many clothes*. Clothes become a symbol of power, in that a woman's ability to attract a man is related to them, so that having too many of them gives a woman the ability to attract too many men!

Dahl works at the Dreamline Fashionwear Company, and the film begins in Joan Crawford territory. Dahl is seen coming out of the factory at the end of a long day, discouraged and weary, anxious to get out of this environment. She and her stepfather argue when she gets home, and the argument couches Dahl's misery in female terms. She tells him about her underdressed childhood: "I was ashamed to go out in the streets," while he snarls, "I dressed ya fine!"

Dahl finds her ticket out of town by winning the Miss Working Girl contest. She wins a trip to Europe and parlays it into her one big chance. ("If I want something bad enough, I'll get it.") She pawns her return ticket and goes to secretarial school. Soon she's a secretary to a married man (Herbert Marshall), watching for her next chance. Dahl enacts the number-three behavioral lesson for women by taking power into her own hands in the following ways:

- Getting her boss (Marshall) drunk in an out-of-town hotel after tricking him into believing he needed a folder she has brought him (as if this weren't enough, she undresses and gets in the twin bed beside him, so that when he awakes he thinks the worst and she makes him promote her)
- Refusing to allow herself to really love any man, as she hates having them touch her; just using her beauty to manipulate them
- Caring only for clothes and money
- Rejecting the man she could possibly love, one who really loves her (Phil Carey)
- Marrying a man she does not love, for his money (Ralph Truman)

Arlene Dahl is as wicked as they come because she usurps power. In fact, she is not the only woman in the film who is in control of things. After Dahl has tricked Herbert Marshall into thinking he slept with her, he actually does fall in love with her, seriously so. Since he is rich and successful, Dahl thinks he might be a good husband, so she tells him he must choose between her and his wife (Faith Brook). This wife, however, is more than equal to the challenge. As she enters the picture, it becomes clear that she, too, is an evil and controlling woman. Tough and experienced, the wife confronts Dahl in a ladies' room, and the two of them conduct one of those typical woman's film face-offs, in which the women decide the fate of the weak and hapless man. The wife explains to Dahl that she is not the first "secretary" that her husband has had, and that Dahl may think he loves her, but there is something she should know. The wife is the daughter of the company's Big Boss (who lives in Paris), and Marshall married her for that reason. There is no way in hell Marshall will divorce his wife, because he would lose everything. Getting out her checkbook with a glamorous flourish, the wife prepares to buy Dahl off. Being wicked as they come, however, Dahl is able to see the wife's ace and up her five. "You don't have to pay me off," she says. "I like my job. I've worked hard for it. Give me a good job in another part of the business, and I won't see your husband again." Dahl is transferred to the Paris office, and the two controlling women understand each other perfectly.

It is inevitable that Dahl must get her comeuppance. Once in Paris, Dahl cleverly woos the Big Boss himself and ends up marrying him. This is the beginning of the end for her, as she finds out that he has, in fact, used her. "I'm sick and tired of being used as a social asset," she tells him soon enough. When she accidentally shoots him, thinking he is a blackmailer who has come to reveal one of her many past secrets, she is sent up on a manslaughter charge. This sentencing is encouraged by Herbert Marshall ("She hated me as she hates all men" is his contribution to her defense). His wife helps out by testifying that Dahl wed her father for his money.

The final woman's-film rule-book sociology is provided for the audience by the character played by Phil Carey, who has been present off and on throughout the film. Showing Dahl an old newspaper he found from her teenage years back in New York, he solemnly reads out the headline that explains what has made her evil. "Teenage Girl Attacked by Hoodlums." "Ever since that happened, you've been treating all men like hoodlums, but it hasn't paid off, Kathy. You've been empty and dead inside . . . been hating so long that you've left no room for love, and that's the one thing you need above all else, Kathy. Love." Here the main point of the film is announced: A woman's job is love. Arlene Dahl is wicked because she forgot her job and did not follow the rules of behavior for women. Instead, she took on power for herself, hurt men, and rejected true love. To restore order, the movie has Arlene Dahl weep and say, "Is it too late for us?" to Phil Carey, who responds cryptically, "I don't know, Kathy. I really don't know."

Dahl's character used deception, but not the acceptable kind, the kind that is placed at the service of others. A woman can lie to get love, or lie to protect others from hurt, or lie by pretending she doesn't really love a man who is better off without her. By giving up her own desires and even her rights, a woman does the right thing. Even expressing anger is all right. But taking on power—Dahl's real crime—is not.

Joan Fontaine's Ivy Lexton in *Ivy* (1947) is a classic example of an evil woman on film. She is evil because she uses her beauty to lure men whom she does not truly love, and she is willing to kill her charming husband for material gain. Her choices all go against the accepted wisdom of the woman's life. She has not become a mother. She has not accepted the role of little wife for a struggling young husband. She is willing to sleep with men other than her husband. It is inevitable that Ivy will be found out for the murderess she is and that the rich man she covets (Herbert Marshall) will ultimately reject her. Ivy's fate is not to become a pampered wife who leads a life of luxury but instead to fall down an elevator shaft. These shafts, suggest the film, yawn ominously out there in the real world, ready to swallow up and destroy the woman who dares to step outside the border of acceptable behavior.

Ivy is standard woman's film fare. Ivy, in fact, dies trying to retrieve her purse, confirming the role that fashion plays in the plots of movies about a woman's life. This purse is a shiny beaded affair, very ritzy and very expensive, and it closes with a clasp that is rumored to have been a cameo that belonged to Marie Antoinette. "Let's hope you'll enjoy it somewhat more than she did," Marshall cheerfully booms out as he presents it to her as a gift. He demonstrates for her the cameo's secret: it snaps open to reveal a hollowed-out space for storing little things. Such as poison. This purchase of the purse for Ivy by the rich man she desires to marry establishes several things in that economical narrative way that old films perfected. Ivy has lured Herbert Marshall's character off his yacht, and he has followed her onto shore and down the little streets where she is shopping. She waits strategically outside a shop, admiring the obviously expensive purse in its window. Seeing her, and not understanding he is being led, he "surprises" her by going in and purchasing the item with wads of bills. "Oh, I shall never dare admire anything again," sweetly protests Ivy, generously accepting his gift. Thus the purse establishes his wealth, her desire for things, and their relationship of clever manipulation on her part and unknowing compliance on his. The fact that the purse is also established as a potential murder weapon as well as a harbinger of feminine disaster (the Marie Antoinette reference) completes the usefulness of the device.

As the film progresses, Ivy keeps this purse always with her. She conveniently fills its cameo with poison on a visit to a doctor who was once her lover. She clutches it beautifully while out shopping or arriving home from walks. She fearfully but surreptitiously picks it up to extract a lacy handkerchief from it, clutching it to her bosom as Scotland Yard explains to her that her husband has been poisoned. She hides it in an old clock when its usefulness is over, and it is this very purse that she has run back to retrieve while the elevator waits for her. What she finds is that the hidden purse is gone, because Scotland Yard has uncannily smelled its existence

Poisoners: Gene Tierney, in *Leave Her to Heaven*

inside the clockworks. Distracted, rattled, and frightened, Ivy runs back
to the elevator, not noticing that the elevator man has responded to another
call while he waited for her. Down the open shaft she goes, dying for her
purse and reminding women everywhere that wanting things and usurping
power can lead a woman to ruin.

    Ivy is interesting because of its method of visual presentation. Set in
England in the early 1900s, it is a beautifully mounted production designed
by William Cameron Menzies. In every way, Ivy Lexton is shown to be a
great beauty, a woman of style and allure. The key word to the visualization
of the character would be "soft." She is softly lit and dressed in soft whites.
She speaks softly, moves softly, and never makes a sound other than the
suitable rustle of silk or taffeta. Ivy is demure, a perfect picture of appropriate femininity. She ducks her head shyly, smiles hesitantly, apologizes,
and even stutters sweetly just a bit when overcome with feeling. She is at
the same time socially confident, well schooled in manners. She knows
how to dress and how to introduce everyone to everyone else with ease.
She is a perfectly-turned-out and polished woman of the period, following
all the rules and conforming to what is expected.

. . . and Joan Fontaine, in *Ivy*

That, of course, is the surface. Under the competent direction of the journeyman Sam Wood, Ivy Lexton is a bi-level visualization. On one level, she is as defined above, the perfect picture of period womanhood. The audience is allowed to see that very clearly. Everyone else in the movie also sees her this way, with the notable exception of certain other women who are equally wise socially. Ivy is functioning within the confines of the plot as a character who is being observed as behaving exactly as she ought to behave.

On the second level, the audience is allowed privileged information. A second line of plot is established visually, in which intense close-ups show Ivy's secret reactions. Little smiles of triumph play about her mouth, and little peeks over her magazine to see what Herbert Marshall's next move will be take the viewer into her private motivations. In addition to these close-ups, the film cuts away to Ivy's reactions, presents compositions that frame her alone with a poison bottle or place her under shadowy lighting—all of which suggest to viewers a second interpretation of her character. In addition, plot sequences, such as one in which Ivy consults a fortune-teller about her future (a sequence that vaguely looks like a visit to an abortionist), show Ivy at work on her true life plans.

These two levels are presented exactly as what they are: two ways of seeing Ivy Lexton. The duality of the character is fully established, but the movie also provides a comment on society's views of women. There is no question but that Ivy Lexton is a villainess, and a classic example of how women ought *not* to behave. However, the film shows viewers how women "get away with it" by conforming on a certain surface level, with their true motivations and true characters well hidden. Society allows this, because men will fall for a woman's beauty and because a clever woman understands that rules do not have to be broken in order to get what one wants, only manipulated.

There are many films about evil, conniving women*—*Leave Her to Heaven* (1945), *Guest in the House* (1945), *Double Indemnity* (1944), *Lady from Shanghai* (1948), *The Strange Woman* (1946), to name a very, very few—but perhaps the most famous, best remembered of the bad-bad-women movies of the 1940s is the kinky *Gilda* (1946). There are enough layers of meaning in its hot presentation of weird sexuality to fuel Ph.D. theses for decades. Effeminate George Macready picks the pretty young Glenn Ford up off the streets by rescuing him from thugs, and the two are thick as thieves until Macready goes on a trip and returns home with a dubious bride, the luscious and radiant young Rita Hayworth. Taking Ford home to meet his wife, Macready calls out cheerfully, "Gilda. Are you decent?" as they approach her bedroom. This turns out to be the central issue of the film. Is she decent? Or not? With perfect Hollywood skill, the film answers the question by indicating that she's not very decent, although she's really decent enough. That is, although she looks and acts as if she's not decent, in the end, she turns out to be decent. Decent is as decent doesn't do.

Gilda uses audience attitudes to present a brilliant depiction of an "evil woman" who is not really evil but who is forced into behavior that *looks* evil because men want her sexually. She's stuck inside herself, her beautiful body, and the roles society thinks match her looks and her body. *Gilda* manipulates the rules of behavior for women by telling a story with a strong subtext. As is true of *Ivy* and many other films about women, *Gilda* sets up a clearly represented double layer for viewers. While we watch

---

* An interesting variation is yet another costume film, *My Cousin Rachel* (1952), starring Olivia de Havilland. In this movie, which will be dealt with in depth in the chapter "Men," the presentation of the leading woman is left totally ambivalent. Is she evil or not? The issue is not fully resolved, because the film is more from the male character's point of view. Since he never really figures it out for certain, neither can the audience.

Gilda behave outrageously, we are allowed to see that she isn't really bad after all. Privileged information shows viewers that she is being driven by her love and passion for Ford to act the way she does and that she truly loves him. The voice-over narration that introduces Gilda to viewers, however, is that of Glenn Ford, who tells viewers that she is bad, no good, a troublemaker. The film becomes a story in which Ford, the narrator, has to find out he is wrong, just as viewers slowly are allowed to shift loyalty over to the side of Gilda, as they, too, realize that Ford is wrong.

The ultimate in this double-layered visualization is the famous "Put the Blame on Mame" number, in which Hayworth attempts a public strip-tease. Slapped around and degraded totally by the man she loves (Ford), Hayworth has more or less given up. In the ultimate "I will be what my man wants me to be," Hayworth goes forward to be as terrible, as loose, as wanton, and as evil as Ford thinks she is. Slightly tipsy and totally defiant, she goes before the nightclub audience and tries to take her clothes off. Can a woman who is willing to humiliate herself for her man, in order to prove him right, be anything other than inherently *Good* according to the movie rules of behavior? Of course not. Hayworth and Ford end up in each other's arms, and Gilda, the quintessence of movie bad women, is understood to have never been really bad. Why? Because she was willing to suffer. Because she was hurt and rejected by her man in the first place, which is why she married Macready. Because all she wanted was love. Because she would do anything her man wanted her to do. Because she understood all too well the rules of behavior for women.

These rules of behavior for women, these investigations into whether the woman is good or bad, are all about the same thing, of course. The character of the woman herself in the woman's genre is a surrogate through which other women learn what the facts of life are. Some of these films are subversive and contradictory; others are more conservative and traditional. But all are teaching women what being a woman is all about if they don't already know and siphoning off anger and resentment about it if they do. A final important purpose for the character of the woman is to use her in an initiation story. This is the cinematic female equivalent of the initiation stories in literature, in which young people, primarily boys, are taught what life is through stories of courage, adventure, and challenge. In these movies about young girls, lovely young actresses cut their hair, put on lipstick for the first time, dress in feminine clothing instead of jeans, and begin to dance, date, and learn what men want from them.

Significantly, these films are often linked to a larger generic family that might be called the sports movie.* In these films, young girls are tomboys, proving that they are excellent baseball players (*Mickey*, 1948), horseback riders (*National Velvet*, 1944), harness drivers (*Home in Indiana*, 1944), or gun handlers (various versions of the Annie Oakley story). These films show women actually giving up not only an active physical life but a definite mastery over men in a sporting activity. They are the opposite of the bad-behavior, evil-woman movie, because they show females *accepting* their roles as women. These women not only do not usurp or covet power, they actively renounce it.

Home in Indiana presents two young teenage girls on the brink of womanhood. They provide a contrast of choices for a woman regarding the attitude she will have toward herself, toward men, and toward her own relationship to them. Neither of the two young girls has a mother. They live completely in the world of men, a world of horse racing and horse breeding, and have only each other to turn to for female advice and knowledge. (There is another woman in the film, Charlotte Greenwood, but she plays a stern religious figure, someone who has no advice for these young girls about sex, men, or life.)

The two girls are Jeanne Crain and June Haver. Crain is introduced in the film by showing her driving a horse and sulky around a track at high speed. Her hat falls back from her head, her braids fly free, and she is joyous, confident, and in control. In our first view of Haver, she is elegantly dressed and coiffed, the complete opposite of Crain. Haver wears jodhpurs, gloves, and a white silk blouse. She is carefully made up, and her entrance is unobtrusive as she rides in on her horse and mingles quietly with the older men watching Lon McCallister, the film's youthful hero. Whereas Crain is the center of McCallister's attention as he watches her drive around the track with consummate skill, McCallister will become the center of Haver's attention in a later parallel sense as she watches him tame a dangerous horse. Crain is established as an admirable figure of control, and the man of the film is placed so that he is watching her accomplish-

---

* The generic linkage of the woman's film to another, more masculine genre will be covered in the chapter "The Woman in the Man's World." The films referred to here are not examples in which women totally take over the male genre. They are films in which there is a link or a relationship to the second, more male-oriented form of story. In addition to the sports movie, there is often a close relationship between the woman's film and two other popular genres—the gangster movie and the musical. It is a logical link. When a woman does not follow the rules of behavior and takes a wrong turn in life, she often ends up outside the boundaries of polite society, which can be visualized as the gangster's world. And if she chooses to work for a living, show business (the setting of many musicals) is an acceptable feminine trade that for various reasons does not seem to count in the usual women-shouldn't-work mode of thinking. If a woman is prancing around a stage in a short skirt singing, it seems an acceptable career.

Jeanne Crain in *Home in Indiana*

ments. The reverse is true for Haver, who is placed in the position of watching him.

These two young women are established as polar opposites. Crain wears blue jeans and denim shirts. Her hair is always in braids, and she wears no makeup. She appears in out-of-door spaces, lying in haystacks, running free across meadows, and sharing in the men's work with the horses. Haver is frequently seen in her frilly bedroom, sitting at an elaborate dressing table, making herself up, plucking her eyebrows, and applying perfume behind her ears.

The two young women are friends, and Haver admires Crain's skill with horses. She tells McCallister, "It takes a lot of driving before you can talk to them with your hands like Char does." However, she takes the role of adviser to the naive Crain, telling her "boys never like it if you show them up. You ought to remember that."

The two girls are contrasted in several scenes. At the swimming pond, Haver in a sexy two-piece suit entices a boy from Lawrenceville to show her how to do his swimming stroke. This necessitates his putting his arms around her. Her pale blue two-piece suit is in contrast to Crain's sensible one-piece tank suit. After Haver returns from boarding school, she arrives at the swimming pond a second time, with her prep-school boyfriend in tow. Crain and McCallister have been having fun together, wrestling and tickling and laughing like children. The arrival of Haver changes everything. McCallister immediately becomes physically conscious of Haver and of himself as a young man. He ignores Crain, who leaves dejectedly. Haver confidently walks out onto the diving board, trim in her new white polka-dot swimsuit, and takes plenty of time to tuck her hair into her bathing cap, so both young men can ogle her. Now the situation is reversed. As a sex object, Haver is entitled to having the two male stars watch her. This is not only the control that she has a right to as the film's leading sex symbol, but it is also the kind of female control that her character is aware of and knows how to use.

While Crain tries to understand what is happening, sneaking looks at herself in Haver's mirror, she receives a key chain for her blue jeans for Christmas from McCallister, while Haver receives perfume called Kiss at Midnight. Haver strikes up a relationship with McCallister that is based on her manipulating his desire for her. She flirts, teases, and invites him to kiss her, but only with her permission and only for as long as she wants. Her relationship with McCallister is, on the one hand, one of manipulation and control as she uses his desire for her against him, and on the other hand, it is one of adoring female as he establishes himself as a successful harness driver. Crain's relationship with him is open, honest, equal. She is a natural woman, and she participates in training a horse and entering him in the races as an equal partner. Having helped to raise the entrance money, she is a facilitator for the men, but not one who serves them in "female" ways as cook or sex object.

Crain tries to learn from Haver. Haver clearly believes that looking good is the way women control things, and teasing men and leading them on is the proper behavior. Crain is not up to that, but she does dress up and put ribbons in her hair, although to no avail. It is only when McCallister looks in at a dance and sees Crain in a different context that his love for her is expressed. In a parallel to the first time he saw her, watching from behind a fence while she drove the horse around the track, he watches from behind a French door while she jitterbugs with a tuxedoed young man. She has her hair up, a long dress on, and she is made up and lovely. McCallister becomes angry at her, and the film's ambivalence is unleashed. He bursts into the dance, grabbing her and telling her, "What are you doing? All the boys are staring at you." She replies, "That's what boys are supposed to do."

McCallister can only realize he loves Crain when she behaves in traditional female ways, but he is also angry at her for becoming someone he no longer likes. In the end, they patch things up and plan to raise and race horses together. Crain has changed, however. She now wears feminine clothes and has renounced her former tomboyish behavior. She has accepted the role of woman in McCallister's life, which apparently means abandoning her free and easy ways, and certainly means abandoning herself as his major competition. *Home in Indiana* shows Jeanne Crain first speaking to Lon McCallister by yelling at him and telling him that he doesn't know how to drive a horse. They have a roaring argument, and she shows him how it is properly done. Her first words to him are "You ought to be ashamed of yourself," but her final words to him, as she looks dewy eyed and adoringly up at him, are "If you say so, Sparky."

Although the film seems to endorse Crain's honesty and capability, it reverses itself at the end. Furthermore, there is additional subversion in the Haver character's presentation. She is the loser in the McCallister sweepstakes (not that she is presented as really caring), presumably because she does not really share his interests in horses and farms. Her affection for him is somewhat false, but we also sense that this young woman has the power to make McCallister do what she wants him to do; she will not dutifully do what he wants. There will be no "If you say so, Sparky" from her. She is our master deceiver, a potential bad woman. Women's having power, unless it is the sexual power they are welcome to have as long as they don't abuse it, is against the rules of behavior. Jeanne Crain is initiated into this knowledge in *Home in Indiana*.

Initiation films like *Home in Indiana* make a woman's awakening the full story. Many other movies physicalize this story as one single major visual event: a young girl goes to her first ball. If the female character's world is too poor for such an outing, then the scene is frequently set at a carnival or fair of some sort. Obviously, such settings represent the Other as a physical place which an inexperienced female enters, leaving her narrow, unsophisticated, even childish world behind. The new space, whether ball or carnival, presents many people whirling loose and free through a world that invites interaction, sexual attraction, and physicality. Young girls who find love and sex at such a ball, whether for good or ill, are presented in countless movies, among them *War and Peace* (1956), *Secrets* (1933), and *To Each His Own* (1946).*

* So well established is the convention that *Lydia* (1941) uses the metaphor effectively in debunking romanticism (while reinforcing it simultaneously, of course). First seen in the film as an old woman—a power figure being honored for her good works—Lydia (Merle Oberon) is soon reunited with three of her former suitors. While she reminisces with them, she talks of a wonderful ball she attended as a virginal young girl. "I entered the room as I entered a dream," she says, articulating the usual woman's film visual presentation of the young-girl-at-ball situation. On-screen, as Oberon narrates, one sees an enormous room with mirrored walls, a huge staircase, hundreds of harpists and full orchestra. As Oberon

The complete book of rules of behavior—or who a woman "should" be—is well illustrated in three Warner Brothers films of the 1930s and early 1940s: *Four Daughters, Four Wives,* and *Four Mothers.* The four daughters are all trying to get married. The four wives are all trying to get pregnant. The four mothers are all trying to protect their homes. Thus, the movies illustrate the motivating goals in the subcategories of the woman's film: young unmarried girls should find love and romance; young wives should learn to get along with their husbands and have babies; and young mothers should fight foreclosures, adultery, disease, and old age. To achieve these goals, the four live out an appropriate mixture of good sportsmanship and deception. All accept their jobs as women, helping to initiate one another properly, and none is evil. The three films represent the conventional approval of the woman's role. Nevertheless, these females *are* controlling figures in their world.

The first movie in the series, *Four Daughters* (1938), was so popular that it inspired two sequels. Originally based on *Sister Act*, a novel by Fannie Hurst, *Four Daughters* is the story of the Lepp sisters, Ann, Thea, Kay, and Emma, the children of an absentminded musician, played by Claude Rains, who has taught them all to play instruments.

In *Four Daughters*, the Lepp household is clearly established as a world of women. The mother is dead—the familiar movie and television-sitcom device by which one parent is placed in a juicier narrative position. The household is run by May Robson, their elderly aunt, who is a surrogate mother. The children, of course, are all females. The father has what was stereotypically considered to be a feminine career, music, and the old aunt is a domineering, though lovable, household force. One lone young man (Jeffrey Lynn) enters this domain to live among them and study music, and his presence naturally disrupts the female world. All four girls fall in love with him, but he chooses Ann (Priscilla Lane). As her wedding day dawns, Ann realizes too late that whereas two of her sisters have recovered from their imagined love of Lynn, her most vulnerable sister, Emma (Gale Page), has not. Ann does what movie women always do in order to solve a major problem: feeling the need to be a really good sport and to sacrifice herself

---

and her escort (Joseph Cotten) literally float upstairs (in slow motion), the music swells, and she sees a long line of handsome, uniformed suitors awaiting her. It is a Cinderella's ball populated with Prince Charmings. Later, Cotten tells his version, the masculine, more realistic presentation. The room is modest in size. There are no mirrored walls. The staircase is present, but appropriate to the size of the room. There is one harpist, an old lady valiantly strumming, and a single violinist, an earnest man sawing his instrument as if his life depended on it. The handsome suitors are not lined up waiting, and there are not many of them. The woman's film thus works as any genre works—it uses what an audience is familiar with, dramatizes it and glamorizes it, and then undercuts it.

Four Daughters: Gale Page and the Lane sisters

for her sister, she tells a big lie and pretends she doesn't really love Lynn at all. To confirm this information, she goes all the way, running off with and marrying a maverick misfit who has also shown up in their world, an angry young man well played by John Garfield. This marriage is doomed. Garfield finally realizes that he is ruining Ann's life for two key woman's film reasons: he cannot earn a decent living (the men in women's films often cannot), and he has taken her away from the loving bosom of her family. Because this is a woman's film, Garfield behaves unlike a male hero. He does what a woman would do under the circumstances: he sacrifices himself. He runs his car off the road and dies to save her, telling his own form of a lie ("it was an accident") and acting out his own form of good sportsmanship.

This type of plot occurrence always brings ridicule down on the woman's film. Why can't these characters just talk things over and get reasonably divorced? But that ignores the point: these films are metaphors for the woman's life. Garfield's sacrifice returns Ann to her home and family, and also to Jeffrey Lynn, who is nobly waiting for her. Emma has come to her senses and has found herself a reliable florist for a husband, and the other older sister, Thea (Lola Lane), has married a wealthy businessman.

In *Four Wives* (1939), the three married sisters concern themselves with two appropriate matters for females: getting pregnant and getting their youngest sister (Kay, played by Rosemary Lane) properly initiated into being a woman by marrying her off. Emma and her florist husband, who have a solid, bourgeois marriage, find that Emma cannot have children, and they are crushed. But they have to be good sports about it. Thea and her wealthy husband find it isn't happening for them, either, illustrating that they may have money and a big house but are no better off in the woman's world than their poorer relations with the flower shop. Thea isn't all that good a sport, so she lays plans for an elaborate adoption, overruling her husband's objections. The widowed Priscilla Lane, as Ann, ironically finds on the eve of her wedding to the ever-faithful and ever-patient Jeffrey Lynn that she is, in fact, going to have her dead husband's baby. Thus we see how it goes in the woman's film regarding pregnancies. Women with husbands don't get, and women without husbands do. Everybody is supposed to be a good sport.

In *Four Mothers* (1941), the family is threatened by two new problems: the sale of the old family homestead and the destruction of the girls' love for one another by imagined adulteries. Money and sex are always problems in stories about women, and here the young women nearly lose the home they have grown up in and nearly lose the men they have married. The homestead story is a subplot, in which the aging father and old aunt are dispossessed when the house is sold out from under them. This becomes a metaphor for the near loss of family harmony. The adultery plots involve two of the daughters. First, Ann works on a daily basis with Clint (Eddie Albert, playing Kay's husband). He is a noble doctor, working with poor people and trying to discover a cure for one of those movie diseases that strike the poor exclusively, providing opportunities for the stars to stay up all night together looking through microscopes. Because Clint and Ann are with each other night and day, his wife, Kay, and her husband, Jeffrey Lynn, believe incorrectly that they are having an affair. Kay's character is used to portray a typical woman's film problem: loneliness. Her doctor-husband works long hours and has no time for her. She is childless and has nothing to do with herself. Her temptation in falling in love with Jeffrey Lynn is thus explained in woman's film terms, and their mutual needs, never actually fulfilled, are presented as warning notes to the audience. The sisters love one another too much for any real trouble, and the film satisfies itself with sending warning signals all around. In the end, the family home has been bought and moved to a new location, and everyone is reunited in harmony and happiness. (The loss of the home and the potential breakup of the family unit struck ominous notes on the brink of World War II, however.)

Four Daughters, Four Wives, and *Four Mothers* were three box-office successes that laid out a conventional, acceptable set of stories for and about women, all reaffirming the correct rules of behavior for women, and all presenting strong women as central to the stories. All three films end optimistically. In *Four Daughters*, Ann is liberated from her sad and doomed marriage and returned both to her loving family and to the man who is right for her. In *Four Wives*, everyone who wants a child gets a child. When Thea's adopted baby arrives, her happiness inspires her own conception. This makes it possible for her to hand over her newly adopted daughter to her barren, poorer sister, in one of those astonishing baby swaps that so often take place in such films. (When Thea gives birth to twins, she is apparently covering any future shortages that may arise in the family.) In *Four Mothers*, the girls are nearly torn apart by both an outside threat (foreclosure and loss of the family home) and an inside threat (adultery). In the end, the home is restored, the marriages are solidly intact, all four girls are married, and all the babies are healthy. This can happen because the four daughters accept their jobs as women, help to initiate one another, and know the rules.

It's all so optimistic and conventional that one hates to point out what the realities of these stories are. There's rivalry, jealousy, suspected adultery, unhappiness, and resentment over one another's homes and wealth. These four sisters have their interwoven stories told as women's pictures, so that even though they are presented as wholesome, straightforward, honest, and good, they also lie to one another, to their respective husbands, to individuals in their community, and to their own father. They stick together, giving each other advice and support (even when it's not needed), but there are limits on their tolerance. They illustrate who women are in movies by showing us their concern with men, marriage, and motherhood, but they also show us deception and lies.

One of the most striking scenes in the three films concerns a traditional dinner party the family stages whenever one of the girls has found the man she wants to marry. Not once but three times the audience is shown how this family of females rallies to deceive the invited man. A routine of careful deception is enacted. First, a seemingly innocent member of the family— not the girl herself—invites the man to dinner. Then the sisters design a presentation that might be entitled *The Perfect Family Life*. Intellectual magazines on various subjects are scattered about the room. Roses are placed in all the vases. Music is playing on the radio. A lamp is set carefully in just the right place in the living room to throw flattering light on the young woman who hopes to become the future wife. A perfect dinner is cooked, with everyone in the house contributing her individual skills, but all claiming that the potential wife cooked it by herself. With great good cheer and remarkable chicanery, they design an atmosphere to showcase the future bride as a female of beauty, grace, intelligence, wit, wide interests, culinary skill, and modesty. In short, they stage for an astonished

viewer a perfect little Hollywood movie about American home life. That
we are shown that it's all phony—that we watch them setting it all up—
is presented as humorous, but also appropriate. It is honest in its deception.
The contradictory idea that this deception is good and right because these
nice young women do it and because they do it together as a family is
presented very straightforwardly. This is Woman's Work, Woman's Business. They are the Perfect Family, because they know how to pretend to
be. Because they can work together in these pretenses, they prove that
they are what they are supposed to be. This scene is presented, as I say,
three times in these movies, as each of three of the young women lures
her husband this way.

What is actually happening in these movies is that four young women
are used to connect viewers to a woman's concerns. The strong young
females in the story survive anything and everything because they know
how to do what is expected of them. All this, however, is also revealed to
the audience to be a clever manipulation, in the great tradition of the
woman's film. An understanding emerges that the woman in the woman's
genre is meant to be strong, capable, and brave. She is central to everything
in the story, and she does not exist for stereotypical purposes but to create
a covert dialogue with women in the audience, which reminds them that
they are women and, whatever else they might wish to do or be, that is a
fact that can never be changed.

DUALITY:
"MY GOD!
THERE'S TWO OF HER!"

THE WOMAN'S FILM found a brilliant device for telling a woman that she ought to conform to the roles society approves for her at the same time as it allowed her the freedom to see and possibly identify, however temporarily, however tangentially, with a female character who did not conform or follow the rules. This device was the story in which there were *two* women, a good one and a bad one, used to represent the conflicting forces in the woman's life, the two things she has to resolve by making a choice. Sometimes the format was varied—a woman had two selves or two women advisers or two different men in her life—but these twosies are always two concrete characters who give substance to the duality and contradiction that fuel movie stories about women.

These two-women-for-the-price-of-one stories were also great for the box office, since audiences got two beautiful stars in the same movie—Greer Garson and Joan Crawford in *When Ladies Meet* (1941), or Jeanne Crain and Gene Tierney in *Leave Her to Heaven*. And sometimes they got their favorite female movie star playing two roles, an idea that most actresses liked very much, since they received more screen time and could play their own competition. It was an excellent way to visualize the polarity of the woman's world, her either-or condition in life.

The variations of this idea follow these patterns:

1. Two different leading women, related or unrelated, demonstrate two different ways for women to live their lives, with one following society's plan and one not following it.
2. One woman has within herself two conflicting personalities, or goals, that need to be resolved in order for her to find happiness.
3. One woman must choose between two different ways of life with these ways represented either by two men who love her or by two female companions who advise her differently. (In both these cases, the woman is choosing between two supporting characters, because the men in these films are seldom front and center.)

There are endless variations of these basic patterns, but all stories of good and bad women, wrong and right men, career versus love, motherhood versus the legal system, or whatever, are contained in them. They present real selves and dream selves, pretend selves, good and bad selves. Although the bad selves frequently seem to be having all the fun—and also all the good clothes—the good selves survive in the end to show everyone how women ought to behave. At the same time, obviously, they allow women a peek at the fun of misbehaving, so that while accomplishing the primary purpose of the cautionary tale, they also provide that unintentionally liberating release that is built into the woman's film.

Of all the doubles and opposites in the films about two women, no version is more satisfying, or more invariably cracked, than the one in which the two women are twins. It's the variation in which we suddenly realize that, as the poster for *Dark Mirror* shouted "My God! There's two of her!"

The idea of a woman as a *thing* is cleverly buried in "there's two of her" stories in which twins are presented. The audience is asked to select, from two identical forms, the one it likes better based on its watching carefully to see which one behaves better. Having made the choice, the audience can conveniently discard the one it doesn't like. After all, there *are* two of them. "That's what twins are, you know," says Lew Ayres in *Dark Mirror*. "Reflections of each other. Everything in reverse." "Reverse" means one of them is going in the wrong direction. Not only is society not going to like that, but the bad twin is going to find it hard to maintain any speed or control while backing up through life. Besides, what safer thing could a strong woman be shown to oppose on-screen than herself?

"There's two of her" movies about twins maintain the woman's film primary concerns no matter what the mood of the movie is, and no matter what other generic family may be involved. Four different types of films about twins from the 1940s demonstrate how this works: *A Stolen Life*, in which Bette Davis appears as twins in a typical woman's film or melodrama;

Here Come the Waves, a musical comedy with Betty Hutton singing duets with herself and portraying twins who enlist in the Waves during World War II; *Dark Mirror*, with Olivia de Havilland in a crime film/film noir in which one twin is an insane murderess; and the camp classic *Cobra Woman*, with the unparalleled Maria Montez cast both as an innocent island girl and as the high priestess of a snake-worshiping cult whose ranks she is rapidly reducing by tossing people one by one into a smoking volcano.

The four films, all of which are set "now," reflect the times in which they were made, although *Cobra Woman*, it might be argued, is set in *no* time. Since it is a fantasy film, taking place in a totally unrealistic world, it has to be considered a part of its own times, and indeed the high priestess seems to be wearing the turbans, high heels, and bare-midriff sequined gowns of its 1944 release date. It is a "now" movie in its own way.

The twins in *Dark Mirror* own and operate a little newspaper-and-cigar stand in a big building, while the twins of *A Stolen Life* are wealthy women who do not work for a living. The twins of *Here Come the Waves* are a musical sister act in a nightclub before they enlist, and the twins of *Cobra Woman* were separated at birth, one becoming a typical "native" girl and the other becoming the cobra queen. The sets of twins are thus utterly different in occupation, life-style, and geographical background, and yet there is fundamental generic conformity. There are four sets of twins, and thus four good women and four bad. What makes one twin "good" and one "bad"? Presumably, since the settings are as far-flung as New England and an imaginary Polynesian island, there might be some significant differences, but there are none. In all these movies, two things always happen. No matter what the root genre or tone of the movie, it is inevitable that there will be a discussion about which of the two women is more beautiful than the other, and a moment in the plot will arise in which one of the two will decide to pretend she's the other one. Both of these things are inherently ludicrous, since a woman can't be more beautiful than herself, and since she is already the other one in the first place. Nevertheless, these actions and discussions are repeatedly put forth as serious plot considerations, and thus they need to be, if not taken seriously, at least taken. Accepted. In accepting them, audiences absorb the sense of a woman as an object, as well as the idea of a movie star as an icon. These two plot events allow the films to become stories about "what makes a woman beautiful" and "why she should behave one way and not the other." These are familiar aspects of the woman's genre. While they are achieving these goals, they also present the opportunity for women to see something else.

These two key elements of the twins story are clearly designed to serve two opposing needs. Discussions in which a man says two identical women differ in beauty because one behaves appropriately and one does not clearly affirm the status quo of good behavior for women. Sequences in which good women pretend to be bad—or bad women pretend to be their better selves in order to steal men's love—animate concretely the idea that a woman would like to be free to act in a way that society does not endorse. The creation of a second self occurs.

In these key elements we can see how the plot allows a viewer to have things two different ways. When a man talks about beauty, he is talking about the desirability of a woman from the male point of view. Since women were being encouraged to view their lives as linked to those of men, any such discussion would presumably be of primary interest to women in the audience. The twins films demonstrate that whereas a man can be lured by a bad twin and temporarily seduced by her, he senses (usually when he actually kisses her) that something is wrong. Evidently his lips can detect insurrection. Beauty is a matter of proper attitude.

On the other hand, when a good woman pretends to be a bad one, isn't she acting out a secret need? Most of these twins movies provide us with a reason that a good woman takes up such a pretense. In *A Stolen Life*, it isn't her fault; people made the mistake for her. In *Cobra Woman*, she's got to save her people from the volcano. However, when a bad woman pretends to be a good one, she always has a *bad* reason for it. It's never because she wants to be good for a while; it's because she wants something she shouldn't have, usually sex, her sister's man, or money.

Seeing one actress, a single person, transfer herself across modes of behavior from good and obedient to bad and murderous or from bad and murderous to good and obedient is a subtle way of allowing viewers to see a woman activate a second self, one that does "the other thing," or makes "the other choice." The popularity of these films about twins suggests that their appeal, like their subject, was twofold, and that one of the appeals was a covert form of liberation.

A Stolen Life (1946), a popular remake of an earlier Elisabeth Bergner film, is the ultimate example of the twins movie. It clearly states why a woman who looks *exactly* like another woman—in fact, let's face it, she *is* the other woman—is not as beautiful, not as sexy, not as desirable. Why? Because she doesn't dress right. She doesn't act right. She doesn't think right.

The irony of this has always fascinated. When I first saw the movie, I was astonished by a scene in which, as the wicked Bette Davis marries Glenn Ford, having stolen him from the good Bette Davis, a toast is offered to "the loveliest bride of the year, or any year." As everyone beams at the beautiful bad girl, her identical twin sister stands alongside as maid of honor. She is *not* the loveliest bride of the year, nor can she ever be, any year, because this other one already is. But she's the same person! Why is Pat, the bad girl, more beautiful than Katie, the good girl? Because Pat is feminine, flirtatious, sexy, provocative, and she wears an off-the-shoulder gown to the barn dance. Why is Katie, the good girl, not as beautiful? Because she is blunt, straightforward, open, often awkward, guileless, and she wears a blouse buttoned up tight and a long skirt that hides her legs. Fashion and glamour. Willingness to be a sex object. These are the things that make one woman beautiful and the other not. After Glenn Ford has married Pat, he asks Katie to go shopping with him, to help him select a gift for his wife. He picks out a filmy, sensuous negligee, and says casually, "Hold it up to you, will you, Katie? It will look wonderful on Pat." He is using Katie as a similar shape, but not as a similar *woman*. Katie is hurt by this, naturally, as the film allows an audience to understand that *she* understands what this means. Pat in a negligee is a very different person from Katie in a negligee. Pat's attitude toward sex and toward Glenn Ford is different from Katie's, and from his man's point of view what he sees when he looks at a woman is not who she really is but what he can get from her that will make him happy.

In *A Stolen Life*, the good twin has had plenty of experience at losing things to her sister. She tries to keep the man she loves from ever meeting her other half because, in her heart, she knows what will happen. There is even a scene in which she more or less begs her sister to leave this one man alone. This only piques the interest of the bad Pat, and when she accidentally bumps into Ford, and he naturally thinks she's Katie, she undertakes the first masquerade of the movie. Since Ford does not know that Katie has a twin sister, there is no reason for him not to think that Pat is Katie. He does, however, notice a difference. "You've really dolled yourself up today," he says. The troublemaking Pat, seeing how handsome he is, enthusiastically enters into the pretense, taking him home to lunch. As they sit talking, Ford defines the difference between the two identical women by saying that being with her today has put him in a whirl. Whereas previously he had felt that he liked her and all that, something had been lacking. She was "a cake without any frosting . . . and most guys . . . they kinda like the frosting." Bad Davis understands at once. "I see. And today I'm well frosted."

Within minutes, poor Good Katie is maid of honor at Bad Pat's wedding to Glenn Ford. Katie accedes to what we know to be one of the important rules of behavior for women: good sportsmanship. She does, however, allow herself one little gesture that reflects how she really feels. When Pat deliberately throws her wedding bouquet to her, Katie steps aside, letting it drop ominously at her feet. Charlie Ruggles, the loving guardian of the two sisters, sympathetically asks Katie what she will do now, meaning "now that you've lost the only man you've ever loved to your evil twin." "Paint," she replies. She decides to do what movies tell us women do when they lose their men—get a job.

Taking up art is frequently a metaphor in the censored films of the 1940s for attempting to loosen up or become sexual. Katie embarks on her "career," in which she begins to paint. Because she has money and can afford it, she soon has an art show of her own. (Alas, she has no talent.) Into her life comes the Real Artist ("A sort of Rasputin of the paint pots"), played by Dane Clark. This character exists to explain in covert terms to an audience just what Katie's problem really is. He tells her that she did not get her man because she is "stiff, ingrown, afraid, and not really a woman." When she becomes terribly upset over his saying this, he smugly adds, "That always gets them. You can criticize a woman's work, but when you suggest that she's not a ball of fire . . . oh, boy!" Clark and Katie ultimately become good friends, and he offers her the possibility of a kind of crude, no-strings sex, but it is not in her nature to respond. This inspires him to more philosophy. "All this art stuff," he says, "that's been a substitute for something else. You're always running away. You'll never land a guy, always closed up inside like this." Despite all the restrictions of 1940s censorship, the point nevertheless gets made that Katie is cold, and Pat is not. In order to trap Ford, Pat has boldly followed him to Boston, openly flirting with him in a suggestive way. An audience is shown how she uses sex to manipulate him and that she is willing to cheat and deceive to get what she wants. The reason Katie will win is established when Clark snorts in disgust that she cannot find happiness, cannot let go, cannot accept anyone other than Ford, because that's how all women are. They want "the grand passion or nothing." "Yes. We do," answers Katie, and the woman's film rule book asserts itself. Love is a woman's career. Not art. Not lovers. Not substitutions. Not even off-the-shoulder blouses. A woman may have to suffer, but if she does not violate the rules, she will get her man.

The inevitable moment comes when Katie must impersonate Pat, Pat having impersonated Katie in order to lure Ford home for lunch. The two sisters go sailing off the New England coast, and a huge storm blows up, in which Pat is washed overboard to her death, conveniently leaving her wedding ring in Katie's hand. When Katie wakes up wearing it, everyone assumes she is Pat, Glenn Ford's wife. In order to have the love of the man she wants, Katie undertakes her own masquerade (although to appease censorship, the plot always finds a reason to keep the two of them from sleeping together until her ruse is revealed). She follows another rule of behavior familiar to the woman's film: deception. Everyone who knew the twins completely accepts Davis as her other self, although Pat's faithful dog definitely knows the difference. (This means that Glenn Ford's character is not as smart as an Airedale, but that's standard for a typical man in a woman's film.)

This masquerade is ultimately a failure, not because Ford or anyone else knows that Katie is not Pat, but because Katie discovers that Pat's marriage had already gone on the rocks. Bad Pat was having affairs, and now Ford hates her, frosting or no frosting. Poor Katie! Furthermore, when (still pretending to be Pat) she meets Dane Clark, he berates her, saying she's probably glad Katie is dead. "You two probably disliked each other from the time you were born. Why shouldn't you dislike one another? It's a perfectly natural antagonism. She said you were so attractive you could have any man you wanted, and you wanted her man." Thoughtfully, he adds, "She said you were prettier. I don't see much difference—except maybe around the eyes." Since he is an artist, he presumably looks beyond the wardrobe, and he is probably almost as smart as the Airedale.

These details from A Stolen Life show how a woman's film contradicts itself. The good woman who lives a virtuous life and who is clearly right for the leading man does not win him. Reason: She does not have fashion and glamour, two prerequisites for women, and she also is too repressed sexually. When the good woman is offered the pleasure of sex from someone who likes and respects her, she refuses. Reason: Women ought to have sex only with men they are married to.

Contradiction number one: If the good woman had been freer, sexier, like her bad sister, she might have won the man she loved, but on the other hand, she shouldn't be freer and sexier, because it's naughty. Contradiction number two is related to the fact that fashion and glamour, two things that are always endorsed by movies, are also shown to be somewhat evil and trivial, in that they are associated here with the bad twin. The good twin trudges around in slacks and old hats, a more honest and decent way for a woman to be.

The main contradiction comes from the fact that, although Pat and Katie are easily told apart by everyone who knows them throughout the film, no one except the Airedale can tell that Katie is not really Pat when she undertakes the impersonation. We are seriously asked to believe that Pat and Katie are totally defined by their wardrobes and sexual attitudes, so that if Katie wears Pat's clothes and is willing to undertake her sex life, there should be no problem. Finally, Katie has to run away, because she cannot go through with Pat's sexual liaisons. The discovery that Pat was having affairs drives Katie out of the masquerade and back to her New England home, where she first met Ford. When he, having finally figured things out, arrives to embrace her, his words to her are, "You were never a liar. How could you think that you could live a lie?" In the end, the good girl is unmasked as herself, who she was all along anyway. The movie, an enormous hit with women, is a classic example of the twins format, reaffirming the need for women to choose love as their career yet allowing them to watch a woman be as bold and evil as she wishes to be, both things perfectly accomplished by one woman. The second self appears, is mean, sleeps around, and then is washed overboard. Convenient *and* satisfying.

In *Dark Mirror* (1946), the psychologist (Lew Ayres) whom the twin Olivia de Havillands fall in love with explains why men think one twin beautiful and the other undesirable. "Not even nature can duplicate character in twins," he explains. It is "character" in a woman that makes men want her, with "character" being further defined as "warmth." In other words, behavior is the key factor. One de Havilland is friendly, open, kind, and nonthreatening, but the other is a domineering menace, full of anger, and a murderess. However, in order to have more time off from their newsstand jobs, these very different twins frequently pretend to be only one person. As a result, one of their customers has fallen in love with them without realizing "there's two of her." Although it is the bad one who actually goes out on dates with him at night, it is the good one, whom he sees each day at the newsstand, that he has fallen in love with. Since they pretend to be one person, he can't figure it out. Why is she so lovely, so acquiescent by day, and so hard to handle at night?

In a bizarre episode in *Dark Mirror*, de Havilland enacts a double-layered scene in which she is the bad twin pretending to be the good twin in a futile attempt to grasp the truth about why men prefer her sister to her. "Why me and not her? We're so much alike. What makes the difference? Am I better looking than she is?" Ayres, pretending he thinks he's talking to the good twin when he knows he's talking to the bad twin, explains it all for the audience: "There's a natural rivalry between sisters. All women are rivals fundamentally, but it never bothers them because they automatically discount the success of others and alibi their own failures on the grounds of circumstances. Luck, they say." (And this man is supposed to be a psychologist!) He goes on to explain that, since sisters are raised in similar circumstances, they have no "alibi" and thus fewer excuses for themselves. "That's why sisters can hate each other with such terrifying intensity," he triumphantly concludes. "Twins . . . especially identical twins . . . well, agonies of jealousy are possible." (No wonder one of these two de Havillands considers killing him.) Later, after her deception is exposed and she is arrested for murder, the bad twin throws an ashtray at a mirror, shattering the image in which she sees her good sister reflected. It's a desperate and pathetic act and, seen today, downright sympathetic. The complications of the woman's film are such that one can almost see the bad twin as the heroine, frantically trying to destroy that dutiful, obe-

The good and the bad Olivia de Havillands in *Dark Mirror*

dient side of herself that men love and thus enslave to good behavior. The movie ends with Dr. Ayres carrying a tray of food into the ailing good twin's bedroom, with a lovely gift on the tray for her. His last words, gazing at the good de Havilland, are "Why are you so much more beautiful than your sister?" Why indeed? Once again, the twins have their beauty evaluated by their behavior, and once again it is implied that goodness in women is related to kindness, acceptance of their female roles, and general obedience. Once again, however, a second self emerges, and this one fights her good self overtly, not only in behaving really badly but also in trying to pin her own murders on her good self.

Here Come the Waves is a musical comedy, and thus the antics of its characters are exaggerated and the presentation is lighthearted. *Cobra Woman* is pure fantasy, pure escapism, and not to be taken seriously on any account. The twins in both *Here Come the Waves* and *Cobra Woman* represent a simpleminded variation on the good/evil, correct behavior/ incorrect behavior scheme.

In *Here Come the Waves* (1944), the two Betty Huttons are a sister act, singing and dancing in a nightclub, until the serious one decides they must do their duty for their country and join the Waves. (She has been inspired by their own recruiting number, which contains such pronouncements to women as "Uncle Sam needs your gam.") Rosemary, the serious twin, tells Susie, the silly twin, that she has already enlisted. Susie protests at first, but comes around when she has time to think about it. ("The Waves are all right. I like their hats.") Since Rosemary is twelve minutes older, she is the one who manages both their money and their careers. Susie, the dependent one, is immature and always follows along. Although the twins of *Here Come the Waves* are opposites, they are not the traditional opposites of good and evil. The twins concept is not much more than a gimmick, with Betty Hutton more or less just playing her own competition, second lead to herself. The two women represent the opposites of sober and responsible womanhood that willingly plays a role well during war, and silly, frivolous womanhood that does not. Since *Here Come the Waves* is a wartime musical, it uses its twins to suggest that women can and even should be serious during the war. After the sisters join up, there is a montage in which we compare the two of them and their abilities to "do a man's job." Susie can't salute properly, can't make her own bed, can't march correctly, and can't remember to follow the simplest of rules, such as the warning on the mess-hall wall: "Remove lipstick before eating." Rosemary, the correct twin, can do it all.

The film clearly comes down on the side of serious, sober behavior for women. Hollywood always had the ability to shift things around to accommodate current thinking, and since women were being asked to do men's work during the war, this film uses its twins accordingly. Yet even in the midst of musical numbers and recruiting propaganda, the "which is more beautiful" and masquerade themes are maintained.

Meeting the sisters again after several years, Sonny Tufts turns *only* to Rosemary to say, "You're all grown up and beautiful." "Gee, thanks!" answers Susie, much to Tufts's surprise, since he wasn't addressing her and does not see her as being as beautiful as Rosemary. Both the film's hero, Bing Crosby, and Tufts fall in love with Rosemary rather than Susie. Here again two women, played by the same actress, do not look alike to men. (This is partly because Betty Hutton wears a red wig over her blond hair for the role of Rosemary.) Inevitably, the moment comes when one twin impersonates the other. Because Susie is herself in love with Bing Crosby, she doesn't want her sister to have him. She puts on a wig and pretends to Crosby that she (her sister, that is) doesn't really love him and is a secret drinker. The impersonation scene is a lengthy comedy sequence in which Crosby is constantly confused and astonished as the two women move in and out of a room, while he thinks there is only one of them. As was true in both *A Stolen Life* and *Dark Mirror*, the wrong-acting twin is undertaking an impersonation with which to steal love away from her sister. The second self is trying to get what she wants (Bing Crosby) and also punishing her annoyingly perfect sister by making her out to be a drunk in public.

Cobra Woman (1944) brings everything down to the bottom line. One Maria Montez, Tolea, is a lovely person about to marry Jon Hall in her island paradise, and the other Montez, Nadia, is busily doing the cobra ritual dance and throwing her subjects into a roaring volcano. (They don't much like it, but they seem to go along with it. "The cobra ritual appeals to their emotions," her prime minister explains. "That's how she holds them.") Good and evil are presented clearly.

This story is the female variation of stories like *The Prisoner of Zenda* and *The Corsican Brothers.* Twin girls have been born on Cobra Island, but when the older one, Tolea, is exposed to cobra venom in the traditional royal ritual, she sickens and nearly dies. This proves that she is not strong enough to become high priestess and eventually queen. Her twin sister, tough and resilient, will have to reign in her place. "By the code of the cobra," Tolea must be killed, but her sympathetic grandmother puts her to sea in a boat with a kindly stranger who raises her on a distant island as his daughter. The film opens just as Grandma sends someone to bring Tolea back to take the place of her evil twin and save the island's people from all ending up in the volcano. Tolea is stolen on her wedding day and taken to the island, with her groom (Hall) following in hot pursuit. It is astonishing that even in the midst of such delicious nonsense, the twin format is maintained. When Jon Hall watches bad Nadia dive into her private swimming lagoon, he naturally thinks she is good Tolea, looking sexier than he has ever seen her. But when he dives in after her to embrace her underwater in a passionate kiss, and she turns out to be bossy and domineering, he muses that "there is some difference here. . . ." He thinks the docile Tolea is more beautiful.*

---

* In both *Dark Mirror* and *Cobra Woman,* the bad woman, after boldly coming on to the man and kissing him, challenges the hero by asking him if he can really tell the difference. Are her lips not the same as her sister's, her kisses just as satisfying? In both cases, the man is able to say "No, they're not." Why? The implication is clearly that when a woman takes on a sexually aggressive role, advancing on the man herself, the man doesn't like it. He will also be able to tell the difference between the two if he kisses them. "By her kisses we shall know her" is proved in movie terms when the real-life Wilde twins, Lee and Lynn, pretend to be each other in *Twice Blessed* (1945). At the moment of final clinch, their two love interests (Jimmy Lydon and Marshall Thompson) sweep them into a loving kiss, only to suddenly break off and reject the twin they hold. Until that moment of lip contact, each had believed he had embraced the one he loved. Kissing is the proof. The film suggests that it is hilarious that each man couldn't tell the woman he loves from her twin, and equally hilarious that kissing her could be that different.

Inevitably, the good twin is forced to impersonate the bad twin, this time in order to try to save her lover from death. Tolea is a good twin put to the ultimate test. She has to face more than the family Airedale: she has to dress up as Nadia and go in front of the whole populace to carry out the cobra ritual dance, in which she swishes around an apparently highly irritated and suspicious cobra. As if this weren't scary enough, she has to go on in this ritual without the prerequisite cobra jewel and certainly without the prerequisite choreographic experience. (The cobra jewel is the source of one of Montez's most delightful film lines, delivered in her thick Spanish accent, in which she demands from herself that she "geef me dat cobra jool.") Because Tolea is the good twin, she does not have the evil, the power, or the sexuality to fool the cobra. Fortunately, Jon Hall and Sabu rescue her in the nick of time.

Cobra Woman represents a slight variation on the twins format in that the bad Montez falls out a window to her death when she is confronted boldly by the good one. The good one's courage, while not intended to be lethal, turns the tide against evil. Tolea orders Nadia to give her that cobra jewel and stop all her nonsense, but the bad girl defiantly removes a spear from the wall and bellows, "You'll have to kill me first!" Finding courage, Tolea orders her twin to "Put that down!" Advancing forward with a determined look on her face, Tolea threatens Nadia, who begins her retreat toward the window. Suddenly frightened, but still evil, Nadia throws her spear, but the power of the thrust propels her backward. Her long skirt and impossibly high-heeled sandals trip her up. She falls off her shoes and out the window. Tripped up by fashion, the woman's fate! After this dramatic finale, the good Tolea is welcomed to her throne by the people of her island, and her lover leaves her there, feeling that he must let her take care of "her people." But this career decision is only temporary, as the good twin runs away from royalty, hiding in Hall's boat to return home. In other words, she gives up her career for him, choosing love and marriage over the queendom. Well, what with that cobra ritual dance and that snorting volcano, it wasn't worth much anyway. Or as her grandma puts it when Sabu asks her if she is the boss of the whole place, "No. I'm just the Queen."

Although *Cobra Woman* is delightfully silly, it has the same purpose as the other twins films. A good woman is seen as more beautiful than a bad one, even though they are the same person, and the second self is activated for nefarious purposes. The evil Maria Montez is clearly a woman of astonishing sexual power. She can intimidate a cobra, a male symbol if ever there was one. She is presented as the single most interesting aspect of the entire film, and the sight of her camping around, pausing only to point dramatically at one of her poor victims, who will then be tossed into the volcano, is a raw and dynamic portrait of unmitigated evil. After we saw this movie, my little friends and I danced around the gravel pit for weeks, taking turns identifying one another for volcanic sacrifice. Nadia was an impressive second self, showing females of all ages that, at least in fantasyland, a woman could call the shots. That Maria Montez inspired Mario Montez and a host of other transvestite imitations is a tribute to the success of the twins format.*

Two women representing opposite behavior in movies are not always found in the twins format, of course. Two women as opposites appear in all kinds of permutations. Sometimes they are simply sisters, as in *In This Our Life* (1942). These two women are southern, and they have men's names, Stanley and Roy. Stanley (Bette Davis) is bad. Roy (Olivia de Havilland) is good. What does Stanley do that defines her as a bad girl? She drinks, dances, flirts, shops, uses sex to get what she wants, interferes with her husband's career, pushing him to earn money instead of finding meaningful work. She, too, wears off-the-shoulder blouses. What does Roy do that proves she is good? She helps black people, supports her man's work, forgives her bad sister, packs for her husband, sews, lectures everyone, wants kids, relates to her man as if she's his mom, suffers, and wears prim suits. What finally happens to bad old Stanley after she has a lot of sex and dancing? She dies in a car wreck, wearing one of her new outfits. And what happens to Roy? Absolutely nothing.

To survive after Stanley decamps with her husband (Dennis Morgan), Roy does two things to keep herself going: (1) she works, because she knows work counts and that it will help ("I've been keeping very busy . . . ever tried working? For yourself? For your self-respect?") and (2) she vaccinates herself with a little of Stanley's attitude. She becomes selfish and hard and throws caution to the winds. When George Brent, the convenient "other man," comes around and tells her she's intelligent, she replies, "That's something every man admires—in another man." Later, however, she tells him she wants "to go somewhere I've never been . . .

---

* The ultimate in twins is probably portrayed by—who else?—Bette Davis in *Dead Ringer* (1964). Davis, near the end of her remarkable career, plays twins (for the second time), *both* of whom are evil. It's a question of degree. One is semi-evil, or semi-good, but both of the women are killers. At that stage of her career, no one was going to take Bette Davis seriously as an innocent little twin half connected to a bad-girl other half. One might say that no one was as good as Bette when she was bad and even badder.

When a movie is about male twins, the issue is not so much one of good and evil behavior as much as of strength and weakness. The primary concern is masculinity. A strong man is good, and a weak man is bad. A man *should* be strong, but he should not be a bully, and he should not be greedy. Therefore, being strong, if strength is equated with too much ambition, and thus greed, is a bad thing. In such cases, a seemingly weak man finds his worth by standing up to a bully or a greedy opponent.

I don't care how far it is or how long it takes . . . there's nothing now but the moment . . . hold me close. I don't want you to think . . . you'll only lose me if you try to hold me." In other words, Roy decides to take her loss like a man. Having been rejected when she was motherly, she learns a masculine role. She embraces her career and uncomplicated sex.

Well, it's a lesson for us all, but what is the lesson? These two women are actually presented as a unit, a pair to be seen as examples in a typical cautionary tale for women regarding proper behavior. Although, again, the good woman will survive, she has lost her husband and hasn't even remained particularly good. In addition to trying to welcome George Brent into her bed, she has suffered terribly and grown somewhat bitter. Morgan, the man she loves, dies, so she doesn't even get him back. Stanley also dies, of course, losing everything, but before she goes she has all the fun and all the clothes. A lesson is taught, there's no doubt about that, but contrasting the two women loosens up the presentation of the film, allowing an audience the pleasure of watching a dynamic woman, played at a very high pitch by Bette Davis, cavort around the screen doing anything she wants to do. The bad girls, like Scarlett O'Hara (who isn't all that bad, of course) have always been more fun to watch than the good ones. Yes, there's a lesson here for us all. The film offsets the visual power of Bette Davis when she's bad by saying that to be bad is to die and to be good is to live and to misuse sex is for sure to die.

In This Our Life is an example of a film in which two sisters represent two behavioral choices, so that the narrative is centered on female characters. A film that presents two women as polar opposites but is actually a story about a man is *Leave Her to Heaven* (1945). These two films illustrate how stories shift emphasis, because although *In This Our Life* has poor Roy being ditched by her man, it is definitely a story about a woman having to make choices. *Leave Her to Heaven* reverses the pattern and becomes a story about a man choosing between two women. Both are women's films, but the organization of audience sympathy is not directed to the men in *In This Our Life*, whereas it is in *Leave Her to Heaven*.

Leave Her to Heaven is one of the greatest of all women's films. It is superbly written, directed, and produced, and its cast members perfectly embody their roles. It has all the glamour and polish of the 1940s films, and its Technicolor look is sensational. It contains a scene that everyone who ever sees the film remembers vividly, in which Gene Tierney, wearing dark glasses, sits calmly in a rowboat allowing a crippled boy to drown in cold water. ("Ooooooh," I once heard a male voice say during this scene at a revival house. "That bitch is chilly.")

The two women the hero, Cornel Wilde, meets are the cousins Ruth (Jeanne Crain) and Ellen (Tierney). They are visually and narratively defined as polar opposites. Ruth is quiet, simple, and honest. She gardens, and this sense of her as a woman who makes things grow and who cares for all things is her major metaphor in the film. When Wilde dedicates one of his books to her, she is called "The Girl with the Hoe." Tierney, on the other hand, is a woman who kills things. She is shown to be a woman who always gets her own way, and whose obsessive love of her own father shuts out both her mother and her cousin Ruth. Two contrasting images of these women define their roles. Ruth is seen from below, trimming the roses on a trellis. The camera looks up at her, and she is framed by both sunlight and wreaths of blossoms. She is smiling, happy in her work, a fair blossom herself. Tierney is shown riding a horse, her father's ashes inside an urn she carries. As she scatters the ashes across a wild landscape in the mountains, she moves the urn from side to side, her face an enigmatic mask, her image one of power and control. She is awesome in her beauty, but cold, even scary, and she is a dynamically moving figure instead of a framed portrait like Crain.

Wilde is overwhelmed by Tierney and marries her, only to find that she now is as obsessed with him as she was with her father. (Wilde is said to look like the dead man.) She does not wish him to work, nor does she wish anyone to live with them or be around them. She does not want him to have anything or anybody in his life but her. His adored but crippled younger brother, who comes to live with them, is the person she allows to drown, ruthlessly removing him from their lives. When she becomes pregnant, she is furious because it forces her to stay home resting while Wilde and Crain go places together. It also spoils her figure. "I hate the little beast," she says, in a shocking statement delivered with great force and passion while she is standing in front of her mirror. She throws herself down the stairs to induce a miscarriage and later poisons herself in order to blame it on Crain and Wilde, ruining and controlling their lives from her grave.

Leave Her to Heaven is about a wrong choice made by Tierney, who will not accept a subservient role, and also one made by Wilde, who chooses a woman for her beauty and the excitement she generates in him. When men make these wrong choices in women's films, it is usually because the bad woman has tricked or manipulated them into it. The underlying message to women is to watch out for one another, and to suggest to women in the audience who perhaps are not beautiful or sexy that their virtues will win in the end.

Old Acquaintance (1943), which was remade as *Rich and Famous* (1981), is an interesting variation on the two-women-as-opposites format because both women are allowed to become successful career women. Two lifelong friends, Bette Davis and Miriam Hopkins, love each other but are nevertheless jealous rivals. Kit Marlowe, played by Davis, is a serious writer. She wears low-heeled shoes, plain suits, and a shirt and tie in the liberated garb of the 1920s when the film begins. She has never married. Her best friend, Millie Drake (Hopkins), wears hair ribbons, bows on her flowered dresses, and floppy hats. She is married, lives in a beautiful home, and has a baby on the way.

As the film opens, Davis is a literary success and Hopkins is a housewife. Hopkins has what the woman's film tells women they should want: a loving husband, a *House & Garden* home, and an expected child. She is not happy, however, and plans a writing career of her own. "There are people who can have both a career *and* a life. I'm sure of it," she says. The film goes on to prove that women can have a career or they can have a life, but they can't have both in the way they *ought* to have them.

Hopkins becomes a huge success writing romance novels with titles like *Lingering Love, Girl Afraid, Ermine and Calico, Married in June, Last Love,* and *Geraldine.* She grows very rich and has no time for either her husband or her daughter. "She has the house, the servants . . . everything a woman wants," says her husband, who has not provided any of them for her on the scale she now has them. He feels useless and diminished, and is clearly neglected.

When Davis, who secretly loves Hopkins's husband, asks her, "Why aren't you more considerate of Preston?" Hopkins replies, "I've been a good wife to him. I've given him everything. I make him a definite department in my life." These words, which might be acceptable from a man, are supposed to be the definition of just how horrible Hopkins really is. The husband laments, "When I married her, she was a sweet, pretty little girl. It was fun . . . but our marriage has been headed for the rocks since she started writing." *Old Acquaintance* demonstrates that if a woman has a career and devotes herself to it, she does not have enough time for her husband or her child. She will not be there when the child is sick, nor will she be able to move to another town with her husband if he is transferred to further his own career.

During this movie, Bette Davis acts as the voice of society. She plays by its rules in that she has not tried to marry or have children because she is a career woman and knows it won't work. She has understood that she must eschew the love choice in order to do her work. She has made the sacrifice. Hopkins is portrayed as a cheater. She tries to have it both ways, tries not to suffer. Finally, however, she can't escape, either.

The two women, both of whom have chosen careers, end up with only each other. Hopkins tells Davis, "My new book is about two women friends." "You mean, like us?" Davis asks. "It's the first sad ending I've ever written," replies Hopkins, "the two women are left all alone. I'll call it *Old Ac-*

quaintance." The two women toast each other with champagne as the camera moves back to reveal what will happen to women who don't accept love or their natural female roles in life. They will be alone—but, of course, they will also be extremely wealthy, well dressed, sought after, successful, and they will be drinking champagne.

Sometimes movies put two women together as a coherent unit, rather than as opposites, and get something that is better than one man. This is "there's two of her and they add up to 1½." These are movies that are indeed made for women only, because the implication is sisterhood. In these films, women who are supposed to be rivals turn out to share the same wonderful qualities of good sportsmanship, beauty, humor, and kindness. They are both let down by the same man. In both versions of *When Ladies Meet*, two worthy women love the same cad, and their interaction brings about their sisterhood and mutual respect. Neither woman becomes a villain.

When Ladies Meet is proof positive that women liked such stories, as it was not only a successful stage play (by Rachel Crothers) that enjoyed a long run and many revivals, but it was also made into a movie twice within a decade. In the 1933 version, Ann Harding and Myrna Loy play two women wronged by one man (Frank Morgan), and in the 1941 version, Greer Garson and Joan Crawford suffer at the hands of Herbert Marshall.

The story concerns a loyal wife (Harding and Garson) whose husband is having an affair with a successful novelist whose work he publishes (Loy and Crawford). When the two ladies accidentally meet at the country home of a friend, they do not realize they are rivals. Staying overnight at the friend's invitation, they strike up a warm friendship, having a lengthy woman-to-woman chat in which they let their hair down. In particular, the unmarried female, who is the first to find out the truth, realizes that her lover's wife is a noble woman who has been putting up with his philandering for years. It is a situation in which women are presented as superior, not only in their morals, but also in their understanding, their patience, their realistic attitudes, and their ability to respect one another's territory. Although one is a traditional wife and one a career woman, they share the same basic problem: they are women. Thus, they are vulnerable to the selfish nonsense of childish men. Their best choice is to understand the truth about that, and at least try not to hurt each other. The ladies meet and bond together in sisterhood, a sorority in which women suffer, are wronged, make the best of it, but don't add to each other's misery if they can help it. Furthermore, the big publishing tycoon (Frank Morgan and Herbert Marshall) ends up looking like he's simply not worth either of these women's time.

• • •

ANOTHER EXAMPLE of "there's two of her" concerns the situation in which one woman assumes another identity. These films break down into two types: those in which a woman's other self emerges without her being able to control it, during sleep or hypnosis, and those in which the woman herself takes control and decides to pretend to be someone else.

The sleepwalking or dreaming woman appears in musicals (*Lady in the Dark*), comedies (*Half Angel*), and melodramas (*Whirlpool*, 1949 version).* The key factor in these movies is the attitude taken toward the woman's other self. Does it control her, or does she control it? If it controls her, the movie can be a drama, a horror film, a musical, or a comedy, but it definitely has a dramatic dimension. However, if the woman herself decides to impersonate another self in order to fool a man, the film is almost always a comedy.

These movies show how women have inner selves that wish to be free, unrepressed, sexual. This *could* be subversive, since it is always a prim and proper woman who dreams this way.† Thus the concept is presented as appropriate, in that a woman is learning to give herself to one man, to allow her "feminine" nature to have love and romance, and to get married. When a woman goes to sleep at night, her other, repressed self can emerge.**

A lavish, even astonishing, visual presentation of the dream self awakening awaits any viewer of the film adaptation of the Moss Hart/Kurt Weill/Ira Gershwin stage hit *Lady in the Dark* (1944). For one thing, all the women in the movie wear hats and carry purses while walking around at the office. (I can imagine some future era of scholars who, without any

---

* We are not talking about movies in which a woman becomes possessed, as in 1944's *The Uninvited*, when Gail Russell's dead mother tries to kill her own child by possessing her. However, other horror films, such as *Cat People* (1942) and the various vampire movies with female vampires do apply. These films depict a second self that emerges at night in purely sexual terms. The implication of *Cat People* is that the self is a man-hating woman, perhaps lesbian, and the vampire movies indicate a woman of rapacious appetites. The second self of these movies is a woman without sexual repressions but one who, when released, is perverse, dangerous, or out of control.

† The woman who goes to sleep and releases herself into a different form is uniformly a good woman whose inner self wishes to be sexier, naughtier, freer in some way. I don't know of any films in which a bad woman falls asleep and dreams that she's taking baskets to the poor.

** This is the plot of the silly movie *Half Angel* (1951) starring Loretta Young in a simpleminded tale of a woman who just gets up and sleepwalks out on the town in order to have a little fun. By day, she's a prim secretary in a large hospital, and she positively *hates* Joseph Cotten, a wealthy, bluenosed lawyer. By night, she rises from her bed à la Vampira and goes on the prowl for him because she subconsciously loves him. At night, she is beautifully dressed and sexy. By day, she's a candidate for the fashion-police squad.

explanation of *Lady in the Dark* to guide them, sagely label it "science fiction," based on the way these women look.) Many women think of this film as an antifeminist tract, since its working heroine is constantly criticized by its hero for having her career. "I know your kind. You have magazines instead of babies" and "Rage is a poor substitute for sex." When she finally abandons her severe, masculine suits for a gold, jewel-encrusted jacket over a simple full-length skirt made of mink skins, he tells her, "You look wonderful. You actually look like a woman."

However, *Lady in the Dark* is like its subject matter, a dreamworld of images that mask their own inner meanings in order to make them acceptable to the dreamer. Ginger Rogers plays the role of Liza that was originated by the elegant Gertrude Lawrence on stage. A wildly successful career woman who edits *Allure* magazine, Liza is suffering from deep anxiety. "There must be something wrong. Why do I have this horrible depression, this panic? Why am I frightened all the time? The nicest man in the world is in love with me. I'm doing the work I adore. The magazine's a huge success. . . ." Why indeed? Her doctor tells her, "All of us hide things from ourselves" and sends her off to a psychoanalyst to find out what her problem really is.

It's on the analyst's couch that the story of Liza is defined for the audience as really being the story of the men in her life. There are four of them:

- Her married lover (Warner Baxter), the "nice man" she referred to when talking to her doctor (Baxter wants to marry her)
- A famous male movie star (Jon Hall), a leading sex symbol of the day (he also wants to marry her)
- Her employee (Ray Milland), a talented man, the one who constantly tells her she is not a real woman (he wants to steal her job)
- Her father (Harvey Stephens), the all-important fourth man, although Liza doesn't realize that he is a daily influence on her behavior (that will be for the analyst to dig out)

Each of the three men whom she sees on a daily basis during the film (her lover, the movie star, and her rival) defines an aspect of Liza's personality, and each has a particular relationship with her. The married lover, Warner Baxter, represents a character that is very familiar in the woman's film. He is the older father figure who is present in a successful woman's life, offering her everything and asking for nothing in return. Although he waits for her in her lavish apartment at the end of each business day, if he senses that she's tired and doesn't feel like company he departs immediately without his dinner. If he drops by her office and senses that she's busy and doesn't feel like talking, he generously says, "You want me

to leave, don't you?", cheerfully departing when she nods. The plot establishes that he cannot marry her because he is already married, and his
wife will not give him a divorce. He feels terrible about this, but Liza
apparently accepts it easily. Their relationship is smooth, calm, dull. Baxter
gives Liza security.

Jon Hall is a figure of glamour and male sex appeal. When he comes
to the magazine to be photographed in a fashion layout, the female staff
goes crazy, running to peek at him and swooning around in girlish fashion.
Liza, however, remains cool and collected, unaffected by his fame and
reputation as a ladies' man, and this appeals to Hall. His attraction to her
restores her self-esteem, and since she is currently questioning herself,
his sexual energy suggests to her that this is what is missing in her life.
Hall gives Liza the promise of sex.

Ray Milland is the man who constantly criticizes Liza. "She shouldn't
be top man. She's flying in the face of nature." Milland makes it clear that
he thinks Liza should quit her job and live more like other women. He
also makes it clear that he wants her job for himself. He is portrayed as
capable and talented, but not necessarily more capable and talented than
Liza. For her part, she recognizes his ability and, after losing her temper
with him and even temporarily firing him, keeps him on because it is good
for the magazine. Milland gives Liza a hard time.

As the film unfolds, the analyst probes "deeply" into Liza's dreams
to find out what is really bothering her. At the same time as the audience
is learning her hidden motives (through several astonishing musical dream
sequences), the plot also reveals the true inner motivations of the three
men in her life. Warner Baxter allegedly wants her for his wife, but what
he really wants is a daughter. Jon Hall allegedly wants her for an exciting
and glamorous sexual partner, but what he really wants is a mother. Milland
allegedly wants to be rid of her so he can run the magazine alone, but what
he really wants is a working equal, a partner, or, if seen negatively, an
employee. These things are revealed to Liza in the nondream portion of
the movie. When Baxter comes to her with the good news that at last he
can get a divorce, Liza realizes she doesn't love him. "I'll fight for you,"
says Baxter, but he doesn't. They both seem relieved. When Liza decides
to date Jon Hall, assuming that he is a man who will protect her, give her
children, take care of her while setting her afire with passion, she is shocked
out of her romantic fantasy when he explains to her that he's happy she's
not like other women—always wanting sex and expecting him to do everything. He is riddled with fears, especially because he has just signed a
big business deal to form his own producing company. "With you behind
me, taking care of me, guiding me," he tells her, "I won't have to worry
about a thing."

This leaves only Ray Milland. Having ruled out the asexual male and learned the sham of the totally sexual male, Liza is left with the jerk who goes around saying "Don't tell me she wears that desk to bed." All he seems to want from her is a decision on what to put on the cover of the magazine's Easter issue. All through the film Liza has been unable to make this decision, to commit herself to what will be seen on the cover, and this becomes a metaphor for her inability to accept herself as a woman. She can't do the woman's thing. She can't make a choice! In the end, Liza realizes that she needs Milland to help her make these decisions, and she asks him to coedit the magazine with her. He is delighted. As they bend eagerly over their work, Liza seems happy, alive, energized for the first time in the movie. They are going to work alongside each other! Suddenly, they look deeply into each other's eyes and kiss. This is as unexpected as it is expected. Because Milland is the leading man, one knows Rogers will end up with him, but because we have seen precious little to indicate that he was the right man in any way, we have to accept it on the terms we have learned from going to the movies: star kisses star.

After their loving kiss, Ray Milland sits down at Ginger Rogers's desk *in her chair*. She herself is trying to sit in it at the same time. As he occupies it, she falls to the floor, an ominous note. "What are you doing down there?" Milland wants to know.

One can ponder this ending. Ginger Rogers has not stopped working. She has not surrendered her magazine to Milland. She has not wed her father figure, nor her sexy little boy. She has decided to share the responsibility of her work with the man who has criticized her for not being a woman throughout the film. He has never said she is not good at her job, however, and he has not asked her in the end to stop working. They have kissed, maintaining the romantic tradition, but what are we supposed to assume? That she will quit and turn the magazine over to him? That he will take it away from her? That she will edit a better magazine now that she has thawed out and found a real man? If each of the three men represents something in this movie about psychoanalysis, a world of hidden symbols, and Baxter represents security and Hall sex, is it not possible to see Milland as representing career?

The explanation of Liza lies in the dream sequences in which an incredulous audience learns her true story as she speaks to an analyst to find out the truth about what lies buried deep, deep inside her. And what does? The favorite emblem of the woman's picture forms the basis of Liza's psyche: a dress. The psychoanalyst asks her, "Does it strike you as significant that in your dreams you are the opposite of what you are now?" He is referring partly to her wardrobe. Liza is shown on-screen to be two people. By day, she is a mouseburger in a mannish suit, but at night, in her dreams, she is a woman with a closet full of feminine clothes. What Liza apparently longs for, as depicted on screen, is not a man but an outfit. We are not shown that she wants to have children or give up her job. She longs to be feminine and loved by a man, but in this particular film that love is represented by the mink skirt, not the apron.

Liza's dreams, which are also musical numbers, are among the most surreal events ever depicted on the American screen. They are lavish, out-of-control, over-the-top visualizations that somehow manage to be both hilarious and frightening. For pure 1940s visual style, *Lady in the Dark* is in a class by itself. The dream sequences are Daliesque, done in pink, gold, pale blue, and lime green. In one of these dreams, Liza approaches a locked chest to search within it for one of her secrets. Suddenly, the chest springs open and out floats a magnificent blue dress. Liza's inner soul is chiffon! The most telling of these sequences is one involving a wedding. Liza visualizes herself marching down the aisle wearing a gigantic hat in the style of Camelot, with cone and wimple. Her bridesmaids are wearing equally odd headgear of a sort that can only be called labial. The look of the wedding party is grotesque, as if the lavish, exaggerated clothing often seen in women's films has been taken to a nightmare level. As Liza moves forward, her wedding gown begins to fall apart, and, in order to reach her groom to complete the ceremony, she has to climb to the top of her wedding cake, layer by layer. As she tries to scale its heights, she is sobbing, and her gown continues to shred. The cake itself seems to be hissing and emitting fog as she proceeds. Everyone on screen watches her with either disapproval or derision, and Liza is shown to be feeling humiliated, degraded. While it is true that this Wedding from Hell is related to Liza's fears of clothes and men, can anyone watch this sequence and ever feel good about weddings again?

Lady in the Dark, having been a highly successful Broadway play, is a good example for examining the terms in which Hollywood addressed the average woman. Although it is frequently thought to be a faithful adaptation, the movie is really quite different from the show. It is less humorous, less musical, and it vulgarizes the original material, moving it toward what Orson Welles once referred to as "dollar-book Freud." In fact, the movie becomes an overt statement of Liza's problems in Freudian terms. These problems are defined for viewers in common woman's movie terms: three different men clearly represent three different choices she might make in life; a dress represents the main psychological problem she has; sex is repressed; and a great deal of dry ice is used to indicate the high seriousness of psychoanalysis. Furthermore, the movie clearly sets up the story as if there were *two* Ginger Rogerses: the one she is, and the one she wants to be. In reading the text of the play, which, of course, doesn't give one the design presentation, it appears that the story is about one Liza, and she has a problem about what she wants to do with her life. The movie has clarified all its issues in movie terms, so that the viewing audience would know where it was. And where it was was the local movie house, not the Broadway theater.

WHAT ALL THESE FILMS that deal with two women—either as twins, sisters, rivals, or the divided self—are about is, quite simply, a woman's desire to be something else. Their popularity had to be partly due to their depicting a woman cutting loose and doing the opposite of what was expected of her. The fact that these films restore order and ultimately endorse the status quo just made the release all the more attractive and pleasurable. It also helped audiences to feel secure to wallow in the fun. One of the best forms for this kind of audience release is the "two of her" comedy format, in which a woman willingly pretends she is another person undertaking an assumed identity for a purpose.

Masquerades of this kind are a popular convention of many screwball comedies of the 1930s and early 1940s. *Midnight, Two-Faced Woman, The Awful Truth*, and *The Lady Eve* are four films in which a woman voluntarily pretends to be someone else. When this happens, there is always trouble ahead for the man in her life, because these are stories of a woman taking on power by leaving all her restrictions behind. And these movies are comedies because comedy unleashes a woman. In comedy, a woman can do terrible things to a man and get away with it. She can set his pants on fire, dump a dish of hot ravioli in his lap, humiliate him in front of his boss, and even marry him without his knowing what is going on. When a woman is unleashed into that kind of violence in a crime film or a horror film, she is clearly bad and must be destroyed for her behavior. But in a comedy, she can get away with it. She can also get drunk, wreck a proper social occasion, and enter into pretense and role-playing, all without society's judging her. Outrageous behavior by women becomes funny instead of frightening.

There is a marvelous inner layer to these comedies that was a kind of bonus for women in the audience. Most of the stars who played in them were also known as performers in serious women's films. When they were then cast in these revenge comedies and were seen to be kicking up their high heels, a second self was carried by the actress's own persona. First, Irene Dunne sits home in *Back Street* (1932) painting plates as a rich man's mistress, and then she comes out in *Theodora Goes Wild* (1936) and defies the conventions of her small-town life. Greer Garson suffers belowstairs as an Irish maid in *The Valley of Decision* (1945) but next thing you know, she's swinging on a trapeze in *Julia Misbehaves* (1948). The liberation of stars like Dunne, Garson, and many others* who played in serious women's films by casting them in comedy roles pleased and delighted all filmgoers, who could revel in the second self of the movie star.

Comedy obviously depends on the release of tension, and the invitation to an audience to laugh at its fears is one of film's most seductive gifts. To take away a man's status as a man—that is, to place a woman in control of what is happening to him by assuming an identity of her own design— provided a wonderful release for women in the audience. They could watch a woman get away with it, do things that polite, well-behaved women never could or would do. She could pretend to be someone else. These masquerades are always liberating, because they allow a woman to step out of her accepted place. And it's hardly surprising that these movies often have revenge plots, in which women activate the fake self in order to punish the men they love. Where men are made less masculine to generate laughter, women are often empowered, made stronger and more destructive.

In such movies, the subversive agenda is not hidden. It is disguised by laughter. In *Midnight* (1939), the heroine (Claudette Colbert) is hired to pretend to be a phony baroness, carrying out the wishes of a cuckolded husband who is paying her to lure his wife's lover away. In *Two-Faced Woman* (1941), a ski instructress (Greta Garbo), who is healthy and straightforward, pretends to be her "sister," a glamorous flirt, to teach her own husband a lesson. In *The Awful Truth* (1937), a divorced wife (Irene Dunne) boldly pretends to be her ex-husband's trashy sister, in order to embarrass him in front of his new fiancée's snooty relatives.

How easy it is for women to deceive! How natural to them is the masquerade! In *The Lady Eve*, Barbara Stanwyck easily seduces the unsuspecting Henry Fonda not once but twice in the same film. When she first deceives him, she is herself, a cardsharping member of a father-daughter team that travels the seas fleecing the wealthy. Fonda is the naive son of the Pike of "Pike's Pale, the Ale that won for Yale." He boards a ship in South America after a lengthy scientific expedition up the Amazon to study reptiles. ("Snakes are my life," he tells Stanwyck. "What a life," she solemnly intones.) Although Fonda and Stanwyck genuinely fall in love, she is revealed to him as the cheat she is before she has a chance to confess. He walks out on her without giving her a chance to explain. Furious and hurt, she decides to teach him a lesson, undertaking the impersonation that is key to the movie.

---

* Claudette Colbert could be serious in *Imitation of Life* (1934) and silly in *She Married Her Boss* (1935), and Barbara Stanwyck, Ann Harding, Norma Shearer, Joan Crawford, Bette Davis, Rosalind Russell all played in such reversals. Also, it worked two ways. A star like Ginger Rogers, known for her comedies and musicals, could suddenly go serious (and win Academy Awards) in films like *Kitty Foyle* (1940).

Stanwyck shows up in Fonda's world as the Lady Eve, a titled British woman. He is so naive, so innocent, that he fails to realize that she is, in fact, exactly the same woman. No such innocence exists on the part of his faithful companion, the magnificent William Demarest. "Positively the same dame" is his view of the matter. As Eve, Stanwyck ruthlessly marries Fonda in a whirlwind courtship, explaining that it will be easy to trick him, because he was made for it, "like the turkey for the ax." On their wedding night, she stages a "confession" to a long list of previous husbands and lovers, which goes on and on and on. ("Hubert? No, Herbert. Hubert came later. . . .") Under the guise of comedy, woman punishes man. Eve not only makes Adam take the apple, she shoves it down his throat.

In all of these movies the goal is the same: punish the man and teach him a lesson. If the films were not comedies, this cruelty and manipulation would not go unpunished, but because the movies are not serious, three of the women end up in the arms of the men they are humiliating, with the fourth, Claudette Colbert in *Midnight*, succeeding in stopping the wife's affair while herself ending up in the arms of a taxi driver who befriended her before she was hired by her wealthy benefactor. What we learn from these films is that when a woman decides to punish a man, she has no trouble doing so. When a woman decides to seduce a man, flirt with him, or make a fool of him, she has no trouble doing so. What will trip her up is the usual thing: love. If she herself falls for the boob she is mugging, she will end up in his arms.

WHEN A WOMAN'S CHOICES are defined by two supporting characters, whether men or women, these characters tend to be undeveloped, even one-dimensional. In *My Reputation* (1946), Barbara Stanwyck has two women in her life who direct her to different ways of resolving the loneliness of her widowhood. Her mother (Lucile Watson) suggests she roll bandages for the Red Cross and accept the life of respectable widowhood that she herself accepted when Stanwyck's father died twenty-five years earlier. The mother figure has done what society expected from her when she had the bad luck to lose her husband. She has worn black ever since and has devoted herself to charitable work; she has buried her emotions and directed any sexual energy into good works. Stanwyck's friend, played by Eve Arden, is a modern woman, happily married to a warm and outgoing man. Their relationship is shown to be frankly and comfortably sexual. She encourages Stanwyck to find her way to a new man, a new love, or, at least, to a new satisfying sexual relationship. These two characters are voices to be heard in the movie, to define for viewers what the choices really are. In *My Reputation*, an excellent film, the voice of society (Stanwyck's mother) is heard to be wrong, and the voice of a full sexual life (Eve Arden) is heard to be right.

In *The Man I Love* (1946), Ida Lupino, the central character, struggles with her own life as a strong loner with a positive self-image. After many years away, she comes home to her family and helps resolve their problems. One of the subplots of the film presents two very different women as models to choose between. Lupino's married sister, played by Andrea King, is a woman who has been a loving wife, making a good marriage. Across the hall in the opposite apartment lives Dolores Moran, a beautiful young woman who is the mother of two small children. She neglects both her kids and her husband and goes out on the town with other men. She wants a good time, good clothes, and plenty of perfume.

These two women, King and Moran, represent a woman's life choices. King is made to suffer deeply, because her husband becomes mentally ill. He behaves badly toward her, even though she is "doing the right thing." Moran does indeed have fun, attract the right men, and live the high life without the burdens of her boring husband and two children. We are shown that, temporarily, things can go wrong for the good woman and right for the bad. In the end, however, King's husband recovers and her life is in order, while Moran has been killed in an automobile accident. Lupino, ever the loner, remains detached from any behavioral labels at the end of the movie, going her way alone.

When a woman's duality is expressed through a choice of two men, the male characters then take on the burden of bad and good behavior. Where females are judged and can be reformed in this regard, men are presented in a more absolute condition. That is, they aren't going to change. Some men are bad, and some men are good—*they* have the choice, and it's up to a woman to use her head and not get a bad one. It's an interesting fact of life in the woman's film that it is almost always true that good women pick bad men, and bad women pick good men. A woman does not select a bad man because she herself is evil, but because she has made a poor choice. An audience is asked to see such a choice as dumb but sympathetic, because love is the woman's career. She was trying to do the right thing and follow the correct rules of social behavior. She just used poor judgment, and films suggest that a woman's poor judgment regarding men is a fact of life, too.

A great many films provide choices between a bad man and a good one. And "bad" where men are concerned does not always mean evil, as it does with women; "bad" can mean weak or sickly or unable to earn a good living. Perhaps the most famous example is the case of Leslie Howard (good) and Clark Gable (bad) in *Gone With the Wind* (1939). They are particularly useful examples because, as it turns out, Howard is good, but bad, because he's weak, sickly, and also loves someone else; his temperament doesn't match that of the fiery Scarlett O'Hara. Gable is bad, but good. He's a wicked man who kicks down doors, hangs around with whores, runs guns illegally; but he's good for Scarlett because he can tame her and match her passion. He understands her; they're two of a kind. Here is duality. Leslie Howard's Ashley Wilkes represents marriage, home, children, fidelity, and respectability. Gable's Rhett Butler represents the opposite in all areas. He is the supreme projection. Is there any woman alive who would choose Howard over Gable? Everyone knows this is the major flaw of *Gone With the Wind*.

One of the most realistic films to use two men is the downbeat *Daisy Kenyon* (1947), starring Joan Crawford. In this grim story, Crawford is a successful fashion illustrator who is not young and who is tired of living half a life with her married lover (Dana Andrews). Andrews is manipulative, cruel to his wife, destructive with his spoiled children; he controls Crawford through sex and male power. (His good side is defined by his desire to defend the Japanese who were deprived of their property during the war.) Crawford's other choice, Henry Fonda, is almost as bad. He, too, is a manipulator, riddled with guilt because his wife died in an auto accident when he was driving. Wanting out of her dead-end affair with Andrews, Crawford's solution is to marry Fonda. When that, too, goes sour, she accuses him of using her. "Yes, I'm using you," he calmly replies. "Aren't you using me?" Few more depressing scenes in popular movies exist than the one in which Andrews, Crawford, and Fonda sit together in a dark and cheerless bar, confronting their mutual needs and weaknesses. In the end, Crawford clears her head by driving off in a snowstorm at high speed and wrecking her car. She decides she'll go with the one who allows her to be herself, to make up her own mind. This presumably is Fonda, but an audience knows he's only the better of the two, not the best deal any woman could want.

"THERE'S TWO OF HER" is one way for movies to polarize feminine behavior. "There's three of her" is another.* The story of women in multiple units became popular early on—the story in which three young women room together (or are sisters). These movies probably emerged as an opportunity for a studio to showcase three lovely young starlets who were all being groomed for top-level success. In *Our Blushing Brides* (1930), Joan

* Multiple-personality films, such as *The Three Faces of Eve* (1957), *Sybil* (1976), and later television versions of this true-life phenomenon, are somehow never very interesting and do not apply here. When the problem becomes clinical, the narrative shifts toward solving a medical problem rather than toward presenting the woman's world.

Crawford, Dorothy Sebastian, and Anita Page are three young women who work as models in a large department store, each one acting out a scenario of her own that illustrates one of the three options available to young women who come to work in the big city.* ("If it isn't one thing, it's another," one of their coworkers comments at the beginning of the movie, which pretty much sums up the plot.) Anita Page articulates the frustrations of her shop-girl life: "Work all day and come home to this dump . . . work in the store until I'm old or I marry some sap and spend the rest of my life washing dishes in the Bronx." Although Crawford figures "I'd do what I wanted if I believed in it, if I were sure it was real" regarding sex, she is a hard-working, virtuous girl: "You've got to be sure it's real, not lie to yourself." Page and Sebastian, however, feel that virtue is getting them nowhere. Page allows herself to be set up in a love nest by a wealthy young man, and Sebastian marries a no-good racketeer who gives her everything—at first. While Crawford models stunning ski outfits, fur-trimmed satin ball gowns, and bathing suits, the other two go downhill. Sebastian says she has "a Fannie Hurst husband—six days out, one day in." When her husband is arrested, she goes back to Ohio. Page drinks poison and dies when she learns that her young lover will marry a girl of his own class. ("She wasn't modern enough," Crawford says bitterly. "She believed him.") Crawford stands off the shenanigans of Robert Montgomery, however, and alone ends up wealthy and married.

"THERE'S THREE OF HER" differs from "there's two of her" in more ways than one. In the twosome format, particularly if the women are twins or sisters, there is always the subtle suggestion that they really are two halves of the same person. The audience is asked to involve itself emo-tionally with the right or wrong half of the duo, suffering alongside the right one when things go wrong for her, but understanding the fundamental dichotomy of the presentation. "There's three of her" clearly develops three different stories, representing three different ways of life, which are in-terrelated only by a shared apartment, a shared occupation. The relationship of the story presentation to the viewer is also somewhat different. In "there's two of her," we are asked to involve ourselves emotionally with the right

* This movie is a reworking of a 1925 silent called *Sally, Irene, and Mary*, in which Crawford, Constance Bennett, and Sally O'Neill play three show girls in a Broadway revue who represent three different attitudes toward love and career. This idea was so popular with audiences that it turned up over and over again for the next three decades, in such movies as *Girls About Town* (1931), *Ladies in Love* (1936), *Three Blind Mice* (1938), *Moon Over Miami* (1941), *Three Little Girls in Blue* (1946), *How to Marry a Millionaire* (1953), *Three Coins in the Fountain* (1954), etc., etc.

or wrong half of the choice. In "there's three of her," there is a more distanced or objectified presentation of three clearly separate women, each acting out one of the three different ways of life that women have open to them. We are not asked so much to identify as to watch and observe. There is very little subversion present in this type of movie, as its goal really does seem to be purely instructional. That is, "good" behavior is rewarded.

Initially, the three young women are seen to be equals in beauty and their opportunity to succeed. By the three different choices they make regarding love and their role as women, they act out the three basic choices open to a woman in life: love and marriage, career, or primrose path. This might be called doing it the right way for a living, doing it the wrong way for a living, and just doing it for a living.

Ladies in Love (1936) is a clear example of how the threesome format works. The three women and the choices they represent are:

JANET GAYNOR: "I'm going to wish for the impossible. A good home. And while I'm about it, I might as well wish for a man—someone to love and look after—and children."

LORETTA YOUNG: "I'm going to wish for a hat shop I can work in. I'm tired of a lot of silly men trying to make love to me. I want to be independent of men."

CONSTANCE BENNETT: "I'm going to wish for a rich husband, one who'll buy me a five-story house, lots of furs and jewels, put lots of cash in the bank, one that's not too hard to look at." (Bennett has been established as a "paid companion" for older wealthy men. Thus, her wish for a rich husband is not a romantic-marriage dream, but a desire to solidify job security in her chosen field.)

Here it is, spelled out: Marry for love; do not marry; "marry" for money. In the end, each girl gets her wish, but not without suffering. Constance Bennett has the misfortune to fall truly in love, but the man she chooses (Paul Lukas, she should have known better) instead marries a very young flibbertigibbet (Simone Simon). Simon has pointed out to Lukas why he ought to pick her instead of Bennett: "In Budapest on your vacations you can find plenty of elegant women [like Bennett], but in South America, where your work is, you want a woman you can count on, someone you know will love you always and always, someone who will share your good life with you." Bennett understands at once what motivated Lukas's decision: "She's [Simon] someone you can believe when she says she loves you." He has chosen a silly young girl without experience over the intelligent but obviously very experienced Bennett, who has been described as the kind of woman society men are found with when they aren't with society women. Bennett ends up marrying the richest man in town on a fair-deal

Ladies in Love—there's three of them: Loretta Young, Constance Bennett, and Janet Gaynor, being directed by Edward Griffith.

basis. She'll have the money she wants, the house, the furs, and the jewels—and he's not too bad looking—but she will not have love. Once having chosen the primrose path, she will always be denied a loving marriage, and her relationship with her man will always be a business deal.

Loretta Young suffers an even worse fate, suggesting that the career choice might be more dire for a woman than the primrose path. Despite her avowed desire for independence, Young's character cannot deny the woman's basic need for love. She falls deeply for a wealthy young man (played by the exquisitely handsome Tyrone Power in one of his early roles). Power returns Young's love, and they enact a Happy Interlude, tipping a skilled viewer off to the suffering that lies ahead. When Power is required to marry a girl from his own class and background, he dumps Young painfully, without telling her of his plans with the other woman. When Young finds out, she tries to kill herself, but is saved by her roommates. In the end, Loretta Young does get her independence. Bennett's rich husband generously finances Young's little hat shop, but it is suggested that this choice—a career—is the most tragic of the three. Bennett at least will have pleasant companionship. Young will only have her hats and her work.

Of the three women, implies the movie, only Janet Gaynor wishes for the right thing. She easily gets her wish, falling in love with a young doctor, played by Don Ameche. He truly loves her, offering her not only an honorable marriage with a professional man but the promise of a loving home with many children. *Ladies in Love* is a "monkey's paw" story, in which three young women wish for something and each gets her wish. For Bennett, it is a form of benign punishment, and for Young, a tragic lesson that nearly takes her life. Bennett and Young are the losers because they did not wish for the thing that women ought to know they should want: a good home, with a husband and children—even though Gaynor has pointed out that she is the one wishing for the impossible. The "three of them" story is one of the least ambivalent of all the types of films about women. As the film reaches its conclusion, Constance Bennett delivers the perfect summarizing tag line about their lives: "Boys 2, Girls 1."

This instructional use of three different women to teach audiences what the right path in life is for females shifts subtly when, instead of three women making three different choices, the plot presents a story in which one woman is trying to choose among three possible men. *Three Guys Named Mike* (1951), *Please Believe Me* (1950), and *Tom, Dick and Harry* (1941) —which was remade in 1957 as a musical, *The Girl Most Likely*—all illustrate this format. The assumption is that she is the good girl of the "there's three of them" phenomenon and thus will choose marriage. The story homes in on the choice. And it *must* be a marriage for love instead of money or security.

Tom, Dick and Harry treats the subject as comedy, but still makes its point. The heroine, Ginger Rogers, is a telephone operator who speculates on marriage with three different men via three dream sequences. Prospect number one is Burgess Meredith, who makes her hear bells when he kisses her, but who has no ambition, no future. Marriage with him looks like a hell of poverty, kids, washing and ironing, broken-down living conditions. Prospect number two, George Murphy, is a go-getter automobile salesman with an unlimited future. Life with him is magazine-ad perfect —little house, picket fence, well-equipped kitchen—but Murphy's ambition causes him to neglect her. Prospect number three is perfect because he's already rich, not to mention handsome and smooth (Alan Marshal). Rogers picks him, but as she's going to drive away in his ritzy convertible, Meredith leans over to kiss her good-bye. As the bells go off, she realizes the truth and reluctantly gets out of the car, presumably to accept a life of poverty. She knows woman's film truth: love is her true career.

FASHION AND GLAMOUR

I suppose that every woman knows
The magic and mystery of clothes.
Often times an evening gown worn at a dance
May be the inspiration for romance. . . .

THIS CHEERFUL, "we're all chums here, girls" patter from the 1936 musical *Colleen* strikes a palsy-walsy relationship with the women in the audience and then immediately takes an ugly turn, warning them:

Oh, how soon the honeymoon can fade away
Without the lure of lovely lingerie.
What would you look like before an altar rail
Without a trousseau or without a bridal veil?

Here is a grim reminder to ordinary women that as a man goes to his ultimate destiny, a woman goes to her final outfit. The movies make it clear: a woman *is* what she wears, so it had better be right. A woman must be F.C. (fashionably correct). She cannot expect to occupy a position at the center of the universe if she isn't properly turned out, and she certainly can't expect to succeed in her natural career of love. Without the right clothes on, she probably can't even think straight, so how can she ever make the right choice? When the prince comes to town, she's got to have a glass slipper. Movies clearly state that fashion and glamour are fundamental to a woman's definition—in her own eyes, in the eyes of the man she loves (whether he knows it or not), and in the eyes of society. A woman shops to live and dresses to kill.

During the golden era of the Hollywood film, audiences, both men and women, were drawn to the movies partly by the luxury they saw on the screen. To satisfy these audiences, Hollywood was always willing to depart from any sense of credibility where fashion and furniture were concerned. Whereas old movies went to great extremes to make sure that a street of shops in Paris had the proper French names above the doors (*pâtisserie*, not "bakery"), they would blow it all by allowing the peasant girl who worked there to suddenly turn up in an elaborate evening gown with matching satin slippers. In the 1930s, 1940s, and into the 1950s, even a movie about a poor little shop girl had her standing behind the counter in a simple dress trimmed in about two thousand dollars' worth of handmade lace. Movies about women of wealth zoomed to the stratosphere with twenty or thirty costume changes, displaying the star not only in a variety of fur coats, but also in fur hats, fur gloves, fur muffs, fur skirts, and fur-trimmed pajamas. Fashion and glamour were direct connections to the audience's need to see things they could never have and to experience feelings absent from their daily lives. As Joan Crawford cries out in *The Bride Wore Red*, ". . . all your life to want things you've seen and heard about and dreamed about. . . ." The place Americans saw those things and heard about those things was at their local movie house, where, as Lina Lamont succinctly puts it in *Singin' in the Rain* (1952), "we bring a little happiness into your humdrum lives."

Not much came down off the screen into the real lives of the movie audience. Fans had to settle for buying movie magazines, collecting autographs of stars, and belonging to fan clubs, but doing those peripheral things in no way satisfied their desires to be *like* the men and women they saw on the screen. To make their fantasies more real, to bring them home with them, as it were, they tried to copycat whatever they saw and heard at the movies. Although they *could* light two cigarettes at once, like Paul Henreid in *Now, Voyager*, and they *could* say "If you want me, all you have to do is whistle," like Lauren Bacall in *To Have and Have Not* (1944), they ran a credibility risk. Their best bet was to try to duplicate the fashions and hairstyles they saw, even if they had to do it on a greatly reduced scale. It *was* possible for women to put their hair in braids like Ginger Rogers in *Tender Comrade* (1943). It *was* possible for a man to stop wearing an undershirt when he saw that Clark Gable didn't wear one in *It Happened One Night* (1934). Women could buy cheap knockoff copies of Joan Crawford's ruffled dress from *Letty Lynton* (1932), and girls who worked in defense plants could imitate Veronica Lake's peekaboo hairdo, even if it did get caught in the machinery. Fashion and glamour were the elements of the woman's film that women could actually get their hands on. They might not be able to find a Clark Gable of their own, but they certainly could get a guy with no undershirt. They could shop for dresses like the ones they saw in the movies, and they could wear their hair the way the stars did. Audiences could become as fashionably correct as their little budget, their little town, or their little world would allow them to be. Knowing this, Hollywood worked harder to manufacture fashion and glamour in a way that might convince women that they could be fashionably correct à la Hollywood.

"Fashionably correct" in movies is thus a high-powered term. It means much more than having gloves that match your hat. Clothing for women in the movies becomes a subtle instrument for several purposes: teaching the need for conformity, stressing the woman's role as sex object or love partner, and showing the viewers consumer goods that they would want to purchase for themselves if at all possible. Thus, what the woman wears and how she looks, as much as what she does, is important to an understanding of the woman's film. Fashion counts.

When I use the word "fashion" here, I am not talking about the sensible little jackets with rolled-up sleeves and the serviceable skirts that women wear on the screen today, as if they really don't care what they have on because, after all, a woman is not defined by her clothes. I am talking about a time in the movies in which women *were* defined by their clothes, and the clothes were fantastic, outrageous, astonishing—designed to stir longings in the hearts of dreamers everywhere and to inspire passion, envy, and, of course, shopping. In those days, when clothes were a large part of the appeal of any film, every movie magazine featured extensive fashion layouts. All female movie stars were required to pose endlessly for stills that showed them full-length in beautiful clothing. This was a world in which all things matched, and everyone was fully accessorized. There were oddball items put forth as basic to good taste and fundamental to a complete wardrobe: scatter pins and rickrack and snoods and hand-dyed shoes. A dress was a "frock," and a coat and dress were an "ensemble." Movie women had dozens of outfits, with special clothes designated for only one specific activity—ski suits, riding habits, tea dresses, tennis shorts, and ice-skating costumes. There was no such thing as wearing the same pair of slacks to ride a horse, take a hike, or work in the garden. Jeans did not exist anywhere outside the neighborhood of farm machinery.

And the hats! Hats that looked like pancakes, and hats that looked like dunce caps. Hats with cabbage roses on top, feathers on the side, drapes under the chin, and veils across the foreheads, with brims that turned up and brims that turned down. Hats bigger than a bread box and hats smaller than a pillbox. Hats perched on the side of the head like rockets about to go off. Insane, calamitous, and even potentially dangerous hats.

These hats mock reason. Did fashion designers hand them over and run away somewhere to laugh themselves silly when Ginger Rogers or Irene Dunne or Rosalind Russell put one on and strode gamely forward? These movie stars deserve all our respect for having to put such things on their heads and then deliver a line like: "Will my husband live, doctor?" (Not if he sees you in that hat!) An explanation of sorts for these hats is humorously offered by one of Danny Kaye's musical numbers in *The Secret Life of Walter Mitty* (1947). Kaye accidentally finds himself the only man at a department-store fashion show in which the famous hat designer, Anatole of Paris, is showing his latest creations. These hats are a joke unto themselves, being made out of mirrors, diamonds, black egret feathers, and ostrich plumes. (One is called the striptease hat because part of it comes off to create a second hat.) Kaye, as the dreamer Mitty, goes into one of his reveries and becomes Anatole. He sings a comedy number about his crazy family. "I'm the result of twisted eugenics of a family of inbred schizophrenics, the end of a long, long line of bats, so . . . I design women's hats!" After showing a hat shaped like a gondola, complete with oars, he adds, "Why do I sew each new chapeau with a style they must look positively grim in? Strictly between us . . . *entre nous* . . . I HATE WOMEN!" This seems to explain movie hats better than anything else could. In a woman's film, a hat is as important as a man. "A girl always tries on lots of hats before she buys one," says Joan Leslie in *Two Guys from Milwaukee* (1946). "I don't see why I shouldn't shop around for a man."

To put in perspective what fashion really meant in those days, one has to focus on what a woman had to have on to be considered properly turned out. Take a random example—Virginia Bruce as a typical 1940s wife, coming down to her husband's office to discuss divorce in *Love, Honor and Goodbye*, an ordinary, minor film of 1945. Bruce wears high-heeled shoes with ankle straps. She has a luxurious fur piece draped over her shoulders, and she carries a large purse. She wears a hat with huge flowers and a filmy veil dripping from it. Her basic outfit is a black suit, well cut, with a long waist and fully draped sleeves. She has a necklace, and she has gloves. She is elaborately made-up, with lipstick, powder, and false eyelashes. Her hairstyle is enhanced with added curls and pompadours. This woman is *dressed*.

It was a full-time job to assemble an outfit like this; it took money and hours of shopping, mixing, and matching to unite a suit, a fur, a purse, a hat, gloves, and jewelry. To put on that much makeup and to shellac that hair would require help and potfuls of materials. Any woman who got up in the morning and constructed such an outfit in order to trot out into the world on those high heels, with those ankle straps cutting into her legs, would take the role of being a woman seriously. Wearing a getup like that,

she wasn't going to look natural or casual or even comfortable. She was
going to be slowed down and inhibited, but she *was* going to be fashionable,
and she *was* going to be glamorous. This was the model that Hollywood
set up for American women. It was an image that spoke of a formidable
power at the same time that it sold hard goods. In addition, it was a model
that gave women something to do—a way to pass their time, a way to use
their energies, as well as a way to define themselves.

Fashion was so important in movies that studios kept on staff their
own costume designers and wardrobe people, famous names like Adrian,
Edith Head, Travis Banton, Irene Sharaff, Orry Kelly, and Bonny Cashin.
Others, like Oleg Cassini, Jean Louis, and later Givenchy, designed only
for one particular star, with people like Hattie Carnegie and Lily Daché
taking on special assignments from time to time. Not only clothes but
hairstyles and makeup required special artists on the payroll, and in many
films such items as jewelry and furs and gloves and hair ornaments received
individual credits. The appropriately named *Vogues of 1938*, starring Joan
Bennett and Helen Vinson, opens up by thanking the "creative contributions" to its presentation from Jackel, Inc., for furs, Irene for Miss Bennett's
wardrobe, Max Factor for Color Harmony Make-up, Sally Victor "for a
great many of the hats," John Frederick for the hats and accessories in the
Fall Fashion Forecast, Trabert and Hoeffer, Inc. (Mauboussin Jewels) for
the jewelry, and, finally, I. Miller and Son for the shoes. This was serious
business, and the audience had a right to know whom to thank—or whom
to blame, as it were. There were even conceits, as when Marlene Dietrich's
character Miss Julie Madden has her credits appear on-screen in *The Lady
Is Willing* (1942) as "Hats for Miss Madden," "Jewels for Miss Madden,"
and "Gowns for Miss Madden."

Why does fashion signify so much about who a woman is? In the
woman's world on film, there is so little freedom possible that a woman's
putting something on her back becomes one of her most dramatic actions.
Clasping a necklace around her neck is the rough equivalent of a man's
destroying an enemy pillbox in a combat film: It's a decisive act, and it
will have consequences. Fashion is so important in a woman's life that
Claude Rains, the villain in *Lisbon* (1956), punishes his straying women
by burning their dresses! When one of his spying servants reports to him
that his latest mistress has been flirting around, Rains commands, "Burn
two of her newest gowns!" When the obnoxious snoop presses his luck and
also reports that the girl kicked him, Rains inquires: "Hard?" When the
servant nods enthusiastically, Rains says, "Then just burn one gown." This
routine turns into a plot device. When Ray Milland later tries to steal this
same woman from Rains, he bargains with her by saying, "For every one
he burns, I'll buy you two." (Ultimately this woman points out that "there

are only two dresses in her life that are really important to a woman. Both are white. Her confirmation gown and her bridal gown." However, neither Rains nor Milland plans to provide her with either of these outfits.)

The fact that fashion and glamour are a fundamental part of the woman's film does not itself mark these movies as different from other genres, of course. Fashion and glamour are a fundamental part of all Hollywood movies—of its musicals, its comedies, its costume films, and even its gangster pictures and westerns. A woman dressed in fringed buckskin is no less beautiful, no less carefully fitted and made-up, than a woman in satin and lace. Men are as well dressed as women, and male stars are photographed with shadowed cheekbones and half-bared chests and bathing suits almost as often as women. (It is called beefcake for men and cheesecake for women.) But it is women's films that reveal best how fashion was used in Hollywood movies and just how important it really was. One can trace this importance across an ever-escalating wave of dramatic madness in the following way:

STEP ONE: Clothes are part of a musical number or a fashion show. They serve no purpose except to look nice on the models and to show people some goods.

STEP TWO: Clothes become the basis of a woman's social testing. Does she look right or not? Can she fit in? Her fashion defines her basic character.

STEP THREE: Clothes shape the entire direction of a woman's life or become the basis for her complete change. By wearing something different, she totally transforms herself into another person with another life-style.

STEP FOUR: Clothes endanger a woman or influence the plot.

It is possible to trace this pattern of escalation as a dress evolves from a pretty frock in a fashion show, to an item that indicates character flaw, to a device a woman can use to better herself, to an instrument of death and destruction.

Nothing accomplishes the goals of the woman's film fashion-and-glamour presentation better than Step One, the simple device of the fashion show, in which a set-piece scene shows the goods, stresses the beauty of women, and subconsciously suggests conformity. It is amazing how many films—and how many different kinds of films—include these fashion parades. There are fashion shows in musicals (*Roberta*, 1935; *Lovely To Look At*, 1952; *Artists and Models Abroad*, 1938; *Fashions of 1934*, for example), dramas (*Vogues of 1938*; *Mannequin*, 1937; *Our Blushing Brides*, 1930; *The Women*, 1939), comedies (*Artists & Models*, 1937 version, *The Secret*

Life of Walter Mitty), and even gangster films (*Nightfall*, 1956) and films noir (*The Pitfall*, 1948).

These parades of attractive women in gorgeous outfits present no problem regarding integration into the plot. If the movie is a musical, a song is performed during the fashion parade. If it is a story about a model who is showing clothes in a department store as part of her job, the story is often continued via the device of having a man who wishes to meet her or date her sit in the audience and try to catch her attention or communicate with her while the clothes pass by. In a serious film like *The Pitfall*, a continuous line of action is maintained while Lizabeth Scott models clothes for the villain. The parade is used to show how Scott is demeaned by the psychopathic Raymond Burr. Although she is doing her job in a safe situation, among a group of other models, he is only pretending he is going to buy the dress she has on. She has to stand in front of him while he instructs her with casual cruelty to "let me see it without the cape." She is forced to partially disrobe in what symbolizes a rape scene. Sometimes the story just stops dead and lets it happen: "And now we'll show you some clothes!"

These fashion shows were accepted by the audience as part of what they were paying to see. Women in the audience could admire the kind of clothes they would never really own but might be able to copy cheaply, while men could enjoy looking at some very beautiful women parading around, frequently in skimpy bathing suits and sheer nightgowns. Why complain? The fact that fashion shows might slow down the story was irrelevant. Who cared? People were there for the fashion and glamour as much as for anything. When a fashion show suddenly appeared in the black-and-white movie *The Women* and was photographed in glorious Technicolor, no one seemed to find that odd. In fact, it not only doesn't seem odd, it somehow seems right. The clothing being shown in *The Women* is so exaggerated that it might as well be from the Land of Oz. One is just as likely to see someone dressed like the Lollipop Kids as to see someone wearing the witch hats and two-foot-long gloves that are paraded past audiences in *The Women*.

The imaginative way these fashion shows are varied reflects how popular they were. *Singin' in the Rain* finds the perfect means of both satirizing the fashion shows from movies of the 1930s and providing one at the same time. As a handsome young tenor of the Dick Powell type sings "Beautiful Girl" in pure 1930s style, a "calendar" of young women unfolds, with each one wearing an outfit appropriate to the month she represents: a wedding dress for June, bathing suit for July, and so on. All the fashions are satiric representations of the late 1920s–early 1930s clothing styles.

The fashion show in *The Women*. Joan Fontaine, Phyllis Povah, Norma Shearer, and Rosalind Russell inspect the goods.

In *Colleen*, the patter quoted earlier is accompanied by a chorus of seemingly hundreds of women who sweep out before the viewer like a veritable women's fashion army in a display of rampant capitalism. There is a militaristic, almost menacing quality to these nubile young women as they step smartly along in time to the music. I always think of them as the fashion troops. First come the Daytime Dress Corps, fetchingly attired in little frocks for afternoon teas, all wearing matching hats and relatively sensible shoes. Next come the Cocktail Sharpshooters, the Riding Habit Cavalry, the Evening Artillery, and the Lingerie Secret Service. There is a sense that this is how women defend their territory—by having the right clothes and the right look; by following fashion dictates. It's satisfying to see how lovely these women all are, and reassuring to realize that one can find the right clothes and have equal success. On the other hand, it's a woman's fashion nightmare. Hundreds of females are wearing the exact same outfit! There's more than a little suggestion of conformity for women here.

Perhaps the most extreme example of how women are defined by what they wear comes in *Billy Rose's Diamond Horseshoe* (1945). "See the leggy lovelies," cried a press release of the day, referring to a musical number in the film in which women in a chorus are dressed as items of food. As a viewer watches in disbelief, one by one they appear, dressed as Cherries Jubilee, Baked Alaska, Banana Split, Chocolate Cake, Pistachio Parfait, Apple Pie à la Mode, Strawberry Shortcake, Cream Puffs, Lemon Meringue, and, my personal favorite, the simple but elegant Bowl of Jell-O.

Sometimes when the fashion show turns up in a musical number or a dream sequence, it is a man who activates the convention by imagining a woman he loves wearing different clothing. Both *On the Town* (1949) and *An American in Paris* (1951) use this device as an excuse for a musical number involving the woman. In *On the Town*, Gene Kelly reads a subway ad about the beautiful Miss Turnstiles of the Month (Vera-Ellen), in which her hobbies and interests are listed. As he reads, the image turns into Vera-Ellen doing an energetic dance and changing from a tennis outfit to boxing shorts, and so on. In *An American in Paris*, Georges Guetary tries to explain to Oscar Levant why he loves Leslie Caron by telling him what she is like. His gushing description of her as "sweet, but not too sweet" and "full of fun, but also intellectual," which contradicts itself in the extreme, is pictured by Levant as a series of changing images. Caron dances against a stylized background, and as her costume changes, the color of the background changes and the style of music follows suit. One moment she is red and jazzy, and the next pink and demure. It is a somewhat frightening demonstration of how men see women as objects, but it is also a fashion parade that was supposed to please women.

These fashion shows were still taking place in one form or another as late as the 1960s in movies like *Made in Paris* (1966), in which Ann-Margret plays a department-store buyer making her first trip to Europe. In *The Nutty Professor* (1963), a modernist film if there ever was one, a mocking mini–fashion show takes place on screen as a subjective fantasy of Professor Kelp (Jerry Lewis in the Dr. Jekyll half of his performance). As Stella Stevens, playing Lewis's dream girl, stands in the doorway of his classroom with her back to him, Lewis pictures her in a series of changing outfits: an evening gown, tennis shorts, a blue bathing suit, and a red, sirenish cocktail dress. Stevens is turned into a cute little paper doll, and Lewis plays with her mentally, changing her outfits in a sly little scene that hints to an audience that what he really wants to do is take all her clothes off. The film uses the established tradition of the movie fashion show, but openly makes it a male fantasy of sex and desire instead of a man's loving dream (Kelly in *On the Town*) or another man's confused attempt to understand a friend's love (Levant in *An American in Paris*). Furthermore, *The Nutty Professor* isn't using the excuse that it is showing the audience a bunch of clothes because women just want to shop.

As years go by, there are a few joking reversals in which women fantasize about men via clothes, or in the case of *Gentlemen Prefer Blondes* (1953), no clothes. In that colorful musical, Jane Russell dances with an entourage of bodybuilders wearing very little while she sings, "Ain't there anyone here for love?" These men don't have any clothes on to be changed, but the idea is the same: viewers see a parade of flesh for whoever in the audience wants to ogle it for whatever reason. A woman does get her chance to fantasize in *The Girl from Jones Beach* (1949), in which Ronald Reagan plays a pinup illustrator, à la Vargas, who pictures every attractive female he meets in the same white one-piece bathing suit. When he falls truly and deeply in love for the first time, he suddenly can picture this woman (Virginia Mayo) only in sensible clothes. Proof of his love is that he can only see her with her clothes on! Mayo, whose character has lamented that "I'm too intelligent for the men I attract, and not beautiful enough for the men who attract me," has her own response to falling in love with Reagan. Striking a blow for equality, she looks at him, sitting near her in his well-cut three-piece suit, and can picture him only in his bathing suit.

At the Step-Two level, clothes begin to take on more significance. Movies begin to use fashion as proof of a woman's social acumen. Fashion becomes a kind of combat zone, or a litmus test for femininity. Tested by the Rules of Fashion, many women are found to be failures. Innocent young girls show up in countless films wearing the wrong thing for the country club dance, the big prom, or the graduation ceremony. Not only do they have to pay for these mistakes on the spot, but they will have to pay for the rest of their lives. They will never be the same. Fashion failure affects a woman's future, even if it has happened to her because she was poor, not stupid. The movies seem to suggest that a woman is entitled to sympathy if she kills her cruel husband but not if she can't dress right. It's a woman's job to know better.

Some of these fashion failures are temporary. When the insecure young wife (Janet Leigh) of a newly successful author (Van Johnson) in *Wives and Lovers* (1963) tries to bolster her self-confidence by buying an expensive dress, in her heart she knows it's not right for her. When her husband's self-assured female agent swoops in, wearing the exact same dress as if born in it, the audience can see clearly that Leigh will never really be comfortable in this new life, but that she still looks good enough to save her marriage. When the poor girls with the wrong outfits are blackballed

by the snobbish sorority in *Take Care of My Little Girl* (1951), they all
come to their senses in the nick of time. The rich girls in town are horribly
cruel to poor Katharine Hepburn in *Alice Adams* (1935) when she wears
the wrong thing at their summer soiree. "Organza!" one smugly whispers
to another. "Well. . . . maybe *we're* wrong." Hepburn ends up with Fred
MacMurray anyway, despite the pain and shame she suffers at their hands.

Other times, fashion failures burn lasting scars into a woman's psyche.
These movies establish the idea that if a woman has been denied good
clothes and has had to suffer socially because of it, she cannot possibly
grow up untraumatized. This idea is put forth soberly, seriously, as a basic
unit of meaning in the woman's world. In *Shadow on the Wall* (1950), Ann
Sothern and Kristine Miller play sisters. Sothern hates her sibling, convinced that she always had to take second best, or as she clearly describes
it, second dress. She berates Miller in an angry speech: "Everything has
to be your way, doesn't it, Celia? Everything I ever wanted, you took.
Everything. Everything I ever tried to do you spoiled. Even when I was
little, the first dress that was really mine, that mother bought just for me.
You remember how you tried it on and wouldn't give it back and cried and
kicked and screamed and you had your way?" Miller feebly replies, "But
. . . that was so long ago. . . ." "Not to me," Sothern fires back.

"You see," says Ruth Chatterton in *The Crash* (1932), explaining why
she is the selfish, desperate creature she is, "when I was little, I had to
wear a badly cut coat." One might have thought it was because she had
nothing to wear and was freezing in an alley, but no—she *had* a coat, but
it was *badly cut*. This is hilarious, but also sobering. Since it is being put
forward as a perfectly logical explanation of a desperate human being, one
realizes that for a woman it would be better to have *no* coat than one that
is unfashionable. If she had no coat at all she would stay home and thus
not offer herself up to ridicule, shame, and rejection.

These scenes illustrate how clothes define women and determine their
status in life. "You wear clothes that another woman can't forgive," Pat
O'Brien tells Josephine Hutchinson in *I Married a Doctor* (1936), and it's
all the explanation either she *or* the audience needs as to why she is
completely ostracized by everyone. It explains her, even to herself, and
that's how important costumes are. Stars were even made famous by costumes. In *Star Spangled Rhythm* (1942), one of those all-star patriotic
musicals of World War II in which every actor the studio had under contract
performs some sort of skit or musical number, three big-name sex symbols
of the day, Paulette Goddard, Dorothy Lamour, and Veronica Lake, sing
a satirical song about what created their successes: "A sweater, a sarong,
and a peek-a-boo bang." In other words, it wasn't talent that put them on
the screen. It was fashion. They aren't comediennes or singers or dancers

or tragediennes and certainly not actresses, they tell us. They are an ordinary item of clothing, a Polynesian wraparound, and a hairdo. What is remarkable about this is that it's true. The three women perform the number with great panache and charm, and it seems utterly acceptable. However, when it is immediately reprised by three men in drag (Arthur Treacher, Walter Catlett, and Sterling Holloway), it suddenly seems ludicrous and demeaning. One realizes that one would never see male stars defined this way. These three men are supporting actors, all associated primarily with comic roles. We aren't watching Clark Gable, Gary Cooper, and Errol Flynn make fools of themselves by singing "big ears, skinny body, and fuzzy mustache." And to make it palatable the three comics are performing it in drag. Here is grim sociology. Thinking they are in control of the joke, the three women have actually laid bare some cold facts about their own stardom, the industry they work in, and the use of fashion in films.

ONE OF THE PRIMARY fashion devices used to explain a woman's character is jewelry. When a woman has jewelry, she is either rich and thus powerful because of her secure economic status, or she has earned enough money for herself to buy her own jewels, freeing herself from male dependency. Otherwise, a man has given her jewelry, either because he finds her beautiful, desirable, and worthy of expenditure, or because he finds her noble and steadfast, or because he loves her madly. Jewelry for a woman is a form of money she can have. She may not control the checkbook or have her own millions in cash, but she can have jewelry.

One can think of countless movies in which a man hangs jewels on a woman . . . around her neck, on her wrist, on her finger. Baubles, bangles, and beads, all designed to do one of several things: to enhance a woman's beauty, encouraging the audience to look at and admire her for physical attributes; to indicate her economic position, a status she might have been born to, married into, or earned on her own; to define her basic nobility of character, as when she refuses jewelry, accepts it under protest as not being what she really wants, or returns it to the man who gave it to her, indicating her true love for him; or to show what a selfish and evil woman she is. Thus jewelry in a woman's film means beauty, power, nobility, or evil, depending on the situation.

The evil woman covets jewelry. A good woman does not really want it, just as she is not supposed to want economic power; that is why, in many films, she returns it to her man in his hour of need. Alexis Smith, wife of Clark Gable in *Any Number Can Play* (1949), saves his gambling casinos by giving him her jewels, and Marion Davies and Billie Burke both give their jewels back to the real men who loved them (William Randolph Hearst and Flo Ziegfeld) in TV-made bio pics of their lives. The implication here is that this is really what the woman *ought* to do. That is, she ought to be willing to work for no pay. It's okay for her to *have* the jewelry, as long as the man insists she take it and she really doesn't want it in the first place. To keep it when the man is in financial trouble, however, would be unseemly. Thus, we are reminded that women really aren't supposed to have their own wealth. Jewels make them look pretty, so those they can have on loan. Even Belle Watling, the prostitute in *Gone With the Wind* (1939), has to give up her presumably hard-earned jewelry, sacrificing it to the Confederate cause and Olivia de Havilland, because Watling, needless to say, has no husband to return it to. When Marlene Dietrich points to a row of medals on the chest of Clive Brook in *Shanghai Express* (1932), she tells him that when she knew him years ago he didn't have those. "Are they for bravery?" Immediately, wryly, he touches the richly jeweled pin on her satin bosom, using the exact gesture she has used, pointing to the same spot on her garment that she pointed to on his. "You didn't have that before either . . ." he comments. One understands that where men are brave in war, women are brave in love. Jewelry is worn as a badge by a woman. Her bravery, her kind of courage and honor, are related to what will happen in her world, the limited world of women. The medals of suffering a woman wears are often jewels—earrings and brooches and bracelets; signs of valor and endurance for a woman who has to survive and suffer in a male-dominated world.

"Have her jeweled and gowned," calls out an old lecher in the musical comedy *The Court Jester* (1956), speaking about Glynis Johns, who has been captured and brought to him dressed in her peasant clothes. "Kitty, prepare me," echoes Lana Turner, at least in control of her own outfits in *The Three Musketeers* (1948), asking her maid, Patricia Medina, to bring her jewels and gowns so that she can gear up to seduce D'Artagnan. "Have her jeweled and gowned" is such a perfect way to say it, implying as it does that the woman stands passively while someone, anyone, puts upon her body the things she must have in order to be considered desirable. In a costume film, even a comic one, when a man calls out "have her jeweled and gowned," he means "get her ready for sex whenever I want it, but to make me want it, she's got to look right, which means well dressed." (It's one step from "have her jeweled and gowned" to "have her enameled and shellacked" to "have her silenced and killed.") The implication is not only that a woman must be beautiful and well dressed to find love but that she must also be aware of that fact.

Time and time again in films, there is a scene in which a plain and unattractive woman is transformed by clothing and makeup into an object of desire. Miraculous! Whether it's a tomboy who suddenly puts up her hair and lowers her neckline (Jeanne Crain in *Home in Indiana*), a guttersnipe who is washed off and who turns out to be a Gainsborough portrait underneath (Paulette Goddard in *Kitty*, 1945, and this applies to all the Eliza Doolittle stories, too), or a mouseburger who becomes a sexpot (Maureen O'Hara in *Do You Love Me?*, 1946), it is a familiar movie situation. A woman's character transformation or change of direction in life is Step Three in fashion progression.

Usually, such a woman is first introduced as associated in some way with success, intelligence, or spinsterhood. Jean Arthur in *A Foreign Affair* (1948) begins the movie as a capable and dedicated though bluenosed congresswoman from Iowa on a fact-finding mission to postwar Berlin. While her fellow junketeers excitedly look out their airplane windows at the ruined Berlin landscape, she primly snaps off her glasses, folds them up with two sharp snaps, shuts them into their holder with yet another snap, places them inside her purse with a definitive, decisive, and very final *snap!* Later, however, under the spell of the loose and immoral German city, and especially under the spell of the even more loose and immoral John Lund, she will put ribbons in her hair, lower her neckline, drape herself in a piano shawl, and put her snap to better use. Miriam Hopkins plays an intelligent and sensible princess in Lubitsch's *The Smiling Lieutenant* (1931). When she has trouble holding the interest of her straying husband, Maurice Chevalier, his mistress, Claudette Colbert (a violinist in an all-girl orchestra), takes pity and advises Hopkins on what to do. "Let me see your underwear," Colbert sings in an outré musical solution to the problem. After careful assessment, Colbert comes up with her solution: "Jazz up your lingerie!" She burns Hopkins's knickers in the fire and transforms her into the object of Chevalier's love with new shoes, new clothes, and new nighties.

In *Funny Face* (1957), Audrey Hepburn works in a New York bookstore, where she is happily studying "empathacalism" and wearing no makeup, straight hair, and functional jumpers. When a fashion layout is photographed in her store, Fred Astaire accidentally discovers what we all know about Hepburn: she has great bones and is as skinny as they come. She is persuaded to become the *Quality* Woman, temporarily posing for fashion photos in return for a free trip to Paris, where the *Quality* magazine layouts will be shot. Although Kay Thompson, as the magazine's editor, is leery of Hepburn ("we're going to have trouble . . . she's a thinker"), Hepburn shows signs of fashion weakness almost from the first moment clothes enter her life. After the models leave the bookstore, she tries on a huge and frivolous hat that was left behind and starts singing about love. In Paris, after dancing with Fred Astaire, she blubbers, "I love Paris and I love these clothes and I love you . . ." She is transformed.

Funny Face is meant to be a satire of the fashion business. Thompson describes herself as someone who helps "the great American woman who stands out there naked and waits for me to tell her what to wear." As to her own advice to them to "think pink," however, she admits, "I wouldn't be caught dead." The fashion models are presented as stupid, and the whole business as utter nonsense. On the other hand, with true woman's film contradiction, Hepburn finds love through fashion, and her initial intellectual interests are ultimately revealed as pretentious. *Funny Face* is a clear case of musical escapism, and perhaps one shouldn't try to read too much into it, but its lesson is clearly that clothes are a woman's ticket to love and happiness. The one woman who pays no attention to fashion, the woman who has no real respect for it, Kay Thompson, is a masculine and loveless figure.

This *Funny Face* concept of how a woman should learn to love fashion and give up thinking is found in the Communist variation in such films as *Ninotchka* (1939) and its musical remake *Silk Stockings* (1957). It is also present in *Jet Pilot* (1957), *The Iron Petticoat* (1956), and the Bob Hope cold war comedy, *Where There's Life* (1947). In all these movies, the leading lady, whether played by Garbo, Cyd Charisse, Janet Leigh, Hepburn (Kate), or Signe Hasso, is a humorless woman who has renounced fashion as a capitalist crime against females. She wears a uniform, quotes Marx, barks orders, and is not interested in love. Sex, yes. Love, no. One touch of silk on her body, however, and she abandons Communism forever.

Fashion is so powerful in a woman's life, suggests these films, that she can completely transform herself through it, not only by becoming beautiful and desirable but also by reversing the process and becoming dowdy and unattractive. In *Pin-Up Girl* (1944), Betty Grable disguises herself by the simple expedient of putting on a pair of glasses. Suddenly, no one knows who she is! The simplicity of it stuns the mind. Who expects Betty Grable to be wearing glasses instead of a one-piece bathing suit? Who expects her to be modestly dressed, sitting behind a typist's desk? The desk is as much a disguise as the glasses, and evidently no one in the film thinks to peek *under* the table for a look at her famous legs, because she gets away with her deception. Grable dressed in a white drawstring blouse, with red rickrack on its ruffles, wearing cherries in her hair, her lips bright red, her hair blazing white-blond, her complexion peachy clear is Betty Grable. With that same hair drawn back, the makeup toned down, wearing a simple buttoned-up navy-blue dress and those glasses, she is someone else. The idea of the glasses, bald in its flaunting of all reason, ends up being a brilliant decision. She is *not* the same person!

One might ask: Can a man be transformed by fashion? In comparing scenes in which men and women are stripped of fashion accoutrements, one sees how fashion is used to transform a woman in a way it does not a man. Even though the stripping of a man is a humiliating act, it does not change him into a different person; it may change his rank, but not him. In *The Life of Emile Zola* (1937), Dreyfus is thrown out of the army and undergoes the painful ritual that is traditional for such removals. Slowly, deliberately, badges of rank and honor are torn from his uniform. Dreyfus stands denuded, his beautiful uniform ugly, debased, a mockery. Suddenly he looks so much *less*. Everything he has worked for in life has been taken away, because a man is defined by his work.

On the other hand, Betty Grable has the opposite occur when she is similarly stripped in *Coney Island* (1943). Grable plays a beer-hall entertainer with plenty of pizzazz. Her costumes indicate perhaps too much pizzazz, as they are always flashy and overdone to match her character's exuberant, peppy, but cheap style of performing. When George Montgomery takes over the saloon, he gives Grable a lesson on how to dress. First he handcuffs her to a fake palm tree so she won't jump around on stage. Then he remakes her costume, a blazing orange sequined gown trimmed in an overabundance of orange feathers. He tears one from the shoulder, one from the hip, snatches off her feathered headdress and removes half of her jewelry. Then he slows down the tempo of her song, forcing her to sing slowly, with meaning and with love. When she becomes fashionably correct, she's no longer just a beer-hall floozy. She has become a star. She's a *somebody*, with a future on Broadway. She's *more*, because her fashion is correct and her female beauty has been exposed. A woman *is* her fashion and glamour, rather than her work.

In *Zola*, a man is stripped of his uniform. He is made less. In *Coney Island*, a woman is stripped of her "uniform." She is made more. Clothes have power in both cases. Dreyfus loses his uniform because he is losing his place in the male hierarchy. Grable is also undergoing a loss of power, in that she is being mastered by a man, handcuffed, and controlled by his vision, but this, suggests the movie, will give her the only power that any woman can have: the power to be seductive, attractive, beautiful . . . and *well dressed*. However, although Grable *is* being controlled, she is also being given subversive power, and, later in the film, when she becomes a star, she uses this power and walks out on Montgomery. She does not need him for any economic or professional support, having been put in touch with her own talent and beauty, so she leaves him behind in the saloon.

The ending of the film returns things to the status quo, resolving the contradiction by having Grable search for Montgomery in a cheap dive because she realizes she truly loves and needs him.

What is the covert message of *Coney Island*? A woman works in a saloon, earning her own living by singing and dancing. She is popular with the rambunctious, low-class crowd, but she is strictly a local success. She has to shout to be heard. A man comes along and shows her how to dress and act in a classy way and make the audience come to her. She discovers the depth of her own talent. She becomes a star. She leaves him, but has to take him back because she loves him. Does this ending mean she will give up show biz to become a little wife? The film does not depict that happening. At the film's end, he's playing piano in the little dive, a ruined man, and she's a big hit on Broadway. Where's the equality? Realistically, one might say that women in the audience are being told that love is more important than anything, and one ought to listen to what one's man tells her. On the other hand, might it not be possible to deduce from this movie that going out on her own is okay for a woman; that a man can be gotten back if one is a star, a success; and that using the help of a man is okay if he has good ideas, but one can still leave him behind? The final uniting of Montgomery and Grable is visualized in a highly significant way. Grable is onstage, dressed in furs and finery, singing her heart out to Montgomery and an adoring audience. She looks down on him, all radiant smiles and confidence. He is playing the piano to accompany her, and no one except Grable is paying him a bit of attention. He is looking up at her from a worshipful, even subservient stance. Grable is the star, in control, although they are performing together. She is still onstage, not renouncing her career, and she is still the center of the universe.*

In the aforementioned *Where There's Life*, Signe Hasso plays a variation of Ninotchka, a tough, disciplined woman who is always, complains her costar, Bob Hope, "shovin' guys around." A particular point is made about the fact that she always dresses in military uniform. Having once established that she is a woman who wears only men's clothing, and who consistently deglamorizes herself, the movie plays with the idea. Chased by villains, Hope and Hasso run into a department store. Suddenly overwhelmed by capitalistic goods—gowns, silk stockings, jewelry, makeup,

---

* Grable's image was feisty. She always played a woman who knew a wolf when she saw him, and she could seldom be pushed around or fooled by one. ("Nobody can hold a grudge for two years," she's told in 1941's *A Yank in the RAF*. "Well, I can," she confidently answers.) She's halfway between a wholesome all-American hometown girl and a hard-bitten small-time chorus girl. The bottom line of her persona is that if a man stands her up, she just goes out with someone else, and he will live to regret it. Where Betty Grable is concerned on film, there is always a someone else.

and perfume—Hasso realizes that she has found the perfect disguise. She not only transforms herself into an elegant and expensively dressed American woman, but also finds a means of escape. Her pursuers naturally no longer know who she is as she walks right past them. When a woman changes her outfit, what villain could possibly recognize her? (Hope, on the other hand, has to disguise himself as a hat dummy, hoping the fact that all men look the same and wear the same hat will camouflage his face among the mannequins.) Marlene Dietrich makes fashion work for her in a similar way in *The Lady Is Willing*. Wearing the *most* outrageous hat, she has found a beautiful baby on the street and has simply brought it home. When authorities try to locate her to take the child away, a policeman naturally remembers the hat, quite possibly the most unforgettable chapeau in film history. When he catches up to Dietrich, she foxily turns the hat around. Backward, of course, it does not look the same, and she calmly explains to the policeman that she cannot possibly be the woman he is looking for because, well, her hat has a feather in the back, not the front. Like all the men of history who have been stumped by fashion, he believes her.

HOLLYWOOD obviously felt confident that audiences paid attention to clothing in movies and that they accepted clothing as something important. Women's movies ultimately go beyond using clothes for characterization, transformation, and escape, and end up using them as real plot devices (Step Four). The way fashion is used as basic to the plot is often very straightforward. The trouble with the bride in *The Bride Wore Red* (1937), for instance, is simply that she wore red. Brides, as we know, wear white (unless they are named Gilda), because brides are virginal and because that is what fashion says they should wear. Actually, this particular bride never gets to the altar, but she does have one fashion indicator of why things will not work out for her in her desire to trap a rich husband: that red, red dress in her closet. *The Bride Wore Red* is a story about a girl who works in a dive on the Trieste waterfront (Joan Crawford). One night she is spotted by one of those aristocratic older playboys who hang around such places in abundance in movies, and he drunkenly challenges a friend (Robert Young): "If I was to take one of those poor things [the waterfront women in the dive] and have her properly washed, dressed and coiffeured, you couldn't tell her from your own fiancée." Young scoffs, but later the count decides to hire Crawford to test his theory. He plans to have her pursue Young at a lavish resort in the mountains, no holds barred and no expenses spared. Within minutes, Crawford is washed, dressed, and coiffed, and, although she was pretty spiffy when she was just a waterfront woman, she is indeed astounding in her new outfits. Meeting her again, Young has absolutely no idea she is the woman from the waterfront dive. (No doubt a great many women in Trieste had faces like Crawford's.)

There's only one problem with the plans to dupe Young. Crawford's lifelong dream has been to have a dress that is red, red, red, with a lot of shiny beads all over it. Being sent out to shop, she does quite well, choosing for the most part a lovely and even appropriate wardrobe. But when she unpacks at the resort, her suitcase contains the proof of who she really is, the telltale outfit that will give her away: a red, shiny dress that is not F.C. It is a dress that brands her as being from another class, another place, as having another set of values, and, it is suggested, too much sexual experience.

Interestingly, the film shows that Crawford can easily handle every social situation tossed at her in the strange environment. Even though she is not absolutely sure which fork to use, she has otherwise perfect table manners. (When asked where she got them, she logically explains, "I go to the movies.") She also is very quick to learn, and shrewd. Meeting the one person of the high-toned social set who instinctively suspects her (Billie Burke), Crawford lets Burke know where things stand: "You're high class, Countess, and very smart. But I'm just as smart . . . so remember that." Her fatal flaw is represented by the appropriate woman's film device, fashion. The dramatic climax of the film comes through clothing, presented as a moment in which Crawford has to confront who she is and why Robert Young will never really marry her. She stands before a full-length mirror, looking at herself in the glittering, red-sequined dress that she couldn't resist buying, and admits, "It's really not beautiful at all. It's too red, too loud, and too cheap. It's a portrait of me." Facing this fashion revelation, Crawford recostumes herself along more suitable lines. She puts on peasant garb and goes out to marry the postman who has been lurking around, trying to win her (Franchot Tone). Out of luck with the rich man, she is at least off the waterfront, larking about in the fresh air in a happy finale.

Note, however, that she does not return to her former waterfront clothes in the end. She makes another fashion change, into dirndl and flowered headgear, and marries for love. The final outfit is used to announce that Crawford was really a nice girl all along and to indicate to viewers the appropriate way a woman should live and, of course, dress.

Jezebel (1938) carries fashion plotting even further. Its subtitle might be *How Society Forces Bette Davis to Conform by Making Her Change Her Dress*. *Jezebel* is basically the story of four outfits: a riding habit, a red dress, a white dress, and a plain gray cape. These clothes define Davis in four climactic scenes:

1. *Her first entrance in the film, which establishes her rebellious character:*
Davis is seen riding sidesaddle on a rearing, bucking horse that she
confidently tames before dismounting. She arrives late to her own
engagement party, walking into a room of women dressed in conventional clothing. These females are all in antebellum gowns with full
skirts, whereas Davis is attired in a riding habit. She stalks in wearing
her boots, her skirt carelessly slung over her arm. She looks modern,
sleek, and stark in this outfit. Although she is told by a maid "I done
laid out your party dress," she doesn't bother to change, shocking
everyone. When she is told "the toddies are for the men," she picks
one off the tray, ignoring the nonalcoholic punch that is for the ladies.
Her clothing immediately establishes that she is different from other
women, that she does not follow convention, and that she aspires to
a masculine freedom.

2. *The famous Olympus Ball sequence, in which she defies society:* This
often-excerpted sequence shows how Davis's character opts to wear
a "saucy" red dress to the annual Olympus Ball, at which young,
unmarried women are more or less required to wear virginal white.
"This is 1852!" shouts Davis. "Girls don't have to simper around in
white just because they aren't married!" The wearing of the red dress
is not only her fashion statement, but also her statement of her own
determination to do as she pleases. It is furthermore a form of defiance
of the need to do as her fiancé, Henry Fonda, wishes. At the dance,
which is dramatically photographed and edited, Davis is shunned by
polite society and humiliated. When she wishes to go home, Fonda
forces her to take the dance floor and complete a dance with him.
Davis has gambled and lost. She cannot defy society. By breaking
the rules and wearing the wrong thing, she is socially ostracized *and*
she loses the man she loves.

3. *Her acquiescence, in which she humbles herself and accepts society's
role for her:* Hearing that Fonda is returning to the South one year
after their Olympus Ball breakup, Davis decides that she will show
him that she can be a perfect wife by accepting her femininity and
her appropriate place as a woman in the social order of the Old South.
To do this, she dresses herself in the traditional all-white, lace-
trimmed gown she was originally meant to wear to the Olympus Ball.
Lace and flowers are added to her hair, and a necklace, bracelet,
and ring complete her outfit as a proper southern lady. By casting
away her former "red dress" self, which caused her to lose the man
she loves, she expects to regain his love by showing him her "white
dress" self. She kneels in front of him, humbling herself by begging

for his love and their marriage, only to find he has already married
someone else.

4. *Her final acceptance of the role of women, in which she prepares to
sacrifice herself:* Placing a plain, gray, totally unadorned cape over
her gown, and thus obliterating *all* fashion, Davis sets out to accompany the desperately ill Fonda to "leper island," where the yellow-
fever victims are sent to die. Davis explains to Fonda's northern wife
(Margaret Lindsay) that only a southern girl can speak Creole, handle
the slaves, and face the horror of leper island. Fonda may be dying,
but if he is to survive, Davis alone has the strength and the knowledge
to save him. His only chance lies in her willingness to sacrifice herself,
demonstrated by her plain gray cape. She puts aside all nonsense in
the form of fashion, all attempts to tempt him through her beauty and
clothing, and settles down to save him. When a woman gives up
fashion, she is truly sacrificing herself.

The entire story of *Jezebel* is a story of fashion mistakes, a woman's tragedy.
The movie contains constant fashion chatter and references to clothing. As
Davis propels her way through the plot, she is frequently heard to call out
such things as "Lay out my dress" or "A party to celebrate! Lay out my
dresses!" She quarrels with Fonda because he is supposed to come and
see her white Olympus Ball gown when she is having it fitted, and he is
too busy at the bank to get there. She talks to her maid about giving her
the red dress after she's worn it, but tells her later that she'll never give
her the white dress. She tells Fonda, "I put on this white dress for you.
To help me tell you how humbly I ask you to forgive me," and after this
apology fails and she is desperate, she tells everyone that there should be
lots of music. "That's why I wore my white dress."

Other than the four outfits described, Davis wears only six costumes.
They are all deemphasized and treated as ordinary: when she stalks into
the bank to get Fonda (another example of unacceptable behavior) in a
daytime dress; when she sits inside her bedroom wearing a negligee while
Fonda tries to get her to come out for a beating; when she sits soberly and
dejected in a simple gown after he has left her but she hears he is to return;
when she is preparing the house in another ordinary dress for his arrival,
before donning her white dress; when, the morning after the big party,
wearing another daytime dress, she hears the news that the second male
lead, George Brent, has been shot; and when she is at the dinner party
where she hears Fonda has yellow fever, while she is wearing a lovely but
not overwhelming dinner dress. These clothes are all pretty, but they are
not dramatic. They are like secondary players in a drama in which the
other four outfits star. *Jezebel* is a story of red dress versus white dress,

with the riding habit and the cape the introduction and the conclusion to their tale of woe.*

The power of clothing is also used in the plot finale of *Sudden Fear* (1952), an underrated thriller starring Joan Crawford as a middle-aged playwright who is married for her money by a sinister actor, well played by Jack Palance. Crawford's character is defined by clothing throughout the entire film. As a somewhat prudish and definitely workaholic author, she first is seen dressed in severe suits and austere dresses. After Palance enters her life, seducing her and thawing her out, she begins to appear in ruffles, even dirndls, and diaphanous negligees. Whereas at first she seemed middle-aged and fierce, strained to the gills from the effort of hanging on to herself, she begins to look radiant, relaxed, and sensuous.

Although Crawford loves and trusts Palance, feeling sexually fulfilled for the first time in her life, she accidentally discovers that he plans to kill her for her money, helped by his former girlfriend, Gloria Grahame, the woman he really loves. Crawford, in the woman's film tradition, at first suffers over this news but then pulls herself together, immediately beginning to plot how she will kill him first, making it look like an accident. (She can't go to the police because her evidence, a Dictaphone recording, is accidentally broken, and she believes they will think she is just a hysterical female.) Since Palance and Grahame have cooked up a scenario of events to be enacted, Crawford retaliates by writing her own counterplot, planning dialogue, motivation, entrances, and exits with great detail and care. Naturally, since she is a world-famous playwright, she can outplot them! She writes a competent little three-act play, and since it is her work that saves her from the dangers of love, we find another of the many subversive contradictions to be found in the woman's film.

The climax of the film comes when Crawford cannot bring herself to actually kill Grahame or Palance. Realizing as she hides in Grahame's closet that she can't go through with it, she runs out into the street to find her way home, wearing a luxurious fur coat over a stark white dress, with a white chiffon scarf on her head. And here it comes: Grahame runs out after her, her own luxurious fur covering her own white dress, her own little white scarf over her head. Palance is lurking up and down the darkened

---

* *Jezebel* is not the only movie that is essentially the story of some costume changes. In *Johnny Guitar* (1954), purportedly a western, Joan Crawford wears the plot and character changes on her back. At first a tough woman in black pants, black shirt, and string tie, with a six-gun on her hip, she moves toward love and a full-skirted, ruffled white dress. Along the way, she goes to the bank in a sensible outfit, talks love with her man in a negligee, changes from her feminine white ruffles into male clothing in which to escape the villains, and takes a moment to doff a wet shirt and hang it neatly over the back of a chair. Picture John Wayne worrying about his laundry!

city streets in his car, planning to run Crawford over in a hit-and-run accident.

Finally he spots her, fleeing through the night, touches of white on her head and at her knees, her high heels clanking across the sidewalks. Identifying her through fashion, he guns his auto and smashes her down. But he runs over Grahame instead! Crawford is saved by the Outfit. You see, a woman really *does* have to have on the right clothes. Nowhere is the faux pas of two women showing up in similar dresses made *more* of a fashion crisis than in *Sudden Fear*, the ultimate use of clothing in the women's film.*

There is one great movie scene in which a woman lashes out at the power of clothes over female lives. Who better to commit this violence than Joan Crawford, a woman who so often played roles in which she was helplessly bogged down in the woman's world? One of the movies' most astonishing sights is that of Crawford, full of power and fury, going on a rampage against consumer goods in her starring vehicle *I Live My Life* (1935). She breaks lamps, shreds flowers, kicks over a tea tray, and finally, in the ultimate gesture, destroys her own wedding gown. Fashion, particularly a wedding gown, is of such importance in a woman's life that Crawford actually addresses the gown as if it were alive, a fellow creature. "Well, look what we have here," Crawford snarls as her maid carries in her beautiful gown. "Aren't you the beautiful thing? All full of sweetness and light, aren't you? Just a big, brave symbol. Two hearts that beat as one. Two souls that called to each other out of the darkness of life. Do you know what I think you are? I think you're just about twenty yards of satin with a lot of lace and doohickeys spread all over you like the coating on a pill, and you can take yourself and fly yourself a kite. So stick it under your pillow. Dream on it, wish on it, cry on it, jump up and down on it." She goes crazy! Ripping, tearing, shredding, shrieking, she enacts the woman's revenge on fashion, an active wrecking of a feminine fashion symbol. When she's all finished (and no woman can watch this scene without her hair standing on end), Crawford does something even more astonishing and scary. She composes herself and begins to rummage calmly through her closet. Within minutes, she finds a suitable new dress, puts it on, goes downstairs, and grimly marries the guy anyway.

* *Sudden Fear* has a serious subtext. Crawford initially fires Palance from her play because she feels he doesn't look handsome enough to play the lead. Thus, a male character is criticized for not looking the way he should, as a woman usually would be. Palance retaliates (after asking if she ever saw the portrait of Casanova with a wart on his chin) by marrying her for her money and trying to kill her. One wonders if any women in the audience thought about how, if he were a woman, he would instead have undergone one of those transformations to turn into a glamour puss, thereby conforming to society's expectations.

In *Morocco* (1930), a Foreign Legion movie, Marlene Dietrich says, "There is a Foreign Legion of women, too. Only we have no flag, no uniforms, no medals. And we are brave." Women are brave in movie terms because they face a world without status, economic independence, or freedom. Love is their only comfort and deceit their only weapon. They do, however, actually have a certain kind of medal—jewels—and a certain kind of uniform—fashion.

GLAMOUR GOES BEYOND mere fashion. Although the concept of glamour includes fashion, it ultimately involves more than what a woman puts on her body. It deals with the lady herself. Movies make a plain statement: women should be physically beautiful in order for men to love them. Behind the scenes, Hollywood was in the business of manufacturing glamour through a complicated process, and this process applied to both men and women. A lot has been written about how ordinary females like Tula Finklea and Ruby Stevens were turned into Cyd Charisse and Barbara Stanwyck, but less has been said about how guys like Marion Michael Morrison and Spangler Arlington Brugh were turned into John Wayne and Robert Taylor. When one studies the still photographs supplied to an eager public by the studio system, one can see that lines were airbrushed away from under men's eyes as well as women's, and that flattering lighting, suggestive clothing (or lack of clothing), and brooding poses were forced on both sexes. The difference was that men were turned into sex objects who did something, and women were often turned into sex objects, period. Men could also be less perfect. They could gawk and gangle like Jimmy Stewart, be too short like Mickey Rooney, or be covered with freckles like Van Johnson. A woman needed glamour. It might be of the homespun variety, but she had to have it. If she didn't have it, Hollywood had to manufacture it for her.

The Hollywood movie clearly tells women they should be beautiful. Being beautiful for women is like being brave and strong for men. Without the basic asset of physical attractiveness, a woman doesn't qualify in the gender sweepstakes; she will be relegated to a drone position. "Well," says Marilyn Monroe in *Gentlemen Prefer Blondes* (1953), explaining calmly to her suspicious prospective father-in-law why she wants to marry his son for his money, "isn't a man being rich like a girl being pretty?"

Of course with its typical perversity, the woman's film often suggests that a woman should be feisty, but not too feisty. Strong, but not too strong. Well dressed, but not overdressed. Glamorous, but not too glamorous. According to the movies, a woman should never be "too" anything, because this might put her in a position of power, a place she should never be. A woman has to know her place. Many films tell stories in which a woman

who is "too beautiful" is destroyed or destroys others. It is sometimes also
suggested that a nice little girl, perhaps played by June Allyson, with hair
in braids and a smudge on her nose, might be a better lifetime mate than
a woman wearing an orchid. No one ever suggests that June Allyson should
be *ugly*, of course, only that everyone should remember that a woman with
too much beauty might get uppity. What is stressed is that a woman should
be beautiful and glamorous and desirable, but as is appropriate to her
situation.

What I am saying here applies to the story line of the film, not to the
audience response. The story might say "not too beautiful" or "not too
many orchids," but the visual presentation may show an audience remarkable beauty, draped with orchids, and invite a viewer to stare at the huge
close-ups of the stars and their astonishing faces. The image invites one
to dream of beauty and to wish to possess it, both for oneself and in one's
love partner. Who needs to be told this? How many times in classic Hollywood films does the star lean back against a pillar, a cushion, or a
blossoming apple tree while the camera provides the viewer with a lingering
close-up? From silent days onward, beautiful young women took lengthy
bubble baths on-screen for no apparent reason. Everyone from Gloria Swanson to Claudette Colbert to Jean Harlow to Joan Crawford to Paulette
Goddard to Betty Grable to Jeanne Crain sat in bathtubs. When Lucille
Bremer finally gets her turn, in *Yolanda and the Thief* (1945), the tub is
the size of an airplane runway, and the bubbles look like hot-air balloons.

In fairness, one has to remember that male stars were forced into tubs
also. Clark Gable, Glenn Ford, Rock Hudson, and Gary Cooper all took
baths on-screen, and back in the 1920s, the men Constance Talmadge kept
falling in love with in *The Duchess of Buffalo* (1926) and *Breakfast at
Sunrise* (1927) were shown in their baths, so audiences could get a peek
at what Talmadge was so excited about. Hollywood was always aware that
there were two sexes to be sold. However, male stars were allowed to be
unusual looking or even almost ugly. Jack Palance, Robert Mitchum, and
Kirk Douglas, all of whom became stars, were unconventional looking and
not handsome by ordinary standards. Few women with such flawed looks
could find themselves being cast 'in leading roles during the golden age of
the studio system.*

In some ways, the concept of an ugly woman is erased by the motion
picture. The stories are always about women who are physically attractive.

---

* What audiences looked for in their beautiful stars is well defined by a comedy song
number in *George White's Scandals* of 1945. In it, Joan Davis and Jack Haley sing about
how they dream about movie stars during the night: "Van Johnson . . . Hedy Lamarr . . .
Victor Mature . . . and Dorothy Lamour. Clark Gable, Betty Grable, Ray Milland and Gene
Krupa's Band . . . but when I wake up in the morning, it'll be you."

The ones who aren't play bit parts or are used as cruel jokes. A woman who is not beautiful cast in a larger part is frequently depicted as a comic-relief character, often a man-crazy type. The nonbeautiful, nonglamorous female plays the role of best girlfriend, the female equivalent of the faithful sidekick role in movies about men. It is possible for female comedy stars who are not beautiful to be the leading women in films, but there are fewer of these than of their male equivalents. Consider women like Cass Daley and Joan Davis. Daley openly flaunted her buckteeth and thus by normal Hollywood standards was considered homely, whereas Davis emphasized her gravelly voice and gawky stature. These two women comics played the leads in minor movies, but they never rose to the box-office equivalent of their male counterparts: nonhandsome comics like Jerry Lewis, Eddie Bracken, Joe E. Brown, Eddie Cantor, and Jimmy Durante, all of whom played the leading man in movies.

Sometimes a comic-sidekick female is played by an older actress, like Helen Broderick, or an elegant "older woman" like Verree Teasdale (not to mention Marie Dressler, a case unto herself). The point is made that an older woman often preys on younger men, but that this is a lost cause. Although comedy variations of this situation abound, there is also the tragic version, with Ruth Chatterton in the 1936 *Dodsworth* (see the chapter "Marriage") or Vivien Leigh in *The Roman Spring of Mrs. Stone* (1961). It is worth noting that, according to movie mathematics, the process of aging does not work with gender equality. Whereas Robert Taylor can stop being a playboy, go to Europe, and become a Nobel Prize–winning doctor without changing a hair on his head (in *Magnificent Obsession*, 1930s version), a woman like Barbara Stanwyck can apparently go to market to sell her artichokes in *So Big* (1932 version) and come home an old woman. These are examples of the Time According to the Movie-Clock Theory, by which one male aging unit is the equivalent of eighteen years, whereas one female unit equals fifty years.

Of course, there are female comedy players who are actually beautiful stars—Carole Lombard, Irene Dunne, and Ginger Rogers, to name a few —but these are not female comics or female slapstick artists. They play in romantic comedies, and although they can do physical comedy if necessary, they do not sacrifice beauty and glamour for laughs. Perhaps the most famous female clown in American show business is Lucille Ball, who, it should be remembered, began her career as a Goldwyn Girl. Ball was really a beautiful woman, and her success in physical comedy came largely on television, not on the big screen. Another female clown, Betty Hutton, was a pretty woman who played a down-to-earth heroine in the tomboy mode. These shadings of attitude toward a woman's looks indicate the standards by which women are judged. A woman who is beautiful is a prize, and she will win the things in life that a woman should have, as long as she does not misuse her beauty or become vain about it.

The woman's film genre sometimes tried to prove it was telling an honest story about a real woman by the simple expedient of having the leading lady remove her makeup and thus deglamorize herself. It was an old joke in Hollywood that if a movie star wanted an Oscar, she should take off her false eyelashes and pull out her shoulder pads. Certainly Olivia de Havilland in *The Snake Pit* (1948), Grace Kelly in *The Country Girl* (1954), and Jane Wyman in *Johnny Belinda* (1948) were all trying to prove that true, with Kelly and Wyman succeeding. A serious performance by an actress molded by the Hollywood glamour school was defined by having her wear no lipstick. A first-rank star appearing on the screen without makeup, elaborate hairdo, or wardrobe was defined as realistic acting, as if putting on flat shoes and a frumpy dress somehow constituted a performance of deep intensity and daring. An acknowledgment of the false nature of the Hollywood image is implied by these "honest performances" in which glamour is erased. There's also an insult to the viewing audience implied. To be like the women in the audience, "real" women on-screen made themselves unattractive. At the same time, those *real* women in the audience were being told that fashion and glamour were everything to a woman, and that they had a God-given responsibility to make themselves attractive.

As if fulfilling some deep need for both audiences and filmmakers, the process through which a woman is made-up and glamorized is often dramatized on-screen. Scenes in which an allegedly ordinary woman becomes a raving beauty are reassuring. It's shown to be an it-can-happen-to-you process. Manipulative human beings in white coats bring out clothes, perfume, furs, makeup, to apply to the woman's body, while she, sitting in a chair, looking almost strapped down, submits to ministrations that include plucking her brows, painting her nails, curling her hair with hot pokerlike objects, and painting her mouth. When it's all complete, her "doctors" hand her a mirror, and she smiles at her new self. Frequently, by today's standards, she looks much worse than she did before, as when the lovely, unspoiled young Lana Turner gets herself made over in *Slightly Dangerous* (1943) and comes out wearing too much makeup, a tight suit that hides her body, and a strictly beauty salon hairdo that does not invite anyone to touch and that also looks as if it weighs fifty pounds. Women, it seems, are not good enough in their natural state. They not only need to be jeweled and gowned, but also plucked, curled, and painted.

Three versions of how a young woman is glamorized in Hollywood and manufactured into a movie star exist in the various remakes of a story that was originally called *What Price Hollywood?* (1932) and then redone as *A Star Is Born* (in 1937 and 1954). (A fourth version, also called *A Star*

Is Born and released in 1976, starred Barbra Streisand in a story about a woman's becoming a pop singing star, which is not the same thing.) These three movies show the glamorizing process across three decades, reflecting changes in women's clothing, makeup, and fashion, as well as changes in attitude toward Hollywood's manipulation of a young woman's life. At first, in 1932, the story is treated as a comedy, with some tragic events, although it ends happily. In 1937, the movie becomes a tragedy, with some comedy, and a sad though upbeat ending in which the woman ends up alone, but strong. In the 1954 version, even though it is a musical variation, the story is told as a tragedy.

These three films show how much things changed from 1932 to 1954. In a short twenty-two years, the business did a complete turnaround. The first movie is in black and white, the second in the new three-strip Technicolor process, and the third in color and the latest technological development, the wide-screen anamorphic process. Each of them stars a woman who is a very big star at the time of the film's release, but whose career will quickly wane. These actresses are Constance Bennett, Janet Gaynor, and Judy Garland, respectively. Each represents the epitome of movie stardom in her own moment, but none can last past her prime. Bennett's type of sleek elegance becomes dated by the time of Gaynor's sweet naturalness, and Gaynor's little-girl charm looks too sentimental by the time of Garland's wiser and sassier performance.

Although each movie is telling essentially the same story, and each demonstrates for viewers how a star is born in Hollywood, the attitude taken toward the actual process of turning a young woman into a movie queen differs. (They all have one thing in common: the accidental meeting of a man who is either a top director, as in *What Price Hollywood?*, or a top movie star—the two *Star Is Borns*—who will facilitate and influence their careers.) In the first film, the process of creating a star is shown to be a system that knows what it is doing and that achieves its effects almost magically. Although Constance Bennett is depicted as a young waitress who will do anything, work any hours, practice her lines over and over again, in order to achieve success, the "star is born" sequence that transforms her from working girl to movie star is presented as an awesome, unrealistic event unattached to practical changes made on her physically. A star is born visually in *What Price Hollywood?* via a glamour montage, which consists of a beautiful close-up of Bennett's face, covered in stardust. Over her image is superimposed a full-length shot of her body. This "person" is at first seen small, in the center of the frame, and then it gradually rises out toward the viewer, getting bigger and bigger until it explodes into a montage of film titles and hands clapping, all topped off at the end by the ultimate symbol of a shining star. A star is literally born.

In the next two films, Janet Gaynor and Judy Garland both undergo an actual typical studio make-over session, and they are also shown being subjected to name changes and publicity plans to exploit them. Audiences are told that Hollywood has skilled technicians who know how to turn attractive young women into the most beautiful and glamorous creatures that can possibly be teased out of their ordinary selves. The magic of *What Price Hollywood?* has become an informed and capable business in the 1937 *Star Is Born* and a silly, misguided system in the 1954 *Star Is Born.* There is an increasing sense that the audience is wising up to the system and thus must be a conspirator in its nonsense rather than an awed recipient of its product.

The 1937 *Star Is Born* shows the process of transforming Gaynor into a star as a form of industrial processing, not necessarily right about how to handle someone new and different, but a system that knows its business and does an overall good job. It's a system that can make mistakes, but that still works. The technicians who work on Gaynor have to study her carefully, trying on different eyebrows, lipstick shades, and hairdos until they get them right. In the end, she looks lovely and radiantly takes her place on the soundstage. The tragic 1954 version treats the process of creating a star as if it is a demented and impersonal set of actions that dehumanize a woman, that destroy her individuality, and that entirely miss the point about what it is that makes her appealing and unique. Judy Garland, pushed and pulled and criticized and rejected, comes out of the make-over looking simply awful. She has been victimized, turned into a typical Hollywood product, a starlet who looks like every other starlet, a dyed blond in a hot-pink dress.

These three movies show how glamour, and Hollywood's ability to create it for average women, goes from being "dreams do come true" to "dreams do not come true." Hollywood inadvertently demonstrates in these films how it self-destructed as the years went by and how audiences became less impressed with the idea that they, too, could be stars, or at least could become glamorous if they just followed the process depicted on the screen. Although plucked eyebrows go in and out of fashion, hairdos get shorter and shorter, and lipstick colors vary, the thing that is constant in all three films is the concept of glamour itself. Bennett is born with it . . . Gaynor gets it . . . and Garland survives it. But all three actresses were, in reality, born with some part of it, and the rest of it, ironically enough, was indeed teased out of them by the remarkable Hollywood system.

ALTHOUGH OTHER WOMEN are sometimes the people decreeing what clothes the woman should wear, it is almost always men who work over a woman in the transformation of her personal beauty. Is it any wonder that horror films often take up the theme of the woman who fears aging or losing her looks? It's a natural step out of the beauty parlor and the steam cabinet over to the mad scientist's experimental lab. It's a short move from applying some Max Factor pancake onto the leading lady's face to the application of synthetic flesh, or creating the bride of Frankenstein out of spare parts.

When a woman is presented on-screen as the epitome of glamour, especially in the 1940s, there is a power to the images that is almost overwhelming. As Bing Crosby croons "Moonlight Becomes You" to Dorothy Lamour in *Road to Morocco* (1942), Lamour appears to the viewing audience as a goddesslike spectacle. Her hair is thick and curly. She wears a negligee with long, flowing sleeves, a piece of clothing that no human being had ever seen in real life, not in Morocco or anywhere else, designed for the express purpose of impressing the audience. To knock them dead, in fact. Lamour and Crosby walk through a gigantic courtyard, with a reflecting pool and fake marble pillars. She is bathed in moonlight as Crosby sings "You're all dressed up to go dreaming. . . . Mind if I tag along?" And tag along seems to be all any man could ever do in this situation. Lamour, no great shakes as an actress, nevertheless knew how to move, wear her clothes, smile sweetly, and just let it happen. She accepts the glamorizing and rises to it, proving why she became a movie star.

Of course, Hollywood's ability to present women as objects needs no proof for anyone who has seen even one of Busby Berkeley's insane musical numbers from his Warner Brothers movies of the 1930s. Berkeley's images show literally hundreds of nubile young women all dressed alike, all moving in exact duplication of one another, and all wearing the same weird blond wig. Berkeley's approach to the female form seems downright mathematical as he moves his salacious camera past these women, as if the instrument itself were some kind of sexual duplicating machine. Berkeley stops at nothing. Sometimes he tracks between the legs of his female chorus, while Dick Powell bellows out "*Ooooooooh,* I'm young and healthy," and other times he has these women bouncing and jiggling through calisthenics while Eddie Cantor sings "Keep Young and Beautiful." Berkeley often defied censorship, showing beautiful female bodies changing clothes behind a screen, their naked silhouettes leaving nothing to the imagination. Hundreds of blonds or hundreds of brunettes stand at ironing boards, sit at white pianos, slide down waterfalls, climb into bubble baths, play illuminated violins, or tap relentlessly forward like a prole army of golddigging females in tap shoes. Berkeley lets viewers look at them from above, as their arms and legs form a kaleidoscopic pattern, or ogle them in profile as they stick their bosoms out and turn their grinning faces toward the camera as it tracks by.

Perhaps Hollywood's essential story of how a young woman is glamorized is the 1944 musical *Cover Girl*, a movie that, with typical contradiction, first transforms a woman into a star, empowering her as a visual
goddess, and then claims that this is a really terrible thing to do, because
it will destroy her chance for happiness by making it impossible for her to
be an ordinary wife. *Cover Girl* is the story of the search for *Vanity* magazine's Golden Wedding Girl. It is a perfect time capsule of 1940s glamour:
red, red lips; long, long fingernails; cascades of hair; and insane hats and
clothes. With the possible exception of the 1960s, in which women were
dressed as if they were little girls, there has been no period in the twentieth
century in which women's fashion expressed so much about the woman's
role as the 1940s. To focus on the outfits women wear during the war years
in movie musicals is to confront the female equivalent of the creation of
Robocop. What women wear is armorlike, and it seems to have a deadly
purpose: reduction of any men they encounter to blubbering idiots. The
colors of the women's suits and dresses are like electric shocks to the
system, perfect hues for the center-of-the-universe position. No one who
saw *Cover Girl* has ever forgotten it. Man and woman, boy and girl, the
audience of the 1940s was galvanized by its glamour, color, musical oomph,
but most of all by its goddesslike star, Rita Hayworth, quite possibly the
definitive sex goddess. Her only real competition would be Marilyn Monroe,
but Monroe's disturbed childhood, mental illness, and ambiguous suicide
give her a dimension of social meaning that changes her into a symbol of
exploitation and/or vulnerability. Hayworth represents more straightforwardly the concept of a Hollywood star simply served up to the public as
a gorgeous physical specimen. This doesn't mean that she was not exploited
or didn't suffer. It just means that her image came along in less-informed
times. *Cover Girl* and *Gilda* are the movies that really solidified her sex-
goddess status, with the 1947 *Down to Earth* proving the point by casting
her as the goddess of dance, Terpsichore. Her marriages to Orson Welles,
the boy genius, and to playboy Prince Aly Khan put the finishing touches
on her legend.

For anyone who wishes to know what 1940s Hollywood was all about,
the glamour montage in *Cover Girl* in which Hayworth is prepared to be
photographed as the *Vanity* Golden Wedding Girl is definitive. "Climb
aboard my magic carpet," says magazine publisher Otto Kruger to Hayworth
when she is chosen to be the *Vanity* magazine cover girl. Immediately, the
audience is shown in detail how the process of glamorization is done. In
a beautiful montage, while Kruger watches like an adoring and approving
father, Hayworth undergoes the special treatment. Luscious clothes are
pulled out of boxes. Minions scurry around at top speed. Six or seven men
in white coats bend over her, concentrating furiously. Her face is creamed,

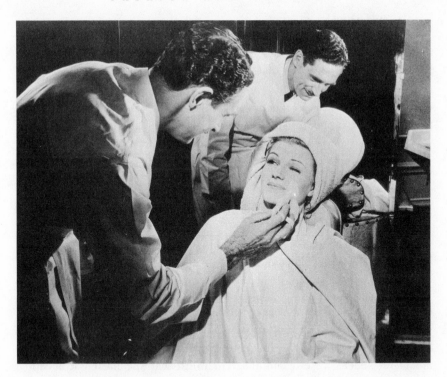

Rita Hayworth is readied for stardom in *Cover Girl*.

powdered, brushed, painted. Her hair is unwrapped, and her hundreds of red curls are pulled out, combed, and teased. Lights are rushed forward and carefully positioned while the photographer studies her intently. Everyone inside the frame focuses on Hayworth, who smiles, dimples, poses, and has her picture taken. Soon the screen is filled with literally hundreds of reproductions of this image, all of which appear on magazine covers all over town. Hayworth looks beautiful, exotic, enviable, desirable. An audience is asked to enjoy the process she is put through and admire its result. Can anyone doubt but that this is how it ought to be for women? All women ought to undergo this process and, of course, come out of it looking like Rita Hayworth.

The film does not culminate with the glamorizing sequence, however. Afterward, Hayworth's face on the magazine cover totally changes her life and marks the beginning of her fall from happiness. She is forced to confront the traditional woman's problem. She must make a Choice. Should she:

1. Choose success, remaining on top as an adored Broadway star, with all the clothes and furs in the world? Or
2. Choose love, going back to Brooklyn and marrying old boyfriend Gene

Kelly, either to perhaps give up her career or at least leave the Broadway spotlight for Brooklyn?

If this was all the story was about, Hayworth's situation in *Cover Girl* would be the traditional love-versus-career movie choice. Subtle layers are woven into this story, however. For instance, Hayworth's dilemma is presented to viewers not so much as a love-versus-career choice as a choice about which of three men she will allow to define her life:

1. The man she really loves, Gene Kelly (he is poor, manipulative, and bossy)
2. The man who really loves her, Lee Bowman (he is rich, manipulative, and bossy)
3. The man who glamorizes her, making her career possible, Otto Kruger (he is very rich and powerful, but also old; he does not offer love, only fame and success)

Hayworth's choices carry baggage. First of all, the choice between the two younger men represents not only two kinds of love—she worships Kelly and Bowman worships her—but also a choice between two kinds of achievement and success. Kelly has told Hayworth that she must not accept a fame that comes as a result of just her physical beauty. "You gotta get there on your feet." The easy way is not acceptable. Since the audience has watched how this success has been at least partially created or manufactured for Hayworth by a team of makeup experts who manipulate her, this argument has credibility.

Bowman represents the success of the *Vanity* magazine cover, and Kelly represents the success of her real talent, dancing, and the hard work he extracts from her. These two men may be seen to be the kinds of men who often turn up in films about women; that is, men who really aren't men but who are just disguised stand-ins for decisions women are trying to make. (See the chapter "Men.") Because Kelly is poor, Hayworth will have to work if she chooses him. If she chooses the extremely wealthy Bowman, she will not have to work. The two men are really covert symbols of career and love, but in reverse of what they seem to be in the simplified plot level.

The third man, Otto Kruger, is the true career choice. If Kelly and Bowman are not to be in her life, Hayworth will be rejecting love of any type as well as a career either dominated by, or given to her by, one of the two men. She will be accepting the life of a career woman won by her own talent and beauty, but—according to the *Cover Girl* story—a career that will not be too much more than just being admired and desired by more men. She will be accepting the life of a sex object.

It is astonishing to consider how contradictory Hayworth's situation really is, as presented in a film that apparently is so clear about where it wants its narrative to end up: with Hayworth in Kelly's arms. For instance, after Hayworth becomes a cover girl she easily becomes a star. She does not have a one-shot success, but instead becomes the star Kelly allegedly wants her to be. She is shown to be truly talented, and her success on Broadway is legitimate. ("If you can better yourself," asks one of her chorus girl pals, "why should [Kelly] object?") The problem beneath the surface of the film is implied, but never stated. Hayworth gets to the top without Kelly's help, rendering him emasculated and unimportant in her life, particularly since the other men she now meets are rich and he isn't. The film doesn't suggest that Rita Hayworth can't succeed without Kelly, only that she won't be happy without his love. Furthermore, what it really shows is how Hayworth becomes powerful in and of herself after she is glamorized. Glamour turns her into a star, the object of adoring gazes and the center of "The Girl on the Magazine Cover" musical number.

In this number, famous cover girls of the 1940s pose in a fashion parade of various outfits and are seen standing beside covers they have posed for on magazines of the day: *Liberty, Woman's Home Companion, Redbook, Coronet,* and so on. (A similar device appears in the 1948 MGM movie *Easter Parade* using magazines of the past, as that film is set in the early 1900s.) Each woman is more or less passive, walking slowly out and, well, *posing,* which is what cover girls do. They stand straight, wear good clothes, smile, and wait to be admired, which is their job. Then they exit. Hayworth's participation in the number is the total opposite. She is a dancing, whirling, twirling, active, and alive force from the heavens, running down from above in a dancing attack, smiling, laughing, with young men dancing out to meet her. Hayworth, in other words, is no stationary cover girl. She is a living, breathing talent. She is also free and unleashed, in control of her dance, the center of the universe.

The justification for Hayworth's giving it all up for love (Gene Kelly) is defined by a parallel story involving the magazine publisher Otto Kruger, who is like a benign father figure. Kruger, in fact, was once in love with Hayworth's grandmother, a show-business performer who captured his heart when he was a young man. Twice, the film returns to the past to show the young Kruger (played by Jess Barker) attending the theater to admire and watch Hayworth's grandmother perform. Although Kruger is too old to play himself as a young man, Hayworth plays the double role. (She is told in the story that she's a double for her grandmother, and she surely *is* a double, since she's the same person.) Beauty, it seems, is both eternal and reproducible; Hayworth, the goddess, is ageless and iconographic. Since this film shows us how the glamorous Rita Hayworth is manufactured, we can only assume that magical men in white coats create one of these every generation. (Which in Hollywood, of course, they did.) The two Hayworths allow an audience to enjoy the leading lady in both modern and period clothes as they also allow a second self to emerge to resolve Hayworth's love conflicts.

Hayworth as her grandmother is a figure of importance and power to the adoring young Kruger. He proposes to her, but his wealthy mother does not approve. Hayworth, as her grandmother, publicly humiliates the young man from the stage by singing a song entitled "Poor John," the words his mother spoke when she first saw Hayworth. This is a movie situation in which a woman is allowed to humiliate a man, even if only through song and dance, and even if she is supposed to be someone who is dead and gone. As it turns out, Grandma gave up marrying Kruger, with all his money and power, in order to marry the man she truly loved, a lowly piano player in the orchestra pit. (Thus the parallel for the granddaughter's life is set.) Kruger admits the truth of this story to Hayworth at the end of the movie, when she is about to marry the wrong man, Lee Bowman (who is *always*, as far as I'm concerned, the wrong man). Hayworth sobbingly says, "I never knew any woman as happy as my grandmother!" and runs back to the arms of Kelly.

Consider how cheerfully *Cover Girl* uses fashion and glamour to contradict itself as it progresses to its final clinch. It does not say that Hayworth should not have a career, but that her career should be dominated by the man she loves, without whom she cannot be happy. It does not say she should not become a Broadway star, but that she shouldn't take a shortcut via her beauty to get there. Then it spends an inordinate amount of time justifying the beauty and glamorizing process, presenting it as not only acceptable but pleasurable for Hayworth to undergo. Then it contradicts that pleasure and says that this process will ruin Hayworth's life, as she begins to drink too much. Its point is that Gene Kelly is the most important thing in Hayworth's life, but it shows how easily she can leave him behind. (He never does reach her level of success.) It also shows how a woman can totally humiliate a man, wielding power over him through song, dance, and beauty. It presents Hayworth as an object of adoration and shows how her beauty empowers her. Then it demonstrates that this is a limited and suspicious kind of power that will not make her happy. However, it shows how happy and free she is when dancing, how joyous and how successful. It says that she needs to achieve success by working hard, but she *is* working hard in Kelly's cheap nightclub. He just bosses her around and treats her badly, and she has to labor as part of the chorus. When the two wealthy men elevate her to Broadway stardom, they are always kind to and considerate of her, thinking of what will make her happy. She is given a gigantic stage that is all her own to dance on and a chorus of men who have to support her, instead of vice versa. Probably no film glorifies glamour more than *Cover Girl* while simultaneously trying to convince everyone in the audience not to accept its false appeals. Quite simply, *Cover Girl* is a perfect example of how women were glamorized and made powerful as images on the screen and then were asked to see this as a total mistake in regard to their personal lives.

The question of a woman's beauty and how she uses it is further presented in a stark drama, *A Woman's Face* (1941), starring Joan Crawford. Directed by George Cukor, the film is a remake of a Swedish movie that featured the very young Ingrid Bergman. The story is told through flashbacks that represent testimony at the murder trial of Anna Helm. Each of the witnesses, one of whom is Anna herself, tells a piece of her story. Although the movie is a tale of murder and blackmail, it is really a story about a woman who is changed from being scarred and ugly into being beautiful and desirable via plastic surgery. In this way, *A Woman's Face* becomes a metaphor for what a woman is supposed to do with her life—that is, fall in love and care for men and children. It shows what happens to her when she is barred from this natural task because she is not beautiful.

In the classic woman's film tradition, Crawford portrays Anna as two different people. As a scarred woman, she is angry, cruel, and hard. She leads the life of a criminal, running a shady roadhouse and indulging in small-time blackmailing of the frequently unsavory customers who turn up in their after-hours dive. As an unscarred woman of beauty, Crawford changes completely. She begins to laugh and have fun. In addition, she becomes a protective governess to a small child, changing into a totally different person.

A Woman's Face is carefully plotted along the lines of duality and contradiction that are common in the woman's film. There are two heroines, a beautiful one and an ugly one, even though they are the same woman. There are two men for her to choose between, a good one (Melvyn Douglas) and a bad one (Conrad Veidt). There are also two ways of life, the criminal and the socially acceptable. After her face is changed, Anna is sent by Veidt to become a governess to a little boy who will inherit the millions that Veidt himself formerly stood to gain. Veidt plans for Crawford to kill the boy after insinuating herself into the household as a trusted servant.

The visual presentation of the film follows what can be seen as a societal attitude toward Crawford's face. When she is scarred and ugly, the camera avoids looking at her. She is seen from the back or from the side. The scarred half of her face is kept in shadows or under the veils of hats. There are no mirrors in her residences, and when she accidentally confronts one, she flies into a rage, smashing it to pieces and trying to kill the member of her gang who hung it there. Each time her scar is shown or revealed, it is a moment of high drama, a recurring shock, presented as a stark reminder to the audience of how she looks and what that means.

While scarred, Crawford wears clothes that are unglamorous, and she wears no jewelry. Her hair looks limp and unwashed, and it certainly is unstyled. She has no makeup of any sort. After she meets Veidt, of course, she begins to shop, coming back to her gang in a fancy new hat and wearing a frilly lace blouse, two representations of her new sexual awareness and sense of herself as a woman.

When her face is changed, she walks out into the sunshine, and a small child smiles up at her. She takes off her hat and walks confidently, stopping two soldiers who turn to admire her looks. When she enters Veidt's building to take him some flowers, since he was the first man ever to bring her any, she stops to look at herself fully and completely for the first time. She stands reflected in a long line of refracting mirrors, her image multiplied a hundred times, both sides of her face perfect. After this, the audience is invited to enjoy countless intense close-ups of Crawford's dramatically beautiful face. Since she is now a beautiful and glamorous woman, she is fit for all of us to look at.

As a beautiful woman, Crawford's character has access to the world of women. She is admired, loved, and included in pleasant social events. When she warns her new little charge that she will be mean to him if he is naughty, the child grins and says, "Aw, you couldn't be mean. You're too pretty." He becomes her little suitor, telling her he wants to marry her (he's four years old) and asking if he can be her escort at the big dancing party his grandfather gives. The old man himself goes gaga over Crawford, smooching her and favoring her in every way. As a beautiful woman, Crawford finds she cannot be vicious enough to kill the child. Mysteriously, she has undergone a complete character change.

In a confrontation scene, Veidt and Crawford discuss this change. Veidt says he hates the doctor who has turned her into a "cooing dove," something "soft" and totally uninteresting. When she says, "I'm a woman," he tells her, "You're a woman, but you're something more. . . . There've been women like you before, but they were queens, conquerors." The issue is clarified as one in which a woman must choose whether to use her power, a form of sexuality or physical beauty, for evil or for good, with the movie saying that good is the only choice that can bring her happiness or satisfaction. In the end, Crawford tells Melvyn Douglas, "I want to get married. I've always wanted to get married. I want to have a home and children. I want to go to market and cheat the grocer and fight with the landlord. I want to belong to the human race. I want to belong."

In other words, Crawford's character does not wish to be powerful.

She wishes to be loved. To be loved, she must be beautiful and desirable and "soft," a "cooing dove." Without the possibility of being a "normal" woman when her face is scarred, she is hateful and destructive. As a beautiful woman, she can become normal and thus be a mother and a wife and a productive member of society.

Perhaps the final comment on Hollywood, women, fashion, and glamour is made by the remarkable moment in *Blonde Venus* (1932) when Marlene Dietrich emerges from a gorilla suit to sing "Hot Voodoo." The setting is a smoky nightclub of the sort that features Cary Grant in a tuxedo at a prominent table. As the orchestra begins to pound out a rhythmic jazz tune, a chorus line of gyrating women in scanty clothes snakes out, with their pelvises locked together in a suggestive dance. They lead a huge gorilla in chains onto the stage. While the music grows wilder and the nightclub grows hotter, the gorilla, menacing the audience with a King Kong stance, suddenly reaches one arm over to the other and pulls off a hairy paw. Out of the ape body emerges a white, white female arm, adorned with a sparkling and very expensive diamond bracelet. As the ape begins to strip, its head comes off to reveal a calm, mocking, and totally ironic Dietrich. She puts on a blond Afro, and as the audience (both in the film nightclub and in the viewing house) goes wild, she begins to sing: "Hot voodoo/I've got my man/hot voodoo/do what you can." What a moment! It contains glamour, transformation, fashion, sex, slapstick comedy, horror, fear, music, filmic references, all laced together by some mad effort that manages to entertain, comment, mock, and frighten. It also satisfies. When one realizes that Marlene Dietrich has emerged out of the hairy presence of an ape in a film in which she plays a sacrificing mother who loses custody of her little boy because she has had to go to work to earn money to pay for her husband's operation . . . well. One can only wonder exactly what viewers were supposed to think about Dietrich, her attitude toward men and motherhood, as expressed through this kind of fashion and glamour.

WHEN ONE THINKS about Hollywood and fashion and glamour, there is one star of the woman's film who stands out beyond any other as representative of those concepts. It is Kay Francis, who became a star *only* because of fashion and glamour, and only because of the woman's film genre. Her career is absolute proof of the importance of clothes, makeup, and jewelry both on and off the screen.

Kay Francis was before my time. I knew her name, and I had seen her in one of her later vehicles, *When the Daltons Rode* (1940), but she had ceased to be a movie star of the top rank when I began going to the movies in the 1940s. Her importance was brought home to me, however, when my sixth-grade teacher, Doris Danielson Dolan, the essence of local glamour, named her firstborn child Kay Francis. The name, she said, was for her favorite movie star, the most glamorous and fashionable woman ever to appear in films. I was suitably impressed, because Doris Danielson Dolan was a fashion oracle of some significance. Every Christmas she wore two astounding items for the annual grade-school Christmas concert: fake cherries in her hair, à la Betty Grable, and gold lamé ballet slippers, à la no one we had ever heard of in Brookings, South Dakota. She was radiant, and she had a rhinestone pin in the shape of a mailbox. When you pulled its little handle, it opened up, revealing not much of anything, but still— opening up! When it came to fashion tricks and astounding attire, Doris Danielson Dolan was in a class by herself. I trusted her judgment and, as soon as I was able, began to track down the films of Kay Francis, who turned out, indeed, to be the most glamorous and fashionable woman ever to be in films.

Sadly, many people today don't know who Kay Francis was, although she herself once said, "I can't wait to be forgotten." People think that the most glamorous and fashionable woman of the 1930s was Carole Lombard, or perhaps her more exotic counterpart Marlene Dietrich. Lombard, however, was a talented comedienne and often a good serious actress. Dietrich was an original, a representation of an androgynous ideal for whom glamour and fashion were tools to be used, but for whom they could never provide the complete definition. Both these women wore clothes well, but their careers have substance beyond the label of "clotheshorse." Kay Francis was *only* fashion and glamour, a true star of the woman's film. She forged a top-drawer career out of nothing but tears and tiaras, a clotheshorse who gave significance to the term.

The camera seems to love Kay Francis. She doesn't look quite like anyone else, and close inspection indicates that she is not a beauty in the usual sense. She is odd looking, really, and she has a slight lisp. But she was born for the bias cut, and she walks through the scuzziest of melodramas as if she were being presented at court. It is often only her modern, almost austere presence that keeps certain weepie movies from going down for the third time. She inhabits the plots as if she were at the Ritz, and she knows how to sacrifice herself and suffer without making you want to kill her. There is a soft loveliness to her voice and body, and a clearly defined line to her shape and head. Her dark hair frames her face, with its generous mouth and broad brow, its luminous eyes. When she's on-screen and dressed right, she's the center of attention, and no one, no matter how much more talented, can take it away from her. When she's cast in a part that uses her ability for sly mockery, for her "isn't this a hoot, but let's enjoy it, darlings" quality, she is terrific (*Trouble in Paradise*, 1932). She has true sophistication and an honest languor, and like all great movie stars, she seems to invite the audience into a conspiracy of some sort. In her case, it's a conspiracy that suggests she knows, and the viewer knows, that what is going on in the plot is sheer nonsense, *but* . . . The "but" is a soupçon of credibility, the hint that it's bad for us but we need it, and we need it because we want to believe in it. Believe in it? Believe in Russian female scientists who pose as whores, and lady doctors who save the lives of dying babies with hairpins snatched from their own heads? Believe in it? "Let's do it," says Kay, and we do. It's her "let's do it and the hell with it, you know we want to" quality that makes her perfect for the woman's film, with its contradiction, its ambivalence, and, of course, its frequently lunatic stories that we all secretly love but feel we ought to be ashamed of.

Obviously, Kay Francis can't act. Acting is not what she is doing on-screen. Being there is what she is doing, and at that she is an Olympic champion. She is presence, not talent. Acting for Kay Francis is a matter of fashion. She depicts boredom by lifting her arm to allow the slow fall of a sleeve off her shoulder. Anger she shows by crushing some roses worn at her waist, and passion is fingering a brooch on her bosom. Defiance is kicking a long skirt around behind her to facilitate and announce her departure, and happiness is lifting up the full skirt of her dirndl with both hands to reveal her lace-edged petticoat. For tragedy, she wears no jewelry, no ruffles, and no flowers, for she knows that a serious situation calls for a plain dress that offers a viewer no distractions, no apologies.

Francis can wear anything. She always looks relaxed no matter what has been draped on her body or stuck on her head. Clothes seem to drip off her shoulders and flow down her body. She is never undone by an outfit or an accessory. She can pick up a fur muff the size of a grizzly bear and make it look like a cloud that has momentarily drifted by. No matter what they put on her, she never looks ridiculous. Clothes cannot intimidate her. She rises above them, putting them in their place, as it were, which is on her body to make her look good, no matter if they have bell cords hanging off them or feathers sticking out of them like daggers. She has the ability to seem to disassociate herself from her clothes. She is a true master of fashion, a woman who is a challenge to the kind of designer whose goal is to make a woman look like an idiot. This is a woman who is always bigger than any mere ensemble, and when she enters a room you're never aware of "what a dress!"—only "what a woman."

The Kay Francis scrapbooks, lovingly kept by and for her during her years of stardom, contain many articles on Francis as a fashion plate. She posed for countless fan-magazine layouts that ran pictures of her in clothes she wore in films, with captions such as "Suggested for summer evenings

—a frock of yellow chiffon with petalled flounce, and if possible, a cape bordered with silver fox." (Probably not very possible for the average reader.) "Here's Kay Francis posing for us in the Grecian-influenced gown she wears in her latest film . . . of ivory brocaded velvet, it has the flowing lines and even the corded girdle of its classic model . . ." For a picture showing a gorgeous close-up of Kay Francis, her eyes wide and her lips slightly parted, with handsome young George Brent beside her, his lips pasted to her shoulder, the caption reads, "And here is Kay's gown in action. For kissable shoulders, this strap effect is strongly recommended!"

Francis's own private life was a woman's film of sorts, the variation in which a poor girl becomes a big star but does not find happiness, ending up awash in booze and pills with no one beside her when death comes. Although she is not too well known today, she really was a big star, and she has the rumors to prove it. No great star can reach the top without being followed by a scandalous story, such as Joan Crawford's stag movie, Clara Bow's night with the USC football team, and Jean Harlow's abortions. Kay Francis was rumored to be black, passing as white, and even today this rumor turns up at dinner parties, shared mostly by people who have probably never seen a Kay Francis movie. Her origins were obscure, and her date of birth shifted in the way birth dates always seem to do for female movie stars. It was said that the woman who worked for her as a servant was actually her mom (in what might be called the Merle Oberon gambit). However, people who knew Kay Francis in Hollywood (both Joan Crawford and Bonita Granville) claimed that Francis's mother was a sweet little woman who often answered the door at Francis's home. It seems unlikely at this point that anyone will ever know very much about Kay Francis's offscreen life, except for what is revealed in her diaries. Written in a garbled mixture of several different methods of shorthand, with an occasional tidbit in regular English script to tantalize the reader ("Hedda here. What a bitch."), they cover only two areas of her life: whom she went to dinner with and whom she slept with. She also had two areas of confession: "Drunk again!" and "Work, work, work, too damned tired to move."

The career of Kay Francis shows how stardom was created in the old studio system. During 1929, 1930, and 1931, Francis appeared in an astonishing total of twenty-one feature films. In some of them, of course, she had only small roles, but in others she was the key romantic lead. It is clear that no one was quite sure exactly how she should be cast or used or sold to the American public during this period. In her first three movies in 1929, *Gentlemen of the Press*, *The Cocoanuts*, and *Dangerous Curves*, she is a villainess, and her very masculine haircut marks her out as someone who possibly will never be a leading lady. By 1930, however, she starts playing sympathetic roles with *Street of Chance*, although *A Notorious Affair* (from the same year) presents her stomping around in riding clothes, brandishing a crop and eyeballing both her groomsman and a man feeding her hounds as possible bedmates. She's also heartless, although soignée, in *Behind the Makeup* (1930).

By the middle of 1930, however, she has hit her stride. In *The Virtuous Sin*, she plays a chemist in the Russia of 1914. She is nobly helping her young husband do research on a serum to cure tuberculosis. When he is suddenly called to his military service, interrupting their important work, Francis volunteers to go to the city to try to influence his commanding officer to exempt him. Here is where the career of Kay Francis begins to define itself. She leaves for the city carrying a suitcase (a crucial tool of the woman's trade) and takes a room at a brothel where she feels confident she'll quickly meet the commander. She doesn't take sensible shoes or register at a hotel for military wives. Oh, no. Once unpacked, she glamorizes herself to attract the attention she wants, and the results are amazing. Her chemistry professor apparently was more of an Elizabeth Arden than a Madame Curie, but who could care? One glimpse of Francis's tiara is all it takes for a viewer to throw credibility out the window. Her glamour *is* credible, and that's all that matters.

In *Scandal Sheet*, from 1931, Francis has a smaller part as the straying wife of a hard-bitten newspaperman played by George Bancroft. ("I print the news no matter who it hurts," he announces, which means, of course, that soon it's going to hurt him.) While he hurries about, perpetrating cheap journalistic tricks on an innocent public and barking out headlines like "Two Bits for Tiny Tot's Tale of Woe," Francis, at home alone and bored, begins to have an affair. She spends her movie time smoking long cigarettes and rummaging in her closet, which is as long as a football field and has fully automated doors.

Toward the end of 1931, she's carrying her own films literally on her back. In the stylish and thoroughly modern comedy *Girls About Town*, directed by George Cukor, she is utterly gorgeous as a gold digger with real character. In *Transgression*, she suffers in the world of clothes and cocktails. When her husband, a mining engineer, goes off to Bombay without her, her virtue is sorely tested. Although a loving wife and honest woman, she soon enough ends up in a beauty salon, being coiffed, perfumed, sprayed, pampered, manicured, and facialed. All the details of this process are carefully shown viewers, even though the running time of the movies is only seventy minutes. After her hair is in place and her velvet is on, she feels sexually alive for the first time in her life. She decides she *must* leave her husband for sleazy Ricardo Cortez, who is tangoing among the potted palms. Having surrendered to his embrace, she speaks the fatal

Kay Francis, always perfectly clad—even as Lenin's
secretary (in *British Agent*, below)

woman's film words: "I've *chosen*." Can anyone doubt that it was the facial that did it?

By early 1932, the studio felt confident enough about the public's acceptance of this unusual woman to cast her sympathetically as a soft-hearted, would-be mother (albeit mixed up with crooks) in *The False Madonna*. This movie is the inevitable variation on the story about a woman who sacrifices her children, only to be reunited with them later. In *The False Madonna*, Francis *pretends* to be such a woman. When the real mother—going home to her rich and long-lost son after his father (her former husband) dies—falls ill and drops dead on a train, a disbarred doctor (William Boyd) and his traveling companion (Francis) decide to pass Kay off as the mom. The boy is seventeen and hasn't seen his mother in fourteen years. Furthermore, he's now conveniently blind ("he was in an air crash two years ago"), so there's not much problem there. His loyal family lawyer, however, knows that Francis is a fraud, but says nothing for the boy's sake. The lawyer *does* tear up the fifty-thousand-dollar check Francis is given by her "son," but allows her to sit loyally and attractively dressed by the dying boy's bedside reading *Vanity Fair* aloud in the one week she spends with him. She finds true peace and satisfaction in the false-mother role, spurning her former criminal cohorts. ("She's gone respectable on us," they wail.) In the end, the boy dies, and the lawyer inexplicably proposes marriage to Francis. "I've got a home, too," he says. "Wouldn't you like a home and peace?" He offers it as if it were a cup of tea and a cookie. "It's what every woman wants, in her heart," responds Francis, accepting it on the same level of commitment. As they go into a discreet clinch, suitable to the recent death of the blind nonson they shared, Francis wears a very beautiful ensemble, with matching shoes and simple jewelry. By now, she's at her peak as a clotheshorse movie star.

By 1933, Kay Francis was making four thousand dollars per week at Warner Brothers. Her face was in every movie magazine and on the cover of many. Her arrival at the pinnacle of stardom was largely due to her work in two of 1932's most successful movies, *Trouble in Paradise*, a delicious and stylish comedy directed by Ernst Lubitsch, and *One Way Passage*, the story of a doomed love affair between a dying woman and a condemned convict who meet on board a ship crossing from Hong Kong to San Francisco via Honolulu. On the one hand, the star of a sophisticated romp that totally stands the test of time (the Lubitsch film) and on the other the leading lady in a tearjerker that can still make audiences cry today (*One Way Passage*, which pairs her with William Powell), Francis hit the top. In 1933, she starred in five movies, and in 1934, four more. In people's minds, she had become what Doris Danielson Dolan told me she was: Hollywood's epitome of style and glamour.

In a sophisticated comedy like *Trouble in Paradise*, she is in her element. In such films—which include *Jewel Robbery* (1932) and *Girls About Town*—she stands out. These few films, however, are the exception in her career. Mostly, she is stuck chugging up the Yangtze on a riverboat, a down-and-outer making her living the way such women have always made their living (*Mandalay*, 1934), or she is huffing up a Tibetan mountainside on a donkey, following a man who doesn't really care about her (*Transgression*). She plays actresses, opera singers, aviatrixes, doctors, magazine editors, and—inexplicably—Lenin's secretary (in the 1934 *British Agent*). As Kay explains it, "If someone didn't take care of details, Lenin would be swamped."

Francis's story is one in which a studio finally figures out how to dress a female star and glamorize her the way an audience wanted to see her. Like the women she played, Kay Francis in the wrong clothes was not a star. In her first years, she seesawed from villain to noblewoman to clotheshorse to little wife until Warner Brothers finally grasped what to do with her: dress her very, very well . . . surround her with good furniture or exotic settings like Russia and Paris and Budapest . . . and let her suffer. Keep the running time short. Let her play a woman who is good but who temporarily acts bad, or who is bad but pretends to be good, but only for about seventy-five minutes. The best Kay Francis film was one in which she could drape around in satin and furs, hop-skip about in dirndls, act naughty, *and* repent. In short, the best vehicle for Kay Francis was that staple of the moviemaking world: the woman's film. A simple setup was created for her in which she played in one of three types of films: elegant and sophisticated comedies, directed by artists and costarring superb actors (*Trouble in Paradise, Girls About Town*); swell-gal movies, in which she assumed a masculine role as a doctor, lawyer, scientist, and had to resolve the old career-love conflict (*Dr. Monica*, 1934; *Mary Stevens, M.D.*, 1933); and the genuine woman's film of the deeply tearjerking variety, in which she has to suffer (*The House on 56th Street*, 1933; *Give Me Your Heart*, 1936). Francis became a top box-office draw and a big, big star in movies that, for the most part, would have sunk the careers of less elegant women. Her films made money for nearly a decade, until finally her high living, difficult ways, and desire for money caused her to be driven out of the business by Warner Brothers.

When one thinks of fashion and glamour, Kay Francis should be the standard by which everything else is measured. Sitting on-screen, as she does at the end of *The House on 56th Street*, wearing a stark evening gown and dealing blackjack with a grace and style that have long since disappeared from American movies, she is the absolute personification of what fashion and glamour meant to the woman's film of the 1930s. She deserves her place in film history.

THE STARS
WHO PLAY HER

THE DEFINITION of the American woman on-screen is made visually concrete by the movie stars who portray her. In order to think about this, it is first necessary to confront the entire concept of "movie star"—who becomes a star, not just in women's pictures but in general, and who tries and fails form a road map to the secrets of the American soul. Lana Turner and Cecilia Parker, two beautiful, blond young women who first appeared on the screen in the late 1930s, are a case in point. Both Turner and Parker were given an opportunity to catch the public's eye by MGM's star-making system. They can be seen together on the brink of stardom in *Love Finds Andy Hardy* (1938), with both of them more or less being groomed for bigger roles. They might be said to be equals at that point, although Turner not only has the showier role in the film, she had already been cast in more movies and in better parts. However, Parker is playing Andy Hardy's sister and had been playing the part earlier in the series, so that audiences were prepared for her and also knew something about her character in advance. Turner's role is not drawing on this previous audience relationship.

What is the difference between them? It is immediately clear that Turner has an impact on any viewer, male or female, whereas Parker does not. Turner can command the attention of the audience no matter what else is going on around her, and when the camera focuses on her beautiful face, she seems to be thinking something that can be specifically understood. Parker does not have this ability. She becomes a kind of surface. She will be noticed but not remembered, even though she is very pretty. Turner can get audiences to respond to her in whatever way their own personalities dictate, and she seems alive, full of juice. Turner is a conduit, an interactive force. This quality has nothing to do with acting but everything to do with film stardom. As a result of possessing it, Lana Turner became one of Hollywood's most famous movie stars, and Cecilia Parker is barely remembered today. A movie star may or may not be able to act by theatrical standards, but he or she must have the ability to create a relationship with viewers. That is the secret of stardom, and the source of the concept known as persona.

"Persona" is the word used to define the quality that a great star projects to an audience and that the audience accepts as being true to the star's nature. John Wayne's persona is that of the all-American active male, while Greta Garbo's would be the mysterious, exotic, and probably European woman. When the entire career of such stars is examined, it emerges that more than a third of the films they have appeared in may contradict this persona in some fundamental way, yet audiences identify these actors and actresses by a particular type of role, the one they most believe them in. We *believe* John Wayne is an all-American hero who never dies in his movies, not the man eaten by a giant squid in *Reap the Wild Wind* (1942). We *believe* Greta Garbo is Mata Hari, from the 1932 film by the same name, and not a loving mother, as in *The Single Standard* (1929). It isn't that Wayne and Garbo are not effective in these other films, but that audiences do not respond to them as much in them. An audience remembers what it wants to remember and discards what it doesn't like or respond to. Who remembers Humphrey Bogart with a skunk stripe in his hair, running around as the villain in *The Return of Dr. X* (1939)? When Garbo played an ordinary woman in the screwball comedy *Two-Faced Woman* (1941), the film was a failure, so that people began to say the public rejected Garbo as a creature of comedy, or as an ordinary woman. Democratized, she was a bore. Yet one of her most successful movies was the brilliant Ernst Lubitsch comedy *Ninotchka* (1939), and Garbo had been cast as wives, mothers, sisters, and sweethearts more than once in her career. It was that her ultimate appeal lay in her exotic quality, as in a movie like *Mysterious Lady* (1928), where she personified love, sex, intrigue, and fantasy, a kind of fur-draped and orchidaceous escapism. This is how people want to remember her, rather than as a ski instructor who danced the chicka-chocka. When a woman like Garbo wraps her head in a jeweled turban and goes out into the pulsing dark of the night draped in gems and sporting one luscious orchid, who is going to remember her sitting beside her son's bed and nursing him through an illness? She was simply too extraordinary to be remembered with a cold compress in her hand; we liked her better

Greta Garbo

when she was willing to die for all our sins, and we were willing to let her.

When actors are unable to establish a persona, either through the roles they are assigned or because they do not possess that elusive quality the audience picks up on, they never become truly famous, no matter how talented or attractive they may be. Beautiful Evelyn Ankers and handsome Richard Denning (who actually married each other in 1942) are a perfect grade-B couple of the 1940s. Each achieved the bottom level of stardom. Ankers was British, but she appeared in such Hollywood films as *The Wolf Man* (1941), *The Mad Ghoul* (1943), and *Spoilers of the North* (1947). Denning was a solid leading man, noted for light romantic roles in *Adam Had Four Sons* (1941), *The Glass Key* (1942 version), *No Man of Her Own* (1950), and *Weekend with Father* (1951). He also appeared in several television series, notably "Mr. and Mrs. North" and "Michael Shayne." Ankers and Denning have the sort of perfect, smooth good looks associated with the concept of movie stardom. Their presence on the screen is pleasant, but perhaps too pleasant. Their physical perfection seems bland, and when the film is over, it is hard to conjure up an exact picture of either of their faces. Ankers and Denning became the type of actors you'd cast to *play* movie stars. Hollywood had so many beautiful faces to cast in movies that sometimes a star was better off having a distinctive feature, something to make him or her noticeable, and thus more memorable. Gable's ears are too big. Jimmy Stewart is too tall and looks gangly. Margaret Sullavan and June Allyson have raspy voices. Norma Shearer has a cast of some sort in one eye. Crawford's mouth is a wide gash, and Davis has bug eyes.

Neither Lana Turner nor Cecilia Parker has such a flaw. Turner's voice, however, is distinctive, and seems too low and husky for her tiny frame. Her potential stardom was also enhanced by the fact she could play in comedies, musicals, or dramas. Once the public picked her out, MGM cast her in all kinds of roles—as a shop girl, an heiress, a cub reporter, and even as a college sociology major! In some ways, Lana Turner as a sex symbol in the 1940s became the equivalent of Joan Crawford in the 1930s. (The studios were always ruthlessly grooming younger women to take the place of the aging stars on their rosters. At Twentieth Century Fox, Alice Faye was replaced by Betty Grable, who was replaced by June Haver, who was replaced by Marilyn Monroe.) Turner and Crawford were not alike physically, but they both came from somewhat tarnished backgrounds, and both were willing to work hard and cooperate with studio plans. Turner even played the Crawford role in a remake of *Grand Hotel* (1932) called *Weekend at the Waldorf* (1945). As Crawford was cast opposite big-name stars like Gable, Tracy, Robert Taylor, and Robert Young to enhance her stardom, Turner was also cast opposite big-name male stars, like Gable, Tracy, Robert Taylor, and Robert Young.*

Both were dream images, beautiful and sexy, but Turner undoubtedly had more of an appeal to male moviegoers than Crawford did, and she did not actually become the same type as Joan Crawford, nor did her career follow the Crawford trajectory. Turner developed a strong and significant persona of her own, and personal tragedies shaped the audience's view of her in a way that was linked only to her. It is also true that no one took Crawford's place. When MGM let her go at the beginning of the 1940s, believing that her time of stardom was over, she moved to Warners and became even bigger, winning an Oscar. Crawford refused to be thrown on the ash heap, keeping her career going for more than twenty-five years beyond the normal span of the typical female star.

For a female star to develop a persona, she first had to last long enough, then had to individualize her roles, breaking free as much as possible from stereotyping by defining herself in some unique way. (She also had to resolve in her own private life the issue her films were always about: what to do about love, marriage, and children.) When scholars oversimplify the image of women on film, suggesting that women were portrayed as either virgins, whores, or mothers, they ignore the fact that many female movie stars created for themselves their own image, a role that was entirely theirs. There was a Janet Gaynor type, a Jean Arthur type, a Joan Crawford kind of woman, a Bette Davis heroine, and a Rosalind Russell comedy career woman. It becomes impossible to think of the career of someone like Jean Arthur as being limited to a simple list of labels like "sex goddess," "mother," "wife," "sister." She was Jean Arthur in a Jean Arthur role, and that was that. She was somebody special, distinctive. She was an actress who could murmur, "Oh, really?" and give it the weight of the Monroe Doctrine.

Furthermore, even an actress associated with one kind of female label got the opportunity to play its opposite. Anne Baxter is a small-town sweetheart in *The Fighting Sullivans* (1944) and an insane nymphomaniac in *Guest in the House* (1944). Janet Gaynor is a virgin in *Small Town Girl* (1936 version) and a whore in *The Man Who Came Back* (1931). June

---

* Longevity was always a problem for female stars, who rarely lasted as long as their male counterparts. When a woman reached the age of forty, she was considered too old to play opposite a twenty-year-old male, whereas a forty-year-old male movie star easily made love on-screen to females half his age. A man with wrinkles and white hair was thought to be sophisticated, elegant, experienced, while a woman in such a condition was over the hill. Women movie stars had a difficult time stretching their careers past even one decade, and the great stars like Crawford, Loy, Davis, Stanwyck, Hepburn, who kept going for thirty or forty years, represent formidable forces indeed.

Allyson is a female doctor in *The Girl in White* (1952) and a destructive shrew in *The Shrike* (1955). Ginger Rogers is supposed to be the spunky American modern girl, and Greer Garson the noble British woman, but Garson plays a flighty flirt in *Julia Misbehaves* (1948), and Rogers is the noble presidential wife in *Magnificent Doll* (1946). Frequently a star goes from virgin to whore to saint all in one film!

The great woman stars, like Crawford and Davis and Stanwyck, began their careers toward the end of the silent era or just at the transition to sound and worked through the next four or five decades. As their careers developed, they were assigned to many different kinds of films, some of which, as I've said, do not match the persona with which they came eventually to be associated. In the beginning, they played roles with different labels. Since only a few women kept their careers going for more than a decade, those who lasted often found themselves playing either caricatures of their former selves, grotesque older women, or television characters that needed to be surrounded by young actors, both male and female (as happened to Barbara Stanwyck in "Big Valley").

If the American woman on film is defined by the stars who portray her, should we try to define what "the woman on film" is by role labeling or by star personae?

In considering this question, it is necessary to face the same hard facts that female movie stars had to face. Personae? If you develop one that presents you as a teenage singing star, what are you going to do when you reach thirty? Deanna Durbin, Jane Powell, and Debbie Reynolds all faced this problem. If you represent an exotic, mysterious woman, what are you going to do when World War II comes along, and heroines are supposed to be wholesome American girls who work in defense plants? Marlene Dietrich and Greta Garbo both faced this, which is how Garbo ended up as that dancing ski instructor and how Dietrich found herself adopting a baby she finds on the street in *The Lady Is Willing*. The persona of a woman star was curbed by age, by changing styles of fashion and glamour, and by limited roles.

Movie stars were movie stars because they connected to individual members of the audience in some specific way. They became figures of identification, rejection, envy, lust, or some response that came from both men and women. In the woman's film, leading women stars might use their persona, or they might play a typical label role, but the most significant thing about the use of an actress in such movies was the purpose she seemingly embodied vis-à-vis the female role in society. It's not just label, which might shift within a film or from film to film, or even just persona, which might never evolve in the star's career or, if it did, might have to change as she aged. The question is, What does the role mean in terms of the woman's place in society? Since the woman's film, more than any other kind of movie, is a covert operation, it's best to step back from labels and even definitions of personae regarding the image of women on film and observe the roles these movie stars played from a slightly different perspective. A pattern of abstraction emerges. The women on film, and the stars who played them, were actually being sorted into three main categories:

1. Unreal women, by which is meant fantasy figures of all types (these stars are dream images, mostly appealing to men)
2. Real women—with the understanding that the term "real" in movies is always subject to discussion, but by which is meant women who are supposed to be like the women in the audience in some way, however tangential (these stars are supposed to appeal to everybody)
3. Exaggerated women, a mixture of the real and unreal, who embody the concept "woman" (these are the true stars of what most people think of as the woman's film; they primarily appeal to women)

I do not mean to suggest that every character ever written for a female on-screen will neatly fit this overview, nor do I suggest that stars only played in one category. I also don't suggest that it is easy to label a role as purely one of the three, without at least a tinge of one or two of the others. Contrary to popular belief, *nothing* about Hollywood is easy to define. We mustn't forget that at the height of the studio system, three to five hundred films per year were made, aimed at all people in the audience. Movies were willing to be all things to all people, to contain comfortable contradictions.

In examining the three categories, a principle emerges. It isn't the role, it's the attitude taken toward it that counts. In the group of unreal women, stars like Greta Garbo and Hedy Lamarr fit. One can also add sex objects like Rita Hayworth and Marilyn Monroe. These are stars whose beauty, elegance, and sexual appeal are somehow beyond the ordinary. They are not really supposed to be role models for anyone, because no one could imagine these women to be duplicated in real life; they are too out of the ordinary, too special. They provide all kinds of escape and yearning for both men and women, but they are the women stars that appeal mostly to men. Granted, it takes a certain kind of intellectual mooncalf to rhapsodize over Garbo today, but these women are not supposed to be the girl next door. Even if they are playing the girl next door, everyone in the audience knows this is crazy. These are the women one puts on a pedestal, the unreal astonishing beauties of the silver screen. Men may lust after them, or dream of them in a noble way, and women can wish they had their beauty, and thus their power. They reduce women to objects of desire.

In the second category, "real women," are the stars who play sweethearts, wives, mothers, or working girls trying to live a good life, whatever that might mean in the context of the film. (It might mean that they temporarily go bad while on this quest.) These women are meant to be seen as ordinary, in that they are supposed to be like something recognized as possible, and thus real. This does not mean that they *are* ordinary and real; what we are talking about is purpose, not execution. These women are role models, and theirs are the films that often tell us the most about what society really thought was appropriate for women. Stars like June Allyson, Ginger Rogers, Myrna Loy, Jeanne Crain, and Jean Arthur play these roles. Rogers, Loy, Allyson, and Arthur represent an American woman who is supposed to be typical or ideal. They are, of course, no more typical than Hedy Lamarr and Greta Garbo, because they are movie stars, but they are the stars who are put forward as typical. Rogers, Loy, Allyson, and Arthur are not exceptionally beautiful, like Monroe and Lamarr. Each has a distinctive voice and the ability to project an instant attitude on-screen. Rogers, Loy, and Arthur are usually wised up, on the ball, feisty. Allyson is also feisty, but she is often presented as sweeter, more innocent than the other three. All but Loy play working girls in the majority of their films. (Rogers, Loy, and Arthur made so many films before becoming stars that there is no way one can simplify the type of roles they played. However, once they reached stardom they usually played a particular type of role, with notable exceptions.) This category has a dual purpose: please the men with attractive women who decide to follow society's main rules at the end of the film, and please the women by presenting nonthreatening, not-too-beautiful, but spunky women facing life with courage, questioning their roles, but at the end of the film finding a life not unlike that of the audience. The purpose is one of reassurance, of reaffirmation of the main goals of society.

The third category, "exaggerated women," is that most often associated with the woman's film when one defines it only as melodrama. These are the ferocious women like Joan Crawford, Bette Davis, Barbara Stanwyck, and Katharine Hepburn, women who throw any film off balance by their frequently neurotic and exaggerated presence. This exaggeration can include excessive nobility, so that Loretta Young and Greer Garson are included.* It's important to remember that a female star cannot begin her

---

* Although Garson personifies the "nobility" of the great women stars, and is perhaps the actress most thoroughly associated with that quality, she is actually only one in a lengthy chain of such types. These women were considered "actresses," not mere movie stars. Garson was preceded by her 1930s counterpart, Norma Shearer, and followed by the 1950s version, Deborah Kerr. And lest anyone think we have left such female characters behind in the liberated 1980s and 1990s, consider Meryl Streep. These women often take a bum rap, but consider how deftly they played these "nobility" roles, and also how capable they

Barbara Stanwyck

career in this group, she has to rise to it. Davis, Crawford, and Stanwyck began by playing real women. Davis was considered too ordinary looking to be a glamour girl, and until Frank Capra got hold of her, no one knew for sure what Stanwyck would turn out to be. Crawford alternated between playing heiresses and girls who worked for a living, with the latter a far more believable niche for her. By the end of the 1930s, Stanwyck had established herself as a capable comedienne . . . Davis as a great actress . . . and Crawford as the ultimate movie star. As the studio system carried them forward into the 1940s and toward middle age, each of them had to deal with the fact that she overwhelmed any story she was in with her powerful presence. Their own accumulated film history of women portrayed began to weigh on their performances. By virtue of their longevity and star power they took on a presence that moved them beyond reality and the

---

were at also playing in an opposite mode. They all did comedies with equal aplomb: Garson in *Julia Misbehaves*, Shearer in *Private Lives*, Kerr in *Dream Wife*, and Streep in *Death Becomes Her*, to name a few such titles.

stance of role model (by which is meant conformity) and into something high-powered, dangerous, exaggerated. And extraordinary.

Here we might pause to consider how a woman who succeeds in a tough business over a long period of time, not dropping out for reasons of love or motherhood or anything else, has to become a grotesque in some way. If a female star endured, she became exaggerated.* Notable. Stars who lived through this process found their personal lives deeply affected. Since movie stars were hardly ever the type of people they played on the screen, their real selves, whatever they might have been, got lost somewhere. Most of them started out as poor girls struggling to be taken seriously. When they finally got to where they could be taken seriously, it was never as themselves but only as the persona they projected. They lost their original personalities and became some kind of confused variation of the other thing. Since they were no longer their original nonfamous self but weren't the other self on the screen either, a strange, hybrid self grew up somewhere in between. This third person, unobserved by the public, limped along through life.

Categories one and three—"unreal women" and "exaggerated women"—are in opposition to each other, with category two the safe territory of social conformity in between. Category two is what audiences are pretending is right, and categories one and three are revealing the truth beneath their surfaces. If exceptionally beautiful and desirable and sexy women are in category one, these women are what men wish them to be. If the women in category two are less intimidating and perhaps not exceptionally beautiful, yet attractive and willing to do what is expected of them, but full of fire and energy, they are who society wishes women were; they are the women with whom we can have it both ways. The women in the third category have moved beyond the term "exceptionally beautiful." They are the women whom the women in the audience *need* to see. They portray characters that the women in the audience wish they were or believe they could be or actually are inside. These are the women no one wants them to be, however.

The heyday of the exaggerated-woman star was the 1940s. At the movies, the woman in the audience learned that she shouldn't ask for the moon—she had the stars. These powerful women acted out the woman's rage and rebellion, got punished for it, and returned to the fold (or not) in time to get the women in the audience home to cook dinner. A group of female stars, formidable in the extreme, emerged as the embodiment of

---

* It is interesting to note that Myrna Loy reversed the process in that she started out playing exotic, Oriental women, fantastical creatures, and ended up playing perfect wives and mothers. Perhaps this is why she was able to keep her career going over nearly six decades.

everything that is both female and intimidating. Each ultimately was taken fairly seriously as an actress, but all played all kinds of roles in all kinds of movies at the start. Each had an identifiable persona on film, and each was a major proponent of the kind of films the general public associates with women. The exaggerations they represented are a natural outgrowth of their long careers. As these great stars aged, they began to portray some exaggerated versions of their younger selves. Once independent of men by choice, Katharine Hepburn began to play a woman who has been left a spinster. Joan Crawford, a powerful, even intimidating presence, began to play women who were either crazy or very, very bad. And Ginger Rogers, who started as the spunky career girl in the real-woman category, began to play an actress or a movie star, to grow exaggerated. These women were being stripped down to the essence of their persona; society's true perceptions of them were being revealed. For instance, Hepburn, never like most women in real society, was shown to be sexless, quirky, weird, and needing a man to thaw her out. Rogers was revealed as a woman who is totally interested only in a career, and Crawford became dangerous: she fought men. Bette Davis, on the other hand, was seen as being bad, but she fought the system for a sense of self, and thus she was fighting in a good way.

Their status as established movie stars combined with their ages, with the need for a great many films about women during the war years (when men were overseas), and with the emergence of a filmmaking approach that would later be called film noir, to bring the public a group of women's pictures that feature powerful women in powerful roles. Today many people think that *only* these movies constitute the woman's film, forgetting the long previous history of the genre and overlooking the fact that certain musicals and comedies are also women's films. Furthermore, not all women's films of the 1940s were shot in the noir cinematic style, which is one of entrapping shadows, claustrophobic compositions, elliptical narratives, and disorienting editing. What is undeniable is that a group of fierce female stars emerged, women who in their offscreen lives had climbed to the top in a difficult profession and who fought to stay there. Fans wanted to see them in stories about women, and most of these women stars were more popular with females than with male moviegoers.

During the 1940s, George Gallup and Associates collected data on the so-called marquee value of specific star names (*Gallup Looks at the Movies: Audience Research Reports, 1940–1950*). These charts were published recently in a book entitled *Women's Film and Female Experience*, by Andrea S. Walsh. The study showed that females in the audience preferred Greer Garson more than men did by the following percentages: 1941–1942, 24 percent to 9 percent; 1944, 58 percent to 37.3 percent; 1946, 56 percent to 38 percent; 1947, 47 percent to 32 percent; and 1949,

40 percent to 26 percent. With Rosalind Russell, a female star whose movies during the period were largely comedies with a wider appeal, the percentages were as follows: 1941, 29 percent to 18 percent; 1944, 34.3 percent to 17.8 percent; 1946, 27 percent to 18 percent; 1947, 33 percent to 21 percent; and 1949, 32 percent to 20 percent. For women stars like Hepburn, Davis, Crawford, Joan Fontaine, and Claudette Colbert, the percentage of appeal increases with the age of the woman viewers, so that women above the age of thirty-one in all cases like these stars more than younger women or men did.*

Joan Crawford and Rosalind Russell, both "exaggerated" and with long careers, make a perfect contrast and an interesting comparison regarding audience perceptions. Crawford, who actually played in many comedies, is mostly remembered as someone in noirish melodramas. Russell, who played in many tragedies and was nominated more than once for an Oscar as Best Actress, is largely remembered as a character who wore pinstriped suits in a series of brittle comedies with feminist implications. Both Crawford and Russell are beautiful women, but their beauty is not soft, or what might be called feminine. They are unconventional looking. Crawford's beauty is all bone structure and suggests nothing pliant. It is rock hard. Russell's beauty is quirky and comes perilously close to caricature. A close observance of these two actresses reveals how much anger is buried in their performances. The exaggeration they embody is linked directly to this anger, which is also the source of their appeal to women viewers and the fuel for the characters they portray. At the beginning of their careers, when they are still young, the anger seems like good old American sass, or personality, but as they age it becomes too powerful a force for such easy labeling, and it has to be channeled somewhere. In Crawford's movies, the anger is turned onto her own characters, and she begins to play suffering, masochistic women. The romantic and stylish comedies she played in early in her career disappear, and melodramas take her over. The opposite happens to Russell. Her anger is increasingly used in comedy as she plays a sarcastic dame with a sharp tongue. Some of her rage is physicalized into knockabout slapstick. Comparing Crawford and Russell illustrates how exaggerated women stars could express anger for women viewers in different but acceptable ways.

Joan Crawford was always "Joan Crawford." She made her way by manipulating her own image with skill and understanding, and managed to update her image whenever the public began to indicate it might be tired of the current one. Her films constituted a minihistory of attitudes toward women, as she marched from flapper to shop girl to sophisticated

* See the Appendix for a list of women stars who were top box-office draws.

lady to comedienne to career woman to older woman victimized by men (who want her money or power) and finally to gargoyle.

Crawford's face has been described as unique, but actually Randolph Scott and Buster Keaton have practically the same face. Crawford's is the female-goddess variation, Scott's the masculine one, and Keaton's the half-female, half-male comic version. As a young woman in her early days at Metro-Goldwyn-Mayer, Crawford was a strikingly beautiful girl, loaded with sex appeal. Pauline Kael once described her as looking in those years as if she were "sexed to the gills." As she aged, Crawford's face became masklike, and a sense of incredible, suppressed rage was conveyed by her presence. As seems to be true for most great movie stars, a self-referential quality entered her work, drawn from two sources: her own life as her public perceived it, and the roles she had played on the screen, which audiences began to believe were who she really was.

Many people think that in the 1930s Crawford played the shop girl who rises to wealth, and that is her image for that decade. Yet in the twenty-six movies starring Joan Crawford released between 1930 and 1940, she played a shop girl exactly twice, in *Our Blushing Brides* and *The Women*. A review of her characters from the decade follows:

Spoiled, willful daughter of a ranching tycoon (*Montana Moon*, 1930)
Shop girl and part-time mannequin (*Our Blushing Brides*, 1930)
Jailbird (actually innocent of charges) who becomes a crime queen
    (*Paid*, 1931)
Cub reporter (*Dance, Fools, Dance*, 1931)
Café entertainer who reforms (*Laughing Sinners*, 1931)
Wealthy socialite (*This Modern Age*, 1931)
Paper-box factory worker who becomes mistress of a powerful man
    (*Possessed*, 1931)
Stenographer in a hotel (*Grand Hotel*, 1932)
Wealthy New York socialite (*Letty Lynton*, 1932)
Prostitute (*Rain*, 1932)
Wealthy British playgirl (*Today We Live*, 1933)
Burlesque dancer who becomes a Broadway star (*Dancing Lady*, 1933)
Housemaid who marries well (*Sadie McKee*, 1934)
Fiancée of a wealthy steamship owner (*Chained*, 1934)
Wealthy girl (*Forsaking All Others*, 1934)
Society girl (*I Live My Life*, 1935)
Historical character Peggy O'Neal (*The Gorgeous Hussy*, 1936)
American heiress (*Love on the Run*, 1936)
Lady Raffles (*The Last of Mrs. Cheyney*, 1937)
Cabaret singer in a dive in Trieste (*The Bride Wore Red*, 1937)

Lower-class button-factory girl who becomes a model (*Mannequin*, 1937)
Nightclub dancer (*The Shining Hour*, 1938)
Aspiring actress who skates (*Ice Follies of 1939*)
Ambitious shop girl (*The Women*, 1939)
Café entertainer (*Strange Cargo*, 1940)

This means that Crawford played an heiress or socialite eight times, or four times as often as she played a shop girl. She was an entertainer of some kind six times, a prostitute once, and a thief twice. She was a working girl three times—once a housemaid, once a reporter, and once a stenographer. Twice she was a factory worker (which is not a shop girl), and in both cases she quickly rose from the factory to become either a successful model or the mistress of a wealthy man. (Once she was an ambiguous character who worked for a steamship line, but who seemed to be independently wealthy.) During the entire decade, Joan Crawford played only one totally unsympathetic role, that of Crystal in *The Women*.

Here is another case of persona misfiring in the audience's memories. Joan Crawford in the 1930s was in movies to provide escape for audiences via stories of wealth that allowed her to wear the fabulous, angular clothes designed for her by the great Adrian. Why does everyone think of her as suffering behind a hosiery counter? In the 1930s, Crawford was young and vibrantly beautiful, and she wore clothes magnificently. But as an heiress or daughter of a wealthy industrialist (as in *Montana Moon*, *I Live My Life*, *Love on the Run*, and *Forsaking All Others*), she was somehow not authentic. The audience sniffed out the common clay in her and recognized her as their surrogate: someone like them who pretends to be an heiress on their behalf. This is the source of Crawford's stardom and popularity. She wasn't going to die for the audience's sins, like Garbo, but she *would* wear ermine and make love to Gable for them. The audience formed an allegiance to Crawford's determined climb, her desperate efforts to shake off the lowdown past she had actually lived. They identified, without realizing it, with her attempt to be something other than what she really was: an ambitious woman, and an angry one.

When she played in screwball comedies during the 1930s, Joan Crawford is like a candelabra on a dinette table: she doesn't look all that bad, but what the hell is she doing there? She is so fierce, so angry. Whatever comedy she is in takes a downward turn, revealing deep questions that lie beneath the surface. In *I Live My Life*, Joan Crawford and Brian Aherne, a movie match ill made, conduct an up-and-down relationship that is supposed to charm but actually appalls. Crawford is an heiress, with all the fashion and glamour that entails, and Aherne is an archaeologist, Hollywood's 1930s idea of a really foolish profession. (Crawford's rich father sees Aherne as a problem spouse because he likes archaeology too much. He ought to like business more.)

In a scene that takes place on the eve of their wedding, Crawford responds to Aherne's concerns about his future with the same kind of cavalier "you'll get over this nonsense" attitude that we are used to seeing men display when dealing with the dreams and aspirations of women in movies. The two stars argue:

AHERNE: I'm not a vice president [referring to the job her father has arranged for him]. I'm an archaeologist.

CRAWFORD: If it's digging you want, we may be able to fix it so you can dig in Central Park. Let's discuss it after the honeymoon. [*She gives him a sexy kiss.*]

AHERNE: [*breaking away*] That won't work anymore!

CRAWFORD: [*focusing in*] Of course, you have a point, and I may be wrong, but I think it's about as selfish a point as I've ever heard. You're saying to me, in effect, give up everything you've ever had, everything you're used to, all your friends, all you've ever wanted, and come with me to a fly-infested village and watch me dig up statues. And then you put on an act about people living your life for you.

AHERNE: But I want to do things *myself!*

CRAWFORD: But what am I supposed to do? Scrape your shovels for you? Or make necklaces out of rocks and sell them to the natives?

AHERNE: It's my life! And I'll live it the way I want! Upside down, catty corner, or sliding down a pole. You're asking me as your husband to give up every interest I have in the world to lead a life that's stupid, dull, and loathsome.

In this exchange, Crawford is much tougher and more passionate than Aherne. She is a woman standing her ground, fighting for her own life, and expressing real anger at the restrictions of the female life. Unfortunately, her "ground" as defined in the movie is the cocktail bar at the Ritz, the fur salon at Bergdorf's, and the massage room at Elizabeth Arden's. Crawford's character's "work" or her "life" is seen as irrelevant because she is idle and foolish, but, more important, because she is female. Her life is not her work, and thus she is in the wrong. The argument becomes a joke, although it does manage to be two-sided. Crawford has all the power in the frame. She is angular, broad shouldered, and smoldering with aggression. Aherne seems willowy, weak, thin, and even quite pretty. Aherne looks "feminine" and Crawford looks "masculine" (using the terms stereotypically), so that the image reverses the male and female roles. This allows an argument in which, while we are clearly supposed to think that Aherne is right and Crawford wrong, Aherne ends up saying what women might be thinking about their roles as wives: "You're asking me . . . to give up every interest I have in the world to lead a life that's stupid, dull, and loathsome." This role reversal is carried forward when Crawford tries to use sex to stop Aherne from disagreeing (her attempt to kiss him). The argument is actually a scene in which both people are saying the same thing, and that thing has to do with one person's having to give up his (or her) life for the other one. Thus, it can be interpreted as either he's right, she's wrong, or she's right, he's wrong. It's either a status quo scene in which women are reminded what their jobs are supposed to be vis-à-vis their husbands, or it's a subversive scene in which women secretly see how they have to sacrifice everything in marriage. The bottom line is that Joan Crawford, the woman, is asking Brian Aherne, the man, to give up meaningful work. He is outraged, and the film tells viewers that for him to give up the work he loves would be crippling and terrible. The fact that this is what women are always asked to do is subversively built into the scene, but only because Crawford's dominant presence, with its authentic anger, validates it.

Crawford's most famous movie role is the one that fused her anger with appropriate woman's film suffering, *Mildred Pierce* (1945). Here she found her true movie niche as a woman who, disappointed and deserted by men, has to battle her own angry way through life. As the waitress-turned-restaurant-tycoon of the title role, Crawford personifies the totally capable but truly furious American woman.

In adapting the James M. Cain novel *Mildred Pierce* to the screen, several key changes were made to the story. These changes are prime indications of what the image of the American woman on-screen was supposed to be. In the book, Mildred is sexual, even incestuous, and nothing ends happily for her. The movie turns the story into one of sacrificial though misguided motherhood, in which a woman tries to do everything for an ungrateful child. To accomplish this, one of Mildred's affairs (with the character of Wally, played in the film by Jack Carson) is eliminated, her long and sexually satisfying adultery with the Zachary Scott character is turned into a one-night stand, and Mildred's younger daughter dies about four frames after their first kiss—apparently a direct causal effect. In addition to being cleaned up sexually, the movie considerably alters Mildred's motherhood. Mildred's older daughter Veda (Ann Blyth) is a more fully developed person in the novel, whereas in the movie she becomes simply a spoiled brat who shoots her mother's second husband. In the book,

Joan Crawford

there is no such murder. On the contrary, it is Mildred, in a hair-raising climax, who tries to kill Veda, attempting to strangle her when she finds her in bed with this same husband. Even more important, Mildred's incestuous feelings for Veda, which are overt in the book, are removed and totally repressed in the movie (although viewers can't help sensing something strange about this obsessive relationship). The movie has also been given an ending that, it is suggested, just might be a happy one, in which Mildred walks out of the police station into the morning sunshine with the man who was her first husband and the father of her children. However, since he was an unreliable breadwinner and she had to go to work baking pies to support the family in the first place, one might wonder just how happy this ending is supposed to seem to married women in the audience. My mother reports to me that when I saw *Mildred Pierce* at the age of eight, I asked why Mildred didn't get a newer, better boyfriend.

The novel has been transformed into a woman's picture, one that can effectively use Joan Crawford's anger to connect to the women in the audience. "I was always in the kitchen," says Crawford's voice on the sound track as she begins to narrate the flashback that will be the story of Mildred's life, "except for the few hours it took to get married. I married Bert when I was seventeen. I never knew any other kind of life, just cooking, washing, and having children." The identification is firmly established with any woman whose experience might have been the same.

Mildred Pierce, as interpreted by Joan Crawford, will reject her life in the kitchen as a female dependent for her living on a male. On behalf of the women in the audience, she channels her anger into a career in which her kitchen skills are put to profitable work. Having intelligence, resourcefulness, and the willingness to work herself to death, Mildred soon owns a chain of restaurants. The film shows women what a woman can do. Then, however, with typical woman's film perversity, it reminds her that she shouldn't do it. While becoming a tycoon, Mildred spoils her only living child, the willful Veda. Mildred's life splits, the mother versus the businesswoman. In one scene, she is begging Veda for love, and in the next she is capably negotiating a loveless marriage for herself with Zachary Scott. Can there be a more chilling moment on-screen than the one in which, having concluded a deal whereby she offers Scott her money in return for his name and social position, she lifts her glass and coldly intones, "Sold"?

Everything Mildred does, she does for Veda. Everything she does for Veda ends up destroying Veda's character, so that the film becomes a tragedy in which Veda commits a murder. Mildred ends up standing out on a pier with a mink and a revolver, wondering if she ought not to kill herself. She survives, however, neither dead nor poor, just relieved of the burden of a serpent's tooth of a child. The film tells us it's Mildred's fault that Veda went wrong, but it shows us that Mildred can take care of herself better than any man she knows can take care of her. Everything about the movie is authenticated by the anger of Joan Crawford, and *Mildred Pierce* connects covertly to viewers by way of this rage.

The career of Rosalind Russell is another example of hidden anger. Like Crawford, Russell is basically a beautiful woman. Seen in repose, seated at a tea table poised to pour, or standing in a draped doorway in one of her voguish outfits, she is stunning, a model of grace and good taste. Once she begins to move, however, something happens. A slightly storkish quality emerges. She's a big, loosey-goosey kind of woman, exaggerated and inherently comic. She squints her eyes, waves her long arms, and lets her long fingers hang down from bent wrists, tosses remarks off as if they were harpoons, or perhaps tiny poison darts, depending on the occasion. She talks out of the side of her mouth, lets out a shriek, or even hauls off and kicks a man's behind, wearing, of course, the highest of heels, the most pointed of toes. She never looks anything but handsome and well dressed, but—something she shares with only Lucille Ball—she can be both elegant *and* ridiculous, holding the two qualities together in a single performance.

Russell found her best film parts in comedy. She was a fine actress, but when she really let herself go in a role what emerged was funny, not tragic, which caused her to be cast in a series of comedies as a nightmare career woman. She herself described these roles:

> I played—I think it was twenty-three career women. I've been every kind of executive and I've owned everything—factories and advertising agencies and pharmaceutical houses. Except for a different leading man and a switch in title and pompadour, they were all stamped out of the same Alice in Careerland. The script always called for a leading lady somewhere in the 30s, tall, brittle, not too sexy. My wardrobe had a set pattern: a tan suit, a gray suit, a beige suit, and then a negligee for the seventh reel, near the end, when I would admit to my best friend on the telephone what I really wanted was to become a dear little housewife.

A look at Russell's career shows what she's talking about. In the decade of the 1940s alone, ten of her nineteen films directly fit this pattern.

His Girl Friday, 1940 (newspaperwoman)
Hired Wife, 1940 (executive secretary)
This Thing Called Love, 1941 (insurance executive)
Design for Scandal, 1941 (divorce court judge)
Take a Letter, Darling, 1942 (coowner of an advertising agency)
What a Woman, 1943 (literary agent)
Flight for Freedom, 1943 (aviatrix)
She Wouldn't Say Yes, 1945 (psychiatrist)
Tell It to the Judge, 1949 (attorney up for federal appointment)
A Woman of Distinction, 1950 (dean of a women's college)

Two of these films illustrate how few differences there are from plot to plot. In *Take a Letter, Darling*, Russell plays the boss and Fred MacMurray her secretary, while in *Hired Wife*, Russell is the secretary and Brian Aherne her boss. In both movies, Russell maneuvers, dominates, insults, deceives, and then captures the love of the man involved. The women Russell plays are exaggerations of working women. They are cartoons. Russell is just as bossy as a secretary as she is as an actual boss, and no matter who says what, she's got a snappy one-liner to throw back. Just to watch her enter the movie in the minor screwball comedy *Four's a*

Crowd (1938) is to see how dominating her comedy performances really are. With great panache and energy, Russell emerges from a taxi and confidently strides into the newspaper office where she works. She slings her purse over her left shoulder, letting it dangle down her back, shoves her stylish hat off her forehead, and sits down at her typewriter. Within minutes, she hears that the paper is folding, and unlike the men around her who are panicky and trying to sell their typewriters, she hurries to confront the paper's owner (Patric Knowles). This scene is another study in male-female contrasts. Knowles is half-dressed and is terrified by her entrance. She barely notices his attire and immediately begins to berate him. "So you're Mr. Buckley. You're the callow, wet-behind-the-ears type." Raising an eyebrow accusingly, snorting in disgust, and planting her hands on her hips, she takes him on. When Knowles's valet enters with the pants to his tuxedo, Russell impatiently snatches them and starts to dress Knowles, bossing him about as he fearfully obeys. "I don't wear the pants," she bellows, "but I'm a newspaperman." The two stand face-to-face, with Russell glaring and Knowles cowering. She is dressed simply, in working clothes, and even though it isn't evening he's attired in top hat and tails. She's dressed like a sensible working woman, and he's more like a silly, fashionable woman getting ready for a long night out. She's the force; he's the weak and confused person being forced. Russell spends the rest of the film two steps ahead of everyone else.

Russell once said, "The frightening thing about those pictures was that the public loved them, and they all made money." What was the appeal? The movies *are* funny. They present the battle of the sexes in a way that both men and women can enjoy. Russell puts men down, her anger serving the needs of comedy yet connecting to something real in viewers, but then she repents. When Crawford repents it's a living hell, but when Russell repents, it's "oh, what the hell." Anger serves the two actresses differently, but well.

The glorious exceptions to the unreal-, real-, and exaggerated-women categories are Marlene Dietrich and Mae West. These two unique creatures inhabit all three categories simultaneously. Their images exist as a kind of questioning of the woman's role or, for that matter, of the man's role. I have often wondered what general audiences actually made of the early Dietrich, putting on her lipstick to face a firing squad at the end of *Dishonored* (1931), or of Mae West, vamping until someone—anyone—was ready. Dietrich was never a top box-office draw, but West was in the top ten in both 1933 and 1934. She is credited with single-handedly saving Paramount Pictures from financial ruin. (Another female, Shirley Temple, was given the same credit at Twentieth Century Fox during the 1930s, as was Deanna Durbin at Universal. It's interesting that such big box-office

Marlene Dietrich

female draws were a child, an adolescent, and a campy joke about women.)*

Dietrich is one of Hollywood's greatest icons. Having had the luck to fall into the hands of Josef von Sternberg, she found herself appearing in films of outstanding quality. Her face was exquisitely photographed by the brilliant Lee Garmes, and her image as an enigmatic, androgynous woman was fully developed by artists. Dietrich stressed that she was only a hausfrau who baked cakes and cleaned apartments for her friends, thus managing to be complex and truly mysterious both on and off the screen. Her persona is a mystifying blend of the male and female, of the real and

* Another interesting star is Marie Dressler, not a glamour figure by anyone's definition. Old, overweight, and mug faced, she became an audience favorite during the early thirties for her portraits of shrewd, tough but tender, and dominant women. Why should Marie Dressler become a star? Was she a favorite with both men and women? Perhaps she was a reassuring mother figure to men and a nonthreatening nonbeauty for women. A similar type to Dressler was the Amazonian Marjorie Main. In the movie *Barnacle Bill* (1941), she hears her lover, Wallace Beery, is two-timing her with a saloon babe. She goes down to the joint, kicks him in the pants, beats up on her rival, busts up the saloon, and even takes off one of her rubber wading boots and beats Beery over the head with it. He takes refuge under one of the tables, begging her to stop. The all-American woman!

unreal. She projects a woman with a sense of humor about the condition of being a woman. When she appears in the frame in a white tuxedo to sing "I couldn't be annoyed," or when she plants a kiss full on the lips of another female while singing "What am I bid for my apples?" she seems to be making it clear to everyone that not only is she a more glamorous woman than anyone else on the horizon but she also is a better man. Who's going to argue? Dietrich seems impervious to the usual female suffering, the usual female choices. Her image suggests that she'll suffer if she feels like it, or choose not to if she feels like it, but that she has some secret inner dimension the rest of us don't have that gives her an insight into life. Sexuality is a matter of costuming. Male or female, take your choice. Pick your own outfit. It's all a joke.

Mae West's image is a similar blurring of sexuality. Her own description of her particular brand of high comedy, which is based on a broad put-down of traditional female roles, was an accurate analysis of the female film image and its duality. "It isn't what I do, but how I do it. It isn't what I say, but how I say it and how I look when I do it and say it."

Mae West built a lifelong career out of making jokes about being a woman, about men chasing women, about sex, and about men and women and their relationships. Her image, highly complex and self-contradictory, was that of a woman freely acting like a man, preying on the opposite sex for physical satisfaction. West openly treated men as if they were sex objects. "Come up and see me . . . anytime," she tells Cary Grant, after appraising his physical assets. West was not a man-eating character, however; she presented herself as a sensual, desirable woman. She combined the idea of woman as submissive sex partner with the idea of woman playing male aggressor. By masking the ambivalence with humor, she got away with it. As many have observed, Mae West may have been the first and best of the female impersonators on film. Her jokes were smutty enough, in a nice way, to appeal to men, and her clothes were glamorous enough, in a weird way, to appeal to women. What she said on-screen and offscreen—and she wrote most of her own material—is really astonishing. "Marriage is nothing more than contracted prostitution. I believe in the single standard for men and women" . . . "Some men are all right in their place—if they only knew the right places" . . . "Men are my hobby. If I ever got married, I'd have to give it up" . . . "I'd like to see a woman elected President. Women have been running men for centuries. It would be easy for them to run a country" . . . "Women want certain things in marriage—the right to a title and a front seat in the lap of luxury."

West is a minimalist. Her action is reduced to two things. Either she humps along with her unusual walk, a kind of female swagger, or she sits on a couch, shifting her eyes back and forth in her head while she utters a suggestive "Ummmmmmmm." She manages to make both these things, the walk and the eye movement, suggest the rhythm of sex. And that, along with some double-entendre dialogue, is about as much actual sex as viewers ever get from Mae West. Although she does indulge in an occasional chaste kiss with a leading man, mostly she's all conversation, innuendo, and minimalist action.

A typical Mae West role is that of Tira the Incomparable, a female lion tamer in *I'm No Angel* (1933, "story, screenplay and all dialogue by Mae West"). Tira's philosophy is simple and functional: "Take all you can get and give as little as possible. Find 'em, fool 'em, and forget 'em." Sashaying out into the lion's den with a pistol and a whip, attired in stark white trimmed in sparkles, Mae barks at her lions as if she were an irate kindergarten teacher with a bunch of naughty kids. "Get up there!" she yells at one of the lions, forcing him onto his stand. "You're holdin' up the whole show." Swaying out of her bedroom in a particularly grand new gown, she asks her black maid, "Is it a flash or is it a flash?" When her maid replies that it's beautiful, Mae says, "I know it's beautiful, but is it a flash?" Flash is everything in Mae's world, because she sells style and not substance. She's a professional tease who picks the pockets of any man she meets. She delivers only if she wants to, never if she has to. After tossing a rival out into the hall, Mae delivers the best line of her career: "Beulah. Peel me a grape."

Mae West and Marlene Dietrich are the two women who never suffer. Dietrich may be distressed or derailed, but her retaliation is always a power move. West makes others suffer, especially men. If anyone messes with her, she takes 'em to court, tries her own case, and wins, as she does in *I'm No Angel*. "Do you feel you did the right thing?" the judge asks her. "Show me a woman who could do any better" is her sage reply, just before she embraces Cary Grant in the final frame, while singing, "I can make it happen when the shades are drawn . . . I'm no angel." Not only can Mae West defeat the double standard, she can kick it around.

Both Dietrich and West took a humorous attitude toward the traditional male and female roles. Dietrich's humor was covert, hidden frequently in sentimental stories about love and motherhood, whereas West's was linked so openly and freely to sex that no one identified it as exactly what it was. Yet both these women sent up the very idea of being a woman as depicted in most other movies. They maintained the glamour and charm of the movie star, but they overturned traditional ideas with their androgynous and amazing personae.

• • •

ALTHOUGH DIETRICH and West sent hidden messages to females in the audience, their overt sexual independence seemed to make them less popular with women. Perhaps their messages were *too* covert, or perhaps their suggestion that women should claim sexual freedom was too frightening. Crawford and Russell, with their righteous anger, had a much greater appeal to women moviegoers.

What *did* make actresses appeal to the female audience? Did women who watched glamorous movie stars want to become them, or want to be the role they played, or want to identify with a story about their own lives as women? All of the above, no doubt, but to be an actress on-screen whom women moviegoers liked required strength, originality in looks and persona, and at least some point of identification. One can speculate that it is a combination of roles, looks, fashion, personal taste, and the times, but beyond that, there will always be some unanswered questions (again one can ask, Why would Marie Dressler become a star?) and some obvious answers to the questions (Claudette Colbert is always on top of things).

Comparing Claudette Colbert and Carole Lombard, two stars who often played elegant women in romantic comedies, shows how subtle variations emerge that draw on possible audience differences. No matter what happened to Colbert, she maintained her cool charm, her throaty chuckle, and her ability to emerge a winner. Even when she was playing a bedraggled poetess on the lam in *It's a Wonderful World* (1939) or was stepping out into a torrential downpour with nothing but a newspaper to shield her gold lamé (*Midnight*, 1939), she looked perfectly turned out, neat, trim, and competent. Whatever it was, Colbert never stepped in it over her shoe tops. No doubt women yearned for that level of subtle mastery and enjoyed Colbert's triumphs.* Lombard, on the other hand, didn't keep herself above it. She fell into it, taking the pratfall, but remaining a good sport. She might shriek and kick at a man (as she did to John Barrymore in *Twentieth Century*, 1934) and she might be socked on the jaw (as she was by Fredric March in *Nothing Sacred*, 1937), but somehow she managed to make it look desirable, appropriate, and not demeaning. Although both Lombard and Colbert played in dramas and were considered serious actresses, they were more appreciated for their roles in these sophisticated comedies about

* Colbert has perhaps the lightest touch of any actress associated with women's films. Even in dramatic roles, such as in *Three Came Home* or *Torch Singer*, she lacks the physical solidity that the great female stars have. She is all charm, delicacy, and finesse. No matter how weighty the issues of her film might be, she never seems to be taking it *too* seriously, yet she has real performance credibility. For this reason, she's often at her best when she has a strong male star opposite her, as in *It Happened One Night* with Clark Gable, or in her films with Fred MacMurray.

women. (Someone might like to do an in-depth analysis of the fact that Colbert, who always triumphed over physical woes, was the more popular star with women. Men preferred Lombard, the woman who took the sock on the jaw.)

Another interesting pair to compare is Katharine Hepburn and Ginger Rogers, the upper- and lower-class versions of the feisty American woman. Hepburn appeals to many modern women, who perceive her to be a strong person who refused to let Hollywood dominate her. These people may not realize that Hepburn could afford her strength. She was rich. She had a family to back her up. Women like Crawford, Davis, Stanwyck, and others had no one to rely on but themselves. Rogers, even though she had her formidable mother, the infamous Lela Rogers, also had to stand on her own two feet. Both Hepburn and Rogers came to Hollywood from Broadway, and although Hepburn appeals to people who see her as an actress who merely dropped in on films when she wasn't busy being aristocratic at home or playing Shakespeare on the boards, Rogers had a much bigger Broadway success in the musical comedy *Girl Crazy* (which opened in October of 1932 and ran for 272 performances). When the two actresses appear in the same film, *Stage Door* (1937), they enact the public's general opinion of who they are. Hepburn is wealthy, elegant, supercool, intelligent, well educated. She speaks in graceful and literate sentences. Rogers is street smart, poor, hard as nails, sassy, tough talking.

What appealed to moviegoers about these two actresses is in some way the same thing. They represent courage and independence; they represent women who wanted to do it their own way. Hepburn became associated with the modern attitudes of feminism, and Rogers with the ordinary woman who fights to work for a living, but both could take care of themselves on and off the screen. On-screen, Hepburn and Rogers, like everyone in Hollywood, played many roles that contradict the remembered personae. Hepburn was a mountain girl in the Ozarks in *Spitfire* (1934), and Rogers played a president's wife in *Magnificent Doll* (1946). Rogers also had a complete minicareer as partner to Fred Astaire. However, both women succeeded in comedies and dramas, and both were Oscar winners. (Both even dated Howard Hughes.) Consider the traits they share in movies. First of all, they wreck men's plans with a willful comic vengeance, as when Hepburn destroys Cary Grant's dinosaur, his engagement, and almost his entire career in *Bringing Up Baby* (1938), and Rogers makes a fool out of Ray Milland in *The Major and the Minor* (1942) by getting him to believe she's an adolescent who needs his help. Hepburn is a protofeminist in *A Woman Rebels* (1936), and Rogers is one in *The First Traveling Saleslady* (1956). They go historical with Hepburn as Queen Mary in *Mary of Scotland*, (1936), and Rogers as Dolley Madison in the aforementioned *Magnificent*

Doll. They are thieves (respectively in *Sylvia Scarlett*, 1935, and *Heartbeat*, 1946), actresses (*Morning Glory*, 1933, and *Forever Female*, 1953), heroines from best-sellers (*Alice Adams*, 1935, and *Kitty Foyle*, 1940), women who marry evil men by mistake (*Undercurrent*, 1946, and *Once Upon a Honeymoon*, 1942), and individuals who fight social problems (*A Bill of Divorcement*, 1932, and *Storm Warning*, 1951). There are "two of them" when Hepburn pretends to be her own nonexistent niece in *Quality Street* (1937) and Rogers subdivides in dreams in *Lady in the Dark* (1944). They try to disguise themselves as boys (*Sylvia Scarlet* and *The Primrose Path*, 1940), enact sympathetic mothers (*Guess Who's Coming to Dinner*, 1967, and *Teen-age Rebel*, 1956), and have problems getting married (*The Rainmaker*, 1956, and *It Had To Be You*, 1947). Where they diverge is in a category that can only be defined as "class." Hepburn seems above it all, keeping herself separate from the ordinary, while Rogers proudly defines herself as one of the crowd, typical. Hepburn's roles often identify her as specifically feminist in her approach (*Christopher Strong*, 1933; *A Woman Rebels; Adam's Rib*, 1949; and so on), whereas Rogers, always tough, always streetwise, suggests that no one can survive who hasn't figured out by the time she is fifteen that she has to stand up for herself. As they age, Hepburn plays more and more spinsters, and Rogers plays more and more famous actresses or movie stars. Their independence finally separates both of them from the pack, so that as older women they are defined as someone different, someone who didn't do it the regular way, by marriage. Offscreen, these women took charge of their own careers, lasting longer than most, and becoming increasingly outspoken as they aged. To women in the audience, they sent signals of freedom and feisty determination, and thus they shared in audience appeal.

Offscreen the great, famous stars of women's pictures were not unlike the suffering women they played on the screen. They were not today's college-educated, more privileged young actresses. The majority of them —with exceptions like the relatively wealthy Katharine Hepburn and professional-class Rosalind Russell and Myrna Loy—came from poor, even sordid, backgrounds. Most of them were without benefit of education or family connections, and many of them had literally no one to teach them about life in any way. In order to become successful, they had to do whatever it was they had to do, and rumors abounded. The truth is that becoming a movie star was not easy, and remaining a star was even harder. Most of them submitted to whatever was necessary, which included everything from capping their teeth to marrying their cameramen.

Part of what was expected from stars in the golden years of the studio system was cooperation with still photographers and fan magazines. Stars posed for endless pictures wearing all sorts of costumes, and the fan magazines aided in the manufacturing of the star image and keeping the image and the name of the woman in front of the public.

The fan magazines of the thirties are particularly interesting, in that they reveal the same duality that the films contain, setting up a second universe of escapism for women readers. Anyone looking into a *Photoplay* or *Modern Screen* of the 1930s is readily reminded that the leading female stars of the decade were *not* wives and mothers for the most part, and if they were, they weren't wives and mothers in the traditional sense. While they were suffering on-screen and acting in stories that suggested love was everything, they were making huge salaries and divorcing a series of husbands. In order to get their faces on the pages of the fan magazines and on the screens of every small town in America, most of them had to put aside home and hearth. There they were in the photos they were forced to pose for, slim, beautiful, well dressed, standing beside their swimming pools and looking radiantly happy. Although the magazines would carry articles from time to time about their foundering marriages ("those two swell kids just can't seem to make a go of it, although they've had six sweet months of happiness and we wish them the best") and their desires to have a family (later), who really thought they were hurting? An astute reader of a typical 1930s fan magazine can see that most of the successful stars either did not have children at all, had them late in life in small numbers, or had plenty of help to raise them. (The male stars, on the other hand, were sometimes fathers of large broods.) Since women who went to the movies and read the magazines often dreamed of becoming these stars, the desire for freedom was an obvious lure of the female movie queen. When a reader learned that Joan Crawford's marriage to Douglas Fairbanks, Jr., had become a tragedy, but she was considering marrying Clark Gable, the woman could keep her own counsel. How many marriages *aren't* tragedies, and how bad can it be if your next husband is going to be Gable?

Articles in these magazines sometimes cater to romantic dreams, as in "Four Rules of Married Love." Other times, they offered explanations, as in "Career Comes First with Loretta," or faced facts with "Why Garbo Has Never Married." They also stimulated escapist dreams of the good life, with "How the Stars Spend Their Fortunes," "Figuring the Stars' Salaries," and "So You'd Like to Be a Star."

Consider the between-the-lines messages the average woman could receive from these interviews in issues of *Photoplay* in the 1930s:

- *"Motherhood—What It Means to Helen Twelvetrees"*: "Today, motherhood is not enough." Twelvetrees sees motherhood as an opportunity to use her substantial movie salary to set up a really good trust fund for her unborn child. If the child is a girl, she wants her to be "young, unspoiled, no matter what her career may be." The interview concludes with Twelvetrees confidently reassuring the reporter that having one child or many will never take her away from the screen.

- *"Joan Blondell: I Want to Talk about My Baby":* This interview takes place on the set of Blondell's latest movie, with the child nowhere in sight. Blondell talks enthusiastically about all the things she has provided back there at home for her newborn son. She also shows off two beautiful bracelets that her current husband (cameraman George Barnes) has just given her as a gift. A reward for her new motherhood? "No," says George, "because she let me photograph her new picture."

- In a detailed interview, Ginger Rogers laments, "I never have time to count my linens, or arrange flowers, to fuss over things. When the maid tells me we need three new tablecloths, I have to phone a shop and tell them to send me three new tablecloths and then I never see them till they are on the table. . . . I'd love to have a baby. Of course I would. Naturally. I shall adopt one. I read in a recent article that a certain star's last baby cost her exactly $150,000 because of her having to be out of production for so long. Time is very valuable to a movie star." Rogers, although married five times, never did get around to affording that adoption.

These articles follow the same format as the films for and about women. They provide details of a rich and wealthy life without husbands or children, but they lament the unhappiness that fame and wealth are supposed to bring. They provide readers with a glimpse of heaven, an escape into wealth and power, and then remind them that this kind of life doesn't hold a candle to their own little lives and families.

These movie stars, particularly the ones who survived to become the screen's exaggerated women, were the nation's first army of prominent career women. They embodied the American woman on-screen, fueling dreams of different kinds of lives, and they also became role models off-screen. Much has been written about how Hollywood exploited women, but most of these women would have had miserable lives without their stardom. They had been exploited long before Hollywood came along, by their fathers, mothers, and other users along the way. In Hollywood, they had their own money and their own clout, and not all of them went down the drain. Some are still wealthy and secure today, and what's even more significant, some found it possible to have it both ways. The stars who play the American woman made her strong and capable both on and off the screen. There's no denying that in both instances mixed messages were being sent, but offscreen, no matter how much the fan mags tried to hide it, movie stars were career women—women who had defiantly and successfully chosen the Other.

WAYS OF SEEING HER

To UNDERSTAND THE American movie, one has to accept its glorious incoherence. Every Hollywood film is a little universe of insanity. Movies are a world of weird juxtapositions, with shocking jumps across narrative time and space that require viewers to assimilate meanings, arcane transitions, and situations that are never explained in dialogue. What is remarkable is how easily an ordinary audience accepts this, gladly taking craziness and contradiction as a model for its own life.

Try these four scenes from typical Hollywood movies for logic:

- An American show girl dressed in a harem costume sings "Boola Boola" in a North African village to a sheik's son while a monkey does a high-wire act over her head and two Nazis watch her.
- A cowboy riding a horse stops under an elm tree just as a Jewish traveling salesman drives up in an open convertible. The cowboy calls out, "Hey, boy, you got any aspirin tablets?" The salesman replies, "Vat's duh matter, your horse got a headache?"
- A headless body walks out of the fog past a peddler with horse and cart, who in turn meets a cheerful man out for an evening stroll and picks him up to deposit him at a tavern door, which is opened by a man in an executioner's mask, while behind him customers discuss World War II, which is raging in Europe.
- A woman wearing high heels, a sparkling headdress, and a long, slinky gown with a train that has twelve inches of fur bordering it is out in the snow on a moonlit night with a Russian cossack in full-dress uniform. They are riding a seesaw, exchanging meaningful lines like "Love is a wave. It comes sweeping over you."

These scenes all exist, in *Tarzan's Desert Mystery* (1943), *Montana Moon* (1930), *The Mysterious Doctor* (1943), and *The Virtuous Sin* (1930), respectively. Each actually does have an explanation for what is happening on the screen, but it is an explanation that is never verbalized. It comes from the accumulation of the situations the audience has been watching. *Of course* there's a Jewish comedian driving through Montana, and *of course* the harem girl sings "Boola Boola." You just had to be there at the beginning. Anyone who ever walked into a cinema in the middle of a movie or turned on the television just as Clarence rescues George Bailey understands this. Things seem a bit strange at first—an angel has apparently come to earth and jumped in the river—but soon enough, seasoned viewers know, it will all make some kind of sense. And, of course, it does. Who has ever started halfway into a movie and had to go all the way to the end without getting it? As a child, I almost always walked in during the middle, and soon enough found out where to look for my explanations—in what was being pictured up there. The bad woman might be *saying* the nicest things to the hero, and she might be *wearing* the very sweetest dress, and she might be *handing* him a cookie, but oh, boy, I could see how bad she really was. The secret of moviegoing is that movie sense is not the same as literary sense. Movie explanations are not the same as book explanations. You have to keep alert. It is a world in which literally anything can happen ("Boola Boola"), but if you keep your eyes peeled, an explanation will appear somewhere.

Nowhere is this more true than in the woman's film, the world of the hidden agenda, the universe of the dual purpose. When the drunken Marlene Dietrich cries out in a woman's flophouse in New Orleans, "Do you think I couldn't get a better bed?" and the film dissolves forward across an ocean to the sight of her as a famous Parisian cabaret singer in white top hat and tails, preening confidently in front of an adoring audience of men, who needs to see how she did it? We know. There is a world of degradation and manipulation implied between her gutter and her triumph, but what is not shown on-screen is as important—and as specific—as what *is* shown. Film is the art of omission, and what is never depicted in the woman's life is as significant as what is. Actually, this is true of all Hollywood movies, but it's particularly useful in a genre that wants to reach its audience's deepest angers at the same time that it seeks to allay them.

Often this anger is transformed into comedy with a subtle, double-layered cinematic alchemy. A typical example is *Standing Room Only* (1944), in which Paulette Goddard, who is bright, energetic, entrepreneurial, and totally impossible, wrecks the life of Fred MacMurray, who is

confused, lost, outmaneuvered, and, finally, hopelessly enamoured. (Over
and over again in popular culture women make fools out of men, which
surely represents women's unwillingness to accept the position in which
society has placed them.) Goddard wants to move up from her factory job
of placing ears on toy donkeys. She spends so much time thinking about
moving up that she messes up and puts the ears on backward. On her way
upstairs to be fired, she overhears that Fred MacMurray is expecting a new
girl to replace his secretary. Goddard can't take shorthand, but she races
into his office, pretending to be the replacement. She's smart enough to
be able to memorize the letters he is dictating to her, "reading" them back
by reciting what she heard. The story then moves forward in a series of
contradictory events:

- *Paulette Goddard destroys MacMurray's life:* she loses his briefcase
  . . . cancels his hotel room in crowded wartime Washington . . .
  causes him to have to sleep all night under a statue in a park . . .
  hires him out as a butler without his permission.
- *Paulette Goddard saves MacMurray's life:* she gets him inside the house
  of the VIP he's trying to see . . . she's a great cook . . . she never
  gives up trying to make things work for him . . . she falls in love with
  him . . . she believes in him . . . and she ends up making it possible
  for him to succeed and become the hero of his company.

Everyone can watch this movie happily. Goddard is sexy and beautiful, and MacMurray is tall and handsome. (No contradiction in appearance!) Goddard is an idiot, and MacMurray is a genius, but MacMurray is
also an idiot, and Goddard is also a genius. Goddard represents how women
are made to look foolish and silly, and MacMurray represents how men are
made to look foolish and silly. He fails; she succeeds. She fails; he
succeeds—and so forth. Film scholarship has too often tried to prove only
one of the two sides available to any interpretation of the ambivalent, sly,
and double-layered Hollywood film that attempted to be all things to all
people.

What has to be considered, then, is the subtle way in which movies
show women doing things they aren't supposed to do and the very specific
ways in which women are photographed, framed, and lit in movies.

How is any one movie asking an audience to see a woman? In addition
to the physical characteristics of the actress who portrays her, there are
other things, such as costuming, the action she's involved in, the camera
angle she's seen with, and the way her character is shaded morally. Is she
Gilda or is she Madame Curie? Is she being carried off and made captive
by the Indians or is she herself driving Indians off as she and a hardy band

of other women defend a wagon train? Is she running a sewing machine or flying a bomber? Is she wearing an apron or an army helmet? Are we looking at her from the ankles up, under a gigantic precipice of bosom, or is she on her knees praying, surrounded by a halo of light? Is there a boa constrictor around her neck or a baby in her arms? Is she running forward to kick and fight an assailant or cowering in terror? No account of content, story pattern, or attitude is to the point unless we also think carefully about how we are being asked to view the woman in the woman's film. The hidden agenda, or the rampant ambivalence, is often contained in ways of seeing her. When Gail Russell thunders up, driving a wagon with a team of horses, in *Angel and the Badman* (1947), she arrives in a whirl of dust and activity. As she pulls back to stop her horses, she is strong and confident. She is standing up in her wagon, a woman of great beauty, and she looks down on the hero. A viewer is asked to see her as the hero, John Wayne, sees her. From his point of view, below her and looking up, an audience sees a woman who is not only beautiful but who can take care of herself, a figure of awe. This character, in fact, will completely change John Wayne's life, remaking him the way she wants him to be, transforming him from outlaw to Quaker, from user of women to respecter of her integrity. Presenting a woman this way has to count for something, no matter how many pies she bakes in the movie or how much of a love story she lives through.

How the viewer is asked to see the woman is defined by the techniques of filmmaking. Images of women are used for many purposes. How women are turned into sex objects or fodder for violence has been written about elsewhere.* What is written about less often is how cultural attitudes about women are used to develop actual narrative events. For instance, in the movie *Unconquered* (1947), Gary Cooper, the hero, and Paulette Goddard, the heroine, are trekking through dangerous Indian country in prerevolutionary America. As they approach a cabin where pioneers have settled, Cooper goes on ahead to scout the situation. What he will find is that the rampaging Indians have brutally massacred the family. The situation is visualized through a clear usage of cultural biases and attitudes toward male and female roles. Cooper goes ahead because he is the man; his job is to face violence and deal with it bravely, calmly. Goddard is left behind because she is the woman, who must be protected from such things. If the scene did nothing else but have Cooper go forward and Goddard hang back it would make the point of cultural attitudes, but it goes further. When Goddard later goes to where Cooper is burying the dead bodies, he solemnly

* See Bibliography for, among others, *Girls on Film*, by Julie Burchill, Carlos Clarens's *An Illustrated History of the Horror Film*, and "An Annotated Working Bibliography," by G. Marchetti.

tells her, "Don't look, Abby. Don't look." By twice repeating these words, "Don't look," he reminds an audience of its cultural conditioning. This massacre is a situation that is too horrible for a woman to deal with. Violence is a man's job. Next, the film goes even further and uses a second cultural attitude, the prejudice that says, "Yeah, but women are nosy gossips . . . they don't obey . . . she's gonna look, she's gonna look." An audience will confidently expect Goddard to come forward and look, and it awaits and anticipates the moment in which she will experience the horror. This enables *Unconquered* to deliver the viewer a slyly uncensored experience. Since American censorship at that time prevented movies from showing mutilated bodies, *Unconquered* allows an audience the vicarious experience of watching Paulette Goddard, representing sensitive feminine values, look on its behalf. Goddard acts out the response appropriate for a civilized society. She reacts in fear and loathing, letting a little scream escape her lips.

Viewers of this scene in *Unconquered* understand several things. First, Goddard is a woman, so civilized behavior becomes a feminine concept. Second, the experience of viewing a woman in distress, frightened and horrified, is made acceptable, even important to the narrative. Third, a woman is a vessel of response or passivity, rather than activity. Fourth, the man is separate from this, because viewing violence does not cause him to react this way. Fifth, the narrative is moved forward, as the audience now understands the event itself—how Cooper saw it and how Goddard saw it—as a unified event. An audience finds out what has happened by watching a woman's reaction to it.

Less complex but even more powerful are the strange images of women that appear suddenly in women's pictures that speak directly to women in the audience about disappointment, anger, and fear. Barbara Stanwyck's inability to pour herself a cup of coffee in *Clash by Night* (1952) makes one of the most powerful images I know of the desperation of women. In the movie, Stanwyck, a tough broad who has led a bad life, has finally settled down with a good husband (Paul Douglas). She has a child of her own and a home of her own. She wants to be respectable. In other words, she wants to lead the life that society tells her is right for a woman. Into her situation, however, intrudes Robert Ryan, a male force that understands all too well the life she used to lead and the appetites it has created in her. As Stanwyck struggles between her passion for Ryan and her desire to be a "proper woman," she tries to do what soap-opera women and real-life women do several times a day every day of their lives: She tries to pour a cup of coffee. What better act to represent the woman's life? As Stanwyck starts to shake and the cup starts to rattle, the scene slowly plays itself out. For what seems like an eternity, Barbara Stanwyck, an icon of the

woman's film, tries to get the coffee into her cup. Finally she sits down in
defeat. It's a superb metaphor of the woman's life. Conformity (pour the
coffee) is expected, but the woman's soul fights the coffee, the coffeepot,
and the whole damned kitchen. Stanwyck's moment says a great deal about
the pressure on women to be "good."

In *This Woman Is Dangerous* (1952), Joan Crawford (who once told
me that the character "wasn't really dangerous, just boring") plays a fake
society woman who is secretly involved in crime. She has undergone an
eye operation to restore her sight, only to fall in love with her doctor (Dennis
Morgan). After her successful surgery, she accompanies the doctor when
he is called to the infirmary of the state women's prison. Crawford once
did time for embezzlement, and she is clearly upset as they drive inside
the walls. She opts to wait in the car, watching a load of women prisoners
returning from an outing. Wearing their uniforms, they are riding stone-
faced and hard, standing up in the back of a truck. Crawford sits inside
the doctor's expensive car, herself dressed in jewels and fur, smoking and
watching. She notices that one of the women is also smoking, hiding the
forbidden cigarette from the guards. The woman surreptitiously pinches
out her smoke by extinguishing it with her bare hands in order to stash it
inside her belt for later use. As Crawford sees this, she unconsciously
pinches out her own cigarette in the same way, burning her fingers. Even
though she's outside now, seemingly protected by wealth and position, her
sense of herself as a woman threatened by the rules has never left her.
Her action speaks directly to women viewers of the restrictions and pressures that all women feel, no matter what their economic circumstances
might be.

How leading ladies are shown to a viewer shapes reaction and thus
determines story. *Double Indemnity* (1944) and *The Lady from Shanghai*
(1948) essentially tell the same basic story. A treacherous, beautiful, blond,
deadly woman of experience lures a willing man into sex and murder. The
men end up ruined (one of them dead, the other one's life forever tainted).
Both stories are narrated by the man, from his own view of the events and
his own memories, and in both cases the film begins after the events have
already taken place. Yet these two films are not at all alike, and people
often express surprise if told they are the same story.

That is because watching them is a totally different kind of visual
experience. Although they are both made in the film-noir tradition, and
both are written and directed by people of exceptional talents (Billy Wilder
and Orson Welles), the two films are different because of ways of seeing.
Double Indemnity is a coherent movie story, constructing a clear meaning
and narrative structure. *The Lady from Shanghai* is an incoherent movie
story, suggesting an almost postmodernist attitude by which one is asked

to grasp a sophisticated level of self-mockery toward the events. *Double Indemnity* is stylish, well shot, and moody, but *Lady from Shanghai* is a masterpiece of bizarre compositions, unexpected sound transitions, and general cinematic experimentation. Looking at the two leading ladies and the way they are presented provides further explanation. Barbara Stanwyck in *Double Indemnity* is the enigma understood. She is mysterious, alluring, possibly evil, but in a way that the audience knows about. She is placed in the frame as all femmes fatales are put there, photographed as a sexually exciting woman with an ankle bracelet, winking at her hapless victim, Fred MacMurray, while he tries to sell her insurance. Everyone knows she's bad from the first moment she slinks downstairs. Rita Hayworth, on the other hand, is presented truly mysteriously in *Lady from Shanghai*. Is she good or is she bad? Is she a joke or is she a leading lady? Is she supposed to be a character in the movie or is she supposed to be Rita Hayworth? Until the end, when multiple images of her in a fun-house mirror make this issue concrete, you can never be sure if the Shanghai lady is friend or foe, good or evil, a real woman or an image representing the concept of advertised movie star.

The double-edged presentation that is common to the woman's film is partly a way of allowing an audience, men and women, to see both what they know to be the truth about things and its romantic counterpart as a simultaneous visual presentation. (This format is, in fact, as stated earlier, the very foundation of Hollywood filmmaking.) For instance, *Tender Comrade* (1943) is a sentimental, overwritten tribute to the American woman and marriage that was released during the depths of World War II. It presents two time frames, the first the now of the film, in which Ginger Rogers and a band of stalwart women work in a defense plant and await the return of their men from war, and the second the past seen in flashbacks that present Rogers's memories of her happy marriage to Robert Ryan. These flashbacks are masterpieces of deception, skillfully and dishonestly written to display the horrors of marriage and then eradicate them in a wash of tears and kisses.

Tender Comrade begins with Rogers spending a loving night with Ryan before he ships out for combat. As she stands looking at him while he sleeps, she says, "Of all the guys I could have married, how come I had to pick out the homeliest one?" Of course, the man she is looking at is the tall, dark, and handsome young Ryan. This establishes the mode of presentation that will dominate the film: let characters say one thing and mean another. As Rogers and Ryan say good-bye at the train station, they mouth a lengthy list of clichés about the postwar American life that they will share: a little house on the edge of town, sleeping late on Sunday, a barbecue in a big backyard that has a vegetable patch, a place for their

kid to play, and her herb garden "with parsley and mint and chives."
Everything about the movie is propaganda, both for the wartime years
themselves and for the promises of what is to come afterward to make it
all worthwhile.

Two of the flashbacks about Rogers's marriage to Ryan show female
unhappiness. The first is the scene in which Ryan proposes to Rogers and
the second is a depressing portrait of their marital discord. Of course, in
both cases, after depicting stress, a false portrait of happiness is reaffirmed.
These ways of allowing the audience to see bad things it knows to be true
about male-female relationships, and then to hear a verbal denial of that
truth, is one of the formats the woman's film uses to connect to its audience
on an honest level and then release it from that honesty.

As each flashback fades to the past, an image appears showing a
gigantic sky full of fluffy white clouds. A chorus of angelic singing voices
goes "ooooh, ooooooh, oooooooh" and down in the lower right-hand viewing
corner tiny figures representing Rogers and Ryan appear. They are shown
in various stages of courtship, embrace, and unity as the story progresses.

The first flashback is triggered by the device of Ginger Rogers talking
to Robert Ryan's photograph. "Hello, you sweet guy," she says. "Remember
me? I'm the girl who almost didn't marry you." (The screenplay is by Dalton
Trumbo.) As the clouds and the chorus appear and then disappear, an
audience sees Ginger Rogers sitting in the backyard of a typical small
house, drying her hair in the sunshine and singing "You Made Me Love
You." Robert Ryan arrives and proposes to her. Rogers becomes furious
at this. "You spend all your time dancing and flirting with other girls and
then when you feel your years creeping up on you, you come back to good
old Jo. You're a wolf!" "Will you stop picking on me?" he yells back.
"You darn fool," she says. After they yell back and forth for a while, Rogers
explains why this proposal, which she considers terribly unromantic because it was straightforward, is unacceptable to her. "A girl likes to plan
on things. If a girl's gonna be in love, she wants to be 100% in love. With
a tightmouth clam like you, she's never safe. She can't act like she's in
love cause she never knows how the guy really feels about it. She can't
come right out with it and she can't even get a kick out of it because the
darn fool may not be in love with her, and she'd just be making an idiot
of herself in front of everybody." Rogers articulates the female reasons for
deception. She expresses the pressures she feels as a woman from society's
view of her. A woman cannot show how she really feels because it isn't
right, and because it isn't right, she might "make an idiot of herself." Her
position is a passive one. She must wait for the man to make the first move
or to express himself, because the prerogative belongs to him. Ryan's
response to Rogers's explanation is simple. "Shut up! I'm sick of hearing

you. Judas Priest, what a crab you're going to be in five years." When Rogers starts to make a feeble protest, he yells again, "I said shut up!"

Naturally, Rogers agrees to marry him. Their conversation is supposed to be terribly honest and cute, and, of course, self-deluding. A viewer is asked to accept that these two swell kids love each other madly, which is why they are yelling this way and why they are so angry with each other.

The second flashback is even more revealing. It opens up after Rogers and Ryan are married and living in a cozy little overdecorated cottage. They are in the kitchen, drying the dishes and putting things away after dinner. When Rogers asks Ryan what he is going to do next, he says he will go sit down and read. As he leaves the kitchen, Rogers frowns deeply and mutters, "Read, read, read." She follows him into the living room, where he sits comfortably engrossed in his magazine. She is bored, restless, and unhappy, although, naturally, dressed in a perfectly sweet little ruffled dress. Rogers tries everything to get Ryan's attention. She turns the radio on. She flops on the chintz couch in a sexy pose. She climbs into his lap while he reads. She tries to remove a splinter from his hand with a needle. Because she won't leave him alone, he finally says that if she has so much time, he wishes she'd spend more of it sewing buttons on his shirts. This precipitates a full-scale quarrel in which the woman's feelings about a dull marriage and her role in it are clearly articulated:

ROGERS: You don't have to carry on so about it. All I did yesterday was just to scrub the back porch *and* clean the basement, take those slips over to Mother's house *and* get you your breakfast *and* get you your lunch and get you . . .

RYAN: [*angry, interrupting*] Will you lay off? You sound like I was making a galley slave out of you.

ROGERS: [That's just] what you're trying to do. All day long, it's just work, work, work, day in and day out, trying to keep the house neat and clean and trying to keep you fed . . . I'm just a cheap substitute for a housekeeper. All you want is somebody to work and slave and scrub and cook and order the groceries and take care of the laundry and the pressing, and clean the house and dust the furniture and lay out your clothes and scrub out the bathtub and then sit with her hands folded in the evening and watch you read!

After this outburst, Rogers runs into the bedroom to cry, but Ryan calmly resumes reading. Later on, they try to talk more sensibly to each other. Rogers tells her husband that she is unhappy because he's only home two nights a week due to working overtime, and when he does come home he just sits and reads and ignores her. He says he's trying to do it all for her.

"Don't give me that woman on a pedestal baloney," she complains. "You want money? Okay, I'll go out and get a job. Either you give up this night work and spend your evenings with me, or I'll go out and get myself a job."

Ryan is horrified. "You'll do nothing of the sort!"

Rogers fights back. "I will so! I'll sling sodas, I'll wait tables. I'll even wash dishes."

Ryan gives up. "Okay, you win." He puts away his reading.

This scene articulates clearly the way that women feel, and it shows audiences why they feel that way. Anger and frustration and disappointment with the little house and the handsome man are put forth in a completely honest and believable way. Rogers utters the battle cry of the future: "You want money? Okay, I'll go out and get a job." The ultimate threat to male happiness. The final nail in the coffin of male control.

The rest of *Tender Comrade*, when it is not spouting wartime propaganda, asks the audience to think of the marriage of Ginger Rogers and Robert Ryan as a perfect example of a happy union. These little quarrels are introduced to prove that this is a real marriage and not one of those fake Hollywood marriages in which the couple never has words or raises their voices. This is war, says the movie, so we'll show you how two people just like you and your own husband yell at each other and disagree with each other. This alleged honesty is the biggest dishonesty of all. What the film really does is act out two scenes in which the woman's disappointment is depicted as being *wrong*. It is neither real (they actually love each other) nor is it appropriate (Ryan is killed in combat). The method of *Tender Comrade* in reaching women in its audience is to connect to their known unhappiness, articulate it, and then refute it.

The flashbacks used in *Tender Comrade* are a common 1940s device. This format clearly influences the way the viewer sees events as they unfold, since the outcome is more or less known at the beginning instead of at the end (barring unforeseen developments and surprises after the final return to present-tense time). In *Citizen Kane* (1941), we begin the story knowing that Kane is dead and how history will see him. The story tells us how he got that way. Films like *Ruthless* (1948), *Edward My Son* (1949), and *Keeper of the Flame* (1942) continue the Kane tradition, as they are all stories about powerful men told in flashback, but in these three instances the stories are really about the women who loved them and how they suffered.

The flashback is a perfect cinematic form for a story about a woman, being in and of itself a rigid, entrapping format that says clearly that there are no choices but the one already made.* When a woman faces her final dramatic crisis, she begins to relive her life. This becomes a review of how she made the choice that got her where she is, and in true woman's film attitude, this choice is always, but always, the wrong one. A flashback is a passive form of storytelling, in that it visualizes events that are allegedly past, inactive, over with, done. When a woman's story is told in such a way, it illustrates her restrictive present, in which all that matters is already predetermined. *Mildred Pierce* (1945), *The Hard Way* (1942), *Letter from an Unknown Woman* (1948), *Leave Her to Heaven* (1945), and *Kitty Foyle* (1940), to name only a few, are told in this format. Other key films, such as *Now, Voyager* (1942), contain major flashbacks that explain important moments in the heroine's past.

How we see things determines a level of understanding that operates both apart from and in connection with dialogue, performance, and event. "Actions speak louder than words," says Cary Grant in *Notorious* (1946) and camera angles speak even louder than actions. "You see," said Hitchcock, "many people think that a little dialogue scene in a movie is motion pictures. It's not." The excellent manipulation of film technique and style in these films changes the way women are seen. It influences viewers regarding not only the character in the story but also the actress and, by extension, women in general. So much that is understood in old movies is implied through familiar images and cinematic techniques. This is very apparent in women's films, in which sex, prostitution, and violence are often suggested visually, hinted at as offscreen events.

In a time of censorship and social limitations, Hollywood found its way of not only implying that sex was happening but, in a way, excusing it. Fireplace flames and fireworks spoke to viewers of "*Wow!* It's happening!"; and heavy rain and high winds added, "But it's okay; nature dictates it." The simple implication is that had it just not been raining, the couple would not have thrown themselves into each other's arms. (This also applies to haystacks, a concupiscent setting if there ever was one.) Furthermore, when heavy rain drives a couple indoors, they have to cohabit in intimate circumstances. This happens to Jennifer Jones and Robert Walker in *Since You Went Away* (1944) when they take refuge in a barn

---

* Flashbacks are also used as devices by which to point up the cautionary-tale aspect of the woman's film. For instance, in both *Maytime* and *The Sin of Madelon Claudet*—to name two otherwise totally dissimilar films—the woman's story is "told" as a flashback. In *Maytime*, an old woman advises a young girl to choose love over career or she will suffer regret, just like Jeanette MacDonald, and in *Madelon Claudet*, an asexual doctor (Jean Hersholt) advises a young wife, Karen Morley, that her husband's career is more important than she is because his mother has sacrificed everything in order for him to have it. In both cases, the young women accept the lessons.

with a haystack (maximum danger!) and to Glenn Ford and Geraldine Brooks in *The Green Glove* (1952—a cozy French inn), Cary Grant and Ann Sheridan in *I Was a Male War Bride* (1949—another cozy French inn), and to Margaret Sullavan and Charles Boyer in *Appointment For Love* (1941). These plot devices excuse women, letting us see their sex lives as not being their fault. Nature made them do it.

One of the differences between today's movies and those from the past is that the old films are about *not* having sex instead of about having it every five minutes. Since society did not condone sex between unmarried partners, many films revolved around a plot device by which the leading man and woman have to pretend to be married to each other and thus end up spending the night in a bedroom together. They would then have to avoid their natural attraction and certainly avoid falling into bed together. This makes a much better story, creating tension and excitement, than yet another ten-minute sex scene during which patrons munch their popcorn and wait for the story to get on with it. Overt sex scenes in effect *stop* the plot; they temporarily inhibit story development while what we are already familiar with from other movies (as well as life) takes place for several minutes. There is only so much variation one can put into these scenes, so audiences wait. In the old days, there were always many lively variations involving misunderstandings, interruptions from other people, and other temptations. This wonderful variety has been well exploited by television in series like "Cheers" and "Moonlighting" and "Anything but Love," all of which have stretched out the plot as long as possible, keeping the two key characters out of bed and maintaining audience interest accordingly.

Sexual agenda regarding women takes all forms, from Marilyn Monroe standing over a grate with her skirt blowing up around her to nun Deborah Kerr sleeping alongside marine Robert Mitchum on an isolated island. When Susan Hayward does a wild Gypsy dance in *Thunder in the Sun* (1959), she is watched by Jeff Chandler. It is a clear metaphor in which a man observes a woman letting herself go, cavorting freely about as an indicator of what she might be like in the act of sex. ("I like the way you *dance*," leers Chandler.) *Thunder in the Sun* also has Chandler watch Hayward when she goes down to the river to bathe, swimming naked under his hidden gaze. (This, in fact, is pretty much all the action and excitement there is in the movie.) In *China Girl* (1942), Lynn Bari comes to rescue George Montgomery from the Japanese, and the two of them act out a metaphorically abusive relationship. Bari is carrying on her body the gun Montgomery will need to escape. She needs to pass the gun to him in front of his guards. To do so, she first triggers his jealousy. He spits out, "You can't wait for me to be dead so you can take up with these monkeys." She slaps him. He slaps back, hard. They start knocking each other around in a little Apache dance of violence. In the melee, enjoyed by the Japanese, she passes him the gun. One might think, Why should these two characters be able to enact such a scenario with such ease and familiarity? One has the depressing sense that this is a real thing with them, that it has happened before. Each is familiar with how the other will react. An audience is asked to enjoy the sight of a male and female who are supposed to have a sexual relationship slapping each other around.

We can also see how movies set up scenes in which strong, beautiful, capable women are humiliated and made to look foolish. Usually this is done in the context of romantic comedy, with the man and woman engaged in a battle royal over love. It is also often set in that particular space that is inevitably associated with women, the kitchen. The movie asks an audience to participate. Come into the kitchen, your mother's place, and take a look at this elegant female movie star in the fur cuffs. Just see . . . this woman *can't even cook.* A judgmental context is visualized. If a woman doesn't know how to make pancakes, what can she actually be worth? Even if she is a federal judge, a nuclear physicist, or a brain surgeon, where's her contribution to things? After all, we've got men to do those jobs. The way to a man's heart is through his stomach, the direction any sensible woman ought to take in life. If a woman can't follow directions along that map, she is simply, well, embarrassing. An audience is asked to watch a woman becoming embarrassed as she is totally humilated. In *Tell It to the Judge* (1949), Rosalind Russell can't cook breakfast at the lighthouse. Robert Cummings has thoughtfully provided her with a nice fish to fry, but she can't clean it, cut off its head, or cook it. The viewer can watch him watch her fail and then triumphantly take it away and cook it himself. Spencer Tracy watches with similar amused tolerance in *Woman of the Year* (1942), while Katharine Hepburn, a world-famous newspaperwoman, tries to make pancakes. Even a cup of coffee is beyond her ability. As Hepburn destroys the kitchen, Tracy shows us how to see her incompetence, and then he rescues her. (At least he has the grace to say that anyone can make breakfast. It's her he wants, not a cook.) In *Skylark* (1941), Claudette Colbert falls on her face, slipping all around the floor, as she tries to cook fish in a boat's galley.

It is perhaps easy to make too much of these humiliation scenes. In all three cases, the women get their men anyway, and they do not fundamentally change themselves. Russell remains a judge, Colbert remains an elegant wife, and Tracy even lectures Hepburn on the folly of her having felt she *should* cook. ("I'm disappointed in you for the first time . . . Sea Biscuit can't be an ordinary horse . . . I don't want you to be Tess Harding any more than I want you to be Mrs. Sam Craig. Why can't you be Tess

Harding Craig?" Why can't she have it all? Why does she feel she ought
to make pancakes?) It is also true that men are similarly humiliated in
movies. Cary Grant has to dress up in a frilly negligee in *Bringing Up
Baby* (1938) and in a woman's army uniform and wig in *I Was a Male
War Bride* (1949). William Powell, who has passed himself off as an expert
trout fisherman in *Libeled Lady* (1936), is forced to enter a stream and
improvise fishing talent in a male-humiliation scene that actually ends in
comic triumph. Comedy films provide humiliation for both men and women,
and tragedy reduces both sexes to tears and defeat. The difference lies in
the fact that when a man is humbled, he can regain his manhood through
action and decisive behavior. When a woman is humbled, there is a lingering doubt left about what is appropriate behavior for a woman, what is
the right way for her to live her life. The doubt, I feel, can be a two-way
street. A woman can think, "Yeah, I ought to know how to make pancakes,"
or she can think, "Phooey on the pancakes, I want to be president."

There is a curious contradiction in the kitchen-humiliation scene that
goes beyond the by-now-familiar contradictory attitude to be found in movies
about women. If a movie is going to make a woman look foolish and as if
she cannot cope, why set it in a kitchen? Why not the boardroom, the
courtroom, or some august corridor of power? Observe the sly manipulation
of subtle cultural attitudes. The kitchen is the woman's territory; therefore
it is a space that doesn't count in the outside world's hierarchy. It is even
a place for servants, children, bums who come begging handouts, and a
general list of powerless and disenfranchised individuals. On the other
hand, it's our false setting of family camaraderie, comfort, and easy reassurances. We have our choice of the cold steel and elegance of the 1930s
kitchen in a large mansion, a setting in which the Celtics could play the
Lakers with room to spare, or the crowded comfort of the farm kitchen with
hot biscuits popping out of wood stoves while everyone plans to save the
crops. There is also a choice of attitudes. Is it Carole Lombard slouching
into the space to flirt with William Powell in *My Man Godfrey* (1936), or
is it Irene Dunne rolling out pie dough in *I Remember Mama* (1948)? If
the kitchen is nothing more than a woman's world, it has no official importance, but if it truly *is* the woman's world, then it is the place in which,
above all else, she has to be able to cope. If a woman can't find her way
to the refrigerator, what can she be counted on for? The kitchen is used
as a visual setting that is the woman's playing field, her testing ground.
Yet it is a kind of powerless space, a place for a woman to enact her
secondary status in society. If she is a good woman, she will know how to
cook in it, but if she is not a good woman, she'll fail her primary task and
her soufflé will fall. A woman who can cook (that is, do the right thing)

finds that her kitchen is a throne room. She becomes a queen, but, of course, only the Queen of the Kitchen. The boundaries of her queendom are very, very small.

It is possible to observe an evolution of cultural attitudes toward women and their roles by tracing changes from original movies to their remakes. There is a subtle difference between the presentation of women in the 1930s and 1940s that can be seen in such films. As is often the case, a minor B film can define those differences sharply and clearly, without pretense. *Two in the Dark* (1936) was remade as *Two O'Clock Courage* in 1945. Both films tell the same excellent little story about an amnesiac man accused of murder and trying to remember what happened. In both films, he is aided by a young woman, but the woman character is presented very differently in 1936 from the way she is in 1945, whereas the male character remains very much the same. In the 1930s, the hero first encounters the heroine while she is sitting on a park bench, alone in the fog at night. She's been locked out of her apartment for not paying the rent. She's unemployed, a perfect Depression image of a woman down-trodden by the economic system. As she begins to help the man, they pretend to be cousins, a ploy that removes sex from their relationship. He asserts himself, always acting as the master, telling her, "Lay off, Maisie, stop butting in. Let me answer the man." In the 1940s version, the young woman is employed. She's a taxi driver (!), with only five payments due before she'll own her own cab, which she calls Harry. She's bouncy, independent, a take-charge type who runs the man and thinks faster than he does, bailing him out in tight spots. Under pressure, they adopt a relationship in which they pretend to be a married couple, and she brings him to her room, unafraid of her landlady's censure. She undresses with him nearby, without any coy pretense at modesty. She is bold, confident, competitive, and also jealous. In other words, she is a true wartime babe, out in the world, doing a man's job and feeling as if she can take the man's role onto herself.

Perhaps the best example of subtle changes in remakes is illustrated by the three versions made of the Fannie Hurst perennial *Back Street*, the story of a woman who devotes her life to the love of a married man.

In the 1932 version, the woman (Irene Dunne) becomes a kept woman. She lives in a little apartment the man provides for her and faithfully awaits his visits, always staying home for him. She has nothing to occupy herself with, although once when her money from him is accidentally delayed for a period of time, she has to paint designs on dinner plates at home in order to earn enough to live on. In the 1941 version, the woman (Margaret Sullavan) has a good job in a fashion shop. She works, although she is not what one would call a hugely successful career woman. In the last version, from 1961, however, the woman (Susan Hayward) has become a fashion tycoon, a wealthy and powerful woman who is the head of a large business of her own.

It is clear that whereas in 1932 an audience was prepared to accept the idea of a woman sitting at home painting plates and sacrificing her life totally to the love of a man, an audience in 1961 was not. In comparing these three films it can be observed that women increasingly are moving out into the world. Step by step, the women gain independence and something to live for or do with themselves other than loving a man. The concept that is built into the first film, that a woman can be ennobled by prostituting herself because it is true love and thus a sacrifice, had become unacceptable by 1961. As the women become progressively more independent, the plots have to establish more clearly a reason that the man would not leave his wife. In the first movie, he just doesn't. Divorce is not mentioned. He's married and has children and his respectable business, and it just can't be done. In the later films, the wives have to be cared for so that the man would look bad if he *did* leave. In the 1941 version, the man cannot divorce his wife because it would totally ruin his career, and in the 1961 version, he has an alcoholic wife who has tried to kill herself. He is responsible for her. There is also a progressive change regarding motherhood. First, Irene Dunne begs and begs, "Give me a child!" She is deeply in love and wants to be a mother. The second version has Margaret Sullavan caring for her sister's child as a surrogate mother in a weak subplot. And in the 1960s version Susan Hayward, in fact, ends up getting the man's two kids to take care of after his death. Finally, the back-street woman gets it all!

Ironically, the best of these three films is the original, beautifully directed by John Stahl and achingly acted by Irene Dunne. Somehow the story makes more sense in this version, because it in no way is masking the basic truth. It is naked in its presentation of a woman sacrificing her life to the love of a man. The point is clearly made that it is love that prevents this woman from accomplishing anything out in the world or from marrying someone else and having her own family. It is love that cripples her.

Shifting attitudes toward the woman's life are also made clear in two versions of another Fannie Hurst best-seller, *Imitation of Life*. Dated 1934 and 1959, the two movies indicate an almost radically different point of view toward a woman who has a successful career. In the first movie, Claudette Colbert plays a young widow who has to go out and sell cans of maple syrup to survive. After a mournful rendering of "Nobody Knows the Trouble I've Seen" over the credits (a tune that might be the official woman's film anthem), the movie opens up on an honest scene of female frustration. Colbert is trying to cook breakfast, bathe and dress her little daughter, get

Styles change, but basic plots go on forever: *Imitation of Life*—1934,
with Claudette Colbert and Jessie Pullman

herself ready to go to work, reassure the child about the day nursery she
hates, answer the telephone and the door—the works. It is an effective
scene in which a woman is trying to juggle two roles, that of the woman
(mother and housekeeper) and the man (career). A solution of sorts presents
itself in the form of a generous, loving black woman (Louise Beavers), who
also needs work, who also is desperate, and who also has a little girl she
wants to keep near her and care for. The two women form an alliance.
Although Colbert cannot afford a housekeeper, the housekeeper can't afford
to keep her daughter, so in return for room and board the black woman
moves in to take the female portion of the burden off Colbert's shoulders.
They, in fact, form a marriage of shared responsibilities.

The two women become real friends. When Colbert arrives home after
a long day selling syrup, Beavers massages her feet. They talk about men:

BEAVERS: You ought to have a man takin' care of you, honey.
COLBERT: I had a man once . . . and he up and died on me.
BEAVERS: Was you very much in love with your late husband, might I
           inquire?
COLBERT: Well, I married him.
BEAVERS: But did you love him?

. . . and 1959, with Lana Turner and Sandra Dee

COLBERT: Oh, Delilah. I think I was too young to know very much about love. Mother was dead . . . he was my father's choice. Father wanted someone to take care of me. So I married him.

After expressing what a pity this is, Beavers tells Colbert that "You's got a big surprise comin' to you, Miss Bea. You need some lovin', honey chile," but Colbert gives the woman's film answer, "I've got Jessie [her daughter]. That's enough."

Thus, the 1934 version of the movie opens up on a frank portrayal of a situation in which a young woman with a child finds herself alone and without financial support, and of how sisterhood can help her. The later version, starring Lana Turner and Juanita Moore, begins with Turner losing her daughter at the beach and meeting the black family because the two children have found each other to play with. Turner's search for her daughter has been photographed by a would-be suitor (John Gavin) who later sells the photo to *Life* magazine, beginning both a romance and a career boost for Turner, who wants to be an actress. Grounded in the very same novel, involving a story of two mothers and two daughters, these films use images and settings to convey two totally opposite meanings. Consider the contrasts of the opening scenes, or the attitudes toward the leading men. The 1934 movie begins by showing us the leading lady inside her home, reassuring her small daughter while bathing and dressing her. She is at home, doing the "woman's" thing. The 1959 film, however, opens up on a crowded beach, and the central action of the sequence finds Lana Turner searching frantically for her small daughter, whom she has presumably let wander off. It is not only a sequence outside the home, but set in a nondomestic space. Turner has to be seen as a neglectful mother, however loving and concerned she might be. The 1934 movie has Colbert meeting the man in her life, Warren William, long after she has become a big success. He is a minor part of the film, not even appearing in the first half of the movie. There is no suggestion that a choice between him and her career need be made. While she was creating her successful empire, there was no love interest in her life. Turner, on the other hand, meets her loved one in the very first scene of the movie. He is a conscious plot presence—the steady reminder that true love would be a better choice for her than a career— from the very first moments of the film. Her career is placed in contrast to his love, and she loses him because she chooses her success over his love.

These films develop further differences while maintaining almost identical basic plots. Claudette Colbert becomes rich and successful because Louise Beavers knows how to make great pancakes. Lana Turner becomes rich and successful because she is a beautiful woman, a desirable sex object, and a great actress. Colbert's success is owed to her friend's talent at making pancakes, since Colbert boxes the flour and puts Beavers's image on it. Turner's success is supported by Juanita Moore, who takes care of the home and children while Turner pursues her acting career. Beavers is shown helping Colbert clean and refurbish the little restaurant they first open together, partner in the work. A scene specifically defines how Colbert gives Beavers 20 percent of the business. Although Turner and Moore are also meant to be seen as friends, there is no way for Moore to become a specific part of Turner's career. In both cases, the black women remain at home, but in one the business success is far more a partnership than in the other.

The second *Imitation of Life* becomes a story about failed motherhood. Under the direction of the remarkable Douglas Sirk, the film takes on a harsh criticism of American materialism, which is brilliantly illustrated by the opening credits in which jewelry—way too much jewelry—rains down on the bottom of the frame.

Lana Turner plays a woman who does not live a life, but who only imitates living a life. Her life is a sham, a performance about feelings instead of real feelings. She is contrasted with her black domestic, a woman of depth and heart, who desperately tries to keep the love of her daughter. While Moore fights for her child, Turner ignores hers. The overt statement is that pursuing wealth destroys people's personal lives, and the covert statement is that a woman shall be a mother, not a career woman.

The selfish materialism that manifests itself in Turner's drive for a career is paralleled by the selfishness of Juanita Moore's daughter, well played by Susan Kohner. Just as Turner does not appreciate the need to be a good mother to her own daughter (Sandra Dee), Kohner does not appreciate the need to be a good daughter to her own devoted, unselfish mother.

Although the earlier film has suggested that Colbert must sacrifice the love of her devoted suitor because her daughter thinks she, too, has a crush on him, this situation comes late in Colbert's life. She and her daughter have a fine relationship, and Colbert, it is implied, can temporarily give up Warren William (while he sails off on a scientific expedition to pass the time) until her daughter grows out of her whim. The ways of seeing the four women characters have been radically adjusted, presumably by and for shifting social attitudes, in these two films.

Stories like *Back Street* and *Imitation of Life* are often laughed at today. They are treated as silly, but they should be seen as metaphors for women's miseries and for the enslavement that women in the audience were railing against. But because these stories are about "women's concerns" and "women's lives," they are thought of as less important, more ridiculous, than stories in which men kill Native Americans and exploit India. On the whole, the woman's film has taken a bum rap.

In the past two decades, feminists have written extensively on the subject of how women are seen in movies and on how women themselves see popular movies, most of which have been made by men. The way women are photographed and positioned inside the frame has undergone considerable theoretical analysis in an attempt to understand how a viewer absorbs filmed narrative and character. One of the first—and one of the best—books written on the woman's film was the pioneering study *From Reverence to Rape*, by Molly Haskell. Gracefully written, warm and funny, Haskell's book is an incisive and historically accurate account of films about women. Haskell points out that there were more positive roles for women in the 1930s and 1940s than there were in the 1960s and 1970s. This is definitely true. The earlier decades were the time of the delicious movie woman. Viewers were asked to enjoy looking at feminine beauty and to consider a woman as a companion, an equal, a challenging opposite who wore great clothes and who always had a comeback for any remark or a suggestion for how to get out of any pitfall. These were the women who had no fear of leopards and who willingly donned disguises and dove off the sides of ships.

Haskell pays tribute to these women and the joy they brought mov-

iegoers, but she also speculates that the tendency of the woman's film was
to show women as self-sacrificing, which she feels is the way in which
popular culture reinforces traditional roles for women. I believe that Haskell
is correct about this, but I would add to it that these movies of hideous
sacrifice, which proclaim that this is the way it is, also subversively reveal
to women the hypocrisy of the repressive social system in which they are
imprisoned. As I have repeated often enough, a woman's film, in order to
tell its story, has to present a central character of great importance who is
out in the world doing something. Since movies encouraged audiences to
identify with characters or dream about having the same experiences as
were shown on the screen, women were inevitably going to project themselves into situations in which they got out and did something.

Haskell's idea that movies reinforce traditional values says frankly
that in Hollywood a patriarchal ideological system was at work. She describes what she sees there without offering theoretical proof, as her book
is an example of individualized sociology, or a form of reception theory.
In a seminal 1975 article called "Visual Pleasure and Narrative Cinema,"
Laura Mulvey posits further that women have been made into passive objects
for male viewing pleasure by male moviemakers. Mulvey suggests that
women on the screen were there to fulfill male fantasies and desires, and
to both relieve and express male anxieties. Films were voyeuristic, and the
voyeurism was male in attitude and execution. When both men and women
looked at movies, they were seeing with a "male gaze." A woman was an
object only to be looked at. Mulvey feels that the female spectator had
been denied power and/or pleasure by these films, because women have
no choice but to form a masochistic relationship to Hollywood's images.
Mulvey's original and challenging essay inspired a wave of feminist film
criticism and theoretical writing that initially supported her analysis, using
as evidence many woman's films, but primarily those from the film-noir or
melodramatic tradition. (This inevitably skewed results.)

Drawing on Mulvey's work, E. Ann Kaplan and Mary Ann Doane
extend feminist scholarship. In *Women and Film*, Kaplan says a woman
"is presented as what she represents for man, not in terms of what she
actually signifies. Her discourse (her meanings as she might produce them)
is suppressed in favor of a discourse structured by patriarchy, in which
her real significance has been replaced by connotations that serve patriarchy's needs." Doane, one of the most influential of the feminists, argues
in *The Desire to Desire: The Woman's Film of the 1940s*, that a woman has
two ways of seeing movies: as herself (a female viewer) or as a "transvestite."
In the former, she identifies narcissistically with the presentation of a woman
as an object, and in the latter, she identifies instead with the male hero.
Thus, movies move women toward identifying with being objects. The

woman's film, according to Doane, removes the male-hero option, because
it is about a woman. Kaplan and Doane say the only pleasure for females
in the movie audience had to come from the refusal of pleasure or "the
desire to be desired." Their ideas define the viewing experience as one in
which a woman finds a trap in the dreamworld of film, because she has no
choice but to project herself onto its characters while remaining passive in
the audience.

The latest wave of feminist scholars has begun to see things somewhat
differently. Their work has begun to address the awareness that the image
of women on-screen may be somewhat more complicated than Mulvey's
essay suggests. Tania Modeleski is one of the best of these writers, and
her excellent book on the work of Alfred Hitchcock, *The Women Who Knew
Too Much*, identifies the ambivalence regarding femininity contained in
his movies. Modeleski begins to argue the great "Yes, but . . ." that logical
people will inevitably ask. She considers the possibility of male and female
viewers seeing things in two different ways, that there may be a "female
gaze," although she clearly believes that women's cultural forms—films,
novels, soap operas, and so on—force repression on women.

Teresa de Lauretis has begun to develop a theory of the female spectator, suggesting that the issue of how women view movies is far more
complicated than what the first wave of feminist theory defined and that
what actually happens to a woman in a movie audience is that she is trapped
in a dual response. (As a character in an old movie might say, "Now you're
talking!") De Lauretis says that, on the one hand, a woman identifies with
the woman in the movie, generally a passive person, and yet at the same
time she is also identifying with the active elements of the movie, that is
to say, with the male characters and subjects.

Can anyone really presume to claim that women's films can be seen
one way and one way only? That all women think alike, react alike, and
see alike? Is there really a difference between female authorship and male
authorship, so that Dorothy Arzner's films can be distinguished from George
Cukor's or Edmund Goulding's? Do films made by men offer limited avenues
of pleasure for women? Is there only one type of female pleasure? And do
women remain the same over different decades? Are they *really* culturally
and historically fixed in time? These questions are important ones, to be
answered by other kinds of studies. This book, which hopes to define the
concerns and typical attitudes of the woman's genre, can at least suggest
the contradictions inside individual visual presentations.

Consider two movies, *Safe in Hell* (1931) and *Roughly Speaking*
(1945). In the former, a nice girl is raped and sexually used by her male
employer until his wife finds out and throws her into the street. Without
references, she is unable to find work and ends up a prostitute. When her

Rosalind Russell takes charge (of Jack Carson) in *Roughly Speaking*.

married abuser tracks her down, she bashes him with an oil lamp, accidentally killing him (she thinks) and setting the hotel on fire. As she
prepares to flee, her childhood sweetheart, now a sailor, returns to shore
to marry her. After she tells him the truth, he at first rejects her and then
helps her to flee to an island in the Caribbean, "the only place with no
extradition laws." In a series of plot complications, she ends up shooting
and killing her married nemesis when he shows up (not dead after all). For
this crime she is hanged. And that's her story. The film ends with her
walking to the gallows. *Roughly Speaking*, on the other hand, is a perky
movie based on a screenplay written by Louise Randall Pierson, who also
wrote the autobiography it is taken from. Pierson's story is that of a young
girl born in 1902 in Quincy, Massachusetts, to wealthy parents, only to
have her father die unexpectedly, leaving them with debts. She goes to
business college and becomes one of the original "typewriters." She is in
every way liberated, determined, and strong.

Audiences first view Pierson as a child, who responds to her father's
comment that her mother is afraid he's "making a tomboy out of her" by
saying, "That's the way it always is. Girls never have a chance." Her father
replies, "Yes. It's a hard world for girls. Maybe you'd better let me manage.
You'll be looked after." "I don't want to be looked after," Pierson replies.

"I want to look after myself. I'm not going to do silly things like knit or embroider or hem dish towels." Father gives her a philosophy to live by ("aim at the stars") and adds, "You've got the stuff in you like these thoroughbreds . . . nothing will ever stop you." Later, Pierson kicks the hat off the head of a rude employer who disrespects her, and tells her roommate, "I wouldn't give up my job for any man living . . . I'm not afraid, I'm not afraid of anything." When a young man proposes to her, telling her that he would like to come home from work and hear the sound of her bustling around in the kitchen, she says, ". . . and if you get home first, the sound of *you* bustling around in the kitchen." She marries, but won't change her name and won't wear white, even though she agrees to have children.

So far, so good. But here's the irony. Or rather, where is the irony? Dorothy Mackaill, in the underrated *Safe in Hell*, fights every man she meets, accepting the true love of her sailor but refusing to save herself from the gallows by sleeping with her prosecutor. When they come to take her to the gallows, she lights a cigarette with the flick of a thumbnail and calmly says, "Let's go." No weeping and no wailing. Behind her she leaves a group of male outcasts who have come to accept her as a friend rather than a sex object, and she has spared her young sailor's feelings by sending him on his way believing she'll join him. Earlier, she was completely honest with him. "I've made my living the only way I could." Now, realizing he really loves the sea too much to settle anyway, she frees him. Although her freedom is death, she makes her own choice.

On the other hand, Louise Randall Pierson's story becomes one of a failed first marriage (he dumps her and their four children for a younger woman), a failure to ever have a career (at least one that is depicted on-screen), and a second marriage to a man who gives her another child and lots of fun, but who is a success at nothing he does. The brave feminist never does have a real job, although she is seen cooking, scrubbing, caring for children, and volunteering in various wartime efforts. In the end, she sees her two older sons off to World War II and witnesses the preparation of her youngest son to join them. She just sits, looking careworn and poor and discouraged. She and her charmingly ne'er-do-well husband cheer themselves by dreaming about their next get-rich scheme.

One of these movies is about a real woman who obviously later becomes a successful author, the other is typical woman's film material about a downtrodden female exploited by men. But the brave words of Louise Randall Pierson are contradicted by the way her actual life is depicted on-screen, and the fictional woman, who, when asked where's her spunk, whines, "I ain't got any," ends up in an in-your-teeth story, a treatise against exploitation by men.

Where does one thing end and the other begin? When do Pierson's brave liberated words outweigh Mackaill's exploitation in a hotel room? When does Mackaill's proudly triumphant lifting of her head as she glares at her island oppressor and stomps past him outweigh the sight of a broken-down Pierson sopping up a beer in a pool hall while her husband, a failure at his door-to-door vacuum-cleaner salesman job, tries to hustle a few bucks to buy food? Ways of seeing can be planned by filmmakers, but not always can they successfully eliminate ambivalence.

What all this adds up to is an attempt by women to understand both the woman's film and the woman's viewing experience. What happens when a woman goes to the movies? Women measure themselves by the cultural norms that are presented to them. What is a woman? How is she supposed to look and act? Movies in the thirties and forties provided models to answer these questions, and women went out and gobbled them up. There were more than five hundred films per year, many of them written by women or worked on by women behind the scenes and almost all of them starring women in some way. To draw the audience, hold it, and draw it back for more, movies had to provide *something* for the viewers that they wanted, needed, and responded to—some hope, some release, some escape. Hollywood succeeded because it did this on a grand scale, and its methods were subversively clever. Connect to reality, and then release. Old-movie magazines often write about the strange phenomenon that although the movie audience contained a larger percentage of women than men in it, male stars were more popular at the box office than female stars. Does this mean that women preferred to view films about men rather than women? There is a lot we don't know about the audiences of the past. What we do know is that women did not surrender their brains, or their prior experiences, when they entered a movie theater. Rather, they used them both to understand and to respond to what was on the screen.

THE WOMAN'S WORLD

It's a woman's world.
It's a woman's world when she's in love.
His hope and his ambitions are the ups and downs she'll gladly share.
She'll give her all without conditions,
When he looks around, she'll be there.
It's a woman's world. Ask any man.
When it's hers, it's his.
It's a woman's world, but only because it's his.
                            —The title song from WOMAN'S WORLD (1954)

JUST AS IN THE MOVIES Paris is designed as a backdrop for only three things—love, fashion shows, and revolution—the movie woman's world is designed to remind us that a woman may live in a mansion, an apartment, or a yurt, but it's all the same thing because what she really lives in is the body of a woman, and that body is allowed to occupy space only according to the dictates of polite society. Hers is an interior world, the only place she can truly call her own, and thus her natural state is mental or emotional, rather than geographic or historical. As a result, the woman's genre is not identified by its settings, as westerns would be, or its time periods, as costume films would be. Instead, it is practically extraterrestrial, occupying no particular place and no specific time other than the now of the viewing experience. Because the woman's film is set in only one place—the woman's world—it can be set anywhere or anytime, since there really isn't any such place. Everyone knows it's a man's world. On the other hand, anywhere

there's a woman, there's a woman's world, because the woman carries her
world around inside her, like an unborn child.

Movies are thus faced with the task of defining visually a world that
exists but doesn't exist. This frees moviemakers to use any background,
put a woman in it as a central figure, and automatically transform the
situation into a woman's film. The presence of a female in any space
automatically feminizes it, rendering it able to provide an audience not
only with a story about a woman and what is happening to her, but with
an attitude toward what she is doing and whether she ought to be doing it
or not.

We all know how movies picture women inside the frame, doing the
things women do, wearing the things women wear. If they are wealthy, they
preside at tea tables and sit at heads of dining tables, well-shod feet poised
above floor buzzers with which they summon reluctant servants. They sit
at dressing tables, staring into huge mirrors, reaching for lavish silver-
backed hairbrushes and tasseled atomizers, clasping diamonds around their
swanlike necks. They rummage through closets where shoes, hats, and furs
are lined up like good soldiers on parade. They go to beauty parlors and
restaurants. They drop in on their husbands at the office, offering cool
cheeks to be kissed in return for hard cash so they can shop. They talk
on the telephone, and they sit in the bubble bath. They stand in the hall
and confidently arrange flowers. If they are poor, they do the same things
in reverse. *They* are the reluctant servants. They run their fingers through
their hair in a steamy bathroom, and there's nothing in the closet but one
plain dress. They go to bowling alleys and carnivals, and their husbands
steal money out of their purses. They have no telephones, and as for flower
arranging, they haven't got the time and wouldn't do it if they did. These
kitchens and dining rooms, bedrooms and bathrooms, closets and beauty
parlors, are all clearly thought of as female spaces. The movies provide
many pictures of them, but movie spaces can be used for contradictory
purposes. If a dressing table in a bedroom is an acceptable female space
and identified as such, a woman who sits powdering her shoulders while
a worshipful male looks on as she selfishly manipulates him is sitting in
negative space. If, on the other hand, she is a good woman, patiently
powdering while her beloved husband pours out his troubles and she offers
wise counsel, it is positive. (Bad woman at negative dressing table: Irene
Hervey in *Manhandled* [1949], as a selfish wife, preening and trying on
her jewelry, admiring herself after an adulterous night out. Good woman
at positive dressing table: Fay Holden as Andy Hardy's mom, listening
patiently to the noble judge while planning pot roast for dinner.)

A boardroom setting can work the same way. A wide-shouldered and

grim-faced female can sit at the foot of a boardroom table, barking orders
to a roomful of dominated males (Joan Crawford in *The Best of Everything*,
1959, or Faye Dunaway *as* Joan Crawford in *Mommie Dearest*, 1981), or
a kindly, open, and generous female can sit at the head of the boardroom
table and dispense wisdom as well as love (Judy Holliday in *The Solid
Gold Cadillac*, 1956). Movie spaces are also not as exclusively gender
specific as one might imagine. You might say there are more women to be
found in kitchens than men, but that might not be true if you take all those
butlers and chauffeurs from 1930s comedies into account. You might say
that the beauty parlor, at least, is exclusively female, but setting aside
Warren Beatty in *Shampoo* (1975) as a fluke, and ignoring all the other
male hairdressers and masseurs, you finally have to admit that although
women are shown in beauty parlors often, men are just as commonly depicted in its male equivalent, the steam room.*

It's interesting how often movie women occupy spaces that might be
thought of as masculine, such as an office desk, an airplane pilot's seat,
the driver's perch on a stagecoach, a lawyer's table, the legitimate stage,
or the operating room. These spaces, however, are never remembered as
female spaces. This is because movies suggest to us that these are men's
spaces that unusual women—remarkable women, wonderful women, *movie
women*—are occupying because of their specialness. They occupy this
space inside the frame on behalf of the women in the audience, who will
never occupy it in real life. On the other hand, there are certain settings
that seem to lend themselves naturally to the story of a woman, and these
are always places with sharply defined parameters. Since one of the primary
goals of the woman's film is actually to define for the audience what the
woman's world should properly be, one sees that this concept can be viewed
as either positive (let a woman find her space) or negative (put that woman
in her place).

These physical spaces of the woman's film—the visualized woman's
world—are generally presented as a series of never-ending traps and prisons
that women rattle around inside of. The woman is trapped in her limited
spaces, and her options for mobility are not presented as horizontal. That
is, she can't move easily from job to job across an occupational landscape
in the movies. What she can do is more spectacular: she can go up, or
she can go down. Thus, one of the most common plot forms of the woman's

* Women go to the beauty parlor to bitch, gossip, and hurt one another—also to get their
hair done and their nails painted. Men go to the steam bath to murder each other, make
big-time money deals, and to sweat out too much drink or food from the night before. Men
say important things in the steam bath. They can risk their lives there. Women say nothing
important in the beauty parlor. They just risk their reputations there.

film is that of the rags-to-riches story (she goes up) or its mirror image, the riches to rags (she goes down).

When a woman goes up, she climbs by marrying or seducing men or by shutting men out of her life. Either way, her mobility is linked to the old problem of men and her relationship to them via her decision about love and romance. When she goes down, it is always because of men. Even if she goes up, she gets nowhere fast. Her rags-to-riches climb takes her from ghetto kitchen to ritzy bedroom, but she's still working for her money. Her determined career fight takes her from the box-factory assembly line to the elegant magazine assembly line, but she's still alone and frightened. As the woman struggles to control, defy, resolve, escape—whatever—her world is a set of boundaries. She struggles to break free of them, with films often suggesting at the finish that only by pulling an even tighter boundary in around herself—accepting marriage and love—can she really find happiness.

Thus, spaces and the concept of space—"a room of one's own," as it were—are important to the woman's film. Since what the movie woman is trying to do is figure out what world she can properly inhabit, and since choosing one world or another is her primary problem, the woman's time on film is frequently marked by an odyssey in which she travels up and down the social ladder, looking for love, solace, lost children, security, or perhaps just her equivalent of Rosebud, the prom date that never materialized.

The woman's world, then, is shown as a series of limited spaces, with the woman struggling to get free of them. The struggle is what the film is about; what is struggled against is the limited space itself. Consequently, to make its point, the film has to deny itself and suggest it was the struggle that was wrong, not the space. The contradiction inherent in the genre asserts itself. What this means is that the physical definition of the woman's world is actually the least ambivalent aspect of the genre. Whatever it is, it's rigid, fixed, and entrapping. The woman's interior or psychological world, the one she lives in emotionally as a woman, is set inside another world, that of society at large. The woman's world on film is a box within a box. The female protagonist has her internal self, desirous of freedom, sex, a job, or a wardrobe, and this is the interior box. The exterior box is the actual setting of the movie, and her private world is contained within it. The easiest way for the movies to tell a story about a woman's world is thus as a personal story about a woman in a specific kind of limited setting with defined parameters.

The way this works can be grasped by considering four typical settings of the woman's film—the prison, the department store, the small town, and the home. They are archetypal: anything else—from the science lab to the nunnery—turns out to be pretty much the same thing. These places are astonishingly alike, on an ascending scale of size. They share one dominant characteristic: clear markers for right and wrong. The small town has the railroad tracks to mark its social boundaries: right side, wrong side. The department store has its employee hierarchy: executive offices and really expensive departments versus the stockroom and the perfume counter. The house has an upstairs and a downstairs, a parlor and a kitchen. And a prison has its inside-the-bars/outside-the-bars division of inmates versus guards and keepers.

The woman starts out on one side or the other. She can begin on the wrong side of the tracks, in the kitchen, down in the stockroom, behind the perfume counter, or in the prison cell. How does she progress? By using her assets, which are beauty (recognized and commented upon) and brains (concealed and used in covert ways). The rich boy in town marries her and moves her across the tracks. The son of the department-store owner notices her, marries her, and removes her from the working world. The homeowner's son notices her, marries her, and makes her the mistress of the home (shifts her over from the kitchen to the bedroom). The prison doctor notices her, realizes she really isn't a criminal at all, and gets her a pardon or rehabilitates her. He'll marry her later, when it's more socially acceptable. (It's one thing for a rich man to marry his employee and elevate her to his status; it's another for a prison doctor to marry a sentenced criminal. Oh, it will work out; it just takes more time.) The spatial progression described here is the rags-to-riches variation on the woman's film. Its opposite is the riches to rags, in which, for example, a wealthy young woman with a good home, perhaps the daughter of a department-store owner in a small town, falls in love with a no-good kind of guy and becomes involved in his criminal activities and ends up in prison.

In the conventional stories about these spaces, the man makes it all possible, and the woman is worthy because of her beauty and, of course, her decency and honesty and her lack of interest in his money. In the unconventional versions, the woman makes it possible by being brainy or brave all by herself, with the man standing by. In the evil, inverted versions of these stories, the bad women *manipulate* it all into happening for all the wrong reasons, the main one being money and the power it bestows. The point is that right or wrong, good or bad, the woman struggles against or moves about in a world defined by fixed attitudes.

One can easily create a typical woman's film plot that goes from limited space to limited space, on a journey to nowhere, using all four of these settings. The film might be set in a small town, in which a girl from the wrong side of the tracks works in the kitchen of the town's richest family. The son (or father) seduces her, or is seduced by her, and she advances to his bedroom. From there she advances through marriage to mistress of the house and out from that into tycoon as she begins dominating his business, which is a department store. However, she is blackmailed by a former low-class lover, and she kills him, ending up in prison. Thus, we see the woman's world as a Board Game of Life, from one limited space to another: from small-town childhood to kitchen to bedroom to the house to the department store to prison. One space is much like another: a woman is finally powerless in a sharply defined set of parameters and she'll never really get control of anything.

Prisons and Department Stores

Here are allegedly two totally different worlds in which to place a woman's film. A prison is an institution set up to punish a woman for breaking society's rules, and a department store is not only a place where she can shop but also a place where she can work to better herself. A prison restricts a woman, deglamorizes her, and cuts her off from the company of men. It takes her jewelry away from her and makes her wear ugly shoes. A department store, on the other hand, not only requires a woman to dress up to work there, but it also surrounds her with fashion and glamour. One setting constitutes a warning to women that if they are bad girls they will be punished; the things they want will be taken away from them. The other is a kind of promise to women that if they are good girls—if they work hard and behave properly—they can be part of a world that contains everything they might ever want. Thus, the prison movie is a cautionary tale and the department-store movie is a fairy tale.

As it turns out, these movies are equally false but also equally true. They are the yes and no of the woman's world, in which all the concerns and attitudes turn out to be the same. Just take a look at the woman's situation if she is in prison:

- She has to follow the rules of the place.
- She has no real money of her own.
- She has no influence and no social status.
- She has to be careful or the men of the place might exploit her, rape her, harm her, or make her pregnant.
- She has to beware of jealousy from other women.

- In order to make her way out, she has to do what is expected of her and resist all temptations, which might include joining an escape gang, sneaking a pet into her cell, or fighting with another inmate.

How will this poor woman survive or cope?

- She will wise up, learning the rules of the situation, knowing who the stoolies or the mean people are.
- She will become humorous, resourceful, and witty.
- She will use her beauty for favors or privileges if she has to.
- She will keep an eye out for someone, a man or a powerful woman, who can help her get what she needs out of the situation.
- She will conform.

All of this is exactly what is going to happen when she goes to work in a department store. She just wears better shoes and gets to clerk behind a counter instead of standing around behind bars. A department-store girl knows that to make her way up the ladder of success, she will have to resist the temptations of theft, falling in with a bad crowd, dating men who will use her, and so on. She will have to know which floorwalker might seduce her and which one might report her if she comes late. She needs to catch the boss's eye and avoid the stockroom boy. It is all absolutely the same where the woman is concerned. What is different is only the purpose of the movie in terms of addressing the women in the audience. One kind of movie is being used to warn women, and the other to con them. Both wear a neon sign saying to females, "This could be you, babe."

In prison, women are beaten and raped. They suffer childbirths in which the baby is forcefully taken from them, and they go insane. They die. In a department store, women fall in love and get promoted. They go to fashion shows and employee picnics. "Look what can happen to you," both these movie settings cry out, and what can happen is related to following the rules. Disobey and you end up behind bars. Play your cards right, and you'll marry the rich owner of the store or his son. A prison setting clarifies exactly what the woman's situation is by stripping it bare of all pretense, whereas the department store sells it to her by dressing it up in beautiful clothes, music, and romance, the escapist finery of Hollywood. The rules of the woman's world are fixed, and whether it's pessimism (prison) or optimism (department store) makes no difference. Examining each setting separately reveals how its world is used to depict a place that can be called the woman's world, which is actually a rigid set of rules and parameters against which a woman plays out her emotional struggle.

Prison was evidently a very popular place to reflect on this struggle

in the woman's films of the early to mid-1930s. A lot of stars found them-
selves behind bars—Kay Francis (*The House on 56th Street*, 1933), Jean
Harlow (*Hold Your Man*, 1933 and *Riffraff*, 1935), Loretta Young (*Midnight
Mary*, 1933), Sylvia Sidney (*Ladies of the Big House*, 1931), and Barbara
Stanwyck (*Shopworn*, 1932, and *Ladies They Talk About*, 1933), to name
only a few.

These films depict a hard world in which a female prisoner is forced
to deal with the woman's life boiled down to its basic terms. In *Ladies They
Talk About*, one of the toughest of the women-in-prison movies of the period,
Stanwyck is confronted with a group of fellow inmates who are *really* hard.
No mothers and sweethearts or innocent victims exist among them. They're
a group of ex-whores, ex-madams, lesbians, thieves, and connivers. When
Stanwyck first arrives ("new fish . . . new fish"), she's given the facts of
prison life by Lillian Roth as they walk together in the prison yard: "Out
here, you're within a few feet of the two things you want most, but you're
always a few feet away . . . freedom and men." The prison setting perfectly
represents that "few feet away" from freedom that is the official position
of women in polite society.

Three major women-in-prison movies illustrate the basic motifs:
Caged, Condemned Women, and *Women's Prison*. Unless they are just plain
nuts, the women in all these movies are in prison because of men, money,
and sex. No matter how extreme their crimes, they all connect in some
way with these issues, with the notable exception of the "normal" Phyllis
Thaxter in *Women's Prison*, who has been incarcerated on a manslaughter
charge for hitting and killing a small child. Presumably she is in a class
by herself because she represents man's greatest fear and society's greatest
menace: the really bad woman driver.

Caged (1950) is the classic women-in-prison situation boiled down
to its essence, which is a story about women shut up in small spaces with
no resources, no connections (other than criminal ones), and no men to
protect or help them. It presents the woman's world in a pure form. There
are almost no men seen from start to finish. The film begins with a scene
in which newly sentenced women climb down from a paddy wagon. A
masculine voice is heard to say: "Pile out, you tramps. It's the end of the
line." This disembodied voice, never identified as to source, represents
the ultimate male judgment as well as the voice of society. It is the source
of all woe. As the film unfolds, the only men who appear in it are an
irritated doctor who arrives during the night to deliver the leading lady's
(Eleanor Parker's) child, and a corrupt politician and his cohort who
threaten the decent prison warden (Agnes Moorehead) when she tries to
censure a cruel matron. And when Parker leaves prison at the end of the

Eleanor Parker (center) and friends in *Caged*

movie, there will be three men waiting for her. One is sitting in the driver's seat of a fancy car, and the other two get out to welcome her and join her in the backseat. One of these men, stepping over Parker as she sits down between them, casually lays a hand on her knee as he crosses over her. Her eyes flicker momentarily, and then she lifts her chin defiantly as the car drives off, and she accepts a light for her cigarette. In a wordless brief moment it is clearly established that she is entering a life of prostitution. Except for the doctor, the politicians, and these ominous criminals, all of whom are seen only briefly, *Caged* is a woman's world.

There are two key women in *Caged* and several minor representational characters. The leading role (Parker) is that of a nineteen-year-old girl, a first offender, who has been arrested when her husband pulled a gas station robbery because they needed money. When the attendant hit her husband over the head, she got out to help, and this act of love made her an accessory to armed robbery. Her husband was killed in the resulting melee, and now she is in jail and two months pregnant to boot. The other key female is the prison warden (Moorehead), a woman of principle. She has reformed the institution as much as she can and disapproves of cruel tactics. She is not without resources or ideas, and is meant to be seen as a strong character, yet she is helpless when it comes to dealing with the various masculine forces that threaten the prison and the women in it. When the baby doctor complains about the hospital's unsanitary conditions, she explains that she has begged for money and supplies, but can't get anywhere. She slyly suggests, "Maybe if *you* spoke to the prison medical board." When prisoners riot and she is criticized, she tells the male politicians, "I told you this would happen when you gave us $8,000 instead of $80,000." She knows that the evil matron defies all rules and browbeats her inmates, but she is unable to do anything about it. When Moorehead finally does discipline the matron, she is victimized by a smear campaign against her in the newspapers. Here is where Moorehead fights back: she tells the politicians that she welcomes their firing her, because she will demand a hearing, which is her legal right, and expose them all publicly. She fights hard and wins, but two significant things are attached to this fight. First, it changes nothing for Parker and the other women, and, second, it occurs only after Moorehead has been thoroughly victimized.

Thus, *Caged* illustrates how the woman arrested and the woman who is the warden are both more or less in the same boat: each in her own way is a powerless female in a man's world. The woman's prison is the box within the larger man's world. Although the movie's surface presentation exists partly to remind women what can go wrong if they disobey, its subtext points up what a lousy situation women have in general, because men dictate the terms of their lives. Prison movies about women subversively carry out this idea by almost always having some negative female figure of authority who is very masculine. In *Caged*, this character is the evil matron played by Hope Emerson, a physically large woman who was frequently cast in quasi-lesbian roles. Emerson was nominated for a Best Supporting Actress Oscar for her portrayal of this matron, who oppresses the inmates by making them pay for her small favors, such as their mail or chocolate bars. She wields her power over them, cruelly punishing them or reminding them that they have no men. In a dramatic sequence, she taunts the inmates as she parades before them, dressed up and ready for a date. "Every time he kisses me good night, I just want to keep on leavin' him . . ." The close-ups of the faces of the lonely and love-starved women are an eloquent defiance of censorship.

The events of *Caged* establish baldly what the problems of the women's world really are:

1. *Men:* "If it wasn't for men, we wouldn't be in here." Or, as one vulnerable woman explains it, when asked why she fell back in for a second time, "Same thing that got me in here the first time—a guy. Sex and love and marriage are all mixed up . . . I loved him too much to walk out on him. You're lucky your man's dead . . . he can't turn you into a two-time loser like my man."

2. *Lack of power:* The women are shown to be without resources of any kind.

3. *Fashion:* The women remember how they used to have black lace underwear, mink coats, and a different pair of shoes for each night of the week. When they go before the parole board, they borrow things from each other, and when Parker asks for a comb before her prison photograph is taken, the impatient photographer snaps: "What's the difference? There's no men in here." When Parker's head is shaved as punishment, she nearly goes mad from the shame, and her entire personality changes afterward.

4. *Motherhood:* Parker gives birth and must sacrifice her child to adoption. Since her husband is dead, she has only her mother to help her. The mother, a weak and silly woman, explains that Parker's stepfather won't have the baby, and if she tries to take him, the stepfather will leave her. "Who will take care of me?" she wails. When Parker finds an abandoned kitten in the prison yard, her desire to care for it is understood by even the toughest of the women cons to be a substitute for her lost child. When Emerson tries to take the pet from her, the women riot and the little creature is killed in the fracas. (It's a hard-knocks world.)

5. *Insanity:* More than one woman goes crazy here, one of them hanging herself and one murdering the evil matron.

The final transformation of Parker from a nice girl, shy and frightened, who says, "I want to do the right thing," into a tough, impatient con who realizes her only chance is to accept the offer of vice-queen Lee Patrick to join her gang is demonstrated by the basic woman's world device: fashion. Patrick has tried to recruit Parker by giving her a lavish compact, studded with jewels ("Rhinestones! Not diamonds!" snaps the newly wised-up Parker, in rejecting it) and embellished with a braided tassel. At her moment of truth, Parker walks to the edge of the prisoners' cage to study closely a young woman who is with a group of well-heeled women touring the prison to "view conditions." While the young girl stands terrified, Parker ogles her long, curly hair (Parker's hair is only just growing back), her manicured nails, her jewelry, but, most of all, her full-length, lavish mink coat.

The camera takes its time in roving over the fur, to make its point. Firmly, decisively, Parker walks back to Patrick and takes the compact, opening it, and sensuously smearing her mouth with the lipstick that Patrick has also provided. The ultimate irony of *Caged*, with all its hard reminders to women of what can happen to them if they break the rules, is that it shows Eleanor Parker, the leading lady, rejecting the lesson herself.

Other prison movies with women carry out the same ideas as *Caged*. Men, lack of power and money, fashion and beauty, pregnancy and motherhood, threat of insanity, and sexual enslavement are also the issues in *Condemned Women* and *Women's Prison*.

In *Condemned Women*, one innocent young girl has actually not committed any crime. She is in prison because she confessed to the theft that her boyfriend carried out; he, she explains, has a chance to finish law school, but not if he has to serve a prison term. "He'll wait," she explains to her very, very skeptical fellow inmates, who roll their eyes. (As it turns out, because this is the movies, he *does* wait, but the girl is killed in a bungled prison escape attempt, so that hardly helps.) Women are shown to be victimized by men even after they are inside. In *Woman's Prison*, one of the inmates has a husband who is incarcerated in the adjacent men's prison. He insists on sneaking over to see her after hours, breaking the rules and risking their both getting caught. She is unwilling, but he wants sex and won't take no for an answer. She ends up becoming pregnant and is beaten brutally by her fellow female prisoners because she gets them all in trouble when she begins to display the overt manifestation of her disobedience. She dies as a result, twice being punished for being a woman —victimized by her man, even though she is presumably shut away from him, and then by her fellow inmates. As one of the women in *Condemned Women* puts it, "There are just two times you oughtn't believe a man— daytime and nighttime."

The relationship of men to the woman-in-prison movie, in fact, determines the fate of the incarcerated women. In *Caged*, there are practically no men, as we have seen, and this leaves Eleanor Parker at the mercy of society. In *Women's Prison* and *Condemned Women*, there are kindly male doctors who fall in love with some of the women and thus rescue them, offering them marriage and society's endorsement. It might be said that the more men there are in a woman's prison movie, the more likely a solution to the woman's problem is to be offered. The male presence allows the movies to be love stories as well as prison movies.

In *Condemned Women* (1938), Sally Eilers plays a young woman who has been arrested for shoplifting and vagrancy because she had been unable to find work. Desperate and ashamed, she tries to kill herself on the ferry that is taking the women to Alcatraz. Once in prison, however, there *is* work for her. She had been a nurse, so she is naturally assigned to the kindly prison psychologist of her particular film (this one played by Louis Hayward). Inevitably, they fall in love.

At this point, the movie shifts its focus away from the traditional prison-film problems onto the traditional woman's film problem, in which the young woman from the wrong side of the tracks is going to ruin the career of the up-and-coming young doctor. When the warden of the prison, a strong male authority figure, finds out through the gossip mill that the two are in love, he calls Eilers in for one of those chats that are so typical of the genre. In a classic woman's film affirmation of the rules of society and a strong demonstration of their force, he tells her plainly that she is going to ruin the doctor's life. It's the familiar "if you really love him, you'll give him up" sequence, in which the woman is asked to sacrifice herself. Give him up. Go away. Die. Or become a famous Broadway star. Do something, but get out of his life.

When Eilers becomes involved accidentally in a prison break and is blamed for it, the film suddenly reverses the stand it has taken on her. The final trial scene, in which the escapees are being judged, exposes to the prison board that the warden had interfered in the love between the kindly doctor and poor Eilers, who isn't a bad woman, just someone who couldn't find work. Where the plot first turned on an affirmation of society's rules and of society's force—the prison warden reminding Eilers she must not wreck the doctor's life—it later turns on an opposite idea. The warden has to be reminded that he should not wreck the woman's *love* life. One social system or attitude exposes the other. Eilers has been truly rehabilitated in prison because she has attempted to sacrifice herself for her man; she has made the right choice for a woman, and the warden is clearly wrong not to see this. Eilers is acquitted, and she and the doctor end up together.

Women's Prison (1955) contains the variation in which the warden is herself a woman. Unlike Agnes Moorehead in *Caged*, this warden (played with all stops out by Ida Lupino) is evil and destructive. She is placed in direct contrast to the film's kindly doctor character (Howard Duff). *Women's Prison* is a movie that is allegedly sympathetic to women, yet here is one of the most hateful female characters ever seen in movies. Women should be treated with respect, the movie is supposed to be saying, yet the idea of a woman like Lupino becoming an authority figure is definitely presented as the worst thing that could happen.

In considering Ida Lupino as the evil warden, one sees several contradictory ideas presented. Lupino is defined as "bad" because she not only has too much power for a woman but also because she uses it freely, without fear. Women with such power cease to be women, the film suggests; it makes men out of them, and that clearly will be disadvantageous for the masculine sex. Lupino's cruelty and dominance define her as inappropriately masculine. More than being seen as a repressed lesbian, however, or a bisexual, Lupino is a kind of pseudowoman, one who becomes a masculine force that oppresses and destroys women.

What makes Lupino so power hungry? The film makes clear that it is because she does not have a sex life. If women are loved, given sex and children, perhaps they would not need this excessive power, suggests the movie.

Lupino's sexuality is ambivalent. She exerts her dominance over the female inmates by forcing them to dress in dowdy uniforms and black stockings, utilizing the crucial women's film device: fashion. She herself, however, dresses luxuriously and fashionably in the very best clothes and jewelry. She is feminine in that sense, and her desire to look good and dress well is supposed to be one of the desired goals of a correct female attitude.

Contradictions such as this make it possible to see Lupino in differing ways:

1. She is representing a male figure in the disguise of a woman, so that no one will realize that the film is actually critical of men. She is thus the male force that destroys women, and she should be destroyed. (She is, in fact, destroyed at the end of the movie.)
2. She represents hidden desires of the women in the audience for liberation or freedom to do as they wish. Viewers are allowed to feel temporarily liberated by watching an evil woman.
3. She is a warning to both men and women that women should neither seek nor have the power of men, nor act as men. They will become evil and destructive, and also unhappy.
4. Men must control women through sex and motherhood, or they go insane, as Lupino does.
5. Women can be allowed to feel liberated by observing and possibly identifying with maleness and the power of men.
6. She's just an exaggerated character in a rather badly written movie.

If one decides Lupino is a warning, the lesson learned is that women should not be men, and men must control women. If one decides Lupino is a covert masculine force, the lesson is that women must fight that force and destroy it before it destroys them. (If one takes the latter viewpoint, one has found a message about men for female viewers put forth in an acceptably disguised form: that of a bad woman.) In the end, Lupino is sentenced to the ultimate women's prison, insanity, since the woman's world is, after all, psychological.

A PRISON is identified with male genres as often as (or more often than) with women's, but a department store is definitely a woman's world. It sells clothes! It also has furniture and appliances and model rooms. In fact, it has absolutely everything that every woman wants, all the stuff she needs to buy. It has *things*. A gal's gotta have what a gal's gotta have, and there's no place like a department store to display it all in one place.

Hollywood obviously found the department store a perfect setting for a movie about women (although not always for the woman's film itself), because department-store movies were never *not* going to involve women as central characters. Women shop, and the opportunity for the audience to sit there having a close-up look at luxury items of all types was irresistible. Where the prison takes away all clothes, perfume, and furniture, the department store puts them all back. Over the years, it has been a staple setting of movies that involve women's issues, providing audiences with plenty of goods to ogle and the freedom to roam up and down the socioeconomic scale. At the same time, a large store is often a setting in which to present various other issues or situate other genres:

LABOR AGITATION: *The Devil and Miss Jones* (1941)
MURDER: *Somebody Killed Her Husband* (1978)
FANTASY: *Miracle on 34th Street* (1947)
SLAPSTICK HUMOR: *Who's Minding the Store?* (1963)
MUSIC: *One Touch of Venus* (1948)
ROLE REVERSAL: *Honeymoon in Bali* (1939, a.k.a. *My Love for Yours*)
VERBAL COMEDY: *The Big Store* (1941)
LOVE AND ROMANCE: *Holiday Affair* (1949), *My Best Girl* (1927)
TRAGEDY: *Sweepings* (1933)
SCREWBALL COMEDY: *Bachelor Mother* (1939)

The cleverness of the department-store movie at creating a microcosm of the entire world is impressive. It is possible to work any type of character into the plot: young, old, male, female, kind, cruel, honest, dishonest, ethnic, WASP. It doesn't matter, because the explanation is simple: he or she works there. Why not? A large department store hires employees of all educational levels and backgrounds, and if it doesn't suit the plot for any given person to be hired, he or she can always come in and *shop* there. It's perfect.

The main cleverness lies in the ease with which women can be involved without the kind of explanation that needs to be set up for certain other movies. The department store is an appropriate setting in which women can easily and accurately be depicted working, as salesgirls, secretaries, and models. It provides a convenient and easy-access mingling of rich and poor, and solves many of those complex "how will the slum girl meet the rich man's son" plot problems for screenwriters. As the rich man's son walks toward the elevator on his way to the top floor to visit his father, what does he see as he glances casually to his right? The beautiful slum girl, standing behind the handkerchief counter. Furthermore, it is both logical and easy for him to walk over and pretend to buy a handkerchief, striking up a conversation.

During the 1920s, when department stores rose to the heights of the shopping experience (all under one roof!), many films used department stores as background settings. These early films were escapist, optimistic tales of love and democracy. Harold Lloyd worked in such a store in *Safety Last* (1923), as did Gloria Swanson in *Manhandled* (1924). Two prototypes of the genre were *It* (1927), starring Clara Bow, and *My Best Girl* (1927), with Mary Pickford and Buddy Rogers. In both these films, the young women stars, playing poor girls, enact the 1920s female version of the Horatio Alger story. They marry rich. The department store is seen as a setting in which it is acceptable for a woman to work, but in which her virtue will be tested. She will meet someone very, very wealthy, but if she does not maintain her own values and her own respectability, she will lose all. Perhaps she will even go to prison, that store with no departments! The department store contains all the rewards that society has to offer a woman. If she goes by the rules, she will be found ready and then removed from it into the proper world of love and marriage. All the stuff in the store will be hers, but she won't have to work for it. The store represents not only what a woman wants, but what she can have. The early films were totally optimistic about her chances.

By the 1930s, a darker side emerged in the setting, although basic optimism wins in the end. *Employees Entrance* (1933) is the other side of the *It* story. In this film, Loretta Young, a poor girl, is actually seduced by the big boss, and so she never really gets past the employees' entrance. Later, after she has married a hardworking fellow employee, she once again lets the boss seduce her at a drunken office party. Ironically, her young husband has let the big boss use and manipulate him, too, and the young couple end up forgiving each other and themselves, ready to return to work at the employees' entrance, the place they belong. (Even when they marry, they enter a huge cathedral after a wealthy wedding party has vacated the premises, begging the priest to marry them, too. It's a kind of employees'-entrance wedding plan.)

Two romantic comedies designed for escapist pleasure with department-store settings are *Honeymoon in Bali* (also known as *My Love for Yours*) and *Bachelor Mother*, both from 1939. They are light entertainment, funny, romantic, and stocked with clothes and all the trappings of wealth. Both also involve children as deterrents to a woman's life of freedom, and both follow the traditional woman's film format of deep-seated contradiction. They maintain the use of the department store as a fixed entity that reflects the rules of the woman's world.

Honeymoon in Bali stars Madeleine Carroll and Fred MacMurray. Carroll plays an enormously successful career woman who is executive vice president of a large urban department store called Morrissey's. She is introduced as happy, successful, kindly, and patient. She has close women friends (primarily the comic relief, played by Helen Broderick) and an ardent suitor (Allan Jones). She is not depicted as a hard-driven, cruel, and selfish career woman who has scrapped her way to the top at the expense of her femininity or her generosity to others; in fact, the audience first sees her *only* as a beautiful and desirable woman. The film begins in a heavy rain, with a window washer (Akim Tamiroff) cleaning windows and looking in on Carroll as she enters her office. (Why he is washing windows in the rain is never explained, although the question is raised by the practical Carroll.) As Tamiroff watches, Carroll straightens her stocking seams, revealing beautiful legs, tries on two different coats, selecting the more sober one of the two, and plops her feet up on her desk to remove one uncomfortable shoe. An audience is clearly placed in the same position as the window washer, that of looking in on a beautiful woman modeling clothes and displaying her physical assets.

As the story unfolds, it becomes clear that Carroll's entire life is the department store. She is still working at two in the morning (wearing an evening gown), and she seldom takes a vacation or thinks of anything other than work. The store is thus not unlike a prison for her, even though she is the boss and happy there. She adheres to what is expected of her from the regime and seldom leaves the premises except for lunches with Broderick or strolls from a restaurant back to her office (her version of chow time and exercise in the prison yard). She might be seen as the warden, due to her lofty position, but she's still in a kind of prison.

Carroll is not depicted as a bad person, just a misguided one. What is going to happen to her in the film is the movie's idea of liberation: getting her out of the department store and into a love relationship with a man who lives in Bali. She will also assume responsibility for a child and thus put her considerable energies and skills toward what the movie suggests is a better choice of a career: motherhood.

The following conversation takes place between MacMurray and Carroll in a posh nightclub, where they have been romantically dancing and dining:

CARROLL: About working girls . . . I suppose you're the kind of man that thinks a woman's place is in the home.

MACMURRAY: Well, isn't it?

CARROLL: I'm not a feminist, but the expression it's a man's world has always irritated me. It's anybody's world that can lick it.

MACMURRAY: I suppose you've got it licked.

CARROLL: Oh, I haven't done so badly.

MACMURRAY: Oh, I suppose you mean you make a lot of money . . . for a woman.

CARROLL: For a woman! The reason men have it over most women is that men use their heads and women use their emotions. That's the attitude that gripes me!

MACMURRAY: What are you going to do when you get married?

CARROLL: I don't believe in marriage . . . not for me or any woman who has the sense to live her own life.

MACMURRAY: I guess I've been out of the world too long. I had a quaint notion that women rather wanted to be married.

CARROLL: Why?

MACMURRAY: Well . . . they need the protection of a man.

CARROLL: I know of more women taking care of no-good husbands and loafing brothers! Protection of a man! I have a salary that makes most men's look sick, and I'm the boss. I have a charming apartment run by a competent maid, and I'm the boss there, too. I have plenty of escorts whenever I want them and . . .

MACMURRAY: I suppose you're the boss there, too.

CARROLL: . . . and I haven't a single encumbrance to worry me, and the most precious thing of all, absolute personal freedom. Now for what reason under the sun do I need a husband?

MACMURRAY: I can think of two . . . or three. Want to hear 'em?

CARROLL: Uh, no . . . I suppose . . . I suppose you think love might be a reason.

MACMURRAY: That's a good start.

CARROLL: I don't intend to fall in love either.

MACMURRAY: You don't?

CARROLL: No, love . . . love muddles you up.

MACMURRAY: What's wrong with that?

CARROLL: Well, it throws you.
MACMURRAY: Have you ever been thrown?
CARROLL: No, and that's not all . . .
MACMURRAY: I'd be afraid to go around making statements like that.
              You're going to feel awfully silly when you have to take
              'em back.

It is interesting how a light romantic comedy maintains not only the
basic point of the woman's film—a woman must make a choice, and her
best choice is for love—but also treats a department store as if it were a
prison, a structure that holds the woman in place until she can learn how
to live her life properly by society's standards. Learning to go by the rules
is the whole point. Suffering the consequences if you don't is the lesson.
Receiving love and protection is the reward for being a good student. The
store, with all its luxury and apparent freedom, incarcerates a woman and
separates her from what she really needs: the other prison of home and
marriage. *Honeymoon in Bali* establishes a plot device by which the woman
can really learn why a career is the wrong choice. A little female child
(Carolyn Lee) is placed in Madeleine Carroll's care, and she wins Carroll's
heart at once, revealing to the audience the truth about Carroll's soul: she
needs love. Becoming a mother even more than becoming a wife will bring
out her true nature. As soon as the little girl enters her apartment, Carroll
undertakes a series of actions with the child that establish not only her
own femininity but the sense that the little girl must be taught only female
things. Within the first sequence involving the child, Carroll puts perfume
on her more than once, dresses her in see-through lingerie, discusses
whether or not the child is too fat, and reassures her that she will, indeed,
be beautiful when she grows up. From then on, the film changes. It has
been feminized. Perfume has been sprayed on the plot. Having stressed
her independence, her desire to eschew love, and her lack of any need for
protection, Carroll tucks the little girl into bed and tells her what prayers
are for. "That's when you ask for love and protection and all the things
that matter . . ." Thus, the film—in a perfectly sensible conversation—
allows a beautiful, wealthy woman to question why she would want a man
or need a man only to undermine her sentiments totally by revealing that
her prayers are for the very things she says she doesn't need.
     The arrival of a child on the doorstep is demonstrated literally in
Bachelor Mother, a department-store movie in which the leading lady,
Ginger Rogers, is not the boss. She's just a temporary employee hired for
the Christmas rush (she's in for thirty days). She spends the early part of
the film emphatically denying that she is the mother of an abandoned child
she finds. Society's attitudes are such, however, that everyone naturally

assumes she is lying. In fact, such assumptions motivate the plot all the way to its conclusion. A series of assumptions—that she's the mother, that so-and-so is the father—create not only the laughs but the forward motion of the story. It is a squeaky-clean little tale that slyly but cheerfully works with events that actually come out of the more serious woman's film. A young woman with a baby and no husband has to find her way in life. *Bachelor Mother* sends up the conventions, but also uses them in its story. The fact that this can happen illustrates how clearly defined the woman's film is and also how clearly defined the woman's role in society is. Inevitably, Ginger Rogers begins to lie to survive and to conform to people's low opinions of women. She has to accept motherhood in order to survive. By doing so, she gets stuck with the baby, but she also marries the boss's son, settling down to a swanky life *outside* of the department store she once aspired to.

The department store in *Bachelor Mother* is a background setting that is constantly reestablished for the viewer. In this case, it is a source of rampant materialism, whereas in *Honeymoon in Bali* it is more representational of the career option in a woman's life. In both cases, however, the story is built to show that women need to accept motherhood, to acknowledge their loving and maternal selves, and in so doing they will be liberated out of the restrictive traps they work in.

The idea that a woman who builds a department-store career is actually building a prison around herself is subtly implied by *Lucy Gallant* (1955), a dull film based on the novel *The Life of Lucy Gallant*, by Margaret Cousins. The story opens up in Texas in 1941, a fact that is stated by a title card on the screen but that is nowhere visible in clothing or attitude. (When the Japanese bomb Pearl Harbor halfway through the movie, it comes as a shock to most viewers, who have totally forgotten that it's 1941.) Jane Wyman plays Lucy, a woman who has been left at the altar by a groom who was appalled when her father was indicted for fraud and embarrassed when the old gent killed himself. She is traveling westward with a set of superbly matched luggage crammed full of expensive clothes with Paris labels—her legacy, her trousseau. When the train is stranded by a washed-out trestle in the town of White Sage Junction, Texas, Lucy meets her fate, which will be two opposing forces: a big man (Charlton Heston) and a small store (the White Sage Emporium). She will transform these by reversing things. Heston will be reduced to a small man by her rejection of his love, and the emporium will be expanded into Gallant's, Inc., a sort of Neiman-Marcus surrogate. This transformation, the film tells viewers, is one hell of a mistake, because all Lucy Gallant has done is build herself a prison in the form of a department store.

"You can't build a fence around yourself," Heston tells Wyman, referring to the way she has built the store and incarcerated herself in it, even living on the premises. "The only thing that stands between you and him are the four walls of this glorified dry goods store," Wyman's best friend, played by Thelma Ritter, tells her. "But it's my dream," responds Wyman. "Well, wake up," retorts Ritter. "Having your own man is better." Thus, the department store, a monumentally successful business in which Wyman functions brilliantly, happily, is defined as a "fence" or as "four walls," a prison of her own construction that protects her from the risk of love. ("Are you off men for life?" Heston asks her after hearing her tale of woe about her fiancé and her father, two offscreen classic cases of male collapse and betrayal of the sort that always fuel the woman's story.)

In the end, Wyman unlocks the door to herself by locking the door on Gallant's, Inc. Along the way, she feebly asks such questions as "Haven't I the right to do two jobs at once?" meaning marriage and career, and "Is there any reason why the women can't get in on this boom town?" She's certainly a champ at business, being seen in not one but two success montages, in which she writes checks, directs employees, straightens up displays, and gets richer and richer. She even takes charge of Heston, telling him that the color of his boots is wrong. "Always wear black with dark gray," she chides, and sure enough, the next time she sees him, he's taken her fashion advice. He's got on snappy new black boots! All of this, however, means nothing. The department store is a prison, and it holds Wyman prisoner. Despite its goods, its economic liberation, its promises of good things, it can be negative if the woman doesn't get her head straight.

THE SMALL TOWN AND THE HOUSE

THE PRISON and the department store are settings that, in film terms, are hermetically sealed off, units complete unto themselves visually and spatially. Although the movie can leave the prison and the store and travel to other places, it does not need to do so to complete itself. The rest of the world influences both settings, but the representational "right" and "wrong" aspects to the two spaces render them self-sufficient.

The small town and the home function differently. The small town can contain a prison and a department store, if necessary, even though that might make it a particularly large small town, but the small town remains the miniature total universe. It is the microcosm that contains all forces, rather than an isolated setting in which to focus the audience on essentials. The home is always treated metaphorically. It is the woman's world that is allowed, the place where the woman is supposed to be, and thus the place where the most personal and psychological stories of women are told.

The small-town story provides a larger, more complicated overview of a woman and her life, one that includes commentary on the man's role, also. The home is the space in which a woman struggles with herself, her own identity, because that is the place where she belongs. These two limited settings may be paired like the prison and the department store, not in terms of the warning and the reassurance, but in terms of the impersonal and the personal. The small-town story of a woman is sociological in its presentation of the woman's world, and the home story is psychological. In physicalizing the woman's world, the small-town film proceeds by creating a roster of female characters that are types who undergo representative disasters and successes. They move about in representative situations and representative spaces.

If I had to define the essence of the American cinema, or even of American popular culture, I would say that it's a particular kind of movie about small towns, one where a bus pulls into a lonely, deserted, ugly little town and an out-of-work, on-the-make stranger climbs out, ready for anything. This is actually the beginning to such films as *Fallen Angel* (1945) and *Double Deal* (1984), and it is a common situation in the books of Jim Thompson. There's an anything-can-happen air to it, and the "anything" doesn't have to be honest. There's a sense that behind this character lies failure, even disaster, but he's going to try again, bringing all that desperate experience into play in this new situation. The people in the story are all tough, hard. It is set in the true Midwest, by which I mean a place populated with people who are wised up as only people who have always had to invent their own excitement can be.

The small town, both real and imaginary, is a frequent setting for American films of all types, not just women's films. It can be candy-box pretty (*Small Town Girl*, 1953 version), mind-bogglingly stupid (*Cold Turkey*, 1971), hypocritical and sinister (*Kings Row*, 1942), threatened by aliens (*Invasion of the Body Snatchers*, 1956 version), allegedly typical (*Picnic*, 1955), archetypal of American history (*Wait 'Til the Sun Shines, Nellie*, 1952), and many other variations, one of which is its usage as a background setting for a woman's film. I think I know why.

In the town I grew up in, there was an old prizefighter called Snoose Box Jimmy who wandered the streets downtown, dependent on the handouts he was given for coffee and pie, bacon and eggs. Everyone more or less took care of him, and my dad always made sure he had a warm winter coat. The interesting thing about Jimmy was his "snoose boxes," little boxes he pulled out of his pockets to show you, the boxes in which he kept his clippings about his former days of glory as a prizefighter. You had to move fast past him to avoid being trapped to look at the clippings, but everyone in town more or less knew that, once in a while, you had to take your turn with the boxes, reading these clippings. There was one important fact about this: there were no clippings. Jimmy was so old no one knew if there had ever been any, but certainly in my time the boxes were empty. It was understood without it being said that the responsibility of the reader was to open the box, take out an imaginary clipping and read it, and then carefully put it back. The whole town did this regularly, in hot weather and cold, in rain and snow. When the Snoose trapped you, you did your duty as a citizen. You accepted the responsibility of pretense. (I hope this puts "Twin Peaks" in perspective.)

A small town is automatically a world of pretense. Since everyone knows everyone else's business, it becomes the job of the populace to act as if they don't know what is going on instead of its being their job to try to find out. There are roles to play, erratic behavior to absorb, and madness to accept. There's nowhere to hide your crazy aunt, and no way to pretend you have money if you don't. To call your lover up means giving the number to the only telephone operator in town, who naturally knows your voice and whose number it is you're asking for. In a world like this, news is not welcome—there is too much of it available. And in a world like this, women have to be very, very careful. The one pretense no one will take on is that a woman is good if she isn't. Thus, the small town is the perfect setting for the woman's film.

As is true for its counterparts—the department-store movie, the home movie, and the prison movie—the small-town movie provides an overt demonstration of the woman's world, with its right side of the tracks and wrong side of the tracks—that is, a right way to live and a wrong way, a rich way and a poor way, a side that society endorses and a side that it rejects. That demarcation point of energetic American enterprise—the railroad tracks—divides the two worlds. The movie small town is used by the woman's film to make the woman's world a geographic space. The small town *is* society, and its streets, stores, churches, and homes reflect a woman's social, moral, and economic status in perfectly clear visual terms.

Many women's films begin with the actual rejection of the small town and its limits for a woman. The woman's story with its mishaps and adventures is sometimes presented as beginning when the woman has the courage to leave the town, or when a misstep she takes forces her to leave. In particular, the act of leaving voluntarily defines the female character as strong, willing to take her chances, and certainly willing to reconsider the limitations that society is forcing on her. When Lana Turner gets out of a

Joan Crawford's progress from Shantytown . . .

taxi at the railroad station in Emporia, Kansas, at the beginning of *A Life of Her Own* (1950), a powerful visual statement is made. "I won't be back," she tells the station attendant, hoisting up her two huge suitcases with a grim determination. She boards the train and never looks back. Behind her lie a hundred women's pictures about just what Lana Turner's life would have been like if she had stayed in Emporia, Kansas.

My favorite of the "I'm blowing this burg" movie beginnings is in *Possessed* (1931). When Joan Crawford walks home from the box factory on a hot summer night, she can't cross the railroad tracks until the luxury train that is slowly passing moves on. Standing, sweaty and exhausted, she looks in the passing windows and, like a member of the movie audience looking inside the frame of the screen, sees a world unlike her own or any she knows.

Here is one of the most overt visual demonstrations of the small-town woman's situation to be found in movies. Crawford is young and beautiful,

. . . to Clark Gable, in *Possessed*

but she is tired and worn-out from her job. She is inexpensively dressed, and her hairstyle is simple and without adornments. As the train pulls slowly by her before stopping, she has time to look carefully into each window. First, she sees the dining car, with linens and napkins being carefully laid out and large silver pitchers of water with tinkling ice cubes being poured. Just the sight of the water cools the hot and sweaty Crawford, who stands with the ice cream she has purchased melting in her hands. She sees cocktails being shaken in the bar car, and a glamorous couple romantically dancing. The woman wears a slinky gown and the man an elegant tuxedo. As they pass sensuously by, the man bends the woman back to kiss her. Next Crawford sees what it takes to maintain that glamour, that luxury. A maid is ironing satin underwear, and a black man is polishing a pair of shoes. In a private railroad car, two silhouettes portray first a couple kissing in a passionate embrace, and next a woman showering. Every image is one of glamour, luxury, wealth, elegance, and sex. Not crude, quick sex, but a languorous and sensuous enjoyment of everything physical and all that money can buy. As the train creeps slowly to a stop, a tuxedoed young man (Skeets Gallagher) is sitting outside at the back on the observation platform. He is holding an ice bucket with a champagne bottle in it, and two glasses. He sees Crawford's hungry look and, appreciating her beauty, offers her a glass. She takes it and drinks the champagne down. The two begin to talk, and when Gallagher asks her what it is she wants out of life and why, she replies that she wants "me," inadvertently giving the feminist cry of "I want to be me" years before anyone ever thought of it. Crawford is straightforward, brave, honest. She talks to Gallagher boldly, without guile. She is not coy, and she does not pretend to be simperingly virtuous. She is naked in her desire and in her dream to be a part of the life of ease she has just glimpsed. Laughing, Gallagher gives her his card and tells her "if you're ever in the city . . ."

Crawford goes home, where her boyfriend and her mother are awaiting her. An argument breaks out when the boyfriend discovers Crawford is slightly tiddly from drinking the champagne. When he criticizes her, she bursts out, "You don't own me. Nobody does. My life belongs to me." Her mother nervously says, "You frighten me when you talk like that." Crawford fires back, "If I were a man it wouldn't frighten you. You'd think it was right for me to go out and get anything I could out of life and use anything I had to get it. Why should men be so different? All they've got is their brains and they're not afraid to use them. Well, neither am I." Crawford articulates a woman's subversive thoughts, and as you watch film after film from these years, it becomes incredibly striking how often you hear a woman cry out such revolutionary speeches. After the argument, Crawford is next seen arriving in New York, where she will pursue a life *Possessed* by Clark Gable. She latches onto some more champagne and some silk underwear of her own. In a large city, she has some space to break a few rules, at least temporarily.

When a girl from the wrong side of the tracks does *not* leave town, she will always be a girl from the wrong side of the tracks, even when she marries rich or makes her own fortune. If there is any gossip connected to her at all, she will never get free of it, such is the power of social approval in a woman's world. "I've lived in a small town all my life, and I know how these people are," a judge tells the family of a young woman who has given birth under mysterious circumstances in *That Hagen Girl* (1947). The resulting baby grows up to be nothing but "that Hagen girl." Not only will a woman who gives birth illegitimately or under unexplained circumstances never get free of that stigma, but the resulting child, especially if it is a girl, will also never get free. "I'm eighteen, and a failure already," says Mary Hagen (Shirley Temple). "I've never done anything wrong except for being born."

One of the best of the small-town dramas that defines the woman's world and its parameters is *The Walls of Jericho* (1948), set in Jericho, Kansas. The thing about Jericho that makes it so appropriate for the woman's film is that, from any woman's point of view, it is an absolutely great place—because in Jericho the women control everything. They know all, see all, hear all, and they certainly tell all. Not only do they understand everything, they have to explain everything to the men. Whatever happens, one of the women explains it to one of the obtuse men who stand around, not getting it. ("Oh, don't you see, Bruce. The reason her husband is running for senator is because she's in love with *you*, and the best way to get your attention is to have her husband defeat you in the election. I knew this the first minute I ever set eyes on her, you silly goose.") Jericho, Kansas, is the woman's world in spades. In Jericho, the women may not be bank owners or senators or leading citizens (reflecting the status quo outside the movie house), but they have *power* behind the scenes. The women of Jericho are only pretending that men rule the world; the story demonstrates that women are really running everything.

Carrying out the established woman's film pattern in which two opposite women are heroines, *The Walls of Jericho* presents two stars in leading roles, Anne Baxter and Linda Darnell. Everything about them is contrasted. The sympathetic role goes to Baxter, but, significantly, she is neither wife nor mother. She is also not a nurse or a schoolteacher. She is a lawyer. Despite the film's turn-of-the-century setting, she is a woman who not only has a career but who is depicted as being exceptionally good at her work. The film never questions Baxter's right to be a lawyer, and never presents a moment in which she has to be rescued or helped with writing a brief. It is suggested that the reason she has become a lawyer is because her father was a famous barrister, but no qualification is offered regarding her occupation or her right to pursue it. Anne Baxter's character does, of course, fall in love with the married hero. This, too, however, is not presented in a conventional way. She shares his life and his work, becoming his friend and companion rather than his mistress. She never suggests—and he never suggests—that she should give up her career for love. Although she chooses not to conduct what she terms a "back street" affair with him, and although she finally decides to practice law in a nearby town rather than have the agony of being near him, she is liberated in every other way. She knows who she is and what she feels, but she does not see love and career as an either-or situation.

Baxter is presented in the film as the heroine, and thus she is its role

model. She is contrasted with the villainess, played by the beautiful Linda
Darnell. On the surface, Darnell's character is the traditional movie heroine:
lovely, gracious, feminine, and a supportive wife. She is certainly everything women are supposed to be in the fashion-and-glamour department.
Like Baxter, Darnell is presented as intelligent and ambitious, but in her
case, too ambitious. One realizes that this character is meant to be seen
as a woman who, had she been a man, would have been president of the
United States in about five minutes. Instead of pursuing her own career as
Baxter has done, Darnell has pursued the traditional female career of wife
by marrying the town's wealthy newspaper publisher (Kirk Douglas). Since
she feels it's inappropriate to get a career for herself (it is 1908), she sets
about getting the career she wants for her husband. She helps her husband
rise to the top, so that she can enjoy the fruits of success on his arm and
at his expense.

 The Walls of Jericho reverses the usual female pattern. The role model
has a career and does not sacrifice all for love. The bad woman does not
have a career and, in fact, is sacrificing everything for her husband. The
heroine is not domestic, dresses plainly, and eschews glamour. Her opposite
is perfect at everything domestic from flower arranging to menu planning,
and she is astonishingly beautiful and desirable. The lesson for women in
the audience would be completely opposite of the normal one except for
one subtle thing: Darnell is bad, not because she is domestic and beautiful,
but because she takes too much power unto herself. She dominates her
man.

 Darnell at first is attracted to Cornel Wilde, but seeing that he is
saddled with an alcoholic wife (Ann Dvorak) and understanding that his
honesty will always slow him down, she sets about breaking up her husband's friendship with him. Then she persuades her husband to run for
public office, and Douglas wins a job that most feel should have gone to
Wilde. To get her doltish husband to run and to win, Darnell lies, cheats,
and manipulates. She does whatever she has to do, including shining up
to the women of Jericho. The movie presents a portrait of how a woman
can make her man succeed. Darnell dresses well, better than anybody,
but she always compliments other women on their clothes, asking where
they bought their frumpy outfits and pretending that she, too, wants to shop
there. She gives great parties, inviting all the right people, but she also
invites all the wrong people, because Jericho is a small town and every
vote counts. Darnell's rise to success is visualized through a series of social
events she plans and executes with consummate hostess skills: card parties,
picnics, teas, dinners, dances, always with Darnell graciously moving
among the guests, skillfully and shrewdly introducing each key person to
the other key person, always covering for her husband and putting him

forward. She flirts when she has to and kowtows when she has to. She is planning her husband's (make that her own) climb toward Washington, knowing that if she does her job well, she'll be out of Jericho forever. This is her ultimate goal.

It is not her way of life that is wrong, but her way of doing it. She is a bad woman because she wields power over others. Baxter, on the other hand, may be a career woman, but she uses what power she has in the service of others, particularly in the service of the man she loves. She saves his life. Thus, her being a lawyer is the right thing, not because it is her career but because it serves the woman's true career, that of love.

The men in *The Walls of Jericho* are typical woman's picture men. That is to say, they are like the women in certain male action pictures: they seem to matter, yet they are mostly window dressing. Everybody *says* how important they are, and how they know things, but there's no real evidence for this. It is the women who understand nuance, who know how to read a gesture, an event, an outfit. They know how to interpret inner feelings, and they can see right through each other. They know there's danger from men and that the primary concerns they must deal with are love, sex, food, clothes, money, and correct society. Politics, which is also what this film is about, is allegedly the world of men, and not women's province. Yet the women are controlling the politics, too, because politics is just love, sex, food, clothes, money, and correct society in a different form.

As is true in *Picnic*, the women in *The Walls of Jericho* become representative of various issues in the woman's film, following the micro-cosmic, sociological pattern of the woman's version of the small-town film. Trading sex and beauty for economic security was the underlying motif of *Picnic*; in *The Walls of Jericho*, the basic concern is larger. What is a woman's appropriate role in life? Whether or not she has a career or marries, she must behave in a suitable way. Darnell and Baxter represent these choices and this behavior-modification program.

The other women in Jericho illustrate women's problems and the suitable and unsuitable solutions open to them:

- Ann Dvorak, as Cornel Wilde's alcoholic wife, has a desperate urge to be accepted socially, to be important in Jericho. She aspires to be like Darnell. This aspiration, coupled with her substance abuse and the fact that she is a liability to Wilde in his career growth, make her "bad." She is villainous because she wants the wrong things out of life, because she does not sacrifice herself enough for her man, be-cause she drinks, and because she shoots at her husband. On the other hand, Dvorak, partly due to her excellent performance, presents

the woman sympathetically, in that viewers are asked to see how sad
all this is. In particular, Dvorak's desire for social acceptance is seen
as tragic yet completely understandable.

- Dvorak's shrewish mother, bossy and calculating. We learn that it is
  she who trapped Wilde into marrying her daughter when he arrived
  in town, lonely and inexperienced sexually, to live in their boarding-
  house. Everyone in town knows that the gullible young man was taken
  in and that the mother was prepared to let anything happen between
  him and her daughter in order to achieve what she felt was a highly
  advantageous marriage.
- A "typical" wife and mother, respected in the town because she does
  exactly what is expected of the perfect woman. However, this idea is
  undercut later in the film when it turns out that she and her husband
  are not actually legally married.
- A young girl threatened by rape, who is emotionally destroyed by the
  experience.

These women offer representative sets of solutions to women's problems with men: trick them, shoot them, pretend to marry them, escape
them by drinking or by going insane. They also provide plot developments
that form a background of women's issues, subplots introduced and resolved
through secondary characters. In addition, there is a great mob of townswomen, a Greek chorus of gabbling, gossiping women who provide color,
comment, humor, and a never-ending flow of verbal observations about
what is really going on around Jericho. (It is the women who know!)

AS HAS BEEN SUGGESTED, the small town exists to physicalize the
woman's social context. The house exists to physicalize her personal world,
her inner self, her private situation, and her deepest needs and desires.
This raises the inevitable question: What does a woman want? One can't
really write about the woman's film without at least mentioning this famous,
if thickheaded, question from a masculine source. More than one movie
shows a man puzzling over this issue. "Women want power, don't they?"
Edward G. Robinson asks Genevieve Tobin in *I Loved a Woman* (1933).
She sagely answers, "Why do you think all women want the same thing?"
This puzzles Robinson so completely that all he can think of doing is
volunteering to endow a university for women in her name. In fact, what
Robinson's character has done throughout the film is mistake his own desire
for power for hers. He explains to Tobin that he wants other women to envy
her power, by which he means the power he bestows on her by making her
a rich man's wife. He asks her point-blank why she doesn't enjoy lording

it over other women with her ability to buy anything she wants. This dismal insight that actually reveals why men want power ultimately drives Tobin out the door. After tucking him into bed one night, she says, "I'm leaving you tomorrow," and sails out the door. She has power of her own, it seems.

Films provide other answers to the question of "What do women want?" "I want things!" cries out Peggy Cummins in *Gun Crazy* (1949), by way of explaining why she and her beloved should embark on a life of crime together. "I want things . . . *big* things!" She utters the battle cry of movie females, the anguished bleat for money, sex, freedom, clothes. *Give me things.* A man's gotta do what a man's gotta do, say movies, but a gal's gotta have what a gal's gotta have, and what a gal's gotta have is things.

When women don't have the things they want, they become unhappy, suicidal, even murderous. "This dime-store china," complains Sheila Bromley to Ronald Reagan in *Accidents Will Happen* (1939), "it's making an old woman out of me." She's unhappy as Reagan's wife because he doesn't earn enough money, and he's never home. He doesn't get ahead. He doesn't buy her things. Bromley, of course, is presented in this particular film as being utterly selfish and evil. She sits home, reading magazines and eating a box of chocolates. In the movies, a woman who sits around with a magazine and a box of chocolates is up to no good. Why isn't she dusting or baking biscuits? Why isn't she Hoovering industriously around the floors or ironing her man's shirts? If she has to eat, let her have a sensible tuna-fish sandwich. Chocolates are decadent; they mean trouble, and so it happens. Bromley gets into trouble because if her husband isn't going to buy her things, she decides she will go out and earn her own money to buy them, even if the way she does it is dishonest. She is clever and can cover up. ("I admire clever women," says the villain. "One sees so few of them.")

From a modern perspective, a viewer sees clearly that Bromley has nothing to do with herself. Her complaints come from the boredom of having to sit home alone day and night while her husband works for long hours for low pay, never advancing himself. She makes this sacrifice for nothing. He can't make enough money to buy her things. Furthermore, it's perfectly obvious that if she had a career of her own, given her brains and ambition, she could easily afford the things she wants.

Things satisfy a woman's needs, but she has to have a place to put them. It's also true that all the things in the world cannot save a woman from society's scorn. Things are things, but respectability is everything, and respectability is measured by one important place, the thing that a woman in a woman's film puts above all else. That place is the house, the single most important movie space that defines the woman's world.

"I want the house," says Hazel Brooks in *Sleep, My Love*, a 1948 melodrama. She has been offered an impressive substitute, a dazzling diamond bracelet that looks to be worth about a cool quarter of a million. Brooks's sleazy lover, played by Don Ameche, is trying to humor her until he can carry out their agreed-upon scheme by which he will drive his superwealthy wife, Claudette Colbert, to kill herself so that they can inherit everything and live very, very well ever after. These two conspirators meet in a dark and dingy dive, and Ameche presents Brooks with the bracelet in a desperate attempt to placate her. Slowly she turns the bracelet over and over on her wrist. She assesses it. It sparkles and winks. She thinks about it. It speaks of glamour and wealth. It's not bad, not bad at all, but . . . "I want the house." She knows true woman's film value. And that's final.

"I want the house" is such a common sentiment in films about women that it is used in a dramatically contrary way to illustrate what a different kind of woman the leading lady is in *H. M. Pulham, Esq.* (1941), based on John P. Marquand's best-selling novel. Hedy Lamarr plays the glamorous and beautiful Marvin Myles, another in a series of 1940s heroines who have masculine names. She is definitely a liberated woman, and as such is both the romantic ideal the hero loves *and* the woman who is wrong, wrong, wrong for him. She has her own apartment, drinks cocktails, and puts makeup on in public, three things that good women presumably do not do. Lamarr knows what she wants out of life: a butler, riches, things, but also the right to work for her own living. Without that, she says, she would "shrink." "There would be nothing left of me."

Of course, in watching hundreds of old movies, one becomes familiar with the female character who wants independence until she falls in love and changes her mind. One inevitably waits for Marvin Myles to change her mind or for the hero to make her see how wrong she is. In *H. M. Pulham*, that moment never comes. When Marvin firmly explains that she was not made to be at sewing circles or out buying drapes, Pulham (Robert Young) tells her, "You're wrong, because you'll have a home of your own someday." Marvin literally yells out, "*I don't just want a house!*"

This brands her a truly subversive heroine, and one who is not destined to be with the man at the final clinch. Marvin explains clearly to Pulham that if there is to be a house, she will buy it herself. She feels she is defined by her work and her independent world. If she marries him and goes to his world, she will be without status of her own; her only status will be *his* status. In the end, they do not marry, and she goes on to get her butler, her riches, her yacht, and even a husband whom she later divorces. She has her success and her money, and although she doesn't look particularly happy, the film doesn't take it away from her. She didn't want the house, which meant she was rejecting the woman's world.

"The house" is a dominant American idea. Americans are promised that each and every one of them can own his or her own home, and homeownership and pride are important parts of the American popular culture. Movies draw on this, placing ordinary small-town families like the Hardys in homes that can only seem palatial by most people's standards. The house, for instance, is a gift his grateful fellow citizens make to Sergeant York for the excellent job he did capturing hordes of Germans in World War I. This was a real fact, and the movie *Sergeant York* (1941), starring Gary Cooper in the title role, makes its finale out of this fact. Gulping and speechless, York is led to a little meadow with a stream in which sits a perfect little home where he and his bride, Joan Leslie, will reside, tax free, mortgage free, forever and ever, till death do them part. The house is York's reward, and the audience's goal.

In the woman's film, the house frequently becomes a character. It is always a metaphor. It represents who the woman is, both as a physical representation of her inner turmoils and a reflection of where she stands on the social scale. It is the space the woman is allowed, her place to dominate. Without it she is powerless, and with it she has a power base of her own. In *Guest in the House* (a 1944 film noir), Anne Baxter, in a forerunner of her portrait of Eve Harrington in *All About Eve* (1950), arrives to do damage to the happiness of the marriage of Ruth Warrick and Ralph Bellamy. Baxter wants the house, which represents stability, love, security, acceptance. Although Bellamy's younger brother, a doctor played by Scott McKay, loves her and wants to marry her, he can't offer Baxter the house, so she sets about telling lies, manipulating men's desires and women's jealousies, and just generally wrecking things. (This problem is solved by an old aunt, Aline MacMahon, who, discovering Baxter's fear of birds, drives her *outside* the house and toward a migrant flock. Baxter conveniently falls over a cliff.)

The house is so important a space in the woman's film world that it is actually a character in *Enchantment, The Enchanted Cottage, Rebecca, Secret Beyond the Door*, and many others. *Enchantment* (1948) is the story of sweet young lovers whose affair is short-circuited by a jealous sister who fears she will lose control of the family mansion if her brother marries. *The Enchanted Cottage* (1945) places a blind man and an unattractive woman in a special world of their own, the cottage of the title, in which they are able to believe themselves and each other to be beautiful. Manderley, the mansion of *Rebecca* (1940), represents not only the dreaded first wife of Laurence Olivier, but also the evil she brought into his life. *Secret Beyond the Door* (1948) uses a house to represent the troubled past of the family into which a woman marries. When the house is burned down, the bride and her groom are freed from the family curse.

Craig's Wife (1936) and *Harriet Craig* (1950) are the original and the remake of a story that illustrates just how much a woman wants a house and what it means to her. In both films, the perfectly kept and ordered house represents the mental state of its heroine, the frightened and repressed Harriet Craig. The perfection of the furniture, the cleanliness of the rooms, and the fact that there is no indication that living, breathing, messy human beings live in this domicile, explain to the viewer both the bad and the good side of Harriet. She *is* her house. The first version, starring Rosalind Russell, was directed by a woman, Dorothy Arzner, but the original material was a play written by a man. Both films tell the story of Harriet Craig, a perfectionist wife, a housewife to end all housewives. In the 1936 version, Harriet boldly states her philosophy of marriage to a young girl (who is properly horrified): "Has it ever occurred to you that love . . . is a liability in marriage? I saw to it that my marriage was a way to emancipation for me. I had no private fortune, no special training. The one road to independence for me was through the man I married to be independent." This attitude, one that many women in the audience in the 1930s might have pursued, is presented as not only wrong, but terrible.

Harriet Craig's character is a treatise on what happens to women when they don't marry for love, but also a solid subversive explanation of why they might not choose to do so. Harriet explains that she believes that having money, even if it is her husband's, gives a woman a certain kind of freedom, whereas marrying for love keeps her enslaved. "Marriage is a practical matter," says Harriet. "A man wants a wife and a home, and a woman wants security." Harriet believes that her only security lies in a good marriage, one that provides things, and that to preserve her marriage she must keep her husband under control.

Controlling her husband, and thus her life, is physicalized by the control she wields over her house. Her fears, which are the same as her strengths, are shaped into a three-layered battle plan for survival:

1. Control the husband by checking up on what he is doing and keeping him from being out and around on his own. Do not let him meet another woman, especially the kindly widow next door, who might give him love and thus take him, your meal ticket, away from you.
2. Control the house; keep it spotlessly clean and in perfect working order, with all meals on time and everything in its place.
3. Control what the neighbors and friends know, and never let them find out the truth about anything in your life.

Hypocrisy is not just Harriet's style, it is a set of clearly thought-out rules by which she lives. "No woman dares to be honest," says Harriet. "She has to think of herself. Who else is going to protect her? I wouldn't trust the love of any man after the things I've seen." She believes that if her house looks nice to visitors, they will believe that her marriage is nice. She believes that if her house is nice for her husband, the marriage will be nice. If she looks nice, he'll think she *is* nice, and so on. The house, the visual space of her woman's world, is the key to everything in Harriet's mind and in her world. "What else does a woman have but her home?" she asks. "I saw what happened to my own mother . . . she died of a broken heart." What had happened to her own mother was that her father had mortgaged their family home in order to give the money to a younger woman. The lesson was not lost on little Harriet, and she'll give her husband the sex he needs in the way he needs it and when he needs it, but she will not allow herself to love him or lose control of him.

Ultimately he rebels. "You set yourself up to control the very destiny of a man," he shouts. "The presumption of you!" In order to show her and put her in her place, he commits two acts, both ludicrous but sadly meaningful in woman's film terms. He breaks her favorite flower vase and smokes in her living room. It would be totally silly if it weren't exactly the way to hurt poor Harriet. His final put-down is "You married a house. I'll see that you'll have it."

At the end of the film, Harriet Craig is left alone in her house, and on the screen appears an ominous title card: "People who live to themselves . . . are generally left to themselves." Let *that* be an appropriate warning to all the women in the audience. And yet, with true contradiction, how many women out there would have been happy enough to have been left to themselves in a substantial house when they got home from the movies? How many thought that what Harriet said made sense? Her subversive words may well have been the voice of many women's true feelings.

The 1950 remake, *Harriet Craig*, stars Joan Crawford. Although it follows the basic plot line of the first version, its emphasis is slightly different. It is even more focused on the house than the first version, and Harriet is played entirely without sympathy. The film is almost a horror picture.

Harriet is still allowed part of her speech about a woman's needing to marry for security, but it is presented as totally unsympathetic. Where Russell was allowed to make the character of Harriet Craig tragically wrongheaded, Crawford is directed to play her as willfully domineering. Russell manipulates her husband in many more ways than Crawford does, and yet there is a sense that she is a person whom audience members should feel is wrong but sad. Crawford's manipulations are linked more directly to her own presence on-screen as a masculine and powerful-looking woman. Russell plays a weak and insecure woman trying to strengthen herself in a man's world, trying to define and preserve her territory, which can only be the house. Crawford is presented as a strong, domineering woman who is trying to take over her man's world, which is represented by the house.

In the 1930s version, Russell's desire for the house is very definitely portrayed as the woman's need to have a place she could not get if she did not marry well. The stated theme—"what else does a woman have but her home?"—is the basic issue. In the 1950s version, times have clearly changed for the viewing audience. Since women had worked during the years of World War II and discovered their own earning abilities, and since homeownership was being touted for everyone in ways that had never existed for the average American family before, the idea that Crawford could not get a home any other way than by marrying it seemed weak. Crawford's desire to have her home perfect is defined as her need to have everything her own way. She is a control freak. She is also a cold woman because "that's how she is," rather than because she fears loss of status or economic security.

Whatever sympathy for the woman's world that the earlier *Craig's Wife* contains might have been generated by its woman director.* Dorothy Arzner was not overtly a feminist, although she did live an unconventional life in terms of her attitudes toward marriage, men, and motherhood. In her movies, she often seemed to present a sense of how hard it was for a female character to sort out the various pressures of her life as a woman. Although Arzner did not suggest an unconventional solution to these problems, other than perhaps suicide or the flaunting of small social conventions, she did at least stress that there *were* problems for women. Whenever she portrayed women lashing out at restrictions, her films had believable emotion.

Another excellent woman's film that clearly depicts the house as representing the main woman character is *The House on 56th Street* (1933), starring Kay Francis. Francis plays a young woman who begins her life on the outside of polite society. She has never had a home of her own, having been raised as an itinerant by her father, a well-known riverboat gambler. (She herself is a skilled card shark.) After her father's death, she becomes a chorus girl in the 1905 Follies, a logical way for her to make her living. The first significant event of her independent life is her need to make her first real woman's film choice. She has two suitors, both wealthy. However,

---

* Many people believe that Dorothy Arzner, director of such films as Hepburn's *Christopher Strong* (1933) among others, was the only woman director in Hollywood. Anthony Slide, a superb film historian, first attempted to set this record straight in an excellent article in *Films in Review* in April of 1976. Slide discusses many women directors, including novelist Elinor Glyn, Jacqueline Logan, Mary Field, Leontine Sagan (who was invited to Hollywood, but never did a feature there), Grace Elliott, Flora LaBreton, Wanda Tuchock, and others. Most people today are aware of Ida Lupino's work, as well as the fact that Lillian Gish was active in this capacity during silent days.

one is young, and one is old. Which should she choose? Her chorus girl
pals offer advice. Some make the practical suggestion that Francis should
string them both along. Others advise her to stick with the older one because
he will be true security, while the younger one will play with her for a year
or two and then marry someone from his own class. Francis, a young woman
of verve, sparkle, and good nature, just laughs and tells her own fortune
with the cards, letting the outcome determine her choice. She goes with
the older man (John Holliday).

Soon, however, the younger man (Gene Raymond) claims her, taking
her riding in a hansom cab and proposing to her. He truly loves her, and
since she has always truly loved him, they agree to wed. Being an honorable
movie woman, Francis explains to her older suitor that she always loved
Raymond but never believed she would receive anything from him other
than a proposition, not a proposal. Although the implication is clear that
she is Holliday's mistress, he graciously releases her, though not without
warning Francis that Raymond's family will never accept her. She will be
hurt, he warns her, adding that she's really swell and had he himself been
the marrying kind, he most certainly would have wed her.

After a mean little marriage ceremony and a luxurious trip to Europe,
where Raymond takes Francis away from the gambling tables, the two
return home to New York City and the central metaphor of the film: the
house on Fifty-sixth Street. From this moment on, Francis is identified
totally with the house, a beautiful mansion Raymond has had built for her
in their absence. The bestowing of the house upon her as a lavish gift
represents his true love for her and his desire to elevate her to full respectability in life. Her moving into it represents her full acceptance of
his love and of her role in life as a proper wife. They beam joyously at
each other as they stand in the nursery, which, as he puts it, "I had added
to the plans as soon as you told me."

In occupying the house on Fifty-sixth Street and giving birth to a
daughter they name for Raymond's mother, Francis becomes her other self:
a respectable matron. Her card-sharking, chorus-girl days are over. Furthermore, this good behavior, in particular the birth of the female child,
has reconciled Raymond's mother to Francis as her son's wife. The two
women become fast friends, and Francis briefly is seen at the center of
New York polite society. "You're a fabulous hostess," says Raymond's mom
to Francis. "I was wrong about you." "Thank you," says Kay.

Because this is a woman's film, however, tragedy strikes as Francis's
former sins come back to haunt her. Her older lover returns, now regretting
that he never married her. He begs her to visit him, for old times' sake,
but when she arrives he tries to make love to her. After her refusal, he
tries to shoot himself, and their ensuing struggle over the gun ends with

him dead and Francis standing bewildered with the weapon in her hand, just as an old servant opens the door to witness her supposed guilt.

Francis now loses her house on Fifty-sixth Street, the house becoming the metaphor for where she stands in society, as well as for how she feels inside. No longer respected wife and devoted mother, she has to leave the house and go to that other woman's world, the prison. Since she has been sentenced to twenty years, she nobly sacrifices herself, telling her husband (who has stood by her) to forget about her and let her disappear, because he has their daughter to raise. Although he believes her to be innocent, Raymond agrees, and Francis tells him that it is best to let the child believe she is dead.

Francis serves her twenty years. Her new house is her prison cell. She sits glumly, looking old and miserable, playing cards day after day as one of those movie montages of newspaper headlines announcing the big events of history flashes by: War, the Armistice, Prohibition, and so on. Raymond is killed in World War I, the war that takes all husbands of that period's leading ladies, and suddenly it is 1925 and Francis is once again out on the street. The old family lawyer tells her that Raymond's mother, now dead, left her five thousand dollars with which to start a new life. She is to go away and never see her daughter, who does indeed believe she is dead. Francis, having entered prison when there were horse-drawn carriages in the streets, stands overwhelmed while automobiles and streetcars rush past her.

What does she do? This is a woman's film, so she takes her money and goes to a beauty shop, saying, "Make me a new woman." Having entered looking old and tired, she emerges as sleek, chic Kay Francis in 1920s fashions and immediately sails for Europe. On shipboard, she meets a card shark (Ricardo Cortez) who tries to fleece her, believing her to be a rich woman. Instead, she fleeces him, and they become a notorious international team of con artists that works all over Europe.

Eventually they return to New York to work in a big gambling house that has just opened. The owners are very eager to have Cortez and Francis, particularly Francis, because there has never been a female blackjack dealer in Manhattan. When she goes to visit the casino, she is amazed to see that it is located in the house on Fifty-sixth Street! Furthermore, her own private gambling room will be in her daughter's former nursery. Francis has come full circle in the woman's film, with the house representing her internal self all the way.

The story concludes with an episode of sacrifice. Francis's daughter (played by Margaret Lindsay) has a gambling addiction that her husband doesn't know about. Francis rescues her by killing Cortez, who is going to tell Lindsay's husband. Francis then puts Lindsay and her husband on a boat to Europe, the daughter having learned her lesson. The crime bosses of the casino dump Cortez's body for Francis in return for her promise to spend the rest of her life working for them in the gambling house. Ironically remembering how she told Raymond when they happily moved in together that she would "stay in that house forever, living the rest of my life there," Francis realizes that now this will really happen and that the house on Fifty-sixth Street is the only place she really belongs.

The house on Fifty-sixth Street is at first Kay Francis's dream, then her nightmare and trap, and then her solace. It represents every step of her career in terms of society's approval. At first, when she has no status, the house does not exist. It is built to accommodate her correct life as wife and mother, and it is taken from her when she breaks with the rules of those responsibilities. After she is tarnished and comes out of jail, it has become a gambling house, losing its own status in polite society. It is a place where she can work, but the work is not legal, not acceptable. In the end, the house is both halves of Francis's life, the place of happy memories of her once-respectable and loving world, and the trap that holds her outside society as punishment for her sins. The movie itself is a composite of typical women's film plots: chorus girl who marries rich; sacrificial mother; prison drama; domestic romance; shipboard glamour; and so on. The house is her woman's world.

THE WORLD OF WOMEN and its frightening limitations are brilliantly illustrated by *The Reckless Moment* (1949). A woman with limited experience, limited mobility, and limited economic flexibility is forced to cope with a serious family crisis during the absence of her experienced, mobile, and moneyed husband. He is off in Germany, doing what men do, which is "their work." She is at home with her wayward daughter, her black maid, and two useless men: her adolescent son (not yet really a man) and her father-in-law (past his prime as a man, which is proved by his living in his son's house).

The Reckless Moment presents the basic woman's world. A decent woman is living in a world of rigid boundaries and rules, with all her options defined by the presence or absence of her husband. If she needs money, he gives it to her. If she has a problem, he solves it for her. And yet— and this is the plot of *The Reckless Moment* and the source of its horror— when the crisis comes in her daughter's life, Mom can't tell her husband about it. The young girl (Geraldine Brooks) has become involved in a romance with a sleazy older man who dies accidentally in the family boat house. The girl is hysterical, and the mother (Joan Bennett) has to cope alone. One reason is that her husband is in Germany, but another, more significant reason is that her daughter, being a female, also lives in the woman's limited world. In order to keep her daughter's name unblemished, and in order to allow her daughter ultimately to take her rightful place in polite society as wife and mother, Bennett knows she's got to hush up the scandal. No one must find out, and that includes Daddy, son, and father-in-law, the men in the situation.

Bennett sets out to do what she can. Driving a small motorboat out in the wee hours of the morning, smartly dressed in coat, scarf, and dark glasses, she dumps the dead body in the ocean. However, the sleazy lover's former "associates" begin to blackmail her, and she is told she must raise five thousand dollars to pay them off and purchase her daughter's letters, which tie her to the death.

The blackmail triggers an extended sequence in which Bennett finds out just how helpless she is in her woman's world. As her husband's wife, she has no money of her own, and no access to any significant money. At first she makes feeble plans to curb household expenses. "Turn those lights off!" She sits at her little French desk, tragically making plans to return her new suit to the store and cut the food budget. She is doing the only financial planning the well-dressed middle-class wife can understand, which is the only kind she ever is allowed to do. She cuts the food budget, her form of the old cookie jar.

Since this obviously won't do the trick, she moves out into the larger world to see what she can do. A visit to the family's safe-deposit box turns up some jewelry and a few bonds, but she needs her husband's signature to cash in the letter. She goes into the city and tries to take out a quickie loan in one of those no-questions-asked establishments. She quickly finds out that, even here, questions *are* asked. She sits nervously, her mink coat partly open, her delicate hands twisting, while a tough and wised-up older woman gently takes her through some key questions of the sort that Bennett has obviously never been asked in her entire life. As the loan officer begins to realize that Bennett has no job, no money of her own, no collateral, and no permission forms from her husband, she sighs and slowly tears up the application form. This is the woman's world, all right. Bennett ends up pawning a few pieces of jewelry that her husband gave her, although she has to accept much less than they're worth. This journey into town, with its visit to the loan establishment and the pawnshop, is presented as a proper woman's descent into economic hell. She is seen walking, clad in her mink, through the seedy streets of a low-class neighborhood, confused and frightened, helpless outside her own home with its safe parameters.

Bennett's natural world is depicted for viewers as being that of her charming little house by the ocean in Balboa. This house initially looks like a perfect upper-middle-class place. It's cozy, all right, but it's also almost posh in its furnishings. It's right beside the ocean, and has plenty of space for the entire family. It has comfy chairs, thriving plants, family photos on tables, artwork on the walls, and little nooks in which to sit and read or have a tasty snack. It is well staffed by the reliable black maid. As the film unfolds, however, this house begins to look less and less like a dream haven and more and more like a trap. Instead of appearing as a place where people relax and unwind, it increasingly is presented as a bastion of repression, carefully maintained as a fortress against sex, violence, and the underworld, but also, as it turns out, against honest conversation, bad manners, and shirtlessness. The reevaluation of the house from cozy nook to ominous trap is a physical demonstration of how viewers have to resee Joan Bennett, who is defined by the house. At first she seems to have it all—a loving family, freedom, a fur coat, and good looks. She seems sensible and reliable. But as the story progresses, one can sense the desperation she holds inside. Just as dark shadows fall over the cozy corners of her house, the noirish elements of her daily life suddenly emerge. Although she is sympathetic in many ways, there are other aspects to her. Bennett's constant and often-repeated remarks to her son to "put your shirt on" or "roll down those pants" or "put your shoes on" are ominous. This concern with conventional appearances sheds a different light on her attempt to cover up things for her daughter. Instead of being just a loving and self-sacrificing mother, she begins to look additionally like a frightened and repressed woman. Her constant tidying up of her world, picking up magazines and straightening pillows, is seen as a direct parallel to her "tidying up" the beach where the dead man has fallen, his body pierced with an old rusty anchor. Whether at home or on the beach, she sweeps guilty evidence off the surface. It is the pattern of her life: take away anything that's not nice; don't mention anything inappropriate.

The family members all seem cheerful and lovingly supportive. As the film proceeds, they seem also to be self-involved, unaware of one another as people with real problems. Bennett mentions more than once that she cannot possibly get away from her family, because she will have to *explain* to them where she is going. She has no freedom of any sort.

The house itself provides no real sanctuary. Everyone knows where everyone else is in it, and it's difficult to find a private place to talk. Spaces are delineated by staircases, doorways, room dividers, and windows. The house seems sliced apart, with areas separated from each other, a metaphor for family relationships. No one in the family seems actually to look at anyone else, and when occasionally they do look at each other, they don't seem to see anything significant. Although a few token "is everything all right?" questions are asked of Bennett, no one seems to realize just how much stress she is really under. No one, that is, except her maid. This character is often seen through windows or room dividers, saying nothing but obviously watching carefully and really seeing what is going on. Her worried face, catching all nuances and responding to mysterious visitors and Bennett's many tensions, is often framed in the corner of the screen. There is a kind of "no one can see what the woman's world is except another woman" aspect to this.

A parallel is pointedly drawn in the movie between the mistress of the home, Joan Bennett, wife and mother, and her black maid, a woman who takes orders from the white people for whom she works. In a sense, she is owned by them, but Bennett is also owned, as we learn, by her family and her husband. Both women are economically dependent, without personal means with which to escape. The two women are actually equals in society, and we see this poignantly at the end of the film when the black woman, understanding trouble and willing to help, goes out with her employer to try to solve the problem in an act of sisterhood.

Bennett is the long-range victim of the sort of romantic dreams that films provide for female viewers. ("No one would ever fall in love if they hadn't heard about it.") She has followed the rules and gotten nowhere. She is saved, ironically, by the involvement of a man—played by James Mason, an underworld figure who is *also* a victim of romantic ideals. To him, she is a mother fighting for her child. He respects this, remarking how lucky the daughter is to have a mother. "Everyone has a mother" is her ironic reply.

Since the story is about repression, the film draws a perfect dividing line between the above-the-line world of polite society, the middle-class world of her household, and the below-the-line world of blackmail and death that her daughter falls into, a world represented spatially by the family boat house, a seedy bar in an even seedier hotel, and the pawnshop. In particular, the family boat house becomes a second home, representing another aspect of their lives. It is dark, poorly lit, off to the side and behind the main house. At night, a light sways outside its main door, swinging ominously as a kind of visual warning to polite people not to enter there. This boat house becomes the setting where two desperate women struggle to maintain the family respectability, to hide their crimes and shame before they can be found out. Both of these struggles end in death, and both of these deaths are covered up or lied about. The first is the accidental death of the daughter's lover, and the second struggle precipitates two deaths. First, James Mason kills the blackmailer who threatens Bennett's world, taking his body away in an automobile. Since Mason himself has been wounded in the struggle, his car runs off the road. Before he dies, he confesses to both earlier deaths, so that Bennett's family can be exonerated from guilt or from fear of detection. Three people die, but the truth never comes out. The boat house is the scene of death *and* deception, the other home that underlies or parallels that of the cozy little nest beside the ocean in Balboa. Thus, Bennett's two houses reflect her life, her internal state, and her family world: the surface house, correct in its perfection, polite in its manners and attitudes, and the undersoul or truth to their lives, the boat house, a scene of assignation and murder.

During the events of the movie, Bennett talks to her husband in Germany three times on the phone, but she never tells him what is going on. She acts as if everything is fine. Once she starts hesitantly to write the truth to him in a letter, and once she starts to say something to him on the phone, but in both instances she catches herself in time. A viewer might expect this man to suddenly arrive home to help her out, to punch out the villains and rescue his daughter, set things straight in the nick of time. But this does not happen. In fact, the husband *never* appears. The final scene does not show him arriving home, with order restored. He just telephones again, and his wife once again reassures him that all is well, saying that they are going to have a wonderful, wonderful Christmas. This is the woman's world. Although Bennett is married and has the responsi- bilities of motherhood, there is actually no man in her life; he's just an unheard voice on the other end of the telephone line, the modern man. Perhaps this is the consummate presentation of the woman's world. The woman is alone inside herself, despite family, despite friends, despite husband. One way or another, the spaces all close down around her.

On its surface level, *The Reckless Moment* might be seen as a story of mother love, in which a respectable woman survives a threat to her middle-class world. Everything about the film, however, introduces the subtext that has been described here, in which a subversive message is being sent. The woman's world is a trap, a place with rigid borders. In her lovely home, Joan Bennett suffers intense psychological distress, and no one notices it except her maid.

A viewer comes to understand that in the woman's life, it doesn't matter whether she's in a prison or working in a department store, or whether she lives in a small town or in her own mansion. She's in the same place, and that place is the woman's world, which is any place the leading woman of a movie inhabits. The curious contradiction of the woman's film, with its empowerment of the female person, dictates the possibility that a place commonly associated with men can suddenly, within the context of the movie itself, be shifted into feminine territory.

Such a shift is illustrated by the opening of the 1932 movie *Shopworn*. After the credits roll, the movie begins in a place that at first seems as if it could not possibly be the setting for a woman's film. If one did not know the movie's title, or that its star was Barbara Stanwyck, one would assume that the audience was about to see a typical movie about the world of working men. Screen time is devoted to a visualization of a group of macho construction workers setting up a dynamite blast. No women are in sight. Heavy equipment, work boots, hard hats, and male camaraderie define the film's universe. The activity of the male workers culminates in a gigantic blast of dynamite, shattering an entire mountainside into a million highly impressive pieces that rain down dramatically across the frame. What more specific situation could there be to set up a film about men doing what they do in their male world?

However, the viewer quickly learns in a sudden shift of perspective that this is *not* the male world, but rather the male world from the female point of view. The men have been having fun blasting the world to bits because that is what men do, but unfortunately they have bungled it. They have blasted the mountain to pieces, but they have accidentally also blasted one of their own workers to death. This man turns out to be the father of motherless Stanwyck. He was her only support and protection in an unsympathetic world, and now he is dead. The film demonstrates clearly how women are left outside of the action, outside of the workaday world, and also outside of the control of their own fates. Men blow things up, and that includes women's security. The opening of *Shopworn*, which truly *is* a woman's film, accurately sets up the woman's world. Women depend on men, and men can't be relied on. As a result, the physical space of the woman's universe, her entire world, can vanish in a minute, usually due to the incompetence, intemperance, or indifference of men.

As Stanwyck's father lies dying, he presents her with her only legacy, his lame and belated advice as to how a beautiful young woman should cope in a man's world: "I have nothing to leave you, Kitty, except maybe a little advice. You're going to find this a tough world, Kitty. Be tough yourself. Then they can't hurt you. Not if you learn to take 'em. Go to your aunt Dot's. Too many men around here. You're grown now. Don't forget. Go to my sister."

Is it any surprise that, after the men blow up the world, Stanwyck goes to the small town her aunt lives in and, within minutes after her arrival, is incarcerated inside a prison? No surprise at all. She lives in a woman's world.

MEN

WITH THE NOTABLE EXCEPTION of the Three Stooges—who cry out
to their fat girlfriends, "Let's go places and eat things!"—men in the movies,
as in life, seem not to know what women want. At the same time, women
in movies *always* seem to know what men want, but they don't agree with
them about it. If movie male and movie female had to go hand in hand
into the ark in the great two-by-two parade, the species would be dead.
From Buster Keaton repressing his urge to strangle his beloved to Cary
Grant's reluctant acceptance of the search for Hepburn's leopard, the movie
screen has been a landscape for the battle of the sexes. As an old man in
Valley of the Sun (1942) advises a young one, "There's only two ways to
handle women . . . and nobody knows what they are."

In the woman's film, this conflict takes on epic proportions. When
we talk of male and female relationships in the woman's genre, we are not
only talking about the romantic ideal of boy meets girl, we are also talking
about woman confronts man. Those sweet romances in which wholesome
love develops, becomes threatened, but is finally restored in the classic
"boy finally gets girl, and this is right for the girl" almost always reinforce
the idea that a woman's best choice in life is love. This will be her basic
career. These movies are an important part of the woman's image on film,
but it is when attention is turned onto men, marriage, and motherhood—
the big three of the women's picture—that the woman's situation comes
into sharp focus. In these movies woman confronts man, and the result is,
to say the least, discouraging. These films, even if comedies, reveal the
true dark and disturbing state of things. And—even more significant—it
is these movies, which are focused on the woman's three most likely concerns in life, that are the ones in which the most covert messages of
unconscious liberation are to be found. These films contain female anger

and frustration, and reveal hidden longing for freedom from biological tyranny.

Yes, films may have been constructed to tell a woman to conform to the status quo: she will at fade-out have understood that her happiness is linked to making the correct choice by settling down with a man. The idea is that a good man will make her life perfect, and certainly socially acceptable, so her job is to locate one of these creatures and marry him, even though, as we all know, a good man is hard to find. As it turns out, he is not only hard to find, but, in the woman's film, he is practically nonexistent, except in a highly suspicious form. If a good man is a "good man" because, in woman's terms, he will take care of her and their children, earn a fine living, worship her and remain faithful to her, never neglect her by going off to fight Indians or settle the planet Mars, keep his mother from criticizing her pie crust, and always remember their anniversary, then there are very few good men in woman's movies.

Once again we find the same contradiction and the same ambivalence. The woman's film cannot be about good men who take care of women and render them plotless, because the movie is supposed to have a woman at the center of the universe confronting disasters of all kinds. Why would she have to confront anything if she has a good man to do it for her? What would be the plot? The importance of a man to a story negates the importance of a woman.* And besides, the most common problem any woman has in her world is obviously a problem with a man.

The very first thing that must be made clear to an audience in any movie in which the central character is a woman is where she stands vis-à-vis men. If she is alone in life, why? Why is she not being cared for by a man? (And that includes not only a husband, but a father, a son, or a brother.) A reason for her not being a conventional wife or mother has to be established. Where is she in the romantic food chain? These explanations are not always put to the viewer as cold facts, but they are woven into the opening scenes of any story about a woman, and whatever form they take, they place the woman sexually, romantically, and maritally. And they also provide another subtext for the audience, constructing a further explanation of exactly why this woman is at the center of the filmed universe.

---

* On the other hand, sometimes men aren't important at all. In the upper-crust, elegant woman's world often depicted in comedies dominated by great woman stars, a cook can be more important than a husband. In *First Lady* (1937), starring Kay Francis, it is a given that if your best friend steals your cook, she has done you extreme damage; you can't easily replace a good cook in Washington, D.C., and your next party may be ruined by soggy canapés. On the other hand, if your best friend steals your husband, you can easily get another one, and where's the loss? It's not tangible, meaning it won't show up on your dinner table.

The only ways to make a film about a woman are to remove the man from the story, to place him in a weak or secondary position, or to turn him into a problem. Thus, men in the woman's film are often depicted as unreliable, destructive, or dead. At best, they are temporary. What emerges are stories in which women have problems, and the problems are usually created by weak men. "They're all alike," says Cleo Moore in *One Girl's Confession* (1953). "They just have different faces so we can tell them apart."

These men are often played by actors like Lee Bowman. This helps define how bad they really are. Actors like Bowman were apparently born to play the weak and unreliable men of the woman's film, to stand behind Jean Arthur and Rosalind Russell, smirking and/or mooning romantically according to the needs of the plot. They aren't handsome enough to distract the eye away from the leading lady's beauty, and they aren't strong enough to pose any threat to her in either the frame or the story line. They can't act much, and they have no particular charm. The best of them, a Paul Henreid or a George Brent, buys the credibility for the least of them, Bowman or Macdonald Carey or John Harvey. They are like furniture. In movies about women, a great deal of attention is paid to things like clothing, makeup, set design, and decoration. These men are part of that background to that world of women and nothing else.

Here's what the woman's film tells us that men do:

1. They die or disappear.
2. They are deeply involved in their work, which is more important to them than any woman, even if she is dying of cancer.
3. They let women down, because they lose their jobs, make women pregnant under adverse conditions, use them or discard them in various ways, or develop amnesia and forget they ever knew them (this happens particularly during World War I, the amnesiac war).
4. They beat, rape, and kill women.

Over and over again, the woman's film shows women as victims of these four categories of trouble with men, in an escalating set of horrors. Sometimes men just die and leave their women widowed, even though they were potentially good men (*So Big*, 1925, 1932, and 1953 versions; *Remember the Day*, 1941; and countless others). Sometimes they can't cope or know in their hearts they aren't good enough, so they wander off and disappear (*Cimarron*, 1931 and 1960; *Show Boat*, 1929, 1936, and 1951, and others). World War I seems to take away a great many of them, a historical convenience. Dying and disappearing define the extent to which these vanishing acts are acceptable to women, in that dying is an act of

God and disappearing is a choice. If a man dies on a woman, she can go forward clean; she's been married or loved, answering society's questions and fulfilling her appropriate choice. She's free to go on to other things, including a career of some sort, unless she has children who need her. If she is a mother, it is obvious that she has to feed and house them, so her working is placed in a different context. Having her beloved man die is a simple way to free the woman in the movie plot to go forward in the story. It also points up the problems women face without economic protection. Such a movie does not say, "Men are terrible providers so you'll be stuck in poverty if you marry." Rather, it says, "Her good breadwinner died and that's why she is stuck in poverty." One is a subversive message, and the other removes any criticism. Nevertheless, men die off on women so often in the woman's film that there is, after all, a hidden message, which is simply that a woman may find herself alone in life and in a difficult situation if her man lets her down.

When a man disappears, it is the motive behind the disappearance that matters. Sometimes elaborate ruses are constructed through which a man thinks his woman is dead, so he goes on without her, and this is, of course, acceptable behavior. If he deserts the woman, however, the lesson is negative. If he develops amnesia and doesn't really know what he is doing, that's another thing. Amnesia is the removal of adult-male responsibility for bad behavior. It is, as Lee Patrick says in *Kisses for Breakfast* (1941), "not a disease, but a plot." It is the screenwriters' handy excuse for wiping out any explanation for why a man is acting the way he's acting. (It seems to me that men get amnesia in movies much more often than women do. Since men are often depicted as being "just little boys," there's a kind of appropriateness to their amnesia: men can become mindless, irresponsible, more easily than women can. If a woman doesn't know who she is or where she's been in life, the sexual implications are unacceptable. A man can knock around and not have to answer for it.)

Dying and disappearing in movie plots are supple ruses. Women in the audience can identify with the removal of a man, if that's what their hearts desire, and the subsequent freeing of the female from the need to be wife, mother, or sweetheart. If that is not what they feel, they can learn the lesson that this *could* happen, and a warning note is struck. If they are perfectly happy with the men in their lives, they can suffer the tragedy vicariously, while thinking how lucky they are. Either response works, but the bottom line of information is simple: men die and disappear on you; you count on them, and they fail you.

The relationship of a man to his work appears in all types of movies, not just women's films. It is made completely clear in such stories that a man puts his work first, and a woman is supposed to accept that.* He can be seen as selfish and villainous for neglecting his home (*Daisy Kenyon*, 1947; *The Power and the Glory*, 1933; *Edward, My Son*, 1949), but even when the movie criticizes the man's values, it shows his neglect as a basic fact of life. Many films overtly spell out to women that this is how it is, and that they have to accept it. "Oh, Tommy," says the heroine of *Murder in the Fleet* (1935). "You've made me understand so many things. The way men feel about each other and their work together. I even learned the way you felt about this ship." In other words, this woman is now ready to be an ideal wife, one who understands about the man's work, his male camaraderie, his ship, all of which take precedence over her in his life. (*Murder in the Fleet* was written by Frank "Spig" Wead, whose own unhappy wife apparently never learned this particular lesson, as is depicted in the fictionalized movie about their marriage, *The Wings of Eagles*, 1957.)

Most of the movies that dramatize problems with men point out clearly that women can just be brushed off when a man is finished with them. Dropped. And there's little to be done about it. When Edward G. Robinson decides to pay off a "dame" he has been "seeing" for years, he says, "I hate to do this, kid. You've been a great pal." She's not surprised: "So the skids are under me, huh? Oh, well. Us dames always get it sooner or later. It's like death and taxes." This brutal exchange comes from a tough Warner Brothers movie of 1933, *The Little Giant*. Robinson concludes with his idea of great good manners. "All the luck in the world to you, Edith," he says magnanimously. But she's not having any. "Aw, never mind the song and dance," she snaps. "I ain't sore. You say quit, so it's quits." She's a realist from the world of women and knows she has no power in the arrangement. Later, when Robinson is asked by one of his gangster pals how Edith took the brush-off, Robinson tersely replies, "Standin' up." And that's how it is in the wonderful world of women on film: woman has to take it both standin' up and lyin' down.

Women get used, even when they themselves are smarter than the

---

* In the male-adventure film *Sky Giant* (1938), the woman (Joan Fontaine) carefully marries a man other than the hero because she sees that for him, mapping the Arctic regions comes first and she comes second. This man not only has missed their engagement party but also keeps postponing their wedding date when duty calls. No fool, Fontaine makes a safe decision and marries the second lead instead. And what happens? She forgot to notice that *all* the men in this movie need to fly and to map, and even the second lead goes off on their wedding night, mapping his fool head off. He, too, is never home and always puts his work first. These movies provide direct information for women in the audience. Not only do men die and disappear, willingly risk getting killed in the line of duty, leaving you broke and probably saddled with kids, but . . . they may even run off with the guys on your wedding night. There may not even be sex! This just isn't worth it.

man, because they can be tripped up by love. Mary Astor plays a smart secretary in *Behind Office Doors* (1931). Because she's a woman and only a secretary, she knows she won't be taken seriously in business, but she also knows she has the brains to succeed. She picks out a pushy salesman and cleverly manipulates him without his fully understanding that he is little more than a front for her. She gives him confidential tips, showing him how to buy out the company she works for and even teaching him what to say and when to say it, what to wear and when to wear it. This latter category of help is designed to touch the hearts of the women in the audience. "The greatest tragedy of my life," he tells Astor, "was graduating from high school with a patch on my trousers, with the other young squirts in tuxedos." Now this is a problem a woman can relate to, so she naturally falls in love with him. It's a fashion problem!

As a result, Astor ends up running both the man's house (standing around arranging flowers in the hall) and his office (keeping him from making disastrous decisions) until he finally announces his impending marriage to another woman, a rich man's daughter. Astor wails, "If it hadn't been for me . . . I made him look like a gentleman. I taught him to speak the King's English. I've shared his troubles and his worries. I've lifted him above the ordinary. I've stood between him and a dozen cheap, designing women, but when it comes to a girl with beauty and money and the glamour of position, I can't do a thing. A girl of his own class—the class I gave him."

This speech is tragic, even though it does sound a bit like a mother's lament ("After all I did for that kid . . ."). But Astor is a woman of brains and courage. ("I'm no drifter. I swim, upstream if necessary.") She has also shown herself to be wise to how treacherous men can be. ("Some say their wives are invalids. Some say their wives don't understand them. Some just say they're not married.") And still she ends up used and abused by the man she loves.

She Had to Say Yes (1933), a smarmy, mean little Depression movie, puts the capper on showing how women are used by men. It's the story of a fashion firm that makes suits and coats of high quality but that is in desperate need of expanding its business. It frankly discusses how the company's "models" are used to help sell the product by "entertaining" out-of-town buyers. *She Had to Say Yes* makes a clear connection between women who put clothes on and parade in front of men and those who also take them off. When the firm's models begin to look tired and jaded, a young wise guy (Regis Toomey) suggests they coerce their secretaries into helping out ("They've got brains that work standing up, too"), even though one of these secretaries is his own fiancée, Loretta Young. At first he wants to protect her from this questionable association with the customers. ("Look out. A bonus is only one of the things you can get from an out-of-town buyer.") Later, however, when an important man takes a fancy to Young, Toomey is willing to change his mind. Young spends the entire film being used by the two men who are supposed to truly love her. Her fiancé sets her up to make money from her looks and sex appeal, and the other one wants to make all her decisions for her and restrict her freedom. Young, disillusioned and fed up, says, "Why doesn't a woman ever get a break? You treat us like dirt under your feet." The low-down morality of *She Had to Say Yes* is revealing in its calm acceptance of the fact that women are going to be used, and there's precious little they can do about it.

The unwed mother, the jilted fiancée, and the wronged wife are subjects that are taken up over and over again by the woman's film. And it's not only the man the woman loves who lets her down, either. Sometimes it's her daddy, and sometimes it's her irresponsible little brother, and sometimes it's her own son. Joan Crawford has to bail her brother out of jail in *Dance, Fools, Dance* (1931) because, weak-willed and callow youth that he is, he gets involved in bootlegging. Barbara Stanwyck is not brought up like "a real gal" in *Gambling Lady* (1934) because she has only a father to care for her, and he's a ne'er-do-well card player. When he kills himself, leaving her destitute, she learns what she considers to be the basic lesson for a woman in life: men desert you when the going gets rough because they aren't strong enough to take it, the way you are.

Men seduce and marry women, using them in their climb to the top, in *Nightmare Alley* (1947) and *Ruthless* (1948). In the first movie, Tyrone Power climbs his way out of the cheap carnival show he works in via a series of love affairs with women who can't resist him. In *Ruthless*, Zachary Scott goes upwardly mobile by inspiring real love in a series of women of increasing wealth. He uses each in turn to gain entrance to the worlds he needs to conquer. First, he proposes to a young girl who is the daughter of the wealthiest man in his small town. Cleverly suggesting that he needs to go to Harvard to be worthy of her, he gets her father to finance his sojourn there. Once on that ladder, he moves on to the superwealthy daughter of influential banking people and gets engaged to her. Next, he seduces the wife of the largest corporation head in the universe and gets her to sell her stock shares to him, and so it goes. Although in both cases, the men end up badly, the women are not rehabilitated either. They've still been used, abused, and abandoned.

The worst thing, of course, is when women are physically victimized. There are far too many examples in which women are raped (*Johnny Belinda*, 1948; *The Outrage*, 1964; *Peyton Place*, 1957), killed (*Psycho*, 1960; *Strangers on a Train*, 1951), beaten and tortured, and treated as horror-film fodder. *Ambush* (1949), a relatively unknown example, shows how easily such attitudes were made a part of normal plot construction. The concept of beating and abusing a woman is a casual part of a sordid subplot.

Ambush is a minor western based on a Luke Short story, and it is in many ways similar to the famous *Fort Apache* (1948), directed by John Ford. Jean Hagen plays a battered wife, married to a drunken, lazy trooper, and her fear of him is naked and open. A second male character in the film, who genuinely loves Hagen, tells her, "When he gets home, he'll beat you again, and if he's not too drunk he'll make love to you." This is her fate. When her husband finally does come home, she tries to stand up to him, saying, "Don't hit me anymore, Tom, I won't stand it." When he gets rough with her, she picks up the frying pan, the woman's weapon, and desperately bops him on the head, then runs outside in fear and confusion. He follows her angrily, but a neighbor woman is passing by, so the couple cover their actions, hiding their shame. At the end of the film, Hagen is still stuck with this man. There is no miraculous reformation. There is no happy ending for her. The man who really loves her doesn't save her. She's just left in her miserable situation . . . with a black eye.

The four rules of what men do define the depressing exploitation and denigration of women in popular culture. Even today, horror films and MTV videos carry on this tradition. What is interesting is how films about women, ostensibly made with at least a covert desire to address the female audience in terms they can respond to, suggest what women can do about these four problem areas. What they do is to show the female alternatives to each of them:

1. A man dies or disappears; a woman can run away.
2. Men let women down and use them; women can use men for sex, marry them for their money, climb social ladders by marrying increasingly richer and more powerful men, or, if pregnant, place the child up for adoption or find another man to marry.
3. A man has his work; a woman can choose to make her own work more important than a man in her life.*
4. A man can beat and rape and kill; a woman can kill.

It is immediately apparent that none of these female alternatives really has society's approval. They aren't even easy to accomplish. Two of them (women using men or killing them) form the basis of tragic stories in which

---

* Stories in which women attempt to replace men in their lives with work, or in which work is placed over love in importance, intersect with all types of movies about women. Since this is one of the major categories of stories about women, their choices, and their worlds, I am only noting it here.

women will be punished for their actions. One (the woman choosing work over love) is almost always a film in which the woman is proved to be terribly wrong in this choice, and the other, the runaway woman, is uncommon until the 1960s and is again almost always a story in which the flight is proved to be an unsatisfactory solution.

When the four basic actions are given sex changes from male to female, it becomes obvious that men have an easier time getting away with them than woman do. These alternative solutions form the basic plots of many women's films, and the films are constructed to point out to viewers that the woman has, in fact, done the wrong thing. The implication is that these four ugly things are what men do. It's not right (although the one involving the importance of his work is okay), but it is how men do things. It's the breaks, babe. But when a woman does these things, she is wrong on all counts.

A brief look at women's films involving these four solutions shows how this works. Take running away. Aline MacMahon plays a woman who owns an isolated filling station/restaurant out in the desert in the 1934 film *Heat Lightning*. She has chosen to leave society behind and isolate herself in a world without men, without temptation, and without fashion. She has done this deliberately because dressing up and looking good, going out in the night after men, used to be her "racket," and she's through with it. "Whatever I was before, I'm different now. I started fresh and clean."

MacMahon plays a strong character, a woman who can do anything she puts her mind to. Although she believes a woman needs both sex and independence, she has found that the two things don't mesh well together. Her experience has taught her that a woman lives in an either-or world, and she has made her choice. The choice requires her to run away to a place where there are literally no men whom she could desire.

What MacMahon has done is transform herself into a man. She dresses in coveralls, with her hair tucked away underneath an old kerchief. (When questioned as to why she always goes around like this, she says she is "dressed to work.") She acts and talks like a man, without sentiment or coyness. She does a man's job, repairing cars and running the filling station, while her sister takes care of the restaurant, the "woman's job."

The action of the film shows just how futile running away like this actually is. What MacMahon has not understood is that there is one thing she can never run away from, and that is the fact that she is a woman. No matter where she goes or what she wears or how many car engines she rescues from the junk heap, she is a woman, and that fact will finally catch up with her. MacMahon's running away is shown to be a sham when the one man she ever really cared about shows up unexpectedly at the filling station. Although she fights the idea, she cannot deny the sexual appeal he has for her. Her running away was not the act of a brave and independent woman, but the slinking off into the desert of a beaten and degraded female who finally just can't resist a bum who puts the make on her. Knowing that she can never resist him, MacMahon changes herself back from male to female. She dons the uniform of the secondary sex. She puts on a dress, loosens her long hair, and smears thick lipstick onto her mouth, but she also retains a sense of what she is doing as dirty and cowardly. As her former lover ogles her, she says, "A few duds make quite a change in a woman, don't they?" He knows her act of changing her clothes means that she has accepted him and his sexual mastery of her.

MacMahon's running away is shown as a failure because she did not truly reject sex, and thus, men. The third category, women's using men, shows females to have ruthlessly detached themselves from caring. They can then use men to climb into a position of power. MacMahon's problem is that she runs away, but she has not really detached herself. She still cares.

Even in films where women don't care and just use men to climb, however, there is usually portrayed the *one* man whom the leading lady really cares about. In these films, women are allowed to make a great many men look like stupid fools, easily dominated by beauty and sex. The woman has learned this lesson by having been herself dominated by the first man in her life, the one she truly loves. *Forever Amber* (1947) is such a story, with Linda Darnell as the virginal young Amber St. Clare falling madly in love with Cornel Wilde, but making her way up the ladder of men after circumstances separate them. Paulette Goddard in *Kitty* (1945) is a guttersnipe picked up, cleaned up, and raised up by the manipulative Ray Milland, who sees her as his own ticket to fortune. He acts as her pimp, really, as she marries herself forward in life, all the while never forgetting that the only man she ever really loved is the bossy Milland. *Gone With the Wind* (1939) has a foolish but spunky heroine whose climb over husbands is necessitated by her having to save herself and her family from the ruins of war. (Scarlett's second and third marriages are motivated by money needs, whereas her first is a face-saving maneuver when her true love marries someone else.) When a woman can be involved in sex without love, she can end up mastering the situation. It is, as always, love that brings her down. Sexual enslavement—a true love—blocks her independence.

Baby Face (1933) is a classic example of a movie in which a woman climbs over men to the top. It demonstrates how these climbs work and shows how futile the woman's efforts always turn out to be. *Baby Face's* climb is motivated by hatred, as well as by poverty. In *Baby Face*, Barbara Stanwyck is a poor girl in the factory slums of Erie, Pennsylvania. Her no-good father runs an illegal speakeasy out of their crummy apartment, and,

Barbara Stanwyck and Theresa Harris in *Baby Face*

it is made totally clear in this pre-Code film, Stanwyck often turns tricks that he sets up for her while he stands outside and waits until the man is finished. Stanwyck in this movie is as tough as you see leading women get in films. She has only two people whom she speaks to in a civil manner: a black woman who works alongside her in the speakeasy and a bookish, older European man who drops in for an occasional beer. The latter acts as her guru, advising her "You have power. You don't realize your potential." Stanwyck's life is sordid, but she's not downtrodden. When her father tries to get rid of her black friend, she stands up to him firmly. He backs down. When he finally leaves her alone with a man she really can't stand, she bashes the fellow on the head. When she and her father quarrel over this, he calls her a tramp. She screams at him, her face screwed up in hideous rage, "Yeah, I'm a tramp and who's to blame? My father! A swell start you gave me. Nothin' but men! Dirty, rotten men, and you're rottener than any of 'em. I'll hate you as long as I live."

This hatred becomes the motivation for her own survival at the expense of the men she meets. When her father accidentally blows himself up with his illegal still, Stanwyck is faced with a choice. Should she accept the nasty proposition one of their ex-customers makes her, or should she go to work stripping at the local grind house? These are her options. "I guess I ain't much of a businessman," she says. Her European guru tells her to fight back, that it's up to her to decide, and that if she stays in Erie she will be lost. While he is telling her this, the camera remains fixed on Stanwyck's intelligent, tough, and calculating face. She is looking up at her friend, and the audience is looking at her from slightly to the right of his vantage point. Her face is seen to be interested in what he is saying, but skeptical. "What chance has a woman got?" she asks. "More chance than a man," he answers. "A woman, young, beautiful like you are, can get anything she wants in the world. But there's a right way and a wrong way. Remember the price of the wrong way is too great. . . . You must be a master, not a slave. Be clean, be strong, defiant, and you will succeed."

Stanwyck considers this thoughtfully, her eyes glittering. "Yeeeeeeaaaah," she says, taking a long drag on her cigarette, suddenly understanding the weight of what he says. She's not sure what the right way to succeed might be (and, Lord knows, *he* doesn't have a plan), but she certainly is experienced in the wrong way. There is one area in her life in which she knows how to be a master. She and her black friend hop a freight train and are off to New York City. The next section of the film, nearly two-thirds of its running time, demonstrates how a woman can succeed. Starting on the sidewalk outside a skyscraper bank, Stanwyck makes her first move toward the top floor. She goes up to a policeman and asks how someone gets a job inside. With his tips, she goes into the personnel office, bottom floor, and finds out that there are no jobs to be had and too many women waiting for them. Spotting a fat southern boy who guards the door to the man who hires, she brazenly says, "I'd like to wait inside," and soon he is following her in for a lunchtime quickie. The climb now begins in earnest, shown to viewers through a series of vignettes in the various departments she climbs up through: filing department, accounting, a vice president's office. The camera moves upward outside the tall building and honky-tonk music accompanies its upward progress.

Along the way, Stanwyck improves herself. She gets a better hairdo, more stylish and expensive clothes, and reads etiquette books in her spare time. As the men make fools of themselves over her, she is able to eliminate each one ruthlessly when the next one, from a higher level, comes along. No matter what happens, such as getting caught in flagrante delicto in an office, she is able to turn it to her own benefit. ("Nothing like this has ever happened to me before. What could I do? He was my boss.") She is finally stopped in her forward march when her vice-presidential-level sweetheart shoots her presidential-level sweetheart and then himself in her posh apartment.

Stanwyck comes forward to the bank to be paid off, but her luck does not hold. The new head of the bank is an ex-playboy, George Brent, who has been around enough, unlike the other bankers, to know that a woman who is being kept is no schoolgirl. He stonewalls her, offering her a ticket to Paris and a job in their French branch. She has no choice but to take it.

Stanwyck's human side has been manifested during all this only by her fierce loyalty to her black friend, now her maid. The film offers an audience a view of a woman who can't be blamed for being the way she is, but who should be blamed for not suffering for it. Although the intention is to show us Stanwyck as a woman doing the wrong thing, her characterization does allow for an understanding of why she does it. This is enhanced when the movie is seen today, because the men are not only lascivious (with the exception of a sincere and eager youth played by John Wayne), but they are also selfish. They are all too willing to use a young woman who works for them, and they know that they are inheriting her from one another. She is able to climb over them not only because she is bad, but also because they are bad. When rejected, they become difficult, even crazy.

In Paris, Stanwyck works, doing a good job. When Brent arrives there some time later, he notices her and soon is romancing her. "I was hoping you wouldn't be like everybody else," she muses, when he tries to get her off on a weekend trip. They do spend three days together, and she comments philosophically, "A yacht or the Albany night boat . . . it's all pretty much the same." When he tells her he'll give her anything—furs, jewels, stocks and bonds, money, an apartment in New York and a house in France— she says there's only one thing she wants, "A Mrs. on my tombstone."

During the romance with George Brent, it is impossible to tell whether Stanwyck is manipulating him or actually falling for him. She is less flirtatious, more thoughtful and silent with him than with her previous male victims. Yet when he marries her and takes her back to New York, the implication is that she has landed her greatest prize. In one of those swift and astonishing plot developments typical of 1930s films, it is suddenly revealed that the bank has failed, and Brent has been indicted. (Evidently this happened while they were asleep on the *Normandie*.) He comes home to tell her he must have everything back he has ever given her: the jewels, the bonds, the cash, the half million, and so on, in order to save himself. To his shock, she refuses. "I'm not like other women," she tells him. "All the gentleness and kindness in me's been killed." Leaving him with the stunned look of a gored ox, she and her maid board a ship for Europe, her leather cases full of jewelry and money.

And now what happens? In the final five minutes of the movie, Stanwyck starts to pace around in her luxury stateroom. Suddenly she's out the door and off the ship, boxes in hand. She races to their apartment—he's not there—and off to the top floor of the bank. He's lying on the floor, a gun beside him, so that she can rush to him and cry, "Oh, no, oh, no, I love you, I've never said that to anyone . . ." He is miraculously revived.

Throughout this film, there has been no indication that Stanwyck is the woman she becomes in the final five minutes. There has been no evidence that she truly loves Brent or, for that matter, that he truly loves her. As she has climbed and succeeded in a triumph of sexual manipulation, only one small indicator tells the audience she's been wrong. This is a letter sent to her inside a book from the old guru. "From your letters," he says, "I can tell you're not doing things the right way. Your life will be ruined." Otherwise, we've observed a strong and conniving woman get ahead in a world of weak and conniving men. All along, until she quits the bank to be kept by the man at the very top, she has worked, and it has been made very clear that she is learning and doing a good job. What we have seen and the way we are asked to view it are not completely matched. In the end, of course, Stanwyck becomes a "real woman." She has wept, given back the jewelry, and accepted her position of slave, not master. Love will now be her career.

The ultimate irony of this astonishing movie is the very ending. Brent and Stanwyck are back in Erie, Pennsylvania, in the same factory slums she began in. The final image of the movie is the identical skyline of the coalfields that was visible in the first moments of the film. Stanwyck has progressed exactly nowhere.

Probably the most famous exploiter of men in the popular fiction of the 1940s is the aforementioned notorious Amber St. Clare, heroine of Kathleen Winsor's *Forever Amber*. "This is the story of Amber St. Clare," announces an opening title card for the 1947 film. "Slave to ambition, stranger to virtue." Amber is a sort of Madame Bovary of 1600s England, who looks in books regarding fashion and tries to dress herself up on her meager budget as a country tavern girl. Although promised in marriage so that she can settle down to her duties as a wife, Amber has other ideas. ("Do you think I'll spend the rest of my life in a pig sty?") She loathes the idea of marriage and motherhood and soon is off to London with the handsome Bruce Carlton, played by Cornel Wilde. Amber's story becomes one of rags to riches, in which a beautiful young woman uses her sex appeal to climb toward power, man by man. This climb is a kind of ugly metaphor for a woman's liberation, but it is again presented as a journey to nowhere because, in the end, the woman finds herself abandoned. She has plenty of clothes and jewels, of course, and she's even been the mistress of a king and a famous stage actress, but without love she might as well be back at the tavern with the pigs.

Four men move Amber forward in terms of money and power. An outlaw, a captain, and a count all die as a result of their involvement with her. Bruce, the man she truly loves, represents the masculine force in all its destructive power. He insists on his own freedom, leaving Amber behind in London, where she will be bilked of the money he gave her to live on. Moral: A woman's dependency on a man is often her ruin. When Bruce turns up again, and Amber stands up the king in order to go off to the country with him, the two of them have a Happy Interlude in a little cottage. Amber is seen running around the little house, wearing an apron and rattling her pots and pans. Bruce cries out in delight, "I had no idea you had such a way with mutton and greens!" Again, however, he lets her down, but when he contracts the plague she goes to him, nursing him, washing his clothes herself by hand, and tying him down when he raves. "Everything I've ever done has been for Bruce," says Amber, but it gets her nowhere.

In the end, Amber's climb is stopped at the king's door. Her final abuse at the hands of the noble Bruce takes place when he arrives to take their son away from her, his dutiful little wife at his side. Bruce's wife is a woman without glitter or idle chatter, a hardworking, sober, and industrious woman. She is in every way the opposite of Amber. When the king, too, rejects Amber, she sees the handwriting on the wall where her future with men is concerned. Bruce has told Amber that their son will have a better, more honest and open life in America with him. "We both want him to get a better start than this," he says pompously, and Amber allows herself to snap, "Bruce, you don't know anything about the start he *did* get." However, she sends the child to him, because when she lets the boy choose for himself, he picks Bruce. It is Amber's final betrayal by the male sex. ("In heaven's name, Amber," Bruce has said, "haven't you caused enough unhappiness?")

Many of these films in which women climb to the top over men are costume dramas—*Forever Amber, Kitty,* and *The Strange Woman.* There are also modern stories, like *Baby Face* and *All About Eve.* In all the variations of a woman's ruthless climb, the women portrayed share three attributes: they are exceptionally beautiful; they have loose morals; they have superb performance skills. These women are going to have to attract their male victims with their beauty, manipulate them by persuading them that they are handsome and desirable males, and they are going to have to put out.

In all of these "climbing" films, except for *All About Eve,* the women begin their lives by being betrayed or seduced in some way by a man. Hedy Lamarr in *The Strange Woman* is left destitute by her drunken father. Stanwyck in *Baby Face* is set up as a prostitute by her father. Linda Darnell is seduced and abandoned in *Forever Amber.* Only Anne Baxter in *All About*

Eve (1950) enters the movie without explanation as a ruthless manipulator. Significantly, hers is the only character that does not end up displaying some kind of sympathetic behavior and earning the audience's pity or respect. When a movie shows the woman to be retaliating against men for some early evil done to her, or if she repents her evil ways and accepts true love at the end of the movie, she can be forgiven. If all she wants is the Sarah Siddons Award, she is not entitled to our sympathy.

MOVIES LIKE *Baby Face* and *Forever Amber* portray a world of greedy, drunken, lascivious, and stupid men. But the woman's film obviously can't make a living that way. Most of these movies are not set up merely to tell women that men are terrible and to be avoided no matter what. That wouldn't work. Since the surface level of most films of this type is a reaffirmation of love and marriage for women, they need to find a way to resolve the problems women have with men in more positive ways.

There is always the simple solution, in which, after involving herself with a bad man, the woman meets a new and better man who does not die, disappear, ignore her, beat her, or kill her. Movies that focus on the problems of women, however, need to keep the woman in the position of importance in the story line. The balance of power must always be in the hands of the woman. The most interesting way that movies find to do this, and still be stories that involve men who are not too disgusting, is one that has not yet been explored in film study. Movies just disguise the true meaning of the story by feminizing the man, making *him* the character that expresses the woman's point of view. Or making *him* the character that actually liberates her into true independence. Or making *him* the character who demonstrates how wretched and silly the woman's world really is. This is a superb ploy, an ideal way to get away with a great many things.

The three ways in which movies accomplish these disguises are:

1. The role-reversal story, in which men are asked to play the traditionally female part of wife or powerless figure, and the woman is asked to play the role of powerful career person or husband
2. The creation of a woman's film in which the central character is not a woman, but a man—the "male weepie" movie
3. The use of an asexual male character in the woman's life, a man who represents a covert liberation of some sort

ROLE REVERSALS

MOVIES FIND a successful and sometimes charming way to call attention
to the silliness of the gender roles assigned to both men and women by
using a plot called role reversal. Originally, it was probably just a clever
way for exhausted screenwriters to vary the stories they were grinding out.
How many basic plots are there? Since so many big box-office names were
females, and since there was a large female audience, why not feature one
of those stars in a story in which she was essentially playing the man's
role, with the man taking on the female's? At the end of the movie, everything could be put back to normal, but in the meantime lots of comedy
and drama could ensue.

Role-reversal movies are fairly common.* Much has been made about
His Girl Friday (1940), because it was an *actual* case where a woman took
a man's role, and much has also been made of the famous role reversal in
Woman of the Year (1942), in which Tracy may be seen as a kind of jealous
wife and Hepburn as a powerful husband. But examples turn up everywhere,
especially in little movies that are clearly written to capitalize on an audience's expectations. For instance, *Man Wanted* (1932) opens up with a
voice saying "the editor is in conference" to a salesman who is waiting to
demonstrate a rowing machine to the editor. As the camera enters the inner
editor's office, a man and woman are seen kissing. The woman is wearing
a white satin blouse with a gorgeous piece of jewelry pinned right between
her breasts, and the man is in a traditional business suit. She looks soft
and feminine and not as if she were dressed for work, but when the phone
rings, *she* is the one who answers.

"Good heavens, Lois, how do you stand it?" the man in the suit asks.

"What, being an editor?"

"The whole racket—telephones, buzzers, crazy-looking people."

* The format is taken to the highest level in 1964 by *Kisses for My President*, in which
Polly Bergen is elected to the office of the presidency, and her husband, Fred MacMurray,
has to assume the role of first lady. *Kisses for My President* becomes a grim and humorless
little endeavor, in which MacMurray, having had to sell his successful business because
it depended on government contracts, is left to do unimportant duties such as entertaining
visiting dignitaries. (In the end, Bergen can't escape biology—"The president is pregnant!!"
She resigns. "It took 15 million women to get me into office, and one man to get me out.")
The role reversal goes nowhere in this case.

"It's all part of the game. And I love it."

This is classic role reversal based on audience expectations. The common assumption would be that *he* is the editor, and *she's* his wife, but he is the lazy, loafing husband and she's the energetic editor. Furthermore, the speeches above would usually be reversed. The husband has dropped in on his mate for lunch the way expensively dressed women often do. As Kay Francis, the editor, explains to the rowing machine demonstrator, "I'm afraid you've jumped to conclusions. The editor of the *400* magazine is a woman."

But not a typical one. Kay Francis really is seen to *be* an editor, sitting behind her desk, swiveling in her chair, barking orders re serial rights. She has no interest in the gossip and fashion of her silly social set. (One of these party types observes, "I don't know how she does it. Works all day. Sleeps all night.") The young salesman with the machine turns out to have gone to Harvard . . . and can he type! He takes shorthand, too, and she hires him to be her secretary. She has decided he is just what she wants because "the work is uncertain . . . it needs a man." The women she has hired keep quitting because they want to have dates instead of working all night the way she does. David Manners plays the young man, who explains his eyebrow-raising job to a friend by saying, "Can't you get it through your fat head that today there are just as many serious-minded women in business as men? When you meet 'em you don't have to treat 'em as if you were out on a party. I didn't talk to her any differently than I would to a man."

Francis and Manners work happily alongside each other, their roles pleasantly reversed, through most of the movie. Soon, however, she is worrying about his ego ("I don't want you to feel you're just a male ste-nographer"), while he's offering to do little unpleasant jobs because "fight-ing a man like Peterson is no job for a woman."

In the end, Kay Francis and David Manners will not only have each other but they will have it all. Since they are both workaholics, they can work themselves to death in each other's arms, sharing the business. It's impossible to tell if *Man Wanted* is a romance, a plea for female equality, or a celebration of the work ethic, but it *is* an example of role reversal, and a positive one for the most part. Viewers are made to realize that they don't *expect* a woman to be boss or a man to be a secretary, but that it *is* possible.

In a serious but lighthearted film based on Ruth Gordon's Broadway success, *Over 21* (1945) presents Irene Dunne as a glamorous, smart, talented, successful, funny, kind, and loving career woman who takes over her husband's role in life while he is in the army. In this movie, Dunne plays a famous screenwriter/novelist who can't bake an apple pie. She is married to a big newspaper editor (Alexander Knox) who can't stand the physical strain of boot camp because he is "over twenty-one." Their gender failures, hers as cook and his as athlete, are appropriate to a time in pop-culture history in which audiences were asked to be supertolerant of one another. It was also a time in which women had to do men's jobs. When the man who owns Knox's paper (Charles Coburn) says he'll sell the paper because without Knox it's nothing, Dunne steps in and writes the editorials herself under her husband's name to buy Knox the time he needs to get through boot camp. Dunne becomes both male and female hero to the story. When her husband finally completes training and finds out his editorials have gone forward, he guesses that it was his wife who wrote them. At his boot camp graduation, he delivers the graduation speech as a tribute to her. He reads her first editorial, "The World and Apple Pie" (the perfect female metaphor), saying that he wanted to give a great speech on this important occasion and someone else had already said what he hoped to say as well as anyone could.

Irene Dunne takes her husband's place, and he is proud of her for it. She is, he says, "the best newspaperman there is." She has helped him through school, mothered him, loved him, covered his job for him, and he loves her for it. She has become a man, and the action is welcome. But only in wartime, and only because the play was written by a woman!

In *Along Came Jones* (1945), *The Paleface* (1948), and *Son of Paleface* (1952), role reversal is cleverly used for western comedy. The first film is a straight western, with romantic emphasis, and the other two are satires. All three, however, play off the idea of the leading men (Gary Cooper in *Jones* and Bob Hope in the two *Paleface* movies) as inept gunfighters. In all three movies, the men are covered in the action by the sharpshooting and quick thinking of the females (Loretta Young in *Jones* and Jane Russell in the other two). The women follow the men around, reaching out from behind trees, barrels, and stairs to blow the enemies away before the inept, and even cowardly, men can be finished off by the villains. These role reversals are made for fun, but they are ways in which women are removed from inactivity. They are not, of course, removed from also playing the romantic leads who end up in the arms of the men.

What role reversal accomplished was a reconsideration of gender activities. Men were demeaned by being put into the woman's traditional position, and women were often made to look cruel and domineering when put in the man's. This did not necessarily in and of itself mean that everything was wrong, but it did point up certain things. It showed that society did not feel that the work women usually do was important; when a man was put in an apron and made to order groceries, it made a servant out of him. It showed that certain qualities that were thought to be masculine were actually bullying and unpleasant when a woman in shoulder pads barked inhuman orders to her staff. But these reversals also showed that women could do the same jobs that men did and behave in the same way. Audiences saw it on-screen. It became a fact, giving women in the audience a new way of approaching their own concerns.

THE MALE WEEPIE

IT IS A CURIOUS FACT of American film history that not all women's films are about a woman. Some of them are about men. Well, why not? If women can invade male-action genres and make female versions of them, why isn't the opposite situation possible, in which a man undergoes the kind of suffering regarding love, family, sex, and children that women do in the woman's film? Of course, it is possible, but the status of women is such, and the attitude toward the woman's film as genre is such, that even as one contemplates the idea, one rejects it. Why would a man, who could be in a nice genre like the western or the gangster film, want to be in a woman's picture? Nevertheless, it happens.

A silent film, *Man, Woman and Sin* (1927), starring John Gilbert, perfectly illustrates this phenomenon. (It actually should have been entitled *Man, Woman and Mom.*) Gilbert, a handsome and talented actor, plays the part of a young and naive newspaper employee who gets an invitation to attend the embassy ball. He becomes giddy and girlish at the thought of his first big social event, and he comes into the newsroom and preens himself, waiting to be seen and admired in his top hat and tails by his fellow newsmen. (Clothes!) He is shown to be totally overwhelmed by the event he attends. The fashion and glamour of the people awe him, and he notices every detail of the room, its furniture, draperies, and so on.

He falls for an older and extremely experienced woman, played by Jeanne Eagels. She is having a torrid affair with a rich married man, but to fill her time and cut down on her boredom, she seduces Gilbert. In this extensive scene, he is shy, virginal, even frightened, while she leads the way, quietly laughing to herself when she realizes he does not understand what she is up to. She gives him an open sexual invitation, but he doesn't pick up on it. Once aroused, however, he falls deeply, madly in love, so that when he finds out about her married lover, he goes crazy and accidentally kills him. This accidental murder is similar to what Ginger Rogers does in *I'll Be Seeing You* (1944). It is the woman's job to kill in moral outrage after seduction. Gilbert is rescued by his mother, who goes to Eagels and shames her into admitting that the killing wasn't really Gilbert's fault. (Mom knows Eagels is bad, because earlier Gilbert has robbed her own sugar bowl to buy "that woman" a bracelet.) Gilbert ends up where a boy belongs, on the arm of his mother, who has his own true interest at heart. This sentimental story, played by a grown man who is an excellent actor and a major star, is an example of a man playing out a story that is more traditionally a story that a woman would play. (In *Man, Woman and Sin* Gilbert is even shown in his bath in exactly the same way one would expect the leading lady to be seen, all glamour and bubbles and sex appeal.)

A male weepie is a film in which the central character is a man, but he is living out a story that would normally star a woman. His concerns are those of love, marriage, parenting. He is forced to choose between happiness and success, and the woman he loves may die or leave him for another man. In movies that can be designated as male weepies, it is apparent that the conventions of the woman's film are fully maintained by them.

Some classic male weepies are *Ten North Frederick* and *Return to Paradise*, both starring Gary Cooper; *Come and Get It*; *Nora Prentiss*; *My Cousin Rachel*; and *Sweepings*. These films all contain the traditional conventions of the woman's film. The men in them suffer. What happens to them is what happens to women. With the exception of Kent Smith in *Nora Prentiss* (1947), all these men are played by strong actors who had long and successful careers in film. In *Ten North Frederick* (1958), Gary Cooper is trapped in a loveless marriage to a cold woman, and he falls in love with one of his daughter's friends. He tries for a political career, but is ruined due to his naïveté and his inability to exploit others. He sinks into alcoholism. In *Come and Get It* (1936), Edward Arnold forsakes his real love, a dancehall girl, for a cold marriage into the boss's family. He becomes a timber baron, only to fall all over again when he meets his former sweetheart's look-alike daughter years later. (Both mother and daughter are played by Frances Farmer, so there's two of her.) Lionel Barrymore in *Sweepings* (1933) spends his whole life sacrificing his personal happiness so that he can build up his department-store business. After his wife dies, all he can think of is providing for his children, so he never has time to take them to the ball game. They grow up to be ungrateful degenerates, but he was doing it all for them, you see. This makes Barrymore the Mildred Pierce of the retail trade. Kent Smith in *Nora Prentiss* is ruined because he is a married man who falls helplessly in love with a lower-class woman (Ann Sheridan). And so it goes. Most of these films are told as flashback stories, the classic passive status of the woman's film. Are there any fundamental differences between these films with a man and those with a woman? Only one: the man stands in for the woman. In *Return to Paradise* (1953), Gary Cooper, an American wanderer, arrives on a Polynesian island where he marries a beautiful native woman and frees the natives from the iron rule of a missionary. When his wife dies giving birth to a baby daughter, Cooper leaves, turning his back on the child. Years later he is reunited with her on his "return to paradise."

My Cousin Rachel (1952), despite its name and despite its having been written by the celebrated female author of books for women, Daphne Du Maurier, is an example of a woman's film that has a man as the central narrative figure of audience response and identification. The story begins with an ominous warning note. Out on the brooding moors, a mature man is calling the attention of a young boy to the dangling corpse of a newly hanged culprit. The man tells the boy to take his time looking and to never forget. That, he warns, is what can happen to you. "A moment of passion, and you pay with your life." This is a warning that might normally be given to a woman, for whom a moment of passion can result in an unwanted pregnancy or shame of some other sort. Although the incident involves two males, it is definitely a woman's film opening.

When this youngster grows up, he becomes Richard Burton. His adviser on the moors, who is actually his cousin, has now become his loving "parent" and guardian, since Burton's own family members are all dead. The two cousins are deeply attached. The older man is crippled and has to walk with a cane, so that he visually represents an impaired adviser, a kind of imperfect male. Since he is neither strong nor vital, nor a natural parent, he is fundamentally nonmasculine in the traditional sense of that term. Burton, in his first major American film role, is presented as a callow youth, not yet experienced in the ways of the world. The two men are almost virginal, and they in no way represent vigorous masculine figures. The opening scenes of the film present a world of clothing, furniture, and concern with moral behavior and good health. (This is particularly true since *My Cousin Rachel* is a lavish costume film.)

The crippled parent figure goes off alone to take the sun in Italy, which is supposed to be good for his health. Italy is a movie territorial metaphor for sex. When movie characters go there from America, England, Scandinavia, they always find sun, warmth, love, and above all else, sex. It is the place where characters go to relax their bodies, their tensions, and their morals. In Italy, we have seen poets become healthy (*Barretts of Wimpole Street*, 1934 and 1957), spinsters get laid (*Summertime*, 1955), virgins get married (*Gaslight*, 1944), independent and willful females bear illegitimate babies (*A Woman Rebels*, 1936), whole families relax and begin relating (*Enchanted April*, both 1935 and 1992), and "dead" couples get reborn.* Sure enough, the parent figure soon sends back word that he has married a beautiful woman whom Burton is to refer to as his cousin Rachel. Almost before Burton has absorbed this, word comes that his wealthy parent figure is dead.

The film then unfolds like a traditional Gothic novel in which an innocent young girl invades the territory of a darkly suspicious, older person of the opposite sex. Burton is Eyre to Olivia de Havilland's Rochester. After journeying to Italy to find out what really happened, he finds himself smitten with his cousin, bringing her back to England with him. Once home, he is seduced by her experience and sophistication. His fever for her makes him incautious. ("A moment of passion, and you pay with your life.")

The high point of this passion is one of the few sequences in which Burton is physically active, as he climbs into de Havilland's room via a balcony. The moonlight pouring in on them, he drapes her naked body with all his family jewelry. She is overwhelmed, and they make love in front of the fireplace. After this love scene, Burton, overstepping himself in his youthful inexperience, announces at a family gathering that he will marry his cousin Rachel. Rachel cries out, "Are you out of your mind?" In an altercation between them later, he, like a young woman, goes crazy and tries to strangle her when he realizes that the lovemaking was not the same thing to her as it was to him. (". . . but that was because you had given me the jewels . . . ," she says.)

Burton now begins to believe that de Havilland is trying to poison him for his money, as she keeps preparing him a tisane she makes herself. Close to dying, he rallies himself as in his fever dreams he imagines they are getting married when he recovers. After he's well, however, Rachel lets him know that they aren't. These plot maneuvers become meaningless, and in the end, Rachel dies because of Burton's mistrust. The film ends with Burton brooding stylishly around the cliffs, looking down on stormy

---

* *September Affair* is a silly film in which Joan Fontaine and Joseph Cotten spend a great deal of time standing by a phonograph listening to Walter Huston sing "September Song." It tells the story of two people who are mistakenly thought to have died in an airplane crash. They seize the opportunity to go to Florence, rent a magnificent palazzo, eat a great deal of spaghetti, and make "fine" love. Italy liberates them into enjoying their physical selves. This movie contains one of the best lines about women: Françoise Rosay, in the traditional Maria Ouspenskaya role, tells Fontaine, "Ah, women. What fools we are. We discover radium, swim the Channel, fly the Pacific, even paint our fingernails . . . all to get a man." This philosophy erupts from her because she has told Fontaine that "it's time you give up this ridiculous ghost life and take your place in the world," and Fontaine has replied, in true woman's-film fashion, "I've made my choice. I don't want a career, and I've never been happier."

water, saying, "Rachel, Rachel, my torment, were you innocent or were you guilty?" (We found this a highly unsatisfactory ending back in South Dakota where I first saw it.)

My Cousin Rachel is a movie about women, written by a woman for other women, and although the central figure who lives to the end is a man, he is a stand-in for female feelings. Audiences are not asked to involve themselves with Rachel, but only to see her as enigmatic, the way he does, and to be confused as to who and what she really is. Burton is in a position of dependency and innocence of a sort usually associated with a female character.

Over the years, the woman's film has been down at the bottom of everyone's critical ash heap. When a film stars a woman in a melodrama, it is taken less seriously than if it stars a man. Making these women's films with men in the central roles was a way of elevating the status of the weepie, but also a way to draw in male viewers. Or perhaps to trick the critics into better reviews. Or maybe just to vary a format. Whatever or whichever, they are again examples of movies in which the woman's concerns are disguised in masculine clothing. They ennoble the woman's concerns by giving them to men. They are different from role reversals in that there is no return to "normalcy" at the end, and the men and women are not trading places in an outer world. Instead, they treat a man's life as if it were the same as a woman's.

THE ASEXUAL MALE

OF ALL THE WAYS in which men are used as disguises by the woman's film, none is as significant as that in which the man is not really a man because the woman is never going to have sex with him. The removal of the sex role from a male character is an obvious form of freeing a woman, and these desexed men appear as a disguised form of liberation for women. They not only suggest in some covert way the idea of a woman's *not* subjecting herself to a man's control, but they also hint that women can control men. And not just men, but also themselves, their own fates. They can be the authors of their own stories.

These "male" characters are not really men. They represent something else. They provide a beard for the woman's secret desire, her hidden needs. If a woman in a film goes about with an asexual male on her arm, she *appears* to be doing the right thing, but her man is really representing something else: freedom, a relationship based on friendship, wealth and power, a career, a need to be a protected child as well as a grown woman, whatever. As might be expected, these characters have their downsides. They may turn on the woman or manipulate her badly. Nevertheless, most of them are helpful, kind, good, generous creatures, and there are a lot of them in women's films. They definitely suggest that women in the audience dreamed of relationships without sex or fear of pregnancy and that they went to the movies to find not only escape but a more serious dream of freedom.

There are five types of asexual men in the woman's film:

1. *The father figure, or Daddy:* A daddy loves a woman without question, dotes on her, and gives her everything, making her the center of all his attention. (You can be intimate with him without sex.)

2. *The asexual "husband":* He is a man invented by the woman's film who enters the woman's life and offers her everything, asking for nothing in return. He is willing to care for children fathered by other men, support any career, accept that he is not loved in return, and provide tons of money. (You can be intimate with him without sex, or at least this is not what he wants from you.)

3. *A ghost or an angel:* He can do anything, period. He brings about all the changes in a woman's daily living situation that she has been longing for. (Since he has no body and technically doesn't exist, you definitely can be intimate with him without sex.)

4. *The family doctor:* Unless a woman falls in love with him, she can tell her doctor anything, and he knows all her secrets anyway. He probes into her anatomy in a chaste and acceptable way. He gives her total reassurance about herself. (You can be intimate with him without sex.)

5. *An impresario:* He discovers the talent a woman has that she didn't even realize for certain was there and develops it so that she becomes world famous, very rich, and totally beloved. (You can be intimate with him without sex.)

There are variations of all these types. Lawyers, grandpas, old family friends, priests, aliens, psychiatrists, faith healers, religious figures, and even a woman's own son, but these are the five basic categories. Daddy is the root figure. He gives life, with the other four types of Daddy giving as is appropriate to their definitions. The "husband" gives economic and social freedom . . . the ghost gives power . . . the doctor gives health, both mental and physical . . . and the impresario gives a career. As usual, these daddies giveth and they taketh away. Sure as hell, they may try to have sex with a woman even though that's not their job. (This includes even her own daddy.) They'll turn ugly and drop a chandelier on a woman while she's singing, and they'll steal her kids and mess with her mind. But, by definition, they are the men with whom a woman can be intimate without sex. These men are a form of freedom, a source of danger, and a unit of repression all in one fell swoop.

DADDY

All around the movie screen in the woman's film the daddy lurks. He casts a big shadow over all kinds of genres and stories. If the movie has a little girl (Shirley Temple, Margaret O'Brien, Natalie Wood), a young singer (Deanna Durbin, Jane Powell), or an exquisite creature on the brink of a luscious womanhood (Elizabeth Taylor in her earliest films), Daddy's there like a truffle hound on the scent. His role, it seems, is to idolize his daughter, make her the center of his life, involve himself in all her projects, and buy her a sensational wardrobe. There's a kind of terrible sadness to this, as clearly the popularity of these films provided dream daddies for millions of neglected young women around the world. In the happy variation of the daddy story (one in which Daddy does not drink, rape, mutilate, inhibit, interfere, criticize, or desert), the most significant factor is that the little girl is the boss. Instead of Daddy controlling her, she controls him. "Do you know what the most important thing in the whole world is?" asks Daddy Herbert Marshall of daughter Anne Shirley in *Make Way For a Lady* (1936). *"You!"* Although Marshall is a busy book publisher who is constantly being chased by glamorous women, his main business in life is his daughter. "Daddy," replies Shirley, "I don't know what I'd do without you." While she fills his pipe, he builds up her confidence, a fair exchange. When it appears to Shirley that her daddy really ought to have a woman his own age in his life, she decides to find him one. It's her job, not his. "He must suspect nothing of my plans," she tells a friend. "Every woman knows that men must be led, not driven."

Little girls in movies are frequently shown as relating to their daddies as if they were their wives. "I have a man to take care of," says little Shirley Temple in *Just Around the Corner* (1938), "and you know how much trouble that can be." The man she is talking about taking care of is her own father. She is busily cleaning their basement apartment, scrubbing floors, doing dishes, and bustling around for all the world as if she's Daddy's little wife, which for all practical purposes in the movie she is. "A man without a woman around the house is quite a problem," she observes, and she's not about to let a problem like that grow up under her own feet.

This theme is played over and over again in Temple's movies. "You're becoming a regular little housewife," she's told in *The Littlest Rebel*

Shirley Temple plays with John Boles, in *Curly Top*.

(1935) as she flurries about, sewing and sweeping. And she doesn't confine her comforts for Daddy to filling his pipe. When Daddy comes home in *The Littlest Rebel*, she cradles him as if he were a baby, his head on her shoulder while she sings "Believe Me If All Those Endearing Young Charms," and he hums along, blissfully content. In *Our Little Girl* (1935), she says, "Maybe if I growed like a weed, I could marry Daddy." In *Captain January* (1936), there is a fantasy sequence in which Temple sings a love song to a man while he is dressed in baby clothes. She is costumed as a nurse and feeding him with a gigantic baby bottle and a huge dish of cod-liver oil. In *Curly Top* (1935), she sits on would-be father John Boles's lap when he visits her orphanage. Her upturned face enchants him in intense close-up, and he begins to sing to her, "It's all so new to me . . ." Soon he has her out to his place at Southampton, and she's riding ponies and wearing new clothes and playing with an impressive set of dolls. He is telling her that, rich as he is, he's looked all over the world for happiness and has never found it until now, with her. It's a love scene! Temple tickles him with a broom straw and climbs on top of him in bed, riding his back to play horsie. "I want Mary [her older sister] and me to get married to you," she instructs him, and so they do, Mary providing an appropriate stand-in for the censors. The topper comes in *Poor Little Rich Girl* (1936), in which Temple actually sings to her daddy, "In every dream I caress you. Marry me and let me be your wife." Even at the age of twelve, when

Temple is looking more mature, she still sits in her daddy's lap and says, "I can't hold you close enough."

In the Temple movies, Shirley's mother is usually dead. The wife/ mother figure has to disappear to make way for the real love union between child and father. Even when the father himself is dead, as in *Bright Eyes* (1934), Temple, dressed like a little masculine aviator in leather jacket and cap, is always kissing Daddy's picture. She is surrounded by her daddy's former flying buddies, who *all* love her and who are *all* Daddy's substitutes. One of them gives her a "magic ring," but first he asks her, "How much do you love me?"

Poor Shirley Temple! Much gets made over these smarmy scenes, and much has been made over her sexy little body, her pouty mouth, her flirtatious ways. No less an authority than Graham Greene pointed out, after seeing *Captain January*, that he thought she had "an appeal interestingly decadent."

All of this infuriates the grown-up Temple, and who can blame her? All she really did was tap her guts out in a series of well-made, unpretentious, and entertaining little films designed to lift a Depression audience out of its worries. These sinister interpretations of her work reflect changing times and changing awareness. What they boil down to is more screenwriting than incest, more plot development than child abuse. Temple is a female superstar, and after her first two or three films she carries any movie she's in. How many times can she be kidnapped or left on a doorstep? To tell a story about her, movies had to deal with the issues that surround any woman, even if she's only three feet tall, and one of those issues is a man. Temple is too young to get married or become a mother, so the movies had to fall back on just one of the big three: men. In her case, that needed to be a daddy.

What is revealing is that when the female is a little girl, one sees things differently. When Temple flirts and waits on her daddy and does anything he wants, it looks like what it is: a form of weird slavery. When a daddy lavishes everything on Temple because he finds her cute and adorable and likes looking at her, it's impossible not to notice that he is reducing her to an object. And there's worse. Females are mistreated and lied to by men even when they are children! In *Little Miss Marker* (1934), her daddy leaves the little tyke behind in a gambling den as security for his debts, and then he goes out and puts a bullet through his brain. She's left abandoned among a bunch of criminals! And this isn't the first momentary lapse on Daddy's part either. "He forgot me once at the circus, and they arrested the man that found me," volunteers Shirley.

Temple's films are actually woman's films. She is always the center of the universe in them, and her concerns are always related to love, family, choices, and all the other usual things. There is often another woman in her films, a grown one, but these females are stooging it for Temple. Sometimes they are allowed to be surrogate mothers, but they are never as important as the daddies and surrogate daddies that Temple hooks up with. Once in a while, one of them is allowed to give Temple some serious advice, as when Dorothy Dell sings to her about the man in the moon and warns her, "Us gals have got to take it from the start, because we're born with heart." Temple looks thoughtful at this, but not intimidated.

The courage and spunk that are really what little Shirley Temple is all about stay with her as she ages, but in a greatly diminished form. When she becomes a teenager, in transition from child to woman, she becomes eligible to be pushed around by a man in the story. Temple becomes old enough to take on shrewish qualities or to nag the daylights out of a man and lay down rules for his behavior. To compare the cheerful and pliant little Temple of *Bright Eyes* with the older girl of *Susannah of the Mounties* illustrates the point.

In *Susannah* (1939) Temple is nearly eleven years old, and showing it. She becomes a virago, revealing her jealousy of the woman the leading man (Randolph Scott) falls in love with, but also engaging in her own first real battle of the sexes with a male her own age. She meets Little Chief, a boy who calls her a squaw. She slaps him. He pushes her down. Shirley's first love scene! And in the great American tradition. In *Susannah of the Mounties*, Shirley still lectures everyone in the story and solves the basic problems all by herself, but for the first time she shows real signs of vulnerability in her film image. As she becomes a woman, she also becomes vulnerable to the woman's usual miseries.

When a girl moves into her adolescence or early teen years, films about her life become treatises on the horrors of womanhood. While gaggles of vicious girlfriends involve her in jealous schemes and wretched plots, and she learns the accepted behaviors of Good Sportsmanship and Deception, the daddy figure becomes a perfect dream figure of a man who provides all and asks for nothing. Daddy becomes an overtly romantic figure. In Jane Powell's *Luxury Liner* (1948), someone tells Powell, who has a worshipful father, "You're a lucky duck to have such a father. Every girl should have a father like that." *Rich, Young, and Pretty* (1951), in which the title tells a young girl what will be expected of her in womanhood, Powell plays the daughter of Wendell Corey. They are a motherless (again!) Texas family that goes to Paris, as do the characters in many films of that time: *An American in Paris* (1951), *April in Paris* (1952), *Gentlemen Prefer Blondes* (1953), *The French Line* (1954), and others.

Powell and Corey go out to see the city, and their evening together is a lavish date in which Corey relates to Powell as if he were her lover.

They dance cheek to cheek, eat a luxurious dinner (during which she fusses over his ulcer as if she were his wife or his mother), and they sing "Deep in the Heart of Texas" together, a musical duet that speaks of their closeness and shared intimacy. As the film progresses, it presents viewers with a great deal of glamour. Not only are the locations beautiful, but Powell changes her clothes constantly, one elegant outfit after another, all fit to her petite frame, all complete with matching hat, shoes, gloves, and purse. Everyone loves Powell, and everything comes her way. Her daddy gives her anything and everything, and he worships her. She is in control of him because of this deep affection. As it turns out, Powell *does* have a mother, but Corey has never admitted this to her. Since her mother is a French cabaret singer, Corey has simply told Powell that she's dead. (Doesn't anyone ever tell the truth?) This mother figure, Danielle Darrieux, enters Powell's life as a surrogate big sister, beautiful and understanding, and willing to make Jane Powell the center of *her* universe, too.

Films like *Rich, Young, and Pretty* are charming escapist musicals. Yet the impeccably turned-out Powell, doted on by everyone, was a cruel role model for young women in the audience. Chances are slim that most young American females were getting that same kind of time and attention from their fathers, but, more significantly, the movie was defining for inexperienced young girls what men ought to do for women. For older women, it was a chance to watch a man doing everything any woman could dream of, but without the pressures of sex and marriage.

These movies about little girls and teenage girls provided a safe context for women to have everything and boss their men around. In the guise of caring for Daddy, a young woman was not overstepping herself if she nagged, bossed, and cajoled. She was not challenging the male, as she would have been if she were his sexual partner, and soon enough, it was hinted, she would have to change her ways when her own man entered her life. These films showed daddies acting out both sides of a man's attitudes toward a woman: they either ignored their daughters because they were too busy working, or they lavished attention on them.

Even grown women are subject to this daddy worship. Jean Arthur plays a relatively tough and savvy newspaperwoman in the 1934 film *Whirlpool*. When she is sent out on an assignment to find a mysterious underworld figure whom hardly anyone has ever seen, she finds him within seconds. (There he is, standing around in a nightclub making dinner plans.) Lo and behold, he is her long-lost daddy, presumed dead in a drowning. Since she was a baby when he "died," he has no idea who she is, but she walks right up and tells him. Wonderful! The two go on the town, staying out all night several nights in a row, arousing the suspicion of her boyfriend and the wrath of her adoptive father. Arthur and Daddy (Jack Holt) embrace, kiss on the mouth, cuddle and hug. She sits in his lap and rests her head on his shoulder. She starts lunch sitting opposite him in the restaurant banquette but soon is close beside him, the two of them laughing like maniacs and looking like lovers. She comes to his apartment to cook him dinner (steak and homemade pie) by candlelight, and, most significantly, they embark on a Happy Interlude. This is the genuine article, in the fine tradition of the woman's genre. They are seen dancing cheek to cheek, riding in a fast speedboat, winning at the races, and, the ultimate, going to a carnival in a lengthy montage. At the carnival, where we know men and women go to fall in love, they ride the roller coaster, shoot at balloons, and play ninepins.

It is clearly a love sequence involving a man and his daughter.* Holt is suave and gray-haired, rich and powerful, attentive, adoring. He is portrayed as any woman's ideal lover, but sex is taboo between them. There is no obligation, no danger for the woman. Everything any woman might want is present—security, glamour, safety, riches, attention—all available with no risk of pregnancy or commitment or loss of freedom. (Of course, this is if one wants to interpret the daddy scenes as wanting what marriage provides without sex. One can also interpret it as a safe way of having sex with Daddy.)†

* In *Holiday in Mexico* (1946), widowed daddy Walter Pidgeon, Ambassador to Mexico, and his only child, Jane Powell, demonstrate another of these love scenes. He sneaks into her bedroom while she is lying on her bed reading, and begins to serenade her by playing her little piano and singing "Goodnight, Sweetheart." She joins him for a duet, and he playfully slaps her butt as they both jump on her bed to cuddle and talk. He comments that she is growing up, and she replies:

POWELL: Glad you noticed.
PIDGEON: I suppose it's only a matter of time till someone will come round here and try to take you away from me.
POWELL: As if anyone could!
PIDGEON: Well, he'll have a fight on his hands. I can promise you that.

They cheerfully plan a trip together, Powell pointing out that she can "go out with you . . . have dinner with you . . . go dancing with you, even. Gosh, it will be just as if I were your girl." She shifts her position on the bed, lying back into his arms, gazing up at him while he says, "You've been my girl for a long time now, since you were about one minute old—and, uh—that's what you'll always be. No matter how grown-up you get—that's what you'll always be." With the treachery of men, however, Pidgeon is soon enough pursuing zaftig Ilona Massey, leaving Powell to find temporary solace with another daddy figure, the middle-aged Jose Iturbi.
† It is possible to observe that stories about young girls with daddies lose their positive edge as the age of the girl increases. As a child female star moves toward womanhood, such stories become more and more those about how the father is a problem, and how his neglect of her—or his attempts to control her life and her sexual choices—destroy her. For example, Elizabeth Taylor's father in *Rhapsody* (1954) neglects her, whereas his in-

Sometimes there is an actual wife and mother on the scene, as in *Out of the Fog* (1941), but the true romance can still be between father and daughter even after the girl is grown-up. Ida Lupino falls for the no-account gangster John Garfield, who extorts protection money from her own little old dad, Thomas Mitchell. Still, Lupino will do as women do. She passes up her reliable, good-guy steady, Eddie Albert, and plans to run off to Cuba with Garfield. She explains this by saying she goes all hot and cold around him, and so she does. When Garfield takes her to a Cuban nightclub to put her in the mood for the trip, it is pure forties sex, all shoved into the hot music, the gyrating dancers, Lupino's tight dress, and her hothouse orchid. She can't help herself where Garfield is concerned, but when he beats up her daddy, Daddy kills him. Lupino has to identify Garfield's body, and she and Daddy reconcile as they walk off arm in arm in the fog together. Daddy is planning on making his own trip to Cuba, financed by Garfield's money, and he and his pal John Qualen would love to have someone like her along—you know—"to cook," and so on. Will she go? You bet, Daddy. They hug.

It doesn't occur to Mitchell to invite his own wife, Lupino's mother, along. The three will go off together, Mitchell ditching his wife and Lupino ditching Eddie Albert. Daddy has killed her sexual lover, has kept his daughter with him both as a little wife and a little girl, and she likes it that way. Daddy will make it nice for her. Here is a film in which the leading lady does not end up in the arms of her appropriate mate but in the arms of her father.

These strange relationships are not restricted to young girls and daddies, of course. Grown young men are often seen hugging their mothers in total body grab and planting wet kisses full on the mouth. James Cagney practically makes open love to his mom in *The Irish in Us* (1935). She gives him money and fusses over him constantly. After one such act of generosity, he takes her in a full embrace, head to head in profile, and kisses her repeatedly, murmuring, "Oh, Mary Ellen, Mary Ellen, you're wonderful." This is the first and only time this character, Cagney's mother, is ever called by her Christian name. Cagney later points out, "What would I want with a wife? I've got you, haven't I? You're my sweetheart." After this outburst, which comes while he is slurping up some hot soup she made for him, he puts his head on her bosom and looks ecstatic. His girlfriend is no fool. She tells his mom, "You're such a sweetheart. I'd hate taking Danny away from you."

This longing also applies to glamorous moms, played by leading

---

volvement with criminals in *The Girl Who Had Everything* (1953), which is a remake of *A Free Soul* (1931), introduces her to a bad man.

actresses, and the sons they bear. In *The Secret of Madame Blanche* (1933), poor Blanche (Irene Dunne) is stuck in prison at the end of the film. When her son, played by handsome Phillips Holmes, comes to visit her, the two of them yearn toward each other, eyes closed, lips pressing together through the prison mesh in a deep kiss, their hands clasping tenderly. It's a love scene! (Is *this* the secret of Madame Blanche?)

The concept of a daddy figure in stories about women, whatever their age, is that of providing a nonsexual source of economic security and emotional happiness for women viewers. The fact that so many of these figures are couched in overtly sexual terms is disturbing, but it is also probably the source of the power of the concept. All these asexual characters are a form of freedom for women, because no matter how much cuddling, kissing, hugging, protecting, financing, or whatever, goes on, the woman has love without sex. Since the three M's—men, marriage, and mother-hood—are a progression toward an increasing sacrifice and servitude, the removal of sex from the equation cuts things back accordingly. When a woman has a man to take care of her with no sex attached, she has no need for marriage and thus no threat of motherhood. The daddy works perfectly in this context.

THE ASEXUAL "HUSBAND"

The asexual husband (or lover or friend or suitor) is a kind of patron for a woman. Since the act of being a woman is both a female's art *and* her job, a man who helps her through it without the usual love and sex component is furthering her profession. And since a man is the important thing in a woman's life, and women see men as having freedoms they don't have, it is inevitable that *a man* can become an acceptable, albeit disguised, form of liberation for a character in a woman's film. Men provide opportunities for women and avenues of escape. Leslie Howard says to the woman he loves in *Berkeley Square* (1933) that he is going to make her see the future, a world unlike the one she lives in. "I must see," she says, dutifully allowing him to project onto her the world he has himself seen, since he is a time traveler. This is a kind of liberation, a transporting of the woman to a world in which society will provide her more freedom than she has, if not enough. He makes her "see." "You have seen the future, Helen," he says, just before he disappears back there himself, leaving her to be an old maid. (He gives her history instead of sex.) Their love becomes a love of souls, or a kind of justification for no sex.

The wonderful thing about these "husbands" is what beautiful timing they have. They always turn up just when a woman needs them most, and their loyalty would make a hound dog cry. They ask for nothing. They are

just *there*, representing an all-consuming love, an unquestioning commitment. They do not criticize, and they do not take away. They are totally
parental, in the best sense of the term.

How are these men defined? First of all, they are almost always old.
If not, the question arises, Why would a young man not want sex? Second,
they are often European, which is an indication that red-blooded American
men would never stand around this way, holding a woman's feather boa
while she sings "Swanee." If these men *are* Americans, they are tycoons,
which means their rapacious, rambunctious days are behind them, not that
this aspect of their lives doesn't exist. Third, these men are good judges
of women. They are connoisseurs. For this reason, they alone can appreciate
how fine the woman is, how good, how true, even if she's been to prison,
killed her former lover, and abandoned her child. Fourth, and this is
crucial, these men are understanding and tolerant. In other words, they
are totally unlike society at large. They will allow a woman to do as she
pleases. Last, they are problem solvers. Because they are rich and powerful,
they have the money and connections to take a woman wherever she wants
to go, and they can help her surmount things that have formerly blocked
her way. If she placed her daughter up for adoption years ago, they can
find her and bring her back. If she can't sing at the Palace because she
once dropped hot soup in the lap of the owner, they can get her the gig
anyway. If the other women in town don't want her invited to the annual
debutante's ball, they will bring her in on the stroke of midnight, shushing
everyone up but good. These are the men who do for a woman what society
will never do: forgive her, raise her to the heights, give her economic
power, admire her no matter what, and make her important in the scheme
of things. Sometimes these men actually marry the leading lady, and sometimes they do not, but always it is made clear that "you'll come to love me
in time" and "I'll be happy enough just being near you." No sex. Or not
enough to matter. They allow a woman *not* to make a choice, but to have
her cake (a safe marriage) and eat it, too (do whatever else she wishes).

A classic example of the asexual husband appears in the 1934 Joan
Crawford movie *Sadie McKee*, the story of a cook's daughter, who is abandoned in the big city by the man she loves, Gene Raymond. Without a
cent to her name, she hangs around the Automat, the Depression version
of both heaven and hell, trying surreptitiously to eat the food that people
have left behind on their plates. (In one tragic moment, a man leaves a
huge piece of lemon meringue pie, only to turn back at the last and put
out his cigarette in it!) Crawford is rescued by Jean Dixon, in one of her
best tough-dame, thirties sidekick roles. Dixon is "no better than she should
be" and realizes that Crawford has been stranded by Raymond. "You're

gonna find out about men, the tripe," she advises Crawford. As the two of
them sway along on the subway, they talk:

CRAWFORD: I'm kinda sick of men.
    DIXON: Aw, you're crazy. They've got what we want, all of it, and
             every gal has her price. Yours ought to be high.

Suddenly Dixon notices that an obviously bluestockinged middle-aged
woman is listening to their conversation, so she leans down to her and
says, loudly and meaningfully, *"Every gal has her price.* I don't know what
you got, but you sure gypped somebody."

Dixon gets Crawford a job dancing in a cheap nightclub, and it is
here that she meets Edward Arnold. As she is dancing around in a skimpy
costume, a rowdy man in the audience grabs her veil and tries to pull it
off. Arnold, a sodden knight in a tight tuxedo, drunkenly reels over and
stops him. In gratitude, Crawford gives him a white rose from the basket
she carries in her number. After Arnold accepts the token, he throws it
onto the floor, saying, "Aw, what do I want with a white rose?" He remembers Crawford's face, however, and asks to have her brought to his
table. ("He's a rich millionaire," Dixon tells Crawford. "Go ahead." One
assumes that if he were a poor millionaire, she wouldn't be so enthusiastic.)

Seated with Arnold at his table is his lawyer, played by Franchot
Tone, who happens to be the son of the family Crawford's mother works
for. Tone has been instrumental in driving Raymond and Crawford out of
town, and Crawford tells him off.

"I had a little world just my size, and you took it away."

Tone tells her that Raymond was bad. "You trusted him, and he let
you down."

"Nothing of the kind," snaps back Crawford. "He was afraid to take
a chance getting married on nothin'. He was just too weak."

During all this arguing, Arnold is barely listening. He is incredibly
drunk, embracing Crawford and hanging on her, babbling about his own
mother having been a cook. He likes Crawford's brutal honesty, and he
takes her home with him. There, he collapses in a drunken stupor, but not
before he proposes to her.

The next day, they go shopping. Crawford not only gets fur-trimmed
outfits and hats and a huge diamond ring, but a new outfit and diamond
bracelet are also purchased for Dixon, her bridesmaid. The newspaper
headlines blare "Working Girl Marries Seventeen Millions." At home on
their wedding night, Arnold is blotto and Crawford tipsy. When they go
upstairs together, the film becomes sordid. Arnold runs to the bathroom to
vomit, and when the door swings open, he has fallen onto his back, unable

to get up. His butler flops him onto the bed on his back and tries to undress him. Crawford watches in fear and disgust. A camera angle offers the audience a view of Edward Arnold from above and to the right of the bed, so that what is seen is his huge, fat belly as he lolls drunkenly, his butler pulling off his pants for him. It is the picture of a eunuch, a man who cannot perform for himself. As the butler continues undressing him, Crawford leaves the room. In the next scene, Crawford and Dixon stand at the foot of Crawford's bed. Eyeing it meaningfully, Dixon asks, "Got all this to yourself?"

"Yeah." Crawford nods.

"*Always* all to yourself?" presses Dixon.

"Yep," firmly answers Crawford.

"Well." Dixon sighs. "A whole lot of us do a whole lot more for a whole lot less."

Crawford has married the asexual male in a film that does not deal delicately with the subject. Where nice men like Ian Hunter stand around in *Secrets of an Actress* and *maybe* could be sexual, Arnold is shown to be incapable of sexual performance. In case viewers don't understand, they are also told in dialogue.

Arnold, however, can do everything else. He has a mansion with twenty-eight rooms and fourteen servants. He has cars and jewels and power around town. He is indeed a "rich millionaire." Most important of all, he adores Crawford, giving her everything and ultimately giving up drinking with her help. (Before this rehabilitation, he socks her cruelly on the jaw, trying to get to his bottle.) During all this time, Tone remains the voice of an unforgiving society, telling Crawford that she's married Arnold for his money, that she really loves Raymond, and that thus she's bad for having made the wrong choice. He refuses to help her rehabilitate Arnold and mistrusts her honesty about doing it. "That's twice you could have helped me and twice you fell flat on me," Crawford tells him. She takes hold alone, shaping up the servants by explaining to them that being a wife is her job just as being servants is theirs. This they can understand.

Arnold remains an asexual husband to the end.* After he is sober,

* There is a distinction to be made between the character being described here and the type played by Paul Henreid in *Casablanca* (1942). This is largely because *Casablanca* is not a woman's film, but Henreid's Victor Laszlo is almost a reference point for such men. The story makes clear that Henreid married Ingrid Bergman, who is much younger than he is, to care for her and protect her. He was a friend of her parents. (Although he did not marry her, but "kept her safe in his house during the war," this is what the Georges Guetary character did for Leslie Caron in *An American in Paris* also.) The Henreid/Bergman marriage is never depicted as having passion, only respect and devotion. They kiss chastely on cheeks, and Bergman's hot embraces are saved for Humphrey Bogart. The asexual male

and still totally devoted to her, Crawford explains to him that she loves Raymond and that she married him only because "I was knocked silly. It was a refuge. There's only one man in my heart and I've got to find him." Love, true love, removes her responsibilities to the marriage. It erases all obligations. Arnold, the perfect asexual husband, understands, calmly offering to take care of all the divorce proceedings himself and asking for "just one last dance."

This is the role of the asexual male. He provides whatever it is that the woman wants. He marries her, but does not expect anything in return. When she is through with him, he waltzes off, just as devoted to her as ever and just as available if ever she needs anything again. He is a figure who conveniently gives a woman all the power that she otherwise lacks. His tycoonship becomes hers, but she doesn't have to do anything for it. He is a figure whom society can approve of for this bestowing of power, because what is he, after all, but a man? Not really a man, of course, but a well-disguised desire for power and wealth and the liberation those things can bring.

GHOSTS AND ANGELS

The very best female fantasies often involve men who are ghosts or angels, because they are all-powerful. They really *can* give a woman anything, because they can do anything. They are magical figures, dream men in the truest sense of the term. These creatures are reasonably common in movies about women. Even today's *Ghost* (1990) is a story about a dead husband who watches over his wife from the grave, dancing with her via the body of Whoopi Goldberg. When movies like this bring handsome men into the lives of women, can anyone doubt the point that these men are fantasies of a romance without sex that provides security and protection?

These ghosts and angels take different shapes for different meanings. In *The Bishop's Wife* (1947), the fantasy male is an angel played by Cary Grant. (Who better to play the part?) Grant enters the life of Loretta Young, the bishop's neglected young wife. The bishop (David Niven) is "terribly busy and tired," intent on building his career and looking after his parish by fund-raising from wealthy and difficult women. Young suffers in silence, but her big eyes look sad, and people notice she's a bit sallow and dragged out. Into her life comes the angel, and suddenly she's joyful and radiant. The angel is really not so much an angel as he is a better,

---

character—an important fixture in many women's films—helps to verify the purity of the Henreid/Bergman relationship for 1940s audiences used to the conventions of many different genres.

Cary Grant as the angel and Loretta Young as *The Bishop's Wife*

more attentive husband, the kind that Young deserves. The film is gentle and sweet, and the audience can watch how a woman blooms under the loving attentions of a man who takes an actual, sincere interest in her. Young begins to come alive. She goes ice-skating and buys a new hat with a great big rose on top of it. This hat, fashion proof of the woman's changed state, is a showstopper.

Cary Grant's mission on earth is twofold. He awakens Loretta Young, and she is like a virgin brought into a happy sensuality, and he wakes up David Niven, who suddenly becomes jealous and realizes he must pay more attention to his wife and less to his career. This angel has come to earth to make a better man of a woman's husband by standing in for him and showing him what to do everywhere except in the bedroom. The angel gives Young love, warmth, and attention, all the things that many women in the audience must have felt were lacking in their own lives. He sets a good example, and the husband learns the needed lesson.

Cary Grant is literally the answer to her woman's prayers. Young's release is beautifully visualized in a scene in which she and Grant go ice-skating. "Oh, Dudley," she says to the angel, "this is heaven." Young and Grant take the ice, whirling and twirling under the emerging lights that come on in the winter twilight, the sound of music filling their ears. Young, always a radiant actress, lights up, as the skating projects a sense of joy, grace, release, and freedom that women clearly would have identified with.

In *Forever Darling* (1956), Lucille Ball's ghost, or fantasy male, is a creature no one but her can see, played by James Mason, who is playing himself. Mason is Ball's inner voice or, as he tells her, the proof that she is dissatisfied with her life. Her unrest takes the form of James Mason because he is her favorite movie star. This is supreme logic by movie standards.

The ghost figure of the successful 1947 movie *The Ghost and Mrs. Muir* is probably the best illustration of the type. This fantasy figure is not a dream husband or a dream lover or a stand-in for the woman's favorite movie star. He is a fantasy figure who represents physically on-screen what Mrs. Muir's inner self really is. Mrs. Muir, played by the exquisite Gene Tierney, is defined as a strong woman who doesn't quite know, at the beginning of the story, how strong she really is. Her story is a true woman's film. The movie begins in turn-of-the century London. Tierney's character is a widow with a small child. She had married her husband when she was barely seventeen years old, and now she is alone except for his domineering mother and unmarried sister. She lives in their home, trapped and miserable, subject to their largess, which makes them feel perfectly free to tell her what she can or can't do. The film opens on her rejecting their domination in a remarkable speech of liberation. Much to their surprise and disapproval, she informs them she is going to take her child and move out on her own, to lead her own life. "I've never had a life of my own," she says. "First it was Edward's life, and then yours. . . ." Her in-laws issue dire warnings, trying to frighten her. However, she is firm. "I've always wanted to live beside the sea," she announces firmly. By speaking the words "I've always wanted," Mrs. Muir liberates herself into the joyous freedom of making her own decisions. Her maid, thoroughly approving, cries out, "It's a bloomin' revolution!"

The first scene at the seashore illustrates both what she is up against as a woman alone and what she plans to do about it. She enters a rental agency and encounters a pure example of the confident male who asserts his masculine authority over her. This man is totally pompous, although not unkind. When she selects from his potential offerings a place called Gull Cottage, he refuses to show it to her. When she persists, he, certain that it is his God-given job to overrule a widowed woman in straitened circumstances, tells her firmly, "I'll have to be the judge of that."

This is Mrs. Muir's trial by combat. When she gamely stands her ground and *really* insists on seeing the cottage, he gives in and takes her to see the lonely, somewhat dilapidated house that is situated out by itself on a spit of land overlooking the rough sea. This is Mrs. Muir's first test as a woman alone, and she passes it—never faltering, never believing for a moment that this man knows better than she does what is right or appropriate for her. When Gull Cottage turns out to be haunted by the raucous sound of rough masculine laughter ("Haunted! How marvelous!"), she shows no fear. In fact, she's delighted.

Into the film, and thus into her life, comes a strong male character, the ghost of the title. This man appears while she is sleeping, because he is, in fact, a character she dreams up, a brave and competent sea captain, a ghost with sex appeal. The ghost is an irascible old reprobate, and he is played with appropriate masculine gusto by Rex Harrison. "I am here," says the ghost, "because you want me to be here."

The Ghost and Mrs. Muir, unlike *Forever Darling*, does not overtly say that the fantasy figure is only a figment of the woman's imagination, there to remain until Tierney, like Ball, gets over her problem. Harrison's character is treated in a much more realistic fashion. He is a ghost, of course, appearing and disappearing, seen only by her, but he is supposed to have once been alive, a flesh-and-blood man.

Now, however, he is a creature of Mrs. Muir's imagination, and because of that, one that she can control. He is the symbol of many possibilities. He might be her need for a man, a strong and lusty one who will not die on her as her weak husband did. He could be her need for a true, deep love, or even for just hearty sex. He can be her need for reassurance as she faces life as a woman on her own, or he could be a covert representative of her desire for a career. He is any and all of these things, but the one that best explains the character of Mrs. Muir is that of career, or independence. He is more or less her "male" side, or that part of her that is brave and independent, fierce and creative. He urges her to value herself. He watches over Tierney as she sleeps, keeping her safe. He guides her, too, and appreciates her. He is a strong husband, an ideal mate. Of course he is also a ghost, so that there is no possibility of sex. He is not only a perfect mate, lover, daddy, friend, mentor, but also the impetus for her to gain in independence and, finally, to have a career as a famous writer. She is allegedly his amanuensis, but what can she really be doing but writing what is inside her?

As she expands and deepens, her very name is altered. Instead of being called Lucy by Harrison, she is called Lucia, which he says is a name for an Amazon, a queen, whereas women named Lucy are always imposed upon. As Tierney's need for money grows pressing, the ghost and

Mrs. Muir write a strong and vigorous book together, the story of his life as a sailor. This period of time in which Mrs. Muir is seen working and creating under the guidance of Rex Harrison is the period in which her independence is completed. When they finish, she says, "When we were writing the book, I was happy." Looking at her, the ghost tells her that she really owes it to herself to see men, but she replies that she has no interest in them.

This is a woman's film, however, so men are not that easily disposed of. When Tierney goes up to London to sell their salty book, she once again enters the conventional world of condescending men. Gull Cottage has been a haven of feminine thinking, a sanctuary of freedom. In London, Tierney encounters two examples of male prejudice. One is her potential publisher, who tells her he already knows all about her book. Twenty million women write them, and they are always love novels of the worst sort. He doesn't publish "feminine literature." In addition to this dismal creature, who soon changes his tune ("It's a man's book!" he will cry out), she meets a suave and sophisticated writer of children's stories, Uncle Neddy, played by George Sanders. He is even more insulting when he learns she has a book. "Is it a cookbook?" he inquires, smirking. When she says no, he adds, "Not another life of Byron, I hope."

George Sanders is in sharp contrast to her ghost. He comes down to Gull Cottage and sweeps her into his arms, observed by the disappointed ghost, who knows instinctively that Sanders is no good. Tierney has not become a fool, however. She realizes that Sanders is conceited, erratic, and childish, but she decides that she needs companionship and "all the things a woman needs." Harrison is contemptuous. "I thought you were a woman with sense, but you're like all the rest. A fool for any man who'll promise you the moon and take everything you have to give."

As Mrs. Muir prepares to once again become a woman in the sense that society approves of, Harrison disappears from her life. "You must live your own life," he says while she sleeps. "You wrote the book, you and no one else. It's been a dream. You imagined it from this house, the garden. . . . It will die as all dreams must die. You will remember it as a dream." When Tierney awakes, she dresses herself in her most feminine clothes and goes up to London to tell Sanders that she will be his. This sequence is in the tradition of the woman's film, the scene in which the woman's heart is broken when she learns the truth about George Sanders, who has lied to her and deceived her, being already married.

Tierney then lives out her life, comfortable on the proceeds of her "man's book." Having filled his purpose, the ghost never reappears. As he instructed, she has no memory of him. She rejects real men and lives a pleasant and useful life, having invented for herself a man who was more than a dream of romantic love, although couched in those terms visually, since that was all society would allow her to know. He was really a manifestation of who she wanted to be, and who she did, in fact, become.

Gene Tierney's character, of course, is never seen writing a second book. When she dies, she rises out of her bed, released from her bondage as a woman. She is young and beautiful again, and Rex Harrison awaits her. Here is a woman's movie moment open to two interpretations. Does it mean that a woman, even after death, can't get free from men or romance? Or does it mean that by living a liberated life, in which she chooses not to be dependent on a man, a woman can finally be united with her true self (with the self disguised as Rex Harrison)?

Another form of ghost is a character sometimes found in American film, the mysterious stranger, a ghost who is not a ghost but who isn't real either. These men come into a town or a situation temporarily to magically change everything for the inhabitants, almost always for the good. They liberate people, let them see themselves in a new way, and sometimes turn the politics of the burg upside down. Mysterious strangers appear in various genres: westerns like *Shane* (1953), or populist small-town dramas like *Johnny Come Lately* (1943). The mysterious stranger can also be a woman—*Mary Poppins* (1964) portrays such a person, after all. The key thing about the mysterious stranger, however, is that there is no sex attached to his or her presence. Thus, the character represents a kind of longing or yearning for something to change, another disguised form of freedom.

One form of mysterious stranger in the woman's film is the character played by Van Johnson in *Miracle in the Rain* (1956). As a young man, Johnson was the classic all-American boy. Freckle-faced, hearty, open, and natural, Johnson projected an uncomplicated, tenderhearted persona that could be wise or smart-ass as needed. During the years of World War II, when he was unable to serve in the armed forces, he rose to major stardom, and his career is still alive today. Johnson could be sexy on-screen, but often, particularly in the war years, he was asked to be boyish, guileless. He plays such a character in *Miracle in the Rain*.

There are four female characters in *Miracle in the Rain*. The first two are close and devoted friends: Jane Wyman, playing a shy, vulnerable, repressed young woman who is totally under the domination of her mother, and Eileen Heckart, an older woman, kindly and humorous, who works alongside Wyman in an office. Neither woman is married. The third woman is Wyman's mother (Josephine Hutchinson), an embittered widow who tried to kill herself when her husband, Wyman's father, deserted her for another, younger woman. She now fears and hates men, and her worst terror is that Wyman will go off with one and she will once again be left alone, untended. Her fears manifest themselves in psychosomatic illnesses that keep Wyman tied to her night and day. The fourth woman is a young and voluptuous secretary (Peggie Castle) in the office, who everyone knows is sleeping with their married boss.

The women share a problem: men. Wyman and Heckart have no men and thus are lonely and unfulfilled, and the mother and the secretary have, in a sense, too much men. These two act out a mirror image of each other's fates: the mother's husband deserted her for a younger woman, and the secretary is caught up in a romance with a married man, who she hopes will leave his wife for her. However, he has no such plan.

Van Johnson enters this world. He is bumptious, charming, kind, and generous. He is the life-giving male force at its best. Thanks to him, the shy and repressed Wyman begins to open up, laugh, and go places. Heckart is allowed to share in this largess, because Johnson is innocent himself and has no ulterior motives toward Wyman. He is happy to include her friend in all their dates if it helps to make Wyman more comfortable. Because Johnson does not fear life or other people, he helps Wyman connect to others. As they fall in love and go through New York City in the time he has before shipping overseas to combat, they meet and interact with various Manhattan types. (This is similar to the plot of another romantic film of the 1940s, *The Clock*, 1945). He buys a "Roman coin" for Wyman as a talisman against the future, a lucky piece to keep him safe in war and her safe at home.

The days the two young lovers spend together have a magical quality, as everything seems to go their way. There is a purity to their relationship, and slowly not just Wyman but all four women find their lives transformed by the presence of this mysterious stranger who takes the form of an all-American boy. Heckart's lonely life is somewhat filled, and she has the joy of seeing her friend find love. The secretary, realizing how true and good Wyman's love is, suddenly realizes what a mean and empty little experience she is having. She walks out on the no-good boss, changing jobs and liberating herself from a demeaning man who is only using her. Most miraculously of all, Wyman's father and mother are reunited through a series of plot maneuvers all motivated by Johnson's presence. Wyman and Johnson agree to marry when he returns from war.

Near the end of the film, when this pseudo–Capra movie turns melodramatic, word comes to Wyman that Johnson has been killed in battle. Already sick in bed with a bad cough, she staggers out into a driving rain to go to the church they once prayed in together. During this extended stagger, Wyman suddenly sees the cheerful Johnson walking toward her, holding the Roman coin, and saying, "Love never dies. I'm here to stay, to love you forever and ever." He kisses her and then disappears. When Wyman is found where she collapsed on the street in the downpour, the

Roman coin that she gave him to take overseas as a good-luck piece is
mysteriously back in her own hand. Johnson has been a force that liberated
Wyman out of her repressed and limited life. She will live on without his
presence physically (no sex), but with the life force he has given her carrying
her forward.*

DOCTORS

The most satisfactory asexual characters are ghosts and angels, followed by the asexual husbands and then the father figures. Two problematic areas are those of doctor and impresario, because both of these
characters keep slipping out of their asexual labeling. Often the doctors
fall in love with the women, and the impresarios are mean to them.
The doctor and the impresario are the positive and the negative of the
asexual type. They are significant because the doctor represents the
woman's acceptance of love (her natural career) and the impresario represents the more unacceptable choice, that of a career instead of love and
marriage.

A doctor is supposed to be a kindly presence in any woman's life.
By virtue of his profession, he should have a superior knowledge of who
and what a woman is. The mysteries of childbirth, for one thing, are not
unknown to him, nor are the secrets of a woman's anatomy or her mind.
Doctors are often secondary characters in women's films, providing counsel
and direction for confused females. When they move forward into romantic
roles, as they frequently do, they, like everything and everyone else, come
in both a good version and a bad version. The bad doctors put women in
asylums, wreck their plastic surgery so they end up looking like alligator

---

* Just as a male character in a film can represent freedom/change/escape in a woman's
life, a woman can represent the same for a man. Sometimes a man keeps in mind throughout
his life the beautiful, sensual dream of a woman he loved in his youth, and this fantasy
figure often has to be rejected so he can be brought to his senses to appreciate the nice
little wife he really has. This is essentially the story of *H. M. Pulham, Esq.* (1941), although
the woman is supposed to be a real person. *Mr. Peabody and the Mermaid* (1948) is an
example of the ghost/angel syndrome for men. In it, the middle-aged William Powell
suddenly sees a mermaid, and his wife has to deal with this problem. It is interesting to
compare this female ghost or unreal figure with those conjured up by female characters, as
the comparison illustrates much about male and female fantasies. The two things are parallel
because both mermaids and ghosts do not exist, and presumably neither can have sex, the
ghost because he technically has no body, and the mermaid because she technically has
no lower half. Where the ghost men are creatures of sublime sophistication and strength
who guide women toward goals that they secretly desire, the mermaid is totally naive,
without experience or knowledge of any sort. Thus, the ghost man teaches, or controls and
directs, and the mermaid is taught, guided, and controlled. Two different kinds of fantasies
for two different sexes occupying two different cultural and social roles.

pears, and abort them under desperate circumstances. The good ones save
a woman's life, freeing her to become who she really is.

The noble Dr. Jacquin of *Now, Voyager* (1942), who totally changes
Bette Davis's life, is such a good character. The psychiatrists who cure the
multiple-personality cases in *The Three Faces of Eve* (1957) and *Sybil* (1976,
made for TV) are such men, as is the doctor who cures Olivia de Havilland
in *The Snake Pit* (1948). When a doctor is a kindly older man, as in the
Dr. Christian movies, he is always helpful to women. When he is young
and sexy, as in the Dr. Kildare movies, he is himself often involved in the
woman's adventures. Technically, however, a doctor is an important man
in the woman's film who does not ask for sex from a woman but who offers
her the explanation she needs about herself that will ultimately free her.

Women constantly go to their doctors in the woman's film. These men
are wise, and they have all the answers. Sometimes the woman doesn't
want to hear the answer, but the doctor always has it. He cures the woman's
cancer, her blindness, her deafness, and her craziness. Doctors *are* a form
of fake men, because they care too much about a woman's concerns. Real
men aren't supposed to do that. The doctor sits and talks with a woman
about her things, her clothes, her children, her worries. He listens and he
cares. He is like a girlfriend. In the doctor category is the fantasy male
who most often represents the woman's desire for a lover rather than for
freedom or a perfect husband or liberation into a career, but when he
becomes a romantic figure he has still played a role that is more feminine
than masculine.

In addition to the father-figure psychiatrists and the destructive psychiatrists and mad plastic surgeons, there are the romantic doctor figures
who end up loving the woman, even though their primary function is asexual
because it is concerned only with the woman's health and well-being. Two
films about impaired women—Loretta Young in *And Now Tomorrow* and
Jane Wyman in *Johnny Belinda*—have romantic doctors. The two women
have the sort of magnificent affliction that movie women are often struck
with, rendering them speechless and thus big-eyed, beautiful, and *silent*.*

* Both Young and Wyman are deaf, a more interesting condition for the woman's film than
blindness. A blind woman may bump into things and suffer, and sometimes be victimized
by killers who sneak up on her, but these events can happen to women who are not blind,
too. A deaf or mute woman seems to be particularly appealing to audiences, a fact that
extends into present times with the success of *Children of a Lesser God* (1986) both on the
stage and the screen. There is something about the woman's inability to communicate by
opening her mouth and talking—about the inability to answer back or speak up for
herself—that appeals. And if a woman does not know what is going on, if she cannot hear
what is being said, she is rendered helpless. Her condition in no way, however, reduces
her beauty, her mobility, her ability to wear makeup and clothes, or her social acceptance.
She can, in fact, spruce up and go anywhere, just sitting silently beside her man. In real

Loretta Young and Jane Wyman make interesting contrasts. Young is rich; Wyman is poor. Young went deaf at an older age from meningitis, so she can read lips and understand all language with remarkable—yes, even astonishing—ease. Wyman was born deaf and has never learned to talk or communicate easily. Both women come under the influence of a doctor who will change their lives.

In *And Now Tomorrow* (1944), Loretta Young meets Alan Ladd, a godlike, omniscient doctor with a cynical sense of humor, a poor boy who has made good and who helps poor people by operating on them on their kitchen tables. He has had excellent luck curing deaf rabbits, so Young begs him to experiment on her, and he does. This film demonstrates the vulnerability of an afflicted woman who becomes totally dependent on a doctor to cure her. She is his patient, his victim, and his object. She is totally in his hands, as he becomes her husband, father, confidant, savior, and god, all rolled into one. By setting this story against a class background—rich versus poor—the film demonstrates that the doctor is stronger than wealth and economic power. The rich woman leads an idle life, not "hearing" what society is telling her. Through the doctor, she gains her hearing, learning that she needs to lead a useful life, putting her millions into his clinic and listening to what he tells her.

When Ladd finally falls in love with Young, she angrily says, "You can't cure me, so you're willing to make love to me." She sees it as his way of retaining mastery over her, since he failed as a medical man. He has constantly insulted her and abused her verbally throughout the film, until she finally bursts out, "Nobody in my entire life has ever talked to me this way." He responds, "Maybe that's what's wrong with you. Why don't you try coming down off that high pedestal of yours and being a human being for a change? Pride isn't enough for even you to live on." This is an invitation that men constantly make to women in films. "Come

---

life, of course, deaf women *can* talk and do. They use sign language and they read lips and they speak aloud. The fact that these communication skills are either ignored, romanticized, or exaggerated on-screen is significant in and of itself.

Presenting a woman as silent, her large eyes trained adoringly or innocently on the man, is one of my least favorite devices. It is a form of something that we have with us on the screen today in an even bigger, less pleasant way, a form in which the woman is, to put it simply, shut up and made uncommunicative or, for all practical purposes, brainless. In today's world, we have entire TV shows ("Twin Peaks") and movies (*Presumed Innocent*, 1990) in which a central female character is dead. There's no better way to make a woman brainless than to make her dead, no better way to render her powerless than to kill her off. In the old days, women characters played by strong and famous actresses couldn't be shoved off the screen so easily. The title character in *Laura* (1944), the inspiration for Laura Palmer of "Twin Peaks," wasn't really dead. She showed up less than halfway into the story and claimed her screen space accordingly.

down, come down" . . . a form of "lie down, lie down." It is both a threat and a promise. Young goes to Ladd for his rabbit injections, willing to become his guinea pig because, as she tells him, "I'm incomplete." Ladd tells her he will keep on working with her as long as she's deaf, until the day "I can give you the only thing you want from me." Symbolically, his injection makes her complete. Because he is the one who has given her "what she needed," he is the man for her, which is lucky, because the one she was supposed to marry is actually in love with her sister, Susan Hayward.

And Now Tomorrow presents a heavily disguised, unpleasant sexuality. Loretta Young is impaired, needing injections to make her whole. Ladd is the great injector, a doctor. A detailed scene in which Ladd injects Young to "make her well" is visualized. Young enters Ladd's office and sits on a stool. He stands, looming over her (despite his short stature). He is an image of mastery and dominance. She is softly lit, so that her face looks innocent, angelic, and what she is wearing, a white blouse with very full sleeves, is designed to enhance a viewer's sense of her vulnerability, her delicacy. As Ladd bends over her ominously, injecting her, he says in his low, throaty voice: "Hurt?"

YOUNG: Yes, a little.
  LADD: More than a little.
YOUNG: All right. More than a little.
  LADD: But you're not afraid of pain, are you?
YOUNG: No. I told you I wasn't.
  LADD: Maybe you even like it.

Young and Ladd are playing doctor in the tradition of the porno film, with more than a hint of pain and masochism. He has been lousy to her all through the film. Using the established persona of Alan Ladd as a slightly kinky sex figure, the film later has him punish Young by making her wait for him while he plays pinball at a joint down the street. This doctor constantly teaches this woman a lesson, putting her in her proper place. The excuse for this is not that she is deaf or female, but that she is rich and upper class; this is supposed to make the lesson acceptable. Young learns her lesson. She begins to obey Ladd and to help him. She holds a lantern high for him while he performs one of his wizard operations in a kitchen on a poor person, inspiring him to tell her, "It's a shame you weren't born poor." She finally says, "Once you said I should have been born poor. You were right. I would have been useful. I would have learned how to work. I started being useful when I became a guinea pig."

And Now Tomorrow is a traditional woman's film. When the story of how Young became deaf is told in flashbacks, there is a traditional moment in which she tells her fiancé, "I'm happier than I've ever been in my entire life." She immediately collapses and wakes up deaf. The film's use of the doctor figure takes Young out of her deafness and out of her idle rich life into an occupation, but only through a muddled and unpleasant love story. The doctor figure is the vehicle through which this happens, and his presentation is in the tradition of the asexual male.

The doctor in *Johnny Belinda* (1948) is kind, totally unlike Ladd. Throughout the film he is teacher, mentor, and doctor to deaf Jane Wyman, who is a poor farm girl in Nova Scotia. She is barely educated, and because of her mute behavior she is more or less isolated from everyone. Subjected to a brutal rape, she gives birth to the baby she names Johnny Belinda. Because he has become her teacher and is constantly with her, the doctor is suspected of being the father. No detailed love development takes place in this film, but at the end the doctor and Wyman are married, with the child happily between them. The doctor functions as the force that transforms Wyman from an untidy, frightened, and illiterate deaf girl into an attractive, happy, educated young matron. He does it without a love scene, and he fathers her child without having sex with her. He is a classic example of the doctor as asexual male.

THE IMPRESARIO

The impresario is the most negative of the asexual men. When a woman has talent and wants it developed, she must have a teacher, someone who knows the ropes and how to develop her potential. There is an obvious sexual implication to this, and movies that tell such stories almost always develop a love-versus-career conflict in the woman's life as part of the story. Usually an impresario is played by an older actor, or if not older, certainly a European, not-very-virile actor. The woman's other choice in life is always represented by a strapping young hulk, often characterized as uncomplicated, unsophisticated, even bumptious. It might be possible to say that the European impresario, who is often cruel, demanding, and possessive, is supposed to represent the unnatural way of life for a woman, while the fresh-faced, openly loving, and generous other man represents nature and the right thing to do. It might also be said, however, that the impresario is a disguised liberating force, showing the woman that such a choice will be difficult and demanding but that it *is* a choice, while the other man represents a barren and even sterile life artistically. It is possible to suggest that films featuring these impresarios speak covertly to a woman's desire for liberation and for her own life. Thus the force that sets her free from the accepted path of marriage and motherhood has to be seen in a film as a man, visualized as the Other Choice.

Films of this type are represented by *The Men in Her Life* (1941), *The Red Shoes* (1948), *Maytime* (1937), and *I've Always Loved You* (1946). *The Men in Her Life*, starring Loretta Young, Conrad Veidt, Dean Jagger, and John Shepperd, is an example of a film in which the impresario dies, leaving the heroine without love. *The Red Shoes* is the type in which, torn between her art and her love, *she* dies. *Maytime* has the woman sacrifice her true love and go to her grave without him, and *I've Always Loved You* has her sacrifice the career and ultimately find happiness as a wife and mother. In *The Men in Her Life* and *The Red Shoes*, the women are ballerinas, in *I've Always Loved You* the woman is a concert pianist, and in *Maytime* she's a singer. Music and dance are "feminine" subjects, and being a musical performer is an acceptable career for a woman. It's not like being a magazine editor or a nuclear physicist. It's not "man's work." Music is a career in which a woman presents herself physically before an audience partly in order to be admired. It is, however, a career, and maintaining it requires a woman to travel, to work, to study, and to make sacrifices. It requires her to be selfish, in that she has no time to make soup for a husband or take the kids to camp in the station wagon. It will also make her wealthy and thus independent and, to a degree, powerful.

Two of the impresarios in these four films are played by foreign actors with accents (Conrad Veidt in *The Men in Her Life* and Philip Dorn in *I've Always Loved You*). Since *The Red Shoes* is British, the accent doesn't count, but Anton Walbrook is a parallel to the John Barrymore character in *Maytime*. All these impresarios are the ultimate in sophistication, good taste, and experience.

And, in fact, these four films define the asexual impresario completely. His role is to represent the career choice, and if he is chosen, there will be no sex, love, or real happiness with him or any other man. If the woman marries him, he becomes an asexual husband. Each of the four stories offers a choice: reject the impresario and find happiness (*I've Always Loved You*); accept the impresario and have a career, but lose true love and happiness (*Maytime*); get neither and end up dead because you can't make the choice (*The Red Shoes*); or have it all ways at once (*The Men in Her Life*).

The Men in Her Life (1941) provides all possible examples by having its leading lady reject love, accept love, reject love, accept love, reject love, and accept love in a particularly muddleheaded series of episodes. In this film, Loretta Young starts out as a bareback rider in a seedy small-time circus. After she rides, she likes to go on in front of the audience and do an impromptu, unschooled ballet dance, because it is her dream of ecstasy to become a famous ballerina. One night, she is seen by a formerly great ballet dancer, played by Conrad Veidt. He tells her that she is beautiful and totally terrible . . . but with potential. He tells her she must go somewhere and learn, and then casually gives her his card.

Young is portrayed as consumed with ambition. She will stop at nothing. She quits the circus and follows Veidt, begging him to teach her himself. He is appalled at this and has no interest in her, trying to throw her out of his home. Young is unstoppable, naked in her ruthlessness. She even follows him upstairs, bursting into his bathroom, begging him, until finally he agrees. What Young does not know is that in agreeing to teach her he has signed his own death warrant, because doctors have told him he must never dance or teach again. Her passion has reached him, however, and he is inspired by her beauty. Veidt is man number one in Young's life, and her ambition will kill him.

While she is studying with Veidt and working very hard, Young has a moment of teenage rebellion with a handsome young man, played by John Shepperd. Shepperd and Young enact a perfect example of the woman's film Happy Interlude, in which they ride off on horses into a forested glade in the rain, seeking shelter and making love. When Young returns home, Veidt understands what has happened and slaps her hard. She immediately apologizes and becomes a famous ballerina. Shepperd is man number two in her life. She uses him and then ruthlessly ditches him, because of her ambition.

After establishing clearly that Young has rejected true love for her career, the movie goes on to present her success. On the night of her greatest triumph, she is shown as surrounded by admiring and doting men, who toast her in champagne and treat her as if she were a queen. She is the center of everyone's attention, and she is radiantly happy, on top of the world. Everything she has ever wanted is hers. Immediately, she is punished for this success. Veidt tells her that, because she is so successful and has reached her own power and potential, they no longer need to be teacher and pupil. She has no further need for him in that capacity, but now they are free to be . . . suddenly, she realizes that he is in love with her, and she knows that she does not and never will love him. At the height of her happiness and triumph her face reveals a moment of deep dismay, but she quickly recovers and pays her debt by agreeing to marry him. She knows she owes him. This marriage is the true acceptance of her career as her life's choice, because she does not love Veidt. He is presented as completely asexual, and the film makes it clear that this choice does not represent love. Rather, it is another step in her career.

The Men in Her Life presents the next few years of Young's life as a montage of her ballet triumphs. She grows more and more famous, more and more successful, and, of course, wealthier and wealthier. Veidt creates a final loving masterpiece for Young, a ballet called The White Rose. This transports her to the ultimate success, and, having completely fulfilled his job, Veidt dies. Young is devastated by his death, because although their marriage was not sexual or romantic it had been full of respect and shared interests. She grieves, so the audience will know she isn't heartless, and then, knowing she is free to find her true love, begins to look for Shepperd. When she finds him, he is engaged to another woman, and Young's heart is broken, more or less. Since Young chose career (Veidt) over love (Shepperd), she cannot expect to find love waiting in the wings.

Young continues with her career, and man number three enters her life (Dean Jagger). He is the typical example of the super-rich man who surfaces in the life of a successful star. After his arrival, Young has now had three men who represent the choices available to women: Veidt, to represent her career; Shepperd, to represent true love and romance; and Jagger, to represent marriage as a metaphor for economic security. When Jagger and Young marry, he wishes her to give up her career, and she agrees to do so. Her ambition is now slaked by her incredible successes, particularly the triumph of her *White Rose* ballet. Since true love is denied her because Shepperd has someone else, she settles for economic security, particularly as she is aware that a dancer cannot keep going forever.

Having once chosen the impresario over love, however, Young's life can never be simple. When she hears, months after her marriage to Jagger, that *The White Rose* is again to be performed in honor of Veidt's memory, she says that no one, but no one, can possibly dance it except herself. Jagger objects, and their argument is a classic confrontation of marriage versus career. Young will not accept his denial of her desire to dance, and she leaves him. She dances brilliantly, but collapses at the end of the performance. Unbeknownst to anyone, she is pregnant. (The woman's film dilemma!) Since she and Jagger are not divorced, naturally she goes away to have the baby in secret. Having the child, a daughter she names Rose, transforms her, causing her to lose all interest in anything but her child. Two years later, she accidentally meets Shepperd and finds out that he did not marry after all. They renew their love. This section of the film shows Young restored to her natural state, the one she would have followed had she not run away from Shepperd after their tryst in the rain. Although she has gone on dancing in order to earn a living, she no longer has any ambition at all, and her concern is always for the happiness of her child.

Young goes to Jagger to ask for a divorce so she can marry Shepperd. Jagger suddenly focuses on the fact that she has a child and that it must be his. He agrees to give her the divorce only if she will give up the little girl to him. Now Loretta Young is faced with the hardest choice of her life. Having rejected true love once, for the sake of her career, she cannot risk that mistake again. Yet how can she give up her child? What kind of a choice is this, she wants to know. (It's a woman's film choice.) Jagger tells her, "It's not a question of whether you love her. It's what are you willing to give up for her." Is Young willing to prove her love for her child by making the maternal sacrifice? Jagger pressures her, telling her that the child will be neglected because of her career. (The child has not been neglected so far, however, but has been shown to be very happy and well cared for.)

Young now makes, by the film's terms, a second wrong choice. Leaving her child behind, she goes off with Shepperd, trying to make up to herself for having made the wrong choice in the form of the impresario in the first place. As soon as she and Shepperd are underway, he is killed by a runaway carriage. She is seriously injured in the same accident, and it is two years before she can dance again. Young is punished for her wrong choice. She loses her true love, her child, *and* her career.

After her recovery, Young resumes a second-rate career performing in places like Australia and Capetown. When she finally returns to New York years later, her child is brought to see her dance and meet her backstage without knowing that this is her mother. When the daughter, too, wants to dance, Jagger unbends and the three are reunited. Young finally becomes a wife and mother, having been fully punished for her ambition.

Young's road to salvation is a long one, but it has to begin with the death of her impresario. He represents the loveless, sexless marriage that a career actually is supposed to be for a woman who marries her career. Only with his death can she go on to true happiness. However, by giving the "career" (man as impresario) so much screen time in so powerful a format, the attractiveness of the career and what it can bring is strengthened and covertly made possible. Actors who play impresarios are usually dominant figures, men like Claude Rains, Conrad Veidt, and John Barrymore, who have beautiful voices, great panache, and strong camera presence. They are to be seen as too old or too experienced for the young woman, but not as ugly or totally unlikable. They represent a viable alternative. It is a choice that a sacrifice must be made for, but the gains that go with it are also shown.

In *Maytime* (1937) the Barrymore character is similar to Veidt in *The Men in Her Life*. Having made it possible for Jeanette MacDonald to have a career, Barrymore becomes, in her mind, entitled to payment in the form of a marriage. Their union is one of mutual respect, but as a result she suffers the loss of her true love, Nelson Eddy.* In *The Red Shoes* (1948),

---

* It is ironic that John Barrymore, famous in real life for his sexual exploits, plays the asexual male here, while the less-than-hunky Nelson Eddy plays the sexual lover.

the young woman is caught between two powerful men, both of whom represent music. One is a composer, and one is a ballet master. Unable to keep herself from her career, symbolized by the red shoes she puts on so that she cannot stop dancing, the woman loses love and happiness and, finally, her life. She dances to her death, or careers herself into oblivion.

Of these four films, the one that presents the most interesting confusion of interpretation is Frank Borzage's *I've Always Loved You* (1946), based on an original story and screenplay by Borden Chase. It is purely and deeply a woman's film, and this seems to create problems for some Borzage scholars, who either ignore it completely or apologize for it. Jean-Pierre Coursodon, writing on Borzage in *American Directors*, calls it "one of the most curious items in his [Borzage's] entire career." Coursodon calls it a "tearjerker" and "so relentlessly maudlin and unreal that no one could be blamed for dismissing it as a piece of idiotic trash." This is the fate of the woman's film. As soon as such a story rears up in the career of a great director, the need either to dismiss it or apologize for it surfaces. Coursodon goes on to admit that in *I've Always Loved You* there is "something disarming and even compelling about the naive silliness of the plot and its total reliance upon the melodramatic paraphernalia of soap opera situations and sentiments." French critic Luc Mollet has the courage to write that the film's "mawkishness and sentimentality are so excessive as to annihilate critical judgment and reach pure beauty." Although Mollet calls the film "perhaps Borzage's masterpiece," he has still found a way to love it without taking responsibility for his feeling. This is equivalent to Pauline Kael's "great trash" category, in which one can conveniently accept movies that touch the feelings without trying to figure out why. There's a wonderful "it's not my fault for liking it" quality to these assessments; they deny the art of film its baroque period.

I've Always Loved You is from a period in American films in which unreal color, massive interior sets, unnatural dialogue, and bizarre clothing expressed attitude and feeling in a heightened manner. Nowhere were such things needed more than in films that took on the responsibility for telling a story about how a woman felt being trapped in the typical role of wife and mother. Such a story is *I've Always Loved You*—a story about the transcendence of love, with music used as a tool by which the woman overcomes the man by proving that her kind of love (family, motherhood, marriage) is even more powerful than his (personal vanity and ego).

It is also possible to see the film slightly differently, in a way that enriches the meaning of the role of the impresario in the woman's life. *I've Always Loved You* tells the story of Myra Hassman, played by the inexperienced young actress Catherine McLeod, who did not go on to major stardom. When the film opens, she is waiting with her music teacher to

Three maestros and their pupils: Philip Dorn conducts Catherine McLeod in
I've Always Loved You; Conrad Veidt instructs Loretta Young in *The Men in
Her Life*; John Barrymore confronts Jeanette MacDonald in *Maytime*.
(Note that each of the men is wielding a sticklike object, and
MacDonald is *igniting* Barrymore's.)

audition for the great Leopold Goronoff (played by Philip Dorn in a performance from the Paul Muni school). Goronoff is bored and impatient with the poor students he is listening to until he spots his former friend, a respected European musician played by Felix Bressart. Bressart has become a farmer and has lived happily with his wife, who is now dead. He regrets nothing, and he has kept his music alive by teaching. As a courtesy, Goronoff listens to Bressart's pupil, a lovely young woman. (When told Bressart has a pupil with him, Goronoff pompously demands, "Where is *he?*" "He's a she," replies Bressart. Goronoff does not believe that women belong in music.) As the young woman comes forward, he tells her what to play for him, as he has told all the other candidates, confusing and frightening them. McLeod is *not* intimidated and says she will play her choice, not his. The *Appassionata.* "I dare you," challenges Goronoff.

These scenes clearly establish what will be their relationship. He will attempt to dominate her but never really succeed. She will assert herself through music. As she plays brilliantly, Goronoff is delighted. "Wonderful! Wonderful! You have a great talent," he exclaims, as his love of music is greater than any petty feelings he has about women. After he has endorsed her talent openly and dramatically, Bressart speaks up with simple dignity and pride, saying, "She is my daughter."

As the film unfolds, it becomes the story of Myra's tutelage under Goronoff. After the maestro, or master, as he is called, follows them back to their idyllic Pennsylvania farm, he and Myra play together on the family's twin pianos. When they play, Myra comes alive and immediately begins to respond to the master. Their playing is their form of sex or love, the only one they will ever share. The master is representative of the part of Myra that places all her passion in music. As they first play at the farm, the sound of the pianos is drowned out by the huffing and chuffing of a tractor that drives past the huge picture window in the room containing the pianos. On the tractor is a young man with no shirt on and with a pipe in his mouth. This subtle entrance introduces Myra's Other Choice: a sexy young farmer named George (William Carter), who is simple and nonmusical, tied to the earth and home.

Goronoff takes Myra away to study with him. He arrives triumphantly at his luxurious quarters in New York, trumpeting out to his grandmother, played by Maria Ouspenskaya, "See what I have! She's mine. I discovered her in Philadelphia." He feels from the beginning that he owns Myra, and he has warned her, with a jolly smile, that when he teaches her it will be difficult. "When I get you at the piano, I will . . . I will . . . I will break your back."

Myra takes up a rootless, musical life with the Goronoffs. As the master plays concerts and conducts around the world, she continues her studies with him, writing letters home to the faithful suitor (William Carter), whose ring she wears in friendship, and to her father, who dies while she is away. Goronoff has many affairs, always with silly women who have to be driven off when he gets bored with them. With Myra, he is like a teacher or a big brother. He is a spoiled and selfish brat, but he is likable in his way. When Goronoff works with Myra, she has to take off the ring that faithful George has given her. Throughout the film, whenever she sits down at the piano she is always shown removing this symbol of conventional love before she begins to play. The two worlds, her farm life and her music, are established as completely incompatible. When she and Goronoff play together during her lessons, Goronoff tells her, "I am the man," but she responds, "And I am the woman." He snaps, "There is no woman in music."

Their relationship, as well as Myra's letters to George, are observed by the sage Ouspenskaya, the quintessential movie crone. Ouspenskaya advises Myra about George: "To like him is all right, but you'd better practice." She also tells her, "Music is bred into you, only music, for you are an artist." She furthers the idea that Myra must make a choice, that a woman cannot have two lives at once. Both the master and his grandmother forget that Myra's father himself had been faced with a similar choice in life and had chosen love.

Finally, Myra is set to play Rachmaninoff at Carnegie Hall, and this event is the climax of the relationship, and conflict, between her character and Goronoff. As the music is being performed, a magnificent war takes place between the two of them, Goronoff conducting and Myra playing the piano. The audience views their conflict through the cinematic devices of cutting, enhanced by voice-overs from Myra that articulate her inner feelings. In addition, cuts to various members of the audience and to stagehands explain in dialogue what is actually happening. Before Myra goes on, Goronoff has said, "We'll show them what Goronoff found on a farm in Pennsylvania. We'll show them what Goronoff can make out of nothing."

During the musical presentation, everything goes well at first. Goronoff has told her, "Watch me always. I am there, always." She is playing with great passion and courage. Suddenly, one audience voice is heard to say, "She's taking over. Stealing the show from Goronoff." A critic sitting beside Ouspenskaya asks, "Why is he fighting her? She plays well." Ouspenskaya, fully understanding, grimly answers, "*Too* well."

A war breaks out between them through music. Myra's voice-over says, "What is it, Maestro? Why are you angry? Don't be angry. Don't fight against me, please. I love you, Maestro. I love you." Various comments trace the progress of their musical conflict, from "Goronoff's takin' a beatin' from a gal" as she ascends and "Goronoff's takin' the play away from her," to "She's not fightin'. She's licked," and finally "What has he done to her? Taught her who's master."

Back at their hotel, Goronoff's jealous rage spills out into an incredible fury. Myra falls into the female pattern of blaming herself and trying to apologize. "I'm sure I acted very stupidly, and I played very badly. Don't be angry with me, master. Whatever I am, you've made it. I was nothing until you taught me." Goronoff won't have it. He literally screams, "You wanted people to say . . . look! Goronoff's pupil is greater than he himself. Trying to steal that which is mine! Well, you can't." He calls her a "little plow girl, good to grub in the earth." Most shocking of all, he tells her to get out, and he means it. As she runs away, completely destroyed, Ouspenskaya puts Goronoff in his place. She tells him that sending Myra away "means that you admit she was greater than you."

The conflict between Myra and Goronoff in their music is an overt demonstration of a woman's fighting for equality and assuming she is entitled to it, and a man's fighting her down, trying to remain master. Goronoff cannot accept Myra if she exceeds him. Myra, loving him, is only trying to make him proud of her by proving she can do what he does, and what he has helped her to learn. In a larger sense, Myra fights for her right to her own career and is rejected.

During the remainder of the film, Myra gives up music, with only three exceptions. All three are directly linked to her feelings about Goronoff. The first occurs when the master is playing at Carnegie Hall, and in an emotional connection to him that is established through parallel cutting, Myra sits down to play exactly as he plays. While the music remains a fluid line between them, representing their feelings and their deep connection, the image cuts back and forth between them. They are one through their music. During this episode, Ouspenskaya, the eternal busybody, arrives at the farm to convince Myra to return. As she drives up, she encounters George, her first eyeful of his masculine pulchritude, although he does have his shirt on this time. As they listen to the music, Ouspenskaya explains that Myra is talking to Goronoff through the piano, and when George says he doesn't understand, she says, "No, you could not understand, nice boy. He will hear her. One hundred miles or one thousand miles cannot stop that voice. Not distance or time." After thinking this over, she decides to keep her mouth shut and gets back into the car, advising George: "You want her, nice boy? Then fight for her. Fight for this woman."

George walks right in and stops Myra from playing. Miles away, Goronoff, too, stops, telling the audience, "I am finished. I will not play for you." As Goronoff walks off the stage, George is telling Myra, "I'm not going to let you do it." The two of them walk among the blossoming trees outside on the farm in the moonlight and discuss what has happened:

GEORGE: I had to stop you, Myra.

MYRA: Why?

GEORGE: Because you've been living a dream.

MYRA: Have I?

GEORGE: Sometimes I think you're in love with a dream.

MYRA: I'm a woman, George. Women don't fall in love with dreams. They fall in love with men, with one man, and when they do, they listen to that man's footsteps in the morning. Their day starts when he smiles, and then they wait to see him again at night. They watch him while he eats, watch the light of the reading lamp as it plays on his face and touches his hair. That's what happens when love comes to a person, George. It'll happen to you.

GEORGE: Maybe it's already happened.

George then speaks the fatal words: "I've always loved you, Myra." When he proposes, she says, "You'd marry me, knowing how I feel about Goronoff? Knowing that I might go running?" When he nods, she runs to his arms, and the image of her with her head on his shoulder fades directly into the image of a small child, their little daughter, with her head on his shoulder.

Both George and Myra have made a sacrifice. Myra has given up her career, in the form of a love for Goronoff, and George has accepted a marriage in which he knows his wife does not truly love him. The world of the farm, with cozy interiors and firelight, is contrasted with the world of the European music circuit, with its cavernous hotel rooms and modern furniture. As the film moves forward in time, however, it is seen that Myra is not happy. She is fulfilling her obligations as a wife and mother, but she has totally given up her music. Her little daughter has never heard her play. As a gigantic electrical storm gathers outside their farmhouse, a perfect device of melodrama, the mother is asked to play for her daughter so she can dance. The radio will not work in the storm. Finally persuaded to play, Myra sits down, and miles away, in New York City, Goronoff is himself mysteriously called to the piano. As the storm thunders and crackles, Myra and Goronoff establish their second musical connection. As they pound away, releasing themselves, Goronoff suddenly says, "I love her! Why didn't you tell me? I must go to her." Ouspenskaya tells him he is too late and makes him promise he will never visit Myra but will leave her alone. He agrees, but says that if she comes to him, that will remove his obligation. While Goronoff makes his promise to Ouspenskaya, the unhappy George and Myra discuss their unsatisfactory marriage back on the farm:

MYRA: I'm happy, very happy. I have you and Porgy [their child] and my home.

GEORGE: It isn't what you have that makes you happy. It's what you give.

MYRA: But I've been a good wife to you. I've given you all I have to give.

GEORGE: All except you.

MYRA: That's not true.

GEORGE: If a man can't have all of a woman, he might as well have none.

MYRA: I wish you'd thought of that a long time ago.

Myra is living in the woman's twilight zone, a world in which she has not committed herself to either choice. Although she has given up one lover (her career, the impresario), she has not really accepted the other (her marriage, husband, and child). She remains in an emotional limbo, and the film indicates that she has no right to do this. Her nonchoice is making everyone unhappy. As he goes unhappily upstairs to bed, her husband tells her to play. He wants to fall asleep hearing her pound the keys. It is a form of challenging her to infidelity. As she plays, Myra weeps and prays, "Dear God. Don't ever let me see Goronoff. Don't ever let me lose the things you've given me." She can only maintain her commitments to these things by totally giving up music, however. She does not play again.

The film goes forward in time, so that Ouspenskaya is dead, and the daughter is grown. Myra has told George's mother grimly, "I've got what I want," and the woman has replied, "Be nice if George had, too." Unbeknownst to Myra, the father has paid for the daughter to have piano lessons, and she is soon to play at Carnegie Hall. Before the daughter exposes herself publicly, the father urges Myra to take her to Goronoff to make sure she is ready. It is his secret plan to confront the situation between his wife and her "master" once and for all.

At Goronoff's, the two see each other for the first time since Myra was told to get out. After listening to the daughter play for about thirty seconds, he politely hands her her gloves and shows her to the door. As the mother realizes what this means, Goronoff tells her, "What difference does it make? This daughter of yours, she will go out in the world and meet a man and acknowledge him to be her master. This is good. This is as it should be. Music is a man. There is no woman in music. A woman is a woman, as it should have been with you, as I am your master." Myra rises to her feet, appalled. "You're wrong," she says, "very wrong." He takes her hands: "These hands. I made them. Without a master, they were lost. They were nothing."

Myra refuses to accept this. She goes to Carnegie Hall to take her daughter's place. She will not only save her child from humiliation, the mother's job, but she will also confront her inner feelings for Goronoff, the wife's job. In addition, however, she seizes the opportunity to bring Goronoff to his knees and prove him wrong. As she replaces her daughter at the piano, Goronoff replaces the conductor on the podium. For the third and last time, Myra plays. As they look at each other defiantly, Goronoff challenges her. "You say I'm not your master? Then play."

Play she does. Music becomes both sex and love. As the stagehand tells us, in case we are lost here, "It's different this time. The shoe's on the other foot." Goronoff's voice-over is heard to say, "I was wrong, Myra. There is a woman in music." Myra polishes him off at the piano and walks directly to the wings, where her husband and daughter await her. She goes to her husband and says, "I love you, George. I've always loved you, always." He replies, "And I've always known you did."

The film is finished with a perfect woman's film duality. Having resolved her need for a career by killing it, or dominating it, Myra accepts the woman's choice—man, marriage, motherhood. However, to do so she has to prove herself the master of a man, the impresario who has told her that there is no place for her in the man's world. She makes him admit he is wrong and frees herself to be happy with the conventional choice.

WHEN AN IMPRESARIO goes mad with his desire to control and/or love the woman, the genre moves away from the woman's film and into the horror category. Horror films are not usually women's films, although they are often films about women. But when a doctor goes mad or an impresario goes mad or, for that matter, a daddy or a friendly ghost goes mad, the genre shifts. The woman becomes fodder for cheap thrills.

There are many impresario-type horror films, such as *Svengali* (1931 and 1955) and *The Mad Genius* (1931), but the granddaddy for popularity is *The Phantom of the Opera* (1925, 1943, 1962, 1983). It has been with us in play and novel form, in silent days, in several sound versions, on television, and in a hugely successful Broadway musical. Each generation is weaned on its own particular version of it. Mine is the 1943 one, starring Claude Rains as the impresario, Susanna Foster as the singer he is obsessed by, and Nelson Eddy as her main love interest. This version clarifies the career issue up front. Susanna Foster is told by the director of her show that "You must choose between the opera and what is called 'the normal life.' You can't do both." Her teacher tells her, "Forget men. Music is everything." Her faithful suitor, a policeman, tells her he's waited two years while she's had her fling, and that it's now time to give it up and settle down. She agrees with her director and her teacher and tells her policeman, "No. I don't want to give it up."

Foster has plenty of suitors, including not only the policeman but also the leading baritone of the opera, Nelson Eddy. In addition, there is her mysterious benefactor, a violinist played by Claude Rains. When Rains is dismissed by the opera because his left hand has gone stiff and he can no longer play well, he tries to get his concerto published. When he mistakenly believes it has been stolen from him, he murders the publisher, but not before a pan of acid is thrown into his face. Rains's desire to have his music published is motivated by his need for money, which in turn is motivated by the fact that he is actually Foster's patron. He has been paying for her singing lessons. Scarred and penniless, he takes up a life underneath the opera house, masked and robed, stealing to survive and dedicating himself to furthering Foster's career. He commits three murders for her and drugs one star and drops a chandelier during the number of another. He is busily clearing the way for Foster to sing the leads. In this capacity, Rains is the absolute king of the asexual males. He is father (in the novel he *is* her father, but this is never clarified in this version of the film), lover, ghost (his phantom guise), and impresario all wrapped up in one. As he leads her underground, he expresses his love for her, calling her "my darling" and telling her to "sing only for me." This version of *The Phantom of the Opera* is true to its 1940s days of the independent, working woman. When Rains dies and Foster survives, her two chief suitors both come to take her to supper after her enormous triumph as an opera star. "You'll have to make up your mind finally and irrevocably between us," they tell her. However, she sneaks out into the hall where she greets her adoring fans, ignoring them both completely so that they realize their only choice is to have supper with each other. Foster rejects love, marriage, suitors, impresario, Daddy, lover, and ghost and goes out into the hall to enjoy the rewards of her own career! After all, her suitors are just two among many, and some of the other stage-door Johnnies are carrying bigger bouquets. Since she has the adulation of all men now, why settle for only one?

THE FUNCTION of all these men, whether ghost, angel, mysterious stranger, doctor, or psychiatrist, is always the same. They are characters who help a woman be what she really wants to be but cannot achieve on her own. They liberate her, take her out of herself. They empower her, and can represent anything and everything accordingly.

MARRIAGE

MARRIAGE HOVERS over the woman's film like a black cloud. It is the "after" of all those "happily ever after" movies, which end with a woman making the right choice, accepting love and the fine print of its social contract, marriage. When the film is a story about that marriage, however, plot development dictates the need for something to go terribly wrong. When the movie begins where the romance leaves off—when it starts after a woman's basic choice is made—it has to be a different story indeed. As far as movie marriages in the true woman's film go, it's a hard-knocks world.

Try to find the perfect movie marriage. All the rapturous talk about Nick and Nora Charles overlooks the fact that the movies of the The Thin Man series are not women's films. They aren't even screwball comedies about marriage. They are stylish, well written and performed murder mysteries, with little touches of quirky behavior and married romance. Nick (the unparalleled William Powell) and Nora (the charming Myrna Loy in her prime) behave like lovers conducting a battle of the sexes in which they both know neither will win because either one could. They are an ideal representation of a male-and-female relationship because they never bore each other, they travel everywhere, they have plenty of money, and they dress very, very well. They sex each other up in discreet ways, and from time to time Nick allows Nora to be one of the boys. Stop and think. Why does Nick keep making all those jokes about marrying Nora for her money? And remember how she has to fight to be included in his adventures? Let's not forget the time he locked her in a closet to keep her from coming with him on a crime caper, and let's not forget that he often points out the dumb mistakes she makes when trying to help him on a case. The plots often turn on how he has to get away from her to conduct his sleuthing business. Given half a chance, he goes off to the races, to the fights, to cavernous nightclubs—to all the *fun*—without her. Loy's definition as "the perfect wife" seems to be related to the fact that she is beautiful, a great pal, very rich, and willing to accept her husband's bohemian friends and errant behavior. There is no argument that Powell and Loy are sensational, or that the films are delightful. But is theirs the perfect marriage? Not from the woman's point of view.

If you want to find a perfect movie marriage, in which the entire film presents the relationship without internal conflict and with both parties as equals, you have to look far afield—to Tarzan and Jane, a couple who really get along and who do, in fact, seem to have an ideal marriage.

Tarzan didn't choose Jane for her wealth. He has plenty of riches of his own—all that elephant ivory and those gargantuan lumps of gold that he comes up with when they need money for Jane to fly home to London so she can fight World War II. He doesn't try to exclude her from his daily life, either. He frequently takes her with him when he goes to work in the jungle, letting her swing right along beside him, and certainly she's always in the thick of the action. Tarzan is that thing our mothers told us to look for, a good provider. He never comes home without meat for the table or some kind of delicious fruit basket, and he often brings Jane flowers. Real orchids! The size of watermelons!

Tarzan is a hunk who *must* be good in bed, and when Jane talks, he listens. He consults her for advice on nonjungle matters, and he does what she tells him to. He is reliable in the fidelity category, resisting out-of-town offers from Amazons, chorus girls, female Nazis, and mermaids. He doesn't change jobs suddenly so that they have to move, and he doesn't come home late or tell lies or pick fights. He doesn't drink, and he doesn't smoke. He doesn't shed peanut shells all over the woven mats, and he's an absolutely perfect father to Boy. He didn't even put Jane through hell by making her give birth to Boy! He went out into the jungle, scavenged a wrecked airplane, and found her a little son, just like the good provider he is. What a man! And, what's more, he's the king of the jungle, which makes Jane a queen, and he has no pesky parents to criticize her cooking. If Jane has any problem, any problem at all, such as her foot in a bear trap or her head in a lion's mouth, Tarzan comes running to the rescue. On the hoof, underwater, from the mountains and the caves and even in New York City, Tarzan finds her, saves her, and takes her safely home again. Tarzan comes through. As for Jane, she's no slouch herself, looking adorable in her little jungle jumper and doing the wife's job by positively worshiping and trusting Tarzan. She never abuses the power her knowledge of the outer world gives her, and she's a perfect mother. Tarzan and Jane

The Perfect Marriage: Johnny Weissmuller and Maureen O'Sullivan, with
Johnny Sheffield as Boy, in *Tarzan's Secret Treasure*

and Boy live in a sweet little house nestled up in the trees, and they have
all the modern conveniences. There's natural air-conditioning, a vacuum
cleaner (a particularly hungry bird), running water (a handy bamboo pole
that runs down to a fresh lagoon), and a rope elevator. They have a gorgeous
swimming pool, deep and clean. It does have a few alligators, but Tarzan
can always wrestle them out of the way. Jane even has reliable help, the
inestimable Cheetah, who is clearly a treasure and who would surely do
windows if they had any.

This is the perfect marriage. It avoids the classic movie marital problems of infidelity, lack of money, interfering in-laws, class differences,
career conflicts, and ungrateful children. Of course, Tarzan and Jane are
not *really* married, so perhaps there's a lesson here for us all. And the
Tarzan movies, like the Thin Man movies, aren't women's films, are they?

In a Hollywood film, there has to be a story, which means there has
to be a problem, which means there has to be a problem with the marriage
if it's a story about a marriage. So most films about marriage end up being
about how the marriage is *bad*, unless the film is really not about marriage
but just uses it as a sort of recognized and appropriate dramatic background

setting. Here is one of the greatest of the ironies to be found in films about women. If a woman's place is in the home and her proper occupation that of wife, and if the job of the movie story is to reinforce those notions, then presumably the majority of movies about women would feature happy marriages. Yet the opposite is true. The woman's film commonly works from the premise of a woman trapped in a wretched marriage (*Traveling Husbands*, 1931), or a woman married to a man she can't count on to provide her with a good living (*Mildred Pierce*, 1945), or a man who is unreliable (*Cimarron*, 1931, 1960), or a man who dies young (countless films, among them *The White Cliffs of Dover*, 1944), or a man who abandons her for a younger woman (*The Power and the Glory*, 1933), or a man who tries to kill her (*Dragonwyck*, 1946), and so on, and so on. *C'est la* woman's *vie*. Things usually turn out well in the end, in the ambivalent tradition that fuels the Hollywood film, but the stories are *about* why marriages go bad.

The woman's film that is primarily about marriage is a story in which the woman's most important choice has already been made. Faced with having to decide between love or the Other, and marriage or the Other, she has already chosen love and marriage. When marriage becomes the "now" of the story, instead of the "after," the plot shifts from showing how a woman makes a choice to an examination of the quality of her choice. This is a plot in which a direct linkage to the viewer in the audience exists. If we can assume that women came to these movies primarily to see the things they dreamed of but didn't have, it must be remembered that marriage, unlike dancing in the moonlight along the Riviera, *was* the thing they had. This was a subject on which many of them were already experts. Hollywood's ability to fool them diminished accordingly.

One can't simply assert that films about happy marriages are never women's films and films about unhappy marriages are always women's films. Nevertheless, this comes very close to being true, for two reasons. First, audiences knew what marriages were like and were familiar with the problems. Second, to build a story around a female character required finding a way to get her out into the world where something could happen to her. If she was married, this meant having her marriage go wrong for some reason. (A happy marriage meant that she was probably content to stay home with her children, wearing her pearls and high heels while delicately pushing her vacuum cleaner over the rug and planning a superb dinner party featuring lobster thermidor. The movie had to get her out of the house!) Even when the woman remained a housewife in a marriage film, there had to be a scene where the wife rejected her life at home and kicked up her heels to capture her husband's attention. This is the "why, Blanche! I didn't know you could water-ski" format, in which Blanche replies jauntily, "Oh, no, Bruce? Well, I was the women's champion in college, and there's plenty else you don't know about me!" Blanche says this over her shoulder, while dancing the cha-cha with Count DuBois.

This does not mean that many portraits of happy marriages do not exist in movies; they do. Most of these movies, however, are not truly what would be called women's films. (Comedies about happy marriages temporarily threatened by another woman or a misunderstanding of some sort are ambivalent presentations, in which a serious problem that many marriages face is treated lightly.)

The happy-marriage film most commonly presents a story in which the union is a background for another, broader story about men. The woman is not the center of the universe. For instance, if the movie is about a crusading newspaperman (who happens to be happily married) and how he fights crime in his city in order to expose the tactics of a hideous crime lord, the marriage can easily be supportive, idyllic, and problem free. (In fact, with so much else going on in the plot, it had jolly well better be problem free.) Such a marriage is actually the Man's Marriage. In it, he finds support, solace, relief from grief, and sex. The wife is there to listen to his troubles and to build him up when he is ground down by events. When the mob warns him to stop his crusade or else, the wife is there to say something like "It seems to me if you do that it will be the end of Western civilization as we know it, and besides I love you, and besides more, little Johnny looks up to his father. You've always been a winner. That's what I married you for, so go out there and stomp those mafiosi." A movie like this suggests that a marriage is happy when it supports the man. When the film is actually about a woman, however, one confronts again the confounding irony of the movie that attempts to reinforce traditional roles for women but in order to do so has to destroy them or define them as unsatisfactory.

Looking at movies that feature marriage as a choice already made rather than as a desired goal, one realizes again how the ever-present either-or ambivalence of the woman's film works. Films about happy marriages tend not to be women's films, and films about bad marriages are almost always women's films.

Happy-marriage movies usually fall into one of six types, all fundamentally using the marriage as a background to tell another kind of story:

1. When the film is not about marriage *at all* (as in the crusading-newspaperman story described)
2. When the marriage is linked to the religious life
3. When the marriage is the story of a "great man" and his accomplishments, with his little wife as helpmate

4. When the married couple work together in a shared occupation, whether it be science, show business, the family farm, or whatever
5. When the film is the story of family life or motherhood, the larger units attached to marriages
6. When the marriage is about to end abruptly (the husband or wife will fall dead in a plot ploy that might be called "happily ever after till your death five minutes from now")

Films like these are set up to move away from being stories about women, with the exception of number six, in which, after the perfect husband drops dead, the woman has to cope alone and thus the movie becomes a woman's film. (If the perfect wife drops dead the film can go in any direction, including that of woman's film.) The death of the perfect mate becomes in and of itself a statement about the impermanence—or implausibility—of happiness in marriage. It is also a plot device by which a woman can be freed from the need to be married. She has already done her time.

Happy-marriage stories are defined by these characteristics: they are primarily about men, they are an idyllic romanticizing of the marital status, they reinforce the status quo of marriage and motherhood for women; and they are mostly about the woman taking the background position (staying home to reassure the crusading newspaperman of number one . . . standing beside the religious man of number two . . . standing behind the "great man" of number three . . . sharing the work load with the man in number four . . . and standing ready to serve the needs of the family of number five). Any time these definitions do not fit the stories being told, the bad-marriage variation of the tales emerges, and the generic family film almost always becomes the woman's film.

There are countless examples of movies in which a man is happily married to a good woman as he goes about his male business. What his business is defines the genre. If he's a cowboy, it's a western, and if he's a dancer, it's a musical. The marriage is *in* the movie and is important to its character definition of the hero, but it is his background, not his foreground. Van Heflin is happily married to Jean Arthur in *Shane* (a 1953 western), and Glenn Ford is happily married to Jocelyn Brando in *The Big Heat* (1953, a film-noir crime movie). Fredric March is happily married to Myrna Loy in *The Best Years of Our Lives* (1946, a socially relevant film), and Gary Cooper is happily married to Dorothy McGuire in *Friendly Persuasion* (1956, a pacifist family drama). Henry Fonda is happily married to Claudette Colbert in *Drums Along the Mohawk* (1939, a historical literary adaption), and Spencer Tracy is happily married to Joan Bennett in *Father of the Bride* (1950, a comedy).

In these movies, the focus is on the male character and his particular problems and adjustments. They are tales about the world outside the home—a larger social context—instead of the private psychological world of women. Even if the story is directly related to marital adjustments, when the man is the central character the marriage problem is defined by a larger problem he has outside the home. For instance, *Half a Hero* (1953), starring Red Skelton, and *Young Man With Ideas* (1952), starring Glenn Ford, both of which are comedies, are focused on the male as protagonist. The wives in the two films, Jean Hagen and Ruth Roman, are not stars of the same rank as Skelton and Ford, and the films follow the action through the experiences of the two men. The plots concern their attempts to achieve the success dream of the 1950s and still do right emotionally by their wives and children. Materialism becomes the problem, along with a man's pride and masculinity, as defined by his earning power. If these films were centered on the woman in the marriage, they would be stories about love, childbearing, jealousy, and the problems inside the home. Instead, they are stories about a man's attempt to rise in a career. Thus, the happy-marriage film bears out the traditional pattern observed for the woman's film: a story about a woman is psychological and personal in nature, and a story about a man is sociological and related to a larger context. A woman's story takes place in the head and the heart, and the man's story takes place in the world itself.

Two socially relevant films, *Teresa* and *From This Day Forward*, provide a good comparison for an understanding of how the background marriage works. Both marriage stories are really about the problems that veterans returning home from World War II find in adjusting to civilian life. In *Teresa* (1951), the young hero, John Ericson, brings home with him an Italian war bride (Pier Angeli, in her film debut). Although the couple love each other, they encounter problems having to do with his inability to find work, her adjustment to a new country, and his family's unwillingness to accept a foreigner. *From This Day Forward* (1946) is a story told in flashbacks by a veteran (Mark Stevens) as he searches for work in the immediate postwar period. He is married to a character played by Joan Fontaine. Once again, the husband and wife, who have a strong love and commitment to each other, find themselves beset by external woes, this time economic.

These two movies were aimed at the postwar American audience, which contained many veterans who were themselves making these adjustments. By using marriage as a background, and setting the adjustment problems in a context familiar to the audience, the films found a suitable forum for discussing some new issues people were facing. The organization of both stories is such that the viewer saw the movies not as stories in which marriages were unhappy because two people couldn't agree on things, but because society was wrong: it ought to give these veterans jobs and accept them as the changed people they were.

The difference between *Teresa* and *From This Day Forward* is a significant one. The latter film stars an Oscar-winning, big-name female star, Joan Fontaine. She is also associated with roles in women's films. Her costar, who was being groomed in the late forties to become a big name, is paired with her to boost his own career, but she is the bigger name of the two. The two stars of *Teresa* are both unknowns. Because of the presence of a female star, *From This Day Forward* has to be much more of a woman's film than *Teresa*. The presence of a woman in the story is enlarged when the woman is played by a star, and accordingly the issues have to concern a woman's world.

This same comparison can be applied to films that involve a marriage to a religious man. In general, films tell us that women can find happiness in such marriages, although not without hardship. The men they marry will be close to saintly, so there can be no worries about infidelity. A religious husband provides a woman with two things: an opportunity to do good in the world herself and an opportunity to support the efforts of a man who is a good provider only in the spiritual sense. Movies have a great respect for these men who make no money. They are presented as moral big daddies, providing directions for living not only to their own families but to entire communities. They seem to know everything and are always without prejudice or small-mindedness. A woman married to such a man finds status as the wife of an important man, and she does have a husband whose concerns are those associated with the woman's world. When a man is in business or politics or some power-oriented occupation, he seldom has enough time for his wife and family. He often loses his values, falls prey to other women or alcoholism, and sometimes even loses the riches he has devoted his time to acquiring. A religious man, however, is home all day. His values are intact and will remain so, and his great wisdom is a solace to one and all. These films reaffirm the concept of marriage as an institution in which the woman works hard, supports the man, accepts sacrifice and lack of material gain—all for a greater good.

Films about marriages to religious men may put the man as the central figure (*Stars in My Crown* and *One Foot in Heaven*), or they may be about the woman (*A Man Called Peter* and *I'd Climb the Highest Mountain*). The same thing happens as with *Teresa* and *From This Day Forward*. When the man is the central figure and the wife a secondary character, the issues of the film do not concern marriage as much as they do religion itself or a larger social issue. *Stars in My Crown* (1950), one of the loveliest Americana films ever made, is about racial prejudice and how the mountain minister Joel McCrea stands up to it, and *One Foot in Heaven* (1941) is an episodic story of how Fredric March leads his family from parish to parish, taking on a significant social problem at each stop. *I'd Climb the Highest Mountain* (1951), on the other hand, is about Susan Hayward, a bride from the city who comes out to rural Georgia to marry her fiancé, a poor minister played by William Lundigan. This film, also a lovely piece of Americana, is narrated by Hayward as a memory of her life. It is the story of how an inexperienced girl becomes a woman, a wife, and a mother. She has to learn to cook and to accept the unsophisticated mountain people of her husband's parish. She suffers the death of her firstborn child and is jolted out of the personal slump she falls into afterward by competition for her husband from a beautiful, well-dressed new woman in the area. Thus, we see how the traditional difference between the man's film (the world at large, with important social issues) and the woman's film (the personal world of a woman, with emotional issues linked to motherhood, sex, and the home) is maintained even by the marriage story involving religion. This comparison shows also how the religious happy marriage is perfectly happy when it makes the man the central character, but how, even though never seriously threatened, it undergoes stress when it is focused on the woman.

A Man Called Peter (1955) reflects a schizophrenic approach. Based on the true-life story of chaplain Peter Marshall as written by his devoted wife, Catherine, the movie is partly a happy-marriage film in which the little woman stands behind the great man, a religious figure. After he dies suddenly, the movie becomes a woman's picture about how Catherine carries on alone, with his sermons to guide her.

The most memorable, uncomplicated happy marriages are found in category number three, the "great man" marriages, most of which are biographical stories about great inventors (*Dr. Ehrlich's Magic Bullet*, 1940; *The Story of Alexander Graham Bell*, 1939; *Edison, The Man*, 1940), great authors (*The Life of Emile Zola*, 1937), great statesmen (*The Magnificent Yankee*, 1951), great personalities (*Yankee Doodle Dandy*, 1942), and great sports figures (*The Pride of the Yankees*, 1942). "Great" is the operative word. A man becomes great partly because he has behind him a loving, sympathetic, supportive, noncompetitive, and certainly noncomplaining wife. In these movies, love and marriage are things a great man takes care of early in life, finding one ideal helpmate and capturing her despite his obvious eccentricities that she alone sees are the marks of genius. The suggestion is that a wife's role should properly be that of caretaker. A woman should see to it that her genius is well fed, well clothed, well dressed, and generally kept on the right track toward inventing, writing, and competing. These films are an attempt to ennoble the role of wife and mother and to imply that the wife of a great man is as important to his success in her way as he is in his, and to further suggest that the most important thing to him is really her, not the work he is doing. All based on real-life stories, these films help sell women on the role of behind-the-scenes influence. If a woman picks the right man and steers him correctly, she will have the ultimate reward: bystander in the paradise of success, enriched by its rewards but free of its pressures. These films show a woman what she can get by playing her cards well and picking "the right man."

What these happy-marriage films establish as proper behavior for wives is that a woman should keep busy in marriage, serve her husband's career, take care of her family, and stay at home. The marriage will then flourish. They depict a division of labor between man and woman and suggest that a man should not be troubled by problems generated by his wife; a man, it is implied, has enough problems out in the world without having to deal with more when he arrives home at night. The subversive side of this story is presented in film comedies through the device of having the man only *think* he is in charge of things. Films such as *Life with Father* (1947) and *Meet Me in St. Louis* (1944) depict an autocratic father who does not realize that he is, in fact, not in charge of anything in his home; he is basically under feminine rule. ("It's enough we let him work and slave to support us," wryly observes the grandfather in *Meet Me in St. Louis*. "He doesn't have to know what is going on here.") The wife and mother in these families is always very clever and, in particular, knows how to trick Daddy into making the decision the family will want him to make while all the time letting him think it's really his own idea.

Films that depict happy marriages in which a couple works together (category number four) are usually about three things: the marriage, the resulting family, and the shared work itself (which determines the genre). A list of famous titles illustrates how this works:

FILM	HAPPY MARRIAGE DEPICTED	GENERIC LABEL
Andy Hardy series (1937–1958)	Lewis Stone and Fay Holden—devoted married couple	Family comedy, teenage adjustment
I Remember Mama (1948)	Irene Dunne and Philip Dorn—devoted married couple	Family drama, teenage adjustment, real-life biography

FILM	HAPPY MARRIAGE DEPICTED	GENERIC LABEL
Mother Wore Tights (1947)	Betty Grable and Dan Dailey—devoted show-business couple	Musical, teenage adjustment, real-life biography
Cheaper by the Dozen (1950)	Clifton Webb and Myrna Loy—devoted married business couple	Family comedy, teenage adjustment, real-life biography
Madame Curie (1943)	Greer Garson and Walter Pidgeon—devoted scientist couple	Inventor drama, real-life biography

Only one of these (the Andy Hardy series) is not based on a real-life couple, which suggests the intriguing possibility that there are more happy marriages in real life than there are on the screen! *Mother Wore Tights, I Remember Mama, Madame Curie,* and *Cheaper by the Dozen* are all based on stories written by the children of the happily married couples. Three of the couples in the films work together, in the fields of show business (Grable and Dailey are a song-and-dance team), science (the Curies, who discovered radium), and the pioneering time-management business (the Galbreths of *Cheaper by the Dozen,* who being the parents of twelve children apparently were forced to learn to manage their time). The real-life mother of *I Remember Mama* was a traditional housewife, but her story is a loving tribute by a daughter who remembers her as a figure of strength and courage.

These biographical films indicate where material for fictional stories about women comes from. The women in these films face death, economic woes, child-rearing pressures, and the need to balance their working lives with their married ones. In both *Cheaper by the Dozen* and *Madame Curie,* the husbands are killed by or in moving vehicles, a blatant plot maneuver of many fictional women's films. These real-life deaths not only conform to woman's film hand-of-fate plots, but also carry out a further tradition of the woman's film story. The death of Pierre Curie at a relatively young age (he is struck by a runaway carriage in the street), frees the filmed version of the Curies' lives to become an actual woman's film. In *Cheaper by the Dozen,* the husband is killed by an automobile accident that isn't depicted on the screen. This event is placed at the very finish of the movie, as it completes the story of the Galbreth family to that date. *Cheaper by the Dozen* is dominated by its male star, Clifton Webb, in the role of the father. This death, however, frees the continuing story of the family to be a woman's film in the sequel, *Belles on Their Toes* (1952), in which Myrna Loy becomes the heroine of a typical woman's film. In these movies, which conform accurately to real-life events, the removal of the male figure once again leaves the woman at the center of the filmed universe.

These films define what a happy marriage is. The men and women are equal partners, sharing both a working life and a family life, with only the fictional Andy Hardy series and *I Remember Mama* keeping the woman inside the home on a regular basis. In all but the story of the Curies, the children in the family constitute an important subplot. In the Andy Hardy series, the teenage son is the central character, with the marriage relegated to the subplot. (There are children in the Curie story, but no significant screen time is devoted to events concerning them.) These films all depict minor marital discords, mostly involving the upbringing of the children. The least discord is depicted in the totally fictional Hardy series. Mrs. Hardy, however, is the least important character in the Hardy family, as the real action takes place between the son (Mickey Rooney) and the father (Lewis Stone). The actress who plays Mrs. Hardy, Fay Holden, is frankly middle-aged and without glamour. The rest of the wives are all glamorous, except for Irene Dunne in *I Remember Mama*, who is presented as middle-aged and physically ordinary. (Dunne wears a wig and padding.) Mrs. Hardy behaves impeccably throughout the series, except in *The Hardys Ride High* (1939), when a sudden influx of wealth temporarily derails the good sense of all the Hardys. Her form of derailment is to start shopping for hideous new hats and forgetting to turn the roast on, but she quickly comes to her senses.

There are subtleties in the presentations of these movies. The two nonglamorous wives, Fay Holden and Irene Dunne, illustrate casting attitudes toward how wives are supposed to look. Holden is a minor actress, cast in support of the two big stars, Rooney and Stone. Therefore, her lack of glamour does not matter, as she is a secondary player. Dunne is a very big star, and her mate is played by a minor actor, Philip Dorn. Her lack of glamour is in the tradition of "I will put aside my lipstick and go for the Oscar." (Dunne was, in fact, nominated for an Oscar, but lost out to Jane Wyman's equally unlipsticked role in *Johnny Belinda*.) The casting of the middle-aged Holden and the deglamorizing of the very elegant Dunne suggest that once women become wives, issues of glamour should be put aside. Of the remaining three happy wives, Loy and Garson (Madame Curie) both look beautiful, but there is definitely no stress on clothes or looks in their roles. Only Grable, as is appropriate for her screen image and for the musical-comedy format of *Mother Wore Tights*, is shown on-screen as a sexy, glamorous woman. Grable is nevertheless more subdued than usual, particularly after her character becomes a mother. The main issue is that these stories present happy marriages in which the husband and wife work alongside each other in shared occupations that require a woman to have knowledge and experience outside of her home life. One wonders why more attention hasn't been paid to movies like this, and what the audience made of the implications. In the two marriages in which the wife remains at home, the purely fabricated one keeps the wife in the background. The biographical one, *I Remember Mama*, places her at the center of the universe. This must have been how her real-life daughter saw her mother's life.

I'll See You in My Dreams (1951) is an interesting variation of this "happy couples who work together" concept. It is a slyly subversive presentation in that the wife actually runs the career of her husband while remaining at home as hausfrau and mother. It is the true story of Gus Kahn and his wife, Grace. Grace (Doris Day) and Gus (Danny Thomas) are presented as a charming mismatch. He's an immigrant with a horse and cart and a liverwurst sandwich. She's an educated woman with a good job plugging songs. His mom has an accent and makes apple strudel. Her father and mother live in a big house in which they set an elegant table. Grace has ambition and drive, and Gus has talent.

Their marriage becomes the background to the story of a great career, with Grace the typical little woman behind the man—except that Grace frequently gets out in front and is criticized accordingly. The crisis in their union becomes the fact that she is too pushy, too domineering, and he leaves her because she is managing his entire life. An audience is asked to absorb and resolve these contradictions:

- Grace is too bossy. This is wrong for Gus and wrong for their marriage.
- But if Grace weren't so pushy, Gus's career would never have taken place. Her belief in him and her ability to get things done have created his career.
- Grace and Gus are terribly happy. Although he never says he loves her out loud, he really does worship her.
- But Grace gets a sock in the eye from Gus, although it's just a big mistake. They argue constantly, and their maid hates *him* and loves *her*.
- Gus is a devoted husband, and he and Grace and their kids hold hands and sing while they stroll through life.
- But Gus goes off to New York alone and falls under the spell of a beautiful Ziegfeld star (Patrice Wymore). He writes "Love Me or Leave Me" for her.

This sequence culminates in the Ziegfeld star and Grace doing what women do in these movies: talking it over between them. Wymore tells Day that Gus never tumbled for her, although she definitely tried to seduce him. Neither woman ever tells Gus anything, of course, and he goes through life not realizing they both are keeping the truth from him. Throughout the movie, there is music and love and romance, but there is also a constant subtext of disappointment, anger, and cross-purpose. Anyone watching the movie picks up on the latter and feels its power. Although the troubles of the Kahns are set forth in the plot, they are easily swept away and treated as jokes (the sock in the eye) or as only temporary (Gus's leaving her). The two end up in each other's arms, singing a duet.

The movies about working couples all merge with the larger genre of the family-life story (category number five). When a man and woman are focused together on rearing their children, and they have common goals and aspirations in that regard, they are a kind of working couple. It's that the business that they share is not a song and a dance, but family life. Many, many such films exist, and lots of them are musicals—*Two Weeks With Love* (1950) and *Meet Me in St. Louis*, for example. But there are also films like *Father Was a Fullback* (1949), *You Can't Take It With You* (1938), and *Father's Little Dividend* (1951). These stories again shift the focus from the woman's concerns to a larger context, which is the adjustment of the children to the outer world or to their growing sexuality.

The main thing about all these films is that the woman involved, usually a minor star, is not front and center to the plot, and she is not faced either with making a choice about her life or questioning her choice in any serious way. Some of these films come very close to being women's films, but they are really stories about social concerns. A happy-marriage film is a film in which the central wife character has already made a choice that is accepted and not questioned.

This almost brings us to the main event, the marriage that is not happy. On the way there, though, one comes upon two kinds of transition films. The first is the movie in which a woman is initiated into marriage, and the second is one in which the woman has both an unhappy marriage and a happy one. These two kinds of movies follow a pattern that might be described as dark/light, but the former kind is a much more optimistic, less subversive movie about marriage than the second. The initiation film seeks to reassure women about marriage and convince them it is a positive way to live one's life. The second type of film speaks to women of the horrors of marriage and then provides a totally escapist release from that truth. The initiation film is the more honest of the two.

I'd Climb the Highest Mountain, the religious-marriage movie mentioned earlier, is also a woman's initiation film. Just as boys are initiated into the rites and passages of manhood in action and adventure films, women are initiated into womanhood in marriage films. Whereas men are taught by men, however, women are not taught by other women, not even by their own mothers. They are placed in a situation in which they are totally on their own (except for their husbands), and they have to figure things out. (Does this mean women are smarter than men?) Such films show a new bride removed from a protective familial cocoon and taken somewhere strange and challenging. She is always beautiful, and she plays the piano, paints watercolors, and treasures lovely things such as her china, her jewelry, or her beloved peacock feathers. Once arrived in her new home, cut off from her family, her things, her conveniences, and, frequently, even civilization, the bride must learn to be a woman. What does this mean? It means she must make a home in the wilderness, doing all the things that are defined as "woman's work." The first thing she is confronted with is an unadorned living space, frequently one that is crude and even dirty. She must not only clean it but also make it beautiful. Next she must learn to cook and sew, to chip ice and pluck chickens. She's got to mush those huskies and plow that corn. After a certain amount of time, she must give birth by candlelight in the cabin, with frequently disastrous results— death for the child or misshapen limbs on little sons. She must learn to accept a world without delicacy or social grace, a world that is, in its larger sense, a world of men to which she has been brought as a civilizing influence, a helpmate, and a breeder. By removing a woman from the "femininity" of civilization and taking her into the "masculinity" of the wilderness, a man puts her to the test. Can she learn her own profession, which is that of being a woman? If she works hard, mastering skills and overcoming dangers and obstacles, she will be needed, and thus valuable. Sometimes she has to be like a man, picking up a gun to fire it at enemies or going alone for help in times of danger, but these things are not her daily work. They only test her mettle. Movies like this remove women from the East, hub of the civilized universe in film terms, and take her to the West (to Indian country), North (Alaskan gold country), and South (mountain country). Films that initiate women like this are many, and they include *Drums Along the Mohawk, Mrs. Mike* (1949), *The Egg and I* (1947), *Secrets* (1933), and *Giant* (1956), which is a definitive example of the type.

They usually begin with a wedding ceremony in the comfortably appointed home of the woman's parents and follow with a wagon train west or a dogsled north. This trip is also one in which the woman may be seen to be leaving behind her girlhood and virginity and going to her womanhood and her sexual awakening. Thus, the new place is "untamed" and "full of promise." If the woman stands up to things, never interferes with her husband's work, and accepts the crudeness of the new world around her, she earns her place as an equal. If she does not accept it, as in *Buffalo*

A W O M A N ' S V I E W

Bill (1944) and *The Howards of Virginia* (1940), she returns home, only to regret it for the rest of her sexless life.*

When marriage becomes a unit of initiation for a woman, if she passes the test, her marriage will be happy. When a man takes a bride to an uncivilized world, there is every chance that a happy-marriage film will ensue, because in the uncivilized landscape, a pared-down representative world, a woman will find useful work and a role to play. Her man will be both her master and her teacher. However, when the opposite is the case, and a man marries a woman from a sophisticated world in which she has known too darn much, and brings her from that world to his own small-town environment, there is likely to be trouble ahead. A wise bride from the world of show business is a particular disaster, as we see when Melvyn Douglas brings Joan Crawford home in *The Shining Hour* (1938) and Jimmy Stewart brings Ginger Rogers home in *Vivacious Lady* (1938). These two women can't fit in. They don't pass the test. They spin not, neither do they weave. They are far too good-looking and too experienced for the worlds their trusting and somewhat naive young husbands live in. These men are too boyish to be masters, and this is no pioneer context calling for the women to contribute. They have also usurped roles that their husbands' doting mothers planned for some other, more manageable female, and the disapproving mothers become their enemies. (The woman in *Shining Hour* is not actually Douglas's mother, but his older sister, a surrogate mother played by Fay Bainter.) Marry your own kind, these films say, and also, speaking to men, don't get a bride with more experience than you and more clothes than anyone else in town. The implication here is that Mother really picks out a man's wife, and even though, again, both films prove the mothers wrong, the majority of the running time is spent demonstrating the problems in detail.

* No one really thinks of movies like *Drums Along the Mohawk*, *Giant*, or even the magnificent silent film *The Wind* (1928) as women's pictures or even as initiation movies of this sort. Nevertheless, they all tell stories that fit the pattern. *Drums Along the Mohawk* and *Giant* are obviously marriage stories, but they are directed by strong male directors (John Ford and George Stevens, respectively), and the marriage is connected to a larger story involving male issues. *Drums Along the Mohawk* concerns the French and Indian Wars and American independence, and Claudette Colbert has to learn how important these issues are. *Giant* concerns the building of male empires and the force of male competition, and Elizabeth Taylor must learn how important that is. Both women exert influence, and both women have power in their marriages, but both are brought out to a wild country from a wealthy eastern background by their men. They provide civilizing attitudes, but first they must learn. *The Wind* is an example of how what is basically an initiation story has been lifted out of any such potentially limiting category as "woman's film" by the greatness of performance (Lillian Gish as a woman from the "civilized" East exposed to the raw elements of the West) and direction (Victor Seastrom).

The transition film that takes a woman from a bad marriage into a good one is really a film about a woman's having made a bad choice in a husband, which is not the same thing as having been wrong in choosing to marry. These films link directly to audience needs. Women trapped in unhappy marriages found escape when they saw the bad marriage removed and the good one put in its place.

One example of this bad/good, dark/light pattern depicting marriage illustrates the method perfectly: *Mannequin* (1937), starring Joan Crawford. Crawford portrays Jessica, a girl from the tenements who sews buttonholes and hems skirts at a factory for a living. Her life is a dreary drag through a long working day, only to come home to more work helping her mother get dinner on the table for her out-of-work father and useless brother. She lives for "Eddie and Saturday night." Eddie (Alan Curtis), this man of her dreams, is a lowlife boxing promoter pushing a no-win fighter named Slug McGoo. What Curtis means in Crawford's life is established in the first half of the film through scenes of dreary work contrasted with scenes of hopeful romance and happiness with Curtis as they go to Luna Park and swim in the moonlight. In this early portion of the film, Crawford is angry but hopeful, in contrast with her worn-out mother, Elisabeth Risdon, who has long since given up.

Despite her optimism and obvious strength, Crawford's life borders on the sordid. She works hard but has little for herself to show for it. She turns her weekly salary over to her mother for household expenses but is aware that her father and brother frequently con her softhearted mother out of it for beer money. An eloquent visual passage defines Crawford's life and her feelings about it as she walks home after her day at the factory. Although it is summer it is already getting dark, and she can't afford carfare. Arriving home, she begins her slow climb up the numerous tenement flights to her own family's cramped apartment. As she climbs, tired, hot, even sweaty, and as darkness falls, she hears a baby screaming and a couple having a desperate argument. On each landing, the sound of some new unhappiness, some new failure, assails her, but since it is no more than her daily portion, she just plows on upward. Arriving home, she immediately dons an apron to help her exhausted mother get the family's meager supper of boiled potatoes and sauerkraut on the table. While the two women rush around in the hot kitchen, the father and brother are lounging impatiently in the living room.

For poor and unhappy women in the audience, this is a clear depiction of a woman in a helpless situation. Furthermore, behind Crawford, who still has her life ahead of her, stands the mother, an ominous example. The visual juxtaposition of the two women in the frame makes a clear statement: Crawford's future could be the same as that of her mother. Later,

Crawford and Curtis discuss this future. Love, the ever-present concept, is talked about as her motivating factor in wanting to marry him. However, she also discusses her loneliness and her need to get free of her family. Cautiously, she defines her own hope for some immediate happiness, however small, and of her desire that she and Eddie might have a home of their own, however small, in some better neighborhood. Suddenly, on their moonlit date, Crawford breaks down and begs Curtis to marry her, promising him that she will go on working, that she will do anything, anything, just to get out of the situation she's in. "What we feel for each other shuts out everything else. What more do we want? What else do we need?" This is the traditional battle cry of love, but *Mannequin* is a movie that will demonstrate in spades what a wrongheaded notion such romantic ideas really are. The extended opening sequence of *Mannequin* clearly illustrates that women marry to get away from the factory, but that getting away from the factory may not be getting far enough away if men are involved.

Crawford and Curtis marry. Their wedding supper ("eleven 85¢ dinners") is held at a Hester Street Chinese restaurant run by a man named Horowitz. This scene is a candidate for the most pathetic wedding supper ever put on film. Crawford is teary-eyed and radiant, trying not to see that her mother's face is a mask of grief, since she alone fully realizes that her daughter has made the same mistake she did. Their little party is small and sad, and the waiter is openly contemptuous that all they can afford is the eighty-five-cent meal even though it's their wedding supper. Although Crawford looks happy and Curtis looks handsome, her happiness has a tinge of desperation to it, and his handsomeness is too slick, too polished and easy. When Crawford gives a wedding toast, saying, "I hope you'll all be as happy as I am right now—always," the film cuts immediately to a shot of her mother's depressed and all-knowing face. A masterpiece of visual tension, the scene manages to portray both a wedding supper with a giddy bride and groom *and* an understanding of what is happening to them that dooms the marriage.

It is in this scene that Joan Crawford's Jessica meets the movie force that will ultimately change her future. As the film sinks to one of its lowest, darkest moments—ironically, her wedding night—into her life comes potential light in the form of Spencer Tracy. Tracy plays a shipping magnate (there were a lot of them in the old days, it seems), who was born and raised in this same neighborhood. Although he is now filthy rich, he likes to come back to his old haunts, particularly to attend meetings of the longshoremen's union, since he's one of those shipping magnates who's really a swell guy, just like one of his own men, whose interests he always has at heart. He's in the Chinese restaurant, presumably for the two-dollar dinner, and he can't help noticing the beautiful Joan Crawford, dancing in her husband's arms and singing "always and always" in his ear. Tracy, implausibly cast in an asexual-male role, meets the young couple and envies Curtis the fact that a beautiful woman like Crawford obviously adores him.

After the party, Curtis surprises Crawford by taking her to an uptown apartment, three little rooms well furnished and cozy, that represents what she has always wanted for herself. She is overwhelmed with joy. The only sunlight seen in this portion of the film, all of which takes place at night or in the dark, occurs on the screen on the morning after their wedding when Crawford arises, reborn as a wife, with all her dreams having come true. "There's nothing in the world I want that I haven't got right now," says Crawford, adding, "I'll work till I drop to keep them [her three rooms]."

As the film progresses, however, the marriage becomes the story of a woman's dreams cruelly shattered. Crawford has saddled herself with a man she cannot rely on. Like her father and brother before him, he does not really work, letting her earn their money by dancing in a cheap vaudeville show. When Crawford's girlfriend points out to her that she's still working, just not in the factory, Crawford snaps, "He took me away from Hester Street." The friend snaps back, "A streetcar coulda done that and cost you less." This realist from the world of women also tells Crawford, "I'm sick of hearing about guys that do the little things. Give me a guy that does a big thing once in a while, like payin' a month's rent."

Soon enough Curtis turns out to be crooked and ends up in jail. Frantic to get him free, Crawford goes to the only source of ready cash for bail money she knows, Spencer Tracy. Tracy, impressed by her loyalty to her obviously no-good husband, gives her the money with no strings attached, but she vows she'll pay it back. After Crawford bails Curtis out, they glumly take the subway home together in the dark, and they begin to quarrel. Finally, she tries to patch it up by saying, "We've still got each other." He replies, "And I suppose that's enough for you?" "Yes, it is," she replies, still clinging stubbornly to her dream of romance, love, and marriage.

After Curtis is free, Crawford is in for an even greater shock. Their little dream apartment was just loaned to him for three months, and they are evicted, ending up in a crummy place not unlike the tenement she thought she had married herself free of. "Who knows what's best for ya?" her husband still insists, asserting his rights as her man. Crawford replies, grimly, "You do, Eddie," and then goes off alone to the bathroom down the hall to cry.

This dark section of *Mannequin*, which pulls no punches, ends only when Joan Crawford finally walks out on her marriage to the man she thought she loved. The film makes an overt rejection of the idea that a woman must accept a life of poverty in an unsatisfactory marriage. The

action is introduced by a conversation between Crawford and her mother
that is astonishing in its outspoken presentation of a liberated viewpoint.
The scene is set in the old family kitchen in the dark and dingy tenement.
In the front room, seen through the doorway in long shot, there are now
three idle men instead of two, all lounging, smoking, telling stories, rocking
in their comfortable chairs. They are father, husband, brother.

Seen in close-up in the kitchen are two women: wife and mother.
They are once again preparing supper in the rudely equipped kitchen,
struggling with leaky faucets, hot pans of steaming boiled potatoes, and
cracked dishes. They are talking:

MOTHER: Jessica?
JESSICA: Yeah?
MOTHER: There are some things I've been wantin' to tell you. I don't
          talk much. Maybe I'm kinda not in the habit anymore.
JESSICA: But what's it all about?
MOTHER: You. You and Eddie. What you've got and what you want.
          What a woman gets. If she wants some say about the life she
          leads. A woman's supposed to lead the man's life. *Her* man's
          life. And women are made that way . . . occasionally.
          Woman's weakness is supposed to fit into a man's strength.
          Her respect pays for the security the man gives her. But now
          you, Jessica. You've got strength of your own. You can do
          things. Not just dream about them like . . . like most women.
JESSICA: What are you trying to tell me, Ma?
MOTHER: Make a life for yourself. Remember what it was that you hated.
          Always remember what it is *you* want. Get it. Any way you
          can. If you have to, get it alone.

The daughter listens to her mother and is soon on her way out of
misery. As Crawford finally leaves Curtis, she turns to him, saying,
"Women are weak and men are strong? My mother wasted a lifetime of
strength trying to prove that."

Once Crawford leaves marriage and love behind, her life changes
instantly. With one cut, the film takes her forward three months in time
to a sunny world in which she, well dressed and elegant, is coming to
Tracy to pay him back the one-hundred-dollar bail money she borrowed
from him. In other words, it looks as if all a woman needs to do to get a
good wardrobe and economic security, and let's not forget to make the sun
shine, is to walk out on a no-good husband and abandon her dreams of
romantic nonsense. Crawford now has a job as a mannequin, and when
Tracy comes to woo her she models a series of stunning outfits. Out she
walks, the center of all attention, swathed in furs, draped in satins, loaded

with jewels in the old woman's film favorite—the fashion show. Soon, she and Tracy are seen at a nightclub, laughing their heads off and agreeing to marry. Next, she's off to Europe with him, and then finally rewed, all in a lovely sunshine of wealth and joy. The two of them end up in a wee cottage in Ireland, with Crawford in an apron, baking a cake and humming. Tracy smokes his pipe in front of the fire, her head in his lap. Thus one marriage, bad and ominously real, is supplanted easily by another marriage, very good and ominously unreal.

This dark-to-light progression illustrates how the woman's film works. First is shown the dark life of an ordinary woman, with its disappointments and lack of security. Then comes the light life with its fantasy of love without strings and wealth beyond dreams. What is significant is that the transition that connects these two sections is a speech of liberation. Lurching out from the screen like a 3-D sock on the nose comes the woman's film zone of truth. "If you have to, get it alone," says the mother, and Crawford sets out to do so, accomplishing it, even though we are not shown that process. Miraculously, after saying she can do it, she does it. Get rid of a man, the film seems to say, and this is what you can do. Yet it then reestablishes the romantic notion it has just undermined through the device of the unreal man played by Spencer Tracy. Curtis, reappearing and hearing about their marriage, comments, "Sounds wonderful. Almost like a fairy story. Swinging through life, hand in hand." Having gone the limit in telling the truth about one bad marriage, the film jumps to an even greater romantic lie than the one that first inspired Crawford to marry Curtis. Crawford does not become an independent force, she just gets a better man. Since this man is totally unreal, it is worth thinking about the message the film really delivers. Is Tracy a form of masking the woman's power, making it acceptable? Or is he a way to erase the message of liberation, rendering it unnecessary? Or is he both things at once?

Is it possible to see this man, the Tracy character, as another suitable stand-in for independence? Possibly, but any images that would show the viewer how Crawford became independent are denied. The audience is not shown how Crawford found her job as a mannequin, learned her trade, and gained her independence. The audience is shown only how she became Tracy's wife. This renders unlikely the possibility of any women in the audience actually emulating what they've seen on-screen. They aren't shown how to find a career, and they certainly won't find a Spencer Tracy. After making a powerful movie that connects directly to audience unhappiness, *Mannequin* releases the pain through a traditional movie escape route.

There is one other strange ambivalence to *Mannequin*. At the end of the film, wealthy Spencer Tracy loses all his money, but Crawford stands by him. Tracy has not believed in her, however, and has failed to trust her at a key moment. For this, she slaps him hard on the face and later tells him, "I'll be reminding you of it the rest of your life." A viewer can believe this. She also starts telling him what he must do to reclaim his wealth. He must work and work and work and start over . . . under her guidance, but also, of course, with her support. *Mannequin* ends with one dominant force and only one dominant force established: Joan Crawford. She's the center of the universe. It seems ironic that films about women, aimed at women, starring women, show the pain to be found in the marriage trap and the luxuries to be found in careers, yet still ask viewers to accept marriage as the ultimate reward available to a strong woman. Presumably, some people in the audience saw through this.

THE DARK/LIGHT pattern of the movie marriage story was still in use at the end of the 1940s. Comedy was a particularly useful format in which to make a transition story that played on the old bad marriage/good marriage have-it-both-ways ploy.

To see how the common and thus recognizable problems of married life are presented and easily resolved one can look at *A Letter to Three Wives* (1949). This movie, a light and sophisticated comedy, first glamorizes the state of marriage, then undercuts it, and then reaffirms it. It conveniently presents in one big movie all the potential problems the bad-marriage movie usually depicts. *A Letter to Three Wives* provides in witty, short episodes the stories of three marriages, each a representative type, pared down, wised up, and served up fresh. First, there is the marriage of a young woman outside her class. Jeanne Crain has married Jeffrey Lynn. She's a poor farm girl with only a five-year-old dress from a Sears, Roebuck catalog to wear to the country club dance at which she will meet all her rich husband's sophisticated friends. (She's got the Fashion Problem as well as the Class Problem.) How did she get into this dilemma? She met him when they were both in the navy, and she was a snappy Wave officer in a uniform. This outfit, as Crain points out, was a "leveler. He couldn't tell if I was Smith, country club, or finishing school." (Kindly Ann Sothern does the thing one usually does in such situations: she cuts the extra flowers off the horrible dress and renders Crain presentable.)

Ann Sothern represents a second type of marriage problem, that of a woman who is paying more attention to her career than to her home. She is ambitious, while her husband (Kirk Douglas) is content to be a school-teacher. Sothern works overtime, on weekends, and late at night as a radio writer, in bondage to her horrible boss (Florence Bates, the female born to play the Helen Hokinson woman). Sothern mothers her twins (who are never seen on-screen) only whenever she can spare a minute.

The third marriage illustrates the Money Problem. A girl from the wrong side of the tracks (Linda Darnell) marries the town's most successful businessman (Paul Douglas) for his money. He is divorced, and quite a bit older than she is, but she knows what she wants. "I want to be in a silver frame on a piano. My own piano in my own house." (She wants the house!) She gets him by flashing a leg at him, giving him a hot kiss, and then walking off, leaving him with his tongue hanging out. He has married her on a similar basis. She wants; he wants. He's got what she wants (money), and she's got what he wants (sex). Both are plenty smart and plenty tough. "We'll do all right, kid," he tells her. "We're startin' out where it takes most marriages years to get. Out in the open. No jokes. You'll see. You made a good deal, Lora May."

Each of these three marriages is jeopardized by an outside force: the other woman, an unseen presence in the movie. The other woman is Addie Ross, a sophisticated, perfect female who does all the things for the men that the women they married can't or won't do. Unlike Jeanne Crain, Addie knows how to dress and to run a house. She's grown up with Crain's husband, part of his smart social set. Unlike Ann Sothern, she remembers Kirk Douglas's birthday and has time for him. She has no career. Unlike Linda Darnell, she has the class that Paul Douglas yearns for, the manners and the elegance, and her own money. Addie sends each of these three men a gift during the movie: a huge bottle of champagne for Crain's husband, to celebrate his marriage (a gracious social gesture showing her elegant manners and upbringing); a thoughtfully selected recording of Brahms for Douglas, a birthday present with a sweet note about the high school play he is directing (Sothern forgot the first and didn't give him time to tell her about the second); a picture of herself in a silver frame to set on the piano of Paul Douglas's posh home (the inspiration for Darnell's own dream). These gifts represent the three things the wives don't give their husbands: social grace, attention, and class. Addie has it all, and one of the three men is going to run away with her. In the end, because the movie is a charming comedy, no one runs away with Addie, and all three couples happily reunite. It might also be noted that, along the way, Crain has become what her husband wants—socially skilled, elegant, and a part of the group. Sothern becomes what her husband wants by cutting back on her career. And Darnell shows all the class any man could want by forgetting her original plan to divorce him and take him for every penny. "I've got everything I want," she says, sticking by her man and showing that, after all, she loves him and not his money.

Thus, one film sums up the basic marriage film problems: class, money, infidelity, career independence, with hints about children (those unseen twins) and in-laws (Darnell's low-class family). Each marriage story gets about half an hour, and since the audience understands the references being made, the filmmakers concentrate on wit, glamour, and sophistication, pulling off one of the few truly elegant films about marital woes. For once, an audience gets to have it both ways and not feel cheated. The problems are honest ones, but they are comfortably resolved.

IN ADDITION to the various kinds of movies that depict happy marriages, and the transitional films that provide the dark/light pattern of showing both happy and unhappy unions, movies about women tell stories about deeply unhappy marriages. In fact, unhappiness in marriage is one of the fundamental plot staples of the woman's film. What the movies show us is that when a woman places her fate in the hands of a man, she's asking for it, because she allows herself to become dependent on him emotionally, economically, and sexually. If he lets her down, as he frequently does, she's in a jam. Jams, these women's movies tell us, are what marriage is all about.

Guidelines about marriage, learned from the movies, teach a woman these things:

1. Marriage fails when you don't have enough money, and marriage fails when you have too much money. (Problem established: money)
2. Marriage fails when you have children and pay too much attention to them, and marriage fails when you have children and don't pay enough attention to them. (Problem established: children)
3. Marriage fails when you get dull and frumpy and lose your attractiveness to the opposite sex, and marriage fails when you get glamorous and well dressed and become too attractive to the opposite sex. Marriage fails when your husband is dull and a failure and no one wants him but you, and marriage fails when your husband becomes exciting and successful and everyone wants to take him away from you. (Problem established: infidelity)
4. Marriage fails when you marry beneath yourself, and marriage fails when you marry above yourself. (Problem established: class differences)
5. Marriage fails if you don't work to help out with economic problems, and marriage fails when you go to work and make money of your own. Marriage fails if you have a career, and marriage fails when you don't have a career. Marriage fails if you are too independent, and marriage fails if you're not independent enough. (Problem established: career conflicts and independence)
6. Marriage fails if your family and in-laws aren't there to help you with

it, and marriage fails if your family and in-laws try to help you with
it. (Problem established: family and in-laws)

The bottom line of all this is clear. Problem established: marriage fails. If
that's the case, how do these films explain exactly why women ever want
to get married in the first place? "I married my way out of South Dakota
once," Una O'Connor tells Jean Harlow in *Suzy* (1936), "but that didn't
mean I loved the guy." Like many women in the movies, she married as
a form of liberation, in her case a way to escape bad geography. Others
have different reasons. "I know what I want," says Linda Darnell in *A
Letter to Three Wives*, and she means the guy's money. Some do it for love,
and some do it for security. Some do it for politics, and some do it to please
their parents. Lots do it because they have to, but the funniest reason I
ever heard put forth is from *Forsaking All Others* (1934), when Rosalind
Russell says, "I'm tired of being a bridesmaid. I wish I could get married
so I could wear a decent hat." (In the world of the woman's film, where
fashion is everything, this is probably the best reason of all.)

Sometimes women on-screen figure out that they themselves were
married for the wrong reasons. In *Coroner Creek* (1948), a drunken wife
bursts out at her husband, "You married me because you thought I was
pretty enough to dress up this house, and wear good clothes, and help your
success go forward." Dorothy McGuire, who has previously gushed out,
"To think I can be married! I can have a home. Someone will love me. I
won't have to be a spinster" in *Invitation* (1952), suddenly finds out that
the only reason Van Johnson wed her is that her father (Louis Calhern)
hired him to do so because he thought her too plain to attract a man on
her own. Besides, she's going to die, and he wants her to be happy, however
briefly. When McGuire finds out that her new groom is an expensive purchase by her father, like a mink coat, she gets so mad she doesn't die after
all.

Since we already know that the woman's world on film is a world of
limited choices, in which women are largely encouraged to see marriage
as a number-one option, why *are* there so many miserable movies about
marriages gone sour? Probably it was because the news of other people's
marital failure was oddly reassuring; such stories certainly provide outlets
for the anger and disappointment some women must have felt. First of all,
these films are saying, "Your marriage may be bad, but take a look at this
one. At least your husband isn't trying to kill you or make you buy ninety-
eight-cent dresses from the dime store." Observing a bad marriage between
Cary Grant and Kay Francis (or Leslie Howard and Myrna Loy) must have
been comforting. If those two, with all their money and looks, can't do
better than you and the guy you married, well. . . . Second, no matter how

bad things get up on-screen, the finale usually finds the couple reunited and the institution of marriage reinforced. Those last-minute happy endings fix it all up, and even when they aren't very convincing, at least they give a viewer something to hold on to. Women in the audience could leave a film about a bad marriage feeling reassured, uplifted, and even superior, confident that, poor though they might be, unhappily wed though they might be, neglected though they might be, they weren't the only ones. And there was hope. When a marriage on film is truly a bad one, then the institution is reinforced by the understanding that fate in the form of some plot development will take care of it for you, and that you can find another, better person to marry. At the very least, there is the temporary escape of the movies. At the movies, the dark would give way to the light.

Who knows how many women truly hated their marriages and enjoyed seeing one go bad on-screen? How many regretted that they ever married in the first place? Having done the job of playing wife and perhaps even having children, could a woman secretly hope her man would die and get out of her life, leaving her free (and, one hopes, well provided for)—free to, as Lucile Watson says in *The Women* (1939), "stretch out in the whole bed by yourself like a lovely swastika"? There's an underlying hint of that in the fact that so many movies contain dead husbands or scenes of runaway brides, interrupted marriage ceremonies, refusals to say "I do." From Claudette Colbert and Clark Gable in *It Happened One Night* (1934) through Cornel Wilde and Ginger Rogers in *It Had To Be You* (1947) to Dustin Hoffman and Katharine Ross in *The Graduate* (1967), men keep rescuing women from marrying no-goods or stuffed shirts, saving them from a life of boredom and regret.

How very secretly reassuring was it for a woman to see Ginger Rogers, dressed in a series of wedding gowns by Jean Louis, reject marriage three times in *It Had To Be You* (1947)? First, Rogers stands at a flower-bedecked altar in a virginal gown with a Peter Pan collar and puffed sleeves and a long veil attached to her high crown of flowers. Suddenly she says, "I can't . . . I can't . . . I'm sorry, I'm sorry. . . ." She cries and runs away in confusion, stopping to reassure her shocked parents. One year later, she's back at the same altar with the same minister, this time in a confidently low-cut satin dress with appliquéd flowers around the bosom. She wears no veil, only a flowered crown. The absence of a wedding veil and the low-cut dress make a fashion statement that says Rogers is now more open, more mature, ready to accept the responsibilities of marriage. Suddenly, again she says, "I can't . . . I can't . . . I'm sorry . . . it's nothing personal." This time she tries to reassure her shaken groom; experienced in disaster, she knows she should comfort him as well as her parents before she exits the room. One year after that, she's back yet again, now austere and resigned in a nunlike outfit in a simple, straight line, with long, full sleeves and a large round halo motif attached to her shawl-like headpiece. She has suffered, but she has a heightened maturity, and a new peace and purity in her role as a woman. Her gown tells us this. But again it's "I can't . . . I just can't" as she stumps off, dejected, without even bothering to apologize to her terrified groom and her distraught parents.

Here is a case of the audience having it all. They get to ogle three gorgeous wedding gowns for the price of one. They get to see three wimpy grooms rejected. And Ginger Rogers is still intact for further plot developments, free and easy and not saddled with a dreary marriage. Was Ginger Rogers striking a blow for women everywhere, who were all secretly thinking, "If only I had just said, 'I can't . . . I can't . . .' "?

This kind of subversion is built into the marriage film. It was not uncommon for women in the 1930s, 1940s, and even 1950s to deliver speeches on-screen that appear to point out the foolishness of the wife's role, some of which seem to come straight from the feminist's handbook. Hedy Lamarr muses on the emptiness of her life as a rich man's wife in *Crossroads* (1942): "You know, darling, sometimes I sit here at home feeling sort of useless and empty. Then I think of you and how important your work is and then I think, well, I'm his wife, and if he's important, so am I, and my ego is all fixed up." As Lamarr delivers this speech, she is fulfilling a totally unnecessary role in the plot, bearing out her own testimony. Smiling brightly, she then says "Tea, darling?" to her husband, played by William Powell, who has been barely listening. Lamarr is seen to be nothing but an object, beautiful window dressing in a plot that has no use for her, allegedly playing a woman in an enviable position with her very own silver tea service. Lamarr ends up looking like a clotheshorse with nothing to do and no one to listen to her.

When Greta Garbo's sister marries and leaves the house in *The Painted Veil* (1934), based on a Somerset Maugham story, Garbo discusses the situation with her mother.

"He'll make Olga a good husband, and a good husband is what every girl wants," the mother says. "What more do you want than a good husband, I'd like to know."

Garbo responds, "Must he be good, Mother? It's not very exciting to be good!"

Garbo is seen on-screen in huge close-up as she and her mother go on talking. The mother's voice is heard from offscreen.

GARBO: Did you love Father very much when you married?
MOTHER: What a question! Of course I did. Your father was a fine man.
GARBO: A brilliant one, wasn't he?

MOTHER: He took a prize every year at the University.
GARBO: And handsome, too. . . . Don't you want me to wait for a man like Father?

This conversation is clearly ironic. Mother is spouting the party line, as it is her job as a vigilant mother to get two daughters married off without mishap to men who will pay the bills and look after them. Garbo longs for more and knows it's a bum's rush to the altar. Allowing the audience to concentrate on the haunting beauty of Garbo, a woman of passion and intelligence, offsets the implausibility of such a woman being happy with the proverbial "good provider" and nothing more.

No movie depicts marriage more dismally than a depressing little minor comedy like *Love, Honor and Goodbye* (1945), starring Nils Asther, Virginia Bruce, and Victor McLaglen. Ostensibly a lighthearted farce about love and reconciliation, its basic plot structure reveals tension, conflict, distrust, doubt, the double standard, and a condescending attitude toward women.

The story concerns a wife (Bruce) who wants desperately to become an actress, although it is firmly, clearly established that she has absolutely *no* talent. Her husband (McLaglen) does not want her even to try, because, as he whines frequently, he wants "a wife." Because he loves her, however, he decides secretly to back her in a show so that she can fail, learn her lesson, and come back home. As it turns out, she really *does* stink, and after her flop she shows up at home chastened and ready for the big romantic evening he has planned (to be followed by a second honeymoon trip).

The insulting nature of all this completely overrides the comedy, which isn't very well written in the first place. Even the fact that it can be presented as acceptable to audiences is offensive. Furthermore, after establishing the wife as an idiot, and humiliating her in her attempts to have a life of her own, the film takes an abrupt turn in which it establishes the proper kind of wife she ought to be. She begins to care for a little orphan girl who is conveniently dropped into the plot. Bruce becomes a model of the sacrificial wife and adoptive mother.

Love, Honor and Goodbye is a minor film, but such movies often reveal more than big-budget hits. The people who made them spent less money and made less of an attempt to create a big fantasy out of life. Often costumes were bought off the rack, and there was a simplicity of presentation. Such films were made swiftly to reflect current attitudes, as timeliness was one of the assets of low-budget filmmaking. Here one sees the depressing truth about common attitudes toward women (they're dumb, keep 'em home, and kids will tie them down) and toward marriage (never tell each other the truth but work subtle scams on each other to get what you want). How could women in the audience fail to grasp the truth about such a movie?

Rage about the marital state emerges overtly in the sometimes charming, frequently appalling Blondie and Dagwood series, which stars the lovely Penny Singleton and the skeletal Arthur Lake. The situation of the Bumstead marriage can be boiled down to a basic premise: Dagwood is an idiot; Blondie is a genius. However, Dagwood is a man and Blondie is a woman, so the idiot prevails. Since they truly love each other, everything will turn out fine, even though their children are contemptuous of them, they don't have enough money, and Dagwood's boss is a venal tyrant who exploits him mercilessly. Throughout these movies, Dagwood suffers and falls over brooms and postmen and dogs, while Blondie sparkles and gets admired and figures things out. Blondie whips up delicious dinners, and Dagwood serves dog food by mistake. Blondie takes charge, and Dagwood takes umbrage. That's how it goes.

The Blondie and Dagwood marital comedies are fascinating in their presentation of what it is that people would like to gripe about through the safety valve of comedy. What emerges is a parallel complaint track. The men see that Dagwood is put-upon, exploited, unappreciated, and tied down. The women see that Blondie is much more intelligent than the men around her but that she is expected to be the "little woman." Since these ideas are presented as exaggerated comedy, and therefore neither honest nor true, they subtly erase their negativity as they appear, waving a cheerful "just kidding, folks" flag at the audience at the same time as they present a veritable cornucopia of horrors about marriage. It's a shell game. Now you see it (marriage is horrible), and now you don't (Blondie and Dagwood love each other).

The concept of the Bumstead marriage is well tested in *Blondie for Victory* (1942), which deals with the issue of the role of women on the home front during World War II. It's comedy, but it's semiserious, because it addresses whether or not women should leave the home to work. The movie opens with its credits presented against a cheerful song in which the two sing:

DAGWOOD: Blondie's not always right . . . I let her think she is.
BLONDIE: All of my thoughts are bright, long as he thinks they're his.

Because it is World War II, Dagwood comes home from work only to find chaos. A baby-sitter is with the baby, and things are a mess. Blondie has organized the "Housewives of America, an organization for the defense and preservation of the American home." Skillfully shoving Dagwood aside, the women decide to "make Mr. Bumstead an honorary housewife" while they pledge themselves "to put the needs of our organization before home and husband." Blondie says, "Now that we housewives have put our homes in order, we must help to put the world in order. Let us get out of the home and into the fight. Let us march right in! In this crisis our families must learn to take care of themselves and I know we'll be pleasantly surprised to see that they are not as clumsy and helpless as they seem." When she finishes this speech, Dagwood immediately falls over the dogs in the kitchen.

This subject matter is carefully presented, because it is wartime and women *are* needed. Yet the subtext tells us this is somehow misguided, a notion further confirmed when Dagwood is summoned to what he thinks is an emergency involving Blondie. Instead, it turns out that she wanted him present for her "defense fashion show" (that old women's film favorite). As he and his boss, Mr. Dithers, watch goggle-eyed, a stern matron booms out that they are about to see "Women on Parade!" Out marches an aston-ishing lineup of women wearing uniforms of all types—one for apparently everything, including the Civilian Defense Summer Uniform, the Civil Defense Canteen Worker, the Red Cross Canteen Worker, the Parachute Nurse, the Defense Factory Worker, and, my favorite, the Bundles for Blue Jackets. Naturally, there is a uniform for Housewives of America, worn by Blondie. (Mr. Dithers, asked to admire her uniform, tells Blondie, "Per-sonally, I've always liked the conservative apron.")

Dagwood and Mr. Dithers discuss things, with Mr. Dithers informing Dagwood that "You're not the only one who should be cooking. I hate to see you get the worst end of this. . . . You're the one who has to be up early, off to the office, slaving all day . . . the first war duty of a woman with a husband and children is to keep up the morale of her home. Then whatever extra time she has can be devoted to victory work." After he says this, however, and Dagwood agrees, they are made to look like total fools as they begin barking like dogs, having eaten dog food for dinner because they're too stupid to cook anything else.

Dagwood organizes the husbands in a reverse Lysistrata-like move. The men are suffering deeply while the women try to do war work. For instance, one has pins in his underwear and one has holes in his socks. (These socks, with those holes in them, occur over and over again in the woman's film when a man wants to prove how hard his life is without a wife to care for him. The American male becomes an outraged figure, holding up his foot accusingly, pointing at his bare toes sticking out of an accusing black sock.)

In the end, Blondie comes to her senses. "We're what America needs," she tells her women. "Housewives!" After she thinks it over, she adds,

"Go home. That's where morale begins. . . . Each one of us is married and responsible for the happiness and welfare of a man. It isn't up to us to do his work for him, but to see to it that he's so well cared for that he's able to do his own work. That's where our duty lies."

Many times movies portray these marriages as if they are just fine, but the subtext is too ugly to ignore. An allegedly happy marriage in a postwar family is presented in *Shadow in the Sky* (1951), with Nancy Davis, soon to become Mrs. Ronald Reagan, as the wife. This marriage features a little house, two kids, and Mom in a chair reading to them. (This is how people who oversimplify the films of the 1950s claim movies always depicted women and families.) There's the house with the picket fence, Mom in her apron whipping up brownies while old Dad smokes his pipe and putters, and the two kids who display perfect teeth, excellent penmanship, and evidence of having attended obedience school. Everything is perfect in the American home. However, if one watches *Shadow in the Sky* all the way through (and I don't recommend it), one finds instead a very different sort of situation. To begin with, Davis's brother is insane, and James Whitmore as her husband is barely making enough money for his family to survive on. One of the kids has nightmares and can't sleep at night, and although her brother *can* be released from his mental hospital, Davis doesn't want him around. She's both ashamed of him and afraid of him. She's lied to the kids about him, too. This family life is no picnic. When things cheer up at the end, with everyone smiling, does this erase the sense of a dark and dismal family life? I think not. Were we a nation of goons forty years ago, who never noticed any subtexts? Film scholarship has a way of making current analysts out to be geniuses, with the audiences of former times cast as idiots.

OVER THE YEARS, there have probably been more Hollywood movies that use adultery as the basic cause of marital discord than any other problem. Adultery is a story problem that easily allows the movie to show glamorous people in romantic situations, and it addresses the in-the-dark yearnings of viewers very directly. Real or imagined, comic or tragic, resulting in reconciliation, divorce, or death, adultery is always a big topic in the world of women. The marriage films that deal with it are legion.

There are three types: the pseudo (the one that never actually happens), the wife's, and the husband's. There is a great deal of difference among these three categories, with the woman's unfaithfulness being truly serious, the man's possibly repairable, and the pseudo evidently considered by Hollywood as a source of great hilarity, a suitable escape hatch, a vicarious and titillating thrill for people who aren't going to do it in real life. Countless light comedies flirt with the topic of threatened adultery, exploring it from all possible angles: the innocent married secretary preyed upon by her boss, or the preying secretary who traps her innocent married boss; the new woman in town whose true love is jeopardized by a wolfish married man's pursuits, or the new woman who sets her sights on one of the town's most contented husbands. The issue is presented from the wife's point of view as well as the husband's, and sometimes the children's. Evidently the fear of losing a husband (and meal ticket) to another woman was very real to the women who stayed home to tend the house and family.

Day-Time Wife (1939), a pseudoadultery film, presents the kind of married life that women in the audience presumably dreamed of. When the wife (Linda Darnell) wakes up in the morning, she is in a twin bed, her makeup and hair ribbon perfectly in place. Underneath the satin coverlet in the bed next to hers is no less a mate than the youthful and gorgeous Tyrone Power. His first words to his wife upon awakening are "My dreams don't do you justice." There's a well-trained dog, an understanding maid, a spacious living arrangement, and plenty of cash. Everything appears to be perfect.

On closer inspection, however, the usual contradictions emerge. Tyrone Power, the gorgeous husband, has forgotten their anniversary, even though it's only their second one. Furthermore, he doesn't show up that night for the surprise party his wife has planned, and when she and the gang go to his office to commandeer him for the festivities, he is not there. When he tiptoes in much, much later, he lies to Darnell and says he *was* working late at the office. What's a nice girl to do? "I'm not going to be like some suspicious old wife, always prying into his affairs and never letting him out of her sight," Darnell pouts to her best friend, the wise Binnie Barnes, who clearly thinks she's out of her mind. "If a woman can't hold her man," says Darnell, "it's her own fault . . . and I'm going to hold mine." But how? Using the usual female-film tool of deception, she concocts a scheme whereby she can do primary research by becoming a secretary and finding out what secretaries have that wives don't. In other words, she means to proceed in harm's way.

In this way the plot follows Hollywood's most highly recommended good-behavior marital ploy: subterfuge. Never Tell the Mate. Darnell becomes a secretary to the lecherous Warren William, but pretends to her husband she's still staying home all day. (Power *does* notice that Darnell has cut her fingernails, but since he pays no further attention to her, she gets away with it.) As a working girl, and a beautiful one, Darnell begins to learn about husbands from the other side. Her married boss asks her to think of him as "a sort of an ineligible eligible bachelor." When she reminds him that he has a wife, he says, "After a while a wife gets to be a sort of a solved crossword puzzle. A man likes to be intrigued . . . likes to fence with someone, someone who might say no."

In plot terms, *Day-Time Wife* conforms to the usual patterns of reinforcing societal concepts, but as usual, describing the surface story, or the bare bones of the plot, does not address the subtext. *Day-Time Wife* reveals in its visual images the ambivalence attached to the idea of a good little wife accepting her husband's behavior, no matter what he does. Where the plot addresses a woman's fear of her man's infidelity, its subtext speaks of a deep desire to punish him for it. What it actually reveals is female anger, however lightly presented, and a need for women to control things. Throughout the movie it is the women who actually know what is going on, while the men don't have a clue. The females hatch schemes and undertake masquerades that they perpetrate on the unsuspecting males. While the women maneuver and shape events, the men accept whatever they encounter at face value. They simply don't get it.

Two scenes demonstrate how this light comedy with glamorous clothes and beautiful stars addresses the subject of adultery, which, of course, is not really adultery but pseudoadultery. These sequences allow the women in the story on-screen and the women in the viewing audience a sense of superior strength and knowledge. In the first, Darnell plays a cruel trick on Power, and in the second, Power and William boast of their mastery over their wives.

The scene between Darnell and Power in which she tricks him is an extended dinner-table sequence. Knowing that her husband is romantically involved with his secretary, Darnell pours a bottle of the secretary's potent and recognizable perfume over their family dog. As the married couple sits down to an elegant evening dinner, the dog comes begging to Power for table scraps. The hapless Power naturally smells and recognizes the scent. Since he has just left the intimate company of his secretary, he immediately assumes that the smell is emanating from himself. As Darnell condescendingly smiles at him from her end of the table, Power begins nervously to try to cover up. Darnell makes silly small talk, pretending innocence. As the action unfolds, Power is humiliated and made to look increasingly immature, foolish, and inept. Darnell, behind the expensive crystal and lavish flowers, is in the narrative position of privileged information and invites the viewers into her conspiracy. Everyone enjoys Power's comeuppance, which is presented as comedy. While Darnell looks coolly beautiful, Power looks less and less attractive as he shrinks before our eyes. While Darnell seems intelligent and even wise (okay, a little smug), Power looks stupid, since he is being reduced to a gibbering idiot by his own dog, not to mention the manipulations of his wife.

In the second sequence, Warren William and Tyrone Power sit down to do men's business together. They believe themselves to be power brokers. They are confident, well dressed, and handsome. They are also both philanderers, and they feel utterly in control of the women in their lives. In the chitchat that precedes their negotiations, Power confidently tells William, "I've got my wife well trained. She's nice and quiet, the home type. I wear the pants in my family." As he speaks these bragging and condescending words, his own wife, unbeknownst to him, is actually sitting outside William's door as his secretary. Furthermore, William has a date with her that very evening! He, of course, doesn't know she's Power's wife. Both men look like posturing fools, victims of Darnell's superior wisdom. As the audience listens to Power speak about his wife in a manner that it knows to be untrue, all sympathy is clearly shifted to her, the more honest and the smarter person. Power is again reduced in the audience's eyes, and his entire approach to marriage is called into serious question. Why should a man be allowed to be unfaithful if he feels like it, while assuming that his wife is safely tucked away at home? Even though *Day-Time Wife* is a silly light comedy, its visual organization and its plot devices suggest that men are both cads and fools and that women must be alert to these facts.

It is astonishing what a sordid tale can be told in a Hollywood movie, all served up as if it were cute and moral, even wholesome. By the time *Day-Time Wife* works its plot line into a frenzy, the audience is asked to accept as normal a scene in which a wife and husband are in a married man's hideaway penthouse, the wife being lured to "the study where the view is better" and the husband being necked onto his back by his secretary. It's all presumably okay because nobody really means it, and nobody is really who or what they say they are. It's just pretend. It's pseudoadultery.

Day-Time Wife clearly supports the idea that married women in the audience need to be on the lookout for straying husbands. When they spot one, and he's their own, they need to get tricky to hold his interest. This is their job, and it's no use blaming other women; it's nobody's fault but their own. "It's not *her* fault," Linda Darnell says, meaning her husband's secretary. "There's a little of the wandering minstrel in every man, and if you don't hold his interest, he's bound to go whistling under other people's balconies." When Darnell and the secretary find themselves cheerfully making up a couch for the out-of-favor Tyrone Power to sleep on, they are downright sisterly in their conversation. "I've been out with him a few times," the secretary says regarding Power, "but I figure he's in love with his wife." (She doesn't know she's actually talking to that same wife.) "Well, then," says Darnell, gratified, "why does he go out with you?" "Ah, it's natural with men, I guess. Makes them feel like they did when they were little boys and stole apples. To him I'm just a nice fresh slice of watermelon." No *real* infidelity ever takes place in *Day-Time Wife*, only the threat of it. The wife retains her virtue, punishes her husband, deals with the threat, maintains the status quo, and has a lot of fun all at the same time.

Pseudoinfidelity is one thing. Real infidelity is quite another. Some women on film can forgive their husbands anything—literally anything— in marriage except real infidelity. Thus it is that Charles Laughton's long-suffering wife in *Payment Deferred* (1932) willingly accepts the news that Laughton has murdered his Australian nephew and buried him in the backyard. In fact, it inspires new closeness between them, and for the first time in years their sex life is interesting. What she can't forgive, however, is finding out that he had an affair with Verree Teasdale during the time she and their daughter were away on vacation. When she hears that news, she goes straight to the cabinet, gets the cyanide, puts it in her fruit juice, and drinks it.

Other wives have no choice but to forgive. What women have to put up with is well illustrated by the infidelity in *Traveling Husbands* (1931), a film about the long-suffering wife of a philandering traveling salesman. When he is shot during a hotel-room party with prostitutes, his wife is sent for because he is believed to be near death. Since the police have not let anyone leave the scene of the crime, the prostitutes and the victim's fellow salesmen are still on the premises. They decide to stage a fashion show to fool the wife and construct a respectable explanation of why these "models" are all present. (What better sham could there be for a woman's film than a fashion show?) When the wife enters the room, the prostitutes are modeling the clothes the men sell, and everyone pretends to the wife that's why they were in the hotel with her husband and his friends. (This is not a comedy, although the plot sounds like a farce.) The wife is not fooled for a minute, and she makes it clear to everyone that she is not an idiot and doesn't want to be lied to.

The prostitute who shot her husband actually loves him, and theirs has been a longtime liaison. She and the wife end up having a talk, in the great tradition of the woman's film. The prostitute laments her life, telling the wife that she, too, would like to have what the wife has: a big house, jewelry, servants, furs. The wife is incredulous. "You think that's what I have? I live in three rooms and worry about paying bills."

"What!" The prostitute is astounded. "With all the money he throws around?" The two women sit and contemplate this as each realizes what a jerk the husband really is, spending his money on sex and booze out of town, refusing to marry the prostitute who loves him, and, at the same time, neglecting the wife who also loves him and who has to scrimp and save to make ends meet. In the end, when it is clear that the husband will survive the shooting, the wife feels she has no choice but to forgive him and take him back. How else can she survive? Like the prostitutes, she is dependent on a man for her living. However, she elects not to press charges against the other woman who did the shooting. Sisterhood prevails. As she prepares to leave, the wife moves toward the prostitute, gallantly offering her hand and speaking the ludicrous words, "Let's both keep our chins up." By using this expression from the stiff-upper-lip tradition of male movies, the wife acts as if she were a brave flier going off to war and saying good-bye to her equally doomed fellow females.

Traveling Husbands presents an infidelity that must be forgiven because the wife is economically dependent on the husband, whereas *Payment Deferred* presents one that cannot be forgiven because the wife is emotionally dependent. Both movies show how women are held in bondage by these situations, but no solutions are offered other than the acceptance of male infidelity. There's an air of "this is one of the facts of life in marriage" to these films. However, this kind of acceptance does not generally apply when the infidelity is on the part of the woman.

There is definitely a double standard. While there is a great deal of tolerance for the straying husband depicted in these films, there is almost none for the straying woman. When a woman betrays a man sexually, it is a matter of cosmic significance, but when a man does it, it may be a casual fling. (Women's infidelity appears most often in movies about the upper class, where idle women have the opportunity and the money to conduct affairs during the afternoons while their husbands do whatever it is that upper-class husbands do all day.)

When a woman strays in marriage, it is seen as justifiable only if her husband is a cad or a killer. Even then, it is best for her to wait until the bounder has been dealt with by society or by fate. It is also justifiable if her straying has been motivated by True Love, but if that is the case she can expect sympathy only from moviegoers, not from the plot of the film itself. She will have to pay.

The Unfaithful (1947) features Ann Sheridan as a wife who has been unfaithful to her husband during World War II while he was overseas and she was lonely and afraid. The film opens in the immediate postwar period, when Sheridan has just stabbed to death her former blackmailing lover who has tracked her to her domestic lair. She has foolishly pretended to the police that she had never met the man before, and now she is stuck with her lie. Desperately she tries to explain to her husband what happened to cause her infidelity: "I didn't want to, but you were six thousand miles away, and I was alone. There was nobody. Paula and her friends now and then. During the day there were things to do, but at night I sat alone. I ate alone. I went to the movies alone. I took a walk alone. Oh, you don't understand. No man could!"

The Unfaithful presents adultery from the woman's side, and no doubt this was a subject that postwar America had on its mind. (The parallel— the man's infidelity while overseas—was dealt with in such films as *The Man in the Gray Flannel Suit* [1956], in which a foreign child the hero fathered turns up in suburbia.) Sympathy for what has happened to Ann Sheridan, a faithful wife gone wrong due to the war and loneliness, is vocalized by her lawyer in an important trial scene. He points out that Sheridan is on trial for murder, not infidelity. Had there been no war, which upset everyone's lives and stability, she would not have strayed. The implication is not exactly feminist. It suggests that had her husband been home to walk with her, eat with her, go to the movies with her— *sleep* with her—he could have kept her in line. Her infidelity, says the lawyer, shall be judged by her husband and society, not the jury.

Just so. It *is* the husband and society who always judge a woman in the woman's film. It is also her bitchy, gossiping female friends. One of them, in *The Unfaithful*, well played by Eve Arden, stands up for her in a somewhat tarnished show of sisterhood. When Sheridan's husband, played by Zachary Scott, comes to visit Arden to talk it all over, he breaks down and cries. Arden tells him she's glad to see him act like a human being for a change. Scott has been a faithful husband, but a neglectful one. He is always promising Sheridan he'll take her on a two-week vacation, just the two of them, but he never actually delivers. (Men are always promising these vacations in movies. The conflict between work and love that a woman faces in life is also presented in the woman's film as a problem she has in marriage. The man's real interest is always in his work, and although he is not praised for his neglect of wife and family, the implication is there that he can be made to see this problem and thus shape up. A little shaping up is all it takes for the man to correct his work-love conflict. For a woman, a little shaping up will not correct that conflict that requires major sacrifices from her, even death.)

Scott and Arden discuss the situation:

SCOTT: I trusted her. You never liked her, did you?

ARDEN: I detested her. She seemed a little too wholesome, but if you came up here because you thought I was going to say something bad about her, you're out of luck. I'm sorry for her. She really loves you. Two and a half years [length of time he was gone to the army] is a long time.

SCOTT: I managed it.

ARDEN: In the South Pacific. Try it on Wilshire Boulevard.

Arden goes on further to chastise Scott by telling him that he married Sheridan only because he was going off to war. She says he wanted a whirl and a memory, a beautiful woman waiting for him, and he didn't want anyone making time with her while he was gone. So he hung a "No Trespassing" sign on her "like you'd stake a gold claim." They had only two weeks together, and *that* was supposed to last her. "You didn't marry her. You just took out an option on her. You wanted her to be perfect."

"What's a wife supposed to be?"

"A human being . . . or is it your manly pride?"

The Unfaithful stands out in its sympathetic presentation of real adultery, not pseudoadultery, on the part of a wife. The other side is represented by one of Hollywood's great films, *Dodsworth* (1936), based on the Sinclair Lewis novel. In this film, the woman's adultery is related to her own foolishness. Dodsworth's wife, brilliantly played by Ruth Chatterton, cannot accept her own aging process, and her desire for European elegance and class wrecks her marriage to her down-to-earth and honest midwestern husband (Walter Huston).

Chatterton's character is not presented as a one-dimensional villainess who does not appreciate her husband. Rather, sympathy is elicited for how she feels, if not for what she does. "I want a new life," Chatterton tells Huston, "all from the very beginning, a perfectly glorious, free, adventurous life. We've done our job." She is referring to the fact that they are middle-aged, wealthy, and their only child is happily married. Huston, as auto magnate Dodsworth, has sold his enormously successful motor company, and Chatterton wants a trip to Europe. He is somewhat reluctant to go, but willing if it will please her. She has explained that life in their midwestern town, Zenith, has stifled her. "Have you ever thought what Zenith means to me?" she has asked. Describing her life there, she tells him it was fine for him, because "you'd go down to the plant and deal in millions and have a marvelous time. I'd go down to the kitchen and order dinner. And then there was the ladies' luncheon and bridge. Always the same ladies. And then dinner. The same people we dined with last week. After dinner, poker for the men and the women for the women. Talk of children, doctors, servants, and the garden club." Mrs. Dodsworth puts it to her husband directly, "I'm begging for life. No, I'm not. I'm demanding it." In Europe, however, her behavior becomes vain and silly. Conflicts arise between them. She feels ashamed of her husband's blunt American ways, while he, for his part, thinks her friends are moochers. But he loves her, and when she tells him, "You've got to let me have my fling," he returns to America without her, giving her the room she needs to make a complete fool of herself. Her resulting adultery, with Paul Lukas, is later exposed by

Dodsworth, who admits, "I wouldn't have gotten where I am if I weren't a bit ruthless."

In the end, Chatterton wants to divorce Huston to marry a young German baron, but his mother, played by the ubiquitous Maria Ouspenskaya, puts it to her directly in female terms when she refuses to give her permission for the marriage. "You are older than Kurt. Have you thought how little happiness there can be for an old wife of a young husband?" Kurt lets her down, telling her that he must think of his mother . . . so she has no choice but to call Dodsworth back. However, he has found a new love in the person of the radiantly beautiful Mary Astor, who gives a performance of great warmth and naturalness. Huston tries to do the right thing, but, face-to-face with his now shallow, silly, and vain wife, he flees back to Astor's waiting arms. *Dodsworth* shows that it is the man who will survive if the woman is unfaithful. Society will never condone her behavior, and the aging process will do her in. Without her reputation and her husband to care for her, the woman will be left alone. Presumably, no adultery could be worth it. *Dodsworth* condemns Chatterton's foolish and adulterous woman, but it shows us why she is the way she is, and that includes the "nice man" who was too busy to pay attention to her for twenty years. A mature film about grown-ups, *Dodsworth* is an interesting portrait of what a woman's life could turn into if she wasn't careful.

THE SECOND LARGEST category of problems encountered in marriage films is that of the woman wanting to have a career. Marriages, films often imply, fall apart when the woman leaves the home and goes out to work. Why? Because the movies show us that these women, who are the central characters of the films, are often very good at it, earning more money than their husbands and thus compromising their masculine mastery. In practical terms, the home falls to pieces. There's no hot food, and dust balls appear under the beds. In psychological or covert terms, these films are about women asserting their right to independence.

When a marriage is bad because of a man's infidelity, it is because a woman might have made a bad choice in a man; still the film tells her to stick with her choice. When a marriage is bad because of the woman's undertaking a career or asserting her independence, however, the film is telling a story about the resurgence of the need for a woman to make a choice. These films are subversive, because, no matter how they end, they are allowing married women to question the validity of their choice, not just of a man but of a direction in life.

The problems a man and woman encounter in marriage when the

woman works have provided the basis of film stories for decades. One of the most astonishing movies ever made on the subject was in place as early as 1932—a little film called *Weekend Marriage*. Based on a story by Faith Baldwin, it tells us how Loretta Young is forced to choose between her marriage and a career, with these choices personified by actors Norman Foster (marriage) and George Brent (career).

Weekend Marriage lays everything about marriage versus career out in the open for the audience. It shows how women trap men, how men left alone at night turn to other women, how men need mothering, and how everything falls apart when women work. At the same time, it shows that women are stronger than men, that they can earn more money than men, that they are smarter than men, that they can get richer men than the ones they already have if they just try. It's a classic example of contradiction and covert liberation, with the usual formulaic dismal ending in which the woman puts the apron back on and gives everything up for her man.

Weekend Marriage begins by establishing immediately what a man wants from a woman. "A man doesn't like his wife working in an office," Norman Foster tells Loretta Young. "He wants to work for her. He wants her waiting for him when he gets home." "Oh, Ken, you're hopelessly dated," replies Young. Young loves Foster and wants to marry him, but he accepts a career advancement in the form of a job in South America. Elated, he tells her he'll be gone for two years, but hopes she'll write. Young laments to her best friend, "Men *are* selfish. What do they care how they mess up our lives? But just let someone interfere with them! *Their* plans. *Their* careers!" ("You're telling me?" replies the friend.)

Young's sister-in-law is played by a sleekly elegant Aline MacMahon. Her character is used to establish what women might secretly want from life. MacMahon has a top job and earns good money. She and her husband have an apartment and a car, and MacMahon wears furs and jewelry. From Young's point of view, MacMahon has it all. In truth, MacMahon and her husband are seen arguing over the situation, and her husband is deeply unhappy with their marriage. He wants to have a baby, and he thinks they could manage even better than they are if MacMahon would quit working. MacMahon bursts out contemptuously: "Yes, I could spend all day taking care of the darned house for you, cooking your meals, washing your dishes and thinking how mahr-vel-ous it will be when you get home at night. Couldn't ever go anywhere because we couldn't afford it. You'd know just *where* I was and just *what* I was doing all the time. We'd see so much of one another we couldn't possibly like each other. It would be indecent. Like not wearing any clothes." Her husband tries one more time, asking her if she wouldn't like to have a baby. "And get a life sentence?" yells MacMahon. "Huh? Not for me. No thank you, Father Davis, not just now."

An Imperfect Marriage: Loretta Young bails Norman Foster out of jail in
Weekend Marriage.

This character of the sister-in-law is presented as being too self-
assured, too strong. It is implied that this woman is not only wrong but
destructive. Yet what she says makes sense, and some of the things she
says must voice the audience's own concerns and resentments. Although
MacMahon's behavior is presented as wrong in the long run, she is a forceful
figure in the movie, liberated, speaking out against men, and stating what
it is she really wants. She is a subversive character in that, yes, she is
proved to be wrong, but not before she raises significant questions.

MacMahon acts as a surrogate mother to Young, advising her on life,
love, and work. She doesn't see any reason why Young should let herself
suffer over her love for Foster or let him decide the future for both of them.
Besides, Foster really does love Young; he just doesn't want to get married
because he isn't earning enough money yet. If he could accept the idea of
Young's working, however, they would have no money problem and could
go ahead and marry without the lengthy separation. MacMahon advises
Young not to let Foster go away, but to use her feminine wiles to get him
to stay and marry her now.

This leads to an astonishing sequence illustrating the ruthlessness of
the woman's life as depicted by movies. With MacMahon as both coach

and cheerleader, Young carries out a plan of subterfuge with which to trap Foster and prevent him from going to South America. Naturally, the bait will be sex. MacMahon instructs Young in the details of how to act when Foster, the man she loves, calls on the telephone to say good-bye. MacMahon lays all the dialogue. She directs the scene, coaching Young in her lines, very much as a scene in a movie would be directed. (It is similar to the staged scene in *Four Wives* that was discussed in the chapter "The Woman Herself.") MacMahon can predict exactly what Foster will say and do based on what she has seen other men say and do. She tells Young how to trigger these responses, and they write the dialogue down on Young's steno pad so she won't forget.

At first, Young is reluctant to undertake this plan. Her "fine" character rejects such chicanery. "I like him too well to trick him into anything," she reminds herself. She does listen, though, when MacMahon begins to tell her what to say. "Darling, how do you think people *get* married?" asks MacMahon. "I don't know," replies Young. "I'll say you don't," MacMahon fires back. In the end, Young can't let Foster leave. She goes through with the lying scenario MacMahon has sketched out, in which she pretends she has another man, another proposal, and will not wait for Foster. He collapses within minutes, and in the very next scene they marry.

After their wedding, Young confidently talks Foster into letting her work, and they embark on a marriage in which the woman is not to be found in the home. Young promises it won't be forever, just "as long as I feel like working, or until I feel like I can afford not to." In the meantime, a telling scene takes place between MacMahon and her husband. He has protested that "I haven't got a clean shirt to my name. I have a hole in the toe of my right sock." MacMahon has a perfect solution: "Wear it on your left foot." When he presses on, "You could send it out, can't you?" she lets him have it: "I can't be bothered with laundry when I get home. I'm too tired. I've worked all day." Her husband begins to mutter to himself: "It's that crazy job of yours. What do we have for breakfast? Mush. What do we have for lunch? Beans. What do we have for dinner? Anything that lives in a can." This dreary exchange is a harbinger of things to come in the Young/Foster household.

Soon enough, Young and Foster are running into practical problems of the same kind. They both work busy jobs with long hours. They cannot coordinate their vacations, so each one has to sit around at home alone with nothing to do all day while the other is working. He leaves the house in a mess and doesn't pick up his laundry. She doesn't have time to cook or shop. They are out of coffee in the morning and eat unhealthy take-out food. He has holes in his socks (evidently a major problem), and they have to leave the bed unmade in the morning. Although they wake up warm and cuddly, there's no time for sex. Soon, her boss is observing that she is dragging around, looking tired, very tired. "It's not so easy," she ruefully tells him, "managing a home, a husband, and a job at the same time." Inevitably, Foster gets a salary cut from forty dollars to thirty dollars per week at the same time that Young gets a raise from thirty dollars to forty dollars. She's relieved and happy because it will all even out, but he's depressed and angry. "You'll be wearing the pants," he says. "Earning more than I am."

Underlining this central story is a depressing second story concerning Young's best friend, Connie, whose Italian family is attempting to choose a husband for her because they want her to marry and have babies. "Don't you be a fool, Connie," Young tells her. "You stick to your job." At Connie's request, Young goes home with her to try to reason with the male authority figure of the family, Connie's tough older brother, Joe. "Things have changed, Joe. There's no reason why Connie should marry someone just because you tell her to. She's not a child and she's not dependent. She can earn her own living just as well as anyone," says Young. Joe is enraged by these words, the clear enunciation of what happens when women go to work and earn their own money: they gain independence. He turns on Connie in a towering rage and yells, "You don't want kids and you don't want housework. You don't want anything that's good for you. You're just a rotten, lazy little fool. . . ." He shoves her hard, adding, "If I had my way, I'd have the whole rotten bunch of you in a sweat shop. I'd make you work so hard you'd be crying for a kitchen and a few babies to take care of just for a vacation."

When Young arrives home late after this unhappy encounter, the articulation of male rage at female independence, she finds that her husband has abandoned the dinner he cooked especially for her and has disappeared. Later, he turns up in jail, arrested for drunken and disorderly conduct. When Young comes to pay his fine, he is deeply ashamed. Young herself tries to be brave. "I've come to pay the fine . . . for my husband," she chokes out. "Which one is he?" asks the hard-bitten desk sergeant. "We've got a great assortment." This sordid little moment, in which the strong and reliable woman comes to bail her weak and childish husband out of jail, must have struck a chord somewhere in the hearts of women in the audience. And there's more humiliation to come. After Young has paid and bailed her man out, a female voice suddenly is heard to call, "Say . . . what about me?" And Young is confronted with the peroxide blond he spent the night with.

After this, things disintegrate fast for Young and Foster. He tells her, "I give up everything for a wife and a home and what do I get? A woman to live with and a lot of dirty dishes. You care more for your rotten job than you do for me." Young's boss steps in and frees her from her impossible marriage. He sends her to St. Louis on an important job, and there she meets the other man, George Brent. Six months later, her husband is out of her life, and she is dictating to her own secretary. Downstairs, handsome George Brent is waiting in an open convertible to take her to the country club where he has planned a surprise birthday party for her. As they drive along in his expensive car, he is muttering about "fall in the Dolomites and the winter in Rome." Although Young protests, "You don't understand. I like being independent," she is seen as on her way to a better life.

Here we have the familiar pattern in which a marriage is bad, and when the wife breaks free of it, she finds a better man. It is like *Mannequin* in that the woman marries a weak man but, when she ditches him, becomes wildly successful and happy within one frame. But it's unlike *Mannequin* because Young is a character who always wanted to work and have a career. Both have fantasy male figures of the asexual type. George Brent is the better man, one with a convertible, who has no problem with Young's working, although he is anxious to provide for her himself. (Money, position, and the Dolomites.) He is the man who is not a man but a figure who exists to provide everything, ask no questions, and demand nothing. As such, he is about to disappear from Young's life. Before they can even get tickets to the Dolomites, Young receives word that everything has collapsed back on the home front. Her brother has left MacMahon, and her own husband is on his deathbed, dying from plot complications. Young weeps, and Brent, true to his job of making everything possible for her, hires an airplane to fly her home and stands waving good-bye gamely as she takes off.

The film has taken its final twist, its final turn in the corridors of ambivalence. The viewer has received the same definitive kind of message that Young has received. With MacMahon now an abandoned wife, the movie has made its final statement about women who work and neglect their husbands: they will come to no good. With Young's husband dying, it has made almost its final statement on what a woman's true role is. What that is has to do with not working, with mothering and nurturing, and, as always, with lying and manipulating.

Back at the homestead, the peroxide blond is camped out with the husband. She is wearing an apron, always a significant fashion statement, and she looks very depressed when she opens the door and sees Loretta Young standing there. In this final scene, the movie goes all out to reaffirm traditional values. First, Young's mother tells her, "In my day, a man had his wife to look after him when he was sick." Second, an established authority figure in the form of the husband's doctor makes a lengthy speech that defines the film's final point of view: "Haven't you brought enough unhappiness to your husband without jeopardizing his life?" he asks. A startled Young, who has just arrived on the scene, asks "I?" The doctor lets her have it. "Let me give you a little advice. One way or another, a man will find a woman to look out for him not only when he's sick but when he's well. That's something you so-called modern girls never seem to count on. You talk about freedom because you think it's something that men have and cherish. But they don't. They hate it. They get along best when they're not free. It's human nature. That's all. They need old-fashioned women looking after their health, nagging them into caution, feeding them properly and giving them families to live for. A great many of these women are just as well fitted as you are for business. But they don't want it. They put their talents to work instead in what people today think is a narrow sphere. Well, I don't think it's narrow. I think it's the most important sphere of all. Not much recognition in it, perhaps, no spectacular publicity, but it's built up nations before now and it will build them up again."

During this speech, which he delivers with the supreme confidence of male authority, Young and the actress playing her mother are seen in close-up, mother behind daughter, their faces masks of grief and regret. "You hear that, Lola?" the mother asks Young. A greatly chastened Aline MacMahon, also standing by, suddenly adds, "Lola, give up anything. The man you love is worth all the jobs in the world. We found that out, didn't we?" Mom and MacMahon sail out the door, adding, "Well, we've done all we could."

While Young goes in to see her husband, who has successfully survived his plot crisis, the blond who has been tending him stands dejected at the window, wringing her hands and worrying. What about her? No one cares. She is society's reject, the woman who has not remained pure. While the blond worries, Loretta Young chooses *to lie* to her husband, in order to restore his self-confidence, telling him she has been fired from her top-level job. (Just how this plot twist differs from the one in which she trapped him into marriage is not made clear. We are to assume that *this* lie is okay, because it's good for him and it puts her down.) As Young completes this therapeutic manipulation, the blond storms in, tearing off the apron and gathering her things. She knows that, with the wife back in place, there's no more room for her. "Don't worry about me," she tells Young. "I'll get along. He's not the only boyo on the block." This ambivalent statement seems to confirm the doctor's words regarding how men can always find available women, but it also is a sad picture of the state of sisterhood in the lives of women. At film's end, Norman Foster, the little boy who needs his mummy in the form of Loretta Young, his nurturing wife, asks her coyly, "What are you going to do?" Picking up the blond's abandoned apron from the floor, she puts it on and tells him firmly, "Be a wife." She accepts both the role and the appropriate costume accessory.

Weekend Marriage was made in 1932, but the problem of a woman wanting things her husband's salary alone couldn't buy her was still around by the time of the 1953 movie *The Lady Wants Mink*. Stripped of its liberated arguments, and updated to television-sitcom format, the movie still presents the basic problem of marriage: What does a woman do when her husband can't earn enough money? This time, the dilemma is kept in the house itself, where—the 1950s are saying—a woman ought to stay. Although the heroine, Ruth Hussey, tries to build her business while remaining a house-wife, her enterprise still ends up wrecking her marriage.

The Lady Wants Mink is the story of a woman who wants a mink coat more than anything else in the world. Since her husband is only a billing clerk in a department store, she knows that she is going to have to find a way to buy it for herself. In this way, a perfect woman's film symbol, a piece of fashion in the form of an expensive mink coat, stands in for the basic problem a woman has in marriage. The scene is set for tragedy in a sad episode in which the husband has lovingly saved his money to buy his wife a beautiful camel-hair coat with fur trim for her birthday. When he proudly presents it, her disappointment and dissatisfaction is obvious to everyone, including him. Hussey's feelings about her desired mink are exacerbated by the fact that her next-door neighbor, played by Eve Arden, has just been given a lavish mink by her very successful husband.

Hussey decides to solve her own problem. She buys a pair of minks, brings them home, and sets about growing her own coat. This act of eco-nomic defiance, although set in the home, brings on a chain of events that are tangible evidence of what movies say will occur in a marriage when a woman asserts herself: Even when she stays at home she will end up not attending to her job as a woman. The first thing that happens is that Hussey has to go out at night, to a meeting at which she will learn how to keep the minks alive. This one event precipitates the following disasters: her tired husband (Dennis O'Keefe) has to cook supper and put the kids to bed, which is treated like the equivalent of World War III; she meets and is attracted to a wealthy older man, who is also at the meeting; a terrible quarrel erupts when she returns home and her husband shouts, "You've turned our lives upside down!" The husband and wife end up sleeping alone after her first and only night out. Here is the news for the viewer: buy two minks and you're practically in the divorce court; let a woman out at night, and she'll meet someone else; give a woman freedom, and you'll have to cook dinner, cope with the kids, and go without sex.

And after all this, there is worse news to come. Hussey's success at mink breeding begins to destroy her husband's masculinity. He loses his self-respect and thus his self-control. He pours water on his boss's head at the office, pulls a chair out from under him, and trips him. Not only does he lose his job but their landlady evicts them when she discovers they are raising minks on the premises. (The landlady is ironically wearing a mink coat when she tosses them out.) Hussey's yen for a coat has totally destroyed their lives.

The Lady Wants Mink is a strange little film, however. Whereas *Weekend Marriage* is fully liberated until its final minutes, *The Lady Wants Mink* is fully unliberated until the woman is let out of the typical 1950s world of tract housing and suburban living. Then she suddenly becomes an equal, taking charge of the family's life and freeing them all from the traditional 1950s life-style.

The Lady Wants Mink resolves itself in an unexpected way. Hussey does not give back the minks and apologize, whipping on her apron and getting out her mixing bowls. Although she does not become a business tycoon either, she sells her first-bred minks and uses the money to buy a run-down house in the country. She keeps her breeders and begins to organize a new life for the family. While the husband fails at being a used-car salesman and begins to dig ditches, she provides a world for the kids (without TV and with plenty of fresh air) and makes the old house into a home with that ease we are all so familiar with in old movies. Instead of dressing like a sitcom joke of a mom, in high heels and pearls, she wears jeans all the time. She becomes productive and happy, instead of dissatisfied as she was before. Her husband drags his feet about this restructuring of their lives, but although he is finally offered his old job back at an increased salary, he realizes that this life, free of materialism and free of the treadmill, and free of the need to keep up with the Joneses, is a better one. "All right, pioneer woman," he tells her, "you win." They settle down happily on a mink farm, their family life intact, out in the fresh air. "Being here with Jim and the boys and just knowing they're happy is my mink coat," Hussey beams.

This film suggests that the world of the 1950s, with its martinis, TV watching, easy credit, and tract housing, is a bum deal. The only way to survive is to get out of it, get away to the country, and—perhaps, just perhaps—let the woman make decisions and become an equal partner. *The Lady Wants Mink* is a status quo marriage film with a kicker and a slightly subversive subtext.

A good way to put career conflicts in marriages in perspective is simply to give the woman the man's job out in the world and put the man at home, idle, with nothing to do but become jealous. In *You Belong to Me* (1941), Barbara Stanwyck plays a doctor and Henry Fonda the rich young man she marries. Stanwyck is out on the job, making house calls to her many male patients, and naturally Fonda becomes resentful. She explains to him that his idleness is ruining their relationship and tells him how important her work is to her. Why should she stop doing good in the world just because he's lazy? He then gets a job in a department store and turns out to be terrific at it. ("All I've needed is work!") However, he gets fired when the store finds out he's rich and taking away a job from someone who *really* needs it. "The work gave me a reason for being on earth. Our jobs are our lives," he tells his gardener just before he decides to disappear.

Stanwyck has been allowed to voice what is usually thought of as important to men, not what is the norm for women. In doing so, she becomes a female voicing ideas that women can recognize not only as feminine thoughts, but also as possible ideas for themselves to consider. This importance of work to a woman, vocalized by a woman's film star, soon enough disappears from the movie's plot. Stanwyck's character changes, beginning to illustrate the usual about-face that denies the way she was originally defined. She closes her office and quits her practice when Fonda first gets a job. She goes all unprofessional and starts worrying about what has happened to him. Love does what it usually does to a woman's career— wrecks it. Money saves the day, however, when Fonda cleverly buys a hospital that is nearly bankrupt and makes her the chief of staff. He is not only giving jobs to people who need them, but he is the bestower upon his wife of the right to work and is the creator of her own job. The film ends with Stanwyck's medical career restored, but now it is seen differently. It is okay for her to work because it isn't compromising him. Man is the power. If he says you can work, you can work. If your husband owns the hospital, it's okay to be his chief of staff. It's kinda like housework then: you're taking care of his place for him.

Films in which married women want careers are about the need for money as well as independence. When a woman wants money and the things it can buy her, what does she do if her man is neither rich nor able to get rich, yet her proper place is in the home? She can stay there and bake pies, like Mildred Pierce, or take in washing or boarders, but having enough money is always a problem for a housewife. The perfectly named movie *Housewife* (1934) is a classic embodiment of the audience's true-life situation in this regard, but it also affords them a fantasy about wealth and power and using their own brains and talent to get money without violating society's rules. The movie follows the usual pattern of having its first half grounded in the familiar (average couple making $175 per month and trying to make ends meet) and its second half moving into a dream (supersuccessful couple with more than $50,000 per year ending up in the divorce court). It is truly a woman's film, because it is the housewife of the title who is the smartest, most capable, and most lovable person in the film, and because it has a light/dark/light motif.

In the beginning, the married couple, Ann Dvorak and George Brent, lives in a little cottage with a picket fence and a welcome mat outside the door. The first image of Dvorak is that of her hands breaking an egg into a bowl, with the camera moving back to reveal her busily beating the egg, supervising an incompetent maid, and dominating the kitchen. She's clearly in control of everything in her domain: her husband, her maid, her child, the dog, the salesman who comes to the door, and the ringing telephone. She is presented as efficient, smart, and capable, with a husband who is thoroughly, overtly dependent on her. "I don't need a shave this morning, do I?" he asks, waiting for her to test his whiskers and tell him. She is not presented as domineering or unloving, however, just as a person who is on the ball, as opposed to her insecure and confused husband. The perfect housewife, she is clearly contrasted with her brother's wife, who lives next door, representing the do-nothing slob wife. While Dvorak is planning Sunday dinner ("a leg of lamb will be nice"), her sister-in-law says, "The delicatessen will cook my Sunday dinner. George will eat ham and potato salad and like it. You fuss too much." This woman, played by Ruth Donnelly, has plenty of observations about Dvorak's devotion: "Lincoln might have freed the slaves, but he didn't do much for the housewife." She also warns, "The worse you treat a husband, the better they like it," to which Dvorak replies, "You have your system and I have mine." In case the audience does not fully understand what the topic of this film is going to be, a voter registration representative comes to the door and asks Dvorak her occupation. Her reply, "Oh, just a housewife," is meant to be roughly equivalent to "Oh, just the president of the universe." Dvorak is ready for anything and can handle everything. Her husband, on the other hand, is afraid of his boss and even afraid to reprimand employees who work under him in the office. He hasn't had a raise in five years, and all their original plans when they were first married ("our trip to Europe . . . our big ideas for the future") have more or less been abandoned.

Things change with the injection into the plot of Bette Davis playing Patricia Barkeley, a twenty-five-thousand-dollar-per-year copywriter from New York City, brought out to Chicago to work in the same office as Brent. Patricia Barkeley turns out really to be Ruth Smith, formerly of Chicago, who went to high school with both Brent and Dvorak. She's a big success now because "I suddenly found out I had some brains and decided to use them." She has never married because she has been in love with football-playing Brent from her high school days. He was then the kind of man she expected later to be "running guns in South America or hunting emeralds in Siam . . . one of those men born to live a glamorous life." It's eight years later, and he's now a meek office manager in a big advertising firm, and Patricia Barkeley is the opposite of Housewife. She is Career Woman, which in a movie titled *Housewife* also means Other Woman.

While Brent has grown weak and out of shape, the two women in his life have both prospered and strengthened. Dvorak clearly has what she wants, although she wishes Brent had more self-confidence and would take risks to get ahead. Davis clearly has what she wants, although she clearly would like Brent to take a few risks with her. But this is the classic example of the woman's film format: two strong women represent opposite life choices, and they will between them determine the outcome of events, especially the man's destiny. Finally, Dvorak talks Brent into going into business on his own. His risk taking is motivated by two events that she herself sets in motion: first, she gets him to make a suggestion to his boss regarding an ad idea that she has, and the resulting brush-off makes him mad enough to quit, and second, she comes up with the $1,749.39 that she has secretly saved out of the household budget to finance his own business.

When Brent starts his own ad agency, its only account is obtained due to Dvorak's ingenuity in pretending to be a rival advertiser on the telephone, so Brent can trick the client into signing. The second big account they receive, the one that turns them into rich people, is due to her getting Brent so drunk he'll be brave enough to chase down a cosmetics tycoon (played by John Halliday) and present the idea she had that got him the original brush-off from his boss.

After Dvorak has herself orchestrated his success, and they are rich and living in a big house, Brent suddenly becomes confident. Money changes him, and thus it changes their marriage. The movie becomes an ironic story in which a wife loses control of her husband when *he* actually goes out to work! While he is weak, and thus childlike, she can tell him what to do. This is seen as an ideal state for women to be in, because the "baby" husband is controlled by the "mother" wife. Bette Davis comes to work for Brent, and they are constantly together, ultimately falling into an affair. ("The minute they get a bankroll," says Donnelly to Dvorak, "they're all alike.") A crisis comes when Brent is fooling around with Davis and forgets to check out the radio show that will advertise their biggest account, Duprez Cosmetics. When the show goes on the air with cornball humor, the last straw is the advertising song:

> *If your skin has got the hue,*
> *Of a plate of Oyster Stew,*
> *Darling, use cosmetics by Duprez.*
> *And if the rings around your eyes,*
> *Are as big as apple pies,*
> *Sweetheart, use cosmetics by Duprez.*

Mr. Duprez is ready to fire Brent over this, but Ann Dvorak, the all-American housewife, saves the day by rushing Duprez home and cooking some crepes suzette for him with her own little hands! ("That must be the first radio contract ever saved by crepes suzettes," muses Brent later.)

Davis and Dvorak square off, having yet another of those conversations in which the women decide everything. Davis forces Brent to ask for a divorce, but Dvorak refuses him, holding on until their little son is conveniently run over in the driveway when Brent backs up at about one hundred miles per hour. (Movie people never look in their rearview mirrors.) In the end, when a woman rings the doorbell of their ritzy home, a reunited Dvorak and Brent grin wildly while little Buddy, the son, healthy again and wearing his military school uniform, tells her wisely, "We don't want anything. We've got everything." Ah, but this woman isn't selling things. She's the voter registration person for *this* district, so what, pray tell, is Dvorak's occupation? "Oh, just a housewife."

George Brent has the last word: "And what a housewife!" he booms out. What a housewife, indeed. A housewife with brains, power, control, and wealth. She's got the house, and she's got the man, and she's carried the average woman with her out of her little picket-fence world into a fantasy that provides every reassurance in the book. Being a housewife is important because she is the real brains of the marriage: if the husband will just listen to her, they can get rich. On the other hand, in case the real-life husband doesn't listen, well, it would just have been trouble with other men, other women, divorce, and run-over kids anyway.

Movies like *Housewife* linked the world of the real housewife in the audience to her favorite reason for coming to the theater, escape, and to the problem that was most on her mind, money. It is a movie in which the woman has a surrogate career through controlling her husband's. Considering a film that is the total opposite of *Housewife*, the 1933 *Our Betters*, one sees how marriage and money remain the basic subjects, even though the movie purports to be a sophisticated comedy about the upper class. During the Depression, stories about men and women with tons of money and shoes to match every outfit were like stories about aliens. A fictional upper class of film was created. Remote from anything real, these people were arch, sophisticated, and useful to Hollywood in depicting purely American concerns. The upper class lived in a world where people had real wealth, and thus they might as well have been living on Pluto as far as the audience was concerned. That meant that all kinds of social questions could be raised in safety in the plots. *Our Betters*, directed by George Cukor and starring the doyenne of draped black, Constance Bennett, is a classic example of an elegant upper-class comedy based on a popular stage play that is actually a way of talking to ordinary moviegoers about things that might be on their minds: money and marriage and adultery.

Our Betters features Hattie Carnegie clothes, especially designed for the film, and has for its technical adviser the famous social humbug Elsa Maxwell, a self-styled recorder of the lives of the rich and famous of her day. Despite the sort of world *Our Betters* depicts, it—just like *Housewife*—is really only about money and how a woman gets it; marriage and what a woman gets out of it; and sex, and how a woman gets it and what she gets out of it. In other words, it's still just a woman's film, even though it carries a theatrical pedigree and a better wardrobe and more expensive furniture.

In *Our Betters*, Constance Bennett plays a rich American woman who marries a titled Britisher, promising, "I'm going to make you a good wife. I feel humble, with all those great ladies in your family." His reply is not particularly reassuring, as he brightly points out, "Well, you're the best looking in the whole crew." Shortly after their wedding, Bennett learns that her groom deeply loves someone else; he only married her for her money, fulfilling his family responsibility. Bennett is crushed when she learns the truth, because the marriage on her part had been sincere: she had truly loved him and was proud to be marrying above herself socially. She lets her disillusionment drive her to a form of rebellion, becoming a "daring wife" who does what she pleases behind the protective covering of a respectable marriage. She also becomes a social dictator who is constantly in the newspapers. Full of natural American wit, character, unscrupulousness, and old fashioned *push*, she forces herself into the highest levels of British society.

Bennett's madcap disregard for her reputation, her repudiation of the notion of love due to her betrayal, are presented in a most sophisticated devil-may-care manner. Yet an audience is asked to see the truth, which is that, underneath, she's a swell gal, laughing in the teeth of her pain; a viewer understands that, after a while, she will straighten out. In the meantime, everyone gets to have it both ways. In general, movies suggest to us that when a woman marries the wrong man, she has to figure things out for herself and cope. Maybe there's a mom or a sister or a good friend or a wiser older woman to commiserate with her about things, but the implication is that it's her own darn fault for making such a bad choice. When a man makes such a mistake, there is usually a kinder, more helpful and loving woman to help him figure it out. He deserves that, it seems, because, after all, marriage isn't his primary business the way it is a woman's. *Our Betters* is well disguised with its glamour and sophistication, but it still questions the choice made regarding marriage. It does not reaffirm much of anything, other than the idea that love is all that matters. Its class setting reveals another important thing about the marriage film, which is how it also uses class to depict the difference between the male world and the female world.

Stories about class in American movies almost always turn out to be about something else, since there really is no class system other than the categories of rich and poor and the swinging doors that lie between them. What passes for a movie about class differences between a man and a woman who decide to marry often turns out to be a story about the differences perceived by people in terms of the male world and the female world. Two films that illustrate this are *Lucky Night* and *The Homestretch*. Ostensibly romances between people with different backgrounds and thus different attitudes, they really are stories about how a woman wants to settle down, control things, make a nest, and have children, and how a man wants to be free and easy and loose and travel here and travel there, taking no real responsibility. This conflict is made concrete as marital stress. These movies are important because within their charming stories and elegant settings they hide the issue that women constantly struggle with in an unliberated world: if they give up their freedom and their chance to earn a good living for themselves in exchange for a home, for a marriage, and for love, what will they do if the man turns out not to be reliable? This is especially painful if children have been born, and the woman has the responsibility for them. These are films in which a woman is not seeking her independence in a career, but is seeking a good marriage with a steady man. Over and over again, marriage movies address this issue, although frequently keeping it somewhat subordinate to another plot question.

In *Lucky Night* (1939), Myrna Loy and Robert Taylor have a marriage conflict over his settling down to a steady job or not, and in *Homestretch*, Maureen O'Hara and Cornel Wilde have a conflict over a racehorse. What the films really depict is the tension between a free (and supposedly masculine) life-style and a tied-down (and thus feminine) one. Both movies show what happens to a woman who marries outside her own world. In both cases, the two women marry "beneath" them socially and economically. They do it for love, but, really, for freedom and for sex. These films show women leaving security and home to stray afield with men who are exciting—who are antithetical to the worlds they've been raised and repressed in.

In *Lucky Night*, Loy is the daughter of one of those sympathetic tycoons whose only wish for their daughters is that they find "a real man." These characters turn up frequently in 1930s movies, especially those made by MGM. (Some have pointed out that this reflects Louis B. Mayer's basic sympathy for such men, since he himself was a tycoon with deep regard for his two daughters and a desire to see them married to strong, successful

men like himself.) What is more interesting from a woman's viewpoint is
that these daughters seldom have mothers to advise them. There is a startling
absence of mothers in many films about females. The films often portray
the significant relationships in a woman's life as, first, her father and then
her husband. A mother doesn't have much of a role to fulfill in one of these
plots unless she is motherly and thus gives wise advice and helps the
daughter with her choices. If she is not motherly, she is an interfering
villainess, either ignoring her child and creating emotional problems for
her or else pushing her toward marrying the wrong man for the wrong
reasons—that is to say, her own private agenda. When a mother character
is in the plot, the power of the maternal is invoked, and an explanation
has to be constructed as to just exactly *why* she is not mothering properly.
It's best just to remove her.

   Lucky Night opens up on a telling image. Myrna Loy, ethereally
gowned in flowing, soft chiffon, is in the arms of a tall, tuxedoed gentleman.
They are standing in a foliage-bedecked atrium with a view of an obviously
spacious mansion behind them in long shot. They are locked in embrace,
lips pasted together, arms entwined. This first sight of Loy is the sum total
of all that Hollywood could ask for any woman, or that any woman in the
audience could ask for herself: wealth, beauty, love, romance, and clothes.
The immediate action is that Loy breaks the embrace, turns from the man,
and walks toward the camera, frame left, her face indicating some vague
dissatisfaction. What unrecorded gongs rang in the hearts of women when
they saw this? Although the rest of the film, a slight effort at best, will be
little more than a story about a woman searching for romance, finding it,
measuring it as wanting, but then pretending she wants it anyway, this
image lingers. What it shows speaks volumes. It says, "Wait a minute,
wait a minute. All this is not enough." In one image is placed all that the
woman's film is supposed to endorse, but the leading lady is shown breaking
away from it, rejecting it, vaguely unfulfilled and dissatisfied by it.

   "What do you want?" her father asks Loy, falling back on that favorite
male question when he learns she has spurned this first perfect suitor.

   "I don't know," she replies. "There's no excitement. They [the men
she knows] don't stand on the bridge of a ship adventuring somewhere.
They don't take my breath away. I can even out-drink 'em. They don't
make me feel like a woman."

   "It's a longing for something that doesn't exist," says Dad.

   On Dad's advice, Loy decides to get a job and live her own life outside
her secure world. Out in the real world she meets a poor and carefree young
man (Robert Taylor) at an unemployment agency. When they share a park
bench later, they become friends and take off on a wild night of drinking.
They have no money, but working together they con a fifty-cent piece out

of a friendly policeman. This leads to a series of adventures that culminate in their capture of a robber for serious reward money. They end up (fully clothed) in twin beds in a fancy hotel room. When they awaken, they have no idea what happened, but the morning papers tell them "Magnate's Daughter Weds Bum." Loy is immediately appalled: "Getting married like some cheap drunk. I don't think I've ever been so ashamed of myself before." When Taylor tries to take the responsibility, she says, "No. I'm a she. That's my business."

Loy and Taylor decide to make a go of it, because they feel they really love each other. They are in a marriage that seems to be about class differences (magnate's daughter and bum), but it really is a marriage about attitude differences. They start out with ten dollars between them. He wants to blow it on a honeymoon, and she wants to bank it and go on a budget. Their differences are depicted in a scene in which they walk down the street together. He stops to spend thirty cents on a rose for her, spouting poetry as he presents it. "Nine dollars and seventy cents," she announces, quickly adjusting their budget.

As the film progresses, it becomes clear that what Taylor wants out of marriage is one long "lucky night," like their first one together. He pretends she has a second persona, "Miss Excitement," the woman he married—full of fun, devil-may-care, and sexy. What she wants, however, is "three little rooms to be kept in . . . a little nest . . . to be safe, safe." This is the presentation of a marital situation in which sex and excitement trapped the man, but now he is bored, unwilling to shoulder his burdens and responsibilities. The woman was happy to be free and easy in the entrapment stage, but now there is life to be lived, curtains to be hung, washing to be ironed. They break up.

How does *Lucky Night* resolve this situation? Drunk, Taylor comes to her father and tells him, "A man can't love a woman more than she loves him." "Why can't he?" asks the father, whose function in the plot is mainly to stand by and ask key questions. "Then he doesn't run the ship," says Taylor. "Gotta be up on the bridge or he won't like himself very much and neither will she. It's the only time he's worth the knowing, it's the only time she can love him. It's the only decent thing he can give her." Hearing the bridge metaphor his daughter has voiced earlier. Daddy knows this must be true love. He keeps Taylor drunk and puts him to bed in Loy's own bed. When she comes home, she finds her husband just where she wants him, and the film ends on their embrace. *Lucky Night* is an odd, contradictory, and unsavory little film. It completely undermines itself, and its happy ending leaves a sour taste. The class and attitude differences, so carefully depicted, are left unchanged, unresolved, and hovering darkly over the final embrace. Its story really speaks to women of the problems they face in life, although its surface is all seedy charm and humor. It attempts to make light of the differences men and women often face *after* the honeymoon.

The Homestretch (1947) tells a similar story, but with a more cohesive, and thus specific, moral presentation. It also represents such a curious generic mix that one might ask: Is this truly a woman's film? Cornel Wilde, a man associated with swashbuckling roles (*The Bandit of Sherwood Forest*, 1946; *Sword of Lancelot*, 1963) as well as with women's films (*The Walls of Jericho; Leave Her to Heaven*), plays the hero, and the movie is really about horse racing, in that it has several long sequences in which close races are played out. Wilde was a pinup boy of the midforties who also had serious acting aspirations. He was nominated for the Oscar as Best Actor for his performance as Chopin in *A Song to Remember* (1945) and was much more than just another weak male actor assigned to fill out the frame in the woman's film. He was at this point in his career a big star, a curious mixture of actor and swashbuckler, but either way, definitely a sex object, due to his good looks and excellent physique. Wilde was on the cover of more movie magazines from 1945 to 1947 than either Tyrone Power or Van Johnson, and inside the fan magazine he was frequently pictured in swimsuits and tights in color photos. *Homestretch* capitalizes on this. When Maureen O'Hara walks in from her dressing room and sees Wilde in his tuxedo, the camera watches while she openly ogles him, registering her approval on her face. "Why, Jock," she says, "you're beautiful." "*You're* beautiful," he replies, "I'm merely very handsome." *Homestretch* understood the female desire to see a beautiful man in beautiful clothes, and like romantic novels and Gothic romances, it provided a romantic man for women to moon over.

By having an acceptably strong male hero, and throwing in the horse racing, *Homestretch* presumably drew both men and women into the audience. It opens up on the man's story, not the woman's, and, in fact, does not introduce the leading female character until several minutes into the film, having already thoroughly established who and what Wilde is. However, once O'Hara enters the picture it becomes her film, and in the end it comes out exactly on her side of the marital argument.

The story is a simple tale of two opposites falling in love and marrying. Wilde is a ne'er-do-well sportsman, who gads around the world, racing horses. His mom went down on the *Lusitania* ("His mother always saw he got what he wanted"), and his dad died in 1927. He's let their old Maryland horse farm fall to ruin, and he hangs about with a drinking, gambling set of international gadflies, among them the traditional other woman played by Helen Walker. O'Hara is from a genteel Boston family. She lives with a maiden aunt and is engaged to William Van Dyke III, a career diplomat with a great future. When she inherits a racehorse that Wilde wants to buy, they are thrown together and fall swiftly in love.

She fights it. "Come away with me, monkey, to the Argentine," Wilde actually says to her, but she replies, after a hot kiss, "This isn't me. It can't be me." "But it is," he insists. "For the first time, it's you, off the string and free." Thus is once again established the idea of a man as a liberating force, a chance for a woman to be herself and out from under parental or societal restriction. When they marry, he takes her to Buenos Aires and buys her a huge bouquet of red roses. Just like Myrna Loy in *Lucky Night*, O'Hara instantly worries about how much it costs and how they are going to pay for it. Immediately after the wedding, she shifts from her love of his poetic freedom to her own sense of the practical. Finally, after putting up with his partying friends, his overspending, and his borrowing money from her rival, O'Hara tells him, "I can't live this kind of life, and you can't go on like this forever. There comes a time when people have to grow up." He promises to take her to Maryland and open the old farm after the next big race, if he wins. She takes him at his word, but when she realizes he really didn't mean it and finds him cozying up to her rival even though they are expecting a baby, she jumps into their convertible and crashes into a tree. (The crash into the tree that erases pregnancies or causes marital epiphanies is a familiar plot maneuver of the woman's film.) When he comes to see her in the hospital, she says words that can only be aimed at the women in the audience. She tells him she's leaving him, and when he tries to kiss her, she says, "That's right. Try to get me that way." Then she gives her big speech: "I've found out that love isn't enough. There's got to be a meeting ground for two people to make a go of marriage, and we're as far apart as the poles. We don't even want the same things. I know in your heart you're really relieved there isn't going to be a baby. That would tie you down." Faithful old William Van Dyke III comes to get her, and she says she will divorce Wilde. Their marriage has failed due to class and attitude differences, but it has really failed in order to speak some truth to the women in the audience about the differences between what men and women want from marriage.

At the end of *Homestretch*, O'Hara gains control of Wilde's winning racehorse, running him under her own colors. She is enormously successful, as a montage shows her horse winning at Hialeah, Belmont, Saratoga, Hollywood Park, each track represented by its own logo and O'Hara represented by a series of astonishing hats, a different one for each race. Finally, at the Kentucky Derby, she will be racing her horse against one rehabilitated by her husband, who has restored the old family farm and is thus in hock to his eyebrows. If he loses the race, he will lose everything he has, including the farm. In the big race, O'Hara finds herself rooting for Wilde's horse instead of her own, but in the end, she wins. Thinking he is ruined, Wilde drives the station wagon up to the posh Maryland homestead for one last visit before foreclosure, but O'Hara is waiting, her horse already in a stall adjoining the one his will occupy. Wilde and O'Hara, the mismatched couple, reunite with kisses on the lawn, happy hunting dogs snapping at their heels.

But what has actually happened? The woman has won, establishing the need for marriage to be defined in her terms. She also proved herself to be his equal, or better, in the racing business. She did not withdraw her horse or throw the race for him. ("I'm not a monkey on a string any longer. I've made up my own mind.") She didn't apologize for winning, and they are back together because he has given up his way of life for hers. All through the film she has said they should go back to Maryland, settle down, and see no more of his gadfly friends. He has laughed it off, but here he is. In Maryland. Settled down. No more of his gadfly friends. This is a film in which the woman slowly takes control and wins, to the obvious viewing satisfaction of the women in the audience. It supports the idea of a woman's role in life as wife and mother, but indicates that this position has the potential of master, not slave.

The contrast between the man's world and the woman's is spoken out loud on the screen more than once in *Oil for the Lamps of China* (1935). Ostensibly a story of how a man goes to the Orient to make his fortune by working for a huge electric company, it is actually a story about the conflicts between a man's work and his marriage. Based on a best-seller by a woman (Alice Tisdale Hobart), it loses focus as a woman's film because its female star, Josephine Hutchinson, seems less important in historical retrospect than its male star, Pat O'Brien. More screen time is devoted to his presence, his dilemma, and his progress than to hers. The film opens up on him, clearly defining itself as *his* story, and she does not appear until nearly twenty minutes of running time has passed. Furthermore, later in the story there is a long action sequence in which O'Brien saves the company funds by escaping the oncoming Chinese Communists and taking a bullet in his arm for his efforts. Her big moment, equal in story terms, is a scene involving childbirth in a remote cabin, but she has to emote offscreen and settle for a sulky aftermath.

As a young man, Pat O'Brien goes to work for a company whose motto on its building is "Light to see the future, power to obtain it" and whose promise to its optimistic, youthful recruits is "The company always takes care of its own."

After three years in the remote Orient, O'Brien travels to Yokohama to collect the bride who has journeyed out to marry him after the long wait. His boss is skeptical, telling him, "I've been in the Orient for years. Being out here doesn't mean pioneering to a woman. It means banishment. The company frowns on marriage. Nine out of ten wives turn their husbands against their work because of a woman's inability to stand up under China. I hope you've got the tenth."

This boss, who later commits suicide when the company demotes him after years of loyal service, is prophetic. O'Brien's bride has turned back on her journey, leaving him a telegram saying she just can't face it. Despondent, O'Brien meets a prim and attractive young woman (Hutchinson) in the hotel lobby, and her fate is equally dreary. She has accompanied her father, a professor of Oriental history, on his first and only journey to the land he has studied all his life, only to have him drop dead on the way over. She is awaiting her own fate, which is to return to America to give violin lessons for a living.

The two make a without-love marriage, a bargain in which she will contribute a home and he will protect it. "I don't need love," she tells him. "I've never had it. I can be useful." She seems grim-faced but willing, and she actually perks up in the tradition of movie females when she sees his unkempt digs full of dust and company furniture. "It'll be fun fixing it up," she cries.

O'Brien and Hutchinson come together physically as husband and wife after the tragedy of the boss's suicide, one month after her arrival. They are then depicted as gloriously happy, grateful for each other's company, support, and warmth. Soon a child is on the way, and the woman's film crisis emerges in the form of a conflict between the man's work and his wife, his male world and her female world. At first, it appears that the conflict can be resolved. When the company ruthlessly sends him to a remote northern outpost, which means she'll be left behind to bear her child alone, she insists on going along even though she knows there will be no hospital and that her life will be even more difficult out there. Once again, she has to fix up a horrid-looking shanty, and once again she transforms it into a comfy paradise. But when the baby arrives, O'Brien has to make the choice between staying with her during the difficult birth or going out to control an oil fire that threatens the company's assets.

When he chooses the company, leaving her to face the death of their child without him, she cannot forgive him. The conflict between the woman's needs and the man's erupts with full force. For him it was the job, and for her it was the child. Although she has been a "perfect" wife throughout the movie, exhibiting good sportsmanship to the extreme, she now begins to just sit, almost catatonic. She hates the company, expressing female rage for all women everywhere who have been neglected because of their husband's work.

After a while, in the kind of inexplicable and unmotivated turn that characterizes these crackpot films, she suddenly greets him warmly when he returns home after a visit to meet the new company head. She has decided to accept her life completely. "My ambition, my emotion, mustn't be mine, but yours. I'm part of you, but you aren't part of me. To a woman that's marriage and a sacrifice, but I made it, Steven, and I'm happy." He replies, looking dumb as only Pat O'Brien can look dumb, "I guess I don't understand." She replies, with triumphant female logic, "No man could."

Actually, it's rather difficult for a woman, too. Where O'Brien has articulated the concept that his work is his identity, Hutchinson has articulated the concept that a woman's work is her marriage. Just as the company is an uncaring, unfeeling, exploitative boss to him, she is prepared for him to be the same to her. Since he's a nice guy, that doesn't quite happen, but it comes close.

Oil for the Lamps of China takes yet another strange turn when, after saying outright in the dialogue that this woman must assume a secondary state in order to be happy and for her marriage to work, she later refutes this by her behavior. Two things happen. She and O'Brien become friends with a young couple whose child falls ill with cholera, and Hutchinson is the only one with the courage and imagination to save him. (The way she does it is unintentionally hilarious. She mixes up a cholera cure, for all the world as if she were making a cake out of a recipe book, standing by the child's bedside and stirring it in a mixing bowl.) The second thing she does is take control of her husband's career. Without his knowledge, she marches herself into the company head's office and threatens him by telling him that she and her husband hold the patents on a lamp the company uses, a lamp actually invented by O'Brien in his first years in China. In this scene, she's a tough realist, calmly negotiating for her husband's job with a courage he has never shown. She admits that her husband, having served the company loyally for years, probably would not sue them, but "I'm a woman and practical." She *would* sue.

The final scene wholly bears out the woman's film world. Her husband bursts joyously into their rooms, crying out that he has unexpectedly been given a wonderful new assignment, although he had been previously told he was to be fired. All it took was for them to wait and have faith, he reminds her smugly. With impeccable woman's film deception, she smiles slyly over his shoulder at the audience, embodying a classic "yes, dear" pose.

Oil for the Lamps of China presents the viewer with a portrait of a woman who is a long-suffering wife, a perfect helpmate. However, she is also an angry manipulator and a liar. She has obviously been her father's slave, and then she becomes her husband's, but her ability to outthink her husband makes one reevaluate her relationship with her father. She ruthlessly usurps the love of another woman's child, shoving her aside to rescue him from cholera, crying out that she has "lost one child and cannot lose another." The conflicts between the man's world and hers are finally erased by her own ruthless manipulations, all of which are presented as not only acceptable but necessary and admirable.

IN ADDITION to presenting viewers with depictions of marital problems they no doubt understood all too well, films about marriages also addressed questions such as Why does a woman marry? and Why does she pick the man she picks? The first issue, why a woman marries, discussed earlier, is answered in a peculiar subcategory of the marriage film, that of the without-love marriage. These strange films seemed to answer some desire for women to be able to have the safety and security of marriage without the pressures of sex. It is possible, these films say initially, that a woman can make an excellent marriage for completely practical reasons. Possible, of course, but not likely. Possible for the short run, perhaps, but not for the long. These weird movies have a kind of perverted presentation of people who have polite society's permission to go to bed with each other, but who can't, won't, or don't. This became a hidden way to look at something that was presumably on the audience's mind or at least within its realm of understanding. That was the question of why a woman would marry in the first place. These movies were probably not created to address a crying need for information on a serious social situation; they were more likely thought up as a clever variation on the boy-meets-girl plot, and they also were a convenient way to introduce some real sexual titillation into the scenarios without threat of censorship. Since they could, would they? A safe way of removing the stop sign from the bedroom was found, while maintaining a romantic courtship falling-in-love story.

Without-love marriages appear in quite a few films, and for various reasons. In the appropriately named *Without Love* (1945), Spencer Tracy and Katharine Hepburn marry because it's hard for him to find accommodations in crowded Washington during World War II, and she has an entire house going to waste. She's also a widow, with time on her hands, and he needs an intelligent assistant to help him with his important scientific experiments. They pool their resources. Her house, his experiments. Her brains, his job. A woman in a movie who marries a man she does not love and does not have sex with is sort of taking him over instead. There's a unisex quality to these films, in which the man and woman fuse into one person, or the woman gets to absorb the man's life while still remaining female.

Without-love, of course, never lasts. In the Tracy/Hepburn film, she starts out as a crisp, sensible woman with a man's name, Jamie. ("I guess they knew I was all they were going to get, so that's why they named me Jamie.") Tracy starts out as a man with a job to do, who won't let any nonsense stop him. Soon Hepburn, with tears in her eyes and hamming it up shamelessly, is explaining to Tracy how she married very young and how her marriage was an idyll of romantic, perfect young love until her husband was thrown by a horse. "It's a bad trick on us, Jamie," he managed to tell her just before he croaked in true woman's-film tradition, "but this isn't the end of it." Hepburn has made those words come true by keeping it alive way past its natural time. For his part, Tracy was once in love with a shallow woman he met in Paris. He describes his passion as "a supremely joyless event with a witch on a broomstick." Since Tracy had the worst of it, and Hepburn had the best of it, neither wants to try again. They are happy with their relationship, which is, by agreement, sexless, based on shared work, good humor, and deep companionship. In every way but one, theirs is a perfect marriage, with no jealousies and no miseries. When all this changes and they suddenly begin to behave like jealous idiots, the film becomes very depressing. This fresh and friendly relationship between two strong individuals changes into a silly mess that demeans them both. It looks as if to become truly married, two people not only have to have sex but also have to make each other miserable.

No initial mutual respect ever appears in another without-love movie, *The Lady Is Willing* (1942). In it, Marlene Dietrich, a single woman who is a famous actress, wants to adopt a baby she has found, and Fred MacMurray, a baby doctor, needs money to finance his rabbit research. She can't adopt if she remains unmarried, so she proposes to him that he marry her for her money. Her adoption will be facilitated, and in return she will gladly finance his rabbits. He is skeptical about how it will work, but she grandly sweeps away his doubts. "I was married in my last play, and I know just how to do it."

This plot boils marriage down to its essence: mutual support. The normal reasons that films tout marriage—for love and sex—are initially excluded, but the plot then busily sets about adding these necessary ingredients into the marriage to make it *right*. In *The Lady Is Willing*, MacMurray plays Chopin on his piano and tends his bunnies while Dietrich wears padded shoulders and tends her baby. Her baby and his rabbits are a perfect parallel.

FILMS ALSO EXPLAIN what kind of men women choose as marriage partners and why. Women, shrewd and schooled in such matters, do not always want the best-looking or even the richest men. What they often want instead is someone they can manage. In other words, a schnook. In *He Couldn't Say No* (1938), Jane Wyman, capably advised by her conniving mother, is openly conning the innocent Frank McHugh into marriage for economic security. McHugh is definitely not the best looking, or even the smartest, but he *is* the most manageable. "Sometimes a woman has to make sacrifices. Take what she can get," advises Mom. Mother also states the primary benefit: "At least, you'll be the boss." Mother, of course, is planning on living with the couple after they marry, and that will include her picking out their furniture and making most of their decisions. All the important ones anyway. The economic security that Jane Wyman is advised to marry into includes security for the mother also.

A perfect cautionary tale for women about the reasons for marriage and for picking a particular man is the 1944 Warner Brothers movie *Mr. Skeffington*, starring the woman's film favorite, Bette Davis, paired with her male equivalent, the sublimely talented Claude Rains. *Mr. Skeffington* is actually a movie about Mrs. Skeffington, but since it seeks to establish the fact that Mrs. Skeffington should have paid more attention to Mr. Skeffington because he was really the center of the universe while she only thought she was, it is appropriately named, after all. *Mr. Skeffington* presents all the various elements of the woman's film as part of its epic flashback plot. It contradicts itself as it moves forward and brings itself to a conclusion on the side of correct behavior for women, using the frivolous Fanny Skeffington as a warning to women of what might happen to them if they live vain and selfish lives and destroy their marriages.

In the subcategory of women's film choices, *Mr. Skeffington* is primarily a marriage movie. The magnificently beautiful and desirable Fanny (Davis) marries the socially unacceptable Job Skeffington (Rains) for his money. Fanny is not Jewish like Job, but she has found herself in dire need of cash because her beloved younger brother has accepted commissions illegally. Fanny has to save her brother from prison by making a financial marriage to a man she does not love, so that the money can be immediately repaid. Here is the first major contradiction of the film's story: Fanny does the wrong thing by marrying without love and for money, but Fanny does the right thing by saving her ne'er-do-well brother. Fanny even articulates the problem clearly for the viewer by saying "I like Job, but I love you" to her brother. Her brother, appalled at her unsuitable marriage, but not, apparently, appalled at the financial rescue, retaliates by joining the Lafayette Escadrille in order to avoid social shame.

Fanny Skeffington is the central character of the film, and thus the identification point for viewers. She is presented as being wrong in her reasons for marrying, but not wrong in her choice of a man. She is vain and silly, overly concerned with fashion and beauty. Nevertheless, in another basic contradiction, she has been married for her sense of fashion and beauty, and not one man she meets is ever interested in her for any other reason. Fanny does her wifely duty by giving birth to a daughter, but she is ashamed of how she looks pregnant, going out of town to hide until the baby is born. After the child (a lumpkin daughter) arrives, she ignores her, proving to be a lousy mother. And having driven Job into the arms of another woman by her indifference, she divorces him, outraged.

In the end, Fanny Skeffington pays for not being a suitable woman —that is, a loving wife and mother. She loses her looks, the one thing she had to use as barter in the world of men. Having suffered a severe case of scarlet fever, she loses her hair and ages dramatically. This reminds women that they must preserve their marriages for economic security because if they lose their looks no other man will want them. Left alone and unloved and unwanted by the very men who had romanticized her and placed her on a pedestal all her life, Fanny suffers the ignominy of losing a young man's love to her own plain and straightforward daughter. In the end, Job Skeffington returns home to her, a man broken by incarceration in a concentration camp. He is, however, blind and cannot see that Fanny is not the beautiful young woman he once loved and married. He carries a picture of her forever in his mind in which she is eternally young, lovely, and desirable. He's perfect! And he and Fanny are reunited in a perfect marriage. Once again, Fanny has a dependent man to care for, as she once cared for her brother. Job can be her child, giving her a chance to redeem herself by becoming a good mother this time. She can always be his beautiful Fanny, since he can't observe her aging process. For his part, his beautiful Fanny is returned, and he will now have the attention and care from her that he never got before. And they are wildly rich. They can live a lie, which is apparently Hollywood's definition of the perfect marriage.

ALL OF THESE marriages, happy or wretched, in the films discussed so far are more or less supposed to be seen by viewers as normal. One other major category of marital experience exists for the woman, however: it's the marriage in which the man a woman promises to love, honor, and obey tries to murder her.

Why does a woman end up marrying a man who wants to kill her? Often enough the movies tell us it's her own fault. In *Dragonwyck* (1946) Gene Tierney keeps saying that she wants to be different. She has dreams, and she wants to get out and see the world. Her mother warns her that "You can't marry a dream," but she has to find out the hard way. Her character is contrasted with that of her dutiful, obedient sister who has docilely accepted the conventional role her family has defined for her.

Tierney begs so passionately for change that she is sent to visit her cousin, where she meets Vincent Price, a married man who presents himself as an upstanding citizen and a model husband. In fact, Price actually hates his wife, and he treats this fat and wretched woman with open cruelty and neglect. Tierney doesn't heed these warning signs, however, even though a local doctor points out that the wife eats to compensate for the lack of love in her life. (Noting how passionately she consumes cream-filled pastries, he muses, "It's as if to . . .") Tierney wants Price because he represents power, money, knowledge of a better, more sophisticated life, and, implicitly, knowledge of sex, all things Tierney does not have back on the farm she came from. Price wants the beautiful Tierney also, killing off his wife in order to marry her.

After the wedding, Price turns out to be an evil version of Mr. Rochester. He, too, has dreams in which he seeks escape, but they are drug-induced dreams. In a sense, a link is thus established between Tierney's and Price's characters that is neither marital nor romantic. Price represents Tierney's worst side. His desires are emblematic of hers, destructive, anti-social, and thus unrealistic. In the tradition of duality in women's films, two men represent Tierney's opposite choices. They may also be seen as representing two sides of herself. First, there is the bad Price, who is her dark inner soul, longing for freedom, escape, and a kind of evil sex. The other man, played by Glenn Langan, is the good country doctor, representing service to society and the woman's acceptance of her duty to become a wife and mother. The film ends up a lesson in obedience for women, and yet it also provides a secret release for their dreams. Price tries to kill Tierney, just as he killed his fat wife, by placing poisoned oleanders in her room. This irony —woman often think of a man who will bring them flowers as a dream man— is preserved in proper feminine terms. When Price eventually dies, his death is more or less the death of the evil (rebellion) in her, just as his attempt to kill her is brought on by her own poor values.

Marriage films establish many different plot motivations for why a man would want to kill his wife. Usually he wants her money, a shrewd reminder to women that having economic power places them in danger. Sometimes a man wants to marry someone else, and, like everything connected with the woman's film, this has a duality. In *The Two Mrs. Carrolls* (1947), Humphrey Bogart wants to kill Barbara Stanwyck in order to marry Alexis Smith. In fact, he killed his first wife in order to marry Stanwyck! For him, it's a case of constant trading up. On the other hand, Charles Laughton kills his wife in *The Suspect* (1944) because she is a total bitch, and he wants to marry the kind and gentle Ella Raines. Bogart wants to kill his nagging wife (Rose Hobart) in *Conflict* (1945), again to marry Alexis Smith, because life with Hobart is hell. A man can also want to kill his wife simply because he's crazy and obsessed, as in *Julie* (1956), where Louis Jourdan has already killed Doris Day's first husband in order to get her free to marry him. Day becomes suspicious and finally decides one night in bed that she just *has* to ask him if he did it. ("I have to think how to do this," she muses on the sound track. "If I'm wrong it could ruin my marriage.") When Jourdan freely admits his crime, Day spends the rest of the movie trying to get away from him, but he is relentless and almost all-powerful in his ability to find her hiding places. His explanation for this obsession: he loves her so much he can't help it. He's *crazy* where she's concerned. There is also a category of films in which men kill their wives just because they like to kill women, and that is what they do. This is the category of "just because. . . ."

All these stories show women that the danger of love is as real and specific as the joy of love.

This phenomenon is further demonstrated in *Shadow of a Woman* (1946), in which Andrea King weds Helmut Dantine after knowing him only one week. Soon she is finding things out. First it's "But, Phillip, I didn't know you had a cabin in the woods," and then, "But, Phillip, I didn't know you had a sister and a nephew." Later it's "But, Phillip, I didn't know you had an ex-wife." Then it's onward to "But, Phillip, I didn't know you had a son." Soon it's a sleeping potion in her coffee, all because she just didn't know. She didn't know because she didn't take the trouble to find out.*

When Andrea King tries to tell the police her husband is trying to kill her, they tell her to "go home and get some rest." Confident authority figures *often* advise distraught women by saying, "Why don't you go home and get some rest." With a few words they dismiss, ignore, reject, and condescend. The key words are "go home," but the subtle implication lies in "get some rest." Inactivate yourself, girl; go lie down. The marriage film itself is one form of "get some rest."

EXCEPTIONS to the usual marriage stories do exist, however. A modern relationship is explored in *Ex-Lady* (1933), starring Bette Davis and Gene Raymond as a young couple who are having an affair *without* marriage. They do not live together openly, although people seem aware of their secret. Instead, he returns to her apartment after guests leave her party and lets himself in with his own key. Davis's character does not wish to marry. She considers it old-fashioned and limiting, and she is suspicious of the position it will place her in. "I went away from home to be on my

---

* As an old doctor points out in *The Two Mrs. Carrolls*, "Women never get their facts straight."

own," she tells Raymond. "I don't want to be like my mother, 'yesing' for some man. I want to be a person on my own. If I like to live with a certain kind of furniture, a certain kind of work, wear a certain kind of clothes, I want to do it, and not hear somebody tell me I ought to do something else. . . . That's what marriage means. You must do what the other person wants. You must please them. It's dull."

A viewer knows in advance that this is not going to be how the movie will end up, that the film will come down, in the long run, on the side of marriage. However, *Ex-Lady* is unusual in many ways. First of all, it does not present Bette Davis as wicked for feeling the way she does. It also does not present Gene Raymond as a cad taking advantage of her, nor as a wimp she shoves around. It simply illustrates the problems a man and woman in love will have when the woman wishes to retain her independence. Of the two, the man is the more uneasy with their situation. "Let's get married," he says, "so I'll have the right to be with you." Davis fires back, "What do you mean . . . *right?* I don't like the word 'right.' No one has any rights about me, except me."

There is no problem about the threat of illegitimate children in *Ex-Lady*. Davis and Raymond are clearly and specifically sleeping with each other, although they are not married, but neither is worried about having children. It is assumed by the movie, and thus presented to the audience this way, that birth control is available. Davis comments about motherhood, "When I'm forty, I'll think of babies. In the meantime there are twenty years where I want to be the baby, and play with my toys, and have a good time playing with them." Again, she is not presented as bad for talking this way, although anyone watching the film knows that this attitude is not going to work out. It is not *just* a career, says Davis. "Sure I want to do good work, but I don't want to be a wife." On that basis, the film is a liberated statement to the audience.

Davis and Raymond marry soon, however, because they both cannot bear the other one going with someone else. Temporarily, their marriage works beautifully. Underneath a fashion magazine photo that features Raymond in a tuxedo, standing by a stove, while Davis in a lavish white gown wields a frying pan for some undisclosed purpose, the magazine gushes about Davis, "She has successfully united a career with marriage." And so she has. Temporarily.

Soon things fall apart. "Don, don't always tell me what to do," Davis directs, finally suggesting, "Let's be lovers again. Let's work separately and do things separately." They seem able to respect each other's individuality better when they are not married. Marriage brings no benefits, but many problems. Davis suggests they should be separate people, so that when they do come together, it'll always be new and exciting and real, and

they return to their original agreement. (Frank McHugh, playing a befud-
dled friend, comments to Raymond: "These modern young people. Give
me the old-fashioned girl. Do you remember the bustle? The hobble skirt?
Hobble skirts. There was an invention. They couldn't walk fast nor far in
the hobble skirt. You could trust them.")

Poor Davis and Raymond, however. Once again, they find they cannot
make things work out. They are back to their original problem: they truly
love each other and cannot bear having each other go with someone else.
Jealousy makes them both miserable, and Davis ends up bursting into a
rival's rooms and demanding that Raymond leave with her at once. Finally,
Davis concludes what many other couples have fully realized: "It may not
be perfect living together all the time, but it hurts both ways. And this
way it hurts less." They reinstate their marriage. "Move over, sweetheart,"
says Raymond to a supine Davis. "Your husband is here to stay."

Ex-Lady is about people with money and position, who have no worries
about children or social ostracism. In this sense, it is totally unrealistic,
yet it poses the problem couples face in a direct and honest manner. This
problem has not necessarily changed in the nineties. When two people love
each other, they need to make a commitment of some sort, and unless it
is marriage, they are going to feel jealous and lonely, so what are they to
do? Evidently, accept the lesser of the two evils, which is exactly how
marriage in *Ex-Lady* is presented to the viewer.

What these bad-marriage films show is that when women marry and
place their fates in the hands of men, they encounter all sorts of problems.
Adultery, alcoholism, impotence, sterility, drug addiction, abusive behavior, gangsterism, illegal business practices, desertion, mental cruelty,
murder, stinginess, insensitivity, disloyalty, homosexuality, neglectful parenting, insolvency, and bad breath. No one, however, encounters anything
to equal the experience of the woman who has to admit "I married a monster
from outer space." The sinister film released under that title in 1958 stars
Tom Tryon as a nice guy whose body becomes inhabited by an alien. Gloria
Talbott plays his bewildered wife. (Apparently filmmakers felt that a perfect
arena for an alien hostile takeover would be a typical American marriage.
Here was a conflict audiences could believe!) In the plot, after one year
of a "horrible" marriage to a young man whose body is taken over on the
night before his marriage, Talbott writes to her mother, "I'm frightened
and bewildered. Maybe it's me, but, oh Mom, Bill isn't the same man I
fell in love with. He's almost a stranger. . . ."

Underneath the surface of this intriguing sci-fi movie is a second
meaning that, like the alien who takes over Tom Tryon's body, seems to
possess the movie for its own purposes. Actually there are several possible
second meanings. The alien possession takes over only male bodies, and

might be seen as a subversive story about homosexuality. ("Well . . . congratulations," softly whispers Tryon, as he moves sinuously toward another man who has just admitted he's in the club, as it were.) There's also the usual interpretation made by American Studies scholars: it's those pesky Russians again. If the interpreter is a leftist, it's those pesky McCarthyites again. However, this truly is a story about marriage, and the metaphor of takeover is a marital one. Tryon is a secondary character, while the central figure of identification is Gloria Talbott, the wife. Although on the surface an example of the science-fiction genre, *I Married a Monster from Outer Space* nevertheless uses a woman and her primary concerns of motherhood, marriage, and love to make its basic points.

From the moment it begins, the movie presents images of sexual encounters between men and women and discussions about how awful marriage is, how limiting. (One character suggests a plan for men to be able to avoid it: mass suicide.) As two men enter a bar, they walk past an open convertible in which a man and woman are locked in a deep, passionate kiss. No matter who walks past, who knocks on the side of the car, or who tries to get their attention, they do not break their clinch. "They are obviously not married," someone observes. Inside, two women of questionable morality are drinking at the bar, discussing the table of men sitting nearby.

"They ain't even given us so much as a look."

"Well, maybe they're married or something."

"If they're willing to overlook it, we certainly are."

Two weddings take place in the relatively short running time of the film, and both women marry aliens. Marriage is on everyone's mind, and women don't seem to have any other plans in life. No women are shown to be working in the film, and an older woman who has been eager for a proposal from her man and who finally gets it says she had gotten so desperate that "I was reading books about Joan of Arc, Florence Nightingale, Madame DuBarry . . . you know," she sneers, "career women." (I like to pause to consider Joan of Arc as a career role model.) Becoming pregnant is a matter of great importance to the women of this movie. It looks almost as if it's their only motivation for marriage. Gloria Talbott goes to see her doctor after one year of marriage, complaining that she is not pregnant yet and wondering if that means there is something wrong with her. She wonders about other things, too. For instance, her husband seems to be able to see in the dark, and he has lost his taste for liquor. Alarmingly, the little dog she gives him for their first anniversary hates him, barking its head off and baring its teeth when Tryon comes near. (Like the dog in *A Stolen Life*, he seems to be smarter than anyone else around.) Finally, Talbott follows Tryon when he goes out at night and learns the awful truth. He is not really a husband. He's a monster from outer space!

As we have seen, these alien monsters inhabit only the bodies of men. They have come to earth to impregnate women with . . . what? Children. What kind of children? "Our kind." Their women were all killed by the power of the sun's rays back on their own planet, and their race is going to become extinct if their scientists can't perfect a way for these aliens to impregnate earth women. So far their scientists haven't got the bugs worked out, but soon, soon. After this news gets out, a scene takes place in which the local bad girl wanders out of a bar and tries to pick up an alien who is inexplicably standing out on the street wearing a hooded jacket and looking into a toy store window at a small doll. Flirting outrageously, she comes on to him, saying, "Want to buy me a doll?" Suddenly, she sees his alien face and screams so loudly that he has to zap her. The idea of this weird-looking creature yearning into a store window at a baby doll is pretty hair-raising for any woman watching, as those unsettling words about children, "our kind," echo in her head. Man, the impregnator, is on the one hand the wife's desired mate, and on the other a frightening alien who destroys a woman.

Tryon has tried to tell Talbott that he is beginning to feel human desires and human emotions and that he is "learning what love is," but she's not having any, and she goes for advice and comfort to that stable symbol of male security and love for women, her family doctor. He, of course, has not been taken over by aliens like the policemen she went to earlier. (They suggested that she get some rest.)

The doctor devises a brilliant plan for finding men who are not yet possessed by aliens. Go to the maternity ward! "I know where to get our men . . . human men!" he cries as he disappears into the labor rooms. If a man can father a child, and has done so, he's a real man. With the help of the town's recent fathers, not to mention the aid of two dogs who jump up and disconnect the alien's air hoses, order is restored, and Tryon becomes his old self again. ("Marge?" he asks, smiling at Talbott. "Bill?" she replies, smiling back, just before they embrace.)

Here is a movie that baldly suggests what the status quo of marriage should be. Men must get their wives pregnant, and wives must keep themselves occupied with child rearing. Its attitude toward marriage can be seen in several different ways: marriage is bad, because it makes a man lose his taste for fun and maybe his virility; or marriage is good, because only through it can a man be redeemed from evil that might possess him; or alien forces are trying to destroy home and hearth; or sex is dangerous; or whatever. But one thing is for sure: a woman who marries a monster from outer space has her hands full. For a woman, it's another example of "l'amour, l'amour, how it *does* let you down," as Mary Boland remarked in *The Women*.

MARRIAGE, all these movies seem to agree, is a flawed institution, vulnerable to all kinds of onslaughts, but you cannot live without it. It's a bad deal, but women must live by the Marriage Rules. Marry for love, not money. Guard your castle against other women and floods. Have children, and don't be silly with other men. Deal with your mother-in-law, and keep 'em flying. Marriage, films whisper out to the women in the audience, is what we know it is, but what could or would we do without it? What choices do we have? Finally, in the 1960s, films emerged that just say no to marriage. They don't discuss all the problems and then conclude that there's no other way to live or provide an escapist fantasy variation of the same thing. As women gained independence sexually and economically, the marriage film underwent perhaps the greatest change in all the categories of the woman's film. Women still went to prison, and men still tried to murder them, and children still gave them fits, but marriage seemed less and less important as it became less and less necessary for a woman's social validation, economic support, and sex life. Two films illustrate the change in marriage films about women, one a serious film in the honest woman's film tradition (*The Happy Ending*) and one a parody of the woman's film (*What a Way to Go!*).

What a Way to Go! (1964) parodies the entire marriage subgenre of the woman's film. (A later comedy, *The War of the Roses*, 1989, simply kills it off, leaving its corpse in front of viewers as a thing to contemplate and wonder at.) "Every man I've touched withers," cries Shirley MacLaine to her psychiatrist in *What a Way to Go!* ("Oh, really?" he replies, eyeballing her body.) She's afraid she's some kind of witch, because no matter what she does, or whom she marries, she ends up richer and richer and the husbands end up deader and deader. Released at a time when there were few big female stars and even fewer women's films being made, *What a Way to Go!* is a harbinger of the feminist movement. It tells the story of a naive girl from a small town in Ohio who never wanted money, only one good man she could love and who would love her back. Jokingly endorsing the old movies that punished women for marrying for money, the story has poor MacLaine *trying* to marry for poverty and never being able to make it stick. Inspired by her body and by their love for her, every man she marries becomes a huge success. Then he dies.

Poor little Shirley tells her story to her psychiatrist in a series of flashbacks, the basic unit of storytelling of the 1940s women's films.

Each of these flashbacks is a satire of a particular branch of the woman's film: the rags-to-riches climb from poverty in which the man loses his values (Dick Van Dyke); the woman behind the "great man" (Paul Newman); the marriage to the rich tycoon in which the woman brings humble, rural, and thus better values to his world (Robert Mitchum); and the show-business musical biography (Gene Kelly). In each, the man is doing fine until MacLaine enters his life and he starts acting like—well —a man, and wanting to prove to her that he can be a success and ending up in a coffin. In the end, widowed four times, MacLaine locates a true failure (Dean Martin) and finds complete happiness with his utter inability to do anything right. *What a Way to Go!* writes finish to the kinds of marriage films that had been around for decades. A time in history had arrived in which couples could live together openly without marriage. The reasons for a woman's needing to see the marriage film collapsed and disappeared, taking the films with them. *What a Way to Go!* satirizes both the woman's film genre and the concept of marriage. In doing so, it announces the onset of liberation. Women were going to have other choices.

One of the first women's films of the post-studio-system years in which a woman made another choice and stuck with it is the neglected 1969 movie *The Happy Ending*, starring Jean Simmons. This is an important movie to consider because in many ways it marks the death of the woman's film genre as it had been previously constituted. Its central character is a housewife, played by Simmons. Instead of being strong and in control like Ann Dvorak or Maureen O'Hara, she is a pathetic creature who drinks too much and who has no self-confidence. In comparing her with the characters played in prior decades by actresses like Crawford, Davis, and Stanwyck, she can only be seen to be a wimp.

Simmons has made her choice in life. As a romantic young girl, she opted for marriage to her dream man, ironically played by John Forsythe, who would go on to become a television icon as that same creature. She is now middle-aged, and her dreams are dead. She revives them, however unsatisfactorily, by getting drunk before noon and by watching romantic old movies on TV. A series of scenes shows her totally unable to cope with anyone, including her husband, her mother, her daughter, and her house-keeper. She is not the center of the universe, and if she were, she would fall down and weep, seeking a place to hide. Furthermore, she lives in a world of similar unhappy wives, one of whom, as they are all sitting around their health club, describes their group as "zombies killing time, till we go home to kill more time."

The women in *The Happy Ending* are all either weak, unhappy, or treacherous. It is a wasteland of women, depicting a world of money and boredom in which women have no real roles to play. As a consequence, they have no self-confidence and no place to go. When Jean Simmons finally runs away from home, in a bungling attempt to save herself, on the airplane to the Caribbean she meets an old college friend (Shirley Jones). This woman seems happy and alive, but her character is used to illustrate the choice of a life opposite to Simmons's. Jones is the mistress of a wealthy man. As she explains to Simmons, she realized her choice would be between that of "a big-mouthed housewife or a big-assed whore," and she chose the latter. Hardly an inspirational choice.

As Simmons acts out her runaway holiday to the islands, she ultimately comes to see that she has lived her life by romantic, foolish notions she learned at the movies (presumably from women's films). She has made the wrong choice. She returns to her home and rejects her marriage. Her husband, who is presented as a nice guy who loves her but doesn't know what to do about her drinking (he is so busy with his work), asks her to return to their home. The scene takes place on the steps of a school, with Simmons holding her books and preparing to enter class. After he asks her to return, she pauses for a moment and then asks him, significantly, "What would you do if we had it all to do over again?" If they could return to their moment of original choice, would he still pick her, still choose to marry? As he instinctively hesitates, betraying himself, she smiles knowingly, turns her back on him, and walks away. Her new choice is made. A new kind of happy ending is about to take over the woman's world.

MOTHERHOOD

IF YOU ask anybody what Hollywood's attitude toward motherhood used to be, you will almost certainly be told, "Positive!" Young mothers, old mothers, fat mothers, thin mothers, *all* mothers are good, and all women should be good mothers. That's the accepted idea, but, like everything else one digs up in movies about women, it is only partly true, and even when true, it is deceptive. In movies about women there are exactly four kinds of mothers:

1. Unwed (who are among the most common in the woman's film)
2. Perfect (who are few and far between)
3. Sacrificial (who are faced with more serpent's teeth and reasons to give up their children than you can possibly imagine)
4. Destructive (who show remarkable talent at their specialty)

These mothers can cross over. An unwed mother can become destructive, then sacrificial, and thus perfect. A destructive mother, on the other hand, can be sacrificial and unwed, but she'll never be perfect. As is true for the virgin who becomes a whore, or the whore who develops a virginal heart of gold, the mothering categories are not fixed. The woman's film is always about a woman on the vertical ladder of society's views about her behavior, so mothers, too, can slide up and down, changing labels as they change behavior. However, each of the four main categories serves a particular purpose, and no matter how much a mother fits in one or two or three of them, her options are most clearly defined by societal evaluation. Unwed and destructive are wrong, but not without redemption, particularly in the unwed bracket. Perfect and sacrificial are right, though sometimes misguided. Each category reflects specific attitudes toward the woman's role, toward the children involved, and toward the men that fathered them.

An overview of the woman's film reveals a logical line of story progression. After the romantic movies in which women fall in love, accept love, and make their choices about men comes the next leg of the woman's journey, the marriage. After the marriage is established, the story of motherhood should follow, though with typical woman's film perversity, the story of motherhood frequently follows the story about a man and a romance, skipping the marriage altogether.

Few people have bothered to watch the films that constitute the true origins of the woman's film in the sound era. This is partly because these movies have not been generally available, and partly because even if they were, no one would want to see them. Most of them are, in a word, terrible. They have no wit, no charm, no grace, and they are often patently ridiculous. Worst of all, they exhibit no cinematic style whatsoever, treating the camera as if its only job is to sit quietly in one place and keep an eye on things. Women's films of the 1940s are frequently models of style and cinematic experimentation, but the majority of the early sound movies about women really *are* trash, which partially accounts for the genre's lack of critical respect. These movies, however, are important to the history of film, in that between 1929 and 1933 so many were released. I am talking about films that star women like Ruth Chatterton and Helen Twelvetrees and Ann Harding. These noble actresses, patient and burdened by plot, carry on as if it all meant something, as if the Oscar were perpetually within reach. They not only portray heroines, they truly *are* heroines. They elevate unworthy material, and at their best they can actually bring a tear to your eye no matter how ashamed you might be of it. These early genre films are the stories of noble sacrifice that most people associate with the woman's genre. There are many forms of noble sacrifice, but the most common one in the early sound period is that of unwed motherhood.

UNWED MOTHERHOOD

HERE ARE the plot synopses of seven such movies from the years 1930 to 1934:

- *Born to Love* (1931):   Constance Bennett is an American nurse during World War I who becomes pregnant by a young aviator who is later reported dead. In order to give her illegitimate child a name, she is forced to marry a wealthy English lord, even though she does not truly love him.

- *Common Clay* (1930):   Constance Bennett is a servant girl who is seduced by her wealthy employer's son. She has to fight a court battle to retain custody of her illegitimate child.
- *Confessions of a Co-ed* (1931):   Sylvia Sidney is a young college girl who becomes an unwed mother.
- *Forbidden* (1932):   Barbara Stanwyck is an innocent country girl who falls in love with an unhappily married attorney when she meets him on a cruise. When she becomes the unwed mother of his child, she allows him (and his crippled wife) to adopt her baby, thus not only ensuring a wealthy home for the child but also allowing her lover to run for governor without scandal.
- *The Life of Vergie Winters* (1934):   Ann Harding is an unwed milliner who, not knowing what else to do, allows her wealthy married lover and his wife to adopt her illegitimate daughter.
- *The Sin of Madelon Claudet* (1931):   Helen Hayes is forced to become a prostitute to earn enough money to raise her little son. When he is grown, she sends him to medical school, never revealing to him that she is the mother he has always presumed was dead.
- *Torch Singer* (1933):   Claudette Colbert is an unwed mother who, no matter how hard she tries, cannot support her daughter financially and care for her at the same time. She is forced to place her out for adoption, but always regrets it.

These stories are about women who have no one to help them. Without the protection of a husband or family and without any economic security or education, they attempt to do what the woman is supposed to do in life: raise children. This is immediately depicted as not only difficult but practically impossible. It is a task that forces women into desperate measures, and they either become prostitutes or famous cabaret singers. They either give their babies over to their married lovers' wives, or they have to marry wealthy Englishmen. This all looks ludicrous today, but if it is soberly considered it reveals that movies offered two polarized kinds of stories to women on this subject. One was cautionary (prostitution and loss of the child) and one was escapist (fame and the peerage).

The unwed-mother story is usually about a young and inexperienced girl who falls in love and has the bad luck to become pregnant. There is also a variation, which is really the same thing as an unwed-mother story, in which the woman is actually married but her husband dies. His family refuses to accept her, and they either take the child from her or leave her in the same position as the unwed mother. The mother raises her child from a distance, paying for his or her education and following his or her progress through life. In some cases, the mother accidentally meets up with the child later in life, rescuing it from some villainy or preventing the youngster from making a grave error in judgment. There is also a variation in which the grown child, now a doctor or lawyer, rescues his own mother without knowing who she is.* These married-mother films include *The Secret of Madame Blanche* (1933), *The Most Precious Thing in Life* (1934), *Madame X* (1929, 1937, 1966, 1981, in all its sound variations), *Wicked* (1931), and *Once a Lady* (1931), which star Irene Dunne, Jean Arthur, Ruth Chatterton (Gladys George, Lana Turner, and Tuesday Weld), Elissa Landi, and Ruth Chatterton, respectively. What these films say to viewers is that when it comes to sex, women are at risk. A woman is not free to express herself in a world that does not have the Pill. She has no sexual freedom or equality, because whatever consequences arise, she will be the one to deal with them. If a woman becomes pregnant, and there is no man to marry her, or even if she is married and he disappears, dies, or catches the Wabash Cannonball, she is out of luck. And no matter how wealthy his family might be, she might not be able to count on them, and she will face an economic and social problem that can overwhelm her.

Not only is a female at risk, but her child will be, too. A woman frequently does not have the education or the background to earn good money, and even if she does, who is to care for the child while she is not home? These pressures, very real and very frightening to women, make superb story fodder for Hollywood, where they churned out variations of all kinds, and because they lay the foundation of the genre, they are of primary importance to an understanding of it. A movie plot in which a woman has to give up her child provided a two-way street of response for viewers who were mothers, perhaps feeling burdened with the difficulties of raising their own children. A woman on film who sacrifices a child suffers and is ultimately punished, reassuring the women watching. At the same time, the woman on film who gives up a child suddenly has freedom. Often, she finds a better life of riches, success, adventure, and, in the end, even an opportunity for love with another man or the same man who caused her problem in the first place. The viewer could watch a woman get free of the burden of mothering without having to feel guilty about it. The woman in the story will be punished, or else she'll get the child back in the end anyway.

* In 1931, reviewing one of the many films in which a child never realizes the woman he is involved with is actually his own mother, *Variety* asked the key question, "Why don't these talker mothers tell their kids the truth?"

So many plots deal with unwed mothers, or the sacrifice of one's child to circumstances, that one has to wonder what, really, was the appeal of such stories to women. Several things suggest themselves. First, having a child without being married might have been a more common experience for women than people realized. Certainly, it was a threat that hung over any woman who decided to have sex without marriage. Seeing it happen on screen was a cautionary tale for anyone contemplating sex, and a cathartic tale for someone to whom it had already happened. Second, the fear of losing one's child—one of the most traumatic things for any woman to face, presumably—would have found response in women. Last, there may have been some covert wish fulfilled here for women feeling beleaguered by too many kids at home, or by someone who did not enjoy the job of mothering. These films just removed the child, freeing the woman for wealth, independence, sex, and good clothes.

Many stories of the 1930s involve women left widowed or impregnated by men who disappeared in World War I. I say "disappeared" because that happens so frequently. Seldom do they simply *die*. According to the woman's film, World War I was a war in which the women got pregnant after one night, the men went blind and forgot who they were, and all the mail got lost. Over and over again, men and women write each other the basic facts the other needs to know. ("Don't worry, darling, I'll meet you at Big Ben on July 8th," or "We'll be married just as soon as my lungs get clear of mustard gas, and in the meantime, I'm just sitting here in the hospital on the Riviera," or "Don't marry Bruce next Thursday, I'm on my way home.") These letters never arrive or don't turn up until a year later. War provides whatever excuses are needed for chaotic plot development.*

The woman's version of heroism in World War I is doing it without being married. The brave young flier who is about to go up in the air in a crate is matched by the female version: the woman who goes to the little inn with the man she loves, daring to risk all. For the times, this *was* an act of bravery, but it never goes unpunished in the movies. In *Born to Love* (1931), Constance Bennett goes to a little French inn with Joel McCrea, and he is pronounced dead and she is pronounced pregnant only seconds later. To give their child a name, she marries the wealthy Wilfred of noble

---

* World War II, on the other hand, a far more optimistic war in terms of film stories, was also more successful where the postal service was concerned. It was a war in which the mail definitely got delivered. Writing letters to soldiers, and the importance of doing so, are stressed over and over again in movies from that period. Such letters form the basis of several movies: *A Letter for Evie* (1945), *Love Letters* (1945), and *Dear Ruth* (1947) are examples. In *A Letter for Evie*, the heroine works in a shirt business, and they are making army shirts, so she puts letters with her name and address in the pocket to get dates.

In women's films of the early 1930s, A leads automatically to B,
particularly if World War I is involved. Constance Bennett
and Joel McCrea in *Born to Love*

birth, who has been standing in the wings waiting, a prototype of the faithful
suitor the women's film often provides for emergencies like this.

Bennett levels with him about the kid, but Wilfred promises her,
"Now life can begin again. I'm not an infatuated boy. There have been
women enough in my life. Think of . . . your baby." She does. They do.
Next thing we know, they are christening little Wilfred, and Bennett is
swanning around in fur, being called "your Ladyship." Just as everyone is
grinning and swilling champagne, however, the phone rings and . . . it's
Joel McCrea! Back from the dead, where he never was in the first place.
As Bennett says, "What happened???" Why didn't he let her know? He
explains, "I was too ill. I didn't even know the war was over." Lord Wilfred
then turns out not to be so noble after all. He's downright annoyed by this
turn of events, and furthermore, a dead Joel McCrea is one thing, whereas
a live one on his doorstep is another. Bennett tries to explain, "I'm his!
With all my heart, with all my soul, with all my body." Wilfred looks cross,
and, as if he just fully got it for the first time, mutters "with . . . all . . .

your . . . *body.*" He throws Bennett out, but he keeps her son. And there's nothing she can do about it, because men have all the money and all the power, and both the law and society's standards are on their side. If she fights, she has to say the child is not Wilfred's, branding the baby as illegitimate and herself as a loose woman. Off she goes into the night, in her hat and furs, carrying her little purse. A wretched though well-dressed sight.

Born to Love further confirms the risk women take in country inns by ending on a sour note. McCrea has gone off to America, leaving Bennett because she has married another man, and for two years she just sinks down and down. Finally, she is invited to see her baby and told she can now see him as often as she likes. When she runs upstairs, full of joy, she confronts Wilfred's last cruel joke: the child is dead! Despite the sheer nonsense of *Born to Love*, this is a truly shocking moment. Poor Bennett has to go out into the fog and stumble home to her sordid digs, but, in the way of the American motion picture, when she gets there McCrea is waiting. He has returned to her. In movies in which motherhood is the main issue, the silver screen giveth and it taketh away. Then it giveth back.

There is something almost magical about the way movie women with children can lose them and then get them back. They don't exactly leave them in a valise in a train station, but they come close. Children die, require adoption because of economic pressures, run away, are stolen, or are just plain farmed out or even ignored. They leave the frame. They go and are frequently not seen again until after the women are rich, famous, loved, and jeweled and gowned. These children then reappear. The lost become found—the sick get well. The adopted return home perfectly turned out, already toilet trained and educated. Do we have to be geniuses to see that these plots allowed women in the audience to have things both ways, to feel relief at seeing the daily burdens of motherhood removed from the story but to be reassured at the end when the mother-child relationship is safely restored? Although such stories are allegedly endorsing motherhood for women with all they've got, they are also conveniently releasing the star and her audience from it.

In *Torch Singer* (1933), Claudette Colbert signs into a charity hospital in a strong state of mind. She admits the truth ("I have no husband") and refuses to give the name of the man who fathered her child. When the female baby is born, she tells her, "Why couldn't you have been a boy? This is such a tough place for a girl to come to." This perspective on the woman's lot is shared by another woman, played by Lyda Roberti, whose husband has died. (If they don't desert, they die.) The two women, in a remarkable presentation of sisterhood, decide to share more than a grim experience with men. They move in together and pool their resources.

While Roberti works, Colbert keeps house and cares for her daughter and Roberti's son.

Ultimately, the women cannot cope, and Roberti feels forced to marry a man "from out west." Unable to manage on her own when she has to both work and care for her child, Colbert finally realizes she must give up her baby and place her for adoption. In leaving the child, she tells her, "Take a mother's advice. Don't ever let any man make a sucker out of you. Anything they get for nothing is always cheap. Make them know what you're worth."

In one of those strange plot movements that old movies seemed to feel were perfectly acceptable, Colbert, the little hausfrau, next becomes a torch singer. At first she is rejected by the nightclub manager, who tells her that she has to suffer to really be able to sing a torch song. Colbert, who understands she is going to have to abandon her child, ironically and dramatically intones, "Watch me suffer!" This can be taken as the key slogan of the early thirties woman's film.

Almost immediately after Colbert has left her child behind, the audience sees her, sleek and chic, singing to an enraptured audience of admiring men: "Give me liberty or give me love," a song that lays out the woman's two basic choices in the film world. Colbert has become rich, powerful, sexy, and tough. "I'm just like glass," she says, "so hard nothing will cut it but diamonds." There is the usual subversive truth in this rise to wealth and fame, because she has abandoned the role of motherhood in order to accomplish it. As a torch singer, she turns pain and enslavement into something defiant, and thus she acts out a form of anger and independence that men can accept, since she is, in fact, still serving them by performing. Having been, she believes, used by a man, she turns her anger on all men, planning to exploit them in return. She knows her cold rejection of them excites them, but she thinks all men are no good for women.

As is almost always true in these films, Colbert finally returns to the fold of nurturing women. The man who fathered her child has gone off to China, sending her a letter telling her to wait, but, as we have seen, the United States postal system cannot be relied upon in matters of love. The letter never shows up, but the man himself eventually does, home from China and still madly in love. The two of them are reunited. Before this happens, however, Colbert has undertaken a second identity. In addition to being a hot cabaret torch singer, she is also Aunt Jenny, a character on the radio who tells stories to children and grants their wishes. It's a case of woman's film duality. Even though Colbert has become suspicious of love and marriage ("some . . . get married and lose their identity that way"), she ends up back in the arms of her lover and with her child restored through an incredible plot development involving lovable Aunt Jenny. *Torch*

Singer is a perfect example of how the woman's film finds a way to remove the child from its plot, so that the woman can do many interesting things, and then finds an equally good way to return the child to the woman in the end.

Unwed motherhood was still a popular story, although in a slightly different format, as late as 1950 in *No Man of Her Own*. A front-runner in the crackpot-plot sweepstakes, this film has one pregnant woman exchanging places with another when they are both involved in a train wreck.

No Man of Her Own begins with an image of a Good Humor truck driving slowly down a sun-dappled street, passing by broad lawns and spacious houses. Barbara Stanwyck's voice on the sound track is heard speaking of "the stillness of perfect peace and security" of this setting, a small midwestern town. As viewers are taken by the camera inside one of the big old houses on the street, it is seen to be well appointed, comfortable, bordering on luxurious. "This is a home," pronounces Stanwyck. Indeed, the image on the screen is one of ladies' magazine perfection, a recognizable movie world of family security. In the living room is seated a happy-looking couple with a beautiful golden-haired child in the arms of the mother. The father reads in front of the fire, and the mother sits beside him, sewing, with the child cradled to her bosom. In a sudden dramatic vocal change, Stanwyck's voice in the narration turns hard and cold as she warns, "This . . . is . . . murder." Everything that an audience sees in front of it immediately takes on a different ambience. The tension that exists between the grown-ups becomes visible. Fear and anxiety are both seen and felt.

As the story that explains this double-layer image is told in flashbacks, viewers learn that the man is not the father of the child, the mother is not the woman she pretends to be, and the child is illegitimate. In other words, "this is a home," but things are not what they seem. The image is undermined by the story.

As the flashback unfolds, its first sequence presents a sordid and disturbing event that can't help upsetting any woman who sees it. Stanwyck, eight months pregnant, drags herself up tenement stairs to pound on a locked door, crying, begging, pleading with the man behind it to open it and talk to her. Inside the room, behind the door, a blond (obviously the new woman in the man's life) says "It's her again" to a cruel but handsome man (Lyle Bettger). Stanwyck's hysterical pleading and weeping extend for what seems to be an eternity until finally the man shoves under the door an envelope with a train ticket out of town for her. He has generously added a five-dollar bill. Stunned, almost immobilized, as she comes to understand fully that he means never to help her, Stanwyck drags herself back down the stairs, the five dollars left behind where she dropped it on the floor.

"Don't ever try to brush me off like that," warns the blond inside the room, but the man doesn't look worried.

On the train west Stanwyck meets a happy couple who are also expecting a baby soon. They befriend her, and she learns that they are on their way to meet his parents, who have never seen the wife (played by Phyllis Thaxter) or even a photo of her. And guess what, this wife has no family of her own! As she and Stanwyck clean up in the woman's dressing room, Thaxter asks Stanwyck to hold her beautiful wedding ring ("See? It has both our names inside") and to slip it on her finger so it won't get lost while Thaxter washes her hands.

"Isn't that bad luck?" asks Stanwyck.

"I couldn't have bad luck," the happy wife replies.

Instantly, there is a train wreck in which the wife and husband are both killed. Stanwyck wakes up in a hospital, with her baby son safely born and tucked into an incubator, and everyone believing she's Thaxter because of the ring she's wearing. Initially, Stanwyck carries out the impersonation for the sake of her child. She knows she has no money to pay for her own delivery and hospital room, but, even more important, the infant in the incubator needs special care. "For you . . . for you," she says to the sleeping infant, just after she's read the letter from her new family, in which they have written, "You're all we have now. You and the little fellow, even though we've never seen you." The helplessness of women in these crackpot plots is significant. Having been used and abused by her lover, Stanwyck tries to find a decent life for her child. She grabs what she can, but it's never *sensible*. It's never a job and a good baby-sitter. She holds up to her cheeks the soft little expensive bootees her would-be family has sent her and decides to pretend she's a woman about whom she knows nothing married to a man she has only seen once.

This sort of story reinforces the sense of desperation that women have when men desert them and they have a child to care for. It shows how limited their options are once they leave the restrictions of polite society behind. Cut loose from secure places, their lives inevitably become crackpot plots.

A woman who is expecting a baby is under time pressure; she can't keep her problem a secret forever. This type of situation is perfect for a movie story, in that it visualizes a dilemma and places it in a highly motivated context that requires the plot to move forward rapidly. Stanwyck in *No Man of Her Own* acts out the full unwed-motherhood problem. Her story is not set overseas, excused by World War I, nor does she become a famous singer or marry an English lord. She has to face up to things on an ordinary street in an ordinary American small town with an ordinary, although reasonably wealthy, family. She takes the plunge.

As Stanwyck is warmly received into the family of her dead "husband," she is in a position to appreciate fully their kindness and generosity. Having had nothing, she is grateful for anything. This makes her a perfect daughter-in-law. She feels slightly guilty, but she always reminds herself of why she is where she is. At her son's baptism, she repeats to herself over and over, "You have a name. You have a name." As she becomes close to her in-laws, particularly the dead man's mother, things go beautifully. The family's other son, played by John Lund, begins to fall in love with her, and his parents, always kind and supportive, are thrilled about that, too. Lund's character is an interesting one. He is obviously not a young man, but he still lives at home with his parents. He has never married, although his mother tells Stanwyck that women are always trying to trap him. Lund is such a wonderful guy that when the family will is remade because of his brother's death, and his brother's "widow and child" are given three-quarters of everything, Lund feels that's okay, because he will inherit the family business (whatever it is).

Just as Stanwyck begins to relax and settle in, a cruel telegram arrives, addressed directly to her. It says simply, "Who are you? Where did you come from? What are you doing there?" These are women's film questions—they ask the questions society always asks a woman. And like all women in these movies, Stanwyck cannot escape her past. It arrives in town in the guise of Lyle Bettger, the man who dumped her after she became pregnant. He is the one who sent the telegram, and now he has arrived to blackmail her and her wealthy family. Determined to save not only her child but also her benefactors, Stanwyck shoots Bettger.

At this moment, the film begins to go seriously askew. A viewer can remember back to the beginning when Stanwyck's voice said on the sound track, "This is murder." It becomes apparent that part of the movie's agenda is a noirish questioning of the old Hollywood ideas about small towns, happy American families, and love affairs. As such it is one of many that mounted an attack on the American home in the postwar period. What is most remarkable is how films like this show upper-middle-class people swiftly and efficiently dealing with murder and degradation. Stanwyck spends a great deal of the movie in a hysterical state, a fate that befell great movie stars as they aged, as we see with Joan Crawford in *Sudden Fear* (1952) and Bette Davis in *Beyond the Forest* (1949). She also constantly invokes the status quo: "I can't do that," "This isn't right," "I can't let you do that," and so on. Having once found herself on the outskirts of respectability, she truly respects the power of the system to knock her down and out; she is slow to break the rules. The normal small-town people she meets up with, however, have no such guilt or worries. John Lund emerges as a perfect opposite to Stanwyck in this. Confident with male power, economic security, and status, he feels free to break laws as necessary for his own personal happiness. In this weird story by William Irish (a pseudonym for Cornell Woolrich), Lund has already fallen in love with his brother's wife (no need to discuss the Freudian implications of this), but when he believes she has committed a murder he loves her even more. He gladly dumps Bettger's dead body on a passing freight train for her. In fact, the only time he comes alive in the movie is when he is involved in murder and deceit. He rises to the ugly side of things, finding an ease of behavior in stepping instinctively back into the dark shadows of a slum doorway, a dead body slung over his shoulder. When Stanwyck feebly objects, he shuts her up, saying that he knew almost from the beginning that she wasn't really his brother's wife but was afraid he'd lose her if he said so. She tries to tell him about her prior life, but he says, "As far as I'm concerned, you were born the day I met you." Lund is the postwar variation of the wealthy asexual man who waits in the wings. He's wealthy enough, all right, but in some perverse sense he seems drawn to her bad past as much as her good present.

Because they live in a small town, and because Lund has a natural instinct for these things, they initially get away with their crime. Three months after the murder, however, during which time Lund and Stanwyck marry, the police turn up. The trail has led directly to Stanwyck. Here is where *No Man of Her Own* remains true to itself as a tale of garbled mother love. As anxious to save her child as Stanwyck has been to save hers, Lund's mother, a sickly woman with a bad heart, has left a letter to be opened upon her death. Since she collapsed and died the night of Bettger's murder, this letter has not been opened, having been forgotten in the crisis. The mother turns out to have written that she herself killed Bettger, believing that her phony confession can be used to save her son, her daughter-in-law, and her grandchild after her death.

It is fascinating and appalling that John Lund is thrilled by the letter and sees it as their ticket to salvation. Stanwyck is horrified. "Do you think I'll let you do that to the only mother I ever had?" she screams at Lund. Embracing her in a brutal close-up, Lund tries to convince her that this, after all, is only what his mother wanted: to sacrifice herself for them. In watching and listening to Lund, a viewer cannot help making a direct visual connection to Lyle Bettger. Both men are blond and fine-featured, and both of them seem perfectly willing to use women for their own ends. Lund utters a cold speech. "Listen," he says to Stanwyck, "I loved my mother. I loved her as much as any man could love his mother, but . . ." His "but" takes the male prerogative and speaks volumes. For a woman watching this movie there is an ominous sense that Stanwyck is out of the frying pan and into the fire.

As it turns out, in another crackpot twist of the plot, the bullet that Stanwyck pumped into Bettger does not match the one that actually killed him. When Stanwyck entered his room and shot him, he was already dead, having been killed by the blond woman who was in his room back in the first flashback scene of the movie. She was the one who had warned him then, "Don't ever try to brush me off like that." When he did, she killed him, and Lund and Stanwyck go free.

No Man of Her Own meshes an unwed-motherhood story with a sacrificial-motherhood story. Stanwyck does what she has to do for her baby's sake, which is assume a false identity. John Lund's mother, played by Jane Cowl in an excellent performance, does what she has to do for *her* baby and for her grandchild. She is willing to sacrifice her good name in the town she has lived in all her life by confessing to a murder she did not commit. She dies believing her fake daughter-in-law *did* commit murder, but she accepts that. Since this daughter is the woman her son loves and the mother of her grandchild, Cowl will go the limit for her. All these two women can do, however, *is* sacrifice themselves, die, bungle it, or wait for rescue. Stanwyck's unwed mother is oppressed, exploited in all ways, and finally finds only murder as a solution, but with one major difference. "The house we live in is so beautiful," her voice says at the end. "Whatever comes we can face together." Stanwyck got the house as well as a name for her son, but only because some other woman solved her problem for her. That nameless blond will now go to prison, living out her own version of the woman's genre.

Three Secrets (1950) is an excellent time capsule of attitudes toward unwed motherhood and the woman's role during the 1950s. Success, it suggests, *is* motherhood. And nothing else. Three women, each of whom has given birth out of wedlock and placed her baby for adoption, come together when they learn that a plane has crashed on a mountaintop leaving only one survivor: a little boy who would have been celebrating his fifth birthday. As a rescue party forms, it is learned that the boy was adopted from a particular home on a specific date. The three potential mothers, each of whom knows he could be hers, turn up to claim him. Three stories, three mistakes—each illustrating choice, each illustrating "what can happen to a woman"—are enacted as flashbacks.

The three woman are (1) a wife (Eleanor Parker), (2) a successful career woman (Patricia Neal), (3) an alcoholic murderess (Ruth Roman). Each made a mistake earlier in life:

1. The wife, in love with the man who fathered her child and deeply innocent, made only the one mistake and has paid for it by the resulting inability to have other children.

2. The career woman willingly gave her child up for her career in an act of refusal "to be a woman."
3. The criminal became involved with a ruthless man, having a sexual relationship outside the safe limits of society's protection.

Each of these three women had a negative relationship with her child's father:

1. Eleanor Parker was fooled by a nice man.
2. Patricia Neal tried to fool a nice man.
3. Ruth Roman was fooled by a bad man.

After each woman's present situation in life is established, their stories are told in flashback, taking viewers back five years from the date of the film, which places the story in the time of World War II. The first story represents motherhood. Eleanor Parker now lives the life of a comfortable upper-class woman with her loving lawyer husband. Her life is idyllic, except that she has no children of her own. She has a maid, roses in all her vases, and silver in all her cabinets, and she has her mother standing by, with whom she can discuss her former tragedy. Her mother, a practical and sympathetic woman, constantly urges her to forget it and not to tell anyone ("What's past is past"). When the news comes about the boy on the mountain, Parker puts on her fur and, ignoring her mother's advice, just goes, remembering her story as she drives to the mountain: It is back during the war, and she falls madly, deeply in love with someone who, as he ships out in the rain, tells her "This hasn't been just another shore leave. If it had I'd have just gotten on that ship and gone." He does, however, have to tell her the truth. There is someone else, his childhood sweetheart, and he is going to marry her, not Parker, after the war. Thus, Parker is seen as having made an honest mistake, probably due to the shifting morality of the country during wartime. She did it for love, and her choice was a decent enough guy; he was just committed elsewhere. When Parker tries to kill herself, her mother intercedes. "You've made one mistake, a bad one. I won't let you make another. No one need ever know. Don't cheat your child. To be brought up in a normal home is his right." Parker is ashamed and confused, but her mother is not. Although she weeps when she sees her grandchild, she remains strong. "This child is never going to its mother," she instructs the nurses. She reminds Parker, "The child would have to live with a stigma all his life. This will be over in a few months." Thus, Parker, a natural mother who says about giving up her child "it's so unnatural," is herself rescued by motherhood, her own forgiving and understanding mother who accepts the ways of the world and fights to save the life of her own child for the future.

Patricia Neal's story is career. She's a big newspaperwoman, Phyllis Horn, called Phil and treated as if she's one of the boys. Her past story takes place in London, where she is covering the war and ignoring the needs of her husband, who says, "I'm getting a divorce. I happen to be a big sentimental guy who comes from a family of eleven kids. I get lonesome without a lot of people around. Or even one." Neal is a frank, open, and sexy woman. She functions like a man, confidently and aggressively dealing with her life. To her husband's remark about divorce, she replies, "So what do you want me to do? Stay home and cook for you? Wash the dishes? I'm not the type. You knew that from the beginning." They have been married for seven years, and during that time she has actively pursued her career to the detriment of their relationship. She tries to win him back with sex, kissing him deeply. "If that's your artillery, you just fired a blank," he says. ("Look out, Duffy, you're limping," she rejoins.) After they part, she returns alone to her office, late one night. The image evokes the loneliness and emptiness of her world. With "I Get a Kick out of You" on the sound track, she throws out the stale sandwich left behind on her desk and looks at a photograph of the two of them from happy days. She realizes she really loves her husband. ("If there's one legit thing about me, it's the way I feel about you.") She goes to his apartment, and as they share a drink, she tells him: "I'd like to speak my piece. I'm scared. I've been ruthless. Stepped all over people. Fought like a man in a man's world, and I made it, but I don't want to lose you." ("Why is it the only time you sound like a woman is in this crummy room?" he asks.) She says she'll give up her job, either write at home or not write at all. "Welcome home, Mrs. Duff," he says.

What follows is an intelligent, although biased, presentation of the career woman's basic problem: Can a woman really have it all? When next we see Neal, she's basting a meat loaf and wearing an apron, humming around the kitchen. However, her editor shows up with a chance to make her "the biggest newspaperwoman since Nellie Bly." "You're asking me to break up my marriage, and I don't want to do that," she says. The editor tells her to "stick a note in the meat loaf." To her husband, she says, "Don't be sore. I've got to do this. It means an awful lot to me. Please understand." He replies, "That's the trouble. I *do* understand. I'm sorry for you, Phil. You tried very hard to be a woman. You just couldn't make it." At the start of the movie, Neal is divorced, and her husband never knew about the child. He has since married another woman. ("She's a simple honest little dope. She thinks taking care of Bob Duff is the most important job on earth.") The grounds for the divorce? Her husband said Patricia Neal wasn't a "woman." (However, she was woman enough to bear his baby without telling him.) This section of the film is one of the most astute presentations of the woman's career problem that appeared on the screen during the 1950s. Although the implication is that Neal clearly did the wrong thing, and she is the only real villain in the film, she will later redeem herself on honest terms. Furthermore, she is presented with some sympathy, and she shows strength and courage regarding her child. She does not attempt to hold the man on false terms, nor does she lie to herself or him about how she feels regarding her career. He, too, is a sympathetic character. Well played by Frank Lovejoy, he is a man whose definition of a woman is someone who doesn't threaten him, who will stay home and take care of him, putting his needs first. In other words, his definition of a woman is a mother. Motherhood destroys Neal, in more ways than one. She does, however, keep her career, and at that she is a terrific success.

The beginning of the Ruth Roman story makes a covert suggestion that she has been ruined by a life of prostitution. She wears cheap, tight clothes and is drinking heavily as the three women await the news about the young boy. As they sit together, Roman tells the others her story, the least interesting of the three and the least honestly presented. "I loved him," she says. "No one figured that. I really loved the guy." The other two listen with the sympathy of sisterhood. ("We're all in the same boat. Three little maids who lost their way, waiting together.") Roman's story represents a double jeopardy. She has borne a baby while unmarried, and she has also killed the child's father, a second act society disapproves of. She has had to be twice punished, and there is no successful present life available to her after the adoption. Where Parker and Neal are motherhood and career, Roman is in the limbo of that third place for women, the wrong life. In her past story, Roman is used by a bad man, an important man with whom she has a romantic idyll, but who ditches her when he's done, leaving the brush-off to be accomplished by a crude employee. When her lover leaves town, she follows, not believing that what they had wasn't true love. When he himself cruelly tells her to "Get smart. This is the kiss-off. The romance is over," she tells him she's expecting his baby. He then sets her up so that another man will pretend to be the father. Roman's response is a classic expression of female rage. She conks him with one of his own fancy and expensive objets d'art and goes to prison for manslaughter. Her baby is born inside the prison and immediately placed for adoption because she is not married and has no family. "They *took* your son away," says Parker. "I gave them mine because I was a coward."

Roman advises Parker *not* to tell her husband about the boy but to just go home, because men don't understand and won't accept. It will ruin her marriage. Parker sends her husband a telegram anyway. When he arrives, his noble reply is overheard by Roman. "Didn't you think I loved you enough? It must have been awful for you. I couldn't deny him to you, not after the years of happiness you've given me." Roman weeps as she listens.

Through her power and influence, Neal is able to find out that the child is Ruth Roman's. When a reporter recognizes Roman as the killer of an influential man, he guesses the truth about the boy.

Neal convinces him to kill the story, telling him the child is really *her* son. "The boy will be hurt."

"Two things I never thought I'd see," he says. "Me killing a story and Phil Horn worrying about someone else."

When the little boy is rescued and brought down off the mountain, all three women are there. Roman, who has been told by Neal that the child is hers, tells Parker, "We cancelled the call [for the information]. We thought it would be better if we never found out. In a way, he belongs to all three of us, and since all of us can't have him, we decided you should be the one to try to adopt him. You can get him. Even if he were mine, I have nothing to offer him. No court in the world would turn you down." Parker worries, "But you can't just leave it like that. You're not being fair to yourselves. You'll blame yourself for not finding out." But Neal backs Roman, and Parker finally agrees to the arrangement. She says, "You'll never have to worry about Johnny again. Either of you." She will act out the role of mother for all three of them. After Parker and her husband leave with the boy, Neal says to Roman, "Come on, champ, I'll buy you a cup of coffee." They are sisters in the problem of a woman's life, their shared secrets bonding them.

The three women have given up their sons for adoption for different reasons: Parker by choice, because she lives in the world of polite society, and there is no place for either an unwed mother or an illegitimate child in it; Neal by choice, because she wants a career and is too proud to use the excuse of the child to bring her husband back and because she cannot both work and be at home; Roman, out of necessity, as society makes the decision for her.

These stories of unwed motherhood ferociously dictate choice. Although they are always on the side of the women involved, they warn brutally what will happen if women stray where motherhood is concerned. They are among the most specific films in criticizing men and society and in questioning the limitations the roles of wife and mother place on women. But by visualizing what can happen, they provide warnings of a dire nature.

The popularity of these stories indicates that women wanted to be reminded about what could happen. It also, however, indicates that they wanted to see women have a child, give it away, and get away with it (with appropriate suffering).

PERFECT MOTHERS

IF YOU WANT to see a perfect mother, look in movies about boys. Andy Hardy has a perfect mother and so does young Tom Edison. So does Little Lord Fauntleroy, and so does Roddy McDowall in *How Green Was My Valley* (1941). Little boys can have perfect mothers as long as they can keep them from dying, but little girls, women, and grown men who are trying to marry leading ladies seldom have perfect mothers. Perfect mothers also turn up in escapist musical films, as when Mary Astor mothers Judy Garland, Margaret O'Brien, and Lucille Bremer in *Meet Me in St. Louis* (1944) or Ann Harding mothers Jane Powell and Debbie Reynolds in *Two Weeks With Love* (1950). Perfect mothers are also a staple of early television sitcoms in the form of Donna Reed or the Beaver's mom, but, perhaps because this was a breed that the real-life women in the audience didn't care for, or had no sympathy for, you just don't see many really perfect moms in movies about women.

When they do exist, they are almost always moms to boys. They bake pies, and they wash underwear, and they understand things. They are also fantasy figures who stand behind great men and presidents, not unlike wives who stand behind great men. They provide everything a man or boy could possibly want. They are idealized, setting the norm by which women can be measured. They are patient, beautiful, and pure. They are often stout and middle-aged, wearing sensible shoes and hats that would never blow off in the wind. They willingly accept their role of slave in the family hierarchy, a role well demonstrated by the Andy Hardy film *You're Only Young Once* (1938). In it, the Hardy family goes on vacation to Catalina. Immediately after they arrive, Andy goes boating and dancing, Dad goes fishing, and Sis goes swimming and out on a date. Mom unpacks, shops for food, cooks dinner, and washes up. As paragons, moms can't do a hell of a lot else, so they present no significant plot development. No doubt this is why we see so few of them.

The trouble with the category is that it becomes clear that a man's idea of a perfect mom just might be the woman's idea of the sacrificial one. These two categories may be interchangeable according to your sex, upbringing, and age. However, there are perfect mothers who are held up as role models in movies, and some of them are not mawkish or annoying.

Such a mother is the real-life woman played by Irene Dunne in *I Remember Mama* (1948).

This mother, although perfect, is an honest human being. She works hard, has a sense of humor, and can manipulate if need be. However, it is not implied that she is a secret conniver for whom honesty is an unknown quality. Mama manages the family's money, but her husband is not a fool or a Milquetoast. She treats her children well, but is firm with them, too. She has their interests at heart, and she does things for them, but she also tries to help them grow and become independent. In short, she is perfect. But she is perfect in a real and acceptable way, suggesting what the job description is and how a woman might succeed if hired for it.

This is about as much as there is to say on the subject of perfect motherhood, except that there are indications that perfection, for some movies, is related to an absence of the man, so that a woman can fulfill the total parental function alone. It is possible for a woman to be really perfect when she has no competition. This stretches the concept of "perfection," but it is a subtle aspect of the movie attitude toward women as mothers.

There is an efficient way in which women's films simply remove the men who father the children, leaving women to carry on alone or with other women, happy to continue in their roles as perfect mothers without the bother of caring also for the fathers. The World War II movie *Tender Comrade* (1943), discussed in the "Ways of Seeing Her" chapter, has the pregnant Ginger Rogers living in a sorority-house environment with a group of women who act out the various roles a husband might play during the nine months of gestation. This group of females constitutes a flawless unit of support and camaraderie for Rogers. In *Music for Millions* (1944), which is also a World War II movie, June Allyson plays in an all-girl orchestra, and when it is discovered she will have her soldier husband's baby, they all rally around and take care of her. (They even write her fake letters from him so she won't know he's missing in action.) There's a sense of good cheer about these male absences, as if all this birthing business is really a woman's job anyway. Since many women gave birth and raised children alone during World War II, this idea turns up especially often during that period. Charles Coburn states it perfectly when he tells Lee Bowman, a returning husband whose baby was born while he was overseas, how he thinks it is for Bowman's wife, Jean Arthur, in *The Impatient Years* (1944). "You see, she's had it her own way so long, and, oh, well, she's been like an old maid, but an old maid with a baby. The way it looks, why, women seem to think that's the ideal existence. They've got their child, but they haven't got a husband to worry about or get in the way around the house." Later on, he adds, "Nice women seem to have a mother complex. A child seems to be natural and necessary for them. Sort of fills up their whole life." Coburn was on to something there, as the movie idea of perfect motherhood so often conveniently removes the father from the scene.

The Great Lie (1941) is another film about motherhood that treats the male lead as a breeder for maternal fulfillment in the most blatantly cynical fashion. Although the two stars, Bette Davis and Mary Astor, are ostensibly rivals for the hero (George Brent, yet again), they are actually rivals in a motherhood sweepstakes in a strange, somewhat appalling story.

George Brent is a playboy who drinks too much. Although he and Bette Davis have been romantically inclined for years, Brent gets drunk and marries a famous concert pianist (Astor). Davis is shattered, and when Brent comes to see her afterward, she bursts out, "Every time I see you I feel like your old gray-haired mother." Their relationship is more mother to son than sexual, like the one he has with Astor.*

Davis acts as a mother adviser to Brent, always helping him be better than he wishes to be. She urges him to further his career in aviation, and tells everyone what a great mapper he is. Like a doting parent, she proudly brags, "He was made a member of the Royal Geographic Society last year." Davis would like to see Brent productively employed, but Astor likes him just the way he is, a naughty, slightly spoiled little boy to play with. In other words, Davis is a perfect mother to Brent. Astor, on the other hand, isn't even a perfect woman, much less a good mom. She's vain and selfish and career driven, although she is sexy. When Brent discovers that Astor's last divorce wasn't final when they wed, he does the gallant thing and offers to remarry her "next Tuesday." She is playing a concert in Philadelphia

---

* Technically, the subject of motherhood in the woman's film also applies to an alarming number of marriages and love affairs in which the primary role the woman is playing vis-à-vis the man is that of mother, not sexual partner or friend or companion or lover. Women's desire to mother men crops up everywhere, in remarks such as "You look just like a little boy caught stealing jam" made to an unfaithful husband found out by Mary Astor in Smart Woman (1931), and in films like the two versions of The Corn Is Green (1945 and 1979), in which a spinster schoolteacher furthers the intellectual career of a young Welsh coal miner. An unusual case is that of The Flame Within (1935), starring Ann Harding as a successful psychiatrist. This woman rejects marriage to a faithful suitor with these words, "No work? No work? Just Mrs. Gordon Phillips, housewife? Oh, what did I give up my youth for? Why did I give up most of my life to this thing if I were just to forget it and throw it away as if it had never been . . . it's more than a profession. It's a religion." Nevertheless, she falls in love with a very young man she is helping, and he becomes an obsession with her. It's obvious he is as much a child for her as a man, particularly since a handsome and successful mature man is part of her life already. Harding, the determined career woman, actually needs to mother someone. In the end, she agrees to marry the older man. While her intended and his best male friend look happy at the news, she looks terrible and sad, defeated. Love and motherhood have wrecked the self-confidence her career gave her.

that day, however, and the conflict makes its own statement. They do not remarry, and instead Brent marries Davis, who is thrilled about it. ("Marriage is a step," Brent's lawyer advises him. "It's a leap," answers Brent, who should know, since he does it twice in a two-week period.) When Davis's faithful servant, played by Hattie McDaniel, hears that the two are going to marry, she begins to sing, "Slumber my darling, thy mother is near." McDaniel is a surrogate mother to Davis, who has no mother of her own. Thus, Davis alternates between being a child to McDaniel and a mother to Brent, until she takes over an actual baby.

When Brent and Davis marry, about twenty minutes of film time has passed. George Brent, having married two women in twenty minutes, now disappears totally from the frame. He does what woman's film men do: he flies off over the Brazilian jungle and gets lost. (If there is one thing we learn from old movies, it is never to fly an airplane over South America.) This liberates the movie to become the story it really is, which is not a romance but a story of a perfect if peculiar motherhood. Just before Brent disappears, Astor meets with Davis to tell her that she is going to have a baby. Astor isn't particularly interested in the child, but she *is* interested in getting Brent back.

After Brent's departure, Davis goes to Astor and presents her with one of the great crackpot deals in the history of the woman's film. Astor only wanted the child to get Brent back, and now he is gone, but Davis wants the child permanently, because it is Brent's. "We both love the same man," Davis points out. "He left us two things. I have his money, and you have his child." She proposes a business proposition—the money for the kid. "You'll ensure my future, and I'll ensure yours." Davis feels that Astor can't go on playing concerts forever, and this will make her financially secure, while she herself will have a purpose in life through Astor's child. "We'll go away together secretly . . . with a truce until it's over," announces Davis firmly.

This generates a truly bizarre episode. Astor and Davis, two great woman stars, both giving terrific performances, go to a shack in Arizona. While Davis stalks around in pants and jodhpurs, Astor lounges around in a chenille housecoat and big sweaters. They argue. They play cards and take walks. Davis acts as a jailer, and Astor is the inmate. Davis mothers Astor in an absurd way, making her take her pills, eat correctly, and cut down on smoking and drinking. Davis treats Astor as if she were a child or her own wife! When she gets up in the night to catch Astor making herself an illegal sandwich, Davis stops her cold. Astor cries out, "I'm a musician. I'm an artist! I have zest and appetite!" Finally, their relationship erupts into a physical fight in which Astor tries to run away. "You make me sick!" she yells at Davis, and even tries to throw a lit lantern to set the house on fire. Finally she stops short and screeches in frustration at the top of her lungs. Davis slaps her, hard, and Astor collapses.

What a scene! If there is a better movie portrait of a woman who is fiercely angry at being pregnant and restricted, I can't imagine what it is. Bette Davis and Gene Tierney abort their babies in *Beyond the Forest* and *Leave Her to Heaven*, respectively, but this is a scene without such a specific purpose. It is a pure, unfocused expression of female rage at the condition of being a woman who must give up her glamorous life and career, however temporarily, and go to live in a cage with a keeper.

While the baby is being born, Davis stalks around outside like the expectant father, which, in essence, she is. Davis becomes both surrogate mother and surrogate father. As they wait, the doctor pontificates, "A woman without a child is like a man without an arm, a right arm. I miss the father standing around and gettin' in everyone's way." Actually, Bette Davis, wearing men's clothes, is standing around and getting in everyone's way, but the doctor doesn't seem to notice.

After the male child is born and Davis returns to Maryland, the heart of the film is over. Its core is the long birth sequence in the Arizona shack. With the child in the picture, George Brent is now free to return to the plot, and back he comes. (He has evidently used his excellent mapping skills to find his way out of the jungle.)

Ultimately, the moment comes when Davis and Astor must fight each other. When Astor arrives in Maryland, she challenges Davis openly for not being honest with Brent. "Why didn't you tell him the truth when he came back?"

Davis tells Astor it's because her only motivation was the child. "Your part was finished the minute you gave that baby to me. From that day on, I had only one purpose in mind, to make that baby mine."

Astor sneers at this. "I'd be too proud to hold a man with another woman's child."

As their conflict unfolds, it is clear that Astor's motive is to retrieve Brent and bring him back to resume their sexual passion and playful life. Davis's is to keep the child, to whom she is a devoted mother. Although Davis is ostensibly in love with Brent, and he certainly is with her, her character is defined by her willingness to accept Brent's child even when he has been born to another woman. Davis is perfect because she is mother to both child and father and willing to accept anything on behalf of both of them.

In the grand finale, Davis explains everything to Brent while Astor sits by. Brent, looking deeply puzzled, asks what Astor wants. Davis explains that Astor wants to take the child because he is hers. "Well," says Brent, "he's a fine little chap, and we'll miss him." Since Astor doesn't really want the child, only the man that fathered him, she stalks to the piano and begins to play a wild concerto. When Davis asks Astor what she will do with the boy, she says coldly, "I'm leaving him with his mother." Davis, the perfect mother, wins back both of her two children, father and son. Perfection in motherhood can exist only when cut loose from a sexual desire like Astor's, and when the woman's primary interest is in possessing the child.

Dr. Monica (1934), a top contender in the crackpot-plot sweepstakes, is another example of a perfect-motherhood movie in which the women do everything and the man is little more than a sperm bank. Kay Francis plays a famous and successful obstetrician, and Warren William is her equally famous and successful writer husband. They are part of a sophisticated set in which everyone, including the women, seems to have a glamorous occupation. In addition to Dr. Monica herself, there is Verree Teasdale, her best friend, who is an architect, and a famous literary critic played by Ann Shoemaker. The only person who has no occupation is the beautiful Jean Muir. ("Have you any profession, Miss Hathaway?" asks the literary critic. "No," says Muir, "I just hang around.")

Dr. Monica and her husband are happy but busy; they have a difficult time finding any time to be with each other. Teasdale tells them, "There's only one way for you two lovebirds to really get together and that's for Monica to give up delivering babies or John to stop writing." "I'm willing," says William, "but how do we decide which?" He inadvertently articulates the larger problem.

Dr. Monica's chief aim in life is to be a mother. Since she is unable to have her own children, she mothers her husband, following after him as he prepares to go outside, tucking his scarf firmly around his neck. "Yes, Mother," he tells her. "I should be your mother," she replies. "You're such a little boy." He is not, as it turns out, such a little boy that he has not fathered a child with someone else. He has been having an affair with Jean Muir, the woman who just hangs around, although he is now going to Europe for six months as a polite way of breaking it off. He really loves Dr. Monica, he has just realized. "I want you to snap out of it, my dear," he tells Muir. "I want you to forget me." He leaves for Europe confident that she will do so, without realizing she is going to have his child.

While William is in Europe, Dr. Monica befriends Muir, seeing her through her pregnancy with the help of Teasdale. When the two of them arrive at the country house where they plan to deliver Muir's child secretly, Dr. Monica accidentally discovers that the father of Muir's baby is actually her own husband. She stomps downstairs to Teasdale, announcing, "It's John's baby." "Oh, no," says Teasdale sympathetically, but when Dr.

Monica says she's not going to do another thing, refusing to deliver the child, Teasdale slaps her smartly on the face. "You're a doctor under oath," she snaps. "Deliver her child!" "Thanks," says Dr. Monica, and goes upstairs to do her job, having been reminded that she's not a woman but a doctor. "I'm a doctor now. A machine."*

At first, neither Dr. Monica nor Jean Muir wants to have anything to do with the little female baby that is born, but soon enough they are both reconciled to their roles as nurturing women. Dr. Monica places the child in Muir's arms, and the two women smile tenderly at each other. They have produced a child, and now they will see that it is well cared for and loved. It is the baby that counts; the man has become irrelevant. A tale of perfect motherhood is being told.

Later, Dr. Monica and Teasdale talk it all over again. Teasdale advises the good doctor to "keep your husband . . . don't give him an inkling [about what has happened]." Dr. Monica, however, has another plan. She will go away with her husband for a glorious interlude of happiness for two weeks, a second honeymoon, and then she will tell him the truth, stepping aside so that he and Jean Muir and the baby can all be together. "But, Monica," says Teasdale, "that's so stupid." The film ends with Teasdale alerting Muir to the impending sacrifice so that Muir is able to get in first licks with her own sacrifice. She sends the baby to Dr. Monica and flies her airplane (she hangs around, but she does have a pilot's license) across the ocean, disappearing forever. This leaves Dr. Monica and the baby and Warren William all together. Dr. Monica calls her husband into the bedroom "for a surprise" and shows him the child lying on the bed.

"Why . . . why . . . what's that?" he asks, since no news of any baby has ever reached him.

"I've adopted her, John," Dr. Monica explains briskly.

The husband inquires as to who the parents are, but the doctor says she really feels it would be better if they never know.

"Monica," says her husband, "you will be so happy."

"Will you?" she asks.

"Your happiness is mine," he responds, so all is agreed upon.

Dr. Monica lifts the baby up and places her lovingly in her husband's arms, saying sweetly, "Hold her, John. She's yours." This leaves Dr. Monica as a woman who has had nothing to do with the biological birth of the baby totally in charge of the situation. Her husband will never know that, indeed, the baby *is* his, because he is a man in a woman's film, and

* This "you're either a woman or a doctor" mentality surfaces in other places in movies, including *Angel on the Amazon* (1948), which puts an audience straight about it. George Brent is bluntly told this about Constance Bennett: "She's not a woman. She's a doctor."

thus what he doesn't know will never hurt him. Dr. Monica and the girl who hung around have had a baby together, and it is not for the man to interfere with their perfect motherhood.

Perfection in motherhood is so powerful that it is apparently a two-way street, along which a child who has never seen his natural mother since he was a baby in swaddling clothes can nevertheless wake up out of a coma and instinctively recognize her. This situation, another worthy of a crackpot award, takes place in *Sarah and Son* (1930), starring Ruth Chatterton as a Dutch immigrant. It is a film that walks the usual woman's film line between sordid truth and delirious escapism. Chatterton is a singer who is trying to get work in vaudeville by pairing up with a lazy hunk she herself characterizes as "a big dumb baby." Her motherly instinct is so overdeveloped that she not only has raised her little sister back in the old country, planning to send for her when World War I ends, but she also mothers and looks after this male ne'er-do-well vaudeville partner. When she receives word that her sister is dead, the emotional collapse this loss brings on drives her permanently into the arms of the silly man she has been mothering.

A cut takes the viewer forward in time, directly from the embrace to the sight of a baby in a crib. Chatterton's life is now the low-down woman's world. While she cries out, "you lazy loafer," her husband lies asleep on their bed. They need rent money, as eviction looms, and the baby needs milk. "Here I am with a little baby and not one dollar," says Chatterton, stating clearly the woman's film dilemma. A sordid situation is depicted in which the couple quarrels, the man wants sex, and the woman just worries about the rent, the baby, and the food. "Why don't you stop thinking about the baby all the time and think of me?" whines the husband, who, to spite her, not only joins the Marines to escape but gives the baby away to rich strangers before he departs. Chatterton, after shrieking and running out into the streets, does the woman's film thing. She becomes a famous opera singer.

The plot ultimately reconnects Chatterton with her son when he is twelve or thirteen years old. Although he does not know she is his natural mother, the two, who have just met, go out on a small boat together. When the boat capsizes, she saves him. As the boy lies in a coma, Chatterton and his adoptive mother stand in the doorway of his room, eyeballing each other. "Mother?" the lad calls out, and though the adoptive mother starts to move forward, she instinctively hesitates, deferring to Chatterton, who graciously indicates that, no, the mother he believes to be his should go to him. "We'll both go," says this woman, not be outdone in the woman's sacrificial sweepstakes. As the two stand hovering over the poor boy, one on either side of his bed, he wakes up, takes a look around, and immediately

recognizes his real mother, reaching out to Chatterton. "He knows somehow." Somehow, indeed. "That's the answer," says the adoptive father.
"He's hers." The power of motherhood, of a woman's responsibility to her
own children that can never be denied, is strongly asserted by films like
Sarah and Son, which empower women as mothers and which suggest that
motherhood is such an awesome force of nature that it can apparently be
read by children no matter what.*

Among my favorite moments in these movies is one that occurs in *A
Child Is Born* (1940), a remake of the 1932 film *Life Begins*. In this
sequence, Gladys George, flat tummied, although she's due to give birth
to twins the next day, gets drunk in the maternity ward and entertains the
other patients with a tap dance. *A Child Is Born* is a series of interlocking
stories about women coming into the maternity hospital to give birth, a
prenatal Grand Hotel. The stereotypes are designed to present an overview
of perfect motherhood in all its guises and to suggest that perfection should
be the goal of all mothers, with each fulfilling the goal to the best of her
individual ability. These stereotypes also link the mothers once again to
the choices a woman has to make and to the sense that female fate is linked
to a choice about men. The women in the maternity ward are as follows:

- *An older woman (Spring Byington):* Every year she comes in to have
  another child. Her family comes with her, all cheerful and bouncy,
  with the mother telling everyone she knows the way upstairs and with
  the nurse on duty heartily explaining, "She's our best customer."
- *A murderess (Geraldine Fitzgerald):* Brought in from prison to give
  birth, she's sort of a fugitive from another kind of movie. To top it
  off, she's got "medical problems."
- *A show-business floozy (Gladys George):* Her husband does not want
  the child and warns her that if she misses their booking because of
  this, he'll go on without her, hiring someone else.

---

* It is interesting to note that this amazing ability of the son to identify his birth mother
by instinct can work both ways. In *The Sin of Madelon Claudet*, Helen Hayes gets out of
prison after ten years and walks into a charity school and automatically knows which young
boy is hers, although he was only three years old when she saw him last. *The Sin of Madelon
Claudet*, for which Hayes won an Oscar for Best Actress in 1932, is a textbook case for
the woman's film. Hayes is deserted by her wealthy young American lover, has a child out
of wedlock, trusts irresponsible friends, becomes the mistress of a wealthy jewel thief, goes
to prison for a crime she didn't commit, is forced into prostitution to send her son to medical
school after pretending to him that "his mother" is dead. A pre-code movie, *Madelon
Claudet* pulls no punches. It's clear that Hayes is a prostitute, and she is shown at first
totally rejecting her newborn infant. Once the child is placed in her arms, however, she's
a cooked goose, sacrificing her entire life to the task of raising him and giving him a chance
in polite society. Hayes also ages into a decrepit old crone, ending up about seventy, while
her son goes from age thirteen to twenty-five.

- *An eighteen-year-old girl (Nanette Fabares, later Fabray):* Her "mother is not coming."
- *A woman who has been trying to have a child for years (Gloria Holden):* She cannot give birth to a live baby. She is nevertheless trying again.

These women represent various stages of perfection, which is partly related to their willingness to be breeders. They also illustrate a subtle subversion, in which women are not rejecting womanhood but are rejecting men. This is a film about motherhood that furthers the concept Charles Coburn was talking about in *The Impatient Years*. That is, that women are not only willing to be mothers, they welcome motherhood—in motherhood, they find perfection. It's men they don't want. Men are useful, necessary to get motherhood going, but after that they become problems, often interfering with the perfection, getting in its way.

In *A Child Is Born*, one man is actively opposed to his wife's impending motherhood, and that is Gladys George's husband. Another, the husband of Geraldine Fitzgerald, is also opposed, because he is forced by the difficult birth to choose between his wife's remaining alive and the child's being born alive. These two men, who try to stop their women's becoming mothers, as it were, are both proved wrong.

The stories are resolved in a torrent of perfection. First, the two unwilling husbands/fathers are dealt with. Since George's husband has told her the baby cannot interfere with her career, she is seen to be rejecting her motherhood initially because she loves her man and her job. However, when she gives birth to the twins, George at first ignores them, refusing to look at them or nurse them. When a welfare worker comes to take them to an orphanage so that George can rejoin her husband and resume her career, she suddenly comes alive, yelling, "You want to know about this mother? Well, I want to tell you about her. I want to tell you about a dame who got kicked around every inch of the way for every little thing. Who met a heel and fell in love with him. Who up to now didn't know what the score was and who almost made her children go through what she did, but who's changed her mind." George takes her twins. Noticing that the poor woman who's tried to give birth over and over again has borne yet another dead baby, she realizes that she has conveniently produced two, so that there's one for her and one for the bereaved woman. She generously shares, and both women are perfectly fulfilled.

The young girl whose mother isn't coming is presented as if she might be an unwed mother. She is actually married, but she and her husband are terribly young, and their parents disowned them because of their elopement. Just before her child is born, this girl's mother bursts into the room, welcoming the impending arrival of her grandchild. "Will you forgive me?"

asks the young mother. "Of course I forgive you. I'm your mother" is the reply. Two generations of potentially perfect motherhood are reunited.

Spring Byington, who might as well be Andy Hardy's mom or Tom Edison's or Roddy McDowall's, gives birth to her latest child, and her entire brood, all of whom are perfectly mothered, welcome the baby and their own mother's return home. This leaves only the poor murderess, Geraldine Fitzgerald, to complete the circle of perfect motherhood for this maternity ward. Fitzgerald's story is one of perfection, but also sacrifice. If she allows her baby to be born, she will die because of her "medical problems." As a matter of fact, she is probably facing the electric chair anyway, but her husband does not want her to die. When asked, "Shall we save the mother or the child?" he chooses the mother. When Fitzgerald hears this, she tells him no, no, no. "I don't think a woman's lived until she has given birth." She forces him to understand that she must be the one to die. The last we see of this man is in a scene in which a nurse is saying to him, "At the very end your wife came to, just so I could tell you, it's her gift to you." The nurse then places a baby daughter in the husband's arms, while he stands there looking bewildered.

During this movie that stresses the strength and courage of women, the men involved all demonstrate weaknesses. They pace nervously while waiting for the birthing to be over, looking terrified. They get drunk or stand around awed and slack jawed over what their women are doing in these hospital rooms. The women are made strong and brave by the sanctity of childbearing. The experience changes them, and their priorities shift, whereas the men remain fixed and inadequate to the challenge. By rising up and accepting nature, the women show audiences how to be perfect mothers. Realizing that the men aren't strong enough to count is a part of that process. This is an aspect to women's movies that cannot be ignored. Although they are geared toward keeping women in the role of wife and mother, they nevertheless tell them that men are useless. They suggest that once a baby is born, a woman doesn't really need a man all that much.

MOTHERS WHO honestly support their daughters in positive ways are interestingly represented in two contrasting cases: Anne Revere as Elizabeth Taylor's mother in *National Velvet* (1944) and Marjorie Rambeau as Ginger Rogers's mother in *The Primrose Path* (1940). Two more different women could not exist, and yet they share ideas and goals for the children. Anne Revere is a mother who in her youth was a champion Channel swimmer, a woman who won a large monetary award for her courage and her ability. She is now happily wed to a grocer, working side by side with him in their store, their chores equally divided in terms of importance. In their pleasant home she is a strong presence, especially in the lives of her daughters, one of whom is the dreamy, passionate Velvet, brought to life exquisitely by the quality and unreal beauty of the young Elizabeth Taylor.

Velvet dreams the impossible dream of entering her horse, Pi, in the Grand National Sweepstakes. No one quite takes her seriously, particularly because there is no way she can obtain the entry-fee money. A dramatic moment arrives in which the mother takes her daughter upstairs into the attic where she keeps her prize money in an old trunk. Slowly opening the trunk, she tells Velvet that *everyone* ought to have a dream and a chance to realize it. Speaking carefully, she tells her daughter that she must remember that entering her horse in the Grand National will *be* her dream, but then it will be over, having to last her a lifetime. It is one of the greatest of all screen moments between a mother and a daughter. (And Revere won a Supporting Actress Oscar for it.)

Rambeau is quite another sort of mother. She is, in fact, a prostitute whose own mother apparently had been in the same trade, a sort of low-grade *Gigi* (1958) operation. Instead of being elegant courtesans who drink champagne, eat ortolans, and sing about it, the women of *Primrose Path* barely keep body and soul together, grateful for a hot meal in their tar-paper railroad shack. Rambeau, however, like Anne Revere, is a mother who understands life, her daughter, and what her daughter's life both should be and will be. Wed to a drunkard and bearing the sole responsibility for feeding herself, her two daughters, and her slovenly mother, Rambeau remains kind, cheerful, and even optimistic—at least on the surface. When she realizes that her oldest daughter, Ginger Rogers, has fallen in love for the first time, she explains her own life: "Pa's weak and he drinks a lot. Anyhow, well, I made my bargain and I'll stick by it. Somebody's gotta take care of the family, and while it might not be the best I asked for, I done the best I knew how." This is her explanation about her own "romantic" life, a few words about why love eluded her, and an oblique reference as to why she goes with men to put bread on the table. After Rogers departs, dressed up for the first time in her life, full of love and desire as she starts out to search down her man, Rambeau goes back into the hovel in which she lives and starts to weep. "Poor Ellie Mae," she cries, "poor little Ellie Mae." It's sisterhood between mother and daughter. Later, as she lies on her deathbed, Rambeau tells Rogers, "It ain't all been fun, baby. I laughed a lot of times when I didn't feel like laughin', and I cried a lot of times when I didn't feel like cryin'." As a mother, she is generous and kind, and as a woman, she does, as she says, "the best" she knew how.

Revere and Rambeau, however, are not typical movie moms. There are two basic types of perfect: the dream moms—the stout, middle-aged makers of pie and washers of underwear—and the mothers that leading ladies frequently turn into: the competent, efficient moms who need no men to stand alongside them in the job.

The difference between these two types lies in purpose. Is the film glorifying the role of motherhood, to sell it to women? Is it celebrating the concept, so more women will do it? Or is it connecting to the kind of woman who really does see motherhood as her only road to power and importance? In other words, is the role of motherhood being defined for men in the audience or for women?

SACRIFICIAL MOTHERHOOD

TWO STORIES of sacrificial mother love illustrate the concept at the same time as they provide an excellent contrast in attitudes toward it. *Stella Dallas* (1937 version) and *Blonde Venus* (1932) are two unquestionably great films directed by cinematic geniuses (King Vidor and Josef von Sternberg, respectively). They star two of Hollywood's most individual women in their title roles, with Barbara Stanwyck as Stella and Marlene Dietrich as the blond Venus. *Stella Dallas* and *Blonde Venus* have been written about and analyzed extensively by scholars from such different angles as auteurism, star power, feminism, Marxism, structuralism. I believe that they are best understood in relation to each other, as they demonstrate clearly how movies provide different attitudes toward what is ostensibly the same thing.

Stella Dallas is a movie worthy of the word "tearjerker." People who watch it and don't cry are probably dead, and if they're not, they should be. Stanwyck's portrait of the poor girl who marries out of her class is a performance of great sensitivity and depth, and it is a crime she lost out on the Oscar for it. (She was beaten by the ridiculous Luise Rainer in *The Good Earth*.) Stella is a woman so disenfranchised by life that she feels she's not even entitled to her own child. Her story illustrates how few options a woman has, and how easily the ones she does have are taken from her. Although she is a loving mother and leads a respectable life, Stella ends up losing everything because she is a woman.

Stella's story is the story of a young and pretty girl in Milhampton, Massachusetts, in 1919. Like all women in all movie mill towns, she dreams of better things, and to try to get them she has taken a business course to improve herself. Her family is poor, and its house is cheap, but she hopes

The Most Precious Thing in Life: Jean Arthur hovers over Richard Cromwell, who doesn't know that she's his mom. (A good example of the theory of accordioning time: Arthur was only about twenty when Sonny was born.)

to catch the eye of the handsome John Boles who is working his way up in the management end of the factories.

John Boles's back story is a woman's film in and of itself. Once a wealthy and irresponsible playboy, he has had to go to work because his millionaire father went bankrupt and killed himself. Although Boles was scheduled to marry his childhood sweetheart, played by Barbara O'Neil, he has disappeared, leaving a note saying that he has to make a life for himself elsewhere. He did not feel he could marry O'Neil while penniless, and as the story begins, she has given up and married someone else. Stanwyck chases Boles, hatching a plot to take her brother's lunch down to the factory so she can meet him. Lonely and sad, he responds to her beauty and spunk, and they impulsively marry. He knows he is marrying out of his class, but Stanwyck is radiant and eager to learn, and he feels he can teach her.

The marriage is briefly shown to be incompatible through the metaphor of their attending a dance right after their daughter, Laurel, is born. Stanwyck wants to have fun and is loud, raucous, and attracted to a table of shady types headed by Alan Hale. Boles is quiet, sticking to the mannered, management set. Boles is a man who does not understand a woman like Stanwyck. He restricts her natural instincts and, in attempting to teach her, represses her. When he tries to tell her to dress more simply, she blurts out that she has "stacks of style . . . allow me at least to know more about one thing than you do."

The marriage drifts apart, as Boles takes a promotion in New York, leaving Stanwyck behind with Laurel (Anne Shirley) in New England. As he goes up in the world, he has asked his wife to "give up a few things, adapt yourself." She fights back by saying, "I don't see you giving up anything. How about you adapting, for a change?" As the years pass, Laurel grows into a lovely young girl. Although Stella is chaste and a devoted mother, she is noisy, common, and badly dressed. She is frequently cranky with Laurel, but always loving, and Laurel adores her. Lonely without her husband, Stanwyck becomes good friends with Alan Hale, but there is no indication that their relationship is physical. He would marry her if she would consider it, but as she tells him, "I don't think there's a man living that could get me going anymore. I guess Lolly [Laurel] just uses up all the feelings I've got, and I don't seem to have any for anybody else."

Four accidents of fate occur in *Stella Dallas*, and each one represents the judgment of society on Stella, a judgment that will ultimately force her to give up her child. Each event brings on a specific social reaction that results in a rejection of Stella as a mother.

- *First Event:* Alan Hale, who has not seen Stanwyck in a long time, drops in on her unexpectedly, bringing a pal with him. Stanwyck, who also has a female friend visiting her, is sitting and feeding the baby.
  Social observation and reaction: Boles comes home, also unexpect-edly, and seeing Hale in his shirtsleeves, holding the child, misun-derstands. He believes he sees a partying foursome.
  Rejection: Boles begins to believe that Stanwyck lives loosely while he is not there and speaks for the first time of taking Laurel away from her.
- *Second Event:* Stanwyck goes with Alan Hale on a train to the city to buy special things for Laurel's birthday party. On the way home, Hale is drinking, and although Stanwyck is not herself behaving improperly, the two of them are loud and foolish.
  Social observation and reaction: They are observed by one of Laurel's teachers from school, as well as the mother of one of the young women invited to the party. They are horrified, believing

Stanwyck to be out drinking with a man who is not her husband. *Rejection:* The teacher sends a note saying she will not be able to attend Laurel's party. Soon phone calls indicate no one else will be coming either.

- *Third Event:*   At Christmastime, Alan Hale again drops in unexpectedly, bringing Stanwyck a turkey. Laurel is now a teenager. Hale is terribly drunk and difficult to manage. While he and Stanwyck are struggling in the kitchen, Boles arrives for his holiday visit with his daughter. Stanwyck puts Hale out the back door and dresses herself simply, the way Boles likes. As he invites her to come out with Laurel and himself, Hale barges back in, falling down and raucous.

Social observation and reaction: Boles again misunderstands, turning cold and taking Laurel away with him.

Rejection: Boles now completely believes wrong things about Stella's friendship with Hale. All possibility of reconciliation or contact between them ends.

- *Fourth Event:*   Stella has been sick while Laurel has enjoyed bicycling and playing games with her wealthy friends at a posh hotel they visit together. Finally feeling better, Stella dresses up in a garish, cheap manner that she herself believes to be beautiful. Going downstairs into the lobby and dining areas, she behaves in what she believes is the manner of a grand lady. Actually, she is too loud, too vulgar, and too obvious. People laugh behind her back. She walks around the grounds, ending up in the little drugstore where Laurel and her friends have gone to have a soda.

Social observation and reaction: As Stella enters the drugstore, with all her bangle bracelets jangling, her cheap fox fur draped over her shoulders, the young people one by one begin to notice her. As they whisper, point, and laugh, Laurel is too busy talking to respond. Suddenly, she looks into the mirror over the soda fountain and for the first time sees her mother as society sees her.

Rejection: Although Laurel never mentions this incident to her mother, she begs that they leave the hotel. The rejection of Stella by the wealthy society Laurel has entered naturally leads to Stella's ultimate rejecting of herself as an appropriate mother for Laurel.

Each of these four events takes Stella Dallas one step further toward the loss of self-respect that will end in her giving up her child. This act of sacrifice is defined by society's view of a woman. In each case, Stella has actually done nothing wrong, but Stella is victimized by social attitudes and, of course, by her own lack of education, grace, and taste. Stella Dallas has to learn the hard way what is expected of her. It isn't enough to *be* a good mother; she has to *look* like a good mother. In other words, she has to conform to society's ideas about motherhood, and this she does not do well.

Laurel twice looks at her mother in a mirror and sees her differently than she did before. The first occasion occurs when the daughter returns home from meeting the perfect mother that John Boles's former sweetheart, Barbara O'Neil, has become. This woman is now widowed, and the mother of three boys. She is also wealthy and the ideal mate for Boles. She is kind and generous and welcomes Laurel as the daughter she doesn't have. When Laurel returns to Stella, she sees her mother smearing cold cream on her face and dying the roots of her peroxided hair. Looking at her mother in the mirror and obviously thinking of the contrast, Laurel kindly and gently says, "Let me do that," and takes the hair dye to touch up the roots herself. Although she is aware of the difference between her perfect "mother" and her real mother in looks, she does not yet see her mother as society does.

This tragedy occurs the second time she sees her mother's reflection—in the drugstore where her friends are laughing at Stella. When she looks up and sees Stella's image in the mirror over the soda fountain, for the first time she truly sees how her mother looks and acts. She runs out in shame and misery, but loyally returns to her mother. As they travel on the train homeward, each in her own Pullman berth, they overhear some of Laurel's friends gossiping about "Laurel's horrible mother." As Stanwyck reacts, she hears that her daughter will never marry the boy she loves because when his mother gets one look at Stella Dallas, "it will all be over." When Laurel creeps down to spy on her mother to see if she overheard, Stanwyck pretends to be asleep. As Laurel wakes her, she says, "It's lonely up there, Mother. I want to come down here and cuddle with you." Laurel draws back from her rich life, down to her mother's level out of love and loyalty, but Stanwyck will have none of it.

Two scenes of sacrifice follow. In the first, Stanwyck goes to O'Neil, and in the second she has to push Laurel overtly away. These scenes of mother love and sacrifice are impeccably performed by all the principals, and they are painful to watch. In the first, Stanwyck and O'Neil talk frankly, as women do in films. When asked if Boles would marry her if he were free, O'Neil says yes. Stanwyck then asks if they would take Laurel, too, if they married. "Oh, no!" cries O'Neil. "I'm a mother. Do you think I could deprive a mother of her own little girl?" But Stanwyck presses on. She says that if they married, and Laurel came to live with them, then "everyone would naturally think she was *your* little girl. You're the kind of a mother that any girl would be proud of." Suddenly understanding what is happening, O'Neil begins to touch Stanwyck's arm, drawing near to her and murmuring, "I didn't know anyone could be so unselfish." "In a little while, she'll forget all about me," says Stanwyck. Without either of them actually saying that Laurel's future will be ruined socially if Stanwyck remains with her, they come to a full understanding. And why not? They are both women, experienced in the social-observation-and-rejection game. Stanwyck says Laurel is a nice girl, and O'Neil replies, "And I know it hasn't come only from her father."

Having made this sacrifice, Stanwyck leaves, but things are not this simple. Laurel loves her mother and feels that she couldn't possibly leave her and come to live with her father and O'Neil. "Your mother will always be your mother," they tell her, but she isn't having any. She realizes her mother is making this gesture because she wasn't asleep on the train after all, and Laurel tries to make her own sacrifice. She cannot live or marry into a world in which there is no room for her mother, no matter how much she might wish to do so. She tells her father that she lived with her mother all those years "when I needed her, and now she needs me."

Laurel returns home, and Stanwyck has to make a second, even greater sacrifice for her child. In a sequence that is almost too painful to watch, Stanwyck gets Alan Hale, now a hopeless drunkard, to pretend that he and Stella are to marry. Letting herself look rough and cheap, Stanwyck lights a cigarette, plays honky-tonk music, and says to Laurel, "A woman wants to be something else besides a mother, you know." Laurel, a sensitive and virginal teenager, is horrified. When she returns to Boles and O'Neil, she shows them a note from her mother in which she is told that Alan Hale and Stanwyck will marry and leave town.

Stella Dallas frees her daughter from loving her by pretending she doesn't want her. She not only has to give her daughter up, she also has to lose her daughter's love. This is the definition of sacrificial motherhood: no matter what, the woman must give up anything and everything for herself so that her child will have a better life. Laurel has said, "My home will be with my mother as long as I live." Stella knows that if Laurel does this, she will end up without any kind of life of her own, and certainly without the life Stella feels she is entitled to.

At the end of the movie, Barbara O'Neil, the sisterhood woman who understands, opens the front curtains of her mansion on the day Laurel is to marry. The wedding will take place in front of this large picture window. Although Laurel wonders why her mother hasn't ever written to her or come for the wedding, O'Neil explains that it is doubtless because she doesn't know. As Laurel is married, Stanwyck stands outside. Dressed in shabby clothes, tears in her eyes, she watches her only child marry, but her face is radiant with joy and pride. Her sacrifice means something to her. Although the pain of being on the outside looking in exists for the viewer, for Stella Dallas it is a triumph of sacrificial motherhood, a job well done.

THAT *Stella Dallas* and *Blonde Venus* could be produced by the same system within a few years of each other, and be aimed at the same general public yet be so different, demonstrates clearly what Hollywood was all about: ambivalence. All attitudes and all opinions, all options and all contradictions.

In *Blonde Venus* (1932), Marlene Dietrich also makes a maternal sacrifice, and what a sacrifice! First of all, her downward journey is undertaken as an act of protest. Her story is the opposite of Stanwyck's in that, from the beginning, she is seen as a potential power figure. She is a woman who works (as a cabaret singer), but she is also a Lorelei who attracts and thus controls the gaze of men. The first sight of her in the film is one of her swimming naked and free. When she later becomes the wife of scientist Herbert Marshall, it is not a case of a woman's slyly tricking a man into marrying her. It is a case of a man naturally falling under the spell of an incredible, seductive woman who chooses to give a man her attention. After their marriage and the birth of their son, Dietrich leads the life of a typical wife and mother. However, Marshall contracts a rare radium poisoning that requires him to go to Europe for an operation or else die. Dietrich overrules his objections and returns to work as a cabaret singer in order to pay for his trip. Unbeknownst to Marshall, she is not only singing "Hot Voodoo" at the nightclub, but she has also undertaken an affair with the wealthy Cary Grant, who advances the money she needs to save her husband.

When Marshall returns from his cure sooner than expected, he discovers that Dietrich is living with Grant and, in a rage, threatens to take their son from her. Dietrich runs away and embarks on a cat-and-mouse game with Marshall's detectives. She travels the country, singing whenever she can, and doing dishes or whatever men force her to do to earn a living. She ends up in Galveston as a streetwalker. Along the way, she cares for her son carefully, teaching him to read and feeding him his orange juice. This solicitous mother love, which is presented sincerely, is nevertheless undercut and contradicted by Dietrich's going out to perform a song called "You Little So-and-So." "You little so-and-so," sings Dietrich. ("Don't forget to lock the door," she has told him.) "Although you know I've lost my control, you sit and talk . . ." ("Finish your orange juice.") "You little so-and-so. Look what you've done to me." ("How about a kiss?") Mother love, and where it puts you in life, are presented in a highly ironic context.

Dietrich finally realizes that she isn't going to be able to care properly for her son while in hiding. She gives her son up, by her own choice.

Dietrich's act of sacrifice, like Stanwyck's, is voluntary, but her story is different. Dietrich has not been pure. She has not lived according to the correct dictates of society and has not merely been misunderstood by its sense of her improper appearance. She has done what she has had to do to keep her child, but she is able to control his destiny until she decides it's wrong for him. Taking the money her husband pays her back for his operation, she gets royally drunk and ends up in a flophouse. She has hated saying good-bye to her child and has felt insulted by Herbert Marshall's pompous presentation of the money. Handing her the cash as if she were a whore, he has said, "It represents my life's work. Had I time to exploit it properly, I could have made a fortune." Instead, he has sold his radium experimentation for enough to repay her so that he can feel rid of her and clean again. (In a cruel parody of what Marshall has said to her, she scornfully repeats his words to a flophouse woman she gives money away to: "It represents my life's work. Had I time to exploit it properly, I could have made a fortune." The entire concept of a man and his pride in his work and ability to earn is mocked by Dietrich's repeating Marshall's pompous, and even smug, speech.)

The surface story of *Blonde Venus* is a conventional tale of sacrificial motherhood. Its cinematic presentation, however, tells—or at least sug- gests—a different story, or a second way of seeing the events. This duality, indigenous to the woman's film, is here a consciously defined part of the movie presentation.

First of all, there is a parallel established between a man's selling his body and a woman's selling hers. The first image of the movie is that of a naked female body swimming in a sylvan pool. Within minutes, Herbert Marshall, now a married man with a child, goes to a doctor and says, "I want to sell you my body." He has come to try to obtain money for his body, either alive or dead—he not only needs money for treatments, but he has to think of how to provide for his wife and child after he is gone. "I want to sell you my body," he says, but unfortunately there is no market for a radiated male body. "I could give you fifty dollars," says the doctor sympathetically, offering charity.

Marlene Dietrich, on the other hand, can sell her body to the highest bidder. She becomes employed to step out of a gorilla suit, wearing prac- tically nothing, while singing and dancing in a nightclub. When spotted by the wealthy Cary Grant, she immediately "earns" more money. Although the film establishes that Grant loves her, and she returns his feelings, it is also made clear that his finances save her husband's life. Dietrich and Grant are shown to be lovers, so that Dietrich has, in fact, sold her body with excellent economic results. Later, Dietrich will have to sell her body with lower economic returns in order to survive, but she is always able to sell it and to make her living accordingly.

Dietrich represents two attitudes in the movie. On the one hand, she is a hausfrau, caring ably for both her husband and her child. She is seen washing her son, picking up dirty dishes and clothes, and scurrying about in her little home. She wears simple blouses and tucks straying hairs back into her sensible bun. On the other hand, she is also seen wearing furs and glittering costumes. She stands in front of men and women, drawing all eyes to her. She keeps a mocking smile on her lips and a hand on her hip as she sings ironic lyrics about love and sex. She is a wife and mother, and she is a sex symbol. She is a little homemaker, and she is a cabaret star. Between these two worlds, represented by the two men, Herbert Marshall and Cary Grant, lies a small strip of transition in which Dietrich muses to Marshall, "I could earn that money by going back to the stage." When he protests that he doesn't want her to work, she finally overrules him, saying, "I'm going to do something to give you a chance to get well." Like a good mother, she will take care of him.

Dietrich activates the Venus or Lorelei inside herself, the part that she has repressed in order to be a wife and mother. Dietrich's duality is, of course, most perfectly represented in the famous "Hot Voodoo" number discussed in the chapter called "Fashion and Glamour." When she emerges from the gorilla suit, she even sings about her duality. "I'd follow a caveman right into his cave. My conscience wants to take a vacation. Make me brave. I want to misbehave. The drums bring out the devil inside me. I want to be bad. Hot voodoo! Burn my clothes!" (When a woman in the movies says "Burn my clothes," something serious is going on.) After her decision to return to work is made, a significant scene occurs. Dietrich, active and energized, flurries around their apartment, packing her clothes and makeup, dictating orders to Marshall about what he should feed their little son and when he should put the child to bed while she's away. The son trails along after his mother, trying to help her, and Marshall stands, inactivated and passive, at the edge of frame left, feebly bemoaning the fact that she is returning to work. "I hate to see you do this," he says, but she overrules him again: "Don't. Don't make it too difficult." All movement and energy, all purpose and direction, are related to the female form in this sequence.

Later, as Dietrich reels around the flophouse, she suddenly says, "I'm not going to stay in this dump anymore. I'm going to find myself a better bed. Don't you think I can? Just wait." This speech dissolves into a series of images that show water, travel, and the rise to stardom of Helen Jones. The next time the audience sees Marlene Dietrich on the screen, she is fully restored to power. As the curtains open on a stage, she walks out to a packed and wildly cheering audience in Paris. Dressed head to toe like a man, in a stark white tuxedo and top hat, Dietrich carries an exceedingly long cigarette holder on which she puffs from time to time. Wearing her very best mocking smile, she casually acknowledges the cheering, pausing to touch one of the chorus girls gyrating by her. She sings, first in French and then in English: "If the moon could waltz . . . do you think I'd care? I couldn't be annoyed. I'd still eat crackers in my bed. What have I got to lose?" Her song is one of a woman totally rejecting everything a normal person ought to get excited over or any rules she might be expected to obey. "I couldn't be annoyed." Back in her dressing room, on her mirror, are the words, "Down to Gehenna or up to the throne, he travels fastest who travels alone."

Marlene Dietrich has been a sacrificial mother, giving up her child to her husband because, as she says, she is "no good for anything except to give up the kid before it's too late." She has heard a judge in a court say to her, "A woman who leads the sort of life you do has no right to the custody of a small child." Dietrich has replied, "I do the best I can." But she knows what the court means, and finally she sacrifices her child. Her husband is a fool with a double standard, but she gives her child to him for the child's sake, because of society's point of view.

Without her child, Dietrich becomes a star, a power figure. She will never stand outside a mansion and watch him marry. On the contrary, she ends up getting him back, as she and Marshall are reunited through the efforts of Cary Grant. *Blonde Venus* acts out the sacrificial-mother motif and undermines it with song, costuming, image, and contrast. It allows a woman to make a mockery of sacrifice and to demonstrate that sacrifice can, after all, be a positive and liberating choice, and not just a decision dictated to her. Sacrifice is as sacrifice does. Onward to stardom, and a white tuxedo. Dietrich turns sacrificial motherhood into a power maneuver.

In the end, Dietrich—restored to Marshall's love—is once again singing her son to sleep and caring for him. In *Blonde Venus*, it is inevitable that the mother will regain her child, because her sacrifice, unlike Stanwyck's, is not a true female sacrifice. *Blonde Venus* is a story of a woman's power, and how she could use it if she chose to. It is in every way a mockery of the concept of motherly sacrifice, a movie that calls into question what the woman's role really is. While appearing to maintain the status quo of the early thirties story of sacrificial mother love, it provides the viewer with an undercurrent of other information.

• • •

THERE IS ONE other type of sacrificial motherhood, that in which the mother is not really the mother but is a surrogate mother. A long line of nannies and schoolteachers appear in movies that are women's pictures. These faithful creatures, who are always established as women who can't have children themselves or women whose lover or husband died, leaving them childless, face a constant pain of sacrifice. From year to year, from job to job, from class to class, they attach themselves to other people's children, only to have to part with them. These stories of sacrificial motherhood are always blatant and shameless tearjerkers. For instance, in *The Blue Veil* (1951) Jane Wyman plays a nanny who goes from family to family, having to leave each time as the child grows beyond needing her care. Schoolteachers like Claudette Colbert in *Remember the Day* (1941), May Robson in *Grand Old Girl* (1935), Jennifer Jones in *Good Morning, Miss Dove* (1955), and Martha Scott in *Cheers for Miss Bishop* (1941) devote their lives to mothering and teaching countless children. In these cases, the children gather at the end of the woman's life to thank her for her teaching, in a kind of gigantic Mother's Day celebration. Colbert and Robson are shown to have taught presidents, and they have the glory of having "given birth" and "sacrificed" a great man to his people. In a sense, these mothers, who are almost always unwed but never destructive, are perfect, because they always nurture and serve, but they are presented to the viewer as sacrificial. This is because they must constantly give the child up for the child's own good or growth. The popularity of these films makes them important to remember. Again, there is an underlying sense that these women can earn money, be independent, and still have the joys of motherhood, although this sense is definitely one that a viewer must impose on the material. The movies themselves present the women as ideal examples of sacrificial motherhood, with the concept defined as an appropriate way for a woman to live her life if she has no man.

DESTRUCTIVE MOTHERHOOD

THE SINGLE GREATEST no-no of the woman's film is that of the destructive mother. Even a woman who kills is shown to have some logical motivation, some trauma that made her that way. Women who go crazy are presented sympathetically, and even nymphomaniacs and kleptomaniacs can have someone, anyone, cluck over them. But the destructive mother, no doubt a phenomenon far too many people had encountered on their own hometown streets, is a character for whom there is a total absence of sympathy in movies.

When a mother becomes destructive to either her son or her daughter, it is always because of some terrible lack in her own life. When Gene Raymond's mother interferes with his love for Barbara Stanwyck in *Shopworn*, she does it by pretending to have a heart attack so that Raymond will have to take her to Europe to rest. While they are away, she has her lawyer arrest Stanwyck on a trumped-up prostitution charge and send her to prison. Why does Mom do this? She fears that she will have no one to care for her in her old age. Mothers are jealous, and mothers are afraid. Mothers fear loss of control, and they fear loss of status and reputation. A destructive mother seen positively becomes a vengeful mother who is out to rescue her child from the clutches of a horrible potential mate, so that she becomes a perfect mother or perhaps a sacrificial one. The destructive mother is, finally, selfish, the one thing that women are always told is wrong for them ever to be.

Mothers who are destructive are either interfering in their children's love lives or in their careers. Where love is concerned, they are always trying to stop it, and where career is concerned, they are always trying to push it ahead. This further endorses the idea that a woman's proper choice in life is love. If her mother blocks it, an audience can see she is destructive. If she is trying to push her daughter into a career, she is also blocking love. Bad mothers of men are always trying to block love, since a man is allowed a career, and his mother wants him to have one.

When a mother does not do her job properly, the child's sex life is definitely ruined, unless the child—like Bette Davis in *Now, Voyager*— gets professional help and a long sea journey. The history of movies is full of crazy killers and nutty gangsters whose mothers have steered them in the wrong direction. From *White Heat* (1949) to *Psycho* (1960), these movies are legion. There are also examples of young women whose mothers have repressed them sexually (*Rachel, Rachel*, 1968), but the most interesting aspect to this phenomenon is the mother who causes her daughter to be *too* sexual. Either she does not love her enough, so the daughter seeks love from too many men, or she uses her daughter as a lure for wealthy men.

In the first category is a film like *Finishing School* (1934). The young Frances Dee is ignored by her society mother, Billie Burke, and shipped off to a school so that Burke is free to live her own life. Feeling unloved and neglected, Dee begins to run around with Ginger Rogers, learning to smoke, drink, cheat, and go out with fast boys. Dee equates the rules of her strict school with the rules of society. She sees the hypocrisy of the people who run things, and she is angry and unhappy. When she meets

up with a genuinely nice guy, played by Bruce Cabot, the school does not
want her to go out with him because he is only a waiter. They turn him
away at the door when he comes to see her. The "acceptable" boys Dee is
encouraged to date are actually drunks who party all night. Dee is disgusted
by this, and she also knows that the reason Cabot is working as a waiter
is to pay his way through medical school.

Dee's destructive mother, Billie Burke, nearly causes a tragedy. Dee
is left alone at school during the Christmas holidays, because both of her
parents have other plans and the other girls have gone to their families.
Dee has received a gift from each of her parents. Her dad has sent her a
letter, with a check for $1,000 so she can buy something for herself. Her
mother has sent her a mink coat. The box contains no card or personal
note of any kind, although the sales slip has been included (a charge for
$2,500). Dee realizes that her mother didn't even pick the coat out herself.

While she sits alone in her room with these two cold gifts, it begins
to snow. Dee looks out the window as her world turns even colder, and
she feels still more alone and isolated. Suddenly, she sees Bruce Cabot
standing outside, signaling her to meet him in the boat house. When she
joins him, they make a fire in the fireplace, creating the first warmth of
her holiday, and he presents her with a gift he has saved up his money to
buy her. It is a box of white handkerchiefs that he has had personalized
by having her name, Virginia, embroidered on each of them. Looking at
this gift, the only one she has received that in any way connects to her as
a human being, she breaks down and weeps. As Cabot is seen kissing her,
the camera moves outside to watch the tracks of their footsteps slowly filling
up with falling snow.

As a result of this one night (of course!), Dee becomes pregnant, an
unwed mother. There is a direct correlation established between her destructive mother's gift and this pregnancy. Dee tries to kill herself by leaping
off a balcony, but she is rescued in time by Cabot and also by her father,
who accepts Cabot and removes Dee from the dreadful finishing school.
Although her destructive mother nearly ruined her life, Dee survives.

ONE OF THE MOST common forms of destructive mother is the one who
drives her daughter toward a career. These mothers are women who want
things for themselves that their husbands cannot get for them. They want
excitement, jewels, clothes, and travel. They use their daughter's beauty,
talent, or sports ability to buy themselves into the world they have no access
to on their own. Because they are keeping their daughters from the natural
world of love, these mothers or mother figures are presented as completely
destructive. There are many examples, including *Hard, Fast and Beautiful*,

Claire Trevor as a Bad Tennis Mother
in *Hard, Fast and Beautiful*

Stage Mother, and *The Hard Way* (in which the mother is actually a sister).

    Hard, Fast and Beautiful (1951), one of the great titles for a film about a woman, is the story of a young girl pushed into a sports career by a destructive mother played by Claire Trevor. As the film opens, the daughter, Sally Forrest, is out in the yard smacking tennis balls against the garage while Trevor is inside cutting out patterns and sewing. Trevor's voice-over introduces the viewer to the story. "From the very moment you were born, I knew you were different. I could see things in you that no one else could. And I knew that somehow I was going to get the very best there was out of life for you . . . I always wanted something better for you, and I made up my mind to get it no matter what I had to do."

    Trevor's story is a common one for women in movies. She married when she was seventeen in order to get out of a crowded, noisy little house. "So then I got married," she says, "and guess what? Things were exactly the same." In other words, her story is just like Mildred Pierce's. But whereas Mildred starts working and baking to give everything *to* her daughter, Trevor starts manipulating and lying to get everything *from* her daughter. Trevor is shown rejecting the sexual advances of her nice-guy husband ("I've got a headache") and wheedling him to spend money beyond what he earns ("Couldn't we look for another house?"). When he doesn't go along with her schemes, she shouts, "Oh, you make me sick. You never cared about pushing yourself ahead. By gosh, my daughter's going to have everything. Everything I missed. She's gonna go places, with the right people." What she really means is that, together, *they* will go places, and Mom will meet the right people.

Trevor begins to manipulate her daughter's life, steering her toward a career as a tennis pro. In order to achieve this, she cuts her own husband out of her life, leaving him behind, sick and dying, and she interferes with her daughter's love affair with a nice young man. Forrest wants to retire and marry this man, but Mother prevents that. "If Gordon's the right kind of boy, he'll want whatever makes you happy," she says, effectively scuttling poor Gordon.

Everything goes wrong in Sally Forrest's life, except for her tennis playing. Eventually that, too, goes wrong, as she and Trevor embark on a European tour, and Forrest begins to drink and party. (Films always depict this as happening to young women who have careers under the dominance of their mothers. It's a format best presented by the story of Lillian Roth in *I'll Cry Tomorrow*, 1955.) Eventually, mother and daughter are screaming at each other. "You must trust me. I've planned your life well up to now," Trevor tells Forrest, adding, when Forrest is insulting, "How dare you talk to me like that? My every move has been for you. You must listen to me. I'm your mother." Like Mildred Pierce before her, Claire Trevor slaps her own child silly.

The destructive mother ends up losing her daughter's love and respect, and she also loses her husband. As she sits at his hospital bedside, the two of them discuss Trevor's life. It's a kind of last chance for the husband to pass judgment, since he will soon die:

H E :   Everything was for Florence [Forrest], wasn't it? You made yourself believe that, but it was all for you. Nobody but you.

S H E :   No! That isn't true.

H E :   You never gave love. That's the most important thing. You took it, used it, but you never gave an ounce of it to anybody.

Having delivered the death blow to her sense of herself, he suddenly goes as hard as nails, turning into a different man. "Beat it, Millie," he tells her. In the end, Trevor is left totally alone in the frame, in the dark of night in an empty tennis stadium. She sits alone, with abandoned programs and papers blowing about her feet, and nothing but the sound of tennis balls being batted back and forth. This is the fate of the destructive mother, the image warns.

Stage Mother (1933) illustrates the same story, but in a show-business format.* The mother—a disappointed performer herself—has a daughter with talent, and she pushes her to the very top of the show-biz world. "Your career is the only thing that is gonna stand by you," she tells the kid, and when the daughter falls in love, Mom breaks it up. "Did you think I was going to let you ruin your career . . . just for a school girl crush?" She begins her life as a destructive mother.

Destructive mothers are not always defined specifically as mothers. For instance, in *The Hard Way* (1942) the mother figure, played by Ida Lupino, is actually the older sister of the child involved (Joan Leslie). In this tough Warner Brothers picture, it is made patently clear that a woman who attempts to gain what she wants for herself through parenting is wrong and must be punished for it.

The Hard Way begins dramatically. As is often true of old movies, the credits themselves establish a harsh and unmistakable statement about women and life. In this case, the titles are written over the medium close-up shot of a headless woman. An audience is faced with the neck, shoulders, and bosom of a glamorous figure dressed in a sharply cut strapless evening gown. This female is never identified as a human being. Rather, she is a set of breasts, shoulders, and fingernails as she drapes herself first with a long strand of expensive pearls. Then she puts on two bracelets, diamonds for one wrist and emeralds for the other. Next, she attaches a huge corsage of double orchids to her bosom and then throws an ermine wrap over her left shoulder. This image totally dehumanizes a woman into a creature who lives for clothes, furs, and jewels. It makes a powerful statement.

Immediately after the ermine wrap is draped and the directorial credit is established, the image fades onto a foggy waterfront pier. This is *Mildred Pierce* territory, and sure enough, out onto the pier bent on suicide comes Ida Lupino, dressed in an expensive evening gown and wearing an ermine. Dropping the fur onto the wharf, she, unlike Mildred, jumps directly into the water. After Lupino is brought to a hospital, the police try to find out who she is. "Why should a good-lookin' number like that want to bump herself off?" one of them asks. "Women!" the other replies. "Who can figure it?" As doctors and policemen hover around her deathbed asking why, the movie shows only Lupino's huge eyes on the screen. Onto them slowly dissolves the image of a dirty, sooty, coal-mining town. If the movie went no farther, this image is really all the viewers would need in order

---

* A true-life story of a stage mother is, of course, the famous Broadway musical *Gypsy*, which was turned into a film in 1962. Both properties were based on the memories of actress June Havoc, who told the story of her ambitious stage mother, Rose, and her sister, the famous stripper Gypsy Rose Lee.

to know Lupino's story. A lengthy flashback—nearly 95 percent of the film's running time—is then presented.

Lupino's story is a classic case of destructive motherhood, and yet it is such a passionate tale of a woman's trying to get her little sister out of the life she herself fell into that it can't help being sympathetic. Leslie wants a graduation dress, but the eight dollars it costs is beyond the family means. Lupino begs her husband for it, but he reasonably says it just isn't possible. Lupino's emotions are raw, and finally, realizing that arguments are useless, she bursts out at him, "The tired man! Dirty and dumb." When he protests this unfair labeling, she replies, "At least I try. I don't sit there like you."

Lupino represents the force of rampant femaleness, which movies are not afraid to portray as powerful as long as it is also presented as wrong or destructive. Lupino starts negotiating Leslie out of town, but not without first telling her, "Don't get taken in like I was. I didn't know what I wanted . . . I just knew I was unhappy. So I married Sam. Well, I'm six years unhappier now, that's all." Leslie is practical enough herself. She asks, "If you can't get out, what makes you think I can?" Lupino's answer defines the destructive mother: "You've got something I never had. And that's me to guide you." Casting her eye over Leslie's physical attractiveness, she adds, "And you've got natural resources."

One might ask why it is so destructive to be a mentor. It's destructive for women's films reasons, which the film goes on to describe fully. It's destructive because:

- Lupino sacrifices her own husband to this mentoring. After the sisters leave town, Sam is neither seen nor heard from ever again.
- Lupino uses Leslie's physical beauty as well as her talent to attract the somewhat naive half of a song-and-dance team (Jack Carson) into marrying her as their ticket out of town.
- Lupino comes between Carson and his partner, Dennis Morgan, taking over the management of their act herself.
- Lupino is not above lying or flirting (and probably worse) with agents to get bookings.
- Lupino actively destroys the career of the aging Gladys George by getting her drunk so Leslie can take over her role.
- Lupino keeps Leslie away from Carson, and when Carson dies on the road alone while Leslie has become a Broadway star, she tells the widow that he was "weak. The only thing you ever did to him was become a success. Do you want to blame yourself for that?"

All of these things add up to the fact that Lupino is not only rejecting love and marriage for herself, but making the same decisions for Leslie.

She is shaping Leslie's life destructively without Leslie's fully realizing it. Dennis Morgan tells Lupino, "I want her to have her own career, not yours." Leslie is like a child, manipulated by Lupino, but half-aware of what is going on. When Carson turns up clumsily to embarrass her at a big opening-night party, Leslie bursts out to him, "Everything is so wonderful for me right now. This is what I've dreamed of all my life. I'm living in a bath of champagne." It's the eight-dollar graduation dress that she never got, finally in her hands and on her back. "What do you expect me to do?" she asks Carson. "Give up everything?"

Throughout the film, Dennis Morgan sees through Lupino. He stands in the wings to make harsh comments on her behavior and to point out to her the truth of her own manipulations. Since this is a woman's film, it is inevitable that this man is the one Lupino loves and would have for herself, and equally inevitable that he will end up with Leslie after Lupino dies. Morgan is a character who cannot ever be brought under Lupino's control or fall prey to her manipulations. This is established by our being shown that Morgan is a ladies' man, someone with a great deal of experience in his own kind of manipulation.

One telling scene stands out. Morgan accuses Lupino of coldness, the most common male form of insult to women in films. "You're like a machine," he tells her. "No heat. No blood. No feelings. I'll bet you couldn't fall in love if you wanted to." She responds to his closeness and to his touching her by murmuring, "Oh, you just don't know." Taking him at face value she lets herself go with him, showing how she feels about him and revealing her desire for the two of them to be together. After he kisses her hotly and she responds, he cynically draws back and says to her the line he gives all his women as he leaves them behind in tank towns across the continent. "Write me. Write me in Duluth." She slaps him hard.

In this scene, Morgan is cruel, using sex against Lupino and openly manipulating her. The film does not necessarily endorse his methods, but it does endorse his attitude. He is right and Lupino is wrong in context. Yet watching the movie today, one is struck by how ambivalent this moment is. Lupino is desperate, vulnerable, and viewers have seen what dreck her life was in the coal town. As her story is being told, audiences know she is lying half dead in a hospital bed, eking out her flashback before croaking. How could a woman watching not feel something for Lupino and her exploitation by Morgan?

Now, Voyager (1942) is a woman's film that could fit practically any chapter of this book. In many ways, it is the definitive woman's film of all time, with a deeply touching performance by Bette Davis.* In every way, it represents the woman's world, the woman's life, and the woman's problems with herself and with men, marriage, and motherhood. However, the primary issue in *Now, Voyager* is really parenting. A grid of interlocking parent-child problems and situations unfolds in the story. Bette Davis has a domineering, unkind mother (Gladys Cooper) so that she has to turn to a kindly, fatherly psychiatrist (Claude Rains) for help. (Davis tells Rains, "I am my mother's servant.") Blossoming under good parenting, she becomes a different person and has an affair with a married man whose daughter, Tina, is a direct parallel for Davis before her transformation. Tina has bad parenting from her own mother (a woman never seen in the film), and she, too, has to go to Claude Rains for rehabilitation. Davis then gets a chance to act as a surrogate mother to Tina, fulfilling two needs at once. She becomes mother to her lover's child in a socially acceptable way, and she relives her own childhood by becoming the kind of mother that she needed but didn't have when growing up. (She mothers herself.)

As *Now, Voyager* opens, Bette Davis (as Charlotte Vale) is caught in a mother-daughter trap. She is a repressed and ugly young woman, the child of Gladys Cooper's old age, an overweight, badly dressed, unattractive spinster, and mad as hell about it. Cooper refers to Davis as "my little girl," adding, "I make decisions for her." Davis is a princess in a tower, living a repressed and angrily unhappy life upstairs in what she ironically refers to as "my castle." Since her family is exceedingly wealthy, Davis's character wants for nothing except freedom and self-esteem.

A flashback soon after the film begins takes the viewer back to when Davis was twenty years old and journeying on a ship with her mother. Suddenly, Davis is seen as a totally different person—vibrant, slim, radiant with life and energy, attractive, and very sexy. On this cruise, her mother catches her passionately kissing a young man who is a ship's employee but who wants to marry her. "I don't care, I'm glad," Davis spits out, but her mother rejects the young man as unsuitable, and she has kept her daughter a virtual prisoner to misery ever since.

---

* Richard Corliss, the film critic for *Time* magazine, wrote in Philip Nobile's book *Favorite Movies: Critics' Choice* the following about *Now, Voyager*: "For far too long, respectable film critics approached the challenge of compiling a 'ten best' list with Kierkegaardian fear and Caligariesque trembling. The interior monologue went like this: 'What will my colleagues think? What will my intellectual readers think? How can I defend film as an art if I include any Hollywood produce among the received masterpieces? After all, *Potemkin* (which I admire but don't really like) is the very stuff of cinema—but *Now, Voyager* (which I love but am afraid to admire) is only a movie!' As a result, the typical ten best list wound up looking like screening selections for an undergraduate course in Seminal Cinema 101. And the *Now, Voyager*s of the film world were relegated to a mind-closet containing all of the critic's secret sins."

Now, Voyager tells the story of how Davis must set out on a second voyage and regain her self-respect, as well as her sexual identity. With the help of one of the world's "foremost psychiatrists," Claude Rains, she begins. Rains takes Davis to Cascade, his country hospital where patients weave afghans and drink springwater. She gains her confidence with his help and sets sail on her second voyage, which is an actual cruise to South America.

The transformation of Davis is proved to a viewer in the terms the woman's film has established generically: fashion. Davis leaves Cascade as slim as she was in youth, but now she is the epitome of mature, sophisticated chic. Her hair is upswept and her eyebrows are plucked. Her nails are perfectly manicured and she holds a cigarette with all the grace and skill of a Balinese dancer. And her wardrobe! Trim suits and Garboesque hats. Long gowns and sequined capes. Smart little sunsuits and afternoon dresses that qualify for that desirable label "frocks." Even though she forgets to unpin a note on the back of a sequined cape, telling her what to wear it with, she cuts a fashionable figure. The note, as it turns out, is what attracts the hero, Paul Henreid, to her.

Henreid at first appears to be the usual experienced European male character, one who is weakly tied to an unhappy marriage out of "honor and commitment." There are, in fact, the usual reasons (or excuses) set up by the plot for why he is married and must remain so: his wife is sick and his daughters would be abandoned if he weren't there for them, and so on. However, Henreid actually does turn out to be a character of honor and commitment. He is a wise man who understands Davis's fears and is tolerant of them. He appreciates her special qualities and slowly draws her out of herself in a manner that is as touching as it is uncommon in the movies.

Everything about the Paul Henreid character and his relationship with Bette Davis has an inevitability and an appropriateness to it, and that includes the attitude of the censors of the day. "Wrong . . . wrong . . . can it be wrong?" asks the lyric of the romantic song on the sound track. To satisfy propriety, the question is asked, but the film supplies the answer. It can't be. And in case that's not enough for the average viewer, another level of excuse is built into the story. It's okay for Henreid to be married and for Davis and him to be thrown together on shipboard and end up sleeping all night together on a mountaintop because . . . it's fate. It's an accident. It wasn't their fault. When they go on an innocent drive up into the Brazilian mountains, their car slides down a cliff and they have no choice but to remain together until daybreak. By taking the decision out of their hands and making it accidental, the film satisfies any form of censorship that might come its way. (And, besides, it doesn't really say they slept together.)

"Wrong . . . wrong . . . can it be wrong?" There's an echo of Madame Bovary to the song, as when she asks, "Is it wrong to want things to be beautiful?" Charlotte Vale has better luck than Emma Bovary because she finds an honest lover. "If I were free," says Henreid, "I'd prove you're not immune to happiness." At this Davis weeps, crying "only tears of gratitude . . . an old maid's tears of gratitude for the crumbs of love." Theirs is a mature love of two needy people. Nobody, not even the censors or the hardest of hearts, can begrudge it.

On her shipboard journey, Davis finds all the things that a woman needs: love, a Happy Interlude, and an opportunity for her own positive motherhood (it will appear later). She has been restored to life, although not to a conventional marriage, since her lover is already wed. (She will also not have a conventional motherhood, since she will have to act as surrogate mother to Henreid's neglected daughter, an ugly duckling, as she herself once was.) Because there is no problem with economic security, Davis appears to be able to come home from her voyage and have it all— love, "husband," "daughter"—but without the usual pressures, problems, or obligations. First, however, she has to deal with Mom.

When Davis arrives home from her voyage a stylish and socially confident woman, Cooper immediately reasserts control by becoming "sick" and needing help. Davis is told that she should occupy her father's room now, the one alongside the mother's, since her mother might need her at any time. "I've moved your things," the mother tells her, and that's not all she tells her. She also directs Davis about what clothes to wear and tells her to put on her glasses, an attempt to make the now-glamorous Davis less attractive. After an argument between them, Cooper falls downstairs, becoming bedridden with torn ligaments. Capitalizing on Davis's guilt feelings, Cooper also warns her that if she doesn't do as her mother wishes, she will be disinherited. Cooper is not only a bad mother, she is also a bad person, one who tries to exert control over Davis through money, a masculine characteristic. "I'll be glad to give a devoted daughter her living," warns Mother, shaking her will in Davis's face.

Now, Voyager reaches a dramatic peak in a scene in which Davis confronts her classic destructive mother on the topic of marriage and motherhood. Davis has just broken off her engagement to a suitable asexual male who has proposed to her. This rejection is a poignant scene in which she obliquely tries to tell him that she has known real sexual passion and could never feel it for him. He doesn't fully understand, but it is clear that they are both relieved. After Davis tells Cooper she is not going to get married after all, the two women talk:

COOPER: Have you no sense of obligation to your family or to me? Here
           you have a chance to join our name, Vale, with one of the
           finest families in the city, Livingston, and you come in here
           and tell me that you're not in love. You're behaving like a
           romantic girl of eighteen.

DAVIS: I don't doubt it. [Davis has sat down in a rocking chair and
           is pushing it back and forth.]

COOPER: And what do you intend to do with your life?

DAVIS: [*ironically*] Get a cat and a parrot and live alone in single
           blessedness.

COOPER: Stop rocking! You've never done anything to make your mother
           proud. Or to make yourself proud either. Why, I should think
           you'd be ashamed to be born and live all your life as Charlotte
           Vale. *Miss* Charlotte Vale.

DAVIS: [Claude Rains] says that tyranny is sometimes an expression
           of the maternal instinct. If that's a mother's love, I want no
           part of it. I didn't want to be born. You didn't want me to be
           born either. It's been a calamity on both sides.

As Davis asserts herself, rejecting her mother's plan for her life, her
mother's evaluation of her accomplishments, and, finally, her mother herself, Cooper's face crumples in horror. She slumps in her chair, having a
fatal heart attack that leaves Davis consumed with guilt. This ugly scene
puts Davis back in Rains's care at Cascade, where she meets the child
whom she can herself mother in a positive way.

The mother's death scene is a confrontation between a very bad,
destructive mother and a woman who is beginning to throw off that tyranny
on her way to becoming a good, perfect mother. Cooper defines clearly
what a destructive mother is. It is a woman who wants her child enslaved
to her own wishes. It is a mother who is, in a word, selfish. A destructive
mother, then, is related to all bad women, because she is yet another form
of the woman who takes power to which she is not entitled. A woman who
wants control of others and has the ability to make decisions is a bad
woman, whether wife, daughter, mother, or cabaret star.

Now, Voyager uses the conventions of the woman's film, but actually
breaks with them or refutes their meaning. Davis has a Happy Interlude
in which she has sex with a man who is married to someone else. Yet she
neither dies nor gets pregnant. Davis loves a man married to a tyrannical
woman who neglects his child and does not love him, but he does not get
free through some plot surprise, such as the wife's falling in a hole. He
does not get free at all. Davis does not throw him over, realizing that the

lovable schnook who has been standing by, all rich and handsome and loving, is really the man for her, one of her own kind. Davis holds on to Henreid, accepting the limitations of their love, rejecting the available husband.

By contradicting these traditions of the genre, *Now, Voyager* makes a powerful, if subversive, statement. "Don't let's ask for the moon," Davis tells Henreid in one of the most famous lines in film history, "when we have the stars." Although Davis will temporarily have sex and love, and ultimately have a child to raise and care about, she will not have them in a way that society condones or recognizes or even, for that matter, is aware of. She will not have a career, either. What will she have? The stars, not the moon. Something a little farther away, a little less tangible, but still there. Most significantly, she will have what *she* wants. She chooses to live life her own way, not by the rules of society, and on that basis, she represents a remarkable heroine, an unusual woman in an unusual woman's film.

How is one to interpret *Now, Voyager*? Some see it as little more than a sop for old maids or an excuse for women with married lovers. Critics say it reaffirms the sense that a woman ought to have her eyebrows plucked and her wardrobe in shape if she wants to be loved, and it also once again has that old favorite daddy/doctor asexual male show her the path she couldn't find without him. It makes love the central choice in a woman's life, and motherhood an important, even necessary goal. (When she is considering marrying the asexual male, she makes it clear her main reason would be that she wants a child.)

Despite these usual societal reaffirmations, however, there are other, important statements. The film also suggests that a woman can change her life, go on a journey, and find a completely new universe . . . that she can throw off the oppression of a domineering mother . . . that she can have sex out of wedlock, for pleasure, without punishment . . . and that she can fill her life with wonderful things, even if she does not marry and produce offspring. Even though this message comes in one of the most deeply romantic films of all time, the movie in which Paul Henreid lights two cigarettes, it is a significant message.

The main issue of *Now, Voyager*, as stated earlier, is bad and good mothering. When Davis's married lover calls her by a name other than her own, one he alone gives her (Camille), he is changing her from the name her mother gave her. He is helping her to be reborn on different terms, to throw off her mother's negative influences. Camille is a romantic, glamorous name, for that is how Henreid sees her. He separates her from her old Charlotte self, and not only is she reborn in his image, but also in her own. "You haven't a very high opinion of yourself," he tells her, helping her learn she has been wrong. At one point, she sees herself in a mirror, chic, slim, elegant, and it is as if she is looking at a stranger. What she is seeing is her new self, Camille.

Davis and her lover are united through his daughter, Tina, whom they call "our child," because they are the spiritual and the physical parent respectively. When Tina blurts out to Davis, "I wish you were my mother!" Davis embraces her, wholeheartedly accepting her role as surrogate mother. "This is Jerry's child in my arms," she thinks to herself. The film becomes a search for appropriate parenting, in which love finally is defined as motherhood.

In the end, she asks Henreid to "please let go." She projects a proud defiance and spirit of independence as she tells him that she can really be Tina's mother only if the two of them stay honorably apart. He can visit them anytime he wishes, but their private relationship must stop. In other words, Davis sacrifices her lover for his child. This is another film that suggests that motherhood replaces any need for a man. The film presents the final choice: the child over the man, motherhood over sex. Was this a connection to an audience of women who were putting up with men in order to keep a child supported, but who had long since rejected sex from them? Most of all, *Now, Voyager* is a story of a strong woman who, having survived and defeated a destructive mother, successfully goes on to live her own life the way she herself chooses.

The Woman in the Man's World

No one has ever seriously questioned the idea that Hollywood has ever had only one real reason for making movies—to generate profits. There has been no other organized agenda, hidden or otherwise. If certain individuals have had ideas or beliefs or political persuasions that were important to their artistic visions, they've had to find a way to steer them past a large committee of executives, writers, designers, producers, actors, and other people. That some could do this was a tribute to their strength of character, determination, talent, and perseverance. Even these people, however, have had to deal with an important fact: if their personal film lost money, the opportunity to repeat the process was probably going to be denied.

Thus we have a situation in which the films being made and released by Hollywood during the golden age of the studio system were, in fact, aimed at the widest possible audience and were designed for the widest kind of appeal. This accounts for their strange ambivalences and contradictions, and it directly addresses one of the main points about the woman's film that has been developed in this book. That is, the woman's film, like many other Hollywood movies, tried to have it both ways at once, to please *all* the audience. *All* movies tried to reach the female audience, just as *all* movies tried to reach the male audience or at least have a little something for everyone or perhaps nothing to offend anyone. All movies tried to reach all the audience. Obviously, filmmakers knew that this wasn't possible, and they aimed their genres and star vehicles at a segment of the audience, but their fantasy was that everyone would go to everything all of the time. Today, films are much more specifically directed to one part of the audience—teenagers, yuppies, or the so-called mature viewer—but back then they went for the hard sell and assumed that if the wife chose the film on Saturday, the husband might get to choose on Wednesday. Furthermore, during the 1930s, 1940s, and into the 1950s, people went out to the movies more often and more loyally than ever again in film history. When one tries to figure out what the image of women was on film, it doesn't make sense to ignore the films that feature women but that are not easily labeled "women's films." To think about the American woman on film, one has to get the whole picture, as it were; one has to think about all the movies. Compare a small, low-budget, black-and-white feature like *Smash-Up, the Story of a Woman* (1947) with a big, Technicolor, heavily advertised feature like *Unconquered* (1947), a western from Cecil B. DeMille. Since more people saw *Unconquered* than saw *Smash-Up*, isn't it possible that the image of Paulette Goddard as a brave "unconquered" female slave who is tortured and then rescued from Indians is as important as that of Susan Hayward as an alcoholic singer who has to rescue her child from a burning house?

If you don't poke around in a wide variety of movies to see what you can see, you miss Ida Lupino's socking the villain right on the jaw in *The Man I Love* (1946), knocking him down the stairs and saving the day while Robert Alda cowers behind her, weak and ineffectual, unable to cope. You miss Gene Tierney's rushing bravely up onto a dangerous parapet to knock out a warning on native drums while Bruce Cabot tries to wrestle with the Nazis down below in *Sundown* (1941) . . . and the determined band of females in *The Secret of Convict Lake* (1951), who collectively beat, club, and pitchfork to death a rapist, leaving his body behind for the vultures with no apologies, no guilt, and no confessions about it later on . . . and the amazing band of peasant women in *Tonight We Raid Calais* (1943), who set fire to their grainfields, throw incendiaries at the enemy, and direct oncoming English bombers to the correct targets. Their faces light up in delight as they rampage across the countryside, and in the end, Annabella, the heroine, calmly hands a baby to the hero, who is returning to England. She'll be too busy fighting the war to take care of a child.

If you stick strictly to "women's" films, you miss the films that show women who duke it out in fistfights, like Una Merkel and Marlene Dietrich in *Destry Rides Again* (1939), or Edna May Oliver coldcocking Blanche Yurka in the big fight scene of *A Tale of Two Cities* (1935). And you miss the countless times the female lead jumps at the villain who's trying to beat up the hero, or the times she bops the bad guy on the head in an attempt to help. The times she twists out of the arms of the coward who's trying to use her as a shield, or even the endless kicking, scratching, and biting that say, "I'll try. I won't take it." None of these instances suggests that a woman is in charge or that she should run the world or be liberated, but they do suggest something to women. Assert yourself, they say. You have a role to play. You don't have to just stand there.

You would miss the moments of comic horror designed to make people laugh but that also must have terrified men and perhaps simultaneously shamed and excited women, such as the one in which Harold Lloyd's mother-in-law threatens him in *Hot Water* (1924). "It's a pity I couldn't enjoy this ride without having to take charge," she tells him, after Harold's driving has careered them around Los Angeles, dangerously out of control in their new car. Here's Doris Day putting on her flats to land the big passenger plane after the pilot is shot in *Julie* (1956), and here's Julie Bishop bravely taking over the driving of an out-of-control bus loaded with innocent people, barking orders to a small boy who is working the hand brake bravely at her side (*Busses Roar*, 1942). (That's a World War II metaphor for you—women and children, without men to help them, have to run the show, take charge, and do a man's job.) The women rise to these occasions, steering bravely onward to triumph.

In countless film plots, women are seen not taking anyone's word for it. They question, and they reject. They are stubborn and determined and suspicious. One has only to see Jack Benny in *The Meanest Man in the World* (1943) shove a little old lady aside to grab her cab . . . and watch her retaliate by smacking him on the head with her purse, snatching back the cab, and confidently calling out "New York Athletic Club" as she speeds away, to realize that the American woman on-screen is a formidable force. As Paulette Goddard says in *The Ghost Breakers* (1940), "Don't worry about me. I'm just a poor working girl. Honest, but tough. I can take care of myself."

Think of all those pioneer women who push west in wagons . . . those molls who gun down their enemies . . . those female sharpshooters in the circus. Remember those women whose curiosity, no matter what, takes them boldly forward. Barbara Stanwyck in *Cry Wolf* (1947) is convinced that Errol Flynn is holding her husband (Richard Basehart) hostage in his laboratory in order to steal his money. She rides up in a dumbwaiter to have a look-see. She clambers out on the rooftop, dropping down through a skylight. She goes searching in daylight and after dark. She tracks, and she traps. She exhibits no fear, no hesitation. In the end, she finds out that Flynn is innocent, and it's her totally crazy husband who's the problem. Chagrined, Stanwyck cries out to Flynn, "It was my fault!"

"Don't blame yourself," he replies.

"I was so stubborn, so suspicious," she continues.

"So hard to convince," he wryly adds.

To completely grasp the image of women in popular movies, one must, then, look at the woman outside her natural habitat of the woman's film. She has to be seen in the man's world, too. There are two ways in which women invade the man's world in films: (1) through movies in which a woman is seen doing what is traditionally thought to be a job for men only, and (2) through female versions of genres that are usually associated with men. In the first, she's still in a kind of woman's film, and in the second, she's in the man's genre. In both, she is somewhere other than in the usual movie place. There's a difference between the first category of movies and those in which women have careers, because the basic purpose differs. A woman who is doing a *man's* job as if she were a man is illustrating the issue of what a woman's capabilities are, rather than the issue of how, if she makes the choice to pursue a career, she will have to sacrifice love. In the second category—hybrid films in which the woman's genre is grafted onto, or fused onto, a genre that would be called "masculine"—an entire masculine genre is feminized, and there is a clear and brutal demonstration of how society and nature restrict women.

WOMEN IN MEN'S JOBS

THESE ARE FILMS in which women take up employment that most people in the audience during the thirties and forties would have labeled "men's work"—the occupations of doctor, lawyer, engineer, architect, political leader, elected official, reporter, business tycoon, manufacturer. These women are not just "working girls" in the tradition of *Kitty Foyle*, and they are not actresses or department-store owners. They are clearly and specifically identified *within the film itself* as doing work that is uncommon for women.

When a movie tells a story in which a woman is doing a man's job, the film begins by addressing the issue of "what is this woman doing here?" A plot explanation of some sort is clearly laid down for the viewer. It may be historic: it is World War II, and nurses are in combat zones because the wounded must be tended. Or it may be fanciful: this woman sails the seas as a pirate because she has no family and her only mentor was a pirate. At the very least, some casual comment is made to tell the audience something about why a woman is in the man's role in the movie. For instance, just as she takes the Hippocratic oath in *Mary Stevens, M.D.*,

Kay Francis taunts her boyfriend: "You said a woman couldn't do it." "Well," he replies, "a woman couldn't. But you . . . you're a superwoman."

When Esther Williams fields a hot grounder in *Take Me Out to the Ball Game* (1949), the action stops for both audience and movie characters to think, "Hot damn! That woman just fielded a grounder!" When Williams goes on to give the ball players tips on how to play their game better and when she turns out to be an expert on baseball and when it turns out that she even has a man's name (K. C. Higgins) and, here's the punch line, she owns their baseball club—*that* is what the movie is about. It constitutes a situation. It makes for the basis of a plot, because the woman is out of place, unusual, dramatic. In looking at *Take Me Out to the Ball Game*, one sees that the plot is not based on the idea that Williams should *not* be part of the ball team, but that it is unusual for her to be and presents a problem for everyone, including her. It throws everything out of whack and, in doing so, provides an opportunity for story surprises and variations on the usual boy-meets-girl stories. ("She's beautiful. She's smart. And she's got a great throwing arm," rhapsodizes Frank Sinatra about Williams.) In the end, Williams falls in love with one of the ball players and enacts a traditional love story, fulfilling the usual female role. Before she steps down to that, the male players have to learn that she is really all right and can, indeed, field a hot grounder. Along the way, Williams looks beautiful, wears gorgeous clothes, allows a love song to be sung to her, and, of course, swims. In other words, she plays a traditional role with something more to it.

Esther Williams is an impressive physical specimen. She's bigger and stronger than the men in the movie, and she's a better athlete than any of them, with the possible exception of Gene Kelly. She *can* field a grounder. She *can* leap around the bases. And she certainly *can* swim, having been a potential Olympic gold medalist in real life. Even in an escapist musical, there is the subversive message: this woman can do things men do; these men ended up liking and accepting her for it; this woman survived in major league baseball.

Okay, so that's not what the film *says* it is about. But what it shows counts, too. There's a credibility to Williams on-screen as a woman of strength, self-confidence, and physical courage. Can that be taken away from her because she's wearing a hat with yellow roses on it and carrying a parasol? Maybe, but I think not. Would it be better if she could take off the hat and not sing? Well, yes. But this doesn't destroy Williams's credibility.

When Esther Williams was interviewed on television by Barbara Walters during the 1980s, she was asked if she had been intimidated by being taken to meet the great Louis B. Mayer when she was a girl of about eighteen. Williams drew herself up, fixed Walters with a stern eye, and said, "I *was* a legitimate swimming champion before I ever walked on a movie set. When you stand on a block and they say, 'Swimmers, take your marks,' you are all alone. Nobody did it for you. The coach can't even do it, and all of those fellas that are so intimidating . . . they didn't intimidate me because *they* couldn't do it. They couldn't get up on a block when they said swimmers take your marks and get to the end of the pool first. . . . I was a legitimate swimming champion."

Working Women on the Hollywood Screen, a filmography by Carolyn Galerstein, names 4,500 features released between 1930 and 1975 in which the leading female character is a working woman. The lists of jobs women are doing in the movies provide a comparison of the number of films in which women are doing the man's job instead of the woman's. A woman is an airline stewardess in 21 movies, and a pilot in 13; she's a nurse in 177 movies, and a doctor in 73; she's a prostitute in 139 movies, and a lawyer in 28. Given the state of things, what is remarkable is that she is *ever* a doctor or a lawyer or a pilot, and when she is, the films are worth looking into.

What happens when a woman is, to take one example, a detective? "A woman detective always looks like a woman detective," comments a bystander in *The Penguin Pool Murder* (1932). Presumably he means that she has breasts. Despite comments like this, however, a woman detective is still doing what is usually thought of as a man's job. A detective is a solver, a superior thinker, a person who walks down mean streets in the dark of night. Two examples of the female detective on-screen are the characters of Nancy Drew and Hildegarde Withers. The first is a teenager, played by Bonita Granville, and the second is an old-maid schoolteacher, played by Edna May Oliver. Both are brilliant, determined, intrepid, self-confident, bossy, and more than able to solve a crime and survive a roughing up. Significantly, however, neither is really in a position to fall in love and have her detecting ability ruined, called into question, or sacrificed for marriage. One is too young, and the other is too old. In other words, these movies offset the fact that a woman is doing a man's job by having the woman in both cases be sexless, or not really a woman. In addition, both women have a man around to help them. Hildegarde Withers has Inspector Piper (James Gleason), who is quite a benign male figure, because he thinks Withers is wonderful. Her ability to solve crimes impresses him, but so, it should be pointed out, does her ability to cook perfect meals and type up all his own notes on a case. Nancy Drew has two men in her life, a malleable young male friend and a doting father. Both these men constantly warn Nancy to be careful, and they are there to help her out of scrapes if need be. Granville and Oliver are women in men's roles, and they frequently deliver lines about a woman's intelligence and superiority to men. But to what extent can they be thought of as providing liberated models for women, and how much do they inspire a sense of a woman's being able to do a man's job in a man's world? "My business is giving orders," says Hildegarde Withers. "If I can handle a classroom full of children, I can handle anything. I've seen enough to know that if this murder is to be solved, a woman's got to do it." Does she mean that solving problems and overruling the masculine police force is truly woman's work? Or is it all a big joke? And if it's a big joke, did the women in the audience take it that way?

Often unusual jobs for women in movies provide a platform for contradiction. Presumably, both men and women could find alliances and reassurances, in either direction, in such films. Miriam Hopkins, as a successful architect in *Woman Chases Man* (1937), delivers this speech to a man who questions whether or not he should hire her for an important job: "I know what you're thinking. That I'm a girl. Yes . . . but I have a man's courage, a man's vision, a man's attack. For seven years, I've studied like a man. Researched like a man. There is nothing feminine about my mind. Seven years ago I gave up a perfectly nice engagement with a charming wealthy old man because I chose a practical career. I left him at the church to become an architect, and today I'm ready and he's dead." Hopkins plays out her role as a career person and does not give up her job at the end of the film. Of course, she does end up in the arms of Joel McCrea, but no one ever suggested celibacy was a sensible goal for a liberated woman. It might be pointed out that Hopkins is defining herself by "a man's vision" and not a woman's, and the film is a comedy in which she is presented as unusual, an eccentric, and not necessarily a role model. However, if we test movies by what we see, we see that Hopkins is shown to be a very good architect, stomping around on floors, knocking on walls, and getting the job done with skill and panache. Her role is not one of an architect who wears lamé and hangs drapes. Although she does occasionally wear lamé (this is Hollywood, after all), she's more often seen up on ladders and out on tree limbs, and when a man makes a pass at her, she totally ignores it. ("Always an architect," he murmurs. "Yes!" she replies. "And a darned good one, too.") Furthermore, it is implied that Hopkins is superior to McCrea because, while she can think like a man, he cannot think like a woman. She can cross over, but he can't, presumably partly because the crossover elevates her but demeans him. Such conversations—and such occupations successfully feminized—are inevitably noticed and thought about, even when presented in a comedy format.

When a woman is placed in a man's occupation on film, it is usually for a purpose that is definitely not liberation; these are not propaganda films suggesting that women should run out and become doctors and lawyers. Rather, they provide the same ambivalence as all women's films do, but ironically they have to work much harder to undermine the power they depict. These films clearly tell women in the audience that being men won't work. They show women that certain occupations are best done by men. Whereas a woman can run a perfume business (*To Each His Own*, 1946) or a restaurant chain (*Mildred Pierce*, 1945) or a pancake empire (*Imitation of Life*, 1934 version), she cannot as easily be a doctor or a traveling salesman or a detective or a lawyer or the head of General Motors. This is a subtle distinction. As we have seen, countless films show women working successfully in all sorts of jobs and achieving wonderful things, and these movies don't seek to say that women can't do these things, only that if they do, they'll be tripped up by love. The films we are talking about here specifically place a woman in an occupation that is not easily open to women in real life. When women hold these occupations, they encounter grief for being in them. They are *told* by characters in the movie that these jobs are not appropriate woman's work. Even though these movies, too, show the woman doing the man's job, and thus provide covert liberation through depiction, their plots are strongly geared to taking the woman out of such jobs for antifeminist reasons. They tell a woman straight out in the dialogue that a man's job is of no use to her if she can't make things work elsewhere in her life—that is, in the part of her life in which she is a woman.

Kay Francis in *Mary Stevens, M.D.* demonstrates this point exactly. Even though Mary Stevens is an excellent pediatrician, women don't want to come to her. "I've got to have a man doctor" and "A woman doctor . . . ugh . . . no thanks!" are two responses from potential female patients. As a result, Stevens has to go into practice with her boyfriend, Lyle Talbot. ("You'll never get him," her friend Glenda Farrell warns her, telling Francis she has "no sex appeal, and neither does any woman in this man's business.") Farrell is right, as Talbot marries a flighty and feminine rich woman, leaving Francis pregnant (after a single illicit encounter, of course) and having to make a sneaky trip to Europe to give birth secretly. On her way home, she tends to sick babies in steerage, and, as a result, her own child catches the fever and dies. She confronts the truth about her medical skills: "My own baby . . . and I couldn't save him." What good is it for a woman to be a doctor if she can't save the life of her own little son? Mary Stevens, M.D., decides to give up her career.

In this way, *Mary Stevens, M.D.*, follows a repressive pattern. First it places a woman in a man's job and shows how very good she is at it— better than the hero is, in fact. Then it punishes her, making her put the job in perspective when compared with the importance of her role as a woman. ("My life stopped when my baby died.") However, Mary Stevens, M.D., has another chapter to her life. As she's moping around her apartment, in a suicidal mood, another medical crisis arises. She is summoned to the janitor's apartment where a child has swallowed that famous invention of Madame Kremiton's, the safety pin. How does Dr. Stevens save the day? By resourcefully removing a hairpin from her hair and fishing the offending instrument out of the little lad's gullet. "They say medicine's a man's game," muses Kay Francis afterward. "Wonder what a man would have done with this." What indeed. Without hairpins—without fashion—he would have been lost. The contradiction is apparent. Mary Stevens is taught that being a doctor is not as important as being a mother, but then the movie reestablishes how important it is for her to be the one, rather than the other. Presumably, the hairpin makes this reassertion palatable, because Mary is wielding a feminine device instead of a scalpel. She is a clever (and well-coiffed) medical woman about the house, resourceful with things the way a woman ought to be resourceful, a kind of handy woman rather than a real doctor. And yet if a woman can rescue a choking child with a hairpin, what, as Francis asks, could any man have done that would have been better? A man *needs* his hospital and his staff. A woman only needs her hairpins.

A telling example of the women-in-men's-jobs movie is the odd comedy *The First Traveling Saleslady* (1956). Traditionally, a comedy places a male hero in a situation in which he is ill prepared to cope, or in which he will have no control. In *Destry Rides Again*, a peaceful man who does not wear a gun or approve of violence becomes a sheriff in a Wild West town. In *Ruggles of Red Gap* (1935), an English butler, trained to be mannerly and calm, is placed in a rude, out-of-control American frontier household. In *The Paleface* and *Son of Paleface*, Bob Hope is a coward trying to survive in a world of outlaws and cowboys. Usually such films involve men, primarily because there are more men comics than women comics in movies, and more of them became stars, but also because the issue of a man's courage is easily satirized against a western background.

The First Traveling Saleslady works a variation on this old comedy theme. Instead of placing a cowardly man where he will have to be brave to survive, the film takes a woman out of her safe context (conventional female role) and places her in a "dangerous" world (the male environment of the western genre). The danger is further defined by two additional things: the woman is doing a man's job, and this represents, in popular-culture terms, a basic joke about sexual freedom.

The First Traveling Saleslady was made in the 1950s, when films had just begun to play with broadly suggestive sexual situations. These movies are peep shows of the worst kind, since the peep doesn't reveal much except a group of reasonably tired innuendos. The very title of this film is a feeble sex joke. A traveling sales*lady*. Oh, boy! Since traveling salesmen represent the idea of men who take their sex for free and easy before bopping out of town to the next woman, will a female version do the same? The prospect exists that, even if the woman is virtuous, she will be vulnerable to the advances of men who assume she isn't because of her occupation and the fact that she is on the road without male protection. A woman who travels for a living is permanently out of town, at the mercy of weather, strange accommodations, unscrupulous men, and suspicious other women. And since a woman like this is always trying to sell something, she is doubly vulnerable.

The First Traveling Saleslady works with all this and adds one further variation, the idea that this saleslady is an ardent suffragette. The entire plot is set against the issues of women's rights. Three basic themes are developed: sex, woman's emancipation, and a woman's right to drive a car, with all three being presented as more or less the same thing. In other words, the idea of a feminist is both enforced *and* treated as a joke.

Ginger Rogers plays the title role. The film is introduced as being set in 1897, when, title cards say, "America was feeling its strength and had come of age as a nation. The American salesman was telling anyone who cared to listen that it was a man's world. The American woman agreed . . . and prepared to take it away from him." The plot tells viewers that men and women are engaged in a terrible war, and that while women pretend to be weak and cooperative, they are actually very dangerous and preparing to take over at any minute. They are about to start driving the car!

As the film unfolds, there is a constant barrage of dialogue about the woman's role. Rogers tells audiences, "Subjugation of women is on the way out" and "Things are gonna change." The men she meets up with tell her, "This is a dog eat dog business, sister" and "I was mourning the woman you could have been if you weren't emancipated." Explaining why women will never be able to drive cars, the hero says, "They're not co-ordinated like men."

Ginger Rogers's character remains calm throughout. She has a simple philosophy of her own: "Don't give away what you can sell." She is not above using her feminine charm to outwit her male sales rival, telling a friend how they will conquer him. "First we charm him. Then we set him up for the kill."

As usual, there is an explanation of How She Got That Way, the story of why Rogers is a suffragette. She tells the hero that her own mother, who was pretty and smart, ended up married to a man who only let her stop cooking long enough to bear his ten children, all of whom are girls. ("Not a vote in the litter.") She makes it clear that she will not under any circumstances live her own life like this. She will earn her own living, avoiding the problem. The man she ultimately falls in love with, however, hates her being a saleswoman. "I figured I'd kill the salesman," he tells her, "and keep the woman." She replies, "You might find it a little difficult to separate one from the other." This is a good honest reply, but the final word belongs to him. He understands that all he has to do is "encourage one and discourage the other," society's usual plan. Finding herself in trouble as a result of this success, Rogers demands a court trial and asks for the right to defend herself. Using her own brains and courage, she saves herself, but not before realizing that she really loves her man.

The pattern of such films is one of demonstrating that women are superior and run everything, but will voluntarily give everything up because otherwise men won't love them. This is an idea that is best expressed through comedy, and many of these films are like *The First Traveling Saleslady*, simpleminded comedies that toy with ideas of liberation and feminism and then undercut them.

A comedy in which a woman has an important man's job is *They All Kissed the Bride* (1942), in which Joan Crawford runs a trucking empire. Meant as a charming confection, *They All Kissed the Bride* was originally supposed to star Carole Lombard, but after her fatal air crash Crawford stepped in as a favor and donated her entire salary to the War Relief Fund in honor of Lombard. A hasty last-minute replacement, Crawford is all wrong for the part. Even though she had starred in comedies in the 1930s, she was never really a comedienne, and the light touch needed for this heroine is not really present. Indeed, Crawford becomes a scary presence hovering over some very dismal events.

In a reversal joke on the famous "what does a woman want" question, *They All Kissed the Bride* openly asks the question, What does a man want? Then it makes the answer clear. He wants a traditional wife, a little woman of his own, and a home. He does not want a woman who runs a trucking empire. Although Crawford is smart, hardworking, rich, and powerful in the movie, this condition is undermined by the plot, which works constantly to take her out of the position of power. The hero, Melvyn Douglas, delivers speeches like: "You're afraid of men, and determined to make the world unsafe for them to live in. You're a machine, not a woman. You have no right to assume any of the feminine graces." With a bunch of violets he sends her, he puts in a note that says, "I debated before sending these. With these you might be mistaken for a girl."

They All Kissed the Bride spends its first half putting Joan Crawford in her place and, ironically, the second half putting Melvyn Douglas in his. In the beginning, he tells her that she hides behind her desk and that she doesn't know how to make love, have fun, or be a woman. "Did you ever go neckin'?" he wants to know. Questions such as this cause her to feel modest and frightened. "I'm afraid of no man," Crawford feebly tries to say, but soon enough Douglas has her under control, dominating her physically, commanding her to put her hand on his neck, then her other hand, and then her head on his chest. "Relax. Take it easy, baby. Nothing to be afraid of," he says, setting forth the idea that all a career woman really needs is good sex in order to find out how misguided she is in wanting to work. Proving that films like this one, which were aimed largely at the woman's market, really *did* provide some covert release for women, however, *They All Kissed the Bride* gives Crawford her own little revenge. Once warmed up, she's hotter than Douglas expected. In the next section of the film, she starts insulting *him*. She tells him *he's* scared, that he always hides behind his typewriter. When Douglas chides her about her immodesty, she stands up and starts to undress right in front of him. He runs out, scared to death.

Both Douglas and Crawford are humiliated and have to question their ideas about sex and their own gender roles. Through various plotting devices, each of them has to end up sleeping overnight in the other's bedroom. Crawford wakes up in a man's pajamas, and Douglas wakes up in a frilly nightgown. In the hands of good filmmakers, this might have been imaginative and meaningful, but in *They All Kissed the Bride* it becomes slightly sordid and almost pointless. Whereas Douglas's questions are perfunctory, Crawford's are clear to the audience. In an extended sequence, she is observed getting drunk, letting her hair go loose, and astonishingly winning a wild jitterbug contest, with her ankle-strap shoes clacking and her padded shoulders flying. Later, as she tries to talk to her staff about new refrigerator trucks, she is shown going into a reverie in which she babbles about "beautiful flowers and babies." As "You Must Have Been a Beautiful Baby" plays on the sound track, *They All Kissed the Bride* completes its takedown of Crawford, who was until then playing a woman extremely good at a very masculine job.

In the end Crawford decides she wants to learn to knit, as she listens to a doctor who tells her that in order for her to be happy she will have to let a man dominate her. She will have to give in to her feminine nature because "better women than you have tried to pooh-pooh it." Crawford thinks things over about her job very carefully, finally saying, "Some mornings I come in very grateful for my job, but around five o'clock I feel something's missing. I'm lonesome." What Crawford learns is that if she doesn't want to end up alone and unloved, she must relinquish *control*.

What *They All Kissed the Bride* has in common with *She Had to Say No*, *The First Traveling Saleslady*, and *Mary Stevens, M.D.* is that, in addition to finding love with a man, the woman has to undergo some form of punishment or humiliation. Crawford is made to look like a fool in front of her board of directors when she starts babbling about flowers and babies. Arden has to make a public apology for herself and all independent women in order to win her lawsuit. Rogers has to be put on trial for a crime that is a result of her having done her job well. Kay Francis has to become pregnant while unwed and then see her baby die from fever.

Each of these problems is directly related to the woman's job itself, showing that women may indeed do a man's work but it doesn't get them anywhere. Since these are the stories in which women usurp the man's role in society, they are the films that most often contain the true put-down of the woman. It makes sense that the stronger the portrait of a woman is on-screen, and the more she is shown as man's equal in the work force, the more dynamic and inarguable the resolution has to be. Thus, over and over again in films about women in men's occupations we have the humiliation scene. Katharine Hepburn, a world-famous newspaperwoman, cannot make pancakes in *Woman of the Year*, and Rosalind Russell, a federal judge, cannot cook a fish in *Tell It to the Judge* (1949). The stronger the visualization, the stronger the evidence against it must look.

Often such movies demonstrate a situation in which the woman deliberately gives up her superiority, renouncing it or denying it in order to please the man. When Annie Oakley (Barbara Stanwyck) outshoots Frank Buck (Preston Foster), she finally figures out she will lose his love. Her only solution is to lose the competition instead. Over the years, the story of Annie Oakley, presented as *Annie Oakley* (1935), followed by its two musical variations, *Annie Get Your Gun* (1950, with Betty Hutton as Annie) and *Calamity Jane* (1953, with Doris Day as an Annie rip-off), has been a perennial favorite. All these films lay out the same scenario: a tomboy who can shoot better than any man alive falls in love with a gorgeous male who also happens to be a sharpshooter. To win him over, she not only has to learn to dress well, wear perfume, and become "feminine." In all but the Doris Day version, she also has to let him outshoot her in a public contest. She has to abandon her ability to beat him. "You cain't get a man with a gun" sings Annie, in the musical version, having heard her beloved himself sing "The Girl That I Marry" ("The girl that I marry will have to be, as soft and as pink as a nursery"). The gun is an appropriate symbol of masculine ego, so that the need to surrender mastery of it teaches women in an audience a sinister lesson, even in a musical comedy.*

* A magnificently stylish film noir, *Gun Crazy* (1949), presents a young couple meeting via a carnival shooting contest. The heroine (Peggy Cummins) challenges the hero (John Dall). Their mutual attraction via their love of guns and shooting is a hot visualization of a true

The ultimate example of how a woman in a man's job is told to get back in her place is the bizarre 1933 movie *Female*, starring Ruth Chatterton. The film introduces viewers to the Drake Motor Company, a busy, bustling place with everyone scurrying around because the president wants things, needs things, demands things. The president is meeting with the board of directors, and the camera slyly shows a portly middle-aged man confidently addressing a round table of business types, while a small woman, perhaps a secretary, sits at the other end of his table. Of course, the president turns out to be the little woman, and the men around the table are all terrified of her. The movie makes a point of how unusual Chatterton's occupation is by implying that anyone who is the president, especially someone of such obvious power, authority, and fear, just must be—a Man. Instead it is—a Woman. "This is unusual" is the inevitable underlying meaning of the opening sequence, and since the unusualness involves a character played by a woman, it will be taken further, so that in the end it is seen to also mean "this is unnatural."

Ruth Chatterton is a real tycoon in this movie. When it comes to worrying about what people think, she doesn't give a hoot. "The things people say about me don't bother me." Furthermore, she boldly does the things that men do, without shame or apology. She has no time for love or marriage, as she explains to an old school friend. As the friend sits by, Chatterton gets a massage to prepare her for her evening of sexual pleasure, and the two women talk:

> FRIEND: Aren't you ever going to fall in love?
>
> CHATTERTON: Romance? Me? I haven't got time. It's a career in itself. It takes too much time and energy. To me, a woman in love is a pathetic spectacle. She's either so miserable that she wants to die or she's so happy that *you* want to die.
>
> FRIEND: Aren't you ever going to marry?
>
> CHATTERTON: No, thanks. Not me. You know, a long time ago, I decided to travel the same open road that men travel. So I treat men exactly the way they've always treated women.
>
> FRIEND: You evidently haven't much respect for them.
>
> CHATTERTON: Oh, I know that for some women men are a household necessity. For myself, I'd rather have a canary.

American romance. Sex and guns and violence. On the surface, *Gun Crazy* says their mutual shooting ability is about sex, whereas *Annie Get Your Gun* tells us it's about love. Underneath the surface, however, *Annie* is about sex and *Gun Crazy* is about love. This is not Derrida. It's fact.

Ruth Chatterton surrounded by her male executives in *Female*

Chatterton lives up to her conversation. Whereas sometimes a career woman in a man's job is portrayed as cold and frigid, just waiting for a man to teach her about sex (like Crawford in *They All Kissed the Bride*), Chatterton gives lessons herself. She likes to follow what her staff calls "the custom of Catherine the Great." She's an active seducer of young men who work in the office, always giving them a pay bonus after their night with her. When she spots a good-looking young fellow and feels like having sex, she inquires about his work, and when he starts to tell her, she suddenly says, "Well, I don't have time to talk about that now. Why don't we discuss it tonight, over dinner at my house. Seven-thirty."

A series of brief episodes portrays Chatterton, the woman, as a typical dabbler in the office clerical pool. She enjoys herself, and the fellows, as if they were the sort of young women who are usually used and ruined by their bosses, react in dismay. If they fuss too much, she exiles them to the branch office "in Montreal." When one of her male secretaries, a former affair, gets emotional in her office, she tells her male factotum "get me two sensible women." She also reminds him that it "takes more than flat heels and glasses to make a sensible woman."

As Chatterton's bonus army grows larger, one of her male bookkeepers expresses horror, but her factotum says, "She's a superwoman. She's the only honest woman I believe I've ever met. There's nothing of the hypocrite about Miss D. And that's more than you can say about the men she comes in contact with. Look at them. A pack of spineless yes men all after her for her money. She sees through them. That's why she tosses them aside." The bookkeeper is skeptical, saying, "Well, one of these days she'll meet a man who'll toss her on her ear."

Growing bored with the "spineless yes men," Chatterton wonders what would happen to her as a woman if men didn't know she was rich and powerful. "What if I were nobody? What would happen?" She gets in her roadster and drives to a carnival to test herself, and there she meets the ear tosser, George Brent. Although they meet as equals and have a fine time together, she will be startled later to learn that he's her new key engineer on a major design project, and he will be even more startled to learn that she's his boss. "I haven't got time to talk about it now," she tells him when he wants to discuss his plans. "Come up to my house for dinner tonight. Seven-thirty."

Brent precipitates a crisis in Chatterton's life as a mogul by rejecting her advances. "I was engaged as an engineer, not a gigolo," he firmly tells her, for all the world like the little girl of virtue from a Victorian novel. Puzzled, Chatterton asks her factotum what kind of women men like . . . how do they want them to act? The factotum, wise to her infatuation with Brent, tells her: "A man like [George Brent] wants a woman who'll look up to him. Gentle. Feminine. Someone he can protect. That's because he's strong and rather primitive, perhaps. The dominant male, my dear." Chatterton thinks this over, and like the smart businesswoman she is, she says, "Gentle and feminine, eh? So that's what they want? Well, we strive to please."

Female then presents yet another of those episodes in which a woman cleverly manipulates and deceives a man. Chatterton tricks Brent into coming to what he thinks is a company picnic. When he arrives out in the country under the dripping willow trees alongside the lovely lake, he finds only Chatterton, dressed in ruffles and a picture hat. Prepared to stomp off in a rage, Brent does, however, take a minute to help her when she pleads, "Oh, will you help me light this fire before you go? I don't seem to be able to." Chatterton soon winds him around her finger, getting him to fetch the water for her coffee and reassure her when the sound of an owl "scares" her. As Brent moves about to help her, Chatterton laughs at him from behind a tree.

The two of them spend a loving night. As Chatterton lies back under a tree, Brent tells her that he has met her "as four entirely different people." They are "the girl at the shooting gallery—she was amusing" . . . "the girl in the factory—she's a very efficient, capable sort of thinking machine" . . . "the girl at your house that night—I didn't like her, perhaps because I'm a man and prefer to do my own hunting" . . . "and the girl you are here tonight." Chatterton sagely asks him which one he likes best—"This one." Then she coyly adds, "Which one do you think is real?" "This one," he says again. Chatterton smiles and kisses him. The one he has chosen has been shown to be purely a performance, the only one that has no truth to her at all. Chatterton is pleased with herself, not realizing that this is a performance she's going to have to end up giving for the rest of her life.

In setting her trap, Chatterton in *Female* is shown to trap only herself. The inevitable ironic moment arrives in which she must be punished for her outrageous freedom. The next day, Brent comes to her office with a marriage license. He has not, of course, thought to ask her first. "I never thought of such a thing," she tells him, totally surprised:

CHATTERTON: Marriage isn't for me! For us! [*hastily correcting herself*] After all, we can be so happy as we are. Don't let us spoil everything.

BRENT: Then you don't love me?

CHATTERTON: Oh, Jim. You're being very unreasonable.

BRENT: I'm just one of the boys, is that it?

CHATTERTON: Don't be absurd. You're being old-fashioned.

BRENT: Is it old-fashioned to be decent? I suppose you think you're too superior for marriage and love and children, the things women were born for. Say, who do you think you are? Are you so drunk with your own importance you think you can make your own rules? Well, you're a fake. You've been playing this part so long you've begun to believe it. The great superwoman! Cracking your whip and making these poor fools jump around. You and your new freedom. Why, if it weren't so pathetic, you'd be funny.

At the end of this speech, Brent is shouting in rage while Chatterton cowers in horror. He rips up the marriage license and stalks out. Having shown a woman to be so incredibly free in her life, the film needs a lengthy speech, strongly delivered, to redress the balance. The operative words are "I suppose you think you're too superior for marriage and love and children, the things women were born for" and "you think you can make your own rules." *Female* pulls back on track by reminding any women in the audience who might have gotten ideas along the Catherine the Great line what their real jobs were, and what the rules for those jobs were.

Female next shows Chatterton slumped and confused in her board-room. As with Crawford in *They All Kissed the Bride*, Chatterton cannot now function properly in her business. Pressed for decisions and answers, which the audience has seen her snappily making throughout the entire movie, she suddenly can't think and can't make up her mind. She bursts out, "I can't go on! I don't belong here. This is no place for a woman. I know I've always thought I was different. I've always tried to beat life the way men beat it, but I can't." Now the film has put its cards on the table.

However, *Female* ends with Chatterton pulling herself together and returning to the boardroom to make the necessary decisions regarding the future of her company. The men are all standing around in fear and con-fusion, with one of them saying weakly, "What are we going to do?" Chatterton says, "Gentlemen, I apologize. Forget that ever happened." She sets up an all-important meeting in New York City for the next day, but instead of flying directly there, she jumps in her car. Shoving her bewildered chauffeur aside, she yells out, "Move over. We're going faster than you know how to drive."

As she careers her car over hill and dale, around curves at high speed, she conducts a masterful search for Brent, finally finding him in a small-town carnival, once again having fun in the shooting gallery, as he was the night she met him. She rushes right up to him and says, "I can't go on without you. I'm not playing a part. I'm not a superwoman. I'll marry you if you still want me to." This, however, is actually yet another per-formance, her last brilliant act of tycoonery. When he ignores her, she adds that she is going to lose her business because she was supposed to be in New York the next day but came looking for him instead. While she watches him shrewdly, his face is to the camera, his back to her. An audience can see her wise look as she waits for him to do exactly what he does: rescue her. It's the firewood trick all over again. When he agrees, the audience can see the knowing twinkle in her eye: she's landed her man the way she ran her factory. As the two of them drive away, she says, "You're going to run it from now on. I don't ever want to see that factory again. I'm going to have nine children." "Is that all?" he asks. "That's all," she replies. Her voice sounds suspiciously like the one she used back in her big office when she was telling everyone exactly how it was going to be.

All these films with women in men's jobs maintain a semblance of telling ordinary love stories in which a woman realizes that love should really be her career. They are *almost* like other women's films in which women just have regular jobs, but instead they clearly declare men the

winners in the battle of the sexes, not because men are better, but just
because they are—well, they're men. Having empowered a woman into an
actual job or role that belongs to a man, these movies knock the woman
down in order to restore order. They are movies with a truly negative agenda,
and yet surely women felt empowered when Ruth Chatterton spoke out loud
the words, "I treat men exactly the way they've always treated women" or
"I know that for some women men are a household necessity. For myself,
I'd rather have a canary."

FEMALE VERSIONS OF MALE GENRES

GENRES WERE ALWAYS looking for ways to vary their basic conventions
in order to keep them new for audiences while still delivering the old
familiar story and characters. At the lowest level, taking a genre and
populating it with women instead of men was nothing but a variation that
freshened up the action or gave the studio a chance to work all its female
stars. But no such variation would ever have been employed unless it fit
the basic generic mold or unless it would have broad audience appeal. So
when female variations of male genres appear, they are worth looking into.
If women weren't supposed to do men's jobs, act like men, or be like men,
why were these movies acceptable? What happens when a woman takes
over a male genre? The feminizing of an established genre was a standard
Hollywood device. Although genres such as the western, the gangster film,
the prison movie, the combat film, the pirate/swashbuckler story, were all
thought of as stories about men in an action-oriented universe, female
versions of all do exist. The woman's film is always a story about a woman,
and when the woman is the protagonist a set of specific feminine problems
and solutions is brought into play, as we have seen. So when a woman's
version of a male genre is created, things that are associated with the
woman's world (primarily issues of love and romance, marriage, sex, rape,
and childbirth) must be reconciled in some manner with the male movie.
The way this is brought about—the construction of the explanation—seems
significant.

There are many examples to consider. There are female combat movies
(*Cry Havoc, So Proudly We Hail!, Flight Nurse,* 1954, *The Wild Blue
Yonder,* 1951), female westerns (*Westward the Women, Johnny Guitar,* 1954;
The Woman They Almost Lynched), prison movies (addressed in the chapter
called "The Woman's World"), gangster movies (*Lady Gangster,* 1942; *Lady*

Scarface, 1941), pirate films (*Anne of the Indies, Frenchman's Creek*), and swashbucklers (*At Sword's Point*). Genres of every sort can be feminized, or made to be about a woman instead of a man. At the simplest level a genre is feminized when the issues become those associated with the woman's daily life instead of the usual ones. For instance, *Money and the Woman* (1940), one of my favorite titles, is a story about banks, embezzlement, and a daring daylight bank robbery. Instead of being an action-packed crime drama, however, with guns and fistfights, the movie restricts itself to a final brief car chase in which the offender is shot and captured. The rest of the movie concerns itself with whether or not Brenda Marshall can actually be trusted in her little job as bank teller. This is a film that suggests to audiences the depressing notion that their bank deposits may only be as secure as the bank manager's love life. While vice presidents stand around in the vault yakking about whether Marshall—the wife of a former employee they know was an embezzler—did or didn't help her husband steal, elaborate ruses are gotten up for putting back into the vault the money that has been embezzled. "If you think it's hard to steal money out of a bank," one of the bank's officers muses, "just wait till you try to put it back in."

Money and the Woman makes its central issue the question of how an audience sees Brenda Marshall. Beautiful and brunette, she wears fantastic jewelry and clothes and seems always to have a ready answer to questions about shortages in her accounts. She is even readier with hatched plots about how to keep her husband out of prison. At a key moment she faints, diverting attention, as it turns out, from her husband as he sneaks into the vault. The movie plays with audience expectations about women. As the leading man becomes suspicious of Marshall, then changes his mind and falls in love with her, then becomes suspicious again, the audience, too, is expected to have these same doubts, mainly based on her wardrobe. Hints are given that she is really okay—she's a mother and a loyal daughter—but she seems entirely too well dressed and too, well, *intelligent* about bank matters to be trusted. As it turns out, the villainess in the piece is actually played by Lee Patrick, and here again audience expectations are practiced upon. Patrick also works in the bank. She is dressed in a plain black suit with a simple white blouse. She keeps her hair (blond) in an unglamorous roll, and she wears glasses. She is stuffy, prim, and always willing to work overtime and take over Marshall's window when she goes to lunch. Naturally, we are not asked to suspect that she is the other woman Marshall's husband loves in place of the exotic, glamorous Marshall. Although Patrick lurks around among the bank books, rolling her eyes and watching everybody, it is made to look as if she suspects Marshall, not as if she herself is a suspect. In the end, Patrick's true character is revealed.

How? When the authorities go to her apartment and she opens the door, she's wearing furs; her hair is loose; she has a cigarette holder and plenty of jewelry. She's all in black, wearing a hat with feathers all over it and a veil. An audience grasps at once that this upgrading in fashion and glamour means that Lee Patrick is the villainess. This movie, made by Warner Brothers, famous for their tight, hard-driving crime and gangster movies, would, needless to say, be very different if its title were *A Man and His Money*.

Another example of how a genre has its issues completely revamped in female terms is illustrated by the dichotomy of the final shoot-out in the western *The Woman They Almost Lynched* (1953). The two female antagonists stalk down the dusty streets. One (Audrey Totter) is attired in typical cowboy gear with boots, pants, hat, and six-guns, and the other (Joan Leslie) wears a simple white blouse and riding skirt, but she, too, has a six-gun strapped across her hips. (It's on loan from her friend in the movie, Jesse James). As they move toward each other in the familiar ritual of the genre, they are watched by groups of men on the street, by males and dance-hall girls who are inside the saloon, and by a gaggle of "respectable" women who are standing around the town's formidable lady mayor, a woman who can tactfully be described only as masculine looking. Everything about the slow walk is traditional, including its culmination, in which Totter pulls her gun, fires, misses, and is then shot in the hand and knocked down by Leslie. These women might as well be Gary Cooper and Jimmy Stewart as far as the visual presentation of the encounter is concerned. However, immediately following the exchange of gunfire, the entire situation is shifted onto female terms:

LESLIE: [*shouting angrily*] Why don't you try acting like a woman? . . . You were born a woman, but look at you. A bloodthirsty female. A disgrace to all women.

TOTTER: [*equally angry*] What about you? Running a saloon! I suppose you're a symbol of virtue.

At this, Leslie turns and stomps back to her saloon, while Brian Donlevy, playing the raider Quantrill, who is inexplicably married to the Totter character, snarls at his wife: "Why don't you give up? She fights better than you. She shoots better than you. She even talks better than you." And one of his henchmen, standing by, adds his two bits: "Yeah! I'll bet she even *cooks* better than you."

The Woman They Almost Lynched is not a comedy, at least comedy was not its intention. It is, in fact, a taut and well-directed oddball western in which women are central to the story. Its shoot-out is a classic example of how a genre shifts its concerns to accommodate a story about women.

Are these females fighting because one is a sheepherder and one is a rancher? Are they fighting because gold has been discovered in the mountains around town? Are they fighting because the frontier needs to become civilized? No. They aren't even fighting over a man. They are fighting over the issue of what it means to be a woman. In fact, the whole story is structured on this very issue. Joan Leslie has come west from Michigan (the apparent center of civilized behavior) to join her brother. He is shot shortly after she arrives, and when the lady mayor refuses to employ her, she is forced into behavior that she feels is not really socially acceptable. She becomes a saloon owner and ends up having to use a gun *and* beat the stuffing out of Audrey Totter in a fistfight. After she cleans up on Totter (in an amazingly realistic and harsh fight), she bursts into tears and runs to the arms of the hero for comfort. Although she has ridden horses and shot guns all her life, and she is smart and a deadeye with a weapon, she feels that this really isn't the right way to behave. "Brawling," she wails, "like a common hussy."

The issue is that since a woman can do what a man can do, should she? Or should she accept her fate and just be a woman? Even as *The Woman They Almost Lynched* reaffirms the idea of a woman's true occupations as love and fashion, it seriously questions that idea by showing that women can do what men do, and do it better than they do, too.

Women, contrary to general opinion, are often found in male roles in western films. Clichés have it that the women all stand around on the porch, wearing aprons and waving good-bye while the men ride off to eradicate the Native Americans. This is ridiculous. In the western frontier world, a woman can easily "be more like a man." The time and place create a setting that provides a logical excuse for it. There are plenty of strong images of women taking action as if they were men in western movies, even when the entire genre is not being feminized as in *The Woman They Almost Lynched*. *Colorado Territory* (1949) ends with Virginia Mayo firing her six-guns at an advancing enemy, her man dead at her feet, until all her ammo is gone and she, too, falls dead and is later seen lying beside her love in the last image of the movie. Barbara Stanwyck rides confidently at the head of her troop of hired killers in *Forty Guns* (1957), while the sound track blares out the title song, "She's a high ridin' woman, with a whip." "It ain't often I meet a lady who can do anything besides look pretty," Wallace Beery tells Marjorie Main in *Bad Man of Wyoming* (1940, originally titled *Wyoming*). And he means it as a compliment. Main handles guns better than a troop of men. She holds Beery off single-handedly when he attacks her home, and she turns out to be a skilled blacksmith when his horse needs shoeing. Even though her masculine skills are treated comically, and Main is not a young beauty but a fat old woman, the point is that we meet such women quite often in the western movie.

Not all these women are respectable. Besides the title characters in *Belle Starr* (1941) and *Dakota Lil* (1950), there are minor characters, like Cheyenne Doolin from *Return of the Bad Men* (1948), the niece of the notorious Bill Doolin, a woman who rides with the gang of the Sundance Kid. When Randolph Scott captures her, he is warned, "Don't take no chances just because she's a girl. She's tough as nails." Cheyenne has contempt for the world of polite society and never misses a chance to say so. She wants only to live her life as an outlaw.

"Women have been known to work," suggests Scott.

"Oh, fine," she replies, "I can just see me waitin' tables six days a week."

"Some women even get married and raise a family, if they're not too busy robbin' banks, of course," says Scott.

At this suggestion, Cheyenne just hoots in disgust. When Cheyenne decides she likes Scott, she is annoyed to find out that he is already planning to marry a sweet widow with a little son. Cheyenne goes to the widow to warn her that she's going to lose Scott because Cheyenne was raised with guns and with men and knows how to handle both. She says she not only knows how to please a man, she's not afraid to do so. This, however, is a western, and this speech in no way wilts the spirit of the well-brought-up widow. She fires right back, "I was raised around guns, too. And I'm tough. I was alone for twelve hours in a farmhouse when my child was born. Don't confuse good manners with softness."

A typical secondary female character in a western movie is that of Jane Wyman in *Bad Men of Missouri* (1941), a film purportedly about the Younger Brothers. As the film begins, Wyman, playing the fiancée of Jim Younger, is a crusading female working on behalf of the farmers in the loan office. Her official job is that of secretary, but she's really there to look after the interests of the "little people." She is a fighter. She argues openly with her loan-shark boss, not only telling him off but slapping him hard. Then she tromps equally hard on the foot of his prissy assistant, just before she sweeps out the door, announcing that she's quitting. This is the American woman of the West on film. She is a thinking, fighting force for good and for change. She is brave and independent, and she has a job to do. Of course, she is also a platinum blond, wearing a snood on her hair, plaid ruffles on her dress, and a bunch of ribbons and flowers on her bonnet. She is a sex symbol who looks good while she slaps her boss and tells him off.

In *Bad Men of Missouri*, Wyman is contrasted with the fiancée of one of the other Younger Brothers. It is made clear that this other woman is weak, feminine, and thus not the woman America needs for the pioneer world. This character dies. Jane Wyman, the slaphappy queen, is the woman for the western world.

When the women are not secondary characters, or love interests, but instead take over the entire western story, the feminizing may make a very strong statement of liberation or it may not. Two useful films to contrast in this regard are *The Harvey Girls* (1946), a musical starring Judy Garland, and *Westward the Women*, starring Robert Taylor and Denise Darcel. Since one is a Technicolor musical satire of a western and one a conventional western, they provide a significant basis for comparison. First of all, setting a story about women going west to find a better life in the musical format automatically suggests that this goal is fantasy. People do not sing and dance down the streets in real life, and the translation of conversation into song, action into dance, and feeling into musical expression is a translation of ordinary human events into an "unreality" or a situation of entertainment, not a situation of "true story told." Thus, *The Harvey Girls* can get away with a lot. It can have its cake and sing it, too, as it can put guns in women's hands as well as any kind of words in their mouths. It can openly question the woman's role, because it so obviously in the long run is going to reaffirm it. A western, on the other hand, is a solidly established genre of "real"-story telling. No matter how comic, how fanciful, how romantic, the western is allegedly taking place somewhat realistically because there was and is a real West. It is an actual place, settled by actual people, so that as a genre, unlike the musical, the western presents something of a real historical context.

The young women in *The Harvey Girls* are journeying west, by train, to find husbands. This is also true of the women in *Westward the Women*, but they go by wagon train. *The Harvey Girls* is set in a later time period, after the West has assumed at least some veneer of civilization, and thus the young women can journey inside a caravan of civilization, with food and drink and comfort, whereas the women on the wagon train are out in the open, having to find their food along the way. Ostensibly, the Harvey girls are journeying west to work as waitresses in the Harvey restaurants, but their secret aim is to get married. The women in *Westward the Women* are openly traveling west to become wives to men in California, a place where there are no women, but their secret aim is to gain respect and independence. *The Harvey Girls* will be about the acceptance of love and marriage by women who want a conventional life in a conventional way, but *Westward the Women*, in which the women will also marry in the end, is about women earning the right to be equals to men and choose their own mates, because on their journey they prove they can do anything and everything that men do.

At the risk of offending women who wait tables, I have to point out that waitresses are servants. In order to marry, the Harvey girls are willing to leave homes and families behind and accept work that is servile in nature, in the thin hope that they will find love, or at least marriage. They have not found mates in the East, in their own world, although they have hoped and have done everything they feel was expected of them as women.

A polarity is established by the movie: some women are good; other women are bad. Across the street from the good girls who work in the Harvey restaurant are the bad girls who work in the saloon, headed up by Angela Lansbury, a very good bad girl. There's no chance for any woman to cross the street for change or reform. This is the opposite of *Westward the Women*, in which the whore, Denise Darcel, is given an opportunity to reform and find marriage. Garland plays that familiar character, the all-American girl with spunk. Spunk is not courage, but at least it allows action. It is one step past sass. Garland is allowed to do more than open her mouth and just talk smart. She takes action by marching into the saloon, gingerly holding a gun, to threaten the saloon people who have stolen the Harvey restaurant's steaks. Although she is able to make the villains return the meat, her handling of the gun is treated as if it's a joke, and she succeeds due to the danger of her incompetence. ("Watch out, men. I'd rather have Dead Eye Dick than a female with a gun in her hand," says a cowboy.) Garland also indulges in a ferocious fistfight with Lansbury. After their fight erupts, all the waitresses come over and beat the stuffing out of the whores. This is the female version of the male shoot-out in the street. Good women aren't wimps in the West! They have to be tough to live there, so they might as well fight like men. (Women punching each other in westerns also happens in *Destry Rides Again*, its remake *Frenchie* (1950), and *The Woman They Almost Lynched*.)

The opening title card of *The Harvey Girls* discusses how these women tamed and civilized the West, "not with powder . . . but with a beefsteak and a cup of coffee." They are, it is said, representative "of the order to come." The women are a symbol of the civilizing influence that men need. In the end, the Harvey girls find their men, although the comedy lead, Virginia O'Brien, sings a satiric song about hers (Ray Bolger). "They say they have hair on their chest but the only thing I've seen is a fancy vest. I'm still looking for something wild in the wild, wild west." The masculine myth of the West just hasn't panned out for her. It has, however, for Garland, who although her spunk carries her past the challenges of guns, fistfights, Indians, fires, and snakes, still swoons when her man kisses her. She

wouldn't have ended up with him, though, without the interference and
help of her bad-girl rival, Angela Lansbury. The one thing that *Westward
the Women* and *The Harvey Girls* have in common is a final show of sisterhood. Garland apologizes for not respecting Lansbury by saying she's
from a small town and probably reacted like a snob. Garland wryly explains
it all through the traditional woman's film device, fashion: "It's only a
matter of style, isn't it? I mean, some people wear one kind of dress and
some another."

Westward the Women (1951) is one of the few films to present overt,
positive sisterhood. It is almost a casebook of traditional attitudes toward
women that will be refuted by the visual presentation. Contained within
its 118 minutes of running time is a gallery of familiar sexual role models.
There is a tough masculine hero, a sex-object female, a "masculine" female
played for comic relief due to her looks and her size, a "neuter" male
comedy lead who can behave positively toward women because he is not
a serious sexual partner, a beardless boy who pays for his sensitivity toward
women with his death, an unmarried mother, a patriarchal father, and a
victimized woman who is first raped and then accidentally killed.

The opening of the film provides a sharp visual contrast between the
free-choice world of the male and the closed-in, limited world of the female.
There is a dual prologue: first, California, 1891, the man's world; and then,
Chicago, the woman's world. Sweeping pan shots from a high vantage point
introduce the masculine universe of Whitman's Valley, California, as the
credits fade and the film begins. The image contains wild horses, riders,
wide-open vistas, and tough men driving herds of newly captured mustangs
into stockades. The sounds and sights are all masculine. The feeling is
one of openness and space, with the men confident and strong in that space.
The two leading male characters are introduced: the hero, appropriately
named Buck and played by Robert Taylor, and Mr. Whitman, the valley
patriarch, played by John McIntire. The two men share a father-son relationship of mutual camaraderie, shared indulgences (they exchange remarks about having both patronized a local whore), and easy control over
themselves and the landscape.

In marked contrast, the second half of the prologue takes place in a
closed room in Chicago, in which all doors and windows are shut, and a
group of women heavily dressed in hats, gloves, and warm clothes sits
primly and correctly on chairs, isolated from each other in their seats.
Their faces are impassive, and many are sewing or knitting while they
await Whitman's decision as to whether or not they will be allowed to make
the trek to California. Above Whitman's head is a sign: "Come to California.
A great country for marrying—find a new home in the west." This patriar-

chal figure deals with the men back in his valley as if they were all equals. He interviews the women, asking them their names, occupations, ages, and the women respond fully, never questioning his right to ask these things. He—and they—see him as the master of their fates.

When Buck, the wagon master, first talks to the women in Chicago, his contempt for them is clear. He talks angrily, in marked contrast to Whitman, who, although he condescends to the women, is at least kind. Buck outlines the horrors and rigors of the two-thousand-mile trip to California. "One out of every three of you will be dead. If you're smart, you'll leave." When the women do not leave, he adds, "Well, you asked for it. You'll get it."

Throughout his talk, the women sit passively, faces hard-set, indicating nothing. They are obviously used to this attitude from men. When Buck barks "Can any of you handle a gun? I mean shoot it and hit what you're shooting at?" two women stand up, each taking one of his guns, and each easily hitting a bull's-eye, appropriately the two eyes of a man's face on a political poster. When the first sure shot hands Taylor's gun back, she says quietly, "Is *that* what you meant?" All the women allow themselves a small bit of laughter.

Buck is what his name implies: tough, sexually successful, and aggressive, devoid of tenderness or sympathy. He is nearly inhuman in his attitude toward his work, which is the dominant source of his pride and his masculinity. He is the very best wagon master there is, and he knows it. His attitude toward women is clear: they are inferior. They are necessary for sex, but, along those lines, it is best to stick to whores, who do a good job and give you no trouble afterward. ("Only two things in this life scare me," he says, "and a good woman's both of them.") That such an unattractive character is designed to be the hero of the film is indicative of accepted attitudes. It is all right for Buck to browbeat the women, for, after all, they are only women. And it is right that the leading lady should fall for him, and that the end of the movie should find them together, even though he has slapped her, whipped her, insulted her, and degraded her throughout the long trek west. The end brings about no character change, no apology from Buck. Such a change could indicate weakness in him, a nonmasculine characteristic.

Fifi Danon is the classic sex-object heroine. Played by French actress Denise Darcel, Danon is never called by her first name after the introduction in the film by anyone but herself. She is big breasted in the mammary tradition of the fifties, and she is clearly a reformed whore. The beginning of the film finds her dressed in ribbons and bows, feathers and fripperies, and huddling with a group of "actresses" (that well-known Hollywood euphemism) planning how to get accepted by Whitman as suitable for his valley. She and her best friend disguise themselves by buying new, plainer clothes and carrying Bibles. A good woman is never, but never, sexy!

John McIntire is a father figure who has grown benign with age, more tolerant than Buck, although the hint of his past is that he was once like Buck. He sees the women as the one natural resource his valley lacks: "My valley is rich. Wheat, cattle, horses, men, ranches. I could see this once. They called it Whitman's folly, but I've made it real. But I forgot one thing. The roots to keep it alive and grow. Women. Good women. Wives. Kids in diapers and the smell of cooking."

Julie Bishop plays Darcel's best friend and fellow former prostitute, Laurie. She represents the classic woman-as-victim figure, the dispensable upstart who dares to dream of a life of her own, of a change that can be real. For her, an honest marriage represents equality, as compared with the relationships she has previously had with men. It is clear that she has always been the loser, the eternal masochist. For Laurie, the trip west means a chance to cease being a victim of men, but life has marked her out as such, and to the end she is exploited against her will. She will first be the victim of rape and then an accidental drowning death.

There are two comic-relief leads in *Westward the Women*: Ito, the Japanese cook hired on by Buck ("I hate women's cooking") and the enormous, masculine Hope Emerson in one of her rock-ribbed roles. These two characters provide humor by being the opposite of what is expected of them as man and woman in "normal" circumstances. Since the film is about a situation in which a man has to learn to accept his own softer side, and women have to learn to be strong, these characters provide a carefully written and structured comic parallel. The woman is physically big, and the man delicate. The woman does a man's work, being strong enough to hold her wagon under control over the worst terrain, while the man is the cook who also entertains everyone by reenacting a melodrama he saw in St. Louis.

The scene in which Laurie dies is one of the first moments in which the women function totally on their own. Heavy rains have endangered the wagon in which Laurie and Danon are sleeping, but the only two men left with the train (the Japanese cook and Buck) are off alone together, getting drunk. (The remainder of the men on the wagon train have deserted, because Buck shot the rapist among them.) When the wagon tips over and is carried into deep water, the women themselves have to band together to chop the bottom out of the vehicle and drag Laurie's body free. As the women pull the tragic Laurie out, they carefully, lovingly hold her dead body up into the rain. There is a sense that, at last, she is being washed clean of her fears and disappointments in life. She is left behind in a grave that carries the simple marker "Laurie." After this event the women are stronger and know they must rely on themselves if they are to make it. Again, in a woman's film, the men have let the women down, being drunk and useless in a moment of crisis.

As the women journey west, they change physically in the frame. Gradually, they grow comfortable with all the difficult tasks they face. Arriving at the edge of the great salt flats, they are seen as if they are individual pillars against the sky, no longer small and frightened in their bonnets and ruffles. Placed against the landscape like giant phallic symbols, the actresses stand tall and confident, assessing the next leg of a journey they now know will never defeat them. As they cross the salt flats, a baby is born to one of them, an unwed mother. "Poor little woman," softly intones the Japanese cook. The women walk silently behind her wagon in the ferocious heat, their faces tense as they listen to the strangled cries of pain that are accompanying the birth. When a wheel falls off the wagon, the horse shies in fear and begins to gallop. Instead of reacting with fear and confusion, the women immediately run after it, lifting the wagon together and holding it up, sweating and straining in the intense heat, listening, listening, saying nothing until, at last, they hear the cry of the newborn baby. At this they smile and at last gently set the broken wagon down. The news is brought out: "It's a boy. It's a he." When the broken wagon is left behind, the camera lingers on it as a symbol as the women journey onward, no longer just taking orders but now in control of their trip. Dramatic images of individual women against an open and stark landscape are rare in American films, and they are memorable.

The women face one other crisis. As the birth of the baby is a crisis in feminine terms, the second is traditionally masculine and generic: an Indian attack. Once again, the hero is not present, having gone off to chase the angry French heroine, with that encounter ending in a hot embrace between them. The women fight alone, and the attack is as violent and difficult as any that would be shown in a standard western film, but with only females to fight it. When Buck and Danon return from their sexual tryst, they join in the battle's finale. When it's all over, Buck asks how many did not survive. In a moving roll call of the dead that is like a roster of sisterhood, the names are called out one by one by the living women, who are, in fact, paying tribute to the courage of fallen comrades.

Westward the Women ends as it was intended to end, with the women all becoming brides. This in no way negates their story as an odyssey of pain toward equality for women. They insist on choosing their own mates, and the men respect their wishes. Since they have had to take the male prerogative in order to arrive in the valley, they are entitled to take it regarding remaining there. As the women select their mates, each finds in

Robert Taylor surrounded by his female wagon crew in *Westward the Women*

some way a counterpart to herself. Emerson, the giant woman, finds an equally bizarre physical specimen of a man, while the Italian woman finds another Italian and the woman with glasses finds a man with similar bad eyesight. Instead of being silly, this finish seems to be a perfect closure, in which the brave women who've traveled west have actually found their other selves, the selves that society has denied them. They have been told they can't cope, can't shoot, can't rope, can't ride, can't fight, and can't endure, and they have proved this to be wrong. Those "masculine" things are now absorbed into them, and they unite to their own other halves at journey's end.

ACTION FILMS that are dramatically feminized are always from a *highly* recognizable and specific genre. Some genres, however, do not have to be adjusted as radically as others in order to accommodate the woman as a leading active force in the story. It is possible just to change the sex of a major character from male to female and more or less go on from there. Such a movie is the swashbuckler *At Sword's Point* (1952), starring Maureen O'Hara. O'Hara, a big, strong-looking woman with a certain amount of athletic ability, made an ideal heroine to do a man's job on-screen. In *At Sword's Point*, a classic adventure film, the key character in the plot is a female musketeer played by O'Hara. Her character is really the story catalyst in the film, and in a deceptive and indirect way the entire movie is about women. Women are everywhere. (Even a queen, not a king, is in power, although she is being controlled behind the scenes by an evil man.) D'Artagnan's son, Cornel Wilde, is first defined as a boy who loves his mother. When the queen's ring arrives to summon him to her aid, it is his mother who further empowers him, taking down his father's sword and giving it to him, saying: "Do it." Aramis's father is dead, too, and Porthos's is old, ill, and weak. Athos doesn't even have a son old enough to fight. It is his daughter (O'Hara) he has to send. Ah, but she's a real pistol and can duel the pants off the other three young musketeers, which is pretty much what she does to one of them.

The movie, however, was advertised to the public in the usual way: "Adventure! Excitement! Danger! Swordplay!" said the ads. They did not say, "A woman's story, Love and Romance, and also some adventure! Excitement! Danger! and Swordplay!" *At Sword's Point* is set in 1648 in France. As the story unfolds, the film does not suggest in any way that O'Hara is not the equal of the three men. On the contrary, she duels Cornel Wilde to a draw, and he openly tells the queen later, "Her sword is the equal of ours." What does happen is that sex becomes an issue, and this is the inevitable separation of men and women on-screen. When all four have to sleep in the same bed, the situation changes. She is no longer one of them; she is different. The next day they face the enemy in a fight, and she becomes equal again. "We will not fight with a lady," one of the villains declares. "I am no lady when I fight," she replies, and proves it. In the end, Cornel Wilde will state, "You are the bravest of us all," and it's seen to be true. The film has made it true.

How does O'Hara, the lady musketeer, demonstrate her bravery? She duels her head off, of course, but she also takes the place of the princess who is being sent off to marry the villain. No man could do that. By offering herself up to marriage, putting on a wedding veil and gown, she is risking her own life beyond anything they could do. She can do the one thing the men cannot do—she can successfully pretend to be a woman. She has also devised a plan whereby she will pose as a barmaid, luring the soldiers with her beauty and femininity, again something the men cannot do. It is always her brains that devise the plan, her beauty that helps carry it out, and her dueling strength that ensures its victorious execution. It is also the *fact* that she is a woman that makes their plans a success.

In films like this, there is often a key moment in which the woman breaks down and tells the villains what they want to know when she sees

Maureen O'Hara and Cornel Wilde in *At Sword's Point*.
Touché!

the man she loves captured. Such a scene is presented in *At Sword's Point*, with O'Hara forced to watch Wilde being hideously tortured. The assumption is that she will break down, because that is the genre convention and because she is a woman. However, O'Hara does *not* break. She will not tell them what they want to know. Later she will be temporarily undone, but not by love. Not by romance. Not by the softness of a woman's heart. She is undone by the treachery of another woman, who tells O'Hara that the other musketeers are dead and convinces her she is a friend who will help rescue the little king. Thus, O'Hara's femininity is not really the problem. It is the other woman's femininity!

The significance of *At Sword's Point* is that it clearly presents a woman as the equal of men in a man's world. The men see her as equal and accept her as such, allowing her brains to solve their problems. They are not worried about letting a woman lead the way. Furthermore, she is not brought down because *she* is a woman, and she does not participate as an equal in the action at the expense of her sexuality. She *is* sexual, and when two of the men fall in love with her, she has no problem choosing the one she wants. No one gives a speech in which it is said, "If only you'd put on a dress, you'd be attractive" or "If only you'd realize you are a woman." She realizes she's attractive even with her sword in her hand, and so do they. She doesn't have to change out of breeches to find out she's beautiful; she already knows it. She doesn't have to find out she's a woman when she's kissed. She is, from the very beginning, both a woman and a swordsperson, and she doesn't have to stop being a woman to be good at dueling. No big deal is made of this, and in that fact lies the importance of *At Sword's Point*, a movie in which the genre is feminized more or less by just turning one character into a woman.

The question of how the woman's film is meshed with the World War II combat film I have previously addressed in *Anatomy of a Genre: The World War II Combat Film*. In short, it is impossible to separate films like *So Proudly We Hail* (1943) or *Cry Havoc* (1943) into one genre or the other. Combat films or women's films? They are either one, or both, or neither. Although the generic setting of such movies *is* combat, the primary issues are those concerned with the woman's world, not the war. The women are worrying about love, romance, sex, and clothing. In *So Proudly We Hail*, there's a dance, a scene of childbirth, a wedding ceremony, and a honeymoon night. Rape becomes the primary combat threat. At the same time, the film is set in an actual combat zone, the island of Bataan, and all the iconography of war is present: guns, ambulances, ships, soldiers, helmets, and a treacherous, mechanized enemy.

What happens is that the basic objective of women in combat is clearly seen to be *taking care of men*, not fighting the war itself. The women are brave, strong, and intelligent, and they behave as real heroes in key scenes. One can see that when a male genre is feminized, it allows women a chance for freedom and heroism but also maintains a status quo in which the women themselves cannot, for example, win the war, only wait for the men to win it for them. The complexity of generic transformation is illustrated by the fact that this film can easily be called either a woman's film or a combat film.

The military-training-camp genre for women is illustrated by *Keep Your Powder Dry* (1945). The pun of the title reveals much. When women go off to camp, one of the problems is sure to be cosmetic. Even though the credits are backed up by a song bawling out "A Wac is a soldier, too," the action of the film at least partially suggests otherwise. A Wac *is* a soldier. She can be trained as one, and as long as love or men do not come along, she will adhere to her military training.

Keep Your Powder Dry demonstrates that, at its root, it is a woman's film by reviving the popular "there are three of them" format of such films as *Ladies in Love*, *Moon Over Miami*, and *Three Blind Mice*. Three very different women come to a Des Moines, Iowa, training center after they join the Wacs during the early days of World War II. "You'll be the best soldier that ever wore a skirt" is said to the one (Laraine Day) who is military to the core, an army-brat daughter of a top officer. The other two represent total femininity, frivolity, and luxury (Lana Turner) and dogged loyalty to whatever society or the situation expects of her (Susan Peters). What happens to these women in training is also revealed in the lyrics to the song: "We came to win the war, but what did we do when we got here? We scrubbed and scrubbed some more."

These women are all trying to compensate for something. Peters, who is secretly married, wants something to do while her husband serves, so she can feel more a part of his own sacrifice. When he is killed, she then knows how important what she is doing is, as it will fill her time and give her something to do with herself. Day is trying to live up to her family's tradition of military success. As it turns out, she is also compensating for what she believes is her lack of sex appeal. She tells how she envied a woman like Lana Turner, "a girl who knew her power as a woman, in high heels and furs." Turner is compensating for finding out she was living a decadent, useless life. Thus, the three women represent:

1. How a woman ought not to be like a man (Day)
2. How a woman ought not to be selfish and frivolous (Turner)
3. How a woman ought to be loyal, reliable, and married (Peters)

Turner makes it as a soldier, proving that World War II really did usher in, however briefly, a new era in which a beautiful sex symbol could find success as a man. Furthermore, the basic issues of the film turn out to be personal integrity, the honor of the corps, and women's ability to do things.

"IF I WASN'T a pirate," says Binnie Barnes in *Abbott and Costello Meet Captain Kidd* (1952), "I'd cry." Lady pirates, however, *do* cry, because love, the inevitable, trips them up and squeezes the tears right out of them. *Anne of the Indies* (1951), starring Jean Peters as Anne Providence, is the story of a female pirate who ends up crying because she can't escape the fact she's a woman.* The man she loves betrays her and lies to her, even though she's a mighty brave lassie. ("She has more courage than you, Pierre.") Unlike Maureen O'Hara in *At Sword's Point*, Anne fails the acid

* In an article called "Femininity and the Masquerade: 'Anne of the Indies,'" Claire Johnston says that this film "marks one of the most radical attempts to explore the fact of sexual heterogeneity in the classical Hollywood cinema, foregrounding the repression of the feminine. . . . [The film] poses the possibility of a genuinely bisexual disposition while remaining a male myth." I would suggest the latter to be common to women's films, rather than uncommon.

test. "You like to play the man. Then act like one," she is told when asked to kill a group of people that include the man she loves. "But I'm a woman," she replies, "as you're so fond of reminding me." Her friend, an asexual-doctor character, tells her, "I used to like you. You were gallant, clean. You've betrayed yourself, my dear." In the end, she sacrifices herself by sailing her ship directly into the enemy. Anne is destroyed by the problem of being a woman.

Anne of the Indies is a female desperado. She sails the seas in her ship, the *Sheba Queen*, wreaking havoc where'er she goes, a feared and respected pirate "whose name for one short year" meant hell on earth. Anne bears scars, however. ("I bear many scars from the English.") Her brother has been hanged by them, and over her breast is literal evidence of the woman's pain, a scar left by the treatment she received from a drunken doctor for a wound suffered. She's cruel and shows no mercy to captives, making them walk the plank without batting an eyelash. The movie is a kind of floating *A Woman's Face*, in which an antisocietal, cruel female outlaw is tamed and reformed by love.

Anne is the notorious Captain Providence. She has chosen to take a masculine name, and her mentor is Blackbeard the Pirate, who has taught her to duel and to live like a man. He is not a sexual figure in her life, being old and ugly and fat, a sure sign we are not to think of him as a romantic character. Anne and Blackbeard duel each other with great gusto and pleasure. He knocks her down, but she gets up and knocks his sword out of his hand. The film provides an action image of a woman openly dueling with a man and taking and giving her knocks as an equal. When things go wrong in her life, and Anne becomes miserable, she carries on in her tough tradition, refusing to knuckle under, demanding of the doctor, "Am I to weep like a woman?" He replies, "You're not to do anything like a woman." But, ultimately, she does. She falls in love with Louis Jourdan, a married man she captures and allows into her crew, not knowing he is a French privateer captured by the English and sent to find Captain Providence for them. If he succeeds, his ship will be returned to him. Anne at first does not change after the Frenchman joins her crew; she remains true to her masculine/pirate self. After Captain Providence successfully overtakes and robs another ship, Anne, the Frenchman, and the doctor each choose one significant thing for themselves from the booty. Anne chooses a sword. The asexual doctor chooses a book. And the Frenchman chooses a dress. The female has chosen the male symbol and the man the feminine one, as the film is a constant questioning of male and female roles. Unbeknownst to Anne, the Frenchman has actually taken the dress because he wants it for his beautiful wife, but his selection of the dress marks the beginning of Anne's transformation from male hero to female heroine. She cannot resist the beautiful garment, eventually trying it on, standing in front of a long mirror and staring at herself. She sees herself as a woman for the first time. The Frenchman discovers her, openly admiring her. When she asks why, he says, "It's the nature of men" to like to see a woman in a dress. As he kisses her, they are interrupted with the news that Blackbeard's ship is coming, the obvious reestablishment of Anne's more masculine side in the plot.

Later, Anne will learn that the Frenchman is not only a spy but married. She is twice betrayed, first as a pirate and then as a woman. When she finally meets the wife, played by Debra Paget, Anne recognizes the contrast between them. Paget is frail, femininely dressed, and socially correct in everything she does. However, she is also feisty. She openly challenges the lady pirate by saying, "You're a disgrace to our sex. Do you consider yourself a woman?" This is always the question to women occupying the man's position in the frame. How can you be a woman if you are a man? Or, how can you be a man if you are a woman? There's a hideous logic to it.

Anne, having been portrayed as cruel and relentless in the first, masculine part of her story, finally accepts the softness associated with the female side of herself. When she has captured the Frenchman's wife, he begs Anne to spare her. He has only one real reason that she should do it: "You're a woman." By this he means that somewhere inside her there must be the mercy and gentleness that is associated with the female sex. Since love for the Frenchman (and the donning of his dress) has proved to Anne that she *is* a woman, she can only respond to his argument. She spares his wife, and him, too. She provides food, supplies, maps, and a boat to set them free, sending her doctor friend along with them. She then covers their escape by sailing her ship directly at Blackbeard's, sacrificing herself for the man she loves. Her female side overrules her masculine self, so she dies. "She's home at last. Let the sea keep her."

Anne of the Indies is a film that only appears to be a pirate movie with a female star. It is actually a movie that is about challenging the traditional male and female roles that we see on-screen. Every plot turn is connected in some way to gender, and the movie refers constantly to the conventions of the woman's film, while apparently set inside a male genre, the pirate film. For instance, Anne is the product of an illegitimate birth, one of the staples of the woman's film. She falls in love with a married man who betrays her, and she sacrifices herself to this love. However, her mentor is a male-outlaw figure, and her ability to *behave* in action like a man is clearly established. In order to clarify for viewers the contrast between the woman's film and the pirate genre, characters discuss male and female roles. "It's the nature of men," says Louis Jourdan to Jean

Peters about why he likes seeing her in a dress rather than in pants. "I should have known a wench couldn't be other than a wench," says Blackbeard when Anne breaks off with him because of her love for the Frenchman. Anne of the Indies is tough, but she is a woman, so she ends up a victim of love, sacrifice, and fashion.

There is no better example of a movie that contrasts the male and female worlds visually than the 1944 *Frenchman's Creek*. Starring Joan Fontaine and Arturo de Cordova, and directed by Mitchell Leisen, *Frenchman's Creek* is written by Talbot Jennings, but it is based on a best-selling novel by Daphne Du Maurier. It is an example of how a pirate movie is feminized.

The first minutes of the film establish Dona as a querulous, petulant, bored, and unhappy woman. Her marriage is shown as empty and loveless, and her husband is seen as a fool whose main interests are gambling, food, and drink. Everything seen in Dona's environment is restrictive: her corsets, her clothing, her small, cramped dressing table loaded with the items she needs to make herself into a woman society thinks beautiful. As she primps and prepares, one sees that all that is natural is contained, covered, powdered, and perfumed. Dona's life is totally devoid of freedom.

The next extended scene takes place at the gambling house itself. In the politest of 1940s terms, due to the censorship code, an establishment that is decadent is visualized. A Brueghelesque swirl of crowded humanity, most wearing masks, is seen reeling through the noisy spaces of the establishment, with the men chasing and lunging after the screeching and laughing women. There is a discreet hint that the gambling house is really a brothel with all the men and women wearing masks in order to conceal their true identities. In this way, they are freed from society's disapproval.

Dona walks among the crowd, a look of distaste on her face. She, too, carries a mask on a stick, and the visual impression is a suggestion that the woman's role is to wear a mask in public. She tells her husband, "I've been playing a part for you. I'm not going to play it anymore." She is clearly unhappy with the emptiness of her life, but not certain what else there is for her to do.

One option presents itself. She can relieve her boredom by temporarily having an affair. The film's chief villain, played by Basil Rathbone, confronts her, smug and confident that, because her husband is neglecting her, she will fall into his arms. She repulses him, but he points out a truth: She is inviting advances such as his "by letting your husband bring you here to sport with him." The movie in this way establishes that the only freedom open to women in this society is that of whoredom or adultery. At this point, the film has clearly established the world in which Fontaine lives and her lack of options in it. She takes the only action she can think of taking: she packs up her clothes and her children and announces she is going "to the country"—that is, their Cornwall estate. Because it is a dull world far from society's pleasures, she and her husband haven't been there in ages. Because of this dullness, she'll get away both from her partying husband and from her would-be seducer.

During the transition trip from London to the country, Dona is warned about a deadly French pirate who raids the Cornish coast. She ignores the warnings and presses on. Upon her arrival, Dona finds the house dusty, uninhabited except for one strange servant she doesn't remember ever having seen there before. This man has an unfamiliar—can it be French?—accent. In a scene that suggests feelings of a newfound freedom, she removes covers from the furniture and gives the servant instructions to open windows, bring in fresh flowers, and so on. At night, she is girlish and happy, alone in her bedroom. Her nightgown is loose, comfortable. Her feet are bare, and she wiggles her toes after flopping on her bed, the bed in which she will sleep without her odious husband. The next day Dona is seen playing with her children, romping with them on the lawn after a picnic, rolling on the ground and laughing. Their idyll is interrupted by the unexpected visit of a pompous neighbor, who again warns about French pirates.

That night, from her bedroom window, Dona observes her mysterious servant meeting an even more mysterious man outside on the lawn, and the next day she sets out to search the woods and rivers near her home. She is captured and taken aboard the pirate ship, where she meets . . . who else? . . . the Pirate Hero. Now Dona enters the world of men, in particular the world of men who live outside society and *all* of its restrictions. She will experience the freedom of the pirate's world and of the ocean, but she will experience it through the device of love for a forbidden man, a man outside her own polite society, even outside her own English nation.

The film begins a series of further contrasts, but not without some conversation that points up the issues for the viewing audience. Dona and her pirate agree to "sup at midnight," long after everyone is asleep, when he can thus arrive safely unseen at her home. Her strange servant, obviously one of the pirate crew, helps Dona plan a late-night snack of "little potatoes roasted in their skins, a cold bird, a bottle, and some wonderful straw-berries." While he, obviously a Frenchman, discusses the menu, Dona tells him, "Oh, I wish I were a man. I, too, would find a ship and sail out to sea and be a law unto myself." After these exchanges, all Dona has to do to get ready is decide what to wear. (She rejects one spectacular gold and red dress. That will be saved for later, the rape scene.)

When the pirate arrives for the romantic midnight meal, he is a schoolgirl's dream of a pirate: a handsome man, with long curls and high boots. He is not coarse, and he is not cruel. On the contrary, he is an artist who draws beautiful sea gulls (thus establishing a link with what are thought to be feminine things), and he wants to spend his whole evening talking about *her*. He flirts. She flirts. She plays the spinet, and he sketches, but mostly they talk—all about the life of Dona St. Columb. The French pirate tells her that he fell in love with her the first moment he ever saw her portrait in her house, months ago, but he sees now that she has ceased to be that youthful and happy person. He speaks of how he, however, can still see the exciting and alive woman behind the mask of polite female society she is forced to wear. "It's too bad you're not a boy," he tells her. "You could sail with me." "Why do I have to be a boy to do that?" she asks, and he realizes the logic of her question. He agrees to take her along on a pirate raid, to allow her to leave the Barbara Cartland woman's genre the film has belabored and to enter the world of the masculine pirate film.

Dona throws off all restraint. Her face radiant, she cries out, "I feel as if I've never been alive before." Dona St. Columb, the leading character of *Frenchman's Creek*, is described as being thirty years of age, married eight years, and the mother of two children. Yet this is her first taste of freedom, her first opportunity to do as she wishes.

As the story has progressed, the stages of her expanding freedom have been represented for Joan Fontaine's Dona through costume change. At first, she is seen loaded with jewels, carrying a mask, moving slowly and heavily under a corseted, layered gown, her hair carefully twisted into precise curls and shapes. After she arrives at her country home, she wears looser garments. And when she joins her pirate lover for a picnic by a stream, she changes behind a tree from an elegant society outfit she wore to visit friends into a simple peasant dress. Wearing this outfit, with her hair loose around her shoulders, a ribbon holding it back, she goes fishing and roasts her catch over a fire. When eventually she boards the pirate ship, she dresses as a boy in stocking cap, pants, shirt, and boots and pretends to be a man on a pirate raid. This progression from restriction to freedom, from female status to masculine, comes visually in appropriate terms for the woman's film: through costuming and fashion.

When Dona returns from her adventure, reality closes in on her harshly. Her husband and a group of his male gambling friends, including the villainous Rathbone, have come down to the coast to capture those pesky French pirates. The task falls to Dona to entertain her husband and the others until midnight, when the pirates will have a favorable tide to sail out of Frenchman's Creek. Dona once again puts on her feminine mask and plays the role of society woman. Gowned in scarlet and gold, red rubies in her ears and at her throat, she does what women do: acts as hostess to a lavish dinner. She flirts, imitates Nell Gwyn, and behaves like a bawd, putting her leg up on the dinner table to show her garter. She is willing to do anything to save the pirates, and to accomplish her goal she uses female weapons: food, clothing, and sex.

The pirates, however, intrude into the dinner, so the hero can have one last embrace and a good-bye from Dona. He says, "I realized our make-believe was over. I am bound to you as you are bound to me." Thus it is suggested that his maleness is covertly a part of her, something that is contained within women that must be repressed or at least dealt with when it surfaces.

The villain, however, sees to it that the pirate is captured. His hatred of Dona erupts in his speech. "You've had at last the love you've wanted all your life. I could kill you for it." She has tasted freedom in that love, the one thing a man like him does not want a woman to have. They struggle as he tries to kiss/rape her, and she ends up killing him. During the fight, she hears one of her babies crying, and at the end of the scene she is seen comforting her little son.

In the finale of the film, the pirate chief is captured, but not the pirates themselves; they have escaped to their ship. It is Dona who devises a plan to rescue their leader, and it is Dona who executes it. In plumed hat and lavish gown, she uses the brains and devices of a female to save her lover, creating a plot regarding a false baby doctor and a pregnancy that requires the doctor's presence. The female part of the character and story liberates the male through feminine ploys and devices. At the very end, dressed as a boy again, Dona engineers her lover's escape or, as it were, gives birth to his freedom. He invites her to Land's End, his home in France, but she cannot go. When her son awoke, she knew then that a man may be free "at all costs if he will, but a woman may escape for only a night and a day." She will remain behind in her old life. He will go forward to his, but he, too, has been trapped by their love. "A pirate who escaped—who loved the sea more than anything in the world, till he found you."

Frenchman's Creek is the story of a woman who finds a man to be not a husband or father but an instrument of liberation. He represents, also, the lure of irresponsibility in terms of her duties as a mother. Dona desires freedom the way men have it, and she momentarily ("for a night and a day") lives life as men live it, but because she is not really a man she must return to her own world, which is defined by the sound of her child's crying for her in the night.

"Women may play and wander for a time," warns her pirate, "but in the end instinct is too strong for them. They must make their nests." She says, "What is the answer?" "There never has been an answer" is his reply.

The character played by Joan Fontaine in *Frenchman's Creek* takes action in the film, leaving her husband, loving a pirate, killing a sexual assailant, going on a pirate raid, and freeing her lover from prison. The men of her societal world cannot do any of this. They are totally ineffectual. The message of the film is a powerful one: women can do anything. They can be full-functioning human beings, the equals of men in any enterprise, and they are welcome to exercise sexual prerogatives for themselves. They can make decisions, and they can make choices. Yet they must understand that, once they become mothers, true freedom is denied them. Once they are mothers, they are in the hands of society and its rules. Their reward? Presumably, their joy in their children. Dona's life shifts back and forth between a male genre (pirate movie) and a woman's film. The pirate genre is thoroughly feminized, yet Dona can never really get out of her own world, her own genre.

WHAT WE LEARN is that, overall, women don't have much luck in the male world, not even when they're out there behaving like men. Lady gangsters die just like men gangsters, unless they're reformed by love and motherhood. Lady pirates don't have much luck either, unless they quit the sea and decide to stay home. Women have better luck in combat, because their cause is noble, and everyone had to do his or her part in World Wars I and II and Korea, and there is a specific role that society has defined for women to play in the combat zone: ambulance driver, nurse, doctor, communications expert, or spy. Thus, the woman's presence in the combat genre is endorsed by reality. Women seem to fare best in the West, where society has not yet laid its heavy hand and where they are needed to pioneer and to help get things civilized.

But why should women in these genres be totally different from men? Men in combat die, and gangsters end up in the gutter. Male pirates have to find love and decide to reform in order to conclude the plot lines, and men run up against having to help civilize the West, too. The point is that if a woman is allowed to enter what is presumably a male genre and participate in it by playing what would ordinarily be the hero's role, then it has been somehow suggested that women can be men. We cannot call this progress, and feminists have posited the concept that one of the few options open to women in film viewing is the transference of their identity into maleness, the loss of themselves as women. These films, with plots in which a woman clearly remains a woman but does what men do, offer a woman the opportunity to experience freedom in a man's world or a man's genre, while remaining a woman.

PROOF:
KITTY AND ANGIE AND JANET

ONE OF THE MOST popular formats of the woman's film, the "this time there's three of them" plot discussed in the chapter called "Duality," offers a good opportunity to test the definition of the woman's film contained in this book. Let's take three typical movies from the 1940s and treat the heroines as three leading ladies in one big woman's film. The films are *Kitty Foyle* (1940), *Smash-Up, the Story of a Woman* (1947), and *The Guilt of Janet Ames* (1947). It is possible to weave their stories together in a "there's three of them" format and demonstrate that all their lives are the same old story about a woman, her world, her fashion and glamour, her divided self, her men, her marriage, and her motherhood. The three women, Kitty, Angie (the woman in *Smash-Up*), and Janet could all be rooming together, which, in fact, they are, in the sense that they share the room of the 1940s woman's film, in which they are living to serve the needs of female moviegoers. "Needs" means that women need something other than the lives they lead, but they also need to have their own lives re-affirmed.

Kitty and Angie and Janet are all nice girls. Angie and Janet don't have any family, and Kitty's old daddy died out from under her. Therefore, they've all three had to take care of themselves one way or another. They've got to put bread on the table, which means either doing it themselves by working or getting married so their husbands can do it for them. Kitty, Angie, and Janet are women with the basic woman's film problem: what to do about the fact that they are women.

First of all, before examining Kitty and Angie and Janet themselves, there is the overview of the three movies as commercial product to consider. Each one has clearly announced its genre by placing the woman at the center of the universe, with two of the movies bearing the names of their heroines, and the other boldly calling itself *The Story of a Woman*. Two of the films indicate the desperate straits that women can get themselves into, via the words "smash-up" and "guilt" in their titles. Each has as its leading lady a major star associated with roles for strong women: Ginger Rogers in *Kitty Foyle*, Susan Hayward in *Smash-Up*, and Rosalind Russell in *The Guilt of Janet Ames*. Both Rogers and Hayward were nominated for Oscars as Best Actress for those performances, with Rogers winning the statuette over stiff competition (Bette Davis in *The Letter*, Joan Fontaine in *Rebecca*, Katharine Hepburn in *The Philadelphia Story*, and Martha Scott in *Our Town*). Hayward lost to Loretta Young in *The Farmer's Daughter*. Each of the films has as its leading man (or men) actors who either never become big-name film stars (James Craig in *Kitty Foyle*, Lee Bowman in *Smash-Up*), or men who were second-echelon stars (Dennis Morgan in *Kitty Foyle* and Melvyn Douglas in *The Guilt of Janet Ames*), following the common pattern of the genre in which the leading men are weak actors. Each film defines itself as an archetypal story of a woman. Kitty is the ordinary working girl. Angie is the extraordinary working girl. Janet is the nonworking girl. Kitty's story is about trying to be a woman by society's standards. Angie's story is about the problems of career versus home and what loss of identity does to a woman. Janet's story is about pretending to be a woman by society's standards, but not actually living up to them—cheating.

Kitty's the one who'll finally understand that settling down with a good doctor to raise a mess of kids is all that any woman could want, while Angie is the poor fool who gets all tangled up in career issues. Janet is the one who goes "bad," although she's an interesting variation, in that her badness, which is not always a form of actual prostitution, leads her to marry. But she's still doing it for economic security because her heart isn't in it. Kitty and Angie and Janet teach us girls all about it. They raise all the questions, suffer all the horrors, release all the tensions and angers, and then return to the fold. They all end up in the arms of their men, but only after suffering failure, alcoholism, death of children, psychosomatic illnesses, fire, and rejection. Poor Kitty! Poor Angie! Poor Janet! If only they had just done the right thing in the first place! But, thank God, they found the true path in time.

The way this works is alarmingly reliable. Although these three films are quite different on the surface, each manipulates the basic tenets of the genre. In order to see how this works, it may be useful first to consider a brief plot summary of each film.

KITTY FOYLE

AS THE FILM BEGINS, Kitty Foyle agrees to marry a handsome doctor. Her former husband, Dennis Morgan, reappears, however, and tells her he is going to South America to live and wants her to come along. They cannot marry, because he will not be able to divorce his current wife, but they will be together. As Kitty packs to go away with him, her second self appears in a mirror and tells her she is foolish. While Kitty struggles with this visualized conscience, her story is told in flashback: Kitty Foyle is an ordinary working girl from the wrong side of the tracks in Philadelphia. Her mother is dead, and her father raises her as best he can. Kitty dreams of romance, which is exemplified for her by the annual Assembly Ball, which all of ritzy Philadelphia attends. Kitty goes to business college and gets a job as secretary to Dennis Morgan, a wealthy young man who has started his own magazine. Their relationship develops, and he takes her to New York to a speakeasy and then to a happy, romantic night at Lake Pocono. When the magazine fails, Kitty assumes Morgan will propose to her so they can remain together, but he only offers to keep her on the payroll until she can land on her feet, nothing more. Kitty's father has warned her that Morgan will never marry out of his class, but Kitty believes it will happen. Now she realizes that Morgan sees her as a young woman from the wrong side of the tracks, so she goes to New York, where she gets a job in a fancy beauty salon run by a worldly-wise Frenchwoman. She meets a handsome young doctor (James Craig) and begins dating him. Later, Morgan appears unexpectedly and tells Kitty he is taking her to the Assembly Ball. It is the night of that annual occurrence in Philadelphia, but he does not take her to the real ball. Morgan realizes he loves Kitty, and they marry. Since they both know that it won't work for them to live in Philadelphia because of the difference in their backgrounds, they plan to live in New York. When they arrive at the mansion in Philadelphia to tell his family that they are married, Morgan's family members are shocked; they had understood that he wanted to marry her, but thought he had agreed to wait one year. During that time, the family planned to make Kitty over by sending her to finishing school. Kitty rebels at this idea and urges Morgan to tell them that it doesn't matter anyway, because they will be living in New York. Morgan's family explains that he will not be able to do this, because his money is held in a trust, and the terms of the trust require him to live in Philadelphia and work in the family bank. Kitty says she didn't marry him for his money. When Morgan hesitates, Kitty realizes it won't work and walks out. The marriage is dissolved just as Kitty finds

Kitty (Ginger Rogers)

out she is expecting a baby. Morgan contacts her, but as she is going to meet him she reads about his engagement to a society belle in the papers. She realizes that he has not called for a reconciliation but to break the news of his engagement in person. She has her child alone, and the baby dies. As her flashback ends, Kitty comes to her senses and goes to marry Craig.

SMASH–UP, THE STORY OF A WOMAN

A BADLY BURNED woman lies in a hospital bed, and as she tosses and turns her story is told in flashbacks. She is Angie, a beautiful and talented young singer, who is seen in the past to have been on her way to major stardom. Performing actually makes her nervous, so that she takes a drink just before she goes on, but she is doing well and has an unlimited future. She decides to give it all up, however, when she falls in love with Lee Bowman. After they marry, Hayward helps Bowman, who has been going

Angie (Susan Hayward)

nowhere in his own singing career, advising him regarding material, what to sing, and how to sing it. As she gives birth to their daughter, he has his first big success, giving birth to his own career. As Bowman's career takes off, Hayward's life goes down. His success isolates him from her, and they are seldom together. He has servants and a beautiful secretary (Marsha Hunt) to do everything for him, including buy his clothes, decorate his house, and plan his life. There is nothing for Hayward to do all day, so she begins to sink into alcoholism. She loses all confidence and becomes a drunken embarrassment. Bowman says they cannot go on, and although she can have anything financial that she wants, he will keep their child because she is an unfit mother. Realizing that she must regain her self-respect, Hayward tries to revive her own career, but it is too late. She sinks into the gutter. In the end, she rescues her daughter from a burning house and is redeemed. Bowman, Hayward, and child are reunited at film's end.

Janet (Rosalind Russell)

THE GUILT OF JANET AMES

THE GUILT OF JANET AMES is a difficult film to summarize. It opens
as a woman is walking along a crowded city street, apparently confused as
to where she is going. As she locates her presumed destination, Barney's
Place, across the street, a man tries to pick her up. As he talks to her,
she barely listens, suddenly starting across the street. While he watches,
the sound of a traffic accident is heard offscreen, and he cries out. The
woman has apparently made a suicide attempt. At the hospital, her purse
is found to contain both a Congressional Medal of Honor and a list of five
men's names. One of the names is that of a former top-notch newspaperman
known to the hospital staff, the police, and other newsmen hanging around.
Although he is now an alcoholic, and has been fired from the newspaper,
he is summoned to try to identify the woman.

When he arrives and sees the medal and the list, he realizes who she
is, producing a newspaper clipping with her photograph and a picture of
the medal. When she is wheeled in, he begins to talk with her and learns

from her doctor that she is paralyzed and cannot walk. The doctor, however, says that her inability to walk is psychosomatic; there is nothing wrong with her physically. This makes her terribly angry.

The former newspaperman (Melvyn Douglas) begins to converse with Janet Ames. He is one of five men whose lives were saved when her husband threw himself on a live grenade during World War II, winning him the posthumous medal. Although this happened two years ago, Russell has continued to mourn his death. Douglas tells her that her pseudoparalysis suggests that she didn't really want to meet the five men, for fear she wouldn't be able to continue blaming them for her husband's death. He also tells her that he knows all five men, and can show them to her via word pictures.

In each of the word pictures, Russell confronts, in abstract form, an issue about the woman's life: a home, the wife's support of her husband's dreams in a marriage, parenting, and a romantic courtship. (There are four word pictures, because two of the five men appear in one.) The pictures are surreal visually, presented with shadows, absence of walls, and blurred backgrounds, partly due to medication that has been given to her.

Russell learns that she feels guilty for her husband's death because she did not really love him. When her husband died a hero, her guilt consumed her and she compensated for it by blaming the five men and mourning him in an exaggerated manner. She now feels that she is healed and also that she loves Melvyn Douglas. Douglas, however, turns out to be the commanding officer who ordered her husband to fall on the grenade. He has become an alcoholic because of his own guilt. When Russell learns the truth, she insists that they must work things out together, and to save Douglas she begins to whisper in his ear her own word pictures, in which they are happily married and he is restored to his position of crusading newspaperman.

KITTY AND ANGIE AND JANET, OR THREE IN A GENRE

POOR KITTY! Poor Angie! Poor Janet! Kitty falls in love with a man who is wrong for her. Her judgment is so poor about this guy that she can't even see that he is weak, dominated by his family, and unable to stand on his own two feet without his inherited money. (Janet could have told her.) What Kitty *can* see is that she may be equally wrong for him, since she comes from the other side of the tracks. With true woman's film humility, she says, "You're Darby Hill and I'm Griskin Street. In Philadelphia, we're two addresses, twenty-three miles and five hundred light-years away." Angie, on the other hand, has the right guy, but she foolishly sacrifices her own career to his, not realizing that his fame will take him away from her and leave her without portfolio in a world of high-living people. (Kitty could have told her.)

Janet could have told both Kitty and Angie what was going to happen to them, because Janet knows that marriage is a tough business. In fact, Janet's guilt is that she married her husband for strictly coldhearted reasons. She didn't really love him. She refused to be a proper wife. She didn't give him a home and children, and she didn't even let him follow his own personal career dreams. She wanted that bread on the table, which, after all, is the reason she married him. Janet could have told Kitty and Angie about men and marriage, but, of course, she would have been wrong, even though right. Kitty and Angie and Janet are three women who have made wrong choices, and now they are going to have to figure out how to make the right ones.

Kitty made the right choice in that she fell in love and got married, but she chose the wrong guy. Angie made the right choice in the guy, but the wrong choice in giving up her career and cutting herself off from life. Janet made the right choice, marriage, but for the wrong reasons. In the woman's film, it's always the either-or, the juxtaposed opposites, the yin and the yang of the woman's world. As is always true in the woman's film, there are further choices to be made. In fact, these movies all open with their heroines on the brink of a required new choice. The films become an examination of the factors that can direct a woman to the correct decision. Two of the movies (*Kitty Foyle* and *Smash-Up*) tell their stories through flashbacks, beginning with Kitty and Angie at crisis points. *The Guilt of Janet Ames* remains in present tense throughout its odd presentation, but Janet's word pictures address the underlying question about her past to get at the reason she is psychosomatically paralyzed and suicidal. The pictures take Janet out of her physical present state into a partially medically induced state, showing an audience images that are not actually happening in present tense but are only being imagined by Janet. The women all have a new and better choice to make. Kitty must choose to marry her doctor, saying good-bye to her Philadelphia lover forever, accepting her role as traditional wife and mother rather than as mistress. Angie must give up drinking and, with her husband's help and acceptance of his own culpability, rehabilitate herself back into the good wife and mother she was meant to be. Janet must purge herself of her guilt by admitting her original wrong choice to be a false wife who refused to be a mother and accept her new role as a mentally healthy helpmate to an emotionally impaired (and alcoholic) new mate. The implication is that Janet will then become his wife and ultimately a mother.

The stories, which could easily take place in one movie, present their three women in crisis. Kitty is about to ruin her life by accepting a kind of whoredom with an unreliable man. Angie is nearly burned to death and may be dying in a hospital. Janet is falsely paralyzed, deeply angry and unhappy, and does not know why. This, say these woman's films, is what can happen to you, ladies. So marry for the right reasons and carry out your duties to home and family.

In true woman's film tradition, these choices are linked to duality. There's two of each of these women, so there's Kitty and Kitty, and Angie and Angie, and Janet and Janet. For instance, Kitty's flashback is triggered by the appearance in her mirror of a *second* Kitty, one who represents her conscience. These two Kittys have an argument over what she should properly be doing with her life. The smart Kitty is reflected in the mirror as an image, and the misguided Kitty stands in her room in front of a chest of drawers while they sort it out. The mirrored Kitty knows that her other self really must not accept the life of a kept woman. Kitty's conscience tells her, "You're making a mistake, you know." As the real Kitty tries to defend herself, her conscience tells her that she must think about the fact that she will not be Dennis Morgan's wife and that people will first describe her as "his girlfriend," and then as "his woman," and finally as "that woman Wynne's mixed up with." Kitty says that she and Morgan will just have to face it. Her conscience corrects her, "*You'll* have to face it." Kitty tries to say that she doesn't care about marriage anyway, because marriage is just "a piece of paper." Her conscience doesn't relent. "You'd better take a little time, sister, because forever is a long, long time."

Kitty's struggle with herself presents in dialogue the warning to women that if they try to live outside the rules of society, it simply won't work. A woman needs to be married, and that is the point of *Kitty Foyle*. Earlier, women who work with Kitty have been heard talking, and one has said, "I want a man and I don't care who knows it. Anywhere from eighteen to eighty is okay with me. They don't come too young or too old."

"Doesn't independence mean anything to you?" she is asked. "After all, what's the difference between a man bachelor and a girl bachelor?"

Her reply: "Men bachelors are that way on purpose."

Kitty also has to choose between two men, another representation of duality. There is the good man, a noble doctor who works among the poor and who loves her deeply and understands everything. He is almost an asexual male. The other man is weak, and he represents the wrong kind of life, sex without marriage. Everything about *Kitty Foyle* is, in fact, a presentation of two choices: the right and the wrong ways for a woman to live, think, love, marry. Although the plot is rather a labyrinth, the point the movie makes vis-à-vis women is a simplified, this-or-that situation, with the choice physicalized as Philadelphia or New York, Dennis Morgan or James Craig, the real Kitty or the conscience Kitty.

Angie's duality is expressed through her alcoholism. She is two different people, depending on whether she is drunk or sober. Sober, she is a sensitive and loving woman who guides her husband well in his career and who adores her daughter. She is a woman who wants the "right" thing, which is a home and family rather than a career. She has all the qualities that society asks a "good" woman to have, including her willingness to place her own needs second to her husband's. Drunk, she is angry, frustrated, and slovenly. She picks fights, makes a fool of herself, and nearly destroys her entire life. Inside the good Angie is this woman who is insecure and frightened, and who, when she has no specific role to play in her husband's life or career world, drinks to give herself courage. When she tells her nursemaid that she has to take a drink before joining her husband at a business cocktail party because she is afraid, the maid asks her what she is afraid of. "Why . . . why . . . I don't know, just people, I guess," she replies. She has the potential to be two different women, and we see both of them on the screen.

Janet's duality is illustrated through the device of word pictures. In the real world, Janet sits in a wheelchair and cannot walk. She is angry and, according to Melvyn Douglas, looks much older than she actually is. This self is the guilty one, the one who tries to live a lie in which she pretends to have been a loving wife. The other self is seen inside the word pictures, which are a form of dreamworld. This self can walk and talk and even laugh and fall in love. She is supposed to be the real Janet Ames, the one that needs to be liberated from inside the other unhappy one. The film is an attempt to unify Janet Ames's two selves into one mentally and physically healthy person. Where Angie in *Smash-Up* has a bad self inside that temporarily comes out and ruins her life before the good self triumphs, Janet Ames has a good self inside that has to be freed through honesty to come out and restore her life to normal. All three of these woman's films clearly demonstrate that women have a dual choice, or dual selves, and that they need to listen to reason and the rules of society in order to allow the good one—that is, the one who conforms—to dominate.

In each of these movies, a man seriously fails a woman. Kitty's guy actually fails her twice. First, he does not propose to her when the magazine dies, although he has been seriously romancing her, and, second, he allows his family to influence him about giving up his marriage. The movie indicates that if Kitty decides to trust this man and go away with him, he will inevitably fail her a third time. He is married to a beautiful woman from his own class and background and is the father of a young son. The movie hints that his wife and child will always claim him, because those are the rules.

Angie's husband fails her by simply ignoring her needs. He becomes so wrapped up in his own success that he forgets she is a person with feelings who needs his love and attention. When she begins to drink to compensate, he does not understand what is happening to her or why. Although he loves her and wants her to be all right, he fails his own responsibilities in the matter. Even when she begs him to pay more attention to her, to go away with her on a second honeymoon, and to realize that she's lonely and afraid, he can't understand. He feels she should be happy because he has provided a high standard of living for her.

The story of Janet Ames is, of course, a story about how *she* failed her husband. However, her husband is dead and never appears in the film in any form, not even in her word pictures. The one man Janet Ames is involved with (the Melvyn Douglas character) fails her by lying to her and by denying his own feelings for her. First of all, he deceives her as to his identity. As he directs her word pictures, she does not know until the last one of them that he is himself actually one of the five men who survived the grenade blast. In fact, he never tells her—she guesses. Even when she guesses, he lies to her and lets her believe that he is still a famous and successful crusading newspaperman instead of the alcoholic he has become. When she confronts him at the finish of the movie, he admits that he also lied about the descriptions of the other four men. He led her to believe that they were (1) half of a loving young couple, (2) a happily married man, (3) a caring father, and (4) a successful nightclub comic. They are in truth (1) a bouncer in a cheap dive with a floozy girlfriend, (2) a man who lives off his wife's rich family, (3) an indifferent father who farms his child out, and (4) a failure who plays the horses every day. The biggest part of his lie is a lie of omission: he neglects to tell Janet that he himself ordered her husband to fall on the hand grenade. In other words, he ordered him to die in his place. This man is a big-time liar! Naturally, he needs Janet Ames to straighten him out.

The problems of Kitty and Angie and Janet are important ones. In fact, the three movies are not just about what these three women should do, but about what all women should do. There is constant discussion about the role of women and constant consideration of just how problematic the woman's world really is. *Kitty Foyle* is practically a treatise. Characters pontificate on what a woman should do, or could do, with her life or what a woman's lot really is where men are concerned. The film actually begins with a lighthearted vignette about the history of women. A little card reads:

"This is the story of a white collar girl. Because she is a comparative newcomer to the American scene, it is fitting that we briefly consider her as she was in 1900." A series of short scenes then illustrate how women have changed since they first "left the home to go out to work." In this sequence, a lovely, turn-of-the-century woman boards a streetcar to go to her job in an office. All the men on the car immediately stand up and offer her their seats. The vignette shows how one of them begins to court her and how he ultimately proposes, much to his own surprise. In the next scene, they are shown to be married, and she is now staying at home. The man arrives at the end of his working day and promptly dumps all his salary into her lap. She takes charge of the money, giving him back a small sum that is a sort of tip. She then salts the rest of it away in her sugar bowl. In the next scene, she is embroidering "Baby" on a sampler while he looks totally awed. However, warns a title card, "she wasn't satisfied." In the final scene, the little wife is once again riding a bus, but this time it is with a group of suffragettes, who are demanding the right to vote. This is followed by the sight of her back on the original streetcar. When one man gets off, she tries to take his seat, but she is pushed aside by a burly man who takes it instead. The final title card now says, "This woman climbed down from her pedestal and worked shoulder to shoulder with men who became so accustomed to her presence during the day that evening brought a new malady to the white collar girl. By 1940 this had come to be known rather gloomily as That Five Thirty Feeling." To introduce a story about a typical woman this way, treating her desire for liberation as a joke, tells us in advance that Kitty Foyle's choice will be a conventional one.

In *Smash-Up*, there are many lines of dialogue that define Angie's problem in terms of what a woman's proper role in life should be. When Angie marries, her agent gives her hell for it: "Any other girl would give her eye teeth for your talent. You belong in the profession, Angie, not playing nursemaid." She replies, "Girls do get married. I'm not just a pair of vocal cords, you know. I've got a heart." When she sinks deeply into alcoholism, the family doctor blames it on her husband, telling him, "Men like you make their wives idle. Useless. You give them servants to clean their houses, nurses to take care of their children. And then you say, now you have everything you want. Sit there and enjoy it. In doing so, you've taken all responsibility away from her, left her life with no value." The doctor says this is wrong, wrong, wrong, and the film certainly demonstrates the truth of what he says. Angie herself says, "I've lost my self-respect." One of the most telling lines is uttered by the other woman of the movie, Marsha Hunt, when she comments on the lives of women: "None of us get what we want."

The story of Janet Ames is nothing *but* conversation about women's

roles. As an abstracted piece set in symbolic terms, it is a series of conversations about what women and men should be doing with their lives.
When Douglas and Russell first meet, Douglas tells her she should be
proud to have the Congressional Medal of Honor. "A President once said
he'd rather have it than be President." She snaps, "Really? I'd rather have
my husband." Douglas tells her, "That's a personal view." She retorts:
"What other view is there if you're a woman?" He coldly answers, "Oh, I
didn't know that women were a separate race of people."

This lecture on the woman's role is the raison d'être of *The Guilt of
Janet Ames*. Melvyn Douglas, in the role of male manipulator and director
of the woman's thinking process, presents his word pictures. "Imagine till
it becomes reality," he says, in a kind of societal directive to the female
to "just keep working on it till you accept it." The four mental images that
are then depicted each teach Janet Ames a lesson about herself, and thus
about the woman's role.

Janet learns that she has been wrong not giving her husband a home,
children, or the chance to do what he wants in life. "I let him die with all
his dreams unfinished," she confesses. "I should have blamed myself . . .
I wish I could pay him back for what I did to him. It was I who refused
to plan our house. It was I who made him stay in that dull job he hated
because I was selfish and afraid to risk my security. . . . My greatest shame
is that I married him and never loved him at all. I married him for all sorts
of reasons, but not because I loved him the way I should have loved him,
and he knew that."

All three women use deception in their dealings with others, and all
three are forced into good sportsmanship. Kitty never tells her husband
about their dead son, but has to be a good sport when he remarries. Angie
lies about her drinking, hiding it from everyone for as long as she can, but
she has to be a good sport about her husband's success and lack of interest
in her. Janet has lied to the man she married about how she felt about
him, and this forces her into the good sportsmanship of having to pretend
to be a happy wife to him. None of these women has a mother to advise
her.

Each film presents a Happy Interlude. Throughout *Kitty Foyle*, her
dreams of love and society life are fulfilled by her romance with the wealthy
Dennis Morgan. The high point of this courtship is reached when he takes
her to the bogus Assembly Ball, the false dream that he palms off on her
in place of the real one at which she would not fit in. This interlude is
presented positively, as Morgan is not treated as if he were a villain during
this time; he is seen as weak, not bad or evil. In their Happy Interlude,
the happiness is real, and this forms a basis for an audience's understanding
of just why Kitty might even consider going off with Morgan for a third

rejection. Morgan's courtship of Kitty has him buying her violets for her woolens, taking her to New York speakeasies, and introducing her to drinking Strega, which becomes *their* drink. ("They say that if two people drink it together," he tells her in perfect woman's film talk, "they'll never drink it apart." Just what this means is rather unclear, and it certainly isn't very reassuring if considered carefully.) Their biggest moment comes when Morgan takes Kitty to Lake Pocono. He reads "The Lady of Shalott" aloud in front of the fireplace, and Morgan and Rogers gamely act out a bit of nonsense in which the two lovers tap out popular tunes on the top of each other's heads in order to guess them. (What fun! "Night and Day" and "Three Little Words" might be all right, but you could seriously disorient someone with "Crazy Rhythm" or "Flight of the Bumble Bee.")

Angie and her husband have a Happy Interlude in the early days of their marriage, when they are still poor and Angie has a dominant and important role to play in her husband's life.

Janet has no Happy Interlude in her past marriage, but she has one on the screen in the fourth word picture. In this bizarre sequence in which she and Melvyn Douglas are shown at an abstractly designed nightclub, they act out a deeply romantic courtship, with candles, wine, moonlight, and dancing. Janet wears a beautiful gown and looks stunningly glamorous. There is the ghost of a screwball comedy in this episode, since both Rosalind Russell and Melvyn Douglas have been associated with such films often enough. The two of them exchange witty repartee as they twirl around the dance floor. And, in yet another example of the insanity commonly found in the Hollywood movie, a floor show begins, and Sid Caesar (yes!) comes out and does his stand-up routine about a crazy psychiatrist who is advising a Hollywood movie about psychiatrists. On the menu, all the dishes are named l'Amour à l'Amour.

Naturally, Kitty and Angie and Janet, who are the center of the universe, must think about what they wear and how they look. Fashion and glamour play the usual important roles. To Kitty, these things represent what she herself can never have. The closest she, an ordinary woman, can get to such things is working in an expensive salon. She can live surrounded by these items, but she cannot have them for herself. Kitty, of course, is supposed to be plain Kitty Foyle, the average American working girl. Her story, based on a best-selling novel by Christopher Morley, was subtitled *The Natural History of a Woman*. Kitty is Everygirl. However, since Ginger Rogers is *a star*, Kitty's little black dresses trimmed in white get pretty fancy from time to time, even though she shares a believable-looking apartment with two other girls.

Fashion and glamour are a part of the glitzy show-business life of Angie. Her husband buys her things instead of loving her, but he doesn't pick them out himself; they are impersonal gifts chosen for her by his self-confident and glamorous assistant (Hunt). One of these gifts, an expensive emerald necklace, is thrown at an imagined rival by Angie in a towering rage—an act that precipitates a fistfight between them. Angie's dilemma as a woman is illustrated by an extended tragic scene involving her purchase of a hat, the typical dramatic use of fashion in a woman's film. With nothing to do but shop, Hayward goes out and buys herself a terribly expensive and thoroughly ridiculous hat. When she comes home drunk, she tries to get both her husband and his best friend to admire her new possession. She wants it to do the fashion thing for her: create a transformation. "It's just what I need. A new personality. Any change would be for the better." The fact that they tell her it's awful after barely looking at it perfectly illustrates why she has become an alcoholic. The rejection of the hat also triggers a hideous bender on her part.

The fashion and glamour of *The Guilt of Janet Ames* are buried deep in the fourth word picture, as already described. The Happy Interlude of the visit to the nightclub brings onto the screen the traditional look and attitude of a light romantic comedy, in which everyone is beautifully gowned. This abstraction represents a woman's happiness, and its usage of fashion and glamour is significant accordingly.

The cinematic presentation of each woman establishes clearly that she is the center of the visual universe. Ginger Rogers is literally in every sequence of *Kitty Foyle*. The camera may leave her temporarily, as when the film cuts from showing Kitty upstairs in her bedroom, typing, to showing her father and Dennis Morgan downstairs talking, or when it cuts away from Kitty selling perfume to a silly older woman to the image of two women discussing how successful a saleswoman she is. In both these cases, cuts immediately bring Kitty back into the action. Kitty is always in the larger context of the sequence, and she is never off camera for long. *Kitty Foyle* is a tour de force for Rogers, the star of a movie that is about nothing else *but* Kitty Foyle.

In *Smash-Up*, Susan Hayward is in the majority of the sequences, approximately 80 percent. Scenes that do not include her are *about* her, in that they depict people standing around discussing her. The few scenes that do not include her involve her husband's work or the other-woman subplot. In the former, Hayward sometimes intrudes in the image via a phone call, and in the latter she is again sometimes on the telephone offscreen or is being discussed. Since scenes involving her husband's commitment to his career, or those that involve the other woman's love for him, are also indirectly linked to Hayward's drinking problem, *everything* is more or less about her.

The Guilt of Janet Ames presents Rosalind Russell in about 90 percent of the scenes. She is not present when the audience first meets Melvyn Douglas at his local bar, or when the police find her list of five names, or when newspapermen discuss her "accident." She briefly disappears when Douglas returns to his bar, before she herself arrives there. However, although there are small parts for doctors, nurses, policemen, and reporters, *The Guilt of Janet Ames* is really only a two-person movie. Melvyn Douglas is important to rescuing the heroine from her guilt, but she is really the entire motivation for the visualizations.

Comparing these three films, one sees how each uses the key elements this book has defined. The woman herself is central to the story, the center of its universe. The films are *her* story. Each is involved in good sportsmanship, deception, and the rules of behavior. Each of the women suffers because each one breaks a basic rule of society for women: Kitty becomes pregnant without a husband (even though she had one); Angie becomes an alcoholic; Janet tries to kill herself. Each woman has something unique about her. Kitty Foyle is strong, a survivor, while Angie is a talented singer, and Janet Ames tries to kill herself—a definitive act, after all. They are on a downward scale of strength: from Kitty to Angie to Janet. This downward spiral is represented by the levels of reality each is able to maintain in life. Kitty lives in a real world, with her mind clear about everything except love. She works, lives a normal life, and copes with her problems, recovering even from the death of her child. Angie is in a similar real world at first, but she slides slowly out of it into a drunken world, losing her grip on her real life, shocked back into it only by having to save her child's life. Janet lives in a totally unreal world, a world in which she lives a lie. Each woman is strong enough to endure in the end, restoring her world to sanity or normalcy or acceptable societal standards. This restoration takes the form of love or happy marriage. Each woman finds her way out of darkness by accepting who she is. For Kitty, that means "plain Kitty Foyle," who will live a typical life as a doctor's wife, forgetting her Emma Bovary dreams of the Assembly Ball and her wealthy first husband. For Angie, it means overcoming the insecurity that made her drink, finding a useful place for herself, something to do that is meaningful. Motherhood seems to be that meaning, but since she had motherhood all along, the film's rehabilitation is a bit shaky. For Janet, accepting herself means not blaming herself for marrying without love and realizing she must never do it again. For all three, normalcy and happiness are related to realizing that, because they are women, marriage and motherhood are their primary sources of happiness.

The woman's world is shown to be entrapping in all three cases. Obviously, Angie is inside the trap of marriage. After the early scenes of the movie, she is seldom seen anywhere except in the expensive apartment her husband has bought for her. She sits around drinking or arrives home from shopping. Her other house is one they had in the country, where she was once happy. This is the house that burns. *Smash-Up* uses the house as the setting of the woman's world. In *Kitty Foyle*, Kitty's place of work is an elegant beauty salon (a sort of department store for cosmetics). However, *Kitty Foyle* does not restrict itself to one world as a setting. Instead, Kitty's world is her lower class, which restricts her from being right for the upper-class world of Dennis Morgan. Janet Ames, since she has rejected the woman's world, is shown to have no world at all. Her problem really is that she doesn't have a world, and thus she is paralyzed. She lives inside her head or her pretense or her neurosis. She is ultimately liberated to have a world, and the final image has her describing her future world to Melvyn Douglas. What she describes is their house, so that will be her woman's world.

Motherhood appears as an issue in each story. Kitty's baby dies, and this is a terrible tragedy for her. Just before her baby is born, her voice is heard on the sound track saying, "This is what a woman wants. It isn't men. Not really. It's something down inside them that's the future." Here is another of those movie moments in which women toss men aside after they become pregnant. In Kitty's case, if she does not marry the doctor she will never have another chance to become a mother. This pressure to accept the normal role of wife and mother is partially driven home to the audience through the death of Kitty's child and a scene in which she meets Dennis Morgan's actual son. This little boy, adorably tricked out in a wee sailor suit, represents what Kitty should have had, what she can have if she marries the doctor, and what she will never have if she hooks up with Morgan again.

Angie is saved from alcoholism by the responsibility of motherhood. As the film unfolds, there is a sequence in which Lee Bowman is out of town, and their child becomes ill. Angie rallies herself, never drinking while she sees the child through a terrible crisis. When she tries to call her husband during the illness, he is too busy to take the call. When the child is well again, he rushes home, having heard about the illness. He finds a nurse in charge and Angie drunk, but he does not realize that the child's life was saved by Angie's sober diligence. In the end, Angie saves her child's life again by rushing into a burning house. Motherhood is the source of her salvation, the thing that can make her strong enough to give up the bottle.

Janet Ames rejects motherhood, and this is a major source of her grief and guilt. When she confesses that she is the one who did not want children, she can be purified and go on to a later life as a mother, since she has learned the error of her ways.

In a basic way, each of these movies is a marriage story. Kitty's marriage fails, and the issue of the movie is whether or not she will remarry correctly. Angie's story is that of a failed marriage, and Janet's story is an example of a poor offscreen marriage made for the wrong reasons. Janet's marriage, a total failure, is never depicted visually on-screen. Kitty's marriage, a love success but a logistics failure, is depicted only briefly, when the newlyweds go to spend five minutes with Morgan's family just before the marriage is dissolved. These two *wrong* marriages thus do not exist on the scene in physical terms for the viewer. Angie's marriage, a right marriage for the right reasons, one that can be rehabilitated to its normal and correct state, is the only one shown on-screen.

THE REAL QUESTION about these three films is whether or not they provide evidence of subversive attitudes, and that is linked to how they make a woman in the audience feel. *Kitty Foyle* and *The Guilt of Janet Ames* are films that strongly support the status quo. *Smash-Up, The Story of a Woman* is different, raising serious questions about the woman's life in its surface story and inviting audience endorsement of its questioning. *Kitty Foyle* undercuts its story of a strong, intelligent woman by its offensive opening, in which the concept of a liberated woman is frankly mocked and turned into a joke. However, the fact that Kitty is bright, capable, and resourceful shows a woman in the audience that she should not accept a weak man in her life. There is an underlying hint that men are not necessary ("This is what a woman wants. It isn't men. Not really.") and that men are unreliable. The good doctor seems like a sensible catch who will give Kitty children and security more than anything else. Kitty Foyle almost seems to be making a Janet Ames kind of marriage.

Kitty Foyle is a film that could only be thought of as subversive after careful examination. But in the long run, it is really a story that tells women they should not believe romantic nonsense. Kitty's father, a sensible lower-class man who worries about his daughter's dreams of wealth and love, tells her: "Judas priest! If ever a man deserved to be hurt, it's that fella who started that Cinderella stuff. Putting crazy ideas into innocent girls' heads, making them dissatisfied with honest shoe clerks and bookkeepers." About Dennis Morgan, he ominously states, "They always finish up by marrying their own kind." Although Janet Ames is liberated through her kind of dreams, Kitty Foyle seems to have to renounce hers and settle for an ordinary life like the one she was born into. Of course she *is* marrying a doctor . . . and she has a good job at which she is successful enough to be sent to Philadelphia to open a new salon . . . and of course her settling is related to the type of settling the audience itself has available, those "honest shoe clerks and bookkeepers."

All three women are sympathetic characters. Kitty is a heroine through and through, and it is never suggested that the dumb things she does should ever be seen as anything but sympathetic. Angie is a deeply sympathetic character, although it is understood that one sympathizes with her situation, not with what it makes her do. Russell's character is the least sympathetic, in that she is presented coldly and without emotional explanation. However, a viewer is asked to feel sorry that she has tried to kill herself, and to hope that she can be saved. Since her story is abstracted and presented in symbolic images, an audience is distanced from it more than from the other two.

The Guilt of Janet Ames is not meant to be subversive, but to reaffirm a woman's traditional role. The fact that it appeared in 1947, just as women who worked during World War II were being asked to settle back down in their roles at home, may be significant (although *Smash-Up* was released the same year). However, as Janet Ames says things like "Children waste ten years of your life" and Melvyn Douglas lies to her, what did women watching it feel? To have Janet humble herself totally, taking full responsibility for not doing everything her husband wanted, might have been appalling. There was an undercurrent of meaning in 1947 that has disappeared today, reflected in a speech of Douglas's when he says that many women must have felt guilty about their unhappy and loveless marriage when their men died overseas.

However one responds to this film, there is a strong moment of subversion in the end. Although Douglas changes Russell's life, he remains weak and broken himself, still guilty and alcoholic, while she returns to herself, jumping to her feet and tracking him down in his bar. There, she takes charge of him, and the final image of the movie has *her* in control, manipulating him to service her own dreams, in which they will live in a little cottage, happily wed, with him a huge success again.

Smash-Up is definitely a movie in which the traditional woman's life is questioned. Since Angie's giving up her career ruins her life, and since this is explicitly stated in the plot, this movie asks serious questions. (It was based on a story co-written by Dorothy Parker.) The following words are spoken on-screen: "I hate to see a promising career interfered with," regarding Angie's own success; "All this leisure. So much of it makes you realize what work really meant"—this is said by Angie's agent as he talks to her while they stand at a bar and he realizes how lost she is and how much she is drinking to fill her time; Angie's doctor tells her husband that she turned to drink in despair, "feeling she has lost you in return for nothing she desired." This man also nails the husband for his own responsibility:

"Her world was built around you and she thought she had lost you. If you accept that it was partly your fault, it will help you both." Angie drinks because she has nothing else to do. Hers is the life that was going to be sold to American women in the coming decade of the 1950s as their dream goal: a rich husband, servants, plenty of shopping money and leisure time. *Smash-Up* shows this life to be a hell in which a woman loses her self-respect. At the end of the movie, Hayward's voice talks about how life is beautiful again because, "It's wonderful to rise each day and fear not, to sleep each night and dream not, and to give one's heart and doubt not." The film subversively implies, "It's awful to rise each day and work not." In the end of *Smash-Up*, Hayward saves her child from their burning country home, a symbolic fire. She is redeemed, and an audience is reassured that now everything will be fine, yet the film fails to indicate *how* this can happen. After showing Hayward slowly disintegrate while her selfish husband rises to fame and fortune, and after showing her drunk and disorderly in public and in private, and after showing her passed out on a city street, picked up and taken home by a guy from the streets whose wife says her sister is a drunk so they felt sorry for her—after all this, how and why should anyone feel better?

If Kitty and Angie and Janet were all in the same film together, Kitty's story could remain the same, with her emergence in the end as a doctor's wife, living in a picket-fenced home with kids all around her. However, either Angie or Janet would have to die. Probably it would be Angie, whose drunken behavior and concern with a career would have to destroy her. Of course, it could be Janet who would die, because she has prostituted herself in pretending to love a man. More likely, Kitty would shape Janet up, and Angie would die nobly in the fire. The point, however, is that these three films, selected almost at random, all easily fit the format of the woman's film. And the same thing would be true if you selected the films about Mildred Pierce, Lucy Gallant, Nora Prentiss, Vergie Winters, Madelon Claudet, Stella Dallas, Mary Stevens . . .

Poor Kitty! Poor Angie! Poor Janet! Their lives are all the same. Their stories are basically all the same. They are women in a woman's film, so variations don't count. They're on a story treadmill to only one place: accept that you're a woman in relation to love, marriage, men, and motherhood, or suffer or become paralyzed or die . . . but at the movies you can be temporarily freed.

These three films fulfill the working definition of the woman's film that was suggested at the beginning of this book:

A woman's film is one that places at the center of its universe
a female who is trying to deal with the emotional, social, and

psychological problems that are specifically connected to the
fact that she is a woman. These problems are made concrete by
various plot developments, and since they are often contradictory, they are represented in the story as a form of choice the
woman must make between options that are mutually exclusive.

One final statement can be added to this definition:

The presentation of the woman's world allows for both an overt
indication that women should lead conventional lives and a
covert form of liberation in which they are shown doing something else or expressing anger about this need for conformity.

Kitty and Angie and Janet all live out this definition, which is proof
of genre, proof of the woman's film and its complicated, contradictory
purpose and attitudes.

Appendix

Bibliography

Index

The Dolly Sisters—there's two of them: Betty Grable and June Haver.

APPENDIX:
WOMEN AT THE BOX OFFICE

Not many women lasted as top box-office draws, and very few even appeared in the top ten as compiled by the motion-picture exhibitors polls. Looking at the years of the 1930s, 1940s, 1950s, and early 1960s, the years of the woman's picture and of the studio system, these are the women who were included by American film exhibitors in each year's list of top ten box-office stars:

1929   Clara Bow, Colleen Moore, Nancy Carroll
1930   Joan Crawford, Clara Bow, Janet Gaynor, Colleen Moore, Greta Garbo
1931   Janet Gaynor, Joan Crawford, Norma Shearer, Marie Dressler, Clara Bow, Colleen Moore, Greta Garbo
1932   Marie Dressler, Janet Gaynor, Joan Crawford, Greta Garbo, Norma Shearer
1933   Marie Dressler, Janet Gaynor, Jean Harlow, Mae West, Norma Shearer, Joan Crawford
1934   Janet Gaynor, Mae West, Joan Crawford, Shirley Temple, Marie Dressler, Norma Shearer
1935   Shirley Temple, Ginger Rogers, Joan Crawford, Claudette Colbert
1936   Shirley Temple, Ginger Rogers, Joan Crawford, Claudette Colbert, Jeanette MacDonald
1937   Shirley Temple, Jane Withers, Ginger Rogers, Sonja Henie, Myrna Loy
1938   Shirley Temple, Sonja Henie, Myrna Loy, Jane Withers, Alice Faye
1939   Shirley Temple, Bette Davis, Alice Faye, Sonja Henie
1940   Bette Davis, Judy Garland
1941   Bette Davis, Judy Garland
1942   Betty Grable, Greer Garson
1943   Betty Grable, Greer Garson
1944   Betty Grable, Greer Garson, Bette Davis
1945   Greer Garson, Betty Grable, Judy Garland, Margaret O'Brien

1946   Greer Garson, Betty Grable, Judy Garland, Margaret O'Brien
1947   Betty Grable, Ingrid Bergman, Claudette Colbert
1948   Betty Grable, Ingrid Bergman
1949   Betty Grable, Esther Williams
1950   Betty Grable, Esther Williams
1951   Betty Grable, Doris Day
1952   Doris Day, Susan Hayward
1953   Marilyn Monroe, Susan Hayward
1954   Marilyn Monroe, Jane Wyman
1955   Grace Kelly, June Allyson
1956   Marilyn Monroe, Kim Novak
1957   No women
1958   Elizabeth Taylor, Brigitte Bardot
1959   Doris Day, Debbie Reynolds, Susan Hayward
1960   Doris Day, Elizabeth Taylor, Debbie Reynolds, Sandra Dee
1961   Elizabeth Taylor, Doris Day, Sandra Dee
1962   Doris Day, Elizabeth Taylor, Sandra Dee
1963   Doris Day, Elizabeth Taylor, Sandra Dee

BIBLIOGRAPHY

Allen, J. T. "The Representation of Violence to Women: Hitchcock's *Frenzy*." *Film Quarterly* 38, no. 3 (1985): 30–38.

Basinger, Jeanine. "Ten That Got Away." In *Women and the Cinema*, edited by Karyn Kay and Gerald Peary, 61–72. New York: Dutton, 1977.

———. *The World War II Combat Film: Anatomy of a Genre*. New York: Columbia University Press, 1986.

Burchill, Julie. *Girls on Film*. New York: Pantheon, 1986.

Cavell, Stanley. *Pursuits of Happiness: The Hollywood Comedy of Remarriage*. Cambridge: Harvard University Press, 1981.

Clarens, Carlos. *An Illustrated History of the Horror Film*. New York: G. P. Putnam, 1967.

Cook, P. "Women in Jeopardy." *Monthly Film Bulletin* 52 (February 1985): 36–39.

Corliss, Richard. "An Obituary Tribute to Bette Davis: She Did It the Hard Way." *Time*, October 16, 1989.

Coursodon, Jean-Pierre, and Pierre Sauvage. *American Directors*, vol. 1. New York: McGraw-Hill, 1983.

Dalton, (Susan) Elizabeth. "Women at Work: Warners in the 1930s." In *Women and the Cinema*, edited by Karyn Kay and Gerald Peary, 267–82. New York: Dutton, 1977.

DeLauretis, Teresa. *Technologies of Gender: Essays on Theory, Film, and Fiction*. Bloomington: Indiana University Press, 1987.

Deming, Barbara. *Running Away from Myself: A Dream Portrait of America Drawn from the Films of the 40s*. New York: Grossman, 1969.

Doane, Mary Ann. *The Desire to Desire: The Woman's Film of the 1940s*. Bloomington: Indiana University Press, 1987.

Erens, Patricia. *Sexual Stratagems: The World of Women in Film*. New York: Horizon Press, 1979.

———, ed. *Issues in Feminist Film Criticism*. Bloomington: Indiana University Press, 1990.

French, Brandon. *On the Verge of Revolt: Women in American Films of the 1950s*. New York: Ungar, 1978.

Gaines, Jane, and Charlotte Herzog. *Fabrications: Costume and the Female Body.*
New York: Routledge, 1990.

Galerstein, Carolyn L. *Working Women on the Hollywood Screen: A Filmography.*
New York: Garland, 1989.

Gallup, George, et al. *Gallup Looks at the Movies: Audience Research Reports,
1940–1950.* Wilmington, Del.: Scholarly Resources, 1979.

Gamman, Lorraine, and Margaret Marshment, eds. *The Female Gaze.* Seattle: Real
Comet Press, 1989.

Gledhill, Christine, ed. *Home Is Where the Heart Is: Studies in Melodrama and
the Woman's Film.* London: BFI Books, 1987.

Greene, Graham. *Graham Greene on Film: Collected Film Criticism, 1935–1939.*
Edited by John Russell Taylor. New York: Simon and Schuster, 1972.

Haskell, Molly. *From Reverence to Rape: The Treatment of Women in the Movies.*
New York: Holt, Rinehart & Winston, 1973.

Huss, Roy, ed. *Focus on the Horror Film.* Englewood Cliffs, N.J.: Prentice-Hall,
1972.

Izod, John. *Hollywood and the Box Office, 1895–1986.* New York: Columbia
University Press, 1988.

Johnston, Claire. "Femininity and the Masquerade: 'Anne of the Indies.' " In
Jacques Tourneur. Edinburgh: Edinburgh Film Festival, 1975.

Kaplan, E. Ann. "Patterns of Violence Toward Women in Fritz Lang's 'While the
City Sleeps.' " *Wide Angle* 3, no. 3 (1980): 55–60.

———. *Rocking Around the Clock: Music Television, Postmodernism, and Consumer Culture.* New York: Methuen, 1987.

———. *Women and Film: Both Sides of the Camera.* New York: Methuen, 1983.

———. *Women in Film Noir.* London: BFI Books, 1978.

Kolbsenschlag, M. C. "The Female Grotesque: Gargoyles in the Cathedrals of
Cinema." *Journal of Popular Film and Television* 6, no. 4 (1978): 328–41.

Lederer, Laura, ed. *Take Back the Night: Women on Pornography.* New York:
William Morrow, 1980.

Marchetti, G. "An Annotated Working Bibliography: Readings on Women and
Pornography." *Jump Cut* 26 (December 1981): 55–60.

Mellon, Joan. *Big Bad Wolves: Masculinity in the American Film.* New York:
Pantheon, 1977.

Moedelski, Tania. *The Women Who Knew Too Much: Hitchcock and Feminist
Theory.* New York: Methuen, 1988.

Mulvey, Laura. "Visual Pleasure and Narrative Cinema." *Screen* 16, no. 3 (Autumn
1975): 6–18.

Nobile, Philip. *Favorite Movies: Critics' Choice.* New York: Macmillan, 1973.

Radaway, Janice. *Reading the Romance: Women, Patriarchy, and Popular Literature.* Chapel Hill: University of North Carolina Press, 1984.

Reed, Joseph. *American Scenarios.* Middletown, Conn.: Wesleyan University
Press, 1989.

Renov, Michael. *Hollywood's Wartime Woman: Representation and Ideology.* Ann
Arbor, Mich.: UMI Research Press, 1988.

Ringgold, Gene. "Rosalind Russell." *Films in Review*, December 1970.

Rosen, Marjorie. *Popcorn Venus: Women, Movies, and the American Dream.* New York: Coward, McCann & Geoghegan, 1973.

Russ, Joanna. "Someone's Trying to Kill Me and I Think It's My Husband." *Journal of Popular Culture* 6, no. 4 (Spring 1973): 666–91.

Sherman, Eric. *Directing the Film: Film Directors and Their Art.* Los Angeles: Acrobat Books, 1988.

Slotkin, Richard. *Gunfighter Nation.* New York: Atheneum, 1992.

Tuchman, Gay, Arlene Kaplan Daniels, and James Benet. *Hearth and Home: Images of Women in the Mass Media.* New York: Oxford University Press, 1978.

Viviani, Christiane. "Who Is Without Sin: The Maternal Melodrama in American Film, 1930–1939." *Wide Angle* 4, no. 2 (1981).

Walsh, Andrea S. *Women's Film and Female Experience, 1940–1950.* New York: Praeger, 1984.

Weibel, Kathryn. *Mirror, Mirror: Images of Women Reflected in Popular Culture.* Garden City, N.Y.: Doubleday, 1977.

Woods, Michael. *America at the Movies.* New York: Basic Books, 1975.

INDEX

Note: Page numbers in *italics* refer to illustrations.

Abbott and Costello Meet Captain Kidd, 478
Accidents Will Happen, 243
Adam's Rib, 185
African Queen, The, 28
Aherne, Brian, 66, 173–5, 178
Albert, Eddie, 80, 288
Alda, Robert, 446
Alice Adams, 124, 185
All About Eve, 17, 245, 271–2
Allan, Elizabeth, 48–9
All That Heaven Allows, 44
Allyson, June, 33, 138, 163–5, 167, 410
Along Came Jones, 275
Ambush, 263–4
Ameche, Don, 113, 244
American in Paris, An, 122, 123, 285, 292n
And Now Tomorrow, 301–4
Andrews, Dana, 109
Angel on the Amazon, 415n
Angel and the Badman, The, 191
Angeli, Pier, 325
Ankers, Evelyn, 163
Ann-Margret, 122
Anne of the Indies, 464, 478–81
Annie Get Your Gun, 457
Annie Oakley, 457
Any Number Can Play, 125
Appointment with Danger, 65
Appointment for Love, 199
Arden, Eve, 107, 108, 355–6, 364, 457

Arnold, Edward, 277, 291–3
Arthur, Jean, 127, 164, 167, 259, 286–7, 324, 395, 410, *422*
Arzner, Dorothy, 209, 246, 248
Astaire, Fred, 127, 128, 184
Asther, Nils, 346
Astor, Mary, 10, 262, 409, 411–14
At Sword's Point, 464, 474–7, *476*, 478
Awful Truth, The, 105, 106
Ayres, Lew, 84, 90, 91

Baby Face, 266–72
Bacall, Lauren, 115
Bachelor Mother, 227, 231–2
Back Street, 56, 105, 202–3, 207 (1932 version); 56, 202–3, 207 (all versions)
Bad Man of Wyoming, 466
Bad Men of Missouri, 467–8
Bainter, Fay, 334
Ball, Lucille, 139, 178, 295, 296
Bancroft, George, 155
Bari, Lynn, 199–200
Baris, Mona, 61, 62
Barker, Jess, 147
Barnacle Bill, 180n
Barnes, Binnie, 350, 478
Barrat, Robert, 60
Barrymore, John, 183, 305, 308, *311*
Barrymore, Lionel, 277
Basehart, Richard, 447
Bates, Florence, 340
Baxter, Anne, 164, 239–41, 245, 271–2

Baxter, Warner, 101–3
Beatty, Warren, 215
Beavers, Louise, 204–6
Beery, Wallace, 180n, 466
Behind the Makeup, 155
Behind Office Doors, 262
Bellamy, Ralph, 245
Belles on Their Toes, 330
Bendix, William, 27–30
Bennett, Constance, 110n, 111–13, *112*, 141, 142, 369, 370, 393–4, 396–8, *397*, 415n
Bennett, Joan, 118, 251–5, 324
Benny, Jack, 447
Berkeley Square, 289
Bergen, Polly, 273n
Bergman, Ingrid, 33, 149, 292n
Bergner, Elisabeth, 86
Berkeley, Busby, 143
Bettger, Lyle, 400, 402–4
Beyond the Forest, 50–4, 402, 413
Bill of Divorcement, A, 185
Billy Rose's Diamond Horseshoe, 122
Bishop, Julie, 447, 472
Bishop's Wife, The, 293–5, *294*
Blondell, Joan, 187
Blonde Venus, 151, 421, 427–30
Blondie for Victory, 347–9
Blue Veil, The, 431
Blyth, Ann, 175
Bogart, Humphrey, 10–11, 161, 292n, 383–4
Boland, Mary, 17, 389
Boles, John, 283, 422–6
Bolger, Ray, 469
Born to Love, 393–4, 396–8, *397*
Borzage, Frank, 309
Bow, Clara, 154, 228
Bowman, Lee, 146, 148, 259, 410, 487, 489–90, 502
Boyd, William, 158
Boyer, Charles, 199
Bracken, Eddie, 139
Brando, Jocelyn, 324
Bremer, Lucille, 138, 409
Brent, George, 44, 59–63, 95, 96,

134, 154, 259, 269, 270, 358, 362, 366–9, 411–13, 415n, 460–2
Brian, David, 51–3
Bride Wore Red, The, 115, 131–2, 172
Bright Eyes, 284, 285
Bringing Up Baby, 64, 184, 201
British Agent, *157*, 159
Broderick, Helen, 139, 229
Bromley, Sheila, 243
Brook, Clive, 64, 129
Brook, Faith, 67
Brooks, Geraldine, 199, 251
Brooks, Hazel, 243–4
Brown, Joe E., 139
Bruce, Virginia, 117, 346
Buffalo Bill, 333–4
Burke, Billie, 125–6, 132, 432–3
Burr, Raymond, 120
Burton, Richard, 278–80
Busses Roar, 447
Byington, Spring, 417, 419

Cabot, Bruce, 433, 446
Caesar, Sid, 499
Caged, 220–5, *221*
Cagney, James, 33, 288
Calamity Jane, 457
Calhern, Louis, 343
Calling Bulldog Drumond, 10
Cantor, Eddie, 139, 143
Capra, Frank, 168
Captain January, 283, 284
Carey, Phil, 67, 68
Carey, MacDonald, 259
Caron, Leslie, 122, 292n
Carroll, Madeleine, 229–31
Carson, Jack, 19, 175, *210*, 437, 438
Carter, William, 312–17
Casablanca, 292n
Castle, Peggie, 299
Cat People, 100n
Catlett, Walter, 125
Cavern, The, 38–9
Chained, 172
Chance at Heaven, 56
Chandler, Jeff, 199

In This Our Life, 95–6
Invitation, 343
I Remember Mama, 201, 328–31, 410
Irish in Us, The, 288
It, 228
It Had to Be You, 185, 344–5
It Happened One Night, 115, 183n, 344
It's a Wonderful World, 183
Iturbi, Jose, 287n
I've Always Loved You, 305, 309, 310, 312–17
Ivy, 66, 68–72, 71
I Was a Male War Bride, 199, 201

Jagger, Dean, 305, 307–8
Jezebel, 132–5
Johnny Belinda, 140, 263, 301, 304, 330
Johnny Guitar, 9, 135n, 463
Johns, Glynis, 126
Johnson, Van, 123, 137, 298–300, 343, 374
Jones, Allan, 229
Jones, Jennifer, 198, 431
Jones, Shirley, 391
Jourdan, Louis, 384, 479–81
Julia Misbehaves, 105, 165, 168n
Julie, 384, 447
Just Around the Corner, 282

Kaye, Danny, 117
Keaton, Buster, 257
Keep Your Powder Dry, 477–8
Kelly, Gene, 122, 123, 145–8, 390, 449
Kelly, Grace, 140
Kerr, Deborah, 167n, 199
Kibbee, Guy, 61–3
King, Andrea, 108, 384
Kisses for Breakfast, 260
Kisses for My President, 273n
Kitty, 127, 266, 271
Kitty Foyle, 106n, 185, 198, 486–9, 489, 493–506
Knowles, Patric, 179

Knox, Alexander, 275
Kohner, Susan, 207
Kruger, Otto, 144–8

LaBreton, Flora, 248n
Ladd, Alan, 24, 26–30, 65, 302–4
Ladies Courageous, 21–3, 22
Ladies of the Jury, 37–8
Ladies in Love, 110n, 111–13, 112, 477
Lady in the Dark, 100–5, 185
Lady Eve, The, 105–7
Lady Is Willing, The, 118, 131, 165, 380
Lady of Secrets, 64
Lady from Shanghai, 72, 193–4
Lady Wants Mink, The, 364–5
Lake, Veronica, 115, 124–5
Lamarr, Hedy, 166, 167, 244, 271, 345
Lamont, Lina, 115
Lamour, Dorothy, 124–5, 143
Landi, Elissa, 395
Lane, Lola, 79
Lane, Priscilla, 78, 79, 80
Lane, Rosemary, 79
Langan, Glenn, 383
Lansbury, Angela, 39–40, 469, 470
Last of Mrs. Cheyney, The, 172
Laughing Sinners, 172
Laughton, Charles, 50, 353, 383
Laura, 302n
Leave Her to Heaven, 70, 72, 83, 96–7, 198, 374, 413
Lee, Carolyn, 231
Leigh, Janet, 123, 128
Leigh, Vivien, 139
Leisen, Mitchell, 481
Leslie, Joan, 19, 117, 245, 436–8, 466
Letter for Evie, A, 396n
Letter to Three Wives, A, 340–1, 343
Letter from an Unknown Woman, 56, 198
Letty Lynton, 115, 172
Levant, Oscar, 122, 123
Lewis, Jerry, 122, 139

Libeled Lady, 201

Life of Emile Zola, The, 129

Life of Her Own, A, 236

Life of Vergie Winters, The, 394

Lindsay, Margaret, 134, 250

Lisbon, 118–19

Little Giant, The, 261

Little Miss Marker, 284

Littlest Rebel, The, 282–3

Lloyd, Harold, 228, 447

Loder, John, 12

Logan, Jacqueline, 248n

Lombard, Carole, 56, 139, 152, 183–4, 201, 455

Long Hot Summer, The, 39–40

Love, Honor and Goodbye, 117, 346

Love Finds Andy Hardy, 160

Lovejoy, Frank, 407

Love Letters, 396n

Love on the Run, 172, 173

Loy, Myrna, 99, 164n, 167, 185, 319–20, 324, 329, 330, 343, 371–3, 375

Lubitsch, Ernst, 127, 158, 161

Lucky Night, 371–3, 375

Lucy Gallant, 232–3

Lukas, Paul, 111, 356–7

Lund, John, 127, 402–4

Lundigan, William, 327

Lupino, Ida, 108, 225–6, 248n, 288, 436–8, 446

Luxury Liner, 285

Lydia, 77n

Lydon, Jimmy, 93n

Lynn, Jeffrey, 78, 80, 340

McCallister, Lon, 74–7

McCrea, Joel, 56, 327, 396–8, *397*, 451

McDaniel, Hattie, 412

MacDonald, Jeanette, 198n, 308, *311*

McDowall, Roddy, 409

McGuire, Dorothy, 324, 343

McHugh, Frank, 381, 386

McIntire, John, 470, 472

Mackaill, Dorothy, 211, 212

McKay, Scott, 245

McLaglen, Victor, 346

MacLaine, Shirley, 389–90

McLeod, Catherine, 309, *310*, 312–17

MacMahon, Aline, 31, 245, 265–6, 358–60, 362, 363

MacMurray, Fred, 124, 178, 183n, 189–90, 194, 229–31, 273n, 380

Macready, George, 72, 73

Madame Curie, 9, 329, 330

Made in Paris, 122

Magnificent Doll, 165, 184–5

Magnificent Obsession, The, 139 (1935 version)

Main, Marjorie, 180n, 466–7

Major and the Minor, The, 184

Make Way for a Lady, 282

Man, Woman and Sin, 276–7

Man Called Peter, A, 326, 327

Man in the Gray Flannel Suit, The, 355

Manhandled, 214, 228

Man I Love, The, 108, 446

Mannequin, 119, 173, 335–40, 362

Manners, David, 274

Man Wanted, 273–4

Man Who Came Back, The, 164

March, Fredric, 183, 324, 327

Marshal, Alan, 33, 113

Marshall, Brenda, 464

Marshall, Herbert, 49, 50, 67–71, 99, 282, 427–30

Martin, Dean, 390

Mary of Scotland, 184

Mary Stevens, M.D., 9, 159, 448–9, 452–3, 456

Mason, James, 254

Massey, Ilona, 287

Mata Hari, 161

Mayo, Virginia, 123, 466

Maytime, 198n, 305, 308, *311*

Meanest Man in the World, The, 447

Medina, Patricia, 126

Meet Me in St. Louis, 328, 332, 409

Men in Her Life, The, 305–8, *311*

Menjou, Adolphe, 56

Menzies, William Cameron, 70

Mercer, Beryl, 33

Meredith, Burgess, 113
Merkel, Una, 446
Midnight, 105–7, 183
Mildred Pierce, 175–7, 198, 322, 452
Milland, Ray, 101–3, 118–19, 184, 266
Miller, Kristine, 124
Miracle in the Rain, 298–300
Mrs. Parkington, 26, 32–5
Mr. Skeffington, 381–2
Mr. Peabody and the Mermaid, 300n
Mitchell, Thomas, 288
Mitchum, Robert, 138, 199, 390
Money and the Woman, 464–5
Monkey Business, 64
Monroe, Marilyn, 137, 144, 163, 166, 167, 199
Montana Moon, 172, 173, 189
Montez, Maria, 85, 93–5
Montgomery, George, 129, 130, 199–200
Montgomery, Robert, 110
Moon Over Miami, 110n, 477
Moore, Cleo, 259
Moore, Juanita, 205–7
Moorehead, Agnes, 34, 220, 222, 225
Moran, Dolores, 108
Morgan, Dennis, 95, 96, 193, 437, 438, 487–9, 494, 495, 498–500, 502, 503
Morgan, Frank, 99
Morley, Karen, 198n
Morning Glory, 185
Morocco, 137
Most Precious Thing in Life, The, 395, *422*
Mother Wore Tights, 329, 330
Mountain Justice, 59–63, *60*
Muir, Jean, 414, 415
Murder in the Air, 56
Murder in the Fleet, 261
Murfin, Jane, 30
Murphy, George, 113
My Best Girl, 227, 228
My Cousin Rachel, 72n, 277–80
My Love for Yours, 227, 229

My Man Godfrey, 201
My Reputation, 44, 107–8
Mysterious Doctor, The, 189
Mysterious Lady, 161

Nancy Drew, Detective, 10
National Velvet, 74, 419–20
Neal, Patricia, 404–8
Newman, Paul, 40, 50, 390
Nightmare Alley, 263
Ninotchka, 128, 161
Niven, David, 293, 294
No Man of Her Own, 163, 400–4
Nora Prentiss, 277
Nothing Sacred, 183
Notorious, 198
Notorious Affair, A, 155
Now, Voyager, 12, *14*, *15*, 16–17, 115, 198, 301, 432, 438–44
Nutty Professor, The, 122–3

Oberon, Merle, 77n
O'Brien, Margaret, 282, 409
O'Brien, Pat, 124, 376–8
O'Brien, Virginia, 469
O'Connor, Una, 343
O'Hara, Maureen, 127, 371, 374–6, 390, 474–7, *476*, 478
Oil for the Lamps of China, 376–9
O'Keefe, Dennis, 364
Old Acquaintance, 97–9
Oliver, Edna May, 37–8, 446, 450
Olivier, Laurence, 245
Once Upon a Honeymoon, 185
One Girl's Confession, 259
O'Neil, Barbara, 422, 425–6
O'Neill, Sally, 110n
One Foot in Heaven, 326, 327
One Way Passage, 158
Only Yesterday, 56
O'Sullivan, Maureen, *321*
On the Town, 122, 123
Our Betters, 369–70
Our Blushing Brides, 109–10, 119, 172
Ouspenskaya, Maria, 312–14, 316, 357

Out of the Fog, 288
Over 21, 274–5

Page, Anita, 110
Page, Gale, 78, *79*
Paget, Debra, 480
Paid, 25, 172
Paid in Full, 5
Painted Veil, The, 345–6
Palance, Jack, 135–6, 138
Paleface, The, 275, 453
Parker, Cecilia, 160, 161, 163
Parker, Eleanor, 220–4, *221*, 404,
    405, 407, 408
Patrick, Lee, 223–4, 260, 464–5
Payment Deferred, 353, 354
Penguin Pool Murder, The, 450
Peters, Jean, 478–81
Phantom of the Opera, The, 317–18
Pickford, Mary, 228
Picnic, 234, 241
Pidgeon, Walter, 10, 33, 287n, 329
Pierson, Louise Randall, 210–12
Pin-Up Girl, 128
Poor Little Rich Girl, 283
Possessed, 17, 172, 236–8, *236, 237*
Povah, Phyllis, *121*
Powell, Dick, 143
Powell, Jane, 165, 282, 285–6,
    287n, 409
Powell, William, 158, 201, 319–20,
    345
Power, Tyrone, 112, 263, 350–2, 374
Power and the Glory, The, 261, 322
Presumed Innocent, 302n
Price, Vincent, 383
Primrose Path, The, 185, 419, 420
Private Lives, 168n
Pullman, Jessie, *204*

Qualen, John, 288
Quality Street, 185

Rachel, Rachel, 432
Rain, 172
Rainer, Luise, 421
Raines, Ella, 383

Rainmaker, The, 185
Rains, Claude, *14*, 16, 17, 78, 118–
    19, 308, 317–18, 381–2, 439,
    440, 442
Rambeau, Marjorie, 419, 420
Rathbone, Basil, 481, 483
Raymond, Gene, 249–51, 290–3,
    384–6, 432
Reagan, Ronald, 56, 123, 243
Reap the Wild Wind, 161
Rebound, 10
Reckless Moment, The, 251–5
Red Shoes, The, 305, 308, 311
Reed, Donna, 55–7, 409
Remember the Day, 259, 431
Remick, Lee, 39
Rendezvous, 10
Return of the Bad Men, 467
Return of Dr. X, The, 161
Return to Paradise, 277, 278
Revere, Anne, 419–20
Reynolds, Debbie, 165, 409
Rhapsody, 287n
Rich, Young, and Pretty, 285, 286
Ritter, Thelma, 233
Road to Morocco, 143
Roberti, Lyda, 398–9
Roberts, Marguerite, 30
Robinson, Edward G., 242–3, 261
Robson, May, 78, 431
Rogers, Buddy, 228
Rogers, Ginger, 56, 101–4, 106n,
    113, 115, 117, 139, 165, 167,
    170, 184–5, 187, 194–7, 231–2,
    276, 334, 344–5, 410, 419, 420,
    432, 454–5, 457, 487–9, *489*,
    499, 500
Roman, Ruth, 325, 404, 405, 407–8
Rooney, Mickey, 137, 330
Rosay, Françoise, 279n
Ross, Katharine, 344
Roth, Lillian, 220
Roughly Speaking, 209–12, *210*
Ruggles, Charlie, 87
Ruggles of Red Gap, 453
Russell, Gail, 100n, 191
Russell, Jane, 123, 275

Russell, Rosalind, 7, 10, 106*n*, 117, 121*n*, 164, 171, 177–9, 183, 185, 200, *210*, 246–8, 259, 343, 457, 487, *491*, 492, 498, 500–1, 504
Ruthless, 197, 263
Ryan, Robert, 192, 194–7

Sadie McKee, 172, 290–3
Safe in Hell, 209–12
Sagan, Leontine, 248*n*
Sally, Irene, and Mary, 110*n*
Sanders, George, 297
Sarah and Son, 416–17
Scandal Sheet, 155
Scott, Lizabeth, 5, 10–11, 120
Scott, Martha, 431, 487
Scott, Randolph, 285, 467
Scott, Zachary, 175, 177, 263, 355–6
Seastrom, Victor, 334*n*
Sebastian, Dorothy, 110
Secret Beyond the Door, 245
Secret of Convict Lake, The, 446
Secret Life of Walter Mitty, The, 117, 119–20
Secret of Madame Blanche, The, 289, 395
Secrets, 77, 333
Sentimental Journey, 56
September Affair, 279*n*
Sergeant York, 245
Shadow in the Sky, 349
Shadow on the Wall, 124
Shadow of a Woman, 384
Shanghai Express, 126
Shearer, Norma, *121*, 163, 167*n*
Sheffield, Johnny, *321*
She Had to Say Yes, 262–3
Shepperd, John, 305–8
Sheridan, Ann, 199, 277, 354–6
She Wouldn't Say Yes, 178
Shining Hour, The, 56, 173, 334
Shirley, Anne, 282, 423
Shocking Miss Pilgrim, The, 45–8, *47*
Shopworn, 5, 220, 255–6, 432
Shrike, The, 165
Sidney, Sylvia, 220, 394

Simmons, Jean, 390–1
Simon, Simone, 111
Sin of Madelon Claudet, The, 198*n*, 394, 417*n*
Sin Ship, 17
Sinatra, Frank, 449
Since You Went Away, 198
Singin' in the Rain, 115, 120
Single Standard, The, 161
Sirk, Douglas, 206
Skelton, Red, 325
Sky Giant, 261*n*
Skylark, 200
Sleep, My Love, 243–4
Slightly Dangerous, 140
Small Town Girl, 164, 234
Smart Woman, 10, 411*n*
Smash-Up, the Story of a Woman, 56, 446, 486, 487, 489–90, *490*, 493–506
Smiling Lieutenant, The, 127
Smith, Alexis, 125, 383–4
Smith, Kent, 277
Snake Pit, The, 140, 301
So Big, 139, 259
Song to Remember, A, 374
Son of Paleface, 275, 453
So Proudly We Hail!, 463, 477
Sothern, Ann, 124, 340, 341
Spitfire, 184
Stage Door, 184
Stage Mother, 434–6
Stahl, John, 203
Standing Room Only, 189–90
Stanwyck, Barbara, 5, 44, 56, 106–7, 137, 139, 164*n*, 165, 167–8, *168*, 184, 192–4, 220, 255–6, 263, 266–71, *267*, 365–6, 383, 390, 394, 400–4, 421–8, 430, 432, 447, 457, 466
Star Is Born, A, 140–2
Stars in My Crown, 326–7
Star Spangled Rhythm, 124–5
Stella Dallas, 421–7
Stephens, Harvey, 101
Stevens, George, 334*n*
Stevens, Mark, 325

Stevens, Stella, 122
Stewart, James, 33, 137, 163, 334, 465
Stolen Life, A, 84–9, 92
Stone, Lewis, 328, 330
Storm Warning, 185
Strange Cargo, 42, 173
Strange Woman, The, 72, 271
Streep, Meryl, 167*n*
Street of Chance, 155
Streisand, Barbra, 141
Sudden Fear, 9, 135–6, 402
Sullavan, Margaret, 56, 163, 199, 202, 203
Sundown, 446
Susannah of the Mounties, 285
Suspect, The, 50, 383
Suzy, 343
Swanson, Gloria, 138, 228
Sweepings, 227, 277
Sybil, 109*n*, 301
Sylvia Scarlett, 185

Take Care of My Little Girl, 124
Take a Letter, Darling, 178
Take Me Out to the Ball Game, 449
Talbot, Lyle, 452
Talbott, Gloria, 386–8
Tale of Two Cities, A, 446
Talmadge, Constance, 138
Tamiroff, Akim, 229
Tarzan's Desert Mystery, 189
Tarzan's Secret Treasure, 321
Taylor, Elizabeth, 282, 287*n*, 334*n*, 419–20
Taylor, Robert, 137, 139, 163, 164, 371–3, 468, 470, 471, *474*
Teasdale, Verree, 139, 353, 414, 415
Teen-age Rebel, 185
Tell It to the Judge, 178, 200, 457
Temple, Shirley, 179, 239, 282–5, *283*
Tender Comrade, 115, 194–7, 410
Ten North Frederick, 277
Teresa, 325–6

That Hagen Girl, 238–9
Thaxter, Phyllis, 401
Theodora Goes Wild, 105
They All Kissed the Bride, 455–6, 459, 462
This Modern Age, 172
This Thing Called Love, 178
This Woman Is Dangerous, 193
Thomas, Danny, 331
Thompson, Kay, 127, 128
Thompson, Marshall, 93*n*
Three Blind Mice, 110*n*, 477
Three Came Home, 43*n*, 183*n*
Three Faces of Eve, The, 109*n*, 301
Three Musketeers, The, 126
Three Secrets, 404–8
Thunder in the Sun, 199
Tierney, Gene, *70*, 83, 96–7, 295–8, 382–3, 413, 446
Tobin, Genevieve, 242–3
Today We Live, 172
To Each His Own, 5, 77, 452
To Have and Have Not, 115
Tom, Dick and Harry, 113
Tone, Franchot, 132, 291, 292
Tonight We Raid Calais, 446
Toomey, Regis, 262–3
Torch Singer, 183*n*, 394, 398–400
Totter, Audrey, 465, 466
Tracy, Spencer, 163, 164, 200, 273, 324, 336–7, 339, 379–80
Transgression, 155, 159
Traveling Husbands, 322, 353–4
Treacher, Arthur, 125
Trevor, Claire, *434*, 434–5
Trouble in Paradise, 152, 158, 159
Truman, Ralph, 67
Tryon, Tom, 386–8
Tuchock, Wanda, 248*n*
Tufts, Sonny, 92
Turner, Lana, 56, 126, 140, 160–1, 163–4, *205*, 205–7, 235–6, 395, 478
Twelvetrees, Helen, 186–7, 393
Twentieth Century, 183
Two in the Dark, 202

Two-Faced Woman, 105, 106, 161
Two Guys from Milwaukee, 19, 117
Two Mrs. Carrolls, The, 383
Two O'Clock Courage, 202
Two Weeks with Love, 332, 409

Unconquered, 191–2, 446
Undercurrent, 185
Unfaithful, The, 354–6
Unfinished Business, 9
Uninvited, The, 100n

Valley of Decision, The, 105
Valley of the Sun, 10, 257
Van Dyke, Dick, 390
Van Dyke, William, III, 374, 375
Veidt, Conrad, 149, 150, 305–8, *311*
Vera-Ellen, 122
Vidor, King, 54, 421
Vincent, June, 21–3
Vinson, Helen, 118
Virtuous Sin, The, 155, 189
Vivacious Lady, 334
Vogues of 1938, 118, 119
von Sternberg, Josef, 180, 421

Walbrook, Anton, 305
Walker, Helen, 374
Walker, Robert, 198
Walls of Jericho, The, 239–42, 374
War and Peace, 77
Warrick, Ruth, 245
War of the Roses, The, 389
Watson, Minor, 52
Watson, Lucile, 48, 107, 344
Wayne, John, 137, 161, 191, 269
Webb, Clifton, 329
Weekend Marriage, 358–65, *359*
Weekend at the Waldorf, 163
Weissmuller, Johnny, 321
Weld, Tuesday, 395
Welles, Orson, 39, 40, 193

West, Mae, 179, 181–3
Westward the Women, 463, 468–74, 474
What Price Hollywood?, 140–2
What a Way to Go!, 389–90
What a Woman, 178
When the Daltons Rode, 151
When Ladies Meet, 83, 99
Where There's Life, 128, 130–1
Whirlpool, 100, 286–7
White Angel, The, 57–9
White Cliffs of Dover, The, 26, 32–5, 322
Whitmore, James, 349
Wicked As They Come, 66–8
Wilde, Cornel, 96–7, 240, 241, 266, 270, 344, 371, 374–6, 475–6, *476*
Wilde, Lee and Lynn, 93n
Wilder, Billy, 193
William, Warren, 206, 207, 350–2, 414, 415
Williams, Esther, 449–50
Wind, The, 334n
Wings of Eagles, The, 261
Without Love, 379–80
Wives and Lovers, 123
Wolheim, Louis, 17
Woman Chases Man, 451
Woman of Distinction, A, 178
Woman Rebels, A, 48–50, 184, 185, 278
Woman's Face, A, 149–50
Woman They Almost Lynched, The, 463, 465–6, 469
Woman of the Year, 200, 273, 457
Women, The, 17, 119, 120, *121*, 172, 173, 344, 389
Women's Prison, 220, 224–6
Wood, Natalie, 282
Woodward, Joanne, 40
Wyman, Jane, 44, 140, 232–3, 298–302, 304, 330, 381, 431, 467–8
Wymore, Patrice, 331

Yank in the RAF, A, 130n
Yolanda and the Thief, 138
You Belong to Me, 365–6
Young, Loretta, 21, 23–30, 34, 35,
   100n, 111–13, *112*, 167, 220,
   228, 262–3, 275, 293–5, *294*,
   301–8, *311*, 358–63, *359*,
   487
Young, Robert, 131–2, 163, 164,
   244
You're Only Young Once, 409
Yurka, Blanche, 446

PERMISSIONS ACKNOWLEDGMENTS

Grateful acknowledgment is made to the following for permission to reprint previously published material:

Barton Music Corp.: Excerpt from "Who Killed Vaudeville" by Sammy Fain and Jack Yellen, copyright © 1945 by Barton Music Corp. Reprinted by permission.

CPP/Belwin, Inc.: Excerpt from "It's a Woman's World" by Sammy Cahn and Cyril Mackridge, copyright © 1954 (Renewed 1982) by Twentieth Century Music Corp., c/o EMI Robbins Catalog Inc.; excerpt from "Westward the Women" by Jeff Alexander, copyright © 1952 (Renewed 1980) by Loew's Inc., c/o EMI Robbins Catalog Inc. World rights controlled and administered by CPP/Belwin, Inc., Miami, Fla. All rights reserved.

Famous Music Publishing: Excerpts from "Hot Voodoo," words and music by Sam Coslow and Ralph Rainger, copyright © 1932 (Renewed 1959) by Famous Music Corporation; excerpt from "I Couldn't Be Annoyed," words and music by Leo Robin and Richard A. Whiting, copyright © 1932 (Renewed 1959) by Famous Music Corporation; excerpt from "You Little So and So," words and music by Sam Coslow and Leo Robin, copyright © 1932 (Renewed 1959) by Famous Music Corporation. Reprinted by permission.

Warner/Chappell Music, Inc.: Excerpt from "Aren't You Kind of Glad We Did," music and lyrics by George Gershwin and Ira Gershwin, copyright © 1946 by Chappell & Co. (Renewed). All rights reserved. Used by permission. Excerpt from "Stand Up and Fight," music and lyrics by George Gershwin and Ira Gershwin, copyright © 1993 by George Gershwin Music and Ira Gershwin Music. All rights administered by WB Music Corp. All rights reserved. Used by permission.

PHOTOGRAPHIC CREDITS

A Note on the Type

This book was set in a digitized version of Bodoni Book, a typeface named after Giambattista Bodoni (1740–1813), a celebrated printer and type designer of Rome and Parma. Bodoni Book is not a copy of any one of Bodoni's fonts, but a composite, modern version of the Bodoni manner. Bodoni's innovations in type style included a greater degree of contrast in the thick and thin elements of the letters and a sharper and more angular finish of details.

Composed by PennSet, Bloomsburg, Pennsylvania

Printed and bound by Arcata Graphics/Martinsburg, Martinsburg, West Virginia

Designed by Iris Weinstein